Third Edition

Health Care Ethics

CRITICAL ISSUES FOR THE 21ST CENTURY

Edited by

Eileen E. Morrison, EdD, MPH, LPC, CHES
Professor, School of Health Administration
Texas State University—San Marcos
San Marcos, Texas

Beth Furlong, PhD, JD, RN
Associate Professor, Center for Health Policy and Ethics
Creighton University
Omaha, Nebraska

JONES & BARTLETT
LEARNING

World Headquarters
Jones & Bartlett Learning
5 Wall Street
Burlington, MA 01803
978-443-5000
info@jblearning.com
www.jblearning.com

Jones & Bartlett Learning books and products are available through most bookstores and online book-sellers. To contact Jones & Bartlett Learning directly, call 800-832-0034, fax 978-443-8000, or visit our website, www.jblearning.com.

Production Credits
Publisher: Michael Brown
Managing Editor: Maro Gartside
Editorial Assistant: Chloe Falivene
Associate Production Editor: Rebekah Linga
Senior Marketing Manager: Sophie Fleck Teague
Manufacturing and Inventory Control Supervisor: Amy Bacus
Composition: Lapiz, Inc.
Cover Design: Michael O'Donnell
Cover Image: © Artifan/ShutterStock, Inc.
Printing and Binding: Edwards Brothers Malloy
Cover Printing: Edwards Brothers Malloy

To order this product, use ISBN: 978-1-4496-6535-7

Library of Congress Cataloguing-in-Publication Data
Health care ethics : critical issues for the 21st century / [edited by] Eileen E. Morrison and Beth Furlong. —3rd ed.
     p. ; cm.
   Includes bibliographical references and index.
   ISBN 978-1-4496-5737-6 (pbk.)
   ISBN 1-4496-5737-0 (pbk.)
   I. Morrison, Eileen E. II. Furlong, Elizabeth.
   [DNLM: 1. Bioethical Issues. 2. Delivery of Health Care--ethics. 3. Ethics, Clinical. WB 60]
   174.2—dc23
                                                                                    2012039134
6048
Printed in the United States of America
17 16 15 14 13   10 9 8 7 6 5 4 3

Dedication

EILEEN E. MORRISON

The third edition of *Health Care Ethics: Critical Issues for the 21st Century* is dedicated to all those who contributed their time and talent to update existing chapters or develop new ones. They shared their insights on topics that will help to balance ethics and healthcare practice in the 21st century. On a personal level, I would like to dedicate the third edition of this text to those who have provided both inspiration and advice. First, there is my family: Grant, Kate, Emery Aidan, and Morrigan Leigh, who listened, loved, and encouraged. There are also my colleagues, relatives, and friends—you each know how much you have meant to me during this process. Finally, there is my publisher, Michael Brown; my coeditor, Beth Furlong; and my Jones & Bartlett Learning editors, Chloe Falivene and Rebekah Linga, whose knowledge, guidance, and patience added so much to the quality and integrity of this work.

BETH FURLONG

Mentors facilitate one's journey. My gratitude goes to Dr. Amy Haddad and colleagues at Creighton University's Center for Health Policy and Ethics. I value the ever-present support of my husband, Robert Ramaley. Furthering the ethical education of others with this book is possible because of the collegiality and support of coeditor, Eileen Morrison. It has been a professional pleasure to work with her.

Contents

Contributors

Karen J. Bawel-Brinkley, RN, PhD
Professor
School of Nursing
San Jose State University
San Jose, CA

Sidney Callahan, PhD
Distinguished Scholar
The Hastings Center
Garrison, NY

Byron Chell, JD
Eugene, OR

Kevin T. FitzGerald, SJ, PhD
Dr. David Lauler Chair in Catholic
    Healthcare Ethics
Associate Professor
Center for Clinical Bioethics
Georgetown University Medical
    Center
Washington, DC

Dexter R. Freeman, PhD
Director
Master of Social Work Program
Army Medical Department Center
    and School
Army-Fayetteville State University
Houston, TX

Janet Gardner-Ray, EdD
CEO
Country Home Healthcare, Inc.
Charlottesville, IN

Glenn C. Graber, PhD
Professor Emeritus
Department of Philosophy
The University of Tennessee,
    Knoxville
Knoxville, TN

Chris Hackler, PhD
Professor of Medical Humanities
Division of Medical Humanities
College of Medicine
University of Arkansas for Medical
    Sciences
Little Rock, AR

T. Patrick Hill, PhD
Senior Policy Fellow
Edward J. Bloustein School of
    Planning and Public Policy
Rutgers, The State University of New
    Jersey
New Brunswick, NJ

Kenneth V. Iserson, MD, MBA
Professor Emeritus of Emergency
    Medicine
The University of Arizona
Tucson, AZ

Nicholas B. King
Assistant Professor
Biomedical Ethics Unit
McGill University Faculty of
    Medicine
Montreal, QC, Canada

Cristian H. Lieneck, PhD, FACMPE, FACHE, FAHM
Assistant Professor
Texas State University—San Marcos
San Marcos, TX

James Lindemann Nelson, PhD
Professor of Philosophy
Michigan State University
East Lansing, MI

Richard L. O'Brien, MD
Professor Emeritus
Center for Health Policy & Ethics
Creighton University
Omaha, NE

Carol Petrozella, BSN, MSN, MSED, EdD
Professor
Miami Dade College
Adjunct Clinical Professor
Nova Southeastern University
Miami, FL

Jim Summers, PhD
Professor Emeritus
School of Health Administration
College of Health Professions
Texas State University—San Marcos
San Marcos, TX

Barbara Supanich, RSM, MD
Medical Director

Palliative Care
Holy Cross Hospital
Silver Spring, MD

Carole Warshaw, MD
Director
National Center on Domestic
  Violence, Trauma & Mental Health
Chicago, IL

Michael P. West, EdD, FACHE
Executive Director and Fellow
University of Texas at Arlington—
  Fort Worth
American College of Healthcare
  Executives
Chicago, IL

Rosalee C. Yeaworth, RN, PhD, FAAN
Professor Emeritus and Dean
  Emeritus
Medical Center and College of
  Nursing
University of Nebraska
Omaha, NE

Carrie S. Zoubul, JD
Borchard Fellow
Center for Health, Science, and
  Public Policy
Brooklyn Law School
New York, NY

About the Authors

Eileen E. Morrison, EdH, MPH, LPC, CHES is a professor in the School of Health Administration at Texas State University—San Marcos. Her academic background includes a doctorate from Vanderbilt University and a Master of Public Health from the University of Tennessee. In addition, she holds the credential of Associate in Logotherapy from Viktor Frankl Institute of Logotherapy and a clinical degree in dental hygiene.

Dr. Morrison has taught graduate and undergraduate ethics courses and provided professional workshops on ethics to physicians, nurses, clinical laboratory professionals, dental professionals, and counselors. She has authored articles and chapters on ethics for a variety of publications. In addition, she is the author of *Ethics in Health Administration: A Practical Approach for Decision Makers, Second Edition*, published by Jones and Bartlett Publishers.

Beth Furlong, PhD, JD, RN is an associate professor in the Center for Health Policy and Ethics at Creighton University in Omaha, Nebraska. Her academic background includes a bachelor's degree and master's degree in nursing, a master's degree and doctorate degree in political science, and a law degree (JD).

Dr. Furlong has taught graduate ethics courses and led continuing education unit workshops for nurses on ethical issues. Her publications are in the areas of health policy, vulnerable populations, and ethics.

Preface

The writing of the third edition of *Health Care Ethics: Critical Issues for the 21st Century* occurred during a time of great change for the healthcare system. In fact, health care is facing its greatest changes since the advent of Medicare and Medicaid. In light of this fact, chapters are included that address healthcare reform and its ethical issues. In addition, authors have contributed new chapters to emphasize the impact of technology and new options in long-term care. Existing chapters were updated; some chapters underwent major revisions to connect better to the challenges faced by health professionals in the post-reform era.

The third edition keeps the organizational model of previous editions to assist students in building their knowledge base of ethics and ability to relate ethics to patient issues across the lifespan. It also provides organizational issues, as well as examples of ethical issues germane to society. In homage to those who greatly influenced ethical thought, the model of a Greek temple organizes the chapters in this new edition (see **Figure FM-1**). The foundation of the temple is ethical theory and principles. Students need this foundation so they can analyze future issues in their practices based on theory and principles and not just on opinion.

The three main pillars of the model illustrate the foundation for the other sections of the text: individual, organizational, and societal issues. An introduction to each section sets the stage for the issues presented in the chapters that follow. Authors with extensive experience in healthcare practice and in ethics contributed their insights in these chapters. At the end of each chapter, discussion questions provide the opportunity for thoughtful analysis and application of the issues raised in the chapter. In addition, a new feature,

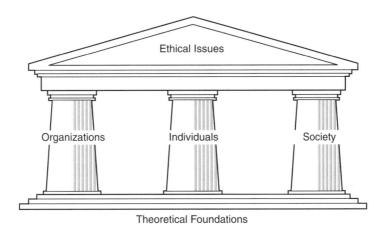

Figure FM-1 Healthcare Ethics Organizational Model

"Food for Thought," gives the student the ability to apply what he or she has learned to healthcare situations. These mini-cases can also lead to lively class discussions.

The authors of this new edition of *Health Care Ethics: Critical Issues for the 21st Century* are experts in their fields, but they are not clairvoyant. Therefore, they cannot predict what will happen in the next 5–10 years, as the Patient Protection and Affordable Care Act becomes the norm for health care. However, one can always apply the principles and theories of ethics to whatever new situation arises. We hope that students will continue to ask themselves, "Is this the best ethical decision to make?" and "How do I know that this is the best decision?" as they progress through their careers. Patients and the community rely on the answers.

PART I

Foundations in Theory

With the advent of the Patient Protection and Affordable Care Act (PPACA), a new era of health care has begun. The changes and proposed changes associated with this law increase the complexity of both patient care and the larger healthcare system. Because of this law, health care will receive even more scrutiny and must provide high-quality, patient-centered, research-based care with fewer or different types of resources. The community will continue to expect a high level of ethics from practitioners and healthcare organizations. In short, you are supposed to "know your stuff" at both a practice and an organizational level if you want to be considered a professional in health care.

To be fully prepared, you need to know your ethics. In today's complex healthcare setting, ethics is not just about doing the right thing, like your Mom taught you. The new healthcare era brings issues that often are exceedingly complex and far from black and white. In addition, society and the health professions themselves often have stringent expectations regarding ethics. In light of these challenges, it seems logical that one must have a solid foundation in the theory and principles of ethics in order to make appropriate professional decisions. The first part of this new edition of *Health Care Ethics: Critical Issues for the 21st Century* contains two chapters that provide this foundation.

The foundation in ethical theory and principles provided in Chapters 1 and 2 also gives you practical tools for analyzing ethics-related issues that you will encounter. Without this foundation in ethics, it would be difficult to develop plausible solutions that you can use to defend your actions or the policies that you help to create. A foundation in theory, principles, and decision making will also enhance your ability to reason and enhance your role as a professional in health care.

The chapters in this part should help you to ask the best questions. For example, as you face ethical dilemmas in the future, ask, "What theory or theories best apply here?" or "If I take this position, what principles will I support or violate?" or "What is the price of not being ethical?" Because ethical issues are usually broader in scope than they appear, you could also think about their effect on individuals, your organization, or on the society in which you live. This type of thinking is and will continue to be necessary in the healthcare environment, where even the smallest issue may have a large impact on professionals and the institutions in which they work.

In an immediate sense, a foundation in ethical theory and principles will be useful to you as a student of this subject matter. You will see the principles and theories explained in this section used in subsequent chapters to examine the issues presented. In addition, at the end of each chapter, there will be questions to encourage you to take your intellect beyond what you have read.

Many of these questions relate directly to the application of a particular theory or principle. By answering these questions, you will enhance the depth of your understanding not only of the specific issue but also of the application of ethical theory and principles. There is also a mini-case called Food for Thought at the end of each chapter that will help you apply ethics to the practice of health care.

In Chapter 1, Summers presents a well-researched overview of the theories commonly used in healthcare ethics. He begins with a model so that you can see where ethics fits into the study of philosophy. Following that, he reviews ethical theories that might not have as much relevance to healthcare practice as other theories, including authority-based ethics, egoism, and ethical relativism. He then presents the most commonly held ethical theories that are applied in healthcare practice. These include natural law, deontology, utilitarianism, and virtue ethics. In his discussions, he uses examples to help you better understand how these theories apply to your professional practice. In fact, he refers to them as part of your *ethics toolbox*.

In Chapter 2, Summers continues his scholarly discussion of ethics by presenting the four most commonly used principles: nonmaleficence, beneficence, autonomy, and justice. Because justice is the most complex of the four, he provides additional material about the types of justice. He also provides information on how you can decide what is just. At the end of Chapter 2, Summers also presents a decision-making model called the *reflective equilibrium model*. This model demonstrates the application of ethical theory and principles in the practice of making clinical and business decisions.

If you read these chapters thoroughly and think about their content, you should be well prepared to discuss the issues presented in the other chapters in this text in a rational way. Remember that many of the issues presented in this text evoke strong emotions in practitioners, patients, and society in general. However, decisions made based on emotions may not be the best decisions for the situation. Therefore, having a foundation in ethics based on these two chapters should be useful in deciding the most ethical thing to do for patients, the organization, the community, and your career.

CHAPTER 1

Theory of Healthcare Ethics

Jim Summers

INTRODUCTION

In this chapter, Summers presents a scholarly account of the main theories that apply to the ethics of healthcare situations. Why bother with such a discourse? The answer is that without a foundation in ethics, you would have to make decisions without a structure to support them. You would not have the wisdom of the theorists to defend your decisions if you needed to do so. In addition, you would not have a knowledge base to analyze the many issues that you will face in health care in the 21st century. For example, the uncertainty of healthcare reform and its impact on the system poses and will continue to pose new ethical issues. Without a foundation in theory, how can you respond to issues that have never occurred before? Therefore, this chapter and the one on the principles of ethics, which follows, will serve as your ethics toolbox.

ETHICS AND HEALTH CARE

From the earliest days of philosophy in ancient Greece, people have sought to apply reason in determining the right course of action for a particular situation and in explaining why it is right. Such discourse is the topic of normative ethics. In the 21st century, issues resulting from technological advances in medicine and science will continue to provide challenges that will necessitate similar reasoning. Healthcare resource allocations will become more global and more vexing as new diseases threaten, global climate change continues apace, and ever more people around the world find their lives increasingly desperate as disease and poverty overtake them. Managers of healthcare organizations will find the resources to carry out their charge increasingly constrained by lack of money and labor shortages. A foundation in ethical theory and ethical decision-making tools can help in assessing the choices that we must make in these vexing circumstances.

Knowledge of ethics can also be valuable when working with other healthcare professionals, patients and their families, and policy makers. In this sense, ethical understanding, particularly of alternative views, becomes a form of cultural competence.[1] However, this chapter is limited to a discussion of normative ethics and metaethics. *Normative ethics* is the study of what is right and wrong; *metaethics* is the study of ethical concepts. Normative ethics examines ethical theories and their application to various disciplines, such as health care. In health care, ethical concepts derived from normative theories, such as autonomy, beneficence, justice, and nonmaleficence, often guide decision making.[2]

As one might suspect, when normative ethics seeks to determine the moral views or rules that are appropriate or correct and explain why they are correct, major disagreements in interpretation often result. Those disagreements

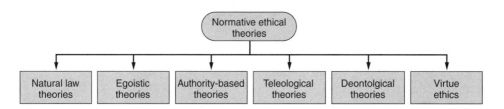

Figure 1–1 Normative ethical theories.

influence the application of views in many areas of moral inquiry, including health care, business, warfare, environmental protection, sports, and engineering. **Figure 1–1** lists the most common normative ethical theories. Each of these theories is considered in this chapter. Although no single theory has generated consensus in the ethics community, there is no cause for despair.

The best way to interpret these various ethical theories, some of which overlap, is to use the analogy of a toolbox. Each of these theories teaches something and provides tools that can assist with decision making. One advantage of the toolbox approach is that you will not find it necessary to choose one ethical theory over another for all situations. You can choose the best theory for the task, according to the requirements of your role and the circumstances. Trained philosophers will find flaws with this approach, but it is hoped that the practical advantages will suffice to overcome these critiques.

All of the theories presented have a value in the toolbox, although like any tools, some are more valuable than others are. For example, I shall argue that virtue ethics has much value for healthcare applications. Before explaining why this chapter has chosen to present particular theories, a quick overview is in order.

- *Authority-based theories* can be faith based, such as Christian, Muslim, Jewish, Hindu, or Buddhist ethics. They can also be purely ideological, such as those based on the writings of Karl Marx (1818–1883) or on capitalism. Essentially, authority-based theories determine the right thing to do based on what some authority has said. In some cultures, the authority is simply "that is what the elders taught me" or "that is what we have always done." The job of the ethicist is to determine what that authority would decree for the situation at hand.

- *Natural law theory*, as considered here, uses the tradition of St. Thomas Aquinas (1224–1274) as the starting point of interpretation. The key idea behind natural law is that nature has order both rationally and providentially. The right thing to do is that which is in accord with the providentially ordered nature of the world. In health care, natural law theories are important owing to the influence of the Roman Catholic Church and the extent to which the Church draws on Aquinas as an early writer in the field of ethics. Several important debates, such as those surrounding abortion, euthanasia, and social justice, draw on concepts with roots in natural law theory.

- *Teleological theories* consider the ethics of a decision to be dependent on the consequences of the action. Thus, these theories are called *consequentialism*. The basic idea is to maximize the good of a situation. The originators of one such theory, Jeremy Bentham (1748–1832) and John Stuart Mill (1806–1873), called this maximization of good *utility*; thus, the name of this theory is *utilitarianism*.

- *Deontological theories* find their origins in the work of Immanuel Kant (1724–1804). The term *deon* is from the Greek and means "duty." Thus, deontology could be called the science of determining our duties. Most authors place Kant in extreme opposition to consequentialism, because he argued that the consequences themselves are not relevant in determining what is right. Thus, doing the right thing might not always lead to an increase in the good.[3] More contemporary deontologists, including John Rawls (1921–2007) and Robert Nozick (1938–2002), reach antithetical conclusions about what our duties might be.

- *Virtue ethics* has the longest tenure among all of these views, except for authority-based theories. Its roots can be traced to Plato (427–347 BCE) and to Aristotle (384–322 BCE). The key idea behind virtue ethics is to find the proper end for humans and then to seek that end. In this sense, people seek their perfection or excellence. Virtue ethics comes into play as people seek to live virtuous lives, developing their potential for excellence to the best of their ability. Thus, virtue ethics addresses issues any thinking person should consider, such as "What sort of person should I be?" and "How should we live together?" Virtue ethics can contribute to several of the other theories in a positive way, particularly in the understanding of professional ethics and in the training necessary to produce ethical professionals.

- *Egoistic theories* argue that what is right is that which maximizes a person's self-interests. Such theories are of considerable interest in contemporary society because of their relationship to capitalism. However, the ethical approach of all healthcare professions is to put the interests of the patient above the practitioner's personal interests. Even when patients are not directly involved, such as with healthcare managers, the role is a *fiduciary relationship*, meaning that patients can trust that their interests come before those of the practitioners. Egoistic theories are at odds with the value systems of nearly all healthcare practitioners.

Before exploring any of these ethical theory tools in depth, it is first necessary to confront the relativist argument, which denies that ethics really means anything.

ETHICAL RELATIVISM

Those who deal with ethical issues, whether in everyday life or in practice, will inevitably hear the phrase "It is all relative." Given that the purpose of this text is to help healthcare professionals deal with real-world ethical issues, it is important to determine what this phrase means and the appropriate course of action. Philosophers have not developed a satisfactory ethical theory that covers every situation. In fact, they are expert at finding flaws in any theory; thus, no theory will be infallible. In addition, different cultures and different groups have varying opinions about what is right and wrong and how to behave in certain situations.[4]

Does the fact that people's views differ mean that any view is acceptable? This appears to be the meaning of such statements as "It is all relative." In that sense, deciding that something is right or wrong, or good or bad, has no more significance than choices of style or culinary preferences. Thus, ethical decision making and practice is a matter of aesthetics or preferences, with no foundation on which to ground it. This view makes a normative claim that there is no real right, wrong, good, or bad.

One could equally say that there is no truth in science, because scientists disagree about the facts and can prove nothing, only falsify it by experiment.[5] However, the intrinsic lack of final certainty in the empirical sciences does not render them simply subjective. As one commentator on the rapid changes in scientific knowledge put it, these changes reveal "the extraordinary intellectual and imaginative yields that a self-critical, self-evaluating, self-testing, experimental search for understanding can generate over time."[6] Why should we expect any less of ethics?

Sometimes there is a claim made that, because there are many perspectives, there cannot be a universal truth about ethics. Therefore, we are essentially on our own. Hugh LaFollette argued that the lack of an agreed-upon standard or the inability to generalize an ethical theory does not render ethical reasoning valueless.[7] Rather, the purpose of ethical theories is to help people decide the right course of action when faced with troubling decisions. Some ethical theories work better in some situations than others. The theories themselves provide standards, akin to grammar and spelling rules, as to when something is properly executed using that theory.

Thus, even though ethics might not produce final answers, we still must make decisions. Ethical theories and principles are tools to help us in that necessary endeavor. The lack of absoluteness in ethical theory also does not eliminate rationality. Often, we simply must apply our rationality without knowing if we are correct. The better our understanding of ethics, the more likely it is that the decision we reach will be appropriate.

ETHICAL THEORIES

Let us begin to examine the tools in the toolbox, knowing that we are fallible, but also that we are rational.[8] The first tool has little application to healthcare ethics; however, it is widely believed and therefore needs to be addressed. It involves the idea of egoism in ethics.

Egoism

Egoism operates from the premise that people either should (a normative claim) seek to advance solely their own self-interests or that (psychologically) this is actually what people do. The normative version, *ethical egoism*, sets as its goal the benefit, pleasure, or greatest good of the self alone.[9] In modern times, the writings of Ayn Rand[10] and her theory of *objectivism*[11] have popularized the idea of ethical egoism. For example, Rand said, "The pursuit of his own rational self-interest and of his own happiness is the highest moral purpose of his life."[12] This is a normative statement, and a reasonable description of ethical egoism.

Although this theory has importance to the larger study of ethics, it is less important in healthcare ethics, because the healing ethic itself requires a sublimation of self-interests to those of the patient. A healthcare professional who fails to do this is essentially not a healthcare professional. No codes of ethics in the healthcare professions declare the interests of the person in the professional role to be superior to those of the patient.

> A healthcare professional who does not understand the need to sublimate his or her own interests to those of the patient or his or her role has not yet become a healthcare professional.

Although occasionally healthcare professionals do not put the patient's best interest first, it is not a goal of the profession to put one's self ahead of the client or patient. A realist might complain, "Yet this is the way most people behave!" Although that may be true, the fact that many people engage in a particular kind of behavior does not make it into an ethical theory. Ethical egoism constitutes more of an ethical problem than anything else. Most people who think of an ethical theory consider it something that is binding on people. However, ethical egoism is not binding on anyone else beyond self-interest. It is not binding on all (i.e., normative), and thus does not meet the criteria of a true ethical theory but is simply a description of human behavior. As such, ethical egoism, if widely adhered to, would lead to a breakdown in social cohesion. How could we trust anyone if they really were ethical egoists and we were as well? Could patients really have confidence in our care for them? Indeed, to care for someone else above your own self-interest, as required by codes of ethics in health care, is antithetical to truly pursuing only your self-interest. The only escape at the societal level leads into the realm of contract theories of the state. Later, we shall see how John Rawls uses the idea that people pursue their own self-interest to develop a theory of a just society in which solidarity seems to be the outcome, as opposed to the extreme individualism ethical egoism typically suggests.

Authority-Based Ethical Theories

Most teaching of ethics ignores religion-based ethical theories, much to the chagrin of those with deep religious convictions. There are several reasons to avoid the use of religion-based ethics in healthcare practice.

A major problem is determining which authority is the correct one. Authority-based approaches, whether based on a religion, the traditions or elders of a culture, or an ideology, such as communism or capitalism, have flaws relative to the criteria needed to qualify as a normative ethical theory. Each of the authority-based approaches, to be an ethical theory, must claim to be normative relative to everyone. Because many of these authority-based approaches conflict, there is no way to sort them out other than by an appeal to reason. Not only do we have the problem of sorting through the ethical approaches, but also arguments inevitably arise concerning the religion itself and its truth claims. If two religions both claim to be inerrant, it is difficult to find a way to agree on which of the opposing inerrant authorities is correct.

In spite of the philosophical issues arising from the use of religion in healthcare ethics, it is quite important for healthcare providers to understand the role of religions and spirituality in healthcare delivery. All religions provide explanations of the cause or the meaning of disease and suffering. Many theologies also encourage believers to take steps to remove or ameliorate causes of disease and suffering. Over the millennia, some of these religions have even formalized their positions by becoming involved with healthcare delivery.

In addition, patients often have religious views that help them to understand and cope with their conditions. Understanding a person's faith can help the clinician provide health care that is more patient focused.[13] For some patients, an ethical issue arises if their faith or lack of faith is neither recognized nor respected.

Beyond direct patient care, a second reason to understand the authority-based philosophies common in the healthcare environment is their effect on healthcare policy. The role of authority-based ethical positions appears to be gaining importance in the 21st century. To be effective working within the health policy arena, whether at the institutional, local, regional, state, federal, or international level, requires an understanding of the influence of the religious views of those involved in the debates and negotiations, which can only serve to strengthen your ability to reason with them. In other words, it is important to understand the "common" morality of those engaged in the debate. The more diversity in beliefs and reasoning, the more important the need for understanding what those beliefs and reasoning might be.

Religion also plays an important role in the creation of healthcare policy because religions have provided a multiplicity of philosophical answers to questions about the nature and truth of the world and how we should act in the world. They explain what is right or wrong and why it is right or wrong. They also help people define their identities, roles in the world, and relationships to one another. Religions explain the nature of the world relative to our place in it.

Thus, as a tool, understanding authority-based philosophical systems has value because it can help in the treatment of patients. It also increases your understanding regarding the positions of persons who may be involved in debates over healthcare issues, such as resource allocations, or clinical issues such as abortion. In addition, it is important to understand authority-based philosophical systems relative to yourself. As a healthcare professional, your role requirements dictate that you do not impose your religious views on patients. At the same time, it is not part of the role for you to accept the imposition of another's values, even those of a patient.

These complex issues relate to professional ethics and are not part of the scope of this chapter. However, it does seem incumbent on all healthcare professionals to evaluate their own faith and to recognize the extent to which they might impose it on others. From the earliest tradition of Hippocrates, the charge was to heal the illness and the patient. More recently, the Declaration of Geneva from the World Medical Association stated that members of the medical profession would agree to the following statement: "I will not permit considerations of age, disease or disability, creed, ethnic origin, gender, nationality, political affiliation, race, sexual orientation, social standing or any other factor to intervene between my duty and my patient."[14] Let us now turn our attention to the oldest non-authority-based ethical theory—virtue ethics.

Virtue Ethics

Virtue ethics traces its roots most especially to Aristotle (384–322 BCE). Aristotle sought to elucidate the highest good for humans. Bringing the potential of that good to actualization requires significant character development. The concept of character development falls into the area of virtue ethics because its goal is the development of those virtues in the person and the populace.

Aristotle's ethics derived from both his physics and metaphysics. He viewed everything in existence as moving from potentiality to actuality. This is an organic view of the world, in the sense that an acorn seeks to become an oak tree. Thus, your full actuality is potentially within you. As your highest good, your potential actuality is already inherent, because it is part of your nature; it only needs development, nurture, and perfecting. This idea is still with us in many respects as part of the common morality.

Finding Our Highest Good

Just what did Aristotle conclude was our final cause or our highest good? The term Aristotle uses for this is *eudaimonia*. The typical translation is "happiness." However, this translation is inadequate, and many scholars have suggested enhancements. Many prefer to use the translation "flourishing." However, any organic entity can flourish, such as a cactus, so the term is not an adequate synonym.

The major complaint about translating *eudaimonia* as "happiness" is that our modern view of happiness would render it subjective. No one can know if you are happy or not; you are the final arbiter. Aristotle thought *eudaimonia* applied only to humans, because it required rationality that goes beyond mere happiness. In addition, *eudaimonia* includes a strong moral component that is lacking from our modern understanding of happiness. In this sense, "happiness" would necessarily include doing the right thing, being virtuous. Others could readily judge if you were living a virtuous or "happy" life by observing your actions. For Aristotle, happiness is not a disposition, as in "he is a happy sort."

Eudaimonia is an activity. Indeed, children and other animals unable to engage self-consciously in rational and virtuous activities cannot yet be in the state translated as "happy."[15] Because it is commonplace to describe children as being "happy," this is clearly not an adequate translation. Given these translation problems, I shall use the term *eudaimonia* rather than its translations of, "happiness" or "flourishing." Essentially, *eudaimonia* can be understood best as a perfection of character nurtured by engaging in virtuous acts over a life of experience.

> Essentially, *eudaimonia* is a perfection of character nurtured by engaging in virtuous acts over a life of experience.

The most important element of *eudaimonia* is the consideration of what it takes to be a person of good character. Such a person seeks to develop excellence in himself or herself. To be excellent, what sort of person should I be? Because Aristotle recognized the essential social and political nature of humans, the answer to this question would necessarily have to include consideration of how we should live together.

Developing a Professional as a Person of Character

Consider what it takes to develop a competent and ethical healthcare professional. The process involves a course of study at an accredited university taught by persons with credentials and experience in the field. It also includes various field experiences, such as clerkships, internships, and residencies or clinical experiences with patients. Part of the education includes coming to an understanding of what behaviors are appropriate for the role, which is called *professional socialization*.

For all healthcare professions, the educational process includes a substantial dose of the healing ethic by specific instruction or by observation of role models. The most fundamental idea behind this healing ethic as a form of role formation is the healthcare professional's sublimation of his or her self-interests to the needs of the patient. This education also includes recognition of the idea that the healing ethic means first doing no harm and that whatever actions are done should provide a benefit.[16]

The Character of a Physician

The goal of professional education and socialization is to produce healthcare professionals of high character. Many professional ethics codes describe the character traits that define high character, or what could be called virtues.[17] For example, the 2001 American Medical Association statement of the principles of medical ethics notes that the principles are "standards of conduct which define the essentials of honorable behavior for the physician."[18] Essentially, the principles define the appropriate character traits or virtues for a physician.

Relative to virtue ethics, these traits or virtues combine to create not only a good physician, but also a person of good character. Like Aristotle's person of virtue, engaging in the activities of *eudaimonia* produces practical wisdom. "Moral virtue comes about as a result of habit."[19] The virtues come into being in us because "we are adapted by nature to receive them, and they are made perfect by habit."[20]

Not only is practice required, but also the moral component is indispensable. Good physicians are not merely technically competent; they are persons of good character. How do we know this? Their actions coalesce to reveal integrity. In addition, a physician or any other person of good character does not undertake to do what is right simply to appear ethical. In a modern sense, the properly socialized physician or person has internalized the ethical expectations. To do the right thing is part of his or her identity.[21]

To use Aristotle's term, physicians have become persons of practical wisdom. In describing practical wisdom, Aristotle says, "[I]t is thought to be the mark of a man of practical wisdom to be able to deliberate well about what is good and expedient for himself, not in some particular respect, e.g. about what sorts of thing conduce to health or to strength, but about what sorts of thing conduce to the good life in general."[22] The mere fact that inculcation of such character traits is so important in all healthcare professions indicates the extent to which these ancient teachings are part of the common morality, or at least the professional morality within the healthcare professions. In short, persons of virtue nurture *eudaimonia* because they believe it is the right way to live and that "[w]ith the presence of practical wisdom [they] will be given all the virtues."[23] Good physicians are living excellent lives; perfecting themselves is part of their self-identity.[24] These persons will, as a matter of course, act on the ethical principles that form the core of their identification of themselves with their role. In health care, principles function as virtues.

Principles of Biomedical Ethics as Virtues

The authors Tom Beauchamp and James Childress have popularized what they call the "principles of biomedical ethics" in a textbook that has gone through five editions from 1978 to 2001.[25] The following list provides brief definitions of these principles.

- *Autonomy* is the ability to decide for oneself. The word derives from the Greek words for "self" (*auto*) and "rule" (*nomos*). It means that people are free to make their own decisions. The failure to respect the personhood of others, making decisions for them without their consent, is *paternalism*.

- *Beneficence* is from the Latin root *bene*, meaning "to do well." More specifically, it derives from the Latin term *benefacere*, meaning "to do a kindness, provide a benefit." It is the practice of doing the good thing. Health care has clearly valued beneficence from its early Hippocratic origins. It is the second part of the dictum "First do no harm, benefit only." Professionalism requires healthcare practitioners to put patients' interests before their own. When combined with beneficence, healthcare professionals hold dear the value, norm, or virtue of *altruism*.

- *Nonmaleficence* derives from the Latin word *mal*, meaning "bad." A *malevolent* person wishes ill of someone. Thus, nonmaleficence means to *not* do wrong toward another. Clearly, this captures the first part of the Hippocratic dictum: "First do no harm . . ."

- *Justice* is a concept with a vast history and multiple interpretations. The etymology is Latin and suggests more than just fairness. The terms *just* and *justice* include elements of righteousness ("she is a just person"), equity ("she received her just due"), and lawfulness ("to bring to justice").[26] A just person is fair, lawful, reasonable, correct, and honest.[27] Most writers in ethics discuss two kinds of justice: distributive and procedural. *Distributive justice* determines the proper sharing of property and of burdens and benefits. *Procedural justice* determines the proper application of the rules in the hearing of a case.

These concepts are foundational principles of healthcare ethics.[28] A person having these virtues as part of his or her character structure, self-definition, and actions is considered a person of good character. In healthcare terms, such a person would be walking the talk of the healing ethic and would be a person of practical wisdom.

Elitism

A person who seeks to nurture *eudaimonia* through his or her actions achieves this goal after long practice of Aristotle's practical wisdom. With this practice of practical wisdom, the person has learned to live well, exemplifying what we would call a person of virtue or integrity, a good person. Such a person also sets the standard for the right action in a particular situation. Thus, virtue ethics has the problem of being elitist. Owing to his view of the hierarchical nature of reality, Aristotle thought that some people were simply not capable of maximizing their potential to reach the highest good.[29]

Aristotle noted the difficulty of encouraging many to a character of virtue, a life of nobility and goodness.[30] Aristotle believed that fear, living by emotions, and pursuing pleasures are the motivations for most people. They lack even a conception of the noble and truly pleasant, having never known it. Aristotle seemed to despair that once these bad traits have long been in place, they are impossible to remove. He concluded, "We must be content if, when all the influences by which we are thought to be good are present, we get some tincture of virtue."[31] The person of practical wisdom becomes the standard for ethical decision making. This leads to an understanding of how virtue ethics can facilitate the management of ethical conflicts.

Balancing Obligations from the Virtue Ethics Perspective

Because different principles of ethics or different virtues conflict, it is not possible to practice in the healthcare professions for long without encountering some kind of ethical dilemma. Some treatments involve harm (we are to do no harm) yet provide a benefit (benefit only). An experienced healthcare professional must be able to explain the relative benefits and risks and gain the cooperation of the patient for such treatments.

Sometimes one principle alone might create conflict. For example, physicians must know how to tell the truth to patients. Even though information can be regarded as therapy, information delivered at the wrong time or in the wrong way can be devastating. Information not delivered at the right time or never delivered at all could mean that the physician is not being honest and is guilty of paternalism. Learning how to deal with these issues effectively takes experience (practical wisdom) and theoretical knowledge.

A major component of the patient–clinician relationship is the patients' trust that their caregivers have their best interests at heart and that they are competent. If patients perceive caregivers as persons of integrity, virtue, or practical wisdom, their confidence in their caregivers will increase. That increase in patients' confidence has documented effects on enhancing the placebo effect.[32] How caregivers communicate, and even how they carry themselves, will do much to influence these perceptions.[33] The caregiver who knows how to do these things, who is an exemplar of the character traits and the virtues in the AMA's Principles of Medical Ethics, is a person of practical wisdom, at least when it comes to medical practice.

Caregivers with practical wisdom, which by necessity includes being of good character or virtuous, will be able to make appropriate decisions about the means to ends. This has significant implications for healthcare ethics. When faced with ethical challenges in medical care, such caregivers will have the practical wisdom to know how to weigh the various issues and concerns and form a conclusion. Because wise and good people can, and do, come to different conclusions about the ethically appropriate choice of action, persons of practical wisdom should consult with one another.

Healthcare organizations have sought to institutionalize this approach by using ethics committees. Those with practical wisdom in health care are far ahead of most professionals and most industries in having a decades-long tradition of ethics committees, ethics consultations, institutional review boards, and the like. These administrative mechanisms make it easier to manage disagreement. The key here is that persons of good character, pursuing virtuous ends, are much more likely to make an appropriate choice than those without such experience or such character. These choices would appear to refute one of the usual criticisms levied against virtue ethics: that there is no clear way to resolve disputes when those who have practical wisdom disagree about the correct course of action. Mechanisms such as ethics committees lead the deliberators to make a decision, even though it may not be unanimous.

Virtue ethics thus leads to the conclusion that, within health care at least, the probability is good that persons socialized to put the patient's interests first will come up with the ethically correct ranking of options. They will also respect the patient's wishes, even if they do not agree with those wishes. Of course, this depiction makes the situation sound much better than it is. Persons well trained in the healing ethic take unethical actions. Is that a fault of the education or the person? Aristotle would fault the person. In Aristotle's view, some people, by nature, are unable to control their passions, their desires, and their emotions. Others are unable to act rationally. Some are just wicked.[34] Yes, the theory results in a form of elitism. However, it seems fair to say that health care has a major advantage over many other fields in that it has a strong educational and socialization process for developing the right character. In a sense, the purpose of the educational process is to develop a cadre of elite professionals. In doing so, they should become persons of high character.

Ethical Theories and Professional Roles

Knowledge of virtue ethics offers one further advantage. Persons of practical wisdom should be better prepared to know when to use a particular ethical theory, depending on the role in which they find themselves. Again, take physicians as an example. Although physicians have a primary obligation to their patients, it is not their only role. Consider the following physician roles, none of which involves patients directly: conducting scientific studies; negotiating with vendors selling equipment and supplies; and hiring, firing, and supervising employees. In addition, physicians might be negotiating with third-party payers, lobbying on behalf of health policy issues, and conducting peer review of other physicians. They might also be involved in the management of healthcare organizations and participate on various advisory and regulatory agency boards. Many other non-patient-related tasks could be listed, such as working with community groups or serving as faculty as needed.

Some of the ethical theories work better in certain roles than others. How do physicians choose the appropriate theory? The socialization process seeks to develop caregivers who are persons seeking the highest good, at least in health care. This foundational process should develop persons of integrity and practical wisdom who can manage the inevitable ethical dilemmas and make the best ethics decisions in any role. They can apply reason to the situation and make the best possible decision within their respective role.

Natural Law

The theory of natural law owes a great debt to Aristotle. Natural law also is important to Roman Catholic theology, given its origins with St. Thomas Aquinas. Many texts on ethics and medical ethics leave out natural law or give it short shrift. Some authors consider the theory a version of moderate deontology,[35] defining deontology as simply any view that defines the right thing to do as dependent on something other than consequences. Thus, there is consequentialism and everything else. In the realm of healthcare ethics, such an approach appears overly limiting. As a tool in the ethical theory toolbox, there are a number of good reasons to know natural law theory. Even if philosophically one can reduce this theory to another, natural law is sufficiently definitive and important to consider on its own merits.[36]

One key to understanding natural law is its assumption that nature is rational and orderly. This theory goes back to the ancient Greeks, who believed that the cosmos was essentially unchanging in its order. Aristotle certainly believed this.[37] This is now a statement of physics—a statement about the nature of the world—rather than a statement about ethics.

*Natural Law's Relationship to Aristotle, St. Thomas Aquinas, and the
   Catholic Church*

Aquinas's beliefs gained prominence in the Catholic Church at the Council of Trent (1545–1563). In 1879, Pope Leo XIII declared Thomism (Aquinas's theology) to be eternally valid.[38] Nearly all writers recognize

St. Thomas Aquinas as setting the standard for natural law theory, just as Aristotle serves as the standard-bearer for virtue ethics.[39] Aquinas developed his theory in his work entitled *Summa Theologica*, meaning "the highest theology." St. Thomas structures the work in the form of a series of questions, which he answers.[40]

The Thomistic conception of *natural law* proceeds as follows: "All things subject to Divine providence are ruled and measured by the eternal law" (ST IaIIae 91, 2). "The rational creature is subject to Divine providence in the most excellent way. . . . Wherefore it has a share of the Eternal Reason, whereby it has a natural inclination to its proper act and end: and this participation of the eternal law in the rational creature is called the natural law" (ST IaIIae 91, 2). This establishes that natural law is given by God and thus authoritative over all humans. Not only can we know the law, but also as rational and moral creatures, we can violate it.

Recall Aristotle's concept of practical wisdom; Aquinas uses the same concept. In fact, he calls Aristotle "the Philosopher" and cites him as frequently as Scripture. The importance of practical reason, how it works, its similarity to Aristotle's conception of it, and the most concise statement of what the natural law compels are all found in Aquinas:

> The first principle of practical reason is one founded on the notion of good, viz. that good is that which all things seek after. Hence, this is the first precept of law, that good is to be done and pursued, and evil is to be avoided. All other precepts of the natural law are based upon this: so that whatever the practical reason naturally apprehends as man's good (or evil) belongs to the precepts of the natural law as something to be done or avoided. (ST IaIIae 94, 2)

Unfortunately, some have stopped at this quote and simply say that natural law means to "do the good and avoid the evil."[41] Because this lacks clarity about what the good might be or about any decision rule by which to decide what to do when goods conflict or when rankings are required, this statement alone does not constitute an ethical theory. It sells the theory short.[42]

Aquinas also drew on Aristotle's idea of potentiality moving to actuality and states that in the realm of what is good "all desire their own perfection" (ST Ia 5, 1). Again, following Aristotle's lead, Aquinas notes that when it comes to practical reason, the rules might be clear, but their application might not be. In short, the details make the principle more difficult to apply (ST IaIIae 94, 4).

St. Thomas then offers an excellent example that shows the difficulty at hand. Everyone would agree that in general "goods entrusted to another should be restored to their owner" (ST IaIIae 94, 4). However, he noted that "it may happen in a particular case that it would be injurious, and therefore unreasonable, to restore goods held in trust; for instance, if they are claimed for the purpose of fighting against one's country. And this principle will be found to fail the more, according as we descend further into detail" (ST IaIIae 94, 4). Taking this practical wisdom approach even further, he generalized that "the greater the number of conditions added, the greater the number of ways in which the principle may fail" (ST IaIIae 94, 4).

Aquinas even went so far as to note that, although all are governed by the natural law, all might not know it or act upon it: "In some the reason is perverted by passion, or evil habit, or an evil disposition of nature" (ST IaIIae 94, 4).[43] So what are we to do? In seeking a principle to determine what is good and what is bad, it is not difficult to find specific behaviors listed in Aquinas. However, an excellent philosophical overview of natural law by Michael Murphy concluded that there are no obvious master principles, but only examples of flawed acts.[44] The *Catholic Encyclopedia* suggests a number of things that would be wrong or right under the dictum to always do good and avoid harm, but nothing about how to resolve conflicts among these requirements.[45] This seems to add a quandary. All decisions are specific and the details will change, so do we have any decision rules?

At this point, scholars disagree on exactly how Aquinas resolves the quandary, and we do not need to follow them in those debates. However, there is still a need for a decision principle when there are disputes regarding which of various actions to take. There are two such principles, and the one most closely associated with natural law theory is that of the double effect.

Principle of Double Effect

The first principle that proposes to distinguish between a good and an evil is the *theory of double effect*. Derived from *Summa Theologica*, the principle has four key points:

- That we do not wish the evil effects, but make all reasonable efforts to avoid them;
- That the immediate effect be good in itself;
- That the evil is not made a means to obtain the good effect; for this would be to do evil that good might come of it—a procedure never allowed; the end cannot justify the means;
- That the good effect be as important at least as the evil effect.[46]

The theory of double effect has use in applied ethics, such as medical ethics, when dealing with abortion, euthanasia, and other decisions where there is a conflict between a good and an evil. For example, under this view, abortion is an evil, but saving the life of a mother is a good. Under this view euthanasia is an evil, but relieving pain by use of morphine is a good. If the person dies, and the death was not intended, then is it acceptable? Major issues arise in the application of the theory concerning how to determine a person's intent. We know that not everyone is a person of practical wisdom who only has a good intent. However, how would we know the intent in a particular case?[47]

At the policy-making level, is it acceptable to cut taxes for the rich at the expense of the poor? What good comes of it? Because there are few rich and many poor, does the good of the rich count more than the good lost by the poor? Note that the further we delve into these types of questions, the more important consequences seem to become, until natural law becomes a form of consequentialism, perhaps rule consequentialism.[48] It is not necessary to resolve these disputes here, because the purpose is to understand the theories for the purposes of making appropriate decisions in health care. Relative to that end, a second decision rule for natural law is available.

Entitlement to Maximize Your Potential

The key to understanding this proposed decision rule relates to metaphysics: "Ethics especially is impossible without metaphysics, since it is according to the metaphysical view we take of the world that ethics shapes itself."[49] The Thomistic ethic draws heavily on the Aristotelian metaphysics that describes the world as a hierarchy of being, with all entities in it striving to reach their own complete state of actualization of their potential. This means that it is a part of the natural order for all entities to strive to maximize their potential. To deny something its ability to actualize its potential is to violate its very nature. Such a violation causes harm to the entity and would be a violation of its nature and of the natural law to avoid harm. Thus, natural law proscribes any activities that would violate an entity's potential.[50] Concerns about termination of potential, at least for rational creatures, are evident in several contemporary healthcare issues.

Many religions and social activists place a considerable emphasis on social and political factors that prevent humans from actualizing their potential. These groups often are at the forefront of social justice movements addressing poverty, ignorance, unhealthy living conditions, and slavelike working conditions. Clearly, healthcare professionals need to understand natural law theory when working with patients who believe in its tenets and with those who advocate social justice. This might include those who are working to improve public health, social conditions, or human rights. Now let us look at another common ethical theory, deontology.

Deontology

The derivation of *deontology* comes from the Greek word *deon*, which means "duty." Thus, deontology is concerned with behaving ethically by meeting our duties. The ethical theory of deontology originates with the German philosopher Immanuel Kant (1724–1804).[51] Although Kant's influence on deontology is significant, many other thinkers are part of the deontological tradition as well.[52] Nonetheless, just as we relied on Aristotle for virtue ethics and on Aquinas for natural law, Kant sets the standard for deontology. Following the review of Kant, we shall examine some of the more contemporary advocates of deontological theories.

Kant's Metaphysics and Epistemology Ground His Ethics

Kant is most well known for his work in metaphysics and epistemology, the *Critique of Pure Reason*,[53] but he also did groundbreaking work in ethics. Kant's writings on ethics appear in several different volumes, with titles such as *Groundwork of the Metaphysics of Morals*[54] and *Critique of Practical Reason*,[55] among others.

The concept of honoring commitments clearly did not start with Kant, but his approach to the issue led to the identification of his ethical theory with deontology. Kant's work in metaphysics and epistemology had a significant influence on this approach and his ethical views. As seen with Aristotle and Aquinas, a complete understanding of ethics often includes a view about the nature of the world and how we know it, in other words, the disciplines of metaphysics and epistemology. In what Kant called a "Copernican revolution for philosophy," he concluded that the belief that perception represented the world was incorrect, or at least incomplete. Instead, the structure of consciousness processes sense data through the means of categories of thought and two forms of intuition: space and time.

Of these categories of thought, the one that relates most directly to ethics is causality. All experiences are subject to causation, which in Kant's view undermines free will. In the Newtonian world of his time, it was widely believed that if you could completely know the behavior of all the matter in existence, you could predict the future behavior of anything material. This did not pose a problem for most people at this time owing to the earlier dividing of mind and matter by Rene Descartes (1595–1650). Like most people, Kant finds free will to be essential for ethics. If a person's every act is determined, how can he or she be held responsible for his or her choices?

At the same time, Kant's reasoning inexorably leads him to conclude that we cannot know what the world is like in and of itself. It is beyond knowing, because we cannot experience anything without use of the categories and forms of intuition. He thus divided the realm of being into the *phenomenal world* of experience and the *noumenal world*. We can think about the noumenal world, but we cannot directly experience it. Thus, we have "an unavoidable ignorance of things in themselves and all that we can theoretically *know* are mere appearances" (B xxix).[56] Relative to ethics, it should be clear from Kant's perspective that the metaphysical issue of whether free will is possible is foundational.[57]

Kant argued that knowledge of the sensible world was insufficient for knowing the moral law.[58] Yet Kant argued that free will makes ethics possible. Free will is the precondition of ethics. If all things are determined by natural causes—causality is one of Kant's categories by which we are conscious of the phenomenal world—then our supposed ethical choices are specious, an illusion. Humans, as a natural phenomenon, are determined by natural laws; causality applies to all natural phenomena. However, the self, in and of itself (the soul), is free from those laws.[59]

Kant recognized that this puts morality beyond the pale of empirical science, and indeed the question about free will is beyond such testing. However, Kant believed that he left a crack in the door that is wide enough to allow for morality. He does this by arguing that the concept of freedom, although not knowable in a scientific way, is something we can think about without contradiction: "Morality does not, indeed, require that freedom should be understood, but only that it should not contradict itself, and so should at least allow of being thought" (B xxix).[60] In this sense, Kant redefines humans as partaking in two kinds of reality: the phenomenal and the noumenal. According to Kant, "There is no contradiction in supposing that one and the same will is, in the appearance, that is, in its visible acts, necessarily subject to the law of nature, and so far *not free*, while yet, as belonging to a thing in itself, is not subject to that law, and is therefore *free*" (B xxviii).[61]

Freedom of the Will

Like Aristotle and Aquinas, Kant certainly thought good character was laudable. However, he was concerned that the properties that constitute good character, without a good will to correct them, could lead to bad outcomes.

For example, we can misuse courage and perseverance without the direction of good will.[62] Kant would go so far as to argue that one should act on the duty of obligation to the moral law regardless of any relationship that might have an outcome such as *eudaimonia*: "A good will is good not because of what it performs or effects, not by its aptness for the attainment of some proposed end, but simply by virtue of its volition, that is, it is good in and of itself" (AK 4:394).[63] In other words, a good will is good because it wills properly. Thus, Kant set a high standard. Some of his language even suggests that the true test of a good will is if the person continues to act out of duty and reverence for the moral law even when it has no personal benefit and might "involve many a disappointment to the ends of inclination" (AK 4:396).[64]

Reason, Autonomy, the Moral Law, and the Will

Kant is distinctive relative to his predecessors in seeking to ground our duties in a self-governing will. This is an appeal to reason itself being autonomous, meaning that we are free to choose, and that if we choose according to reason, we shall conform to the moral law: "If reason completely determined the will, the action would without exception take place according to the rule" (AK 5:20).[65] One can see the extremely prominent principle of autonomy coming into play here.

Typically, an autonomous agent is one who makes his or her own rules and is responsible for his or her actions.[66] To violate that autonomy is to violate a person's innermost selfhood, something Kant develops as one form of the categorical imperative (taken up below). Thus, one does not seek the foundation of ethics in the development of a person of good character seeking to actualize his or her intrinsic nature, seeking the end of *eudaimonia*. Instead, the subject matter of ethics is not character, but rather the nature and the content of the principles that determine a rational will. Free will is determined by moral principles that cohere with the categorical imperative. This abstruse approach, for many, simply disconnects the moral law and free will from real life.

The idea of autonomy here is not the view that individuals make their own laws. It means that the laws that bind you in some sense derive from your own making, your own fundamental nature as a self.[67] For Kant, the will is free in the sense that you choose to be bound by those principles of reason. This capacity to make such a choice is what makes humans members of what he called the "kingdom of ends." The person has chosen freely to bind himself or herself to the constraints of the categorical imperative and the dictates of reason.

The requirement of the duty to obey the moral law to express a good will brings the notion of intent into the discussion. Why a person acts in such a way as to conform to the moral law is an important component of ethical evaluation in the Kantian scheme. Let us turn to what Kant thought would count as rational principles that would ground ethics or the moral law.

Kant attempted to discover the rational principle that would ground all other ethical judgments. He called this principle the categorical imperative. The *categorical imperative* is not so much a rule as a criterion for determination of what ethical principles meet the test of reason.[68] The imperative would have to be categorical rather than hypothetical, or conditional, because true morality should not depend on individual likes and dislikes or on abilities and opportunities. These are historical "accidents." Any ultimate principle of ethics must transcend them in order to meet the conditions of fairness. We shall later see how Rawls used similar ideas in developing his concept of a veil of ignorance. Kant developed several formulations of the categorical imperative. The most commonly presented ones follow.[69]

- "Always act in such a way that you can also will that the maxim of your action should become a universal law" (AK 4:421).[70] This principle often is caricatured as the Golden Rule: Do unto others as you would have them do unto you.[71] This does not capture the full meaning of what Kant had in mind, and may indeed miss the essence of his teachings, as he specifically disavowed that this was his intended meaning (AK 4:430).[72]

- "Act so that you treat humanity, both in your own person and in that of another, always as an end and never merely as a means" (AK 4:429).[73] Kant spoke of the good society as a place that was a kingdom of ends (AK 4:433–434).[74]

The Categorical Imperative as a Formal Decision Criterion

Although Kant believed that these two statements of the categorical imperative were formally equivalent, the first illustrates the need to apply moral principles universally. That a principle be logically consistent was important to Kant. This principle of universal application is also what allowed ethical egoism to be dismissed as something humans do when making decisions, but not as something that is an ethical theory. The second formulation points to making the radical distinction between things and persons and emphasizes the necessity of respect for persons.

Kant's theory evaluates morality by examining the nature of actions and the will of agents rather than goals achieved. You have done the right thing when you act out of your obligation to the moral law, not simply because you act in accordance with it. Note the fundamental importance of intent as compared with any concern with outcomes. One reason for the emphasis on duties in Kant's deontology is that we are praised or blamed for actions within our control, and that includes our willing, not our achieving. In terms of the common morality, most people think that there is something wrong with saying that people are good when they do not have a good will and their good outcomes were merely happenstance. Kant did care about the outcomes of our actions, but he thought that, as far as the moral evaluation of actions was concerned, consequences did not matter. As Kant pointed out, this total removal of consequences "is strange enough and has no parallel in the remainder of practical knowledge" (AK 5:31).[75] Let us now look at the second version of the categorical imperative, which is foundational in healthcare ethics.

The Categorical Imperative as Respect for Persons

The second version of the categorical imperative emphasizes respect for persons. According to Kant, you should "[s]o act as to treat humanity, whither in thine own person or in that of any other, in every case as an end withal, never as means only" (AK 4:429).[76] People, unlike things, ought never to be merely used. Their value is never a means to our ends; they are ends in themselves. Of course, a person might be useful as a means, but you must always treat that person with respect. Kant holds this view because of his belief that people are rational and that this bestows them with absolute worth: our "rational nature exists as an end in itself" (AK 4:428).[77] This makes people unique in the natural world. In this sense, it is our duty to give every person consideration, respect, and dignity. Individual human rights are acknowledged and inviolable in a deontological system. The major emphasis on autonomy in health care springs from these considerations and others like them. Although most people who defend autonomy and treating people as ends and not merely as means do not use these formalistic Kantian reasons, this principle of autonomy is foundational in healthcare ethics. It is part of health care's common morality.

The Categorical Imperative and the Golden Rule

According to the categorical imperative, if the maxim or the rule governing an action is not capable of being a universal law, then it is unacceptable. Note that universalizability is not the same as universality. Kant's point is not that we would all agree on some rule. Instead, we must logically be able to accept that it could be universal. This is why the concept seems very much like the Golden Rule: Do unto others as you would have them do unto you.[78] If you cannot will that everyone should follow the same rule, your rule is not a moral one. As indicated earlier, many think Kant's first formulation of the categorical imperative implies or even is a restatement of the Golden Rule. However, Kant specifically repudiates the Golden Rule interpretation (AK 4:430, note 13).[79]

Kant saw the justification for the Golden Rule in terms of consequences and fairness. If it is fair for me to do something, then it should be fair for everyone. Alternatively, in consequential terms, we typically hear officials, merchants, managers, and parents, when they are considering exceptions to policy, say that "If I do X for you I have to do X for everyone." If one made exceptions for each individual, then the consequences would be bad and unfair.

Kant wanted to get beyond such issues. He wanted to know whether a person performed an act out of duty to moral law and thus expressed a good will. He stipulated that the moral agent acting solely out of a good will should ignore empirical considerations such as consequences, fairness, inclinations, and preferences. For Kant, an act carried out from an inclination, no matter how noble, is not an act of morality (AK 4:398). Indeed, he went so far as to say that the less we benefit from acting on the moral law, the more sublime and dignified it is (AK 4:425).[81]

Acts take on moral worth if the person acts solely from duty to the moral law, absent any emotional inclinations or tangible benefits. This sets up the very difficult standard that we can only know if persons are morally worthy or obeying the moral law when there is nothing in it for them. Their actions would be opposed to their desires, inclinations, even their self-interest. Taking such an extreme position essentially disconnects Kant from the real world in which people live and make ethical judgments.

Virtue Ethics and Kant's Moral Law

Although likely controversial, it seems, for purposes of healthcare ethics, that the best way to make sense of Kant is to conceive of the person of good will in a manner akin to Aristotle's virtue ethics. Thus, to make Kantian deontology useful, you could say that a person of good will also is a person of practical wisdom as described by Aristotle. Does this inclusion of Aristotle reject Kant's work? No, but a critical analysis and comparison to virtue ethics is warranted.

Although Kant's theory suffers from disconnection from any normal motivational structure in human life, it still has applications in healthcare ethics.[82] The deontological theory emphasizes the attention to duty found in all codes of ethics in health care. Kant put into sharp relief the ethical idea that it is wrong for people to claim they can follow a principle or maxim that suits their interests but would not want others to do the same. Most important for health care is the recognition of human dignity and autonomy. To use people solely as means to an end, whether as teaching material in medical schools, prisoners in research experiments, or slaves, is fundamentally a violation of all being.

Deontology poses two problems that lead many to reject it. First, the statement of categorical imperatives, maxims, duties, rules, or commandments yields only absolutes. Kant really has only one absolute. His absolute is that you must act solely on the basis of a good will: a reverence for, and an obligation to, the moral law formalized by the categorical imperative. However, the lack of prescriptive content leaves many unsatisfied. Actions either pass or fail, with no allowance for a "gray area." Virtue ethics handles the gray areas by depending on the wisdom of the person of practical wisdom. This is one reason why as an ethical tool virtue ethics enables us to handle the problems of healthcare ethics more robustly.

The inability to make distinctions between lesser evils or greater goods is the other problem. Moral dilemmas are created when duties come into conflict and there is no mechanism for resolving them. Kant, with his very limited description of only one ethical duty—to obey the moral law—can claim to escape this problem within his philosophy. He used the radical view that such decisions are outside the bounds of morality if based on inclinations or consequences. Defining the real world of ethics in this radical way does not help much when faced with decisions that involve your inclinations and the weighing of consequences. Even if you have, as Kant seemed to think, only one duty, it is a formal one, and its various manifestations could conflict.

Virtue ethics and the natural law theory face this problem of conflicting duties as well. For example, whereas abortion is clearly wrong under the natural law theory, the outcomes of unwanted children, starving children, child abuse, overcrowding, malnutrition, and so on also have a moral bearing. Duties often conflict in healthcare situations. For example, if I tell the truth in some situation, it may lead to someone getting hurt, whereas a lie could have prevented it. My duty is both not to lie and not to do things that lead others to harm. No matter what I do, I violate a duty. Pure deontology theory does not allow for a theoretically satisfying means of ranking conflicting duties. However, most duty-driven people are not going to be so literal with the Kantian version of deontology that they find themselves unable to rank conflicting duties. Virtue ethics offers the guidance of a person of practical wisdom using the available tools of considered judgments, common morality, ethical theories, and ethical principles to resolve the difficulty and move on.

Of the theories presented so far, virtue ethics offers a much more useful and helpful approach in achieving ethical processes and ethical outcomes in the realm of health care. Virtue ethics is more interested in the development of ethical persons than in the development of maxims and imperatives. The normal understanding of the Golden Rule works perfectly well in ethical decision making within the framework of virtue ethics, even if Kant himself disavowed it.

The policy implications for deontology are significant because of the emphasis on duty and the training of most healthcare professionals in the duties incumbent upon them. The emphasis on duty leads most clinicians to consider themselves deontologists. However, most would balk at the pure Kantian version of duty and would more readily assent to the duties experienced by a person of practical wisdom, following the virtue ethics tradition. Duty-driven clinical staff can walk into a meeting and know in advance what the right thing to do is: to maximize the benefit to their patients. This is their duty, and their professional code of ethics codifies this duty. If they had to rank their duties, they would be patient first, their profession second, other clinical professionals third, with maybe their employing organization a distant fourth.

Having such a clear sense of their duties and having only a few duties on the list makes it very easy for clinicians to talk about their obligations to patient care. In contrast, healthcare managers and officials who make policy have a much more difficult ethical chore. They must balance competing claims among many groups. Their loyalty is not simply to one group, such as patients. For healthcare managers, even if their loyalty is only to patients, that loyalty is in the aggregate. Managers represent the organization, whereas clinicians represent the individual patients. The ethical obligations of managers are much more complex; if the organization fails, the clinicians will not be able to help the patients. Let us now look at two deontologists whose theories have more practical bearing on the issues involved today in deciding about healthcare policy. Such concerns are important owing to the need to allocate burdens and benefits such as access to health care that is of high quality and that is not delivered in a way that denies us other social goods because of its high costs.

Non-Kantian Versions of Deontology: John Rawls and Robert Nozick

This section takes up two influential and relatively recent theorists from the deontological tradition. Rawls and Nozick have different ideas of what is right and argue that by following their principles of what is right, a more just society will result. Of course, as philosophers do, they disagree over not only what is right, but also what is just. These two thinkers have influenced the debate on the provision of health care in our nation, including the recent healthcare reforms.

John Rawls (1921–2002)

John Rawls's *A Theory of Justice*, published in 1971, is considered a seminal text. Knowledge of his ideas is part of the common morality of most policy makers, even if many expressly reject those ideas. The basic idea behind Rawls's theory of justice is "justice as fairness."[83] Rawls limits his plan to a theory of justice that would apply to a society where the rule of law is respected.[84] People in such a society will differ on their goals and on their views of what counts as just. Yet, they recognize agreed-upon methods to arbitrate disputes so that they are capable of continued functioning within the society. In other words, a disappointment or a disagreement does not lead to violence or to call for rebellion. Rawls identifies himself as being in the tradition of social contract theorists and as a deontologist, even a Kantian. Rawls says that his theory is essentially deontological because it is not consequentialist.[85]

The idea of a social contract as the origin of society goes back to Thomas Hobbes (1588–1679), John Locke (1632–1704), David Hume (1711–1776), and Jean Jacques Rousseau (1712–1778). All of these thinkers conceived of the beginnings of civil society as a compact or contract made among consenting adults to give up certain things in order to achieve others, such as order, harmony, trade, security, and protection. They agreed in establishing the idea of a hypothetical situation that could be altered by persons acting to obtain some rights and privileges in exchange for others without the use of coercion. Rawls used a similar hypothetical situation and called it the original position, in which rational people are behind a veil of ignorance relative to their personal circumstances. The decisions about the principles of a just society that they select when they know nothing about their circumstances are what Rawls says are the principles of a just society.

Rawls emphasized that people seek to protect and maximize their self-interest. He argued that fundamental to that goal is liberty. He further argued—his most controversial point—that to have a just society requires an infrastructure and a system of rights that protect the minority and those who have fared less well in life's lottery than others. The key to his theory is the situation in which the bargaining about the nature of society takes place and what those who are bargaining know about their society and themselves. Rawls called this the original position.

The Original Position and the Veil of Ignorance In explaining the original position, Rawls takes as rational the ethical egoist's position that everyone would want to maximize his or her personal self-interest. However, while negotiating the most just society for yourself, you are asked to voluntarily draw a veil of ignorance over yourself. This veil of ignorance is, from a personal perspective, absolute. You know nothing about yourself at all. You do not know your station in life, your preferences, your motivational structure, your willingness to take risk, your age, your health, your socioeconomics, your intelligence, your demographics—nothing.[86] In one fell swoop you have lost all the reasons for protecting your particular advantages or for hedging your bets to protect you from your disadvantages. You know you want to be in the best possible circumstances when the veil of ignorance is lifted and you leave the original position.[87] Not knowing exactly what to protect, we are then inexorably forced to the kind of considerations that are common in medical ethics when treating patients for whom we lack information of any useful sort.

It is not unusual in healthcare settings to have patients who are in need of treatment but are completely unable to communicate their wishes to us. We know nothing of their family, their station in life, and so forth. Often, we cannot find anyone to speak for them, and they cannot speak for themselves. We have no clues what they would have wanted. Normal notions of informed consent, durable power of attorney, and substituted judgment fall away as tools for us. We are forced back onto the idea of deciding what to do for such persons based on the idea of what the rational person would want in such circumstances, or what is sometimes called the best interests standard.[88] We could say that persons with such a complete inability to speak for their own interests as individuals are in the original position. In this situation, this original position, we are all truly equal, because we know nothing of our circumstances.[89]

Now, although we are behind this veil of ignorance relative to our personal circumstances, we nonetheless have a considerable amount of knowledge about other things. Rawls allows those who are behind the veil of ignorance to know general laws pertaining to political affairs and economic theory and to know something of human psychology.[90] Indeed, he allows that the parties will "possess all general information"[91]—just no information about their own particulars. Thus, they have no way of calculating the probability that they will wind up in a certain position as a result of their choices. Only by such extreme means does he believe one can ensure the fairness of the result. It is a hypothetical thought experiment that, he argues, guarantees that whatever principles are chosen are just.

In his view, everyone should get an equal share of the burdens and benefits unless there is a material reason to discriminate. If our job is to come up with a set of principles that will decide what those material reasons are, then we should carry out our job with the least bias. If we go back to the ideal of justice as blind, we see that the blindfold has become a veil of ignorance. Rawls does not at all advocate that we would seek an equalitarian outcome. He assumes we are persons who want to maximize our self-interest, but he does not assume concepts such as benevolence or even nonmaleficence.[92] Once we determine the principles of a just society, then we can use them to develop material reasons to discriminate in the distribution of burdens and benefits.

Two Basic Principles of Justice The first principle of justice meets with little objection, but the second inspires considerable debate. Rawls orders these principles serially in that liberties in the first principle cannot be rationally traded for favorable inequalities described in the second principle.[93] The prioritizing of liberty above other principles of justice is one of the reasons Rawls distinguished himself from consequentialists. Their perspective, according to Rawls, is that there is only one principle: the greatest good for the greatest number.[94]

Rawls described the first principle of justice as follows: "[E]ach person is to have an equal right to the most extensive basic liberty compatible with a similar liberty for others."[95] This type of right is similar to the liberties protected in the U.S. Bill of Rights and can be called a process right. He described these rights as follows:[96]

- Political liberty (the right to vote and to be eligible for public office)
- Freedom from arbitrary arrest and seizure (which goes back to *habeas corpus*)
- Freedom of the person along with the right to hold (personal) property
- Freedom of speech and assembly
- Liberty of conscience and freedom of thought.

Rawls took a controversial position relative to the distribution of inequalities of office, income, wealth, and of goods. He called this the "difference" principle.[97] In this second principle of justice, social and economic inequalities are appropriate if they are arranged so that the inequalities actually help out the least fortunate persons in society. In addition, the inequalities should be connected to positions, offices, or jobs in society that everyone has an equal opportunity to attain.[98] The inequalities that Rawls sees as permissible are (1) inequalities in the distribution of income and wealth and (2) inequalities set up by institutions that use differences in authority and responsibility or chains of command. Rawls also said that society cannot justify a decrease in liberty by an increase in social and economic advantages. In this sense, liberty is the most important of the principles.

A classic example of how Rawls's principles might apply relates to physicians. Physicians often command superior incomes and social status, which are clearly inequalities. This circumstance requires an explanation. Once everybody is out of the original position and back in the real world, the hope is that anybody can become a doctor if he or she has the talent.[99] Suppose a person decided that he or she wanted to become a physician. However, obtaining the education needed to actually become a physician requires an inequality: less fortunate people help pay for this education with their taxes. In the just society envisioned by Rawls, the person desiring the education would have to compensate the less fortunate in some way once he or she became a physician. The physician is free to keep the wealth, or at least some of it. But, because gains in wealth are allowed only if they benefit the least advantaged along the way, the physician would never escape an obligation to help the less fortunate.

Some Concerns with Rawls's Theory According to the difference principle, inequalities may be justified, but only if they are to the advantage of the least well off. Rawls considers it "common sense" that all parties should be happy with such a principle.[100] Rawls also states that "the combination of mutual disinterest and the veil of ignorance achieves the same purpose as benevolence."[101] However, it is not difficult to imagine that many would voice concerns over forced beneficence and the government mechanisms and taxing schemes that would be needed to identify what counts as a natural gift or talent and is therefore unearned. Consider the relatively bitter discussion about reparations to the descendants of slaves.[102] Recall the still active debates over affirmative action or over how to treat illegal immigrants or their American-citizen children. Many if not most of the wealthy would also be unlikely to assent to the thought experiment of putting on a veil of ignorance because they would not accept the forced benevolence that the difference principle imposes. Simply put, many are less interested in justice than in keeping their advantages for themselves and their children. Thus, Rawls's position, although just, runs into human nature.

Some might argue that because Rawls is running up against human nature his theory should be dismissed. Rawls addressed such arguments. He was perfectly aware of the imperfections of the real world outside the veil of ignorance; that is why he invented the thought experiment. The fact that the distribution of burdens and benefits by nature is unequal is not an excuse. "Occasionally this reflection is offered as an excuse for ignoring injustice, as if the refusal to acquiesce in injustice is on a par with being unable to accept death."[103]

Rawls believed that "the natural distribution is neither just nor unjust."[104] As Rawls stated it, "[T]hese are simply natural facts. What is just and unjust is the way that institutions deal with these facts."[105] Thus, it is up to us to decide the principles of a just society and to take steps to create that society.

Rawls concedes that one might affirm his contract approach but eschew the difference principle, or vice versa.[106] To understand Rawls's theory and its application, we need to examine his most famous opponent: Robert Nozick, the philosophical defender of libertarianism. Nozick neither accepts the contract approach of the original position nor the difference principle.

Robert Nozick (1938–2002) and Libertarianism

Robert Nozick and John Rawls both worked in the Harvard Philosophy Department at the same time, but their philosophies disagreed considerably. However, both authors described themselves as coming from the deontological tradition relative to ethical theory in that they rejected consequentialism. Nozick's first and most famous book, *Anarchy, State, and Utopia* (1974), was an attack on Rawls's work that focused on the extensive state envisioned as necessary to bring about Rawls's ends.[107]

In the healthcare field, Nozick's work in political theory would have great significance in providing theoretical underpinnings to the side of the debate that argued that there are no positive rights to health care, nor should there be any.[108] On the other side, Rawls's difference principle can be used to argue for health care as a component of the primary social goods.[109] Thus, Rawls and his followers represent the liberal tradition that government should step in to help people disadvantaged in life's lottery. Nozick and his followers represent the conservative tradition that if you want something you should obtain it yourself.

Like Rawls, Nozick claimed roots in Immanuel Kant. However, Nozick focused on the second formulation of the categorical imperative. You may recall that Kant said "So act as to treat humanity, whither in thine own person or in that of any other, in every case as an end withal, never as means only" (AK 4:429).[110] Nozick drew on this formulation, earlier described as the emphasis on autonomy. In the very first sentence of the book he stated his approach clearly: "Individuals have rights, and there are things no person or group may do to them (without violating their rights)."[111] He said that this imperative put a constraint upon how others may be used. He stated that this version of autonomy can "express the inviolability of others."[112]

Nozick argued that Kant, in his categorical imperative, did not simply say we should *minimize* the use of humanity as a means. Rather, he said we should treat others as ends in every case, never as means only.[113] The word "only" leaves the meaning of this statement open to alternate interpretations that would suggest that minimization is all anyone could really mean in the actual world. People obviously are means to ends. If people are means to ends, then how is it possible to treat them only as ends?

Nozick also said that if we take his view of Kant and the inviolability of persons seriously, then we misspeak when we say that someone must make a sacrifice for the social good. He argued that there is no social entity to whom we can make a sacrifice; there are only other persons. Social entities are simply abstractions. "Using one of these people for the benefit of others uses him and benefits others. Nothing more. . . Talk of an overall social good covers this up."[114] To use a person in this way is to fail to respect him or her as a separate person: "No one is entitled to force this [sacrifice] upon him—least of all a state or government."[115]

Nozick also objects to Rawls's difference principle. He opposed the forced redistribution of benefits and burdens so that the less fortunate are made better off as the price for the more fortunate being more fortunate: "Holdings to which people are entitled may not be seized, even to provide equality of opportunity for others. In the absence of magic wands, the remaining means towards equality of opportunity is convincing persons each to choose to devote some of their holdings to achieving it."[116] Simply put, if you do not like what you have, take steps to get more. If you want people to help others, convince them to do it. Is this justice? Is it distributive justice? Are we really being just if we tell people who are severely disadvantaged and who have little capacity for work to simply choose to improve themselves?

Rawls would hold that such outcomes are arbitrary—not just—in that they are based on the natural lottery, over which we have no control. The veil of ignorance is intended to get us to think about the principles of justice that would follow if we did not know our personal circumstances. For Rawls, what is just is what persons in that original position would choose.[117] The principles that result are the distributive justice principles of a just society. Nozick claimed that theories like Rawls's could be defeated by voluntary agreements. Indeed, he opposed the use of the term "distributive justice" because it implied a central distribution authority. This is not the reality of free adults, so he preferred the term "holdings" and talked of how they are acquired and transferred.[118] Nonetheless, he was unable to escape completely from the long tradition of the term "distributive justice" and continued to use the term. He specified three conditions that meet the requirements of distributive justice:[119]

1. "A person who acquires a holding in accordance with the principle of justice in acquisition is entitled to that holding."[120]
2. If a person is entitled to the holding and transfers the holding, the person to whom it was transferred is now entitled to it.
3. No one is entitled to anything except by gaining a holding from a previously unheld state (principle 1) or obtaining it from such a person by voluntary transfer.

A very interesting outcome of Nozick's reliance on these three principles is that it is unnecessary to argue that anyone deserves the outcome that results.[121] Nozick thus rejects the basic idea of distributive justice; the principle is that everyone should get an equal share unless there is a material reason to discriminate. He complained that any reason to discriminate resulted in an inappropriate end state or patterned outcome.[122] What was appropriate was the three principles that he enunciated relative to historical entitlement and then subsequent transfers of holdings.

Most puzzling, at the very end of his chapter on distributive justice, Nozick did take up what to do to rectify the problems of historical injustices. Justice only prevails in following the three principles noted earlier that described proper acquisition and transfer. If these are followed, there is no injustice in the resultant outcomes, whatever they are. "If, however, these principles are violated, the principle of rectification comes into play."[123] He then allowed that a specified (he uses the term "patterned") outcome might be appropriate to rectify the past injustice. Nozick provided the following view of how this could be done: "A *rough* rule of thumb for rectifying injustices might seem to be the following: organize society so as to maximize the position of whatever groups end up least well-off in the society."[124]

This remarkable statement by the champion of libertarians sounded very like the difference principle.[125] However, it left out Rawls's idea that the better off can be better off, but only if the less well off benefit as well. In Nozick's formulation, it seems we have moved back to equalitarianism, because our only interest, when tasked to correct injustice, is maximizing the position of the least well off. The only possible outcome of this logic must be a leveling or raising of everyone to the average.

Because what happened historically is what counts as justice, it would be hard to find a significant case in which the original holdings were justly gained. For example, when Thomas Jefferson made the Louisiana Purchase it was certainly a great surprise to the Native Americans who had been living there for thousands of years that they had no ownership rights in their land. This loss of ownership rights ended up being true for them no matter how much labor they had mixed in with the land.[126]

As a libertarian, Nozick's principles resonate loudly with those who emphasize the free market and a meritocracy. Typically, these will be the same people who resist calls for allocation of resources to healthcare needs, especially if this is done by taxation. The extent to which these libertarian views are part of the common morality has a great influence on healthcare policy.

At this point we have examined all but one of the major ethical theories. Let us now examine the ethical theory that describes how most managers work: consequentialism.[127]

Consequentialism

Consequentialist moral theories evaluate the morality of actions in terms of progress toward a goal or end. The consequences of the action are what matter, not their intent. This is in contrast to previously noted theories (e.g., deontology, virtue ethics, and natural law) that take intent into account. Consequentialism is sometimes called *teleology*, using the Greek term *telos*, which refers to "ends." Thus, one finds that the goal of consequentialism is often stated as the greatest good for the greatest number. Consequentialism has several versions, the best known of which is utilitarianism. *Utilitarianism* defines morality in terms of the maximization of the net utility expected for all parties affected by a decision or action. For the purposes of discussion, *consequentialism* and *utilitarianism* are used here as synonyms.

For the consequentialist, the person's intentions are irrelevant to the ethical evaluation of whether the deed is right or wrong. Outcomes are all that matter. The consequentialist will agree that intentions do matter, but only to the evaluation of a person's character, not the evaluation of the morality of his or her acts. In natural law, virtue ethics, and deontology, part of the ethical assessment concerns the person's intention. The consequentialist would say that intention simply confuses two issues: (1) whether the act itself is leading to good or bad outcomes and (2) whether the person carrying out the act should be praised for it or not. Consequentialists consider the second issue to be independent of moral consideration relative to the act. It is relevant only to the evaluation of the person's moral character. Of course, to leave out intentions completely seems to violate a deep sense of our understanding about what it means to be ethical. Most people find something wrong with saying an act is ethical if it happened by accident.

Types of Consequentialism

The two major types of consequentialism are as follows:[128]

- *Classical utilitarianism (or act consequentialism).* Each act is considered based on its net benefit. This version of utilitarianism has received the most criticism and is not supported by modern ethicists. Nonetheless, it makes a convenient target for those who dislike consequentialism. For example, determining the consequences of something is often an exceedingly data-intensive undertaking, and the data may be lacking. The facts regarding the consequences are also themselves in debate. Imagine the difficulty if such an approach must be followed for each decision anew.
- *Rule consequentialism.* The decision maker develops rules that will have the greatest net benefit.[129] The development of rules to guide conduct is clearly similar to the actions of managers who develop policies. This rule version of consequentialism includes two subspecies: negative consequentialism and preference consequentialism.

In organizational healthcare settings, policy making is an important component of the work, and consequentialism is often used as a basis for decision making. For example, one could readily construe that the construction of a diversity policy is justified by rule consequentialism, as could policies to further informed consent. Lawmakers and administrators who set health policies at the national level also use consequential arguments to justify decisions, such as requirements to provide indigent care or emergency services. We first look more deeply at act or classical utilitarianism and later consider rule utilitarianism.

Classical Utilitarianism

Classical utilitarians spoke of maximization of pleasure or happiness. Classical utilitarianism is most often associated with the British philosopher John Stuart Mill (1806–1873). He developed the theory from a pleasure-maximizing version put forward by his mentor Jeremy Bentham (1748–1832). As clearly stated by Mill, the basic principle of utilitarianism is that actions are right to the degree that they tend to promote the greatest good for the greatest number.[130]

Of course, it is unclear what constitutes "the greatest good." For Bentham, it was simply the tendency to augment or diminish happiness or pleasure.

Bentham, being a hedonist in theory, did not try to make distinctions about whether one form of pleasure or happiness was better than another form.

For Mill, however, not all pleasures were equally worthy. He defined "the good" in terms of well-being and distinguished not just quantitatively, but also qualitatively, between various forms of pleasure.[131] Mill is closer to the virtue theory idea of *eudaimonia* as a goal in that he specifies qualitative distinctions rather than simply adding up units of happiness or pleasure.[132] Indeed, Mill said that one is duty bound to perform some acts, even if they do not maximize utility.[133]

A defining characteristic of any type of consequentialism is that the evaluation of whether an outcome is good or bad should be, in some sense, measurable, or that the outcomes should be within the realm of predictability. Thus, in the realm of consequentialism, ethical theory attempts to become objective, seeking a foundation that is akin to the sciences. This principle is enshrined in the world of commerce, trade, management, and administration as the *cost–benefit analysis approach*.

As a theory, consequentialism is not as closely tied to its founder as are the previous three theories discussed. Thus, rather than probing the depths of Mill's writing, a more free-ranging approach is used, and the section presents various versions of consequentialism that are in play today. This approach will avoid the considerable controversies surrounding what Mill meant by his theories[134] and draw out of consequentialism tools that are useful to persons dealing with issues in healthcare ethics.

Relative to what consequentialism means, Bentham insisted that "the greatest number" included all who were affected by the action in question, with "each to count as one, and no one as more than one."[135] Likewise, in Bentham's version of the theory, the various intrinsic goods that counted as utility would have an equal value, such that one unit of happiness for you is not worth more than one unit of happiness for me. Quite clearly, to talk about "units of happiness" is far-fetched, and indeed that is one of the criticisms of the theory.[136] However, numerous correctives to the theory have been advanced over the years, and some of these are helpful.

Unlike deontology and natural law with their conflicting absolutes, consequentialism of any form allows for degrees of right and wrong. If the consequences can be predicted and their utility calculated, then in such situations the choice between actions is clear-cut: always choose those actions that have the greatest utility. For this reason, the theory has had great appeal in economic and business circles. However, in healthcare decision making the economic view of utility is not fully satisfactory. For example, how do you compute the suffering of someone whose spouse has become disabled? Although attorneys do calculate the monetary value of life years lost when a there is an injury , whether monetary settlements can really compensate for a lost livelihood or a broken future is debatable.

In spite of this objection, managers of healthcare organizations, including clinical managers, must often think in terms of the aggregate when evaluating their decisions. Persons taking the tack of a deontologist and trying to fulfill their duty can readily say that their obligation is to the patient. Managers have to consider patients in the aggregate, the organization, the larger community, and their employees in their decision making. Managers' divided duties and obligations are part of their job descriptions, as opposed to the single obligation to the patient that clinicians enjoy. Managers also are trained to consider their decisions in terms of maximization—the best outcome for the resources expended in the greatest good[137]   or as managers say, the "biggest bang for the buck." Of course, in management, as in ethics, problems arise:

- It is not always clear what the outcome of an action will be, nor is it always possible to determine who will be affected by it.
- The calculation required to determine the right decision is both complicated and time consuming.
- Because the greatest good for the greatest number is described in aggregate terms, the good might be achieved under conditions that are harmful to some, so long as that harm is balanced by a greater good. This leads to the attack that consequentialism means "the end justifies the means."[138]

The theory fails to acknowledge that individual rights could be violated for the sake of the greatest good, which is sometimes called the "tyranny of the majority." Indeed, even the murder of an innocent person would seem to be condoned if it served the greater number. The complaint is that consequentialism ignores the existence of basic rights and ethical principles such as autonomy and beneficence. The fact that Mill would categorically deny this by saying some acts are wrong regardless of the consequences is held as a violation of his own stated philosophy. Of course, we are not seeking doctrinal purity, but useful tools to help us in healthcare ethics.

Finally, who has time to run endless computations every time a decision is needed? "Analysis paralysis" would be the predicted outcome, which would not maximize any version of utility. In any case, because of these problems few philosophers today subscribe to act consequentialism.[139] The proposed improvement to several of these problems is rule consequentialism.

Rule Consequentialism

The idea behind rule consequentialism is that behavior is evaluated by rules that would lead to the greatest good for the greatest number. At this point, the theory begins to tie in more clearly to virtue ethics and to the person who has achieved practical wisdom. It takes a person of some experience to know how to develop rules that will likely lead to the greatest good for the greatest number. Managers and government officials would call these rules *policies*.

Once a policy is developed, presumably by evaluation of its likely outcomes, then the person who needs to make a decision refers to the applicable policy instead of having to make endless evaluations and calculations. Indeed, a person of practical wisdom might well conclude that long-term utility is undermined by acts of injustice. He or she would then develop a policy that recognizes and respects autonomy. Rule utilitarianism thus could use the utility principle to justify rules establishing human rights and the universal prohibition of certain harms. Such rules would codify the wisdom of experience and preclude the need for constant calculation.

Thus, rule consequentialism looks like the very same activity in which managers and policy makers engage when they make policies and procedures. A policy is a general statement meant to cover any number of situations.

The person creating it makes the decision that following the policy is the best way to achieve the organization's goals. The person then uses procedures as the means to carry out the created policies. Managers and government officials have been using this process for a long time. Overall, it works well, even though rules or policies do not work fairly in every situation.

Indeed, the failure of the rules to fit every situation is one of the reasons to have humans in charge instead of machines. At this point, the inclusion of a person of practical wisdom, from the virtue ethics tradition, comes into play. Managers or clinicians (persons of practical wisdom) can decide if the special circumstances warrant making an exception to the rule when they need to make judgments. If so, they could modify the rule to consider these special circumstances. In this way, fairness is preserved.

These exceptions might be justified by such material reasons as need, merit, potential, or past achievement. The manager or policy maker will also have to recognize, and be willing to accept, that sometimes the enforcement of a rule will lead to unfair outcomes. However, the principle is still sound and much better than the chaos of trying to evaluate the probable consequences of a situation each time a decision is required.[140]

Rule consequentialism can also incorporate the goals of negative consequentialism. The idea behind *negative consequentialism* is that alleviation of suffering is more important than the maximization of pleasure. Further, to have as a goal alleviation of suffering incorporates into the goal the protection of the powerless, the weak, and the worse off. Thus, from a social policy point of view, rules that operate as safety nets can accomplish this goal. Allowing access to emergency treatment regardless of ability to pay is an obvious healthcare example. Now let us look at the last version of consequentialism, *preference consequentialism*.

Preference Consequentialism

Preference consequentialism argues that the good is the fulfillment of preferences, and the bad is frustration of desires or preferences. People in this sense are not seen as having preferences for pleasure or happiness per se; their preferences are left to them. Thus, autonomy becomes a bedrock value. For example, persons preferring to suffer great sacrifices to get into medical school are seeking to fulfill their preferences.

In another example, a patient could have termination of treatment as a preference, even if it leads to his or her early death. It is hard to imagine how that leads to happiness or pleasure when the person is not alive to experience such states. Other preferences could be losing weight, making a new friend, or rearing a healthy child. Note the similarity of this point of view to the emphasis in health care of respecting people's wishes that forms part of the general attack on paternalism. The theme here is to find out a person's expectations and then seek to meet them. Within preference consequentialism, any number of states or conditions might be preferred, owing to the vast variability among people's desires. Consequentialism of this form is compatible with many different theories about which things are good or valuable.

How can someone know another person's preferences when making decisions that involve that person? Health care has developed clearly enunciated procedures in the area of informed consent to answer this question. One can speak of *substituted judgment* when one knows the preferences of a person who is now incompetent.[141] In cases in which the person has not communicated his or her preferences, we are forced to fall back on what is called the "best interests standard," or, more commonly, the "reasonable person standard." What would a reasonable person want in the circumstances at hand?[142]

Healthcare ethicists have done a decent job in trying to discern what the preferences are of an individual who has become incompetent. However, policy-making decisions have an impact on large groups of people, most of whom will be personally unknown to the decision makers. Development of the tools to ascertain the preferences of a large aggregate of individuals is a much different task.[143] The tack that seems to occur is that the decision maker applies the "reasonable person standard" to the aggregate. However, considerable evidence suggests that such a standard may fall considerably short of meeting a specific person's actual preferences, whether it is what a reasonable person would want or not.[144] Simply put, the preferences that humans have are so diverse and so changeable that it might not even make sense to use them as a standard for maximization. Compared with the "reasonable person," a number of people may have preferences that are not "reasonable." Thus, although this preference standard may work at the individual level, it seems to have less value as a policy statement to use in the aggregate. This happens because the primary way to institutionalize it as a rule is to invoke the reasonable person standard, which may run roughshod over individual preferences that are "unreasonable."

Evaluation of Consequentialism

One of the most common criticisms of consequentialism is that it appears to allow some to suffer mightily if the net outcome is an improvement for a greater number. This argument is specious. The concept of respect for autonomy is presupposed by the very statement that the good sought is the greatest good for the greatest number. Although consequentialists might talk about utility, the good in mind has to include respect for the personhood of others as a minimum requirement. If not, why would they even be included in the prescription? If respect for the other is not presupposed, then it seems the theory would really devolve into a form of egoism. Thus, respect for the wants, preferences, hopes, and choices of others must be implicit for the theory to remain intact. Lack of this foundational component would mean that the theory really does boil down to the ends justifying the means, as noted earlier. However, such a view is off base relative to the intent of the theory.

Mill himself stated this quite clearly in his classic essay "On Liberty": "The only freedom which deserves the name is that of pursuing our own good in our own way, so long as we do not attempt to deprive others of theirs, or impede their efforts to obtain it."[145] It is difficult to think of a more obvious reference to respect for the autonomy of others and their liberty to pursue it. Some argue that this meant that Mill was really a deontologist. However, such arguments seem arcane, academic, and irrelevant to our purposes. Thus, I consider it a compliment to Mill that he recognized the need to temper his "greatest good for the greatest number" with respect for basic principles of autonomy and freedom.

ETHICAL THEORIES AND THEIR VALUE TO HEALTHCARE PROFESSIONALS

Over thousands of years, no ethical principle or theory has survived criticism by trained philosophers without serious flaws emerging. Nonetheless, healthcare professionals cannot throw up their hands. They must make decisions and give reasons for those decisions. Leadership often means choosing a course that you know some will not support.[146] Healthcare professionals understand the need for picking and choosing among the theories to work with the circumstances at hand.[147] This is why the person of practical wisdom, from the virtue ethics tradition, serves as the best model and is the model that various healthcare professions have sought to produce. In the case of physicians, the tradition goes back for millennia. For other healthcare professions, the time period for development of a sense of professionalism, for production of persons of practical wisdom, has been much shorter.[148]

Clinicians and healthcare managers will use their practical wisdom to advance the interests of specific patients, patients in the aggregate, the community, and the organization by drawing on principles and theories as necessary to advance these interests. For managers, having rules that tend to provide the greatest good for the greatest number over the long term functions as a guiding principle in the same way that duties do for the clinician. Both clinicians and managers can come to the table with some clear ideas about what is appropriate to do in a given situation. The clinician has the emotional upper hand, because most people respond better to appeals based on helping a specific individual rather than protecting a policy. Nonetheless, the manager is well equipped by understanding the proper role of rules or policies.

People in the policy-making arena can enhance their evaluation of the behavior or motivations of various stakeholders if they determine the ethical system these stakeholders are likely to be using. Clinicians are likely to take a deontological approach, because their training makes their primary duty to the individual patient. They will not be as concerned with the external consequences of a decision (e.g., costs, inconvenience to the family) as they are with whether they are doing the right thing for the patient's medical care. The right thing is that which allows them to meet their duty and therefore support their sense of themselves as upholding the integrity of the profession. In other words, they want to uphold their sense of themselves as virtuous persons, persons of practical wisdom in the field of medicine or health care, doing the right thing for their patients. The right thing includes not only meeting their duty, but also evaluating the consequences of their decisions on patients and their families.

Managers are in a more difficult position because they have obligations to many stakeholders, not just to the individual patient. Those obligations are often unequal, sometimes conflicting. Sometimes their best strategy is to recognize that they lack the luxury of having obligations that are pure and easily defined. Instead, they have to think of multiple and conflicting stakeholders and try to develop a solution that will generate the greatest good for the greatest number. All the while, they must respect the principles of autonomy, justice, beneficence, and nonmaleficence.[149] In their experience, the rules they adhere to have had those positive results; therefore, they suggest them in the current case. It is clear that the ethical challenge for a healthcare manager is more difficult than for those working from a strictly clinical perspective.

SUMMARY

This chapter makes it clear that no one ethical theory is sufficient for all healthcare decisions. However, a review of the principle features of the main ethical theories used in health care provides a toolbox for decision making. After a brief explanation of authority-based ethics, there was a description of virtue ethics as something common in the socialization of healthcare professionals. Next, the chapter provided a discussion of the features and use of natural law theory. The chapter also included two prominent ethical theories used in health care: utilitarianism and deontology. Finally, there was a discussion regarding the merits of considering virtue ethics as a healthcare professional.

The 21st century promises challenging healthcare ethical issues for individuals, organizations, and society. Therefore, a deeper understanding of and the ability to apply ethical theory will be even more necessary for appropriate responses to these challenges. Ethical theory did not develop in a vacuum. Each theorist studied the works of those who went before and provided his or her own wisdom. Similarly, theories form the basis for the main ethical principles used in healthcare practice and decision making. You will find a discussion of these principles in Chapter 2. In addition, subsequent chapters will apply both theories and principles to current and future healthcare challenges.

QUESTIONS FOR DISCUSSION

1. Why should you have a foundation in ethics if you are involved in health care? Are you not already a good person?
2. How can you use the tenets of natural law in your practice of health care?
3. Why is virtue ethics advocated as the best model for persons who work in healthcare professions? Does this argument succeed in helping manage inevitable ethical dilemmas?
4. Why is deontology still important in contemporary healthcare practice? How can you use the categorical imperative to make decisions in today's healthcare practice?
5. How does utilitarianism affect healthcare decision making? Do you think this theory will be useful for making decisions about future issues?
6. How does Rawls's theory connect to the movement for healthcare reform? How would Nozick argue against it?

FOOD FOR THOUGHT

The only certainty we seem to have in today's healthcare realm is that profound changes are coming. What their extent will be is undetermined, but we do know that we are facing the greatest change in the system in 46 years. The demands that these changes will make on the system will also make demands on our application of ethics to the practice of health care. What demands on ethical practice do you see for the future? How can knowledge of ethical theory assist you with meeting these demands?

NOTES

1. For a good overview of the value of cultural competence in health care, see J. R. Betancourt, A. R. Green, and J. E. Carillo, *Cultural Competence in Health Care: Emerging Frameworks and Practical Approaches* (New York: The Commonwealth Fund, 2002). Retrieved from www.cmwf.org/usr_doc/betancourt_culturalcompetence_576.pdf. Accessed November 26, 2011.

2. T. L. Beauchamp and J. F. Childress, *Principles of Biomedical Ethics*, 5th ed. (New York: Oxford University Press, 2001). Beauchamp and Childress popularized these four concepts, starting with the first edition of their text in 1979. The concepts, or "principles," as these authors call them, appear later in this chapter. The authors consider these principles more valuable than the theories. For purposes of clinical medical ethics, this ordering may be appropriate. It seems less suitable for the more general category of healthcare ethics, which includes policy making well beyond the bedside.

3. Some authors distinguish deontology from consequentialism solely by the fact that it places total or some limits on the relevance of the consequences in the deliberations. See T. A. Mappes and J. S. Zembaty, eds., *Biomedical Ethics*, 2nd ed. (New York: McGraw Hill, 1981), 4.

4. R. Benedict, "A Defense of Moral Relativism," *Journal of General Psychology* 10 (1934): 59–82. Written by a leading figure in 20th-century anthropology, this work is one of the most influential contemporary defenses of ethical relativism. Numerous anthologies, including *Everyday Life*, 3rd ed., ed. C. Sommers and F. Sommers (San Diego: Harcourt, Brace and Jovanovich, 1992), include reprints of this work. This reference was found at http://public.clunet.edu/~chenxi/Phil315_031.pdf/. Accessed November 26, 2011.

5. See K. Popper, *The Logic of Scientific Discovery* (New York: Basic Books, 1959) for the defense of falsifiability as a criterion of scientific knowledge.

6. V. Klingenborg, "On the Recentness of What We Know," *New York Times*, August 9, 2006. Retrieved from http://nytimes.com/2006/08/09/opinion/09talkingpoints.html. Accessed November 26, 2011.

7. H. LaFollettee, "The Truth in Relativism," *Journal of Social Philosophy* (1991): 146–154.

8. The lack of certainty and infallibility disturbs many. See M. J. Slick, "Ethical Relativism," Christian Apologetics and Research Ministry, 2003. Retrieved from http://www.carm.org/relativism/ethical.htm. Accessed November 26, 2011. This organization renounced relativism because "right and wrong are not absolute and must be determined in society by a combination of observation, logic, social preferences and patterns, experience, emotions, and 'rules' that seem to bring the most benefit." According to this group, reliance on scripture improves this messy process.

9. In an introductory chapter, a complete account is not possible. However, for an extensive bibliography, see L. M. Hinman, "A Survey of Selected Internet Resources on Ethical Egoism," Ethics Updates, http://ethics.sandiego.edu/theories/Egoism/index.asp.

10. See, for example, A. Rand, *Virtue of Selfishness* (New York: Signet, 1964).

11. The Ayn Rand Institute website recommends L. Peikoff, *Objectivism: The Philosophy of Ayn Rand* (London: Meridian, 1993). Retrieved from http://www.aynrand.org/site/PageServer?pagename=objectivism_intro. Accessed November 26, 2011.

12. A. Rand, *Introducing Objectivism* (Irvine, CA: Ayn Rand Institute, 1962). Retrieved from http://www.aynrand.org/site/PageServer?pagename=objectivism_intro. Accessed November 26, 2011.

13. The spiritual dimension is one of the nine elements of the patient-centered care model championed by the Planetree model. See S. B. Frampton, L. Gilpin, and P. A. Charmel, *Putting Patients First: Designing and Practicing Patient-Centered Care* (San Francisco: Jossey-Bass, 2003). Retrieved from www.planetree.org/about/components.htm. Accessed June 5, 2006. See also the Duke University Center for Spirituality, Theology, and Health, http://www.spiritualityandhealth.duke.edu/. This site contains an extensive reference to the literature in this area.

14. World Medical Association, "The Declaration of Geneva," originally adopted in 1948 and most recently amended in 2006. Retrieved from http://www.wma.net/en/30publications/10policies/g1/. Accessed August 16, 2012.

15. Following tradition, the citations for references used to locate classical passages are by the name of the work and the particular line number. See *Nicomachean Ethics*, Bk. I, Chap. 9, 1099b32–1100a5. The actual edition used is R. McKeon, *Basic Works of Aristotle* (New York: Random House, 1971).

16. Very substantial arguments arise over just what *harm* and *benefit* mean, but those are not necessary to consider here. The exact words noted do not occur in the Hippocratic Corpus. However, *Of the Epidemics* (Bk. I, sect. II, pt. 5) states it clearly: "The physician must . . . have two special objects in view with regard to disease, namely, to do good or to do no harm." Retrieved from http://classics.mit.edu/Hippocrates/epidemics.html, an online collection of the Hippocratic Corpus. Accessed November 28, 2011.

17. There is considerable debate about the definition of virtues, including which ones are important. I shall have to leave that discussion aside and simply hope the reader has an ordinary conception of what a virtue is.

18. See American Medical Association, *Principles of Medical Ethics* (Chicago: American Medical Association, 2001). Retrieved from www.ama-assn.org/ama/pub/category/2512.html. Accessed November 28, 2011.

19. *Nicomachean Ethics*, Bk. I, Chap. 2, 1103a17.

20. Ibid., Bk. I, Chap. 2, 1103a25.

21. The following material on honesty was inspired by R. Hursthouse, "Virtue Ethics," Stanford Encyclopedia of Philosophy, 2007. Retrieved from http://plato.stanford.edu/entries/ethics-virtue/. Accessed November 28, 2011. I have rewritten it to fit healthcare professionals from its original, more general appeal.

22. *Nicomachean Ethics*, Bk. 6, Chap. 13, 1140a–1140b.

23. Ibid., Bk. 6, Chap. 13, 1145a2–3.

24. This seeking of self-perfection has a major influence in Western culture, extending from the Greeks into the Roman Stoics and then into Christianity. In some interpretations, Islamic jihad means a similar struggle with the self, a striving for spiritual self-perfection. Muslims knew of Aristotle's teachings far in advance of Christendom. After the decline of Rome, Aristotle's work was lost in the West. However, in the ninth century, Arab scholars introduced Aristotle to Islam, and Muslim theology, philosophy, and natural science all took on an Aristotelian cast. After the Crusades, Arab and Jewish scholars reintroduced Aristotelian thought in the West. The correct interpretation of jihad is a matter of considerable debate and is not a topic here.

25. Beauchamp and Childress, *Principles of Biomedical Ethics*, 5th ed.

26. "Justice," in *The Concise Oxford Dictionary of English Etymology*, ed. T. F. Hoad (New York: Oxford University Press, 1996). Retrieved from www.oxfordreference.com/views/ENTRY.html?subview=Main&entry=t27.e8229. Accessed June 19, 2006.

27. For example, a teacher might say, "Your response did the subject justice," meaning that it was right and that it was a more than merely adequate response; it was good. Or one might say, "The person showed the justice of his claim," meaning it was a proper and correct claim.

28. Beauchamp and Childress, *Principles of Biomedical Ethics*, 5th ed.

29. Aristotle thought slavery was okay because some persons could comprehend the rational principle but not possess it. They acted from instinct (*Politics*, Bk. II, Chap. 5). Aristotle described barbarians as brutish, along with people of vice (*Nicomachean Ethics*, Bk. VII, Chap 1, 1145a30 and Chap. 5, 1148a15–30). By nature, some people should rule and others

be ruled. He thought Greeks should rule barbarians, "for by nature what is barbarian and what is slave are the same" (*Politics* Bk. I, Chap. 2, 1252b8). Women were inferior by nature to men as well: "The relationship between the male and the female is by nature such that the male is higher, the female lower, that the male rules and the female is ruled" (*Politics*, Bk I, Chap. 4, 1254b12–14). The hierarchy of being and value had significant importance politically for millennia, and continues to do so today. Obviously, metaphysics influences our lives. The common morality has changed relative to many of these views.

30. *Nicomachean Ethics*, Bk. X, Chap. 9, 1179b5–10.

31. Ibid., Bk. X, Chap. 9, 1179b18. The other sentiments are written directly preceding this line. A tincture of something seems to suggest that it is not quite the real thing, although it could do some good. So many various definitions of the term *tincture* exist that it is difficult to get a precise understanding of the meaning of the phrase.

32. See B. Justice, *Who Gets Sick: How Beliefs, Moods, and Thoughts Affect Your Health*, 2nd ed. (Houston: Peak Press, 2000). This book reviews the scientific literature on the subject and provides an excellent introduction to the field.

33. In the realm of healthcare management, providing cues to quality to assure patients that the services are appropriate is part of the management of the dimensions of quality. See V. A. Zeithaml, M. J. Bitner, and D. D. Gremler, *Services Marketing*, 4th ed. (New York: McGraw Hill, 2006). See also Frampton, Gilpin, and Charmel, *Putting Patients First*.

34. Some of these issues are discussed in *Nicomachean Ethics*, Bk. VII, Chaps. 1–10, 1145a15–1154b30.

35. Mappes and Zembaty, *Biomedical Ethics*, 2nd ed., 7. The brush that paints all ethical theories as either more or less consequentialist seems much too wide.

36. For an extremely informative philosophical overview of natural law theory in general and Aquinas's version of it in particular, including an excellent defense of how natural law does not neatly fall into either deontology or consequentialism, see M. Murphy, "The Natural Law Tradition in Ethics," Stanford Encyclopedia of Philosophy, 2002. Retrieved from http://plato.stanford.edu/archives/win2002/entries/natural-law-ethics/. Accessed November 28, 2011.

37. On how the heavens have never changed in their orderly cycles, see *On the Heavens*, Bk. I, Chap. 3, 270b10–17.

38. See G. Kemerling, "Thomas Aquinas," PhilosophyPages.com, 2011. Retrieved from www.philosophypages.com/ph/aqui.htm. Accessed November 28, 2011.

39. For more modern writers in the field of natural law, see, in alphabetical order, T. D. J. Chappell, *Understanding Human Goods* (Edinburgh: Edinburgh University Press, 1995); J. Finnis, *Aquinas: Moral, Political, and Legal Theory* (Oxford: Oxford University Press, 1998); P. Foot, *Natural Goodness* (Oxford: Oxford University Press, 2000); J. E. Hare, *God's Call* (Grand Rapids, MI: Eerdmans, 2001); M. Moore, "Good Without God," in *Natural Law, Liberalism and Morality*, ed. R. P. George (Oxford: Oxford University Press, 1996); and M. C. Murphy, *Natural Law and Practical Rationality* (Cambridge: Cambridge University Press, 2001).

40. St. Thomas Aquinas, *Summa Theologica*. The entire work (Benziger Bros. edition, 1947, trans. Fathers of the English Dominican Province) is available online at the Christian Classics Ethereal Library. The online index can be found at http://www.ccel.org/ccel/aquinas/summa.toc.html. Accessed November 28, 2011. Question 94 is found at http://www.ccel.org/a/aquinas/summa/FS/FS094.html#FSQ94OUTP1. The standard reference format for something in *Summa Theologica* is, for example, ST IaIIae 94, 4. This is interpreted to mean that the citation comes from the first part of the second part of *Summa Theologica*, question 94, article 4.

41. B. B. Longest Jr. and K. Darr, *Managing Health Service Organizations*, 5th ed. (Baltimore: Health Professions Press, 2008); K. Darr, *Ethics in Health Services Administration*, 5th ed. (Baltimore: Health Professions Press, 2011), 19.

42. For a better account within the healthcare literature, see J. W. Carlson, "Natural Law Theory," in *Biomedical Ethics*, 2nd ed., T. A. Mappes and J. S. Zembaty (New York: McGraw Hill, 1981), 37–43, and M. C. Brannigan and J. A. Boss, *Healthcare Ethics in a Diverse Society* (Mountain View: Mayfield Publishing, 2001), 23–25.

43. This also contradicts some commentators, who say that it assumes all rational beings will agree on the content of the natural law. For this error, see Brannigan and Boss, *Healthcare Ethics in a Diverse Society*.

44. M. Murphy, "The Natural Law Tradition in Ethics," *Stanford Encyclopedia of Philosophy*, 2002. Retrieved from http://plato.stanford.edu/archives/win2002/entries/natural-law-ethics/. Accessed November 28, 2011.

45. V. Cathrein, "Ethics," *Catholic Encyclopedia Online*, ed. K. Knight, 2003. Retrieved from http://www.newadvent.org/cathen/05556a.htm. Accessed November 28, 2011.

46. For an extensive discussion of this approach in the healthcare literature, see Beauchamp and Childress, *Principles of Biomedical Ethics*, 5th ed., 128–132.

47. To go further into such controversies, see, as examples, P. J. Cataldo, "The Principle of the Double Effect," *Ethics & Medics* 20 (March 1995): 1–3; B. Ashley and K. O'Rourke, *Healthcare Ethics: A Theological Analysis*, 4th ed. (Washington, DC: Georgetown University Press, 1997), 191–195; and D. B. Marquis, "Four Versions of Double Effect," *Journal of Medicine and Philosophy* 16 (1991): 515–544.

48. A similar insight was noted by Beauchamp and Childress, *Principles of Biomedical Ethics*, 2nd ed. (New York: Oxford University Press, 1983), 115.

49. Cathrein, "Ethics."

50. This theory does not appear to protect nonhuman animals, plants, dammed rivers, strip-mined mountains, and the like. Given their lack of rationality, the fact that they are not made in the image of God, their lower level in the hierarchy of being, and their being a means to our ends, their potential would matter less. In the Aristotelian scheme, only angels were between humans and the unmoved mover, or God. Later on, Descartes, although not favored by either Catholics or Protestants in his time, made a fundamental distinction between mind and matter. Only humans were believed to be endowed with mind capacity. *Mind* easily translated into concepts such as *soul*. Thus, the rest of the natural world, being without mind or soul, did not require us to worry about whether its potential would be circumscribed by our actions upon it.

51. Most of Kant's works appear to be available free online at http://oll.libertyfund.org/Intros/Kant.php, along with works of many other authors. I do not know whether the translations are those most accepted by scholars. Retrieved November 28, 2011.

52. Although in near complete disagreement about the substance of their respective views, John Rawls and Robert Nozick are considered deontologists. Their views are essential to understanding current political debates.

53. I. Kant, *The Critique of Practical Reason*, trans. L. W. Beck (Indianapolis, IN: Bobbs-Merrill, 1956).

54. I. Kant, *The Moral Law*, trans. H. J. Patton (London: Hutchinson University Press, 1948).

55. Kant, *Critique of Practical Reason*.

56. I. Kant, *Critique of Pure Reason*, trans. N. K. Smith (New York: St. Martin's Press, 1965), p. 29. The "B xxix" refers to the standard paging of the work. The "B" indicates that this passage is in the *Critique*'s second edition only.

57. There is vast literature on the issues involved in whether free will exists. Different flavors of determinism are discussed, and different perspectives on what it means to say that someone acts freely. Although these issues are important, they simply cannot be broached here. For a good overview of the issues and the approaches taken by various religions, as well as various thinkers, see W. K. Frankena, *Ethics: Foundations of Philosophy Series* (Englewood Cliffs, NJ: Prentice Hall, 1963), 54–62, and T. O'Conner, "Free Will," *Stanford Encyclopedia of Philosophy*, 2005. Retrieved from http://plato.stanford.edu/entries/freewill/. Accessed November 28, 2011.

58. What the moral law is will be taken up with the discussion of the categorical imperative.

59. Kant, *Critique of Pure Reason*, 26–29 (B xxv–B xxx).

60. Ibid., 29.

61. Ibid., 28. If you find this argument hard to follow, you are not alone. It takes a considerable study of philosophy to understand the argument, which by no means suggests you would agree with it.

62. I. Kant, "Fundamental Principles of the Metaphysics of Morals," trans. T. K Abbott, in *Basic Writings of Kant*, ed. A. L. Wood (New York: Modern Library, 2001), 151.

63. Ibid., 152.

64. Ibid., 154–155.

65. I. Kant, *Foundations of the Metaphysics of Morals*, trans. L. W. Black (Indianapolis, IN: Bobbs-Merrill, 1959). The "AK 20" is the conventional page numbering used in Kant scholarship, locating this quote within the 22 volumes in the Preussische Akademie edition. Different pagination is used when referring to the *Critique of Pure Reason*.

66. Beauchamp and Childress, *Principles of Biomedical Ethics*, 5th ed., 57–112, provide a good discussion of autonomy in the context of medical ethics. E. E. Morrison, *Ethics in Health Administration: A Practical Approach for Decision Makers* (Sudbury, MA: Jones and Bartlett, 2011), 27–45, provides a discussion tailored to healthcare managers.

67. R. Johnson, "Kant's Moral Philosophy," Stanford Encyclopedia of Philosophy, February 26, 2004. Retrieved from http://plato.stanford.edu/archives/spr2004/entries/kant-moral/. Accessed November 28, 2011.

68. Beauchamp and Childress, *Principles of Biomedical Ethics*, 5th ed., 348–351, provides a useful summary of these issues.

69. Kant posits a third version of the categorical imperative, "The Idea of the Will of Every Rational Being as a Universally Legislative Will" (AK 4:431). See Kant, "Fundamental Principles of the Metaphysics of Morals," 188. However, since this seems to restate the emphasis on autonomy found in the second version, I shall not take up analysis of it separately.

70. Kant, "Fundamental Principles of the Metaphysics of Morals," 178.

71. For a sampling of sources stating or suggesting that Kant's categorical imperative is the Golden Rule, see Longest Jr. and Darr, *Managing Health Service Organizations*, 5th ed., 103; Darr, *Ethics in Health Services Administration*, 5th ed.; Brannigan and Boss, *Healthcare Ethics in a Diverse Society*, 29; J. O. Hertzler, "On Golden Rules," *International Journal of Ethics* 44, no. 4 (1934): 418–436; S. B. Thomas, "Jesus and Kant, a Problem in Reconciling Two Different Points of View," *Mind* 79, no. 314 (April 1970): 188–199; P. Weiss, "The Golden Rule," *Journal of Philosophy* 38, no. 16 (July 31, 1941): 421–430; and J. E. Walter, "Kant's Moral Theology," *Harvard Theological Review* 10, no. 3 (July 1917): 272–295, esp. 293. Those who write about ethics without having philosophical training are even more likely to make this mistake. A website on engineering ethics simply indicates that the categorical imperative is the Golden Rule; see http://www.engr.psu.edu/ethics/theories.asp. Accessed November 28, 2011. I have even made the error myself in discussing ethical theories in the healthcare literature. See the following articles, which were part of a column on healthcare ethics: J. Summers, "Managers Face Conflicting Values," *Journal of Health Care Material Management* 7, no. 5 (July 1989): 89–90; J. Summers, "Clinicians and Managers: Different Ethical Approaches to Honoring Commitments," *Journal of Health Care Material Management* 7, no. 4 (May–June 1989): 62–63; J. Summers, "Determining Your Duties," *Journal of Health Care Material Management* 7, no. 3 (April 1989): 80–81; J. Summers, "Duty and Moral Obligations," Journal of Health Care Material Management 7 no. 2 (February–March 1989): 80–83; and J. Summers, "Ethical Theories: An Introduction," *Journal of Health Care Material Management* 7, no. 1 (January 1989): 56–57. The fact that something looks like something else does not make it that something else.

72. The disavowal occurs in a footnote in Kant, "Fundamental Principles of the Metaphysics of Morals," 187, note 13. To the normal reader the footnote would not clearly indicate that it references the Golden Rule, because Kant cited it in Latin and none of the terms resemble the English version of the Golden Rule.

73. Kant, "Fundamental Principles of the Metaphysics of Morals," 186.

74. Ibid., 190–191.

75. Kant, *Foundations of the Metaphysics of Morals*, 31.

76. Kant, "Fundamental Principles of the Metaphysics of Morals," 186.

77. Ibid., 186.

78. For a good history of the Golden Rule, including versions that precede the Christian formulation of Matthew 7:12, see J. O. Hertzler, "On Golden Rules," *International Journal of Ethics* 44, no. 4 (July 1934): 418–436.

79. Kant, "Fundamental Principles of the Metaphysics of Morals," 187, note 13.

80. Ibid., 156.

81. Ibid., 183.

82. Some of the ideas in this section were drawn from F. Feldman, "Kant's Ethical Theory," in *Biomedical Ethics*, ed. T. A. Mappes and J. S. Zembaty (New York: McGraw-Hill, 1981), 26–37, esp. 36–37.

83. J. Rawls, *A Theory of Justice* (Cambridge, MA: Harvard University Press, 1971), 11.

84. Ibid., 4–5.

85. Ibid., 30.

86. Ibid., 136–137.

87. Ibid., 142–143.

88. Beauchamp and Childress, *Principles of Biomedical Ethics*, 5th ed., 101–103.

89. Rawls, *Theory of Justice*, 17–19.

90. Ibid., 137–138.

91. Ibid., 142.

92. Ibid., 17.

93. Ibid., 43, 61.

94. Ibid., 43–44.

95. Ibid., 60.

96. Ibid., 61.

97. Ibid., 75–83.

98. Ibid., 60–61, 75–83, and elsewhere.

99. For purposes of the argument, we have to leave aside the very real issue that equal opportunity is simply not available to large swaths of the population whether they have the talent to be a physician or not.

100. Rawls, *Theory of Justice*, 104.

101. Ibid., 148.

102. For two of many articles favoring reparation to descendents of slaves, see D. T. Osabu-Kle, "The African Reparation Cry: Rationale, Estimate, Prospects, and Strategies," *Journal of Black Studies* 30, no. 3 (2000): 331–350 and W. William Darity Jr. and D. Frank, "The Economics of Reparations," *American Economic Review* 93, no. 2 (2003): 326–329. For an article showing public opinion about such reparations, see M. R. Michelson, "The Black Reparations Movement: Public Opinion and Congressional Policy Making," *Journal of Black Studies* 32, no. 5 (2002): 574–587.

103. Rawls, *Theory of Justice*, 102.

104. Ibid.

105. Ibid.

106. Ibid., 15.

107. R. Nozick, *Anarchy, State and Utopia* (New York: Basic Books 1974), xi.

108. E. Feser, "Robert Nozick," Internet Encyclopedia of Philosophy, 2006. Retrieved from http://www.iep.utm.edu/n/nozick.htm. Accessed December 9, 2006.

109. Rawls, *Theory of Justice*, 62, 92–93.

110. Kant, "Fundamental Principles of the Metaphysics of Morals," 186.

111. Nozick, *Anarchy, State and Utopia*, ix.

112. Ibid., 32.

113. Ibid.

114. Ibid., 33.

115. Ibid.

116. Ibid., 235.

117. Rawls, *Theory of Justice*, 42.

118. Nozick, *Anarchy, State and Utopia*, 149–150.

119. Ibid., 151.

120. Ibid.

121. Ibid., 156–160, 217.

122. Ibid., 156–157.

123. Ibid., 230.

124. Ibid., 231.

125. Such statements made truly hard-core libertarians turn against Nozick. See M. N. Rothbard, *The Ethics of Liberty* (New York: New York University Press, 1998), esp. section 29, "Robert Nozick and the Immaculate Conception of the State." For other criticisms of Nozick cited by Rothbard in the libertarians' own journal, see R. E. Barnett, "Whither Anarchy? Has Robert Nozick Justified the State?" *Journal of Libertarian Studies* 1 (Winter 1977): 15–21; R. A. Childs Jr., "The Invisible Hand Strikes Back," *Journal of Libertarian Studies* 1 (Winter 1977): 23–33; J. T. Sanders, "The Free Market Model Versus Government: A Reply to Nozick," *Journal of Libertarian Studies* 1 (Winter 1977): 35–44; J. Paul, "Nozick, Anarchism and Procedural Rights," *Journal of Libertarian Studies* 1, no. 4 (Fall 1977): 33-40; and J. D. Davidson, "Note on *Anarchy, State, and Utopia*," *Journal of Libertarian Studies* 1, no. 4 (Fall 1977): 341–48. The website for the journal is http://www.mises.org/jlsdisplay.asp.

126. The same is true in recent times. The Bushmen of the Kalahari in southern Africa, after living in the area for 35,000 years as hunter-gatherers, were ejected from the land as having no tenure rights. See E. M. Thomas, *The Old Way: A Story of the First People* (New York: Sarah Crichton Books, Farrar Straus Giroux, 2006), Chap. 20, esp. 294–295.

127. Healthcare managers do have a fiduciary duty to the organization and its patients. Such duties are described as the duties of care and loyalty created when a person undertakes to act for the benefit of another to whom he or she has a relationship implying confidence and trust and creating the expectation that he or she will act with a high degree of good faith.

128. For a very good overview of these views and a critical review as well, see A. Gandjour and K. W. Lauterbach, "Utilitarian Theories Reconsidered: Common Misconceptions, More Recent Developments, and Health Policy Implications," *Health Care Analysis* 11, no. 3 (September 2003): 229–244. A different source lists ten versions of consequentialism; see W. Sinnott-Armstrong, "Consequentialism," Stanford Encyclopedia of Philosophy, 2011. Retrieved from http://plato.stanford.edu/entries/consequentialism/. Accessed November 29, 2011. At least three versions of rule consequentialism are described; see B. Hooker, "Rule Consequentialism," Stanford Encyclopedia of Philosophy, 2008. Retrieved from http://plato.stanford.edu/entries/consequentialism-rule. Accessed November 29, 2011.

129. Deontology can also be divided into rule and act deontology, although I did not find the distinction useful here. See Frankena, *Ethics*, 21–25.

130. J. S. Mill, *Utilitarianism* (1863), Chap. II, para. 2. Retrieved from http://www.utilitarianism.com/mill1.htm. Accessed November 29, 2011. Owing to the many printed versions, I am citing this work by reference to chapter and paragraph.

131. Ibid., Chap. II, para. 2. Accessed November 29, 2011.

132. *Eudaimonia* was discussed previously and is human happiness that necessarily includes pursuit of the good for humans qua humans.

133. See D. Lyons, "Mill's Theory of Morality," *Nous* 10, no. 2 (April 1976): 101–120, esp. 103–104. He draws this conclusion from Mill's discussion of duty and punishment in *Utilitarianism*, Chap. V, para. 14–15, where Mill finds that punishment is necessary for persons not fulfilling their duties, without regard to any specific calculation of consequences. The fact that this begins to sound like deontology we shall leave unchallenged.

134. For example, Lyons, "Mill's Theory of Morality," 101–120, notes the considerable debate over whether Mill was an act utilitarian or a rule utilitarian and whether considerations other than utility entered into Mill's decision calculus. Lyons cites considerable sources on both sides of the debate.

135. Discussed by S. Gosepath in "Equality," Stanford Encyclopedia of, Philosophy, 2007. Retrieved from http://plato.stanford.edu/entries/equality/. Accessed November 29, 2011.

136. For an extremely well-written, even witty, analysis of this difficulty, see M. Sagoff, "Should Preferences Count?" *Land Economics* 70, no. 2. (May 1994): 127–144. For a very abstruse and technical paper reaching essentially similar conclusions, see D. M. Hausman, "The Impossibility of Interpersonal Utility Comparisons," *Mind* 104, no. 415 (July 1995): 473–490.

137. See J. Summers, "Managers Face Conflicting Values," *Journal of Health Care Material Management* 7, no. 5 (May–June 1989); J. Summers, "Clinicians and Managers: Different Ethical Approaches to Honoring Commitments," *Journal of Health Care Material Management* 7, no. 4 (May–June 1989): 62–63; J. Summers, "Determining Your Duties," *Journal of Health Care Material Management* 7, no. 3 (April 1989): 80–81; and J. Summers, "Duty and Moral Obligations," *Journal of Health Care Material Management* 7, no. 2 (February–March 1989): 80–83.

138. One of the common texts used for teaching healthcare managers the principles of management includes a section on ethics. Although much of the section is on point and the overall text is excellent, the discussion of consequentialism does not even mention that the typical understanding is "the greatest good for the greatest number," but instead simply says "a summary statement that describes utilitarian theory is 'the end justifies the means.'" See Longest Jr. and Darr, *Managing Health Service Organizations*, 5th ed. The author of the statement, Kurt Darr, had previously written *Ethics in Health Services Administration*, 5th ed. In that text he did mention the idea of "the greatest good for the greatest number" along with "the end justifying the means," but thought both attributable to utilitarians, although not to be "applied without qualification" (p. 17). He did not discuss those qualifications. Unfortunately, many healthcare managers, only exposed to the more general management theory book, will never know about the greatest good for the greatest number. They would likely perceive consequentialism as inherently allowing an evil to seek a good. For one of many other examples of misunderstanding consequentialism, see G. Koukl, "Means and Ends," Stand To Reason, 1994. Retrieved from www.str.org/site/News2?page=NewsArticle&id=5444. Accessed November 29, 2011. Like Koukl's, many of the sites making the claim that utilitarianism means the end justifies the means are religious sites. For an example of a business misreading of Mill's consequentialism, see R. Scruton, "Thoroughly Modern Mill," *Wall Street Journal*, May 19, 2006, A10. Available at http://online.wsj.com/article_email/SB114800167750457376-lMyQjAxMDE2NDI4MjAyMDIxWj.html. Accessed November 29, 2011. Scruton considers Lenin, Hitler, Mao, Stalin, and common criminals as "pious utilitarians." To define a theory by one of its criticisms is exceedingly off base.

139. B. Hooker, "Rule Consequentialism," Stanford Encyclopedia of Philosophy, 2008. Retrieved from http://plato.stanford.edu/entries/consequentialism-rule. Accessed November 29, 2011. Hooker provides the reasons for this rejection and cites a large body of scholarship to support his contention. See also E. Millgram, "What's the Use of Utility?" *Philosophy and Public Affairs* 29, no. 2 (Spring 2000): 113–136, esp. 126.

140. A criticism in the philosophical literature is that revision of the rule to deal with exceptions leads inevitably back to act consequentialism. See Hooker, "Rule Consequentialism." Practical experience as a manager and an educator of managers suggests that any manager worth his or her salt learned long ago not to let this happen.

141. Beauchamp and Childress, *Principles of Biomedical Ethics*, 5th ed., 98–102, discuss the substituted judgment approach and find it lacking. They promote the phrase "pure autonomy standard" for what I understand as the substituted judgment approach. Their change in terminology is not used in the healthcare literature as a replacement for "substituted judgment."

142. See E. E. Morrison, *Ethics in Health Administration: A Practical Approach for Decision Makers* (Sudbury, MA: Jones and Bartlett, 2011), 28; and Beauchamp and Childress, *Principles of Biomedical Ethics*, 5th ed., 102–103.

143. In political decision making, we fall back on the idea of having an elected person who represents us. Those representatives collect information about what their constituents think in a number of ways. In the organizational setting, the entire discipline of market research can be involved in this process. However, these information-gathering methods are seldom quick or inexpensive.

144. See Sagoff, "Should Preferences Count?" and Hausman, "The Impossibility of Interpersonal Utility Comparisons."

145. Mill, *On Liberty*, Chap. I, para. 13.

146. I refer the reader to P. Tillich, *The Courage to Be* (New Haven: Yale University Press, 1952) for helpful thoughts on coping with difficult quandaries about the meaning of life and difficult choices in life.

147. See Longest Jr. and Darr, *Managing Health Service Organizations*, 5th ed., 106. The authors stress the balancing and eclectic nature of the work of the manager in drawing on ethical theories and principles. See also Brannigan and Boss, *Healthcare Ethics in a Diverse Society*, 28, for a similar view. See Morrison, *Ethics in Health Administration*, 20–22, for thoughts on what it means to healthcare managers to draw these ideas together into a personal ethic.

148. For example, the professional society of healthcare managers, the American College of Healthcare Executives, traces its origins to 1933. The organization was founded to develop the profession of healthcare managers. See http://www.ache.org/CARSVCS/wesbury_fellowship.cfm. Accessed November 29, 2011. Many other healthcare professions are even more recent in origin.

149. See J. Summers, "Doing Good and Doing Well: Ethics, Professionalism and Success," *Hospital and Health Services Administration* 29, no. 2 (March–April 1984): 84–100, for an early discussion in the healthcare literature about the integration of these values and approaches.

CHAPTER 2

Principles of Healthcare Ethics

Jim Summers

INTRODUCTION

Chapter 1 of *Health Care Ethics: Critical Issues for the 21st Century* presented the major ethical theories and their application in health care as part of a foundation for the study of ethics. This chapter extends that foundation by showing how those theories inform the principles used in health care and apply to the issues in that field. The principles commonly used in healthcare ethics—justice, autonomy, nonmaleficence, and beneficence— provide you with an additional foundation and tools to use in making ethical decisions. Each of these principles is reviewed here. The concept of justice is presented last because it is the most complex. In addition, this chapter presents a model for decision making that uses your knowledge of the theory and principles of ethics.

NONMALEFICENCE

If we go back to the basic understanding of the Hippocratic ethical teaching, we arrive at the dictum of "first do no harm, benefit only." The principle of *nonmaleficence* relates to the first part of this teaching and means "to do no harm." In healthcare ethics, there is no debate over whether we want to avoid doing bad or harm. However, the debate occurs when we consider the meaning of the word *harm*. The following ethical theories come into play here:

- A consequentialist would say that harm is that which prevents the good or leads to less good or utility than other choices.
- A natural law ethicist would say that harm is that which is opposed to our rational natures, that which circumscribes or limits our potential.
- A deontologist would say that harm is that which prevents us from carrying out our duty or that which is opposed to the formal conditions of the moral law.
- A virtue ethicist—a person seeking *eudaimonia*, a person of practical wisdom—would find that harm is that which is immoderate, that which leads us away from manifesting our proper ends as humans.
- An ethical egoist would define harm as that which was opposed to his or her self-interest.

What Is "Harm" in the Clinical Setting?

In the clinical setting, harm is that which worsens the condition of the patient. However, deciding what *harm* or *worsen* means is no simple matter. Much of health care involves pain, discomfort, inconvenience, expense, and perhaps even disfigurement and disability. Using the natural law theory of double effect, we justify harm because there is a greater good. A consequentialist would say that the greater good, the greater utility, occurs from accepting the pain or dismemberment as part of the cost to get the benefit the healthcare procedures promise. The due care standard to provide the most appropriate treatment with the least pain and suffering sounds almost like a deontological principle.[1]

Most healthcare workers consider harm to mean physical harm, because the long history of healing has focused primarily on overcoming bodily disorders. However, harm can occur in other ways. For example, healthcare managers can cause harm by failing to supervise effectively. The result may be inadequate staff or a lack of equipment that is maintained or kept up-to-date. Either of these can lead to adverse patient outcomes. Harm also comes from strategic decisions that lead to major financial losses and jeopardize the ability of the organization to continue. At a different level of harm, making the decision to dispose of hazardous materials without taking proper precautions puts the community at risk. In another example, healthcare policy makers can cause harm by changing eligibility requirements that lead to patient populations being unable to afford or to access the care they need. The ways in which harm can occur are infinite.

Harm as Negligence

Given the vast number of ways in which harm can occur, healthcare workers have developed numerous protocols to protect patients, families, the community, and themselves. Failure to engage in these protocols is an act of omission, as opposed to directly doing harm, which is an act of commission. A substantial body of law and ethical understanding supports the view that such a failure is *negligence* (omission). The person has not exercised the due diligence expected of someone in his or her role.

Healthcare financial managers also face a number of laws to ensure that they are not engaging in fraud and abuse, which also cause harm. For example, failure to follow the expectations of good financial management is essentially *malfeasance*. This term is very close to *maleficence* and represents neglect of fiscal responsibility. Medical professionals find a similar term with *malpractice*. Part of the education of all healthcare professionals concerns what it takes to avoid doing harm, to ensure that due diligence is followed.

Part of the development of a healthcare professional is to create a person of integrity who would consider it a violation of self to put those who trust in him or her at risk. Persons who avoid this violation are persons of practical wisdom. They have achieved *eudaimonia* in their professions and in their lives. They can sit down together and discuss what they should do in a complex ethical situation. In the healthcare community, we believe that persons working within the healthcare ethic share a common understanding of the mission, vision, and values of health care. They are able to reason together, even if they get to their conclusions by different ethical theories and principles. The shared values of "first do no harm, benefit only" provide a foundation that is often lacking in ethical disputes outside of health care.

Harm as Violations of Autonomy

An exceedingly large number of issues come to the surface as soon as you begin to address the issue of what harm is in a thoughtful way. For example, quality-of-life issues come into play. If a person elects not to receive a treatment because of a loss of life quality, then many people believe that imposing the treatment on that person is wrong. This would violate the principle of autonomy and evidence paternalism. Using the principle of autonomy, persons own their lives.

However, if the person is incompetent, the ethical approach is to determine if one knows the person's wishes from the time when he or she was competent, and, if known, to follow them. This practice is termed *substituted judgment*. If the person's wishes are unknown, then the usual approach is called, the *best interests* or *reasonable person decision*. The assumption is that the reasonable person would choose what is in his or her best interest.

BENEFICENCE

The other part of the Hippocratic ethical dictum is "benefit only." The principle of beneficence addresses this dictum. The *bene* comes from the Latin term for "well" or "good."

Beneficence and a Higher Moral Burden

Beneficence implies more than just avoiding doing harm. It suggests a level of altruism that is absent from simply refraining from harm. The ethical principle of having to engage in altruistic or beneficent acts means that we are morally obligated to take positive and direct steps to help others. Relative to the ethical theories, the underlying principle of consequentialism, the greatest good for the greatest number, is itself a statement of beneficence.[2] Early writers in the consequentialist tradition argued for the theory because of their belief that human nature was benevolent.[3]

Because beneficence is a fundamental principle of healthcare ethics, ethical egoism (i.e., the belief that our primary obligation is to ourselves and that selfishness is a virtue) is disconnected from health care. This is true because most people enter health care as a profession because they want to help people. Health care also is different in terms of the common morality. The larger society does not necessarily hold people as negligent or deficient for failure to perform beneficent acts. However, in health care the professional roles carry that expectation.

Acts of kindness and courtesy not expected by typical strangers are expected of healthcare workers. Failure to open a door to help someone in a wheelchair may be discourteous in most settings or perhaps even rude. However, it is unprofessional if you are a healthcare worker. Beneficence is part of the common morality of health care.

Nonmaleficence and Beneficence Are Insufficient Principles

Historically, the main problem that has emerged from emphasis on nonmaleficence and beneficence is that in most healthcare situations the physician was the person who defined "harm" and "good." Historically, most people were ignorant of what the physician was doing or talking about or why he or she prescribed certain treatments. Thus, the physician defined the patient's self-interest and carried it out. When the person who is receiving benefit or avoiding harm has little or no say in the matter, that person receives paternalistic treatment. The term *paternalism* comes from the Latin *pater*, which means "father." Paternalism, by definition, means that one treats the patient as one would treat a child. However, one of the major developments in health care over the last several decades has been patients' assertion of their desire to make decisions for themselves. Thus, we have to move beyond nonmaleficence and beneficence to include the principle of autonomy.

AUTONOMY

If you make a decision for me from the "first do no harm, benefit only" perspective without involving me in the decision, then my autonomy has been violated. Even if your entire intent is to put my interests before your own, leaving me out of decisions about myself violates my "self." Your intention to execute an act of beneficence does not mean I experience it as such an act.

Autonomy and the Kantian Deontological Tradition

Autonomy as a concept means that the person is self-ruling. The term *auto* is from the Greek and means "self." The rest of the term comes from the Greek *nomos*, which means "rule" or "law." The derivation of terms such as *normative* comes from this Greek word. Thus, one can understand autonomy as self-rule. Underlying the concept of autonomy is the idea that we are to respect others for who they are. This view is honored in the medical tradition as far back as the Hippocratic writings. Therefore, the duty of the physician is to treat people's illnesses, not to judge them for why they are ill. It might be necessary for the physician to try to get patients to change what they are doing or who they are, but that is a part of the treatment, not a character judgment.

Autonomy in Health Care

In the healthcare setting, it is often unclear whether the patient does or does not possess the conditions required for autonomy. Two important conditions must be met for autonomy: Are patients competent to make decisions for themselves? Are patients free of coercion in making the decision? These questions reflect the idea that autonomy implies the freedom to choose. Typically, people have an understanding of what it means to be competent and be able to make choices on their own behalf. However, that is not all there is to competence and autonomy.

The competent person also needs to be free of coercion. Coercion could mean they are trying to please someone—their parents, their children, or the providers—and thus are hiding their "real" choices. Forms of coercion that might prevent free choice in health care are myriad. Providers often encounter patients whose choices are compromised or coerced. For example, an abused spouse may not feel free to discuss the causes of bruises. A raped daughter may avoid discussion of a sexually transmitted disease. Drug abusers may hide their condition for fear of job loss.

An interesting approach to competence is the idea of specific competence, as opposed to general competence.[4] Competence can be understood as the ability to complete a task. This may mean you are able to do and understand some things, but not others. For example, a person with a transient ischemic attack might be unable to balance a checkbook. However, that same person might be able to understand the consequences of medical procedures and thus assent to them or not. This is an example of specific competence. A person may be intermittently competent owing to his or her medical condition. Thus, the person is competent to assent to treatment right now, but was not two hours previously, and might be unable to do so two hours in the future.

At this point, we have seen the importance of nonmaleficence, beneficence, and autonomy as principles of healthcare ethics. Now we move to the last of the four principles of healthcare ethics: justice.

THEORIES OF JUSTICE

In general, to know something is unjust is to have a good reason to think it is morally wrong. We can ask, "What sorts of facts make an act unjust rather than simply wrong in general?" Several reasons are available.

People use the term *injustice* to mean unfairness in treatment. Injustice in this sense occurs when similar cases do not receive similar treatment. Following Aristotle, many believe that we are required, as a formal principle of justice, to treat similar cases alike except where there is some relevant or material difference. The equity requirement in this 2,400-year-old principle is critical. Now I shall break down the concept of justice into its components.

Justice usually comes in two major categories: procedural and distributive. *Procedural justice* asks, "Were fair procedures in place, and were those procedures followed?" *Distributive justice* is concerned with the allocation of resources. In some cases, both of these issues will be in play at the same time. Both justice principles start from the idea that in the distribution of burdens and benefits the allocation should be equal unless there is a material reason to discriminate.

Procedural Justice

Procedural justice can be defined as "due process." For example, in the legal system, we speak of being equal before the law as a part of procedural justice. In the legal sense, then, procedural justice or due process means that when you get your turn, you receive the same treatment as everyone else. One can apply this concept to health care. For example, if you are waiting to see your primary care physician, did others get to go ahead of you without any clear medical reason?

Procedural injustices occur in health care, but they are more common when dealing with employees. For example, if a healthcare manager has to terminate employees due to economic considerations, are the procedures for determining who will go applied without bias? In such cases, the issue is not so much whether what happened was in itself just or fair, but whether the method used followed the stated procedures. No one would claim that it is fair to terminate good employees with long careers of service who have done nothing wrong. However, if economic circumstances dictate that there must be terminations of employees, the procedural justice question emerges as to whether there were standards and procedures for making the selection and whether they were followed.

Failures of due process can also occur in the health policy arena, and those participating in policy making carefully watch for these failures. For example, suppose that at a public hearing, the time limit for speaking is 3 minutes. You will not think justice is done if some are allowed to speak 10 minutes, whereas others are constrained to 3, or perhaps told to sit down after only 1 minute.

We now turn to a review of the principles of distributive justice.

Distributive Justice

The concept of distributive justice relates to determining what is fair when decision makers are determining how to divide burdens and benefits.[5] Kaiser Family Foundation data suggest the extent of the resource allocation disparity in healthcare demand and spending.[6] One percent of the U.S. population consumes 23.7% of healthcare resources. Half the U.S. population consumes only 3.4% of healthcare resources. The other half consumes 96.6% of healthcare resources. This is an extraordinary mismatch in the use of healthcare resources. Is it fair?

When it comes to distributive justice, several questions can emerge. Why are so many using so little? Are they healthy or simply unable to access the system? Are we seeing an improvement in the lives of that 1% who are taking up nearly 25% of the spending, whether measured by the patients or by the medical community? Are there less expensive ways to achieve healthcare goals? Do the healthcare goals, whatever they are, make sense relative to the world in which we find ourselves? Such questions are debated endlessly; however, they will not sidetrack us here. The point is to see the difficulty of the task of distributing the burdens of healthcare costs while seeking the holy grail of affordability, availability, and quality all at the same time.

To understand distributive justice, you must first understand that resource allocation issues occur at all levels. For example, a physician has to decide how much time to spend with each patient. Busy nurses have to decide how quickly to respond to a call button relative to the task they are engaged in when it sounds. Nurse managers have to allocate too few nurses to too many patients. Healthcare managers hire employees. If they are going to increase pay, they must decide what method to use. Should the increase be across the board or by merit or seniority? If by merit, then who decides whether employees deserve it, and is the method fair? The latter question is one of procedural justice. This is an example in which the two types of justice often occur together.

Organizational leaders have to decide whether to spend scarce money on capital improvements on buildings and equipment, new employees, more money for the current employees, new services, or advertising, or whether to save the money. In health care, allocation of scarce resources can be a matter of life and death. For example, in Texas, persons with AIDS and HIV infection pleaded at a Texas Department of Health public hearing that funding not be cut. On the line was a drug-assistance program facing budget cuts. The drugs for this treatment cost $12,000 per year, and the state was considering only allowing coverage if income levels were not in excess of $12,400. If a person made $13,000 a year, he or she would have only $1,000 on which to live. Desperation prevailed, as people told the panel to look them in the eye so they would know who they were killing. Attendees promised "not to slip quietly into their graves."[7]

Regardless of the outcome of that policy decision, in the midst of such emotions the need for the reflective equilibrium (discussed later in this chapter) is high. Decisions are difficult when you are facing people who claim they are in such a crisis. One can explore many related issues to understand why decisions are made with regard to distributive justice.

Material Reasons to Discriminate

The basic principle of distributive justice is that each person should get an equal share of the burdens and benefits unless there is a material reason to discriminate. What are the reasons to discriminate?[8] The multiple reasons to discriminate typically boil down to two different concepts: that the person deserves it or the person needs it. Society believes that those who work hard and do well deserve their success. That is the common morality in the United States. In contrast, a person who breaks the law and hurts people deserves prison. Health care shares this common morality but also includes a more complex element—need. The following list includes the most common candidates for material reasons to discriminate, all of which are subsets of need or being deserving.

1. Being deserving or worthy of merit includes one's contribution or results and effort.
2. It also includes the needs of individuals or groups, such as the following:
   - Circumstances characterized as misfortune
   - Disabilities of a physical or mental nature or, more generally, unequal natural endowments
   - A person's special talents or abilities
   - The opportunities a person might have or might lose
   - Past discrimination against a group that is perceived as having negative effects in the present
   - Structural social problems perceived as restricting opportunity or even motivation

In the larger society, there is also a need to discriminate based on material need. One of society's views of distributive justice is that you get what you deserve or merit. Your results or contribution is what counts the most in getting what you deserve. The most common form of getting what you deserve in the larger society comes from the market. Therefore, if you are good at what you do, the market rewards you. If you are not, the market does not reward you, or even punishes you. For example, the physician who sees the most patients is sometimes the one with the higher income. Healthcare managers who meet revenue or productivity goals should get higher pay than their peers who fail to do so.

In the larger society, effort matters too. Many want rewards based on effort, and often this effort is what our culture and our institutions reward. Kant, for example, thought we should be praised or blamed for actions within our control, which includes our willing, not our achieving. In some cases, we cannot determine whether the results that did or did not occur were within the person's control. However, we can observe their effort, and it translates as reward. Thus, the healthcare manager who supervises the more complex healthcare system receives more pay than a department manager does. Researchers in biomedicine might work long and hard without necessarily getting the results they seek, yet they are compensated for their expertise and their labor.

Many of us are willing to help a person whom we perceive as putting forth effort and will give up on the one who is not. This applies to healthcare treatments as well. For example, patients who follow "doctor's orders" to the letter and are clearly working hard to solve their health problems will likely elicit more support and effort from the clinical team. These situations are common in the management of chronic diseases and in behavioral health. Now let us take up the reasons to discriminate based on need.

Discrimination Based on Need

It is exceedingly difficult to put an upper limit on the concept of need. For example, the World Health Organization (WHO) defines *health* as "a state of complete physical, mental and social well-being and not merely the absence of disease or infirmity."[9] This definition sets up a model of need that is theoretically impossible to meet. However, some approaches are more useful than others. These include the following.

Need Based on Misfortune In health care, the common morality is to discriminate for or against patients based on their need for care. For example, persons with emergencies are treated first, no matter how long one has waited in line. Persons in accidents, regardless of whose fault it is, are seen as having experienced a misfortune. Victims of natural disasters generally are perceived the same way. However, many of the conditions we treat in healthcare organizations are not owing to an infection, a bad series of decisions, or a natural disaster. People may suffer from genetic defects that vastly restrict their functioning. Others have reduced abilities in physical or mental capacity. One can consider these conditions a form of misfortune.

Even in the healthy population, significant disparities exist between people as to physical and mental ability, including factors such as motivation. For example, one could consider a person's special talents or abilities as a potential area for discrimination. Although we normally do not think of discriminating in favor of someone owing to special talents or abilities, it does occur. In health care, the clinical team may make more efforts to help someone with a special talent. For example, during cancer treatment, Lance Armstrong, who later was a seven-time Tour de France bike race winner, was administered a different chemotherapy than the protocol to protect his aerobic capacity.[10] Although that may not sound significant, it is a special treatment.

Healthcare managers make hiring and promotion decisions on perceived ability, speculating that past performance will be a guide to future performance. In that sense, the criteria are a mix of something you have done and a gamble that you will continue to perform. Policy decisions sometimes are made this way as well, such as when awarding a contract or grant, or funding a program. It appears that those involved have the ability to accomplish the goals of the policy makers.

Children and the elderly also receive special consideration based on abilities or talents. For example, the argument for spending money on children's health care ties into the idea of their future abilities. This echoes the natural law argument to maximize potential. Many clinical workers will go to great lengths to help a child become whole, because the child has so much life yet to live. Advocates for the disabled and the elderly also are concerned with ability. They worry that the reduced potential and ability of the elderly can lead to discrimination and thus loss of opportunity.[11]

Need Based on Past Discrimination Other forms of need might include redress of past injustices to social groups, which overlaps with the need to provide opportunity and prevent the loss of ability. Such thinking led to the Civil Rights Act of 1965 and affirmative action. It could also be argued that past discrimination means that the protected groups deserve special dispensations. Clearly, the opportunities of many persons in those groups were restricted. Many special talents went undeveloped.

In the United States, health care long ago gave up the institutionalization of segregation by race or gender. Nonetheless, in health care we have seen the nation respond to special groups and their needs by development of entire healthcare systems for them. For example, the Veterans Administration system is the largest healthcare system in the world. In addition, the design of the Indian Health Service is to provide care to a very limited and specific group.

For some disadvantaged groups, the effects of adverse discrimination have led to structural problems that prevent some of the members from taking advantage of available opportunities. These structural burdens, such as poverty, poor educational and housing systems, and even poor transportation systems, often receive blame for the difficulties experienced by some. Regardless of what led to the problems, one knows that structural burdens have adverse health consequences.

Many people who claim to have a need also say they have a right to our services. Let us look at the concept of rights, because they are intertwined with the concept of justice.

Distributive Justice and Rights

In the United States, debate continues over whether access to health care is a right or a purchased commodity. Much of the language is confusing, because there are many types of rights. One thing is clear: to claim a right means that you believe there is some legal reason you are entitled to something or that there is at the least a moral claim that your right is supported by ethical principles and theories. Rights range from ideal rights to legal rights. When someone makes a claim that something is a right, the typical reaction of the other party is to consider the basis of the claim. Is it a legal one? Is it moral? Alternatively, is it simply a wish or a statement of a preference?

Ways of Categorizing Rights

The diagram in **Figure 2–1** shows the types of rights and their relationships. One can find all the rights within the circle of ideal rights, which are rights we wish we had. Rights that are within another circle are subsets of that right. Rights that are partially within one or more other circles are rights that share common characteristics with their shared circles. For example, natural rights include elements of substance rights and negative rights. Some of the substance rights and negative rights have become legal rights. A positive right is a certain type of thing or social good to which you have a legal right. All positive rights are a subset of legal rights.

The size of the circle also indicates the relative importance of each type of right within the common morality of the United States. For example, in the United States our common morality puts more emphasis on negative rights than on substance rights. Some other nations place a greater emphasis on the collective welfare as opposed to individual opportunity. In these cases, the substance rights category would be larger, and more of it would fit inside the legal rights circle.

The list of rights here is by no means exhaustive. The following discussion of the types of rights in Figure 2–1 provides a synopsis of the issues involved.

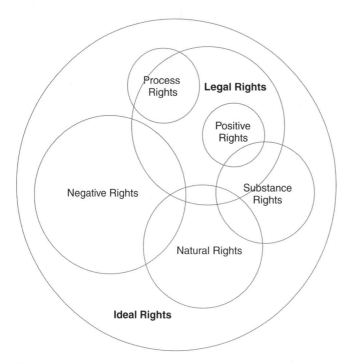

Figure 2–1   Types of rights and their relationships.

Major literature exists on the topic of rights and includes others that are not part of Figure 2–1.[12] The best of all rights, from the point of view of the claimant, are enforceable and legal rights.

Legal and Positive Rights

Margaret Mahoney notes that positive rights used to be called "social goods," which society may or may not provide. The change to calling them "rights" was part of a rhetorical technique to give them a greater sense of legitimacy to the public.[13] A *legal right* means that someone has a legal obligation to fulfill your right, whatever it happens to be. A *positive right* is a narrow example of a legal right, because it is a specific social good. For this reason, it is shown in the diagram in Figure 2–1 as a circle completely within the set of legal rights. These rights are written into the law and are described as *entitlements*. However, a legal right can include more than simply entitlements. For example, the legal system protects the right to due process, but it is not the provision of a good. One could say the same of the legal right to privacy under HIPAA (Health Insurance Portability and Accountability Act) laws. Thus, like due process, a right to privacy is not a positive right even though it is a legal right.

When rights are under pressure because of budget shortfalls, political pressure to cap government spending, or the like, the real meaning of a legal right is that you can go to court to get it enforced. Legal rights are not as strong as they were once thought to be in protecting the person with the right. For example, you may have a legal right to abortion or to Medicare and Medicaid, but if no one is providing it, your right has little value. Apparently, even the strongest version of a right does not mean that you will be able to exercise whatever rights you have.

Substance Rights

Substance rights can be legal rights or not. They are rights to a particular thing, such as health care, housing, a minimum wage, welfare, food stamps, safe streets, a clean environment, and the like. In this sense, they are similar to positive rights, but not necessarily legal, as with an entitlement. This is somewhat of a nuanced difference, because a substance right might imply that it is a right to something basic needed to maintain life. Nations, such as those in Europe, can be concerned with substance rights and attempt to guarantee an outcome or a basic minimum for their citizens. In those nations, the substance rights became legal rights. The positive legal rights noted earlier for health care also are substance rights, as would be the right in the United States to get treatment, or at least be stabilized, at an emergency department regardless of ability to pay.

Negative Rights

In Figure 2–1, based on the common morality of the United States, the circle for negative rights is relatively large and extends into the legal rights domain. The terminology used for negative rights comes from the British tradition and essentially means that you have the right to be left alone. You have the right to do anything not strictly forbidden by the law.

Negative rights are clear and enshrine liberty. For example, the Bill of Rights is primarily a list of negative rights, such as that speech and assembly will not be restricted. The Bill of Rights also includes the idea that a state will not enforce a religion. It also reinforces the negative right that allows people to have weapons because "a well-regulated militia, being necessary to the security of a free state, [means] the right of the people to keep and bear arms shall not be infringed."

In the realm of health care, one major negative right is that we have the freedom to pursue our lives as we see fit. For example, motorcyclists claim they have a negative right to be free from having to wear protective helmets. Another negative right enshrined in law in some places is the right not to have smokers in your workplace, eating area, or public areas generally. Smokers maintain this is a major affront to their freedom. One person's negative right to be free of smoke is the cancellation of another person's negative right to be free to smoke.

Other legal protections that ensure you are left alone involve the protections against sexual harassment and hostile work environments. The privacy protections in HIPAA are yet one more legal negative right. Your medical information cannot be accessed unless you authorize it or for medically necessary reasons related to your care. As in the case of positive substance rights, the costs on the part of those who must honor or take responsibility for ensuring you are free of these hazards can be large.

Process Rights

Given the Bill of Rights, many laws relate to ensuring that due process is followed, at least for most people. As noted in the discussion of the layout of the diagram in Figure 2–1, process rights do overlap with natural rights. In the United States and in most developed nations, process rights also are legal rights.

Natural Rights

Natural rights have a long history. The concept of a natural right means that we should respect attributes that humans have by nature.[14] For Aristotle and St. Thomas Aquinas, these features would be those that best support our achievement of our highest good. The appeals to natural rights within our common morality that are most well known go back to the Founding Fathers. Drawing heavily on John Locke, Thomas Jefferson proclaimed in the Declaration of Independence "We hold these truths to be self-evident, that all men are created equal, that they are endowed by their Creator with certain unalienable Rights, that among these are Life, Liberty, and the pursuit of Happiness."

One practical advantage of the natural rights approach to determining a person's rights is that people from very different perspectives use the same language. Thus, even if their views are philosophically inconsistent, they can agree that someone has a natural right. For example, many will say that there exists a natural right to that which is necessary to move toward one's full potential, and health is important to this. To the extent that health care is related to health, one should be able to sustain the argument that morally one has a right to health care. Note that the philosophical reasons for why anyone should be able to develop his or her potential are manifold. However, people of differing religious and philosophic views could agree about having a natural right to develop potential without having to argue or even acknowledge their underlying philosophical differences. Thus, simply as a matter of rhetoric, the language of natural rights plays an important role in making right claims within our common morality.

Ideal Rights

An *ideal right* is a statement of a right that is meant to be motivational, a goal to seek. The WHO definition of health and its subsequent claim that everyone has a right to the highest attainable health care falls into this category.

Reflections on Rights

One element of the reflective equilibrium model (discussed later in this chapter) that comes into play is the weighting of rights. The fact that we have a right seldom means that it trumps all other considerations. Consider the issue at the policy-making level. Assume there are rights to national security, education for the young, transportation, protection of property rights, and health care. Does one right trump the others at all times? Probably not, even though sometimes people think that their right claim should trump all the others. Even within health care, do the healthcare needs of the old trump those of the young?

What Does Having a Right Mean?

The U.S. Supreme Court has noted that you have no rights unless they are legal rights backed by statute. The fact that a strong moral case can be made is not sufficient. This applies directly to the example healthcare case that follows. Recruiters for the military sold military service to World War II and Korean War veterans by stating that if they put in 20 years or more of service, they could obtain free medical care at VA hospitals. However, the Pentagon ended those benefits for veterans over age 65 in 1995 because they were eligible for Medicare. However, Medicare is not a complete healthcare system, and it is not free. Further, some veterans over age 65 say they cannot afford the premiums, deductibles, and co-payments of supplemental programs.

When the veterans filed suit to stay in the VA program, they learned that a promise by a recruiter does not equal a law on the books. Thus, in one sense they had a right to something because they were promised it, but in the strictest sense of the word they had no rights if a law did not compel their treatment. A review of the laws dating from just after the Civil War found that the VA was treating people without statutory authorization. The Supreme Court ruled 5–4 that although the recruiters had made the promises in good faith, there was no contractual obligation. Thus, the federal government had no contractual obligation to the veterans.[15] This ruling is very significant, because it enshrines the idea that the only rights you have are strictly legal ones. As the nation and the world struggle increasingly with resource allocation issues, concerns about rights and distributive justice will become ever more common.

REFLECTIVE EQUILIBRIUM AS A DECISION-MAKING MODEL

Figure 2-2 depicts the reflective equilibrium model. The middle of Figure 2–2 shows the basic facts of the situation for a healthcare issue in which there is a need for a decision. In discussions of ethics, those making decisions about what to do use what are called *considered judgments* as decision-making guides.[16] Another term for such considered judgments is *ethical intuitions*, although the terms are not exactly the same.

A considered judgment implies that a degree of thinking and reasoning occurs before making a decision. To many people, an intuition is simply a feeling, but to ethicists a moral intuition includes an element of reasoning. In moral reasoning, we test our considered judgments against our feelings, and vice versa. Clearly, the common morality will have a considerable influence on these judgments and intuitions as well.

Intuitions or considered judgments, as understood by ethicists, are essentially moral attitudes or judgments that we feel sure are correct.[17] These are of two types: (1) intuitions or considered judgments about particular cases (e.g., letting people stay in the New Orleans Superdome during the Hurricane Katrina incident without doing anything to supply or protect them adequately was not a good thing) or (2) regarding general moral rules (e.g., people whose lives or property are threatened by a natural disaster should be helped). Many such considered judgments exist in health care. For example, a person with a medical emergency should receive treatment regardless of his or her ability to pay.

Ethical theory comes into play in examining people's motivations. Some people may believe they should do something because they have a duty to help others. Others may believe that assisting in a decrease of suffering is appropriate, and that the more people our decisions can help the better. Still others might appeal to our basic inclinations as humans to do the right thing or suggest that God or some deity or deities want us to fix the problem. When asked to justify their actions and decisions, these same persons might rely on these explanations or they might rely on ethical principles.

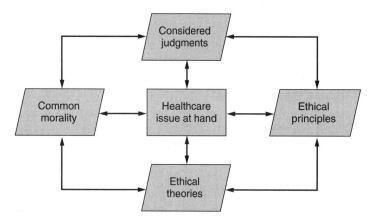

Figure 2-2   Reflective equilibrium at work.

As discussed earlier, ethical principles include advancement of liberty, respect for autonomy, and acting out of beneficence to advance welfare. They also include ensuring that we do nothing to cause harm by following the principle of nonmaleficence. We try to do this all fairly by upholding principles of justice. The typical portrayal of the healing ethic—first do no harm, benefit only—captures at least two of these principles: nonmaleficence and beneficence. The questions become just what to do. In the midst of all the decision making, the people involved are unlikely to consciously draw on ethical theories or principles. They have internalized these foundations for making decisions and simply do so. This is what it means to be a person of practical wisdom, a person exhibiting *eudaimonia* as described in Chapter 1.

The term *reflective equilibrium* describes this back-and-forth process of coming to a coherent solution. John Rawls has described this method,[18] and its hallmark is its lack of dogmatism. The person involved in making the decision revises the decision as new information becomes available. The person may choose to draw on one principle or ethical theory more heavily than he or she did in previous decisions.

Such movement back and forth among competing ethical theories and the quick reweighing of the importance of ethical theories and principles can sometimes look like incoherence or arbitrariness. However, people making healthcare decisions are not as troubled by the requirements of doctrinal purity as they are by the need to come to a decision. They need to have a sound ethical basis to explain that decision, get action on that decision, and get on to the next task. Ethical theories and ethical principles can help them to reach those decisions, explain them, and motivate others to act decisively, urgently, or passionately on them. With this foundation, the outcome is better, assuming the decision was sound. If not, the reflective equilibrium begins again. For this reason, the author chose the toolbox approach to better equip healthcare decision makers with an understanding of the principles and theories of ethics, so they can better decide, better explain, and better motivate. As Beauchamp and Childress put it, disunity, conflict, and moral ambiguity are pervasive features of moral life. Thus, it should be no surprise that untidiness, complexity, and conflict should be part of the process, too.[19]

SUMMARY

The principles of healthcare ethics complete the elements necessary for the reflective equilibrium. The primary principles of healthcare ethics are autonomy, beneficence, nonmaleficence, and justice. Justice is by far the most complex principle, because it includes various conceptions of rights and there is greater dispute about what justice is and how to achieve it. Understanding the various nuances of rights and justice is of considerable importance in making resource allocations at the bedside, at the organizational level, or at the health-policy level of government.

In using the reflective equilibrium model, a person will have to use reason to pick from among the principles, the theories, the common morality, and the considered judgments to apply them to the issue at hand. In health care, we have a great advantage over most organizational approaches to dealing with ethical issues. Given the tradition of ethics committees and consults, a group of persons who are skilled and experienced in applying the reflective equilibrium is more likely to reach a decision that is reasonable than is a single person. This process will be messy; it will be error prone. That is the human condition, and there seems to be no way around it.

Ethics is a complex field. Over thousands of years, humans have yet to develop an ethical theory that will satisfactorily handle all the issues. Nonetheless, some approaches have proven more satisfactory than others and have led to the development of principles. You might ask, "Now what?" Are there any final answers for healthcare issues now and in the future? The answer is "no." However, the important role of the study of ethics and ethical issues and the use of the reflective equilibrium model is to keep the inquiry going. The process matters as much, or even more, than the products. Although there was acceptance of certain beliefs for relatively long periods, the process eventually leads to a change. Let us hope the changes will result in improvement to our lives and an increase in the good. It is the job of each of us to keep the process going.

QUESTIONS FOR DISCUSSION

1. What do you think is the most important principle for clinical healthcare professionals? Explain.
2. Why is beneficence a more complex principle than nonmaleficence?
3. Why is respecting autonomy so important to the future of health care?
4. Why is justice in health care more complicated than just doing what is fair?
5. How can the reflective equilibrium model assist you in making practical ethical decisions in the future?

FOOD FOR THOUGHT

Today's healthcare system presents and will continue to present ethical challenges. Consider what Summers teaches us about the principles of ethics. How can you make these principles part of your day-to-day practice of medicine? Will you have to make some difficult choices to remain an ethics-based practitioner?

NOTES

1. See E. E. Morrison, *Ethics in Health Administration*, 2nd ed. (Sudbury, MA: Jones and Bartlett, 2011), 48.
2. J. J. C. Smart, "Distributive Justice and Utilitarianism," in *Justice and Economic Distribution*, ed. J. Arthur and W. Shaw (Englewood Cliffs, NJ: Prentice Hall, 1979), 103–115, esp. 103. In contrast, Richard Hare, also a consequentialist, specifically disavows that intuitions are

a sufficient base for an ethical theory; R. M. Hare, "Justice and Equality," in *Justice and Economic Distribution*, ed. Arthur and Shaw, 116–131, esp. 117.

3. D. Goleman, "The Roots of Compassion," *New York Times*, December 19, 2006. Retrieved from http://happydays.blogs.nytimes.com/2006/12/19/the-roots-of-compassion/?8ty&emc=ty. Accessed November 29, 2011. The author of the article surveys brain research and finds that humans may be hard wired to have empathy, compassion, and thus beneficence. T. L. Beauchamp and J. F. Childress, *Principles of Biomedical Ethics*, 5th ed. (New York: Oxford University Press, 2001) point out this early history on page 166.

4. This approach was pioneered by Beauchamp and Childress, *Principles of Biomedical Ethics*, 5th ed., who point out this history on pages 70–72.

5. Robert Nozick, in *Anarchy, State, and Utopia* (New York: Basic Books, 1974), 149–150, argues that the very language of "distribution" implies a central organization deciding who gets what and why. To him this improperly frames the discussion to imply a state and its attendant mechanisms when the problem is the state itself and its inevitable oppression.

6. Kaiser Family Foundation, "Illustrating the Potential Impacts of Adverse Selection on Health Insurance Costs in Consumer Choice Models," November 2006. Retrieved from http://www.kff.org/insurance/snapshot/chcm111006oth2.cfm. Accessed November 29, 2011.

7. M. A. Roser, "Don't Cut State Drug Funds, AIDS, HIV Patients Plead," *Austin-American Statesman*, January 17, 2003, B1, B6.

8. Arthur and Shaw, eds., *Justice and Economic Distribution*, 1–11 was helpful here.

9. World Health Organization, "About WHO." Retrieved from http://www.who.int/about/en/index.html. Accessed November 29, 2011.

10. L. Armstrong, *It's Not About the Bike* (New York: G.P. Putnam's Sons, 2000), 108–109.

11. For a sampling of complaints, see K. Hausman, "Mentally Ill Workers Rarely Prevail in ADA Discrimination Claims, Survey Finds," *Psychiatric News* 37, no. 16 (2002): 6. See also M. Weiss, "Study Finds Discrimination Against Disabled Patients," ABCNewsHealth.com. Retrieved from http://abcnews.go.com/Health/story?id=2633167&page=1&CMP=OTC-RSSFeeds0312. Accessed November 29, 2011. See also R. Longley, "Disabled Face Discrimination in Rental Attempts," About.com. Retrieved from http://usgovinfo.about.com/od/rightsandfreedoms/a/disablerents.htm. Accessed November 29, 2011.

12. See L. Wenar, "Rights," Stanford Encyclopedia of Philosophy, 2011. Retrieved from http://plato.stanford.edu/entries/rights/. Accessed November 29, 2011.

13. M. E. Mahoney, "Medical Rights and the Public Welfare," *Proceedings of the American Philosophical Society* 135, no. 1 (1991): 22–29, especially 23.

14. Wenar, "Rights," was helpful here. See especially section 6.1 on status rights. Retrieved from http://plato.stanford.edu/archives/fall2006/entries/rights/. Accessed November 29, 2011.

15. Associated Press, "Veterans Lose Health Care Suit Against Pentagon," *Washington Post*, November 20, 2002. Retrieved from www.americasveterans.org/news/112002.html. Accessed November 29, 2011. For a sample of unhappy commentary, see M. Marquez, "Government Must Honor Promises from the Past," *Austin-American Statesman*, January 21, 2003: A11.

16. J. Rawls, *A Theory of Justice* (Cambridge, MA: Harvard University Press, 1971), 47–48.

17. Arthur and Shaw, eds., *Justice and Economic Distribution*, 10.

18. Rawls, *Theory of Justice*, esp. 20–21, 48–51.

19. Beauchamp and Childress, *Principles of Biomedical Ethics*, 5th ed., Chap. 9, especially 389–390.

Critical Issues for Individuals

Part II of *Health Care Ethics: Critical Issues for the 21st Century* is concerned with issues that affect individuals. Given that health care is a personal business, it is not surprising that this is the largest section of the text. Topics in this section range from gametes to death, with the majority of the chapters focusing on issues concerning the beginning of life and its end. These stages present many ethical concerns for patients, families, practitioners, and organizations.

Chapters 3 through 6 are concerned with ethical dilemmas related to reproduction and prenatal care. Today and into the immediate future, the part of life concerning reproduction and prenatal care will continue to present critical concerns for practitioners who wish to be ethical and honor patient needs and desires. Ethically thorny issues such as the use of assisted conception and abortion promise to continue to be part of professional decision making in the future. In addition, advances in technology complicate decisions surrounding care during this stage of life because they offer more options for creating life than were previously available. For example, Chapter 6 provides an update on the technology of cloning, which had previously been the purview only of the science fiction writer.

The subsequent discussion (Chapters 7 and 8) present issues related to the treatment of adults, particularly as they age, examining the current thinking on the ethics of determining who is competent and who can make decisions to refuse treatment (Chapter 7), and examining the ethical issues faced by older adults who are involved in the long-term care system (Chapter 8). It describes the growing concerns about the increasing numbers of people who may need long-term care, the quality of that care, and the ethical issues faced in the industry.

The next topic (Chapter 9, new to this edition) addresses the current issues in assisted living, including a description of what assisted living is and what it offers. The author relates problems of access to the principle of justice. She also discusses the regulation of assisted living and its effect on autonomy beneficence/nonmaleficence, and justice.

Next, there is a discussion (within Chapters 10, 11, and 12) on the ethical concerns surrounding the process of death and dying. They deal with who makes the decisions about how dying happens and what procedures are involved in the dying process. Issues in these chapters will become even more critical as the population bolus of Baby Boomers reach this stage of their lives; their sheer numbers will increase its ethical concerns. As we saw in earlier chapters, technology will also add to the decision-making process in the area of withholding nutrition (Chapter 10) and assisted death (Chapter 12).

This portion of the text (contained within Part II) challenges your thinking about the ethical issues that you will face in providing health care in the 21st century. It also assists you in applying the theory and principles that you learned in Part I to future situations involving individuals. For some readers, the situations discussed will be personal, and many of you may deal with them as part of your work in the healthcare field.

CHAPTER 3

The Moral Status of Gametes and Embryos: Storage and Surrogacy

Glenn C. Graber

INTRODUCTION

Technology sometimes complicates issues regarding human reproduction by increasing the number of choices available to us. **Table 3–1**, which I have whimsically entitled "41 Ways to Make a Baby," illustrates this idea.[1]

Technology has made possible a separation of the role of the genetic mother (who contributes germ cells, perhaps for in vitro fertilization) from that of the gestational mother (in whose uterus the fetus develops). In addition, the social mother (who cares for the child after its birth, perhaps through adoption or foster parenting) might be different from either of these. The roles of genetic and social father have always been separable.

Line 32 of the chart expresses the situation in which the baby has five parents—or perhaps six if you count the technician who delivers the sperm to the ovum as a sort-of father. In line 34 (male cloning), the source of the enucleated ovum might be different from the gestational mother, and the social mother might be still a different woman—or perhaps the genetic father might choose to raise the child in a life partnership with another male, giving the child two male and two female "parents."

Who among these four or five or six are *really* the parents of the resulting baby? Who should be given authority to make decisions about whether to continue the pregnancy if complications develop? Who should have a say in decisions about terminating treatment of a newborn if he or she is severely compromised?

Not only are these relationships complex, but also they multiply decision points beyond the traditional possibilities. Until the advent of the birth control pill, no safe way was available to stop the process between fertilization and implantation, because this took place in the inaccessible regions of the woman's reproductive tract. Now we have ways to access the reproductive tract safely. Microinvasive surgical techniques allow physicians to manipulate ova within the fallopian tubes or the uterus, including assisting a sperm in penetrating the wall of the ovum. These techniques give rise to some of the more exotic possibilities on Table 3–1, such as those in lines 39 and 40. In addition, many of the early steps in the reproductive process can be carried out in the laboratory (e.g., in vitro fertilization, twin fission, and genetic therapy), and we may have to decide at each stage whether to move forward to the next stage as well as with whom to consult about the decision. One dramatic example of this is the practice of removing one cell from a pre-embryo created through in vitro fertilization to test for genetic anomalies that might help the parents decide which pre-embryo to implant.[2] All these situations are possibilities with which we are not conceptually, emotionally, or ethically prepared to deal. We must sort out myriad questions about the status of the entity at each stage and the relationship of the other parties to this entity.

Table 3–1   41 Ways to Make a Baby

		Source of Germ Cells		Delivery of Sperm	Site of Fertilization	Site of Gestation	Social Parents	
1	Traditional	SF	SM	SF	SM	SM	SF	SM
2	AIH	SF	SM	Technician	SM	SM	SF	SM
3	IVF	SF	SM	Technician	In vitro	SM	SF	SM
4	ICSI	SF	SM	Injection	In vitro	SM	SF	SM
5	Rent-a-womb	SF	SM	Technician	In vitro	Surrogate	SF	SM
6	Artificial womb	SF	SM	Technician	In vitro	Artificial womb	SF	SM
7	Adultery—a	GF	SM	GF	SM	SM	?	SM
8	AID	GF	SM	Technician	SM	SM	SF	SM
9	AID + IVF	GF	SM	Technician	In vitro	SM	SF	SM
10	AID + rent-a-womb	GF	SM	Technician	In vitro	Surrogate	SF	SM
11	AID + artif. womb	GF	SM	Technician	In vitro	Artificial womb	SF	SM
12	Adultery—b	SF	GM	SF	GM	GM	SF	?
13	Surrogate (AID)	SF	GM	Technician	GM	GM	SF	SM
14	Ovum donor	SF	GM	Technician	In vitro	SM	SF	SM
15	Surrogate (IVF)	SF	GM	Technician	In vitro	Surrogate	SF	SM
16	No. 14 + artif. womb	SF	GM	Technician	In vitro	Artificial womb	SF	SM
17	Fornication	GF	GM	GF	GM	GM	?	?
18	Bachelor motherhood	GF	SM	GF	SM	SM	—	SM
19	No. 18 + AID	GF	SM	Technician	SM	SM	—	SM
20	No. 18 + IVF	GF	SM	Technician	In vitro	SM	—	SM
21	No. 19 + rent-a-womb	GF	SM	Technician	In vitro	Surrogate	—	SM
22	No. 19 + artif. womb	GF	SM	Technician	In vitro	Artificial womb	—	SM
23	Bachelor fatherhood	SF	GM	SF	GM	GM	SF	—
24	No. 23 + AID	SF	GM	Technician	GM	GM	SF	—
25	No. 23 + IVF	SF	GM	Technician	In vitro	GM	SF	—
26	No. 24 + rent-a-womb	SF	GM	Technician	In vitro	Surrogate	SF	—
27	No. 24 + artif. womb	SF	GM	Technician	In vitro	Artificial womb	SF	—
28	Adoption	GF	GM	GF	GM	GM	SF	SM
29	No. 28 + AID	GF	GM	Technician	GM	GM	SF	SM
30	No. 28 + IVF	GF	GM	Technician	In vitro	GM	SF	SM
31	Embryo adoption—IVF	GF	GM	Technician	In vitro	SM	SF	SM
32	Five Parents (or is it 6?)	GF	GM	Technician	In vitro	Surrogate	SF	SM
33	No. 29 + artif. womb	GF	GM	Technician	In vitro	Artificial womb	SF	SM
34	Clone—male EO	SF	—		In vitro	?	SF	?
35	Clone—female EO	—	SM		In vitro	?	?	SM
36	Cytoplasmic transfer EO	SF	SM	Technician	In vitro	SM	SF	SM
37	Twin fission (blastomere separation)	?	?	?	Twin fission	?	?	?
38	Embryo transfer	GF	GM	GF	GM	SM	SF	SM
39	GIFT / ZIFT / DOST / IPI	SF	SM	Technician	SM	SM	SF	SM
40	LTOT	SF	SM	SF	SM	SM	SF	SM
41	Genetic Therapy	?	?	?	Gene therapy	?	?	?

KEY TO ABBREVIATIONS

SF   =   social father
SM   =   social mother
AIH   =   artificial insemination by husband
IVF   =   in vitro fertilization and embryo transfer
ICSI   =   intracytoplasmic sperm injection
GF   =   genetic father (merely)
GM   =   genetic mother (merely)
?   =   unknown (indicates multiple possibilities)
AID   =   artificial insemination by donor
—   =   none

EO   =   source of enucleated ovum (germ cell source contributes cell *nucleus* only; mitochondrial genes are *not* transferred)
GIFT   =   gamete intrafallopian transfer
ZIFT   =   zygote intrafallopian transfer
DOST   =   direct oocyte–sperm transfer
IPI   =   intraperitoneal insemination
LTOT   =   lower tubal ovum transfer.

THE MORAL COMMUNITY

I am convinced that the thorny question of the moral status of the materials of human reproduction can be settled, if at all, by decision rather than by discovery. It is less an ontological question than a political one (in the broadest sense of the term *political*, referring to the conventions and agreements among the members of a community or a society). Information about the entities in question may, of course, be relevant to the outcome—but not in anything like the way in which further analysis of the molecular structure of a soil sample retrieved from Mars may furnish evidence for or against the question of whether there is life on that planet.

The issue here is to establish the boundaries of the moral community—who counts, morally; who stands to us (i.e., to those of us in the acknowledged moral community) in a way that requires us to consider them directly in our decisions and actions. These boundaries are ones that the community draws for itself, not lines that we discover embedded in the ontological landscape.

This issue transcends the usual divide in ethical theory between teleological and deontological theories. Before teleologists begin to calculate the consequences of their actions, they must determine *whose* welfare is to count; only then can they begin the process of calculating which action is optimal. I have elsewhere[3] distinguished between several characterizations of what I call the "moral reference group" (**Table 3–2**).

"Human" designates a biological feature; whereas "person" designates a social role. A *person* is an entity who can enter into certain sorts of social relations with us. A *human* is the genetic offspring of human parents. The movie character E.T. was a person, but he certainly was not human. A fetus in the womb, immediately before birth, is human, but is not—yet—a person because it is not available for social interaction.

Two teleologists with identical theories of value may come up with very different assessments of a given course of action if they approach their welfare calculations from the perspective of different moral reference groups. For example, a thorough-going sexist who refuses to take into account the interests of one gender would come to a very different conclusion about the optimal division of household tasks in a typical family a person who took the interests of all members of the household into account. More seriously, a personalist would be willing to withdraw life support from a permanently comatose individual

---

Table 3–2 Moral Reference Groups

Label	Scope
Personalism	Persons and only persons
Humanism	Humans and only humans
Vitalism	All and only living entities
Racism	All and only members of one race
Nationalism	All and only citizens of one nation
Sexism	All and only those of one gender
Universalism	All and only sentient creatures

(because the capacity for social interaction is no longer present); whereas a humanist would point to the continuing humanity of the individual as a reason for continuing support.

Determination of the moral reference group is also a meta-theoretical issue for deontologism. Kant's categorical imperative, for example, glosses together the moral reference group of personalism with that of humanism when it is phrased to read "Act so that you treat humanity, whether in your own person or in that of another, always as an end and never as a means only."[4] It might be unclear whether this definition applies to persons only or to all humanity, but it is clear, on the one hand, that it does not countenance sexism, racism, or nationalism, and, on the other hand, that it does not include sentient nonhuman animals in the moral community. Kant was no animal-rights advocate.

The debate about animal rights can help to illuminate the issues here. Animal-rights advocates point out the features of nonhuman animals that are similar to human attributes (especially sentience, including especially the capacity to suffer pain). They accuse us of inconsistency if we uphold moral rules against certain sorts of treatment of humans at the same time that we allow similar treatment of nonhuman animals. I contend that, even if successful, this argument is not enough to establish so-called rights in any full-blooded sense or to establish genuine moral standing for nonhuman animals. Even if we are persuaded by these arguments that we have been needlessly cruel in our treatment of animals in food production, research, and other activities and resolve to treat them in less cruel and more humane ways in the future, we are still a long way from granting them genuine moral standing or membership in the moral community.

Moral standing goes beyond describing actions as cruel or inhumane. For members of the moral community, another, more serious category of wrong is possible: the wrong of moral affront, indignity, or disrespect. One can show disrespect without being cruel (e.g., through diffidence), and one can cause pain (and perhaps even be cruel in a sense) without showing disrespect. For example, a father refrains from rescuing his son from a painful experience in the interest of allowing him to experience the natural consequences of a mistake he has made so that he will learn the wrongness of it. The common element in instances of disrespect or affronts to dignity has to do with the breakdown in an established system of cooperative mutual interaction. Instead of treating you as a peer engaged in a joint enterprise, I fail to acknowledge your interests or concerns and "use" you to further goals of my own. This notion of indignity or disrespect is the core notion in moral standing. If nothing we do to an individual qualifies as an indignity, that individual lacks full moral standing.[5]

Individually, some of us may form such a strong bond with our pets that we admit them to our moral circle, and thus we regard a slight to them as an indignity. However, as a society we are a long way from having this sort of regard for nonhuman animals generally. The day might come when we do, and we might then look back on our current treatment of nonhuman animals with the same disdain as we hold for the institution of slavery in our nation's past. However, unless and until we reach this sort of general understanding of their status, we cannot say that nonhuman animals are truly admitted into the moral community.

It is difficult to say precisely when (if ever) there will be an established status of moral standing for nonhuman animals. It is not enough for one or two visionaries to treat them in this way and to urge us to follow their example. At the other extreme, it is probably not necessary that each and every member of the moral community acknowledge their standing. Some (ill-defined) threshold of acceptance exists that would lead the moral anthropologist to say that this entity has become a full-fledged member of our moral community.

We can raise questions in this regard as to whether children are currently fully established members of our moral community. Child abuse statutes are on the books throughout our society, but they are not always seriously enforced. Authorities all too often condone gross abuse of children by their parents or caretakers as acceptable discipline or as falling within the domain of the privacy of the family and therefore none of the community's business.

If we are still at this stage with regard to children well over a century after the establishment of humane societies to campaign against cruelty to children and animals, it is not surprising that we are uncertain about the moral standing of reproductive materials or of the embryo at various stages of its development.

One aspect of this issue faced a concrete political test in November 2011. The State of Mississippi put on the ballot a constitutional amendment that would extend legal protection to the earliest forms of human life. The amendment read as follows:

> **SECTION 33. Person defined.** As used in . . . Article III of the state constitution, "The term 'person' or 'persons' shall include every human being from the moment of fertilization, cloning or the functional equivalent thereof."[6]

If enacted, this amendment would have made illegal all forms of abortion—including those when the mother's life is at stake—as well as any forms of birth control, which prevent implantation of the fertilized ovum. Although polls before the voting indicated that the amendment might pass, when they reached the privacy of the voting booth, the citizens of Mississippi defeated the measure resoundingly. Fifty-eight percent voted against the measure; only 42% favored it. Proponents promise to carry this issue to other states, and perhaps to introduce it as an amendment to the U.S. Constitution, so we may see this debate on the issue at the heart of our discussion here continue in the months and years to come.

Technological developments in the reproductive area not only increase the points at which we may (and perhaps must) make decisions, but they also have an impact on our attitude toward the developing embryo. On the one hand, the use of ultrasonography gives the expectant parent(s) prenatal contact and experience with the embryo. I have heard more than one couple describe the ultrasound images of their fetus in utero as "our first baby pictures." In contrast, however, the greater awareness of the uncertainties of pregnancy that has come to our attention through our diagnostic technologies has led to what one commentator has called "the tentative pregnancy."[7] In this instance, women do not fully acknowledge that they are pregnant (especially to their friends but also attitudinally to themselves) until early ultrasounds, amniocentesis, or both have established that the fetus is free from the sort of significant problems that might lead to miscarriage or to a decision to have an elective abortion.

MAKING DECISIONS

How does one make decisions about the separation of roles within the reproductive process that affect the stake of the various parties? It is far from clear. Parents I know who have both one or more children who are genetically theirs (e.g., lines 1–4 on Table 3–1) and one or more who are adopted (e.g., line 28 on the table) uniformly insist that there is no fundamental difference in their commitment, emotional attachment, or sense of parenthood toward these children. Indeed, after a while, they may have to stop to remember which children are genetically theirs and which are not.

Similarly, when the case was in the news a few years ago about a child who had been switched at birth with another baby some dozen or so years earlier, I asked many of my friends who have children how they would feel if they were to learn after many years that the child they had been caring for was not genetically their child. I could not find anyone who would even begin to countenance the possibility of returning the child they now had to his or her genetic parents and taking on responsibility for the child who was genetically theirs. They uniformly and emphatically said that they considered the child currently in their household as *their* child, and that the other child, although having genetic links to them, would be a stranger to them.

Yet infertile couples expend enormous resources and effort in attempts to have a child who is genetically theirs, whereas many adoptable children languish in institutions or foster homes. To these people at this stage of the career of parenthood, genetics matters a great deal; to people at a later stage of the career, it seems to matter a great deal less. The child for whom I have cared and established a relationship with is clearly *mine*, no matter whether he or she is genetically mine; the child that I *propose* to care for is less obviously mine merely because I am entrusted to care for him or her. I suggest that identification comes with extended contact with the child and getting to know that child *as a person*. Until that point, the child is, in a way, an abstraction—but I may more nearly identify the abstraction with myself if I am aware of a genetic linkage. All this suggests that genetics, not to be discounted entirely, are far from fundamental to the long-range bond between child and parent.

The interest of adopted children in learning about their genetic parents raises similar ambiguities. Most (but not all) adopted children report a strong interest in learning about their genetic parentage, but most also insist that this interest does not interfere with or diminish their emotional ties to the parents who have cared for them since birth (what I call their "social parents" in Table 3–1).

New technologies introduced one more complication. Even if the notion of the zygote or fetus as a *potential* person could be given sense in traditional reproduction—perhaps in terms of the course of development that would occur naturally if nature were left without interference to follow its course—this makes little or no sense nowadays. The natural course of events for a frozen pre-embryo[8] is inertial—it will remain in suspended animation until some intervention occurs to change its status. Little practical difference exists between the potential for personhood of a frozen pre-embryo and that of an individual germ cell that has not yet been joined with another. Only one additional laboratory step is required to move the individual sperm or ovum onto the path toward becoming a person (i.e., in vitro fertilization). Only one additional step is required to move the frozen pre-embryo onto the same path (i.e., implantation). Without technical intervention, the potential is nil in both cases.

Several ambiguities cannot help but be reflected in our valuation of the entity in question and in our decision making about it. A pre-embryo is not the same as a child. In fact, a vast gap exists between the ways we experience and think of these two stages of the reproductive process. The way we think about what constitutes a child also varies based on the time of gestation and the change in status from embryo to fetus to birth.

It is argued by some that the pre-embryo is already genetically individuated and thus that it should be accorded the respect due to any human being;[9] however, this overlooks at least two respects in which a pre-embryo falls short of full human status. For one thing, twinning could occur after this stage, so we may have here the proto-stage of two persons (i.e., identical twins) instead of one individual. Second, the cells at this stage are not yet differentiated in terms of which cell will become one organ and which another—and, indeed, some of the cells that form part of the unified organism at this point of development will differentiate into placental material and thus will ultimately be discarded. Thus, it flies in the face of genetic fact to insist at this stage that the person who will (perhaps) come into being is present in some inchoate form. Furthermore, the probabilities of carrying the pre-embryo to term are only in the neighborhood of 5% even if implantation occurs, so the odds are decisively against having a child develop from this clump of cells.

At what point in development shall we rule that a baby becomes a member of the moral community in her or his own right? **Table 3–3** sketches some key candidates for the transition point, together with the underlying philosophical rationale for each. It might not be the case that a bright line comes to be established; instead, an increasing value may be placed on the entity as it develops, culminating finally in a full-fledged sense of dignity or moral personhood.

These sorts of considerations led the Ethics Committee of the American Fertility Society to conclude the following:

> We find a widespread consensus that the pre-embryo is not a person but is to be treated with special respect because it is a genetically unique, living human entity that might become a person. In cases in which transfer to a uterus is possible, special respect is necessary to protect the welfare of the potential offspring. In that case, the pre-embryo deserves respect because it might come into existence as a person. This viewpoint imposes the traditional duty of reasonable prenatal care when actions risk harm to prospective offspring. Research on or intervention with a pre-embryo, followed by transfer, thus creates obligations not to hurt or injure the offspring who might be born after transfer.[10]

Table 3–3 The Beginning of Moral Personhood

Transition Point	Underlying Philosophical Rationale
Preconception	Transmigration of souls. Reincarnation—the personal identity (soul) exists before and independent of embodiment.
Conception	Identification of personal identity and/or potentiality with genetic integrity.
Conception + 14 days	Past twinning limit; assumes that individuation of soul, identity, or life is established once genetic integrity is firm.
Implantation	Acknowledges the high frequency of spontaneous abortions before this stage; thus, individual identity or potentiality is tied to the *probability* of live birth.
Organ function	The beginning of "life" is sometimes dated from the initiation of the functioning of certain key organs, such as the heart or the brain. This is an attempt to make the criterion of the beginning of life parallel to the operational criterion of death.
Quickening	Reflects the ancient view that the fetus was inert matter until a certain point and then it "came alive." The change was usually ascribed to ensoulment (see next item).
Ensoulment	Infusion into the fetus of a soul.
Viability	Emphasizes the possibility of independence as the identifying feature of a person.
Birth	Emphasizes actual independence as the crucial feature of membership in the moral community.
"Personhood"	Usually correlated with certain landmarks in mental and social development, such as a concept of self. Usually based on an analysis of rights.

Reproduced from G. C. Graber, A. D. Beasley, and J. A. Eaddy, *Ethical Analysis of Clinical Medicine*: A Guide to Self-Evaluation (Baltimore: Urban & Schwarzenberg, 1985), 197.

I am convinced that applying this reasoning to the various decisions that might arise leads to a sensitive and morally serious approach.

All the parties affected by choices ought to have some significant voice in decisions, and all parties should take into account the special respect owed to these entities at every stage. In addition, special precautions should be taken if there is a possibility that the entities are to be implanted and allowed to develop. For example, surrogacy contracts ought not to be regarded as indistinguishable from, for example, a contract that a woman might enter into to keep some piece of property in trust for a period of time. In addition to fiduciary duties to the contracting parties, the surrogate mother has special obligations of due care to protect the life that, it is hoped, will result. However, if her life or health were threatened from continuing the pregnancy, it would be unreasonable to expect her to jeopardize her future in order to continue the process. Thus, she would retain her right to abortion in this sort of situation. The legal right to elective abortion might remain even if her reasons for ending the pregnancy were less weighty (e.g., the notorious case of pique over a late expense payment by the contracting parties), but ethically we would surely criticize an individual in these cases for failure to show the special respect that is due to the fetus.

Surrogacy arrangements ought to be developed with caution, recognizing that we are not dealing with a mere material possession, but rather with an entity that merits special respect and that may well generate intense emotions in the gestational mother, thus making it difficult for her to carry through agreements to give the child up and sever all ties once the child is born. Several notorious court cases have dealt with these matters, but even more common are hurt feelings by surrogate mothers who had expected to continue to be involved in the child's life after birth. All these issues require a thorough discussion throughout the gestational process, and clear-cut agreements negotiated in detail.

It may be too much to expect the law to be responsive to all these ambiguities, at least immediately, but our ethical thinking in this area is that they need to be taken into account. We are dealing here with issues for which we must stretch our thinking to provide nuanced, sensitive ethical guidance. It would be too heavy-handed to prohibit development of this technology because we do not have a ready set of rules for dealing with its ethical dimensions. It is simplistic to thrust these decisions into the Procrustean bed of our moral rules for dealing with already-born children. Instead, we must undertake the task of sorting through the complexities and ambiguities of these unprecedented human dilemmas and attempt to come to consensus on the courses of action that maximize all the values involved. In the best sense, casuistry (resolving moral questions by using ethics principles) is called for, because we have a moral landscape before us that has been heretofore uncharted and must be filled in through the most careful and sensitive analysis of all its features.

SUMMARY

In this chapter, Graber discusses the many reproduction options that will be a part of the creation of human beings in the 21st century. Although these options are a tribute to the progress of reproductive technology, they pose serious ethical issues in terms of the moral status of gametes and embryos and the need to identify the boundaries of the moral community. Graber uses ethical theories to show how to define the members of this community.

In addition to complicating the definition of a moral community, reproductive technology also creates ambiguity about how one sees the nature of an embryo. The chapter discusses these issues and presents information about parents' attitudes toward the personhood of children whether they are their genetic offspring or not. Finally, it points out the gap between the advances of reproductive technology and the moral decisions they will generate. The 21st century will require the courage to travel this moral landscape and map our course though ethical reasoning and discourse.

QUESTIONS FOR DISCUSSION

1. How important is the definition of *moral community* to defining the moral status of gametes and embryos?
2. What elements of deontology apply to making ethical decisions about this topic?
3. How can teleological thinking apply when defining the moral status of gametes and embryos?
4. Autonomy seems to be a theme in this chapter. What are the ethical issues relating to autonomy for the surrogate mother?
5. What ethical issues exist for the different stages of moral personhood? How can this concept assist you with ethical decision making?

FOOD FOR THOUGHT

This chapter introduces new ways of thinking about reproductive technology and how its use can challenge our ethical thinking. In fact, this technology may even redefine who we are as humans. Suppose a person told you that using reproductive technology was not ethical because it does not respect persons. Using Table 3–3 and the material in the chapter, how would you respond to this person?

ADDITIONAL READINGS

American Society for Reproductive Medicine. *Ethical Considerations of Assisted Reproductive Technologies: ASRM Ethics Committee Reports and Statements.* Available at http://www.asrm.org/EthicsReports/.

Genetics and Public Policy Center, Washington, DC (www.dnapolicy.org), reports on:

- *Reproductive Genetic Testing: Issues and Options for Policymakers* (2004)
- *Preimplantation Genetic Diagnosis: A Discussion of Challenges, Concerns, and Preliminary Policy Options Related to the Genetic Testing of Human Embryos* (2004)
- *IVF, Egg Donation, and Women's Health* (2006)
- *The Genetic Town Hall: Public Opinion About Research on Genes, Environment, and Health* (2009)

Glover, J. *Ethics of New Reproductive Technologies: The Glover Report to the European Commission.* DeKalb, IL: Northern Illinois University Press, 1989.

Humber, J. M., and R. F. Almeder, eds. *Bioethics and the Fetus: Medical, Moral and Legal Issues.* Totowa, NJ: Humana Press, 1991.

Post, S. G., ed. *Encyclopedia of Bioethics*, 3rd ed. New York: Macmillan Reference USA, 2004. See especially the following articles:

- "Embryo and Fetus"
- "Fetal Research"
- "Genetic Testing and Screening"
- "Moral Status"
- "Reproductive Technologies"

Walters, W., and P. Singer. *Test-Tube Babies: A Guide to Moral Questions, Present Techniques, and Future Possibilities*. New York: Oxford University Press, 1982.

NOTES

1. For an earlier version of this chart, see G. C. Graber, "Ethics and Reproduction," in *Bioethics*, ed. R. B. Edwards and G. C. Graber (New York: Harcourt, Brace, Jovanovich, 1988), 635.
2. See, for example, N. Fost, "Conception for Donation," *Journal of the American Medical Association* 291, no. 17 (2004): 2125–2126.
3. G. C. Graber, A. D. Beasley, and J. A. Eaddy, *Ethical Analysis of Clinical Medicine: A Guide to Self-Evaluation* (Baltimore: Urban & Schwarzenberg, 1985), 256–258.
4. I. Kant, *Foundations of the Metaphysics of Morals*, trans. Lewis White Beck (Indianapolis, IN: Bobbs-Merrill, 1959), 47.
5. For a fuller account of this argument, see R. B. Edwards and G. C. Graber, *Bioethics* (New York: Harcourt, Brace, Jovanovich, 1988), 16–18.
6. For the actual submission of the language of this proposed amendment, see http://www.sos.ms.gov/Elections/Initiatives/Initiatives/26text.pdf. Accessed June 13, 2012.
7. B. Katz Rothman, *The Tentative Pregnancy: Prenatal Diagnosis and the Future of Motherhood* (New York: Viking/Penguin, 1986).
8. J. Lejeune, *The Concentration Can: When Does Human Life Begin? An Eminent Geneticist Testifies* (San Francisco: Ignatius Press, 1992).
9. Graber, Beasley, and Eaddy, *Ethical Analysis of Clinical Medicine,* 197.
10. American Fertility Society, "Ethical Considerations of the New Reproductive Technologies," *Fertility and Sterility* 46, no. 3, Suppl. 1 (1986): 35S.

CHAPTER 4

The Ethical Challenges of the New Reproductive Technologies

Sidney Callahan

INTRODUCTION

How should we ethically evaluate the new reproductive technologies that treat human infertility? National debate over this issue continues as the incidence of infertility increases and new techniques become available. Without a consensus about what is morally acceptable, a huge, profitable, and virtually unregulated "baby business" has grown and expanded.[1] At this point in the United States, legal lacunae and regulatory inconsistencies exist amidst contested ethical views.[2] One cause for the confusion arises from the rapidity of technological innovations and the burgeoning market practices serving the growing demand.

Another factor is the existence in our society of large conflicts over the morality of sex and reproduction. Ongoing bitter debates exist over abortion, stem-cell research, the status of embryos, and, to a lesser extent, contraception and sex education in the schools. Lacking societal consensus on the morality of using medical technology to plan, limit, or interrupt pregnancies, we confront difficulties in evaluating the newest assisted reproductive technologies aimed at producing births. To add to the uncertainty, the developed world is experiencing cultural changes in attitudes toward women, children, gender, and the family. These interrelated social and technological changes have produced a pressing need to develop an ethic of responsible reproduction.

My focus here is on some of the newest challenges. How should we ethically assess the innovative array of recent techniques developed to assist reproduction, such as in vitro fertilization, embryo transplants, egg and sperm donations, and surrogate mothers?

TWO INADEQUATE APPROACHES TO EVALUATING ALTERNATIVE REPRODUCTIVE TECHNOLOGY

Two inadequate approaches to the ethical assessment of the new alternative reproductive technologies are mirror images of each other in the narrowness of their focus. A conservative approach adopts as a moral requirement an "act analysis," in which the biological integrity of each marital heterosexual act must be preserved without artificial interference. In this view, a heterosexual married couple's act of sexual intercourse and union must always remain open to procreation.[3] Morally, marital "love making" and "baby making" must not be separated. This view forbids separation of sexual acts from their procreative potential in order to obtain a contraceptive or reproductive effect; ergo, artificial techniques that separate conceptions from acts of marital intercourse are wrong. It also does not support third-party sperm and eggs ever being used for assisted reproduction. The fact that many alternative reproductive technologies do not protect embryonic lives gives further cause for condemnation. Although the use of medical knowledge of human fertility for interventions that increase the probabilities of in vivo conception are approved, achieving procreation through in vitro fertilization, artificial insemination, cloning, or third-party egg and gestational surrogacy is judged to be unethical.[4]

At the opposite end of the ideological spectrum, another form of act analysis focuses on the private acts of autonomous individuals for reproduction by medical technologies as exercises of procreative liberty and the intrinsic human right to reproduce. One must permit competent adult persons to exercise their reproductive rights at will, without interference. As long as due process and informed consent by these adults are safeguarded through appropriate contracts, they should be free to engage in any safe alternative reproductive technology that can be procured from providers.[5] This permissive stance toward individual-willed choices and the acceptance of market transactions is held to be morally justified on the basis of an individual's right to privacy and autonomy. In this perspective, those who would limit acts of reproductive liberty must bear the burden of proving or demonstrating concrete harm from an innovative practice. Therefore, in effect, almost any alternative reproductive technologies will be allowed as ethically acceptable because long-term negative consequences can hardly be shown beforehand.

One can evaluate both of the above approaches to the ethics of using reproductive technologies as too narrow to address the breadth and complexities of the moral challenge. In a multifaceted, intergenerational, socially critical, and conflicted situation, no single good can be decisive. A reproductive ethic based solely on private liberty or on preserving the biological integrity of each marital act of genital intercourse will hardly be adequate or satisfactory. Humans are both biologically evolved creatures and socially embedded rational persons living within overlapping cycles of familial cultures. Mastery of biological nature through technological interventions is an essential characteristic of the human species. Religious believers will add that the exercise of reason and technological discovery fulfills the call of the Creator to further human survival, human flourishing, and the relief of suffering. Yet either as believers or unbelievers, rational human beings observing their own historical record must acknowledge that innovative technologies can also produce harm.

That the unrestricted use of new technologies has resulted in ecological and ethical disasters is an unfortunate but incontestable truth. In too many cases, such as the invention of lethal weapons of war, the ends were destructive and intended. In other cases, well-meaning innovative technologies have inadvertently produced unforeseen harms. Often harms arise from ignoring the ecological and social environment or from failing to foresee that long-term side effects will outweigh immediate advantages. There is a grain of truth in the warning that control of nature by some people can end in producing oppressive control of other people. Because technological innovation is rarely value free or neutral, there must be a prudent and ethical assessment. Consequently, according to a precautionary principle, one should ask those proposing innovations and change to show that no biological or social harms would ensue.

Innovative reproductive technologies are particularly worrisome because the stakes are so high for both individuals and society. New human lives are at risk, and the children conceived and born are nonconsenting third parties who are completely vulnerable to the desires and decisions of adults. Reproduction is not only central to family formation but also carries significant cultural values. Highly intelligent humans are "the self-interpreting animals," who live in sociocultural groups governed by symbolic meanings. Endorsing particular reproductive technologies will have cultural effects beyond fulfilling an individual's private desire to become a parent. Unfortunately, individual human desires, even good desires, may not serve the good of others.

Faced with new assisted reproductive technologies, the technological imperative (i.e., what can be done should be done) must not be allowed to govern individual and group reproductive practices and policies. The question is whether certain practices are right, good, and conducive to human flourishing for all the individuals and social groups concerned. One must address complex moral and social concerns as well as technological effectiveness.

A BASIS FOR DEVELOPING AN ETHICAL POSITION

In the case of reproductive technology, ethical positions should be grounded on consideration of what furthers the future good of potential children, their individual parents, their families, and the moral standards of worth of the larger society. What will benefit the various individuals involved as well as the common good? Conflicts will assuredly arise, and priorities and limitations will be enforced. It seems right and just that in conflicts of interest, one should give precedence to the good of the potential and newly existing child. The nascent human life is the most vulnerable party in the reproductive process and cannot give consent. Practically and politically, it is also clear that the physical and psychosocial welfare of a population's children determine the future welfare of the whole society. The protection, care, and education of children is a central moral obligation of humanity, and it is also collectively necessary for survival and social flourishing. The 1989 United Nations Convention on the Rights of the Child recognizes this moral and social truth. Human communities have a moral and social imperative to protect children and to institute practices that will provide for their well-being.

Prudent decision makers respect the biologically built-in social needs that evolution has produced for the successful reproduction of the species, as well as recognize the advantages that scientific knowledge and technological interventions bring. Evolved biological processes, sociocultural norms, and altruistic ideals have served human reproductive success. Parental altruism and protective caretaking is the foundation of group survival. In the human struggle against biological and social dangers, achievements have produced wonderful progress against disease, mortality, and social oppression. Yet, when scientific and social innovation involves unknown risks to vulnerable lives without their informed consent, precautionary principles should prevail. In the pursuit and practice of parenthood, given the intensity of emotional desires mixed in with profit motives and discrepancies in personal power, vigilance and safeguards are necessary. *Do no harm* is the primary moral mandate, always and everywhere.

One ethical justification for taking risks and adopting new assisted reproductive technologies claims that they should be permitted because they are analogous to, and just an extension of, the socially accepted practice of adopting children. Adoption is an ancient and widespread human practice that continues to flourish in modern societies. Evidence abounds that without ties of genetic kinship, one can incorporate children successfully into families by legal adoption. Therefore, why not allow and encourage innovative infertility treatments that break genetic ties and involve collaboration from third parties, such as egg and sperm donors or surrogate mothers? The claim is that the psychological intent and social commitments of parents are the most important and essential characteristics for family success. Therefore, achieving parenthood and founding a family through reproductive technological assistance should, like adoption, be open to infertile heterosexual couples, single parents, and homosexual couples. Moreover, individual children can prove to be resilient and manage to cope with step-families, single-parent families, and other cases where nonbiologically related "fictive kin" step in to rear children.

However, arguing from the example of adoption and "after the fact" crisis management is flawed and hardly justifies initiating or accepting any and all innovative reproductive technologies. Emergency adaptations make for poor standard operating procedures and norms.[6] In the case of adoption, a child already exists and is in need of parental care. Adoption rescues a child through an altruistic and committed action that benefits a child in need of a parent.[7] Regulations are placed on adoption by law, and there are many social protective measures aimed at preventing abuses. A rescue situation differs greatly from deliberately conceiving a child in order to give it up to others for monetary or other rewards.

Commercial sale or intentional breeding of human beings has been legally and morally unacceptable in Western society since the outlawing of slavery. In the interest of preserving the human dignity inherent in embodied integrity, there has been a prohibition on the purchase of brides, children, sexual intercourse, or bodily organs. Society considers the selling of children for sexual trafficking and pornography as a monstrous abuse. Existing moral norms regarding personal bodily integrity safeguard the moral mandate to treat a human being as an end and not as a means to another's purpose. To fabricate, make to order, or sell a baby to satisfy another individual's reproductive desires for parenthood reduces a human life to a product or material commodity.

Admittedly, no child can consent to its own birth, and a child once born generally would rather exist than not. A person can be grateful for life but also disapprove of his or her means of conception, even wanting such future acts to be banned. A child conceived through rape or incest could adapt well in a good adoptive family environment, but surely it would be wrong to plan or approve of such conceptions. Children kidnapped at birth from pregnant prisoners in Argentina's dirty war could have experienced good family care but feel deeply wronged. It is also no argument for employing an innovative procedure to point out all the failures and family dysfunction that beset children conventionally conceived. Yes, genetically related families can produce suffering, but existing dysfunction hardly justifies risk-taking practices because the outcomes could be no worse. Ethical decisions for employing an alternative reproductive technology should be justified on the grounds that it will strengthen, rather than threaten, basic operating moral and cultural values. What ethical norms should be proposed and defended?

A PROPOSED ETHICAL STANDARD

With the aim of safeguarding the well-being of the child, individual parents, family structures, and positive moral values of society, the following ethical standard for the use of alternative reproductive technologies can be proposed. It is ethically permissible to use an alternative reproductive technology if it makes it possible for a socially adequate heterosexual married couple to have a child that they would normally expect to have but cannot because of their infertility. The innovative techniques used should be proved medically safe and not harmful to nascent life or to the health and well-being of individual women and men.

Infertility does not seem strictly classifiable as a disease, and is never life threatening. Nor is infertility or childlessness a bar to living a worthwhile, happy life. One does not prove or enhance one's masculinity or femininity by producing a child. However, procreation and founding a family is an important natural good and an expected outcome for a young adult married couple. Infertility can cause intense suffering, and one can aptly view it as a dysfunctional burden. The moral dedication of medicine is to correct human dysfunction and relieve suffering by effective and ethical interventions. Consequently, it can be a great benefit when scientific knowledge and medical technology can assist an infertile couple to fulfill their normally expected reproductive functions.

As in any practice of medicine, the techniques used must be ethically acceptable; they should correct, remedy, and restore without doing harm—to the infertile who suffer, to the child, or to others. Important values of the society at large need to be respected and encouraged. Ethically acceptable assisted reproductive technologies that meet these requirements would include artificial insemination by husband (AIH), in vitro fertilization (IVF) of the couple's egg and sperm, or various tubal transfer methods that neither use third-party donors nor deliberately destroy embryonic lives. It seems morally contradictory to destroy human life to create new life. Such a remedial ethical standard for reproductive technology is based on evolved biological and developed sociocultural norms in which the genetic parents, the gestational mother, and the rearing parents are not separate and are adequately prepared to rear the child that results from remedial medical intervention. To this end, potential parents who are to be medically assisted to reproduce should be presently alive and well, in an appropriate period in their life cycle, and possess average psychological and social resources to care for a potential child.

Helping the severely retarded, the mentally ill, the genetically diseased, the destitute, the aged, or widows with a dead spouse's sperm to have a child they otherwise could not have would be ethically unacceptable. It would also be ethically suspect and medically risky to alter average expectable reproductive conditions by using techniques that intentionally produce multiple births that endanger the health of the prospective children. Such methods also lead to selection and destruction of "excess" embryos in the womb or to the use of genetic screening to obtain a desired gender. (The practices of sex-selective and other forms of abortion, genetic screening, and selection produce a whole range of other ethical problems that will not be dealt with in this chapter.)

One can generally acknowledge that the power to intervene in such a crucial matter as the procreation of a new life puts medical professionals and institutions in a fiduciary relationship with the potential child and not just with the adults involved. As causal agents, professionals have an ethical duty not to take serious risks on behalf of nonconsenting others. Agency brings moral responsibility and produces unavoidable moral obligations for professional practitioners. They, like other members of society, have moral obligations to uphold larger social goods and values as well as their duties to individuals in their care. Moreover, the fact that we employ medical resources and professional skills for hugely expensive remedial infertility treatments means that larger questions of distributive justice cannot be ignored. The huge profits that arise from unregulated marketing and innovative infertility services raise other ethical and political concerns.[8] Other developed countries have instituted far more regulation and legal safeguards for use of reproductive technology than the United States, which is often derided as "the wild west" of reproductive medicine.

The claim that there is a violation of an individual's right to reproduce if infertility treatments are not available to any individual who can pay for them seems wrongheaded. A negative right not to be interfered with (e.g., the right to marry, which itself is not absolute) does not entail a positive right (e.g., that society is obligated to provide a spouse). Moreover, as a society, we have already decided that when child welfare is in the balance, social, legal, and professional interventions and curtailments of liberty are justified. Adoption procedures, custodial decisions, and child abuse cases require that professionals make judgments on the fitness of parental capacities. As the frequent cases of child abuse leading to death attest, it is better to err on the side of safety than to take risks with children's lives. Should not medical professionals and clinics be similarly responsible and cautious in carrying out the interventions that will create new children? The emotional desperation of many infertile persons (most often women) can be conducive to abusive but unregulated practices in a multibillion-dollar industry.

Employing third-party donors or different forms of surrogates is not, in this author's judgment, an ethically acceptable use of reproductive technologies. The practice of selling eggs and sperm is equally suspect and belies the meaning of a "donor" as a gift giver. It is possible to variously combine collaborative procedures using procured surrogates or sperm and eggs to produce embryos that may gestate in hired gestational wombs purchased through contract. Such separating and fragmenting of the reproductive process poses social and psychological risks arising from diffusion of responsibility and fragmentation of identity. To understand the problems with third-party donors, we need to consider the evolution of values, goods, and safeguards in the biological and cultural norm of having two heterosexual parents who are the genetic, gestational, and rearing parents of their biological children, who will be cared for over an extended family life cycle.

Many proponents of third-party donors in alternative reproduction—whether for infertile married heterosexuals, single men and women, or homosexual couples—ignore what happens *after* the conception, production, and procurement of a baby. There has been little account taken of the fact that individuals live out their lives within complex familial ecological systems.[9] The assumption seems to be that why and how one gets a baby makes no difference in what happens afterwards in the years of childrearing and family life. This might be true when breeding dogs and horses, but it is hardly true of complex thinking, feeling, imaginative, self-aware humans interested in their origins and narrative destinies in the world. Knowing your family history and kinship ties can be important in constructing one's self-identity, especially in adolescence. Identifying one's father, mother, and extended kinship group is critical in understanding and finding one's place in the world.

When a young person becomes sexually mature and wishes to marry and procreate, thoughts turn to his or her own progenitors and life story. The difficult challenges of developing into adulthood can become more confusing when collaborative reproduction has been employed. In old age too, genetic family relationships become more salient in the arc of a life. Legitimizing and morally sanctioning third-party or collaborative reproductive technology puts at risks the well-being of the child, the parents in families, the donor(s), and important moral goods of our culture.

THE FAMILY

The advantages and safeguards for children in having two married heterosexual parents who also are the genetic, gestational, and rearing parents are manifold and becoming more evident in new sociological research.[10] This kind of family produces biological and cultural advantages for its immediate and extended members. From an evolutionary point of view, mammalian "in vivo" reproduction and primate parent–child bonding provide an effective means for the protection, defense, and complex long-term nurture and socialization of offspring. Survival is endangered when a species lays eggs that are left floating unprotected in the sea or buried in the sand to take their chances with passing predators.[11]

With the advent of long-living rational animals such as human beings, the basic primate models of parenting were broadened and deepened; they are constituted by committed pair-bonded parenting and extended kinship bonds, such as siblings and grandparents.[12] Two heterosexual parents supported by their respective kin can engage in more arduous parental care-taking over an extended period of time. Grandparents give aid to the third generation, or their children's children. The mated pair who reproduces is also embedded in a larger social network that gives protection and generates the culture that furthers human flourishing. Society bases the foundation of present families on biological realities along with the cultural norms of commitment that produce altruistic bonds and mutual caretaking between the generations.[13]

Slowly the Western cultural family ideal has become less patriarchal as the equal moral worth and rights of women and children have been recognized. Families ensure far more benefits than simply maintaining law, order, and stable continuity. As the mated couple freely chooses each other, they make a commitment to share the task and joys of life. Bonded by love and legal contract, a man and woman mutually exchange exclusive rights to each other and give each other emotional, sexual, and socioeconomic support. Sexual mating results in children who concretely embody the marital union and have an equal claim to parental care from father and mother. In addition, the extended families of both parents are important resources for the couple; they can serve as backup caregivers, especially in cases of death or disaster.

No analysis of one procreative act in a marriage can do justice to the social fact that a reproductive couple and their children exist as a unit within an extended family of kin. Siblings, cousins, aunts, uncles, grandparents, and other relatives are important in family life for both practical and psychological reasons. Individual identity is rooted in biologically based descent and cooperative kinship networks within larger social groups. The family is one remaining institution where one is given or ascribed status by birth; one cannot earn or achieve the provision of unconditional altruistic care. Psychologically and socially, the family provides emotional connections and opportunities for altruism and gives meaningful purpose to life. Those individuals who do not marry or found families of their own still have strong connections to their kin through their families of origin.[14] Human beings exist within familial and social envelopes and must do so to flourish. However, as a human, culturally constructed commitment, why must genes and biology be the basis for the family? Cannot any persons who intend and declare themselves to be a family, be a family?

Although the internalized conscious psychological identification and commitment to be and supportively act like a family is the foundation of human families, one cannot deny the powerful bond created by genetic relationship. Biological kinship ties are important in other primates, and one should not underestimate them in human societies.[15] One working definition of the family is that a family consists of people who share genes. Sociobiologists and evolutionary psychologists emphasize the power of genetic relationships to generate altruism and human bonding automatically.[16] In fact, the willingness of infertile couples to continue the struggle to procreate their own biological child is testimony to the existence of strong innate urges to reproduce oneself genetically with a beloved mate. Even half of a genetic tie may be preferred to none. When an adoption is initiated, the legal system uses the template of genetic kinship ties as a model for legal relationships.

One understands that the genetic parental relation to their offspring of two married persons is the synthesis of two equal genetic heritages, with the child situated within both lineages. Members of both families give support, or one set of kin may by choice or chance become more important. But having two sets of kin provides important social resources or social capital. The child is heir to more than money or property when situated in a clear and biologically rooted kinship community. Siblings and collateral kin take an interest and help their biological relatives who share their genes and progenitors. In old age, younger generations of families take responsibility for caring for their older relatives.

Filial piety is an ancient virtue that still has force. The genetic tie is a powerful motivating factor because it is unique, localized, embodied, and an irreversible connection existing through time and space. One cannot undo it by changing circumstances and intentional commitments.

The search by adopted children for their biological parents and possible siblings reveals the psychological predisposition of humans to know of their birth origins and history.[17] Social movements toward greater transparency and openness of information regarding biological origins respond to the child's right to know. The children resulting from third-party donations increasingly seek out knowledge of the third-party donors. When there are one or more third-party donors—of sperm, eggs, or embryos—a child is distanced or cut off from either half or all of his or her genetic origins and heritage. If there is secrecy or deception concerning the child's origins, then there are wrongs to the child. The child's biological relatives remain unknown to him or her, and for their part, the grandparents and half-siblings are deprived from knowing their descendants and family members. Because family secrets are difficult to keep and seep into a family's atmosphere, delayed disclosures can produce distrust among those kept ignorant or overtly deceived. Even when a child and his or her relatives know the truth, the identity of the donor (or donors) can become an issue for all concerned. Are there other siblings and relatives out there?

Evolutionary psychology has come to see genetic factors as being increasingly important in mating, parent–child interactions, and childrearing outcomes.[18] When rearing parents and genetic parents differ and the donor is unknown, there is a provocative void. If there is knowledge of the donor and he or she is part of the rearing parents' family or social circle, other potential psychological problems and conflicts may emerge regarding who the real parent is and who has primary rights and responsibilities. When the third-party donor is also the surrogate mother, combining genetic and gestational parenthood, the social and legal problems can be profound. The much-discussed Whitehead–Stern court struggle indicates the divisive chaos and suffering that is possible in third-party surrogate arrangements and contracts.

In the average expectable situation, two married parents possess equal genetic investment in the child. The mutual and equal genetic relationship to the child can become a unifying force for the parents. They are irreversibly connected and made kin to each other through the child they have jointly procreated. This new life is the concrete embodiment of their love, commitment, and sexual bonding. A pregnancy with mutual monitoring of the developing child unites the couple and prepares them for their joint caretaking enterprise.[19] Each parent shares his or her genetic link with the child with his or her own extended family. Common genetic inheritance produces a family likeness and sense of belonging. Biological sharing of genes leads to empathy and easy affective attunement for family members. The child's genetic link to the other partner and to each marital partner's own kin can work to strengthen the marital and family bonds.

At the same time, the fact that the child is also a new and unique life formed by a random combination of a couple's genetic heritage gives the child enough difference so that he or she is seen as a separate and unique person. The child possesses what has been called an "alien dignity" as an irreplaceable, unique human life that must be recognized.[20] (Cloning one's self or another would be wrong because of its denial of and infringement on a child's possession of a new and unique identity.) Because we are embodied creatures, the psychological bonds of caring, empathy, and social commitments are built on the firm foundation of biological ties and bodily identity.

Assisting two parents to have their own biological child through technological interventions without third parties can further the bonding of a couple. Medical treatments and other procedures to remedy infertility can be an arduous process that tests personal commitment to each other and to the potential child. When techniques such as AIH or IVF or tubal ovum transfer are used to correct a couple's infertility, the time and money spent, the shared stress and discomfort, and the cooperative efforts required can serve to strengthen the couple's union. Seeking to bear their biological child can focus two persons upon their marital relationship and their mutual contribution to parenthood. The psychological bonding can increase and transcend the stress and unpleasant procedures that intervene in their sexual and social lives. Mutual sacrifices are necessary. When successful, the resulting baby will be a new person in whom there is mutual investment and to whom the parents are equally related. Given the equal investment in their child, both parents are equally responsible for childrearing and support.

Unfortunately, in assisted reproduction, the success rates for the arduous and expensive treatments of infertility are low and often disappointing.[21] The advancing age of men and women with infertility conditions is one obstacle; the expense of treatments is another problem. A couple has to be able to withstand frustration and burdens together and not become danger-ously obsessed with the quest. Otherwise, the temptation is strong to move to ethically and medically problematic methods offered in unregulated mar-ketplaces. So-called baby hunger can produce emotional pressures that cloud judgment and produce so-called genetically clouded children who will bear the risks.

When employing third-party genetic donors, one parent will have a biological relation to the child, and the other parent will not. True, the non-related parent can give consent, but even when consent is free, there is never an equalization of the imbalance. Although there is certainly no question of adultery in such a situation, the psychological intrusion of a third-party donor can have an effect on the couple's union. Even if there is no jealousy or envy, the situation dramatically defines the reproductive inadequacy of one partner, and reliance is placed on an outsider's genetic heritage and superior reproductive capacity. Asymmetry of biological parental relationships within a family or household has always been problematic, from Cinderella to today's stepparents and reconstituted families.[22] Children who are unrelated to one of their married parents have less positive social outcomes and are in greater danger of abuse.[23] The most frequently cited cause of divorce in second marriages is the difficulty of dealing with another person's children.[24] The empathy and irreversible identification and tie that come from a knowledge of shared biological kinship seem to buttress parental authority and commitment. In disturbed families under stress, one finds more incest, child abuse, and scapegoating if biological kinship is asymmetrical.[25]

Biological ties become psychologically potent just because human persons in families engage in imaginative subjective relations with one another, whether as children or adults.

Parents' fantasies about a child's past and future make a difference, as all students of child development or family dynamics will attest. Identical twins might even be treated very differently because parents project different fantasies upon them.[26] Third-party donors and surrogates cannot be counted on to disappear from family consciousness, even if legal contracts can control other ramifications and overt interventions. A child conceived by new forms of collaborative reproduction is part of a biosocial experiment without his or her consent. Although, as noted, no child gives informed consent to conception, a biological child of two parents is begotten and born in the same way as his or her parents. Even if there is no danger of transmitting unknown genetic disease or causing physiologic harms to the child, the psychological relationship of the child to his or her parents is at risk by third-party technological innovations. A child confronts the fact that his or her creation was made to order as a contracted product by third-party strangers—for pay. Treating a child like a commodity—something to be fabricated and procured to satisfy the desires of purchasing parents—infringes upon the child's alien dignity as a gift of nature's biological bounty.

As ideals of parenthood have developed, those who seek a child not as a gift received for its own sake but to satisfy some personal parental need or desired extrinsic end are judged ethically lacking in altruism and commitment. Unfortunately, we are still struggling to overcome residual beliefs that see children as a kind of personal property or as an adult entitlement that provides a "life-enhancing experience." Only gradually have we welcomed children as new lives given to their parents in trusted guardianship. Children are now valued as equal in moral worth to adults, despite their dependency and powerlessness. Having a child solely for some selfish purpose has now become as morally suspect as marrying solely for money or status. In the past, people have wanted children to secure domestic labor, to have caretakers in old age, to increase social power, to prove sexual prowess, or to have someone of their own to possess—or scapegoat. A person or a couple obsessively driven to procure a child might not be prepared to rear the actual child once born. Being wanted and being well reared are not the same. Parental dreams of the optimal baby or perfect child, the overinvestment in "gourmet children," also can be psychologically burdensome for a child.[27] Adolescent problems of anorexia, depression, and suicide have been viewed as related to the dynamics of parental overcontrol.[28] A young person must achieve a separate identity in order to interrelate adequately with others and to become autonomous-in-relationship. More ominously, the child who was desired for all the wrong reasons may not be accepted if born with problems. Outright rejection of imperfect or nonoptimal babies cannot be safely avoided by contracts. There may also be some health risks for IVF children, mainly due to multiple births and prematurity.

In the course of a child's development, psychologists note that thinking and fantasizing about one's origins seems to be inevitable in the search for self-identity. In alternative reproduction, the question "Whose baby am I?" becomes inevitable.[29] "Why was my biological parent not more concerned with what would happen to the new life he or she helped to create?" The need to know about possible half-siblings and other kin might become urgent at some point in development. The first infants conceived from sperm donors are now entering young adulthood, and they have started new Internet support groups and blogs to address their issues. Similarly, young adopted adults also search for their biological relatives and support movements for transparency and access to information. One concern is the problem of inadvertent incest, but the main focus is on the issue of achieving identity and integrity.

DONORS AND THE CULTURAL ETHOS

Procuring donors of sperm, eggs, embryos, or gestational wombs is an essential component of collaborative reproduction. Brokers, individuals, and clinics advertise and sell sperm, eggs, and gestating surrogate services in competitive marketing. The multibillion-dollar business has grown as infertility has increased. Reproductive marketing has been clothed in a "gauzy shroud of sentimentality," where misleading terms such as "donors," "surrogate mothers," "family building," or "forever families" are used to describe highly profitable enterprises.[30] Affluent infertile persons shop for sperm, eggs, and womb services in competitive markets with fluctuating prices. Brokers advertise and search for donors to recruit them for a profit; clients shop for the eggs and sperms they want and that they can afford. Donors, too, shop for the best deal.[31]

However, in this burgeoning enterprise, little research has examined the effect of the baby business on the donors. Women's physiologic health is one growing concern, as the complicated, arduous process of egg donation has increased the dangers posed by powerful drugs and invasive procedures. In addition, there has been little critical analysis of the morality and psychology of what a donor is doing. When persons are being paid, they are not strictly donors but are selling their genetic and bodily resources. There is an effort to have such transactions assimilated into the model of blood donations or organ donations, but this analogy is misleading.

When young persons sell their eggs and sperm, they are selling the unique genetic identity that they received from their own parents and grandparents. This is not like donating a kidney, because sperms and eggs contain the unique information and inherited generative potential that is basic to identity—one's own, and a future other. When an individual treats this inherited gift of unique genetic identity and generative power as less than personally inviolate, or contracts to sell it, he or she breaks an implicit compact to respect and practice "procreative stewardship."[32] An egg donor is selling the reproductive capacities of the eggs that she inherited from her mother while still in her mother's womb. A gestational surrogate mother sells her reproductive capacities much as one sells bodily sexual function in prostitution. The poor will need money, and the rich can offer to pay.

Occasionally there will not be an exchange of money, and donors or surrogates can consider that their voluntary participation in another's assisted reproduction is an act of unalloyed altruism, perhaps undertaken for a relative or close friend. But this altruism is clearly being directed to fulfill the desires of adult(s), not of the child who will be born. No donation, unpaid or not, of either sperm or eggs avoids the serious problem in the practice of donation of sperm or eggs by third parties: such practices counter a basic principle of morality, that is, that you take responsibility for the future consequences of your actions as a causal agent. Adult persons are held morally responsible for the effect of their words and deeds. In serious matters that bring about powerful effects, such as sex and reproduction, which have irreversible lifetime consequences, we rightly hold competent persons to a high standard of moral and legal responsibility. Specifically, to counteract tendencies toward sexual irresponsibility and child neglect, Western culture has insisted that men and women are accountable for those sexual acts that create new life. Donors, whether male or female, who take part in collaborative reproduction abdicate their future responsibility for their reproductive acts that will enable the births of their own biological children.

In fact, in most cases the donor contracts to avoid any future personal interventions. A person is specifically enjoined not to monitor or carry through on what he or she initiates or causes to happen. Instead, sellers hand over control of their generative resources and potency to physicians, brokers, or others, usually strangers. By design and contract, persons abdicate all consequences for their reproductive cooperative actions. Yet procreative responsibility is a basic demand of the natural responsibility arising from the causal efficacy inherent in the possession of power by rational human agents.[33] Taking part in the procreation of a new life incurs moral obligations and moral claims from the life engendered. It seems doubtful that a legal convention devised to further an innovative technology can undo such obligations. Certainly, contracts cannot undo the unique genetic linkage with biological parents.

Donors who abdicate reproductive responsibility also deprive their own parents of grandparenthood. They also keep other closely related family members from knowing their biological relatives. Future children of the donor, or other children of a surrogate mother, might never know their half-siblings. To disregard the biological reality of genetic relationships promotes a mistakenly disembodied, fragmented view of how human beings actually function. Moreover, when a woman donates her eggs or gestational capacity, or both, there is a grave danger of exploitation, as feminists have warned.[34] The physiologic risks attending the drastic intervention in a woman's reproductive system needed for egg retrieval and surrogacy are considerable.

If a woman is offered a great deal of money, she will be tempted to sell her bodily resources and suffer the consequences. Poor third-world women are already recruited to the gestational surrogacy market. Middle-class young women with desirable looks and high IQs can command high prices for their eggs; affluent bidders now advertise in college papers. When eggs are commodities sold to the highest bidder, a woman's identity as an integrated whole person is under the threat of reduction to a material supplier of parts. Similarly, with the sale of sperm, we sanction fragmented integrity and male abdication of responsibility for their biological offspring. Society allows the profit-making commerce in sperm, also complete with competitive advertising, despite social epidemics of male sexual irresponsibility and father-abandonment of children.

Many young males think nothing of masturbating and selling their sperm for cash until later in life, when they begin to rear their families. Popular published accounts of a donor finding out that he has over 70 children out there are unsettling—as are the prospects of being confronted by these children or having the half-siblings organize through Internet connections.[35]

When there is commercialization of reproduction, governed by contract and the purchase of body parts and functions, familial culture becomes even more fragmented and alienated. There is endangerment of the great primordial civilizing reality of invested parental commitment, mutual dependency, and irreversibly bonded genetic kinship. There is a weakening of commitment to support and care for one's own children when we legitimize the isolation of genetic, gestational, and social parentage. Those individuals who disregard the biological and cultural values that have previously evolved in our societies are engaging in a risky experiment with their children and their family lives. Most often, as persons of good intentions, they do everything they can to normalize and fulfill their desired parental roles. Their argument is that the great good of having children justifies the means employed. Often, they may refrain from deception and even encourage extended familial relations with donors and surrogates. However, in the end, can children comprehend, without anxiety, the fact that men sell their sperm, women market their eggs, and mothers make babies and give them away for money? Nothing could be more risky to human welfare than to enable men and women to distance themselves emotionally from their own bodily being, from their own family heritage, or from their future offspring.

One of the requirements for a responsible ethic of sexuality and reproduction is to acknowledge sexual acts as personal acts involving the whole person. Lust is wrong outside of committed loving relationships because it disregards the whole person in the pursuit of sensual gratification. If money is involved, a person is reduced to a means to fulfill another's desire, and exploitation follows. So, too, it seems wrong and dangerous to isolate, purchase, and intentionally use a person's reproductive capacities apart from his or her own family existence.

SUMMARY

An approved practice of isolating sexual and reproductive acts from personal responsibility for the outcomes is a form of moral abdication that can only increase existing problems within the culture. Society already faces a challenge to its traditional norms of moral obligation, responsible reproduction, and parental commitments to caretaking. Cultural norms, based on reason and natural evolution, have mandated the unity of genetic, gestational, and rearing parents. A mated and committed pair-bonded couple exists in an acknowledged extended biological kinship system. Families exist as dynamic intergenerational institutions that are embedded in the larger society; through procreation and altruistic adoption, families fundamentally enable human health, economic well-being, and emotional flourishing.

In Western societies, new scientific knowledge has brought new techniques of assisting infertility dysfunctions, but these interventions require ethical assessment. Morally, the parental role is correctly understood as basically an altruistic endeavor—parents procreate and rear children so that these new lives can develop and flourish. Children are no longer ethically viewed as personal property or as a means to satisfy adult desires, needs, or purposes. When adults make individual reproductive decisions, or groups enact public policies, the good of the potential child should be the primary consideration. Children will most safely flourish in a society that culturally endorses socially committed, biologically related families upheld by personal moral responsibility in their procreating.

This author has argued for an ethical standard that limits alternative reproductive techniques to those that remedy the infertility of a committed couple in average expectable conditions that can adequately support child care. To this end, she argues that the unity of genetic, gestational, and rearing parents should remain intact. Collaborative reproduction risks the good of the child, the good of families, the good of donors, and the important norm that agents uphold personal moral responsibility for their reproductive actions. Certain limits should be set on using new technological means for assisted reproduction. As Gandhi wisely said, "Means are ends in the making."[36]

QUESTIONS FOR DISCUSSION

1. According to Callahan's ethical reasoning, why would a business to create "gourmet children" be unethical when the potential parents are able to provide informed consent?

2. What ethical principles would apply in a decision to limit the use of current and future reproductive technologies?

3. How is Callahan's position on reproductive technology different from Graber's view in Chapter 3?

4. What ethical theories support Callahan's position in this chapter? What theories would not support it?

5. What ethical principles could be used to support Callahan's position in this chapter? What principles would not support it?

FOOD FOR THOUGHT

Suppose a woman is a celebrity whose income depends on her being "body ready" for her next role. She also wants to be a mother and has unlimited income to invest in a child that will meet her specifications of the "right baby." Also suppose that the technology that she desires is now readily available.

1. From an ethics standpoint, how do you defend her decision to have the baby she desires? How would you refute the ethics of such a decision?

2. How could being a baby created by technology and according to specifications affect the child? How could it affect the child as he or she becomes an adult?

3. What, if any, limitations should be placed on the baby business?

NOTES

1. See D. L. Spar, *The Baby Business: How Money, Science, and Politics Drive the Commerce of Conception* (Cambridge MA: Harvard Business School Press, 2006); D. L. Spar, "The Business of Babies," *Science & Theology News* (July–August 2006): 43–46; and D. L. Spar, "Buying Our Children, Selling Our Souls? The Commodification of Children," *Conscience* 27 (2006): 14–16.

2. See B. Steinbock, *Life Before Birth: The Moral and Legal Status of Embryos and Fetuses*, 2nd ed. (Oxford: Oxford University Press, 2011); and E. Marguardt, *The Revolution in Parenthood: The Emerging Global Clash Between Adult Rights and Children's Needs* (New York: Institute for American Values, 2006).

3. Congregation for the Doctrine of Faith, *Instruction on Respect for Human Life in Its Origin and on the Dignity of Procreation* (Washington, DC: United States Catholic Conference, 1987).

4. A statement of these principles can be found in Roman Catholic Church teaching: see Congregation for the Doctrine of Faith, *Instruction on Respect for Human Life*. Also see P. Lauritzen, *Pursing Parenthood* (Bloomington, IN: Indiana University Press, 1993).

5. J. A. Robertson, *Children of Choice: Freedom and the New Reproductive Technologies* (Princeton, NJ: Princeton University Press, 1994).

6. J. Wallerstein, J. Lewis, and S. Blakeslee, *The Unexpected Legacy of Divorce: A 25-Year Landmark Study* (New York: Hyperion, 2000).

7. M. Stewart Van Leeuwen and G. Miller Wrobel, "The Moral Psychology of Adoption and Family Ties," in *The Morality of Adoption: Social-Psychological, Theological, and Legal Perspectives*, ed. T. P. Jackson (Grand Rapids, MI: William B. Eerdmans, 2005), 3–31.

8. M. Ryan, *Ethics and Economics of Assisted Reproduction: The Cost of Longing* (Washington, DC: Georgetown University Press, 2003). See also D. L. Spar, *The Baby Business*; D. L. Spar, "The Business of Babies"; and D. L. Spar, "Buying Our Children, Selling Our Souls?".

9. A classical statement of this process can be found in E. H. Erickson, *Childhood and Society* (New York: Norton, 1950); also see J. Heckhausen, "Psychological Approaches to Human Development," in *The Cambridge Handbook of Age and Ageing*, ed. M. L. Johnson (Cambridge: Cambridge University Press, 2005), 181–189; and R. Martinson and S. A. Martinson, "The Nature of Parenting," in H. Anderson, D. Browning, I. S. Evison, and M. Steward Van Leeuwen, eds., *The Family Handbook* (Louisville, KY: Westminster John Knox Press, 1998), 63–89.

10. Institute for American Values, *Why Marriage Matters: 26 Conclusions from the Social Sciences*, 2nd ed. (New York: Institute for American Values, 2005); Marguardt, *The Revolution in Parenthood*.

11. See J. Altman, "Sociobiological Perspectives on Parenthood," in *Parenthood: A Psychodynamic Perspective* (New York: Guilford Press, 1984); and E. O. Wilson, *Sociobiology* (Cambridge, MA: Harvard University Press, 1975). See also M. Daly and M. Wilson, "Evolutionary Psychology and Marital Conflict: The Relevance of Stepchildren," in *Sex, Power, Conflict: Evolutionary and Feminist Perspectives*, ed. D. M. Buss and N. M. Malamuth (Oxford: Oxford University Press, 1996), 9–28.

12. The role of the father has been seen as critically important in both the female and male child's intellectual development, moral development, sex role identity, and future parenting; for a summary of relevant research, see R. D. Parke, *Fathers* (Cambridge, MA: Harvard University Press, 1981); and S. M. H. Hanson and F. W. Bonett, *Dimensions of Fatherhood* (Beverly Hills, CA: Sage Publications, 1985).

13. See K. Gough, "The Origin of the Family," *Journal of Marriage and the Family* (November 1971): 760–768; P. J. Wilson, *Man the Promising Primate: The Conditions of Human Evolution*

(New Haven, CT: Yale University Press, 1980); G. P. Murdock, "The University of the Nuclear Family," in *A Modern Introduction to the Family*, ed. N. W. Bell and E. F. Vogel (New York: The Free Press, 1968); and M. J. Bane, *Here to Stay: American Families in the Twentieth Century* (New York: Basic Books, 1976).

14. S. P. Bank and M. D. Kahn, *The Sibling Bond* (New York: Basic Books, 1982); I. Arnet Connidis, "Sibling Ties Across Time: The Middle and Later Years," in *Cambridge Handbook of Age and Aging*, 429–436.

15. Wilson, *Man the Promising Primate*, and Daly and Wilson, "Evolutionary Psychology and Marital Conflict."

16. D. S. Browning, "Adoption and the Moral Significance of Kin Altruism," in *The Morality of Adoption*, 52–77.

17. C. Nadelson, "The Absent Parent, Emotional Sequelae," in *Infertility: Medical, Emotional, and Social Considerations*, ed. M. D. Mazor and H. F. Simons (New York: Human Sciences Press, 1984); M. Stewart Van Leeuwen and G. Miller Wrobel, "Moral Psychology of Adoption."

18. Twin studies and the recognition of inherited temperamental traits have followed studies showing a genetic component to alcoholism, manic depression, schizophrenia, antisocial behavior, and IQ. For a popular discussion of the findings concerning schizophrenia and criminal behavior, see S. Mednick, "Crime in the Family Tree," *Psychology Today* 19 (March 1985): 58–61. For a more general discussion by an anthropologist, see M. Konner, *The Tangled Wing: Biological Constraints on the Human Spirit* (New York: Holt, Rinehart & Winston, 1982). See also Daly and Wilson, "Evolutionary Psychology and Marital Conflict."

19. A. Macfarlane, *The Psychology of Childbirth* (Cambridge, MA: Harvard University Press, 1977); M. Greenberg, *The Birth of a Father* (New York: Continuum, 1985).

20. H. Thielcke, *The Ethics of Sex* (New York: Harper & Row, 1964), 32ff. Later analyses of the ethics of having children can be found in J. Blustein, *Parents and Children: The Ethics of the Family* (Oxford: Oxford University Press, 1982); O. O'Neill and W. Ruddick, eds., *Having Children: Philosophical and Legal Reflections on Parenthood* (New York: Oxford University Press, 1979); and S. Callahan, "An Ethical Analysis of Responsible Parenthood," in *Genetic Counseling: Facts, Values, and Norms; Birth Defects*, Original Article Series 15, no. 22 (New York: Alan R. Liss, 1979).

21. Centers for Disease Control and Prevention, American Society for Reproductive Medicine, and Society for Assisted Reproductive Technology, *2003 Assisted Reproductive Technology Success Rates: National Summary and Fertility Clinic Reports* (Atlanta: U.S. Department of Health and Human Services, Centers for Disease Control and Prevention, 2003). See also D. L. Spar, *The Baby Business*; D. L. Spar, "The Business of Babies"; and D. L. Spar, "Buying Our Children, Selling Our Souls?".

22. Daly and Wilson, "Evolutionary Psychology and Marital Conflict."

23. Institute for American Values, *Why Marriage Matters*.

24. B. Maddox, *The Half Parent: Living with Other People's Children* (New York: M. Evans and Company, 1975); R. Espinoza and Y. Newman, *Stepparenting: With Annotated Bibliography* (Rockville, MD: National Institute of Mental Health, Center for Studies of Child and Family Mental Health, 1979).

25. See "Explaining the Differences Between Biological Father and Stepfather Incest," and "Social Factors in the Occurrence of Incestuous Abuse," in *The Secret Trauma: Incest in the Lives of Girls and Women*, ed. D. E. H. Russell (New York: Basic Books, 1986).

26. D. N. Stern, *The Interpersonal World of the Infant: A View from Psychoanalysis and Developmental Psychology* (New York: Basic Books, 1985).

27. See "The Child as Surrogate Self" and "The Child as Status Symbol," in D. Elkind, *The Hurried Child* (Reading, MA: Addison-Wesley, 1981).

28. S. Minuchin, B. L. Rosman, and W. Baker, *Psychosomatic Families: Anorexia Nervosa in Context* (Cambridge, MA: Harvard University Press, 1978).

29. L. Andrews, "Yours, Mine, and Theirs," *Psychology Today* 18 (December 1984): 20–29; Marguardt, *The Revolution in Parenthood*.

30. See Spar's descriptions in D. L. Spar, *The Baby Business*; D. L. Spar, "The Business of Babies"; and D. L. Spar, "Buying Our Children, Selling Our Souls?". See also Lisa Mundy,

Everything Conceivable: How Assisted Reproduction Is Changing Men, Women, and the World (New York: Knopf, 2008).

31. Donor 15, "Ova Sale: The Art of the Deal in the Gray Market for Human Eggs," *Reason*, October 2006. Retrieved from www.reason.com/news/show/36867.html.

32. B. Waters, "Adoption, Parentage, and Procreative Stewardship," in *The Morality of Adoption*, 32–51.

33. H. Jonas, *The Imperative of Responsibility: In Search of an Ethics for the Technological Age* (Chicago: University of Chicago Press, 1984).

34. B. Rothman, *The Tentative Pregnancy* (New York: Viking Press, 1986); H. Holmes, B. Hoskins, and M. Gross, *The Custom-Made Child: Women-Centered Perspectives* (Clifton, NJ: Humana Press, 1981); A. M. Jagger, ed., *Living with Contradictions: Controversies in Feminist Social Ethics* (Boulder, CO: Westview Press, 1994); Michelle Goodwin, "Assisted Reproductive Technology and the Double Bind: The Illusory Choice of Motherhood," *Journal of Gender Race & Justice* 3 (2005–2006).

35. R. Romm, "All His Children: A Sperm Donor Discovers His Rich Unsettling Legacy," *The Atlantic*, December 2011, 22.

36. M. Gandhi, *The Essential Gandhi: An Anthology of His Writings on His Life, Work and Ideas* (New York: Random House, 1962).

CHAPTER 5

Abortion: The Unexplored Middle Ground

Carol Petrozella

INTRODUCTION

In 1998, R. A. McCormick wrote about abortion as an unexplored middle ground.[1] His words have withstood the passage of time and textbook editions and remain the model for this chapter. Petrozella's discussion provides an update on the issue of abortion and notes that it continues to divide the country. During the Republican National Convention in August 1988, McCormick listened to an interview with fundamentalist minister Jerry Falwell and Faye Wattleton, then president of Planned Parenthood, on the subject of abortion. Falwell insisted that unborn babies were the last disenfranchised minority— voiceless, voteless, and unprotected in the most basic of civil liberties. Wattleton's statements all returned to the concept of privacy and the woman's right to decide whether she would or would not bear a child. It was a tired old stalemate; neither party budged an inch. The moderators identified their only common ground as the ability to disagree.[2]

Unfortunately, the Falwell–Wattleton exchange is still an example of the current discussion on abortion. Each side makes one point that is central and absolute. The discussion accomplishes nothing except perhaps to raise everyone's blood pressure. All remarks are based on this single absolute starting point. Thus, Falwell saw nonviolent demonstrations at abortion clinics as signs of hope for a transformation of consciousness and a growing rejection of abortion. Wattleton saw them as unconstitutional and violent disturbances of a woman's exercise of her prerogative to make her own choice. In 2012, the BBC presented a series of arguments against abortion that opposed an automatic right for women to have this procedure. They are framed from a slightly different perspective than Falwell's, but share an absolute nature.[3]

Are we doomed forever to this kind of dialogue of the deaf? Perhaps, especially if the central principles identified by both sides are indeed central. However, one should note an important difference in these "central issues." Falwell and those who currently share his view speak primarily of the morality of abortion and only secondarily about public policy or the civil rights of the unborn. Wattleton and her successors say little about morality (although they imply much), but put all the emphasis on what is current constitutional public policy. On his level, Falwell was right. On her level, Wattleton was right (in the sense that *Roe v. Wade* does give women a constitutional right to abortion). The discussants are like two planes passing in the night at different altitudes.

In such heated standoffs, the idea of what public policy ought to be, especially which morality to choose, still remains to be fully discussed. The linkage of these two issues in a consistent, rationally defensible, humanly sensitive way usually becomes victim to gavel pounding and vote getting. Unless the public consciousness can make a more satisfactory linkage than it has thus far, any public policy on abortion will lack supportive consensus and continue to be seriously disruptive to social life. The terms *pro-choice* and *pro-life* will continue to mislead, label, and divide our citizenry.

Is it possible to enlarge the public conversation so that a minimally acceptable consensus might have the chance to develop? McCormick thought so and called his proposed area of conversation "the unexplored middle ground."[4] Despite McCormick's hopeful stance, the middle ground continues to be unattainable. Funding for women's health and family planning continue to be controversial and a focus of national and international debate. All agree that women's health is a United States and United Nations priority. The Earth Charter, the UN Millennium, and *Healthy People 2020*[5] (which states U.S. priorities for a healthy population) all address women's health issues and the disparity of health care and gender discrimination.

Currently, the abortion debate and women's reproductive rights have been in the political spotlight. Fueled by the funding debate, access to legal abortions has been hampered. Dorothy Samuels, in her article "Where Abortion Rights Are Disappearing," states: "Opponents of abortion rights know they cannot achieve their ultimate goal of an outright ban. . . [s]o they are concentrating on enacting laws and regulations narrowing the legal right and making abortion more difficult to obtain."[6]

Some level of middle ground was reached when President Obama issued an executive order "ensuring enforcement and implementation of abortion restrictions in the Patient Protection and Affordable Care Act."[7] The order states that "[f]ollowing the recent passage of the Patient Protection and Affordable Care Act ('the Act'), it is necessary to establish an adequate enforcement mechanism to ensure that Federal funds are not used for abortion services (except in the cases of rape or incest, or when the life of the woman would be endangered), consistent with a longstanding Federal statutory restriction that is commonly known as the Hyde amendment."[8] The order further states that these policies extend to the health insurance exchanges that are part of the act and reinforces that healthcare facilities and providers of care cannot be discriminated against because of "an unwillingness to provide, pay for provide coverage or refer for abortions."[9]

The issue of women's rights still is paramount in the discussion of abortion. According to Gloria Steinem, cited by Hill in an *Oakland Tribune* article of March 6, 2012, "Reproductive freedom is a fundamental human right—to decide what happens to our own bodies is as basic as freedom of speech and freedom of assembly."[10]

ELEMENTS OF A MIDDLE GROUND

1. There is a presumption against the moral permissibility of taking human life. This means that any individual or society sanctioning this or that act of intentional killing bears the burden of proof. Life, as the condition of all other experiences and achievements, is a basic good, indeed the most basic of all goods. If it we take a life without public accountability, we have returned to moral savagery. For this reason, all civilized societies have rules about homicide, although we might disagree with their particulars.

McCormick considered the presumption stated above to be the substance of the Christian tradition.[11] The strength of this presumption varies with times and cultures. Cardinal Joseph Bernardin noted that the presumption is stronger in our time.[12] By that he meant that in the past, the public saw capital punishment as a legitimate act of public protection. Furthermore, in war, killing was justified on three grounds: national self-defense, the recovery of property, and the redressing of injury. Now, however, many people reject capital punishment and view only national self-defense as justifying violent resistance. Although such applications remain controversial, they are not the point here. The key principle is the presumption against taking human life.

The debate about personhood continues. The definition of personhood is that it occurs "at the time of conception." In November 2011, Mississippi attempted to enshrine this idea into law through a referendum. However, the measure failed by a narrow margin. If laws defining personhood pass in state legislatures, then even certain types of birth control will be illegal.[13] As noted by an editorial in *USA Today*, the proposed Mississippi law would have made abortions "illegal period":

> [T]he measure would effectively ban abortion under virtually any circumstances, including rape and incest, and quite possibly to save the mother's life. Interpreted strictly, it would outlaw any birth control method that interfered with a fertilized egg, such as the morning-after pill and IUDs. It would stop embryonic stem-cell research and could severely restrict in vitro fertilization for infertile couples, because unused fertilized eggs are often discarded.[14]

2. Abortion is a killing act. Many discussions of abortion gloss over the intervention as "the procedure" or "emptying the uterus" or "terminating the pregnancy."[15] In saying that abortion is a killing act, McCormick did not mean to imply that it could not be justified at times. He meant only that the one certain and unavoidable outcome of the intervention is the death of the fetus. That is true of any abortion, whether it is descriptively and intentionally direct or indirect. If the death of the fetus is not the ineluctable result, we should speak of premature delivery. To fudge on this issue is to shade our imagination from the shape of our conduct and amounts to an anesthetizing self-deception. All of us should be able to agree on this description, whether we consider this or that abortion justified or not.

To support this idea, the Partial-Birth Abortion Ban Act was passed into law in 2003.[16] Over half the states in the union had already passed bans before the act was finally passed and signed into law. Physicians perform this now-banned procedure on fetuses 20 weeks or older. According to Senator Rick Santorum, there was no need for a health exception with this bill, because the research showed no indication for this. Senator Santorum introduced the bill in the Senate.

Eric Eckholm examined the new restrictions on abortions being enacted by several states. He noted, "Dozens of new restrictions passed by states this year have chipped away at the right to abortion by requiring women to view ultrasounds, imposing waiting periods, or cutting funds for clinics."[17] He further stated that "six states, in little more than a year, ban abortions at the

20th week after conception, based on the theory that the fetus can feel pain at that point."[18] The article pointed out that the viability of the fetus is usually 24 weeks, and that the Supreme Court has decreed "that abortion cannot be banned until the fetus becomes viable."[19]

3. Abortion to save the life of the mother is morally acceptable. Certainly, the issue of abortion to save the life of the mother remains controversial and does not achieve universal agreement. Often a distorted interpretation of a "fundamental individual right to life" exists that comes close to editorial hucksterism. Those who formulate their convictions in terms of a "fundamental right to life" by no stretch of the imagination deny a similar right to the mother. Nor does such a general statement about fetal rights even address situations of conflict. In thinking about common ground, it would be useful to recall the statement of J. Stimpfle, bishop of Augsburg: "He who performs abortion, except to save the life of the mother, sins gravely and burdens his conscience with the killing of human life."[20] The Belgian bishops made a similar statement.[21] Agreement on this point may seem a marginal gain at best. However, in the abortion discussion, any agreement is a gain, especially when it puts caricatures to rest.

4. Judgment about the morality of abortion is not simply a matter of a woman's determination and choice. Pro-choice advocates often present their position as though the woman's choice were the sole criterion in the judgment of abortion. McCormick believed that very few people, if any, really mean this, at least in its full implications.[22] It is simplistic and unsustainable. Taken literally, it means that any abortion, at any time, for any reason, even the most frivolous, is morally justified if the woman freely chooses it. That is incompatible even with the admittedly minimal restrictions of *Roe v. Wade*. No official church body and no reputable philosopher or theologian would endorse the sprawling and very unlimited acceptance of abortion implied in that criterion. It straightforwardly forfeits all moral presumptions protective of the unborn. In this formulation, the fetus becomes a mere blob of matter.

Conversation about the fourth point will not bring overall agreement on the abortion issue. However, it might lead to a more nuanced formulation on the part of those identified with the pro-choice position. It might also lead to a greater sensitivity on the part of some pro-life advocates to the substantial feminist concerns struggling for expression and attention in the pro-choice perspective.

Controversy concerning the pro-choice perspective is complicated by the availability of the ability to self-induce abortion and the laws against such actions. In the United States, Jennie McCormack was arrested in Idaho for using RU-486, which was purchased over the Internet for $200.00 to self-induce her own abortion.[23] Idaho has a law that prevents a woman from performing a self-induced abortion. Later, the case was dropped for lack of evidence. However, the community ostracized Jennie. Jennie made her decision because there is no Medicaid funding for abortions and she could not financially pay for the abortion. In an article, Nancy Hass stated that the case exemplified what pro-choice groups "have been warning of for years: as clinics become inaccessible, poor women are more likely to take abortion into their own hands. In the era before Roe v. Wade, that meant backroom abortions; now it conjures images of a lonely woman in a small town at her keyboard performing an internet search of the term 'abortion pill.'"[24] Hass cites Women on the Web, noting that "Hundreds of online merchants will send RU-486 without a prescription."[25] This organization provides the abortifacient to women in countries where abortion is illegal.

5. Abortion for mere convenience is morally wrong. This statement only makes explicit the previous point. Once again, agreement on this point might seem to represent precious little gain. Agreement might even be fugitive because of the problem in defining the phrase "mere convenience." For example, technological advances in the use of ultrasound to determine the sex of a child have begun to change the population dynamics in certain countries that prefer male children to females. Several areas in India have had a "sharp decline for unborn babies who are found by ultrasound clinics to have a female gender."[26] Clinics who perform ultrasounds for gender identification have been banned in India. However, the law can be bypassed by using mobile ultrasounds. According to UNICEF, "Inequality is always tragic and sometimes fatal. Prenatal sex selection and infanticide, prevalent in parts of South and East Asia, show the low value placed on the lives of girls and women and have led to unbalanced populations where men outnumber women."[27]

In an article entitled "UN Using Sex-Selection Abortion Problem to Push for Abortions," Florencia Cadagan stated, "A recent United Nations inter-agency statement on imbalanced sex ratios calls for unrestricted access to abortion as a human right. The statement recognizes that sex-selective abortion is a form of gender discrimination against girls and women, but nonetheless proclaims that ensuring access to services for safe abortion is crucial."[28] It is difficult to prove that a woman is having an abortion for sex selection, so it is argued that this possibility should not negate the availability of safe abortions. Cadagan further notes that the issue of sex-selective abortion

> affects many countries worldwide, especially Asian countries. The UN statement states that restricting access to certain reproductive technologies in order to prevent an imbalanced male-to-female ratio in a given society should not result in the curtailing of human rights of women. However, sex-selective abortions have become so intense that by 2020 an estimated 15–20 percent of men in northwest India will lack female counterparts.[29]

In addition to sex-selective abortions, one must consider the moral implications of abortions for disabilities. As technological advances have provided the means to detect disabilities, should these fetuses be targeted for abortion? Nancy Flanders poses the question, "What if the debate was instead about the unborn child with cystic fibrosis or Down syndrome [rather than sex selection]?"[30] Is advising parents to abort the child with a disability "really about compassion or is it about convenience?"[31] She states, "The fact is that aborting a baby based on a disability is the same as aborting a child based on sex or race. It's discrimination and it sends the message that people with disabilities are less than human and don't deserve a chance at life."[32] She believes that this form of discrimination will continue until society becomes educated about disabilities.

6. There should be an abolishment of conditions that lead to abortion insofar as is possible. The abolished conditions could include poverty, lack of education, and lack of recreational alternatives to sexual promiscuity among teenagers. Nearly everyone agrees with these prescriptions, but there is little effort to address them. In other words, we have tended to approach abortion too exclusively as a problem of individual choice rather than a social problem. Left at that, it tends to divide people. Were it also approached as a social problem, it could easily bring together those in opposition and move the issue beyond the level of individual choice.[33]

7. Abortion is a tragic experience to avoid if possible. Regardless of one's moral assessment of abortion, most people could agree that it is not a desirable experience. It can be dangerous, psychologically traumatic, generative of guilt feelings, and divisive for families. Of course, it is invariably lethal to fetuses. No amount of verbal redescription or soothing and consoling counseling can disguise the fact that people would prefer to achieve their purposes without going through the abortion procedure. It is and always will be tragic.

8. There should be alternatives to abortion. This is a corollary to the preceding point. Its urgency is in direct proportion to the depth of our perception of abortion as a tragic experience. It would seem likely that the need for alternatives should appeal above all to those who base their approach on a woman's freedom of choice. If reproductive choice is truly to be free, then alternatives to abortion should be available. Alternatives include all the supports—social, psychological, medical, financial, and religious—that would allow a woman to carry her pregnancy to full term should she choose to do so. Expanding the options is expanding freedom.

Bishop Skylstad's letter to the secretary general of the International Secretariat of Amnesty International, dated September 12, 2006, supports this statement. Bishop Skylstad, president of the U.S. Conference of Catholic Bishops (USCCB), stated:

> [A] far more compassionate response [than abortion] is to provide support and services for pregnant women and to advance their educational and economic standing in society. The Catholic Church provides these services to many women around the world and commits itself to continuing to do so. The Catholic Church will also continue to advocate greater attention to these needs in all relevant international assemblies.[34]

This letter was in response to a proposal by Amnesty International to support what the bishop called an "assertive policy of advocating abortion on demand as a 'human right.'"[35] The bishop urged Amnesty International to maintain its neutral stance on abortion and to "not dilute or divert its mission by adopting a position that many see as fundamentally incompatible with a full commitment to human rights and that will deeply divide those working to defend human rights."[36]

9. Abortion is not a purely private affair. *Roe v. Wade* appealed to the so-called right of privacy to justify its invalidation of restrictive state abortion laws. In public debate, assertions about a woman's "control over her own body" often surface. Such appeals either create or reinforce the idea that abortion is a purely private affair. It is not; at least not in the sense that it has no impact on people other than the woman involved. It affects husbands, families, nurses, physicians, politicians, and society in general. We ought to be able to agree on these documented facts. McCormick argued that the term *privacy* is a misleading term used to underline the primacy of the woman's interest in abortion decisions.[37] Communal admission of this point, which is scarcely controversial, would clear the air a bit and purify the public conversation.

10. *Roe v. Wade* offends many people. So did previous prohibitive laws. On these matters, those who acknowledge facts must agree. However, to place these facts together invites people out of their defensive trenches. In other words, it compels them to examine perspectives foreign to their own.

11. Unenforceable laws are bad laws. Unenforceability may stem from any number of factors. For instance, a public willingness to enforce the law may be lacking. Alternatively, the prohibited activity may be such that proof of violation will always be insufficient. On the other hand, enforcement attempts might infringe other dearly treasured values. Whatever the source of the unenforceability, most people agree that unenforceable laws undermine the integrity of the legal system and the fabric of social life.

Our own American experience with Prohibition should provide sufficient historical education on this point. Its unenforceability stemmed from all the factors mentioned above and more, and it spawned social evils of all kinds. In this respect, Democratic Senator Patrick J. Leahy of Vermont once remarked that the use of amendments should not be to create a consensus but to enshrine one that exists. He added:

> The amendments that have embodied a consensus have endured and are a living part of the Constitution. But where we amended the Constitution without a national meeting of minds, we were forced to retract the amendment, and only after devastating effects on the society.[38]

12. An "absolutely prohibitive" law on abortion is not enforceable. By "absolutely prohibitive," McCormick meant two things.[39] First, such a law would prohibit all abortions, even in cases of rape and incest and in cases where the life of the mother is at stake. Second, "abortion" would mean the destruction of the human being from the moment of conception.

Such a prohibitive law is unenforceable. First, it has no consensus of support, as poll after poll over the years has established. Even religious groups with strong convictions against abortion have noted its unenforceability. For example, the Conference of German Bishops (Catholic) and the Council of the Evangelical Church (Protestant) issued a remarkable joint statement on abortion some years ago.[40] After rejecting simple legalization of first-trimester abortions (*fristenregelung*), they stated that the task of the lawmaker is to identify those conflict situations in which interruption of pregnancy is not punishable (*strafloslassen*).

The second reason an "absolutely prohibitive" law would not work concerns specification of legal protection from the moment of conception. If this were enshrined in the penal code and attempts made to enforce it, we would be embroiled in conspiracy law (the intent to abort). Why? This is because in the preimplantation period, there is no evidence of pregnancy. Lacking such evidence, one could not prosecute another for having performed an abortion, but only for having intended to do so. That is just not feasible.[41]

13. There should be some public policy restrictions on abortion. This point may seem to lack bite: after all, those most polarized could agree on this "middle ground," and even *Roe v. Wade* admitted "some" control. This tiny island of agreement is not important in itself. By focusing on it, discussants must face these two questions: "What kind of control?" and "Why?" Discussing these questions could take us right back to square one, but it could also lead to a more nuanced and sophisticated notion of public policy in a pluralistic society.

A phenomenon occurring today that supports the issue of public policy restrictions is the use of abortion for sex selection. According to Florencia Cadagan, the United Nations recognizes the problem of sex-selective abortions and that it is "a form of gender discrimination against girls and women, but nonetheless proclaims that ensuring access to services for safe abortion is crucial."[42] The UN report cited in this article noted that "[f]ollowing an ultrasound examination, a woman can go to a different clinic to have an abortion while providing a reason that is acceptable within the legal framework."[43]

14. Witness is the most effective leaven and the most persuasive educator concerning abortion. McCormick did not mean to discredit the place of rational discourse.[44] We abandon such discourse at our own risk, and often the result is war. Only genuine education is eye opening. The most effective way of opening eyes is often the practical way of witness; we come to understand and appreciate heroism much more by seeing heroic activity than by hearing or reading a lecture on it. We are more selfless when surrounded by people who are concerned for others. We are more fearlessly honest when friends we deeply admire exhibit such honesty.

Those with deep convictions about freedom of choice for women or about the sanctity of fetal life would be considerably more persuasive if they emphasized what they supported rather than what they opposed and did so in action. Pro-life advocates (whether individuals, organizations, or institutions, such as dioceses) should put resources into preventing problem pregnancies, and when those pregnancies occur, they should support them in every way. Paradoxically, the same is true of those who assert the primacy of free choice. For if the choice is to be truly free, genuine alternatives must exist. In summary, "putting one's money where one's mouth is" is an effective alternative to other means, such as bombing and picketing.

15. Abortion is frequently a subtly coerced decision. As ethicist Daniel Callahan pointed out, "a change in abortion laws, from restrictive to permissive, appears—from all data and in every country—to bring forward a whole class of women who would otherwise not have wanted an abortion or felt the need for one."[45] The most plausible interpretation of this phenomenon, according to Callahan, is that the "free" abortion choice is a myth. He stated:

> A poor or disturbed pregnant woman whose only choice is an abortion under permissive laws is hardly making a "free" choice, which implies the possibility of choosing among equally viable alternatives, one of which is to have the child. She is being offered an out and a help. Nor

can a woman be called free where the local mores dictate abortion as the conventional wisdom in cases of unmarried pregnancies, thwarted plans, and psychological fears.[46]

Interestingly, agreement that many abortion decisions are coerced might result in cooperation between pro-choice and pro-life advocates. The concern of "pro-choicers" for true freedom would lead them to attempt to reduce or abolish coercive forces by offering genuine alternatives. The pro-life faction should rejoice at this provision of alternate options because it would reduce the felt need for abortion and thus the number of abortions.

16. The availability of contraception does not reduce the number of abortions. In 2012, President Obama modified the birth control rule in the Patient Protection and Affordable Care Act and granted an extension to religious-affiliated employers. Under the act, religious employers would be required to include birth control free of charge as part of their health plans. Richard Wolf reported, "Obama announced that the rule would be tweaked so that in cases where non-profit religious organizations have objections, insurance companies would be required to reach out to the employees and offer coverage directly."[47] Wolf quoted President Obama's statement: "Under the rule, women would still have access to free preventive care that includes contraceptive service no matter where they work. That core principle remains."[48] President Obama also commented that "if a woman's employer is a charity or a hospital that has a religious objections to providing contraceptive services as part of their health plan, the insurance company—not the hospital, not the charity—will be required to reach out and offer the woman contraceptive care free of charge without co-pays, without hassle."[49]

Arguments against this policy cite religious freedom as the underlying issue. House Speaker John Boehner is quoted by Richard Wolf as saying, "If the president does not reverse the attack on religious freedom, then the Congress, acting on behalf of the American people and the Constitution . . . must. This attack by the federal government on religious freedom in our country must not stand and will not stand."[50] Jeanne Monahan, director for Center for Human Dignity at the Family Research Council, stated: "Some people have moral or ethical objections to contraceptives. They should not be forced to violate their conscience by paying premiums to health plans that cover these items and services."[51]

The morning-after pill is included as part of the services for reproductive health. Secretary Kathleen Sebelius of the Department of Health and Human Services restricted the use of the morning-after pill without a prescription to women 17 years of age or older. However, government scientists recommended that this pill be available to all ages without the need for a prescription. There are issues concerning the lack of physician care and the increase in appropriate sexual behavior that could occur with the availability of the morning-after pill. International issues also exist. For example, the United Nations issued a manual in 1999 that the Vatican condemned because it recommended "the distribution of emergency contraception—the morning after pill—in refugee camps. The UN has never insisted that refugees be forced to swallow this pill, only that it be made available to women facing the risk of rape."[52] An additional comment regarding the Vatican's position on birth control was that "[t]he Holy See approves only the natural method of birth control for use in refugee camps."[53]

Whether for prevention of abortions or for birth control, contraceptives are not without risk to women. The Food and Drug Administration (FDA) has recommended stronger labels on the contraceptive patch and some best-selling classes of birth control pills that contain drospirenone, warning about the possibility of blood clots. An FDA study "estimated that 10 in 10,000 women taking drospirenone containing drugs would get a blood clot per year, compared with about 6 in 10,000 women taking older contraceptives."[54]

The Institute of Medicine (IOM) Advisory Panel submitted a report to Secretary of Health and Human Service Sebelius regarding coverage for contraception. In this report, the panel stated that "nearly half of all pregnancies in the United States were unintended, and that about 40% of unintended pregnancies ended in abortion. Thus, it said greater use of contraception would reduce the rates of unintended pregnancy, teenage pregnancy and abortion."[55] The report further stated that "contraception is highly cost-effective."[56] The IOM panel recommended that contraception be provided at no cost because women without insurance could not afford birth control. The panel recommended coverage of sterilization procedures, education, and counseling as well as emergency contraceptives such as Plan B and Ella.

Healthy People 2020 includes a goal for family planning: "Improve pregnancy planning and spacing, and prevent unintended pregnancy."[57] These services include "contraceptive and broader reproductive health services, including patient education and counseling."[58] The overview of the goal discusses the benefits of family planning for the prevention of unwanted pregnancies and teen pregnancies. This section further discusses the cost savings to Medicaid and the public costs of unwanted pregnancies. *Healthy People 2020* recommends preconception care that includes a reproductive life plan. "A reproductive life plan is a set of goals and action steps based on personal values and resources about whether and when to become pregnant and have (or not have) children."[59] This definition is derived from R. Gold's work *An Enduring Role: The Continuing Need for a Robust Family Planning Clinic System.*[60]

The section on family planning in *Healthy People 2020* contains 15 objectives. A selected list that is pertinent to this discussion includes the following:[61]

- Family Planning objective 3 deals with the availability of emergency contraception at family planning clinics and calls for an "[i]ncrease [in] the proportion of publicly funded family planning clinics that offer the full range of FDA-approved methods of contraception on site."[62]
- Family Planning objective 4 calls for an "[i]ncrease [in] the proportion of health insurance plans that cover contraceptive supplies and services."[63]
- Family Planning objective 6 deals with contraceptive use at the most recent sexual intercourse. It calls for an "[i]ncrease [in] the proportion of females or their partners at risk for unintended pregnancy who used contraception at most recent sexual intercourse."[64]
- Family Planning objective 9 deals with an increase in abstinence. One of the targeted objectives is to increase the percentage of adolescents under the age of 17 who have never had intercourse. The use of condoms to prevent pregnancy and protection against sexually transmitted diseases (STDs) is also included in this objective.[65]

- Family Planning objective 14 targets Medicaid eligibility for pregnancy-related care. It calls for an "[i]ncrease [in] the number of states that set the income eligibility level for Medicaid-covered family planning services to at least the same level used to determine eligibility for Medicaid-covered, pregnancy related care."[66] Currently 21 states have met these criteria; the target for *Healthy People 2020* is 32 states.

- Family Planning objective 15 deals with publicly supported contraceptive services and supplies. Its objective is to "[i]ncrease the proportion of females in need of publicly supported contraceptive services and supplies who receive those services and supplies."[67] The use of condoms to prevent pregnancy and protection against STDs is also included in this section. There is an emphasis on education in this and in several of the objectives.

In addition, the Maternal, Infant and Child Health (MICH) section of *Healthy People 2020* includes an objective with a developmental focus on preconception health. "Recent efforts to address persistent disparities in maternal, infant, and child health have employed a 'life course' perspective to health promotion and disease prevention."[68] An emerging issue in MICH occurred when "[a]t the start of the decade, fewer than half of all pregnancies [were] planned. Unintended pregnancy is associated with a host of public health concerns."[69] The report noted that "[t]he risk of maternal and infant mortality and pregnancy-related complications can be reduced by increasing access to quality preconception (before pregnancy) and interconception (between pregnancies) care."[70]

The irony is that *Healthy People 2020* is advocating for access to family planning as part of a vision of "a society in which all people live long, healthy lives" and has identified family planning as one of the priorities, with 15 targeted objectives.[71] However, the trend to remove public and private funding from Planned Parenthood would seem to negate this effort. In addition, the controversy over religious freedom and women's health in the Patient Protection and Affordable Care Act is compromising access to family planning.

Finances are still a major barrier for access to family planning services. The issue remains: Do women have the right to family planning, and if so, who pays for the cost of the services? Questions regarding coverage remain unanswered. To be covered without cost sharing, a prescription must be obtained. Another issue occurs when a women has her tubes tied and there is no cost sharing or deductible. What if there are complications and the procedure requires hospitalization? Will male vasectomies and condoms be covered? The Department of Health and Human Services will need to address these questions and many others.

17. Permissive laws forfeit the notion of "sanctity of life" for the unborn. This is a harsh statement, but that does not make it less true. Here ethicist Daniel Callahan is at his best—and most tortured. He grants a woman the right not to have a child she does not want. However, he is unflinchingly honest about what this means. "Under permissive laws," he notes, "any talk whatsoever of the 'sanctity of life' of the unborn becomes a legal fiction. By giving women the full and total right to determine whether such a sanctity exists, the fetus is, in fact, given no legal or socially established standing whatsoever."[72] Callahan does not like being backed into this corner. However, he is utterly honest. His legal position does not allow for any pious doublethink. The law "forces a nasty either-or choice, devoid of saving ethical ambiguity."

18. Hospitals that do abortions but have no policy on them should develop one. McCormick introduced this proposition as a contribution to the unexplored middle ground because non-Catholic healthcare facilities have approached the problem almost exclusively in terms of patient autonomy.[73] Some hospitals have grown nervous about this posture because it amounts to simple capitulation to patient preferences. They have begun to see that theirs is not a carefully reasoned moral stance on abortion, but an abdication of the responsibility to develop one. The counsel to develop a policy is relatively nonthreatening because it does not dictate what that policy ought to be. It is promising because it suggests that ethical complexity and ambiguity might become more explicit, which would represent an advance in the dialogue.

19. One should take the "consistent ethic of life" seriously. McCormick[74] borrows the phrase *consistent ethic of life* from Cardinal Joseph Bernardin. Many have observed that those who are most vociferous about fetal rights are among our most hawkish fellow citizens. Something is amiss here. One must consider abortion within the larger context of other life-and-death issues, such as capital punishment and war making.

20. Whenever a discussion becomes heated, it should cease. This is the final proposed piece of middle ground. McCormick knew from long experience that shouting sessions on abortion only alienate and divide the shouters.[75] Nothing is illumined, not because the arguments being offered are not illuminating, but because nobody is either listening or being heard.

The idea of an unexplored middle ground and the invitation to explore it will please few. Yet the abortion problem is so serious that we must grasp at any straw. A nation that prides itself on its tradition of dignity and equality for all and the existence of civil rights to protect that equality cannot tolerate a situation denying human fetuses this equality and these rights. We must at least continue to discuss the problem openly. Quite simply, the soul of the nation is at stake. Abortion's pervasiveness represents a horrendous racism of the adult world. When it is justified in terms of rights, all rights are endangered because their foundations have been eroded by arbitrary and capricious application.

For this and many other reasons, it is important that abortion continue to occupy a prime place in public consciousness and conversation. If we settle for the status quo, we may be presiding unwittingly at the obsequies of some of our own most basic, most treasured freedoms. That possibility means that any strategy—even the modest one of keeping a genuine conversation alive by suggesting a middle ground as its subject—has something to recommend it.

THE CONTINUING RELEVANCE OF DISCUSSION REGARDING ABORTION

Abortion issues continue to be in the forefront of public consciousness and conversation. Examples include the arguments regarding late-term abortion heard by the Supreme Court. Linda Greenhouse, in her article "Justices Hear Arguments on Late-Term Abortion" stated that Justice Kennedy's comments reflected arguments that the doctors challenging the law have made. They say that "partial-birth abortion—known medically as both "intact dilation and evacuation and D and X for dilation and extraction—is often safer because removal of an intact fetus avoids injury to the uterus. The more common method of second-trimester abortion, in which the fetus is dismembered, can leave behind bone fragments."[76]

Another issue that garnered attention was the approval and signing by then President George W. Bush of a law that made the morning-after pill (Plan B) accessible to women older than 18 without a prescription. Garner Harris, in a *New York Times* article published August 25, 2006, noted that "abortion rights advocates argue that the wide availability of Plan B may reduce abortions: abortion opponents assert that Plan B will cause them."[77] Harris quoted Kirsten Moore, president of the Reproductive Technologies Project in Washington, D.C., as saying, "We are pleased that a common sense, common ground agenda for reducing unintended pregnancy and the need for abortion finally won out."[78]

The Pontifical Academy for Life "Statement on the So-Called 'Morning-After Pill'" stated that the morning-after pill used "within and no later than 72 hours after a presumably fertile act of sexual intercourse has a predominantly 'anti-implantation' function, i.e., it prevents a possible fertilized ovum (which is a human embryo), by now in the blastocyst state of its development (fifth to sixth day after fertilization), from being implanted in the uterine wall by a process of altering the wall itself. The final result will thus be the expulsion and loss of this embryo."[79]

Plan B remains controversial. In an article about Shippensburg University's Plan B vending machine, Reming reported that the vending machine in the university's clinic dispensed condoms, pregnancy tests, and the morning-after pill. The university installed the machine after a survey supported the idea (85% approval) and the student government asked that it be installed. The university stated that no one younger than 17 would be allowed access to the machine, in compliance with FDA regulations that any female younger than 17 must have a prescription.[80]

Other issues for consideration in abortion discussions and in finding the common ground include the wide availability of family planning methods and the reimbursement of insurance companies for these services. Other areas of discussion might address questions such as "Should churches that oppose contraceptive use be required to include these services in their employee health plan benefits?" Finally, questions such as "Should politicians whose religious beliefs are in conflict with their public duty as they see it be sanctioned by their religions if their vote conflicts with their religious teachings?" may have to be included in the discussion about common ground. Certainly, the issue of abortion and abortion policy will still be an area for discussion in health care well into the 21st century.

SUMMARY

This chapter helps the reader understand why there is still difficulty in finding a middle ground on the issue of abortion. It began with the presentation of the two current and very divergent positions. Using McCormick's ideas as a starting point, Petrozella then described the need to expand public conversation to include points of consensus or middle ground on this difficult issue. She presented new information to be considered for establishing this middle ground. Although some elements of her argument might be controversial for the reader, examples and ethical reasoning support each element. The issue of abortion will continue to challenge ethics in the 21st century.

QUESTIONS FOR DISCUSSION

1. According to the author, why is it difficult to discuss the concept of abortion?
2. What is the role of the healthcare professional in relation to abortion?
3. How can the principles of ethics (autonomy, beneficence, nonmaleficence, and justice) assist in finding a middle ground on abortion?
4. What is the impact of new legislation on finding common ground on abortion?
5. How does your personal view on abortion affect your care for patients in this area?

FOOD FOR THOUGHT

Abortion remains a controversial topic even in clinical practice. Patients and clinicians often have different ethical positions on this procedure, and conflicts can occur. Some patients find it difficult to discuss their medical history concerning abortion. From a practical point of view, how can you obtain information from patients on abortion-related areas without seeming to make judgments? Remember that nonverbal communication is a powerful communicator.

NOTES

1. R. A. McCormick, "Abortion: The Unexplored Middle Ground," in *Health Care Ethics: Critical Issues for the 21st Century*, ed. E. E. Morrison, 2nd ed. (Sudbury, MA: Jones and Bartlett Learning, 2009).
2. Ibid., 87
3. BBC, "Arguments Against Abortion," BBC Ethics Guide. Retrieved from http://www.bbc.co.uk/ethics/abortion/mother/against_1.shtml. Accessed April 28, 2102.
4. McCormick, "Abortion," 88.
5. U.S. Department of Health and Human Services, *Healthy People 2020*. Retrieved from http://www.healthy people.gov/2020. Accessed May 23, 2012.
6. D. Samuels, "Where Abortion Rights Are Disappearing," *New York Times*, September 9, 2011. Retrieved from http://www.nytimes.com/2011/09/25/opinion/sunday/where-abortion-rights-are-disappearing.html?_r=1&pagewanted=print. Accessed April 28, 2012.
7. Alliance Alert, "Executive Order: Ensuring Enforcement and Implementation of Abortion Restrictions in the Patient Protection and Affordable Care Act," March 22, 2010. Retrieved from http://www.alliancealert.org/2010/03/22/executive-order-ensuring-enforcement-and-implementation-of-abortion-restrictions-in-the-patient-protection-and-affordable-care-act/. Accessed April 28, 2012.

8. Ibid.

9. Ibid.

10. A. Hill, "Gloria Steinem Speaks Out in East Bay About 'War on Women,' Rush Limbaugh," *Oakland Tribune*, March 6, 2012. Retrieved from http://www.insidebayarea.com/oakland-tribune/ci_20107187. Accessed April 29, 2012.

11. McCormick, "Abortion," 89.

12. J. Bernardin, "Call for a Consistent Ethic of Life," *Origins* 13 (29 December 1983): 491–495; J. Bernadin, "Enlarging the Dialogue on a Consistent Ethic of Life," *Origins* 14 (5 April 1984): 707–709.

13. "Editorial: Mississippi "Personhood" Measure Goes Too Far," *USA Today*, November 6, 2011. Retrieved from http://www.usatoday.com/news/opinion/editorials/story/2011-11-06/personhood-abortion-vote-Mississippi/51097728/1. Accessed May 23, 2012.

14. Ibid.

15. McCormick, "Abortion," 89.

16. Partial-Birth Abortion Ban Act of 2003, S. 3, 108th Congress. Available from http://www.govtrack.us/congress/bills/108/s3. Accessed May 23, 2012.

17. E. Eckholm, "Several States Forbid Abortion After 20 Weeks," *New York Times*, June 26, 2011. Retrieved from http://www.nytimes.com/2011/06/27/us/27abortion.html. Accessed May 23, 2012.

18. Ibid.

19. Ibid.

20. F. Scholz, "Durch ethische Grenzsituationen aufgeworfene Normenprobleme," *Theologish-praktische Quartalschrift* 123 (1975): 342.

21. Les évêques belges, "Déclaration des évêques belges sur l'avortement," *Documentation Catholique* 70 (1973): 432–438.

22. McCormick, "Abortion," 90.

23. N. Hass, "The Next Roe v. Wade? An Abortion Controversy in Idaho Inflames Controversy," *Daily Beast*, December 12, 2011. Retrieved from http://www.thedailybeast.com/newsweek/2011/12/11/the-next-roe-v-wade-jennie-mccormack-s-abortion-battle.html. Accessed May 23, 2012.

24. Ibid.

25. Ibid.

26. A. Nusrat, "Sex-Selective Abortion, Gender Discrimination, Threaten Girls in Kasmir," Women News Network, January 19, 2012. Retrieved from http://www.trust.org/trustlaw/news/sex-selective-abortion-gender-discrimination-threaten-girls-in-kashmir. Accessed May 23, 2012.

27. Ibid.

28. F. Cadagan, "UN Using Sex-Selection Abortion Problem to Push for Abortions," LifeNews. com, July 3, 2011. Retrieved from http://www.lifenews.com/2011/07/03/un-using-sex-selection-abortion-problem-to-push-for-abortions/. Accessed May 23, 2012.

29. Ibid.

30. N. Flanders, "Sex-Selection Shocks Us But Abortion on Disabled Babies Don't" LifeNews.com, February 10, 2012. Retrieved from http://www.lifenews.com/2012/02/10/sex-selection-shocks-us-but-abortions-on-disabled-babies-dont/?pr=1. Accessed May 23, 2012.

31. Ibid.

32. Ibid.

33. McCormick, "Abortion," 91.

34. W. S. Skylstad, "Letter to Irene Khan, Secretary General Amnesty International," September 12, 2006. Available from http://old.usccb.org/sdwp/international/2006August29AI.pdf. Accessed May 24. 2012.

35. Ibid.

36. Ibid.

37. McCormick, "Abortion," 92.

38. Cited in M. C. Segers, "Can Congress Settle the Abortion Issue?" *Hastings Center Report* 12 (June 1982): 20–28.

39. McCormick, "Abortion," 92–93.

40. Conference of German Bishops and the Council of the Evangelical Church, "Fristenregelung entschieden abgelehnt," *Ruhrwort*, December 8, 1973, 6.

41. McCormick, "Abortion," 92–93.

42. Cadagan, "UN Using Sex-Selection Abortion Problem."

43. Ibid.

44. McCormick, "Abortion," 93.

45. D. Callahan, "Abortion: Thinking and Experiencing," *Christianity and Crisis*, January 8, 1973, 296.

46. Ibid.

47. R. Wolf, "Obama Tweaks Birth Control Rule," *USA Today*, February 10, 2012. Retrieved from http://content.usatoday.com/communities/theoval/post/2012/02/source-obama-to-change-birth-control-rule/1. Accessed May 24, 2012.

48. Ibid.

49. Ibid.

50. Ibid.

51. R. Pear, "Panel Recommends Coverage for Contraception," *New York Times*, July 19, 2011. Retrieved from http://www.nytimes.com/2011/07/20/health/policy/20health.html?_r=1. Accessed May 24, 2012.

52. J. Manning, "Pope's Assault on UN Refugees," *The Globe and Mail*, November 29, 2001.

53. Ibid.

54. A. Yukhananov and A. Selyukh, "Contraceptive Rulings Spark Concern," *Sun Sentinel*, December 25, 2011, 9A.

55. Pear, "Panel Recommends Coverage."

56. Ibid.

57. U.S. Department of Health and Human Services, "Family Planning," HealthyPeople.gov, 2011. Retrieved from http://www.healthypeople.gov/2020/topicsobjectives2020/objectiveslist.aspx?topicid=13. Accessed May 25, 2012.

58. Ibid.

59. Ibid.

60. R. Gold, "An Enduring Role: The Continuing Need for a Robust Family Planning Clinic System," *Guttmacher Policy Review* 11, no 1 (Winter 2008).

61. U.S. Department of Health and Human Services, "Family Planning," FP-2–FP-12.

62. Ibid., FP-2.

63. Ibid., FP-3.

64. Ibid.

65. Ibid., FP-4–FP-5.

66. Ibid., FP-12.

67. Ibid.

68. U.S. Department of Health and Human Services, "Maternal, Infant, and Child Health," HealthyPeople.gov, 2011. Available from http://www.healthypeople.gov/2020/topics-objectives2020/overview.aspx?topicid=26. Accessed May 25, 2012.

69. Ibid.

70. Ibid.

71. U.S. Department of Health and Human Services, "About Healthy People," HealthyPeople.gov, 2011. Retrieved from http://www.healthypeople.gov/2020/about/default.aspx. Accessed May 25, 2012.

72. Callahan, "Abortion," 296.

73. McCormick, "Abortion," 95.

74. Ibid.

75. Ibid., 95–96.

76. L. Greenhouse, "Justices Hear Arguments on Late-Term Abortion," *New York Times*, November 6, 2006. Retrieved from http://www.nytimes.com/2006/11/09/washington/09scotus .html?_r=1&adxnnl=1&adxnnlx=1337972550-YWvD896nWReP99JMIudnkQ&pagewanted= print. Accessed May 25, 2012.

77. G. Harris, "F.D.A. Approves Broader Access to Next-Day Pill," *New York Times*, August 25, 2006. Retrieved from http://www.nytimes.com/2006/08/25/health/25fda.html. Accessed May 25, 2012.

78. Ibid.

79. Pontifical Academy for Life, "Statement on the So-Called 'Morning-After Pill,'" October 31, 2000. Retrieved from http://www.vatican.va/roman_curia/pontifical_academies/acdlife/documents/ rc_pa_acdlife_doc_20001031_pillola-giorno-dopo_en.html. Accessed May 25, 2012.

80. A. Reming, "Shippensburg University Plan B Vending Machine: What Is Plan B?" *International Business News*, February 8, 2012. Retrieved from http://www.ibtimes.com/articles/295098/ 20120208/shippensburg-university-plan-b-vending-machine.htm. Accessed May 25, 2012.

CHAPTER 6

Proposals for Human Cloning: A Review and Ethical Evaluation

Kevin T. FitzGerald

INTRODUCTION

In August of 1975, Dr. John Gurdon, a British scientist, reported the first successful cloning of frogs using nuclei from adult frogs transplanted into enucleated eggs.[1] This success generated great enthusiasm among scientists for developing techniques for cloning animals. Over the next two decades, the initial enthusiasm greatly declined, because not only did the cloned frogs never develop into adult frogs, but also further experiments seemed to indicate that cloning a mammal from either adult or fetal tissue might never be possible. As scientific interest in cloning waned, so, too, did the apparent need for extensive ethical discussion concerning the possibilities of human cloning. At times, it seemed as though only Hollywood was still interested in human cloning, with movies such as *The Boys from Brazil* and *Multiplicity*.

On February 22, 1997, Dr. Ian Wilmut and his team of researchers from the Roslin Institute in Scotland regenerated scientific enthusiasm for animal cloning with their announcement of the successful cloning of a sheep. The media reignited speculation about human cloning and its moral implications. In the wake of this renewed interest came various proposals concerning what could, what might, and what should be done with regard to applying this new cloning technique to human beings. It is the intent of this chapter to review some of these proposals and to evaluate them as to their scientific probability and ethical justification. Before evaluating these proposals, the wise course is to clarify the currently known facts about human cloning.

THE STATE OF THE SCIENCE OF HUMAN CLONING

The remarkable scientific article published by Wilmut et al. in the February 27 issue of the journal *Nature* demonstrated that it was now possible to use cells from the differentiated tissue of an adult mammal to produce a clone of apparently normal characteristics.[2] Differentiated tissue is primarily composed of cells that have taken on specialized functions, such as those performed by liver and muscle cells, and, consequently, have turned off all the other genes not needed to perform these specialized functions. Many researchers had feared that it would never be possible to turn these genes back on so that specialized cells from an adult mammal, or even a fetal mammal, could be used to produce a cell that acts like a single-cell embryo, or zygote. Zygotes are considered to be "totipotent" cells because the one cell has access to all the genes it needs to make all the different types of cells and tissues required for development. Hence, for a viable clone to be created, the adult cell had to be returned somehow to a state of totipotency. Using a kind of nuclear transfer similar to that used by Dr. Gurdon, the researchers in Scotland were able to revert an adult mammary cell to totipotency and create a mammalian clone.

One can divide the idea of what constitutes a viable clone into two categories: reproductive clones and research clones. If one is cloning for reproductive purposes, then the concept of a viable clone is that one generates an infant animal unburdened by significant health problems so that it might live a relatively normal life. Currently, few researchers or ethicists argue for reproductive human cloning.[3] The vast majority of experts and biomedical societies are against attempting reproductive human cloning at this time.[4] Research cloning is currently the most intense focus of debate. This process is designed to create cloned human embryos that either will be experimented on directly in research on human embryonic development or will be destroyed in order to study the embryonic stem cells that can be isolated from these cloned embryos. Although stem cells taken from the embryo are not totipotent, they are of great interest to some researchers because they are still pluripotent—that is, able to make all the various tissues and cells that are present in the human body after birth. In either case, research or reproductive cloning, one creates the cloned human embryos in the same fundamental manner as Dolly the sheep was created.

Although the cloning of Dolly was rightly heralded as a major breakthrough in science, many obstacles remain to the application of this technology in humans. The research done in South Korea and published in the journal *Science* that was internationally touted as the big breakthrough in human cloning turned out instead to be a complete hoax.[5] In fact, as of November 2011 no research group has presented verifiable evidence of the creation of a stem cell line that has been derived from a cloned human embryo created by nuclear transfer into either enucleated eggs or zygotes.[6]

In light of the lack of success in achieving human cloning, why is there still so much excitement about it? A variety of articles and reports enumerate the reasons for pursuing human cloning. As mentioned earlier, these publications focus primarily on the benefits achievable from research on cloned embryos. These benefits include (1) creating tissues, organs, or other treatments that can be matched to individual patients or diseases; (2) creating cloned embryonic stem cell models for research on specific human diseases, such as how they arise during development as well as how they might be more successfully treated; and (3) using cloned embryonic stem cells for research on human reproduction and development in general.

The next sections of this chapter review these proposals, with the pursuit of human cloning for research reviewed first because it is currently of greatest relevance to the public discussion and debate. Reproductive human cloning is reviewed second because the likelihood of pursuing reproductive cloning will depend on the success, or lack of success, researchers have with their attempts to clone human embryos for research.

HUMAN CLONING FOR RESEARCH PURPOSES

The goal of research cloning is to create human embryos that will develop up to the blastocyst stage. At this stage of development, usually around five to seven days after fertilization has occurred, the embryo is a small, hollow sphere with some cells in its interior, called the inner cell mass. The entire embryo may be about 200 cells at this point of development. The cells of the inner cell mass are the cells that are of interest to researchers, because they are pluripotent and can become embryonic stem cell lines. These cells must be separated from the rest of the embryo in order to become a cell line.

Currently, destruction of embryos must occur in order to create embryonic cell lines. This destruction of human embryos is one of the main points of contention in the public debate concerning human cloning for research. There is a more detailed examination of this issue in the later ethics section of this chapter.

What do researchers propose to do with the cloned human embryonic stem cell lines they wish to create? As mentioned previously, several things. First, the primary advantage researchers think these cell lines will have is that they can come from an individual with a specific disease or condition. The idea then is that the underlying genetic or biochemical cause of the disease might be investigated more precisely by using the cloned embryonic stem cell line to produce the different types of cells affected by the disease and to observe how their proper functioning is disrupted by the disease during the process of differentiation and afterward.

Using this information and the particular cloned cell line, researchers might then be able to attempt different types of interventions aimed at preventing, reversing, or compensating for the disease condition. If an intervention is efficacious, then there might be manipulation of the cell line to create cells, tissues, or even organs that no longer have the disease. If a given manipulation demonstrates success and safety, then the tissues or organs created might be useful for transplantation back into the person whose adult cell was used to create the cloned embryo that was the source of the embryonic stem cell line.

Although the creation of transplantable tissues and organs might be the ultimate goal, researchers could also claim that, even if they do not achieve that goal, they might still learn some very important basic biology about disease processes from this research, such that it would help treat diseases in some other way. Hence, the fundamental emphasis put forth as justification for human research cloning is the widely accepted idea that research is done primarily to benefit people. In other words, if the research will benefit people, we should do it. Whether this justification of human research cloning is legitimate is analyzed in the upcoming section of the chapter on ethical issues. However, currently many of the purported benefits of research cloning are still speculative, because no cloned human embryonic stem cell lines have been created.

Recently, cell lines that have many if not all of the key features of cloned cell lines have been created by a revolutionary technique that does not use human eggs to transform adult cells into cells that act like embryonic stem cells. This technique induces pluripotency in adult cells and so creates "induced pluripotent stem cells," or iPSCs.

HUMAN INDUCED PLURIPOTENT STEM CELL RESEARCH

iPSCs are the result of reprogramming adult cells to act like embryonic stem cells. This reprogramming is done by adding factors to the cells that change the expression pattern of the genes in the cells to mimic gene expression patterns found in embryonic stem cells. In the 2006 publication of the breakthrough research led by Dr. Shinya Yamanaka of Japan, scientists reported that by forcing the overexpression of four genes linked to pluripotency, they were able to make adult fibroblast cells change into cells that behaved like embryonic stem cells.[7]

Although the cloning of Dolly had reinvigorated the idea of directly reprogramming mammalian adult cells into embryonic-like cells, many scientists were surprised at how rapidly this goal was achieved and how few genes were needed to achieve the reprogramming. Since this breakthrough experiment, researchers around the world have reprogrammed a variety of human cells using a variety of gene combinations and techniques. Some research groups have even produced iPSC lines from patient samples in order to have pluripotent cell lines that reflect the genetics and biology of a particular disease. In addition, one collaborative international group of researchers used a mouse iPSC line with a known genetic mutation to demonstrate that it is possible to perform genetic repair on the mutation in the iPSCs.[8] Such genetic treatments could result in the creation of large numbers of patient-specific healthy cells and tissues that could be given to the patient to treat a particular disease.

The importance of iPSC research for the human cloning debate is that it might well provide an alternative to research cloning. All the benefits that human cloning research is purported to bring to patients are already being pursued by iPSC research. What impact this stem cell research advance has on the ethical arguments surrounding the issue is considered in the ethics section of this chapter. The next section contains a review of the current state of human reproductive cloning.

HUMAN CLONING FOR REPRODUCTIVE PURPOSES

To address the issue of reproductive cloning, one must first acknowledge the significantly higher level of control over the cloning process that will be required for reproductive cloning relative to that required for the research cloning process. Basically, the reason for this difference is safety. Proponents of research cloning need not be nearly as concerned about the loss of embryos or the creation of useless embryos than proponents of reproductive cloning need be regarding the creation of cloned children. Proponents of research cloning might well be satisfied with the creation of one useful cloned cell line out of several or many attempts, whereas those who desire to pursue reproductive cloning would likely be dissatisfied with the creation of one healthy child out of several or dozens that are born, or even carried in pregnancy. This safety issue is one that leads many research cloning proponents to back away from supporting reproductive cloning at least for the foreseeable future.

If these safety issues could be adequately addressed and human cloning technology perfected to an acceptable level (again, there is no evidence of this progress currently), what reasons are then given for the pursuit of reproductive cloning? Can parents who face both genetic and reproductive obstacles to having their own children use it? Some have proposed that human cloning could be another alternative in the array of assisted reproductive technologies

(ART) offered to such couples. One could imagine the possibility that no alternatives are available to a given couple except attempting to clone one of them. Of course, the question arises at this point: What do we mean by having one's "own" child? A cloned child would actually be biologically more like the much-delayed identical twin of the parent used for his or her cloning. Because one's biological children are actually only half related to each parent, one could argue that any cloned child would be as biologically different from a natural child as an adopted child is.

When pushed to an extreme, it becomes evident that a genetic reductionism underlies this reproductive cloning perspective. Are genes the only possible basis for the parent–child relationship? Are human identity and personality merely genetic? What of adopted children who call their parents "Mom and Dad," or those who look to teachers or mentors as the ones who have been most instrumental in forming their identities? A consistent response from most scientists regarding the furor about the possibility of human cloning has been to remind people that we are more than our genes, even on a physiologic level. One's environment plays a significant role in shaping one's identity and characteristics. Examining still another proposed use for reproductive human cloning will help elucidate this point.

Some have proposed that human cloning be employed so that a couple could "replace" a dying child or a person could replace a dying spouse. As in the previous case, there is a dangerous biological reductionism inherent in this proposal. No human being is replaceable—not even physiologically. We are all unique, including identical twins. The desire to clone a child or spouse to "replace" the lost loved one may well indicate a misguided attempt to find a biological solution to the age-old problem of dealing with the grief and trauma of death. Even if parents successfully deal with the psychological struggle of the loss of a loved one, the cloned child or spouse would always have to live with the reality of being cloned in an attempt to replace another.

From this brief overview, one can see that even if the immense safety issues could be surmounted with regard to reproductive cloning, many other significant issues remain concerning what exactly the purpose would be in pursuing human reproductive cloning. In addition, there are ethical issues, which the next section addresses.

ETHICAL ISSUES IN HUMAN CLONING

Before one can address the ethical issues surrounding human cloning, it is necessary to clarify some details that are often confused in the mass media and the public debate. One can see evidence of this confusion in the different answers that are obtained when people are polled about whether they agree with human cloning or not. Depending on how one phrases the questions asked, one can reliably get the majority of respondents to be either in favor of human cloning or against it. Comparing two past polls will help demonstrate this point.

On March 25, 2005, the results of a poll done by the Opinion Research Corporation and commissioned by the Coalition for the Advancement of Medical Research (CAMR) indicated that "a strong majority of Americans solidly support embryonic stem cell and therapeutic cloning research."[9] As stated on the CAMR Web site:

> Of the 1,045 people responding, the specific breakdown of responses was as follows: 59% said they favored medical research that uses stem cells from human embryos (30% strongly favor, 29% somewhat favor); 33% are opposed (13% somewhat oppose and 20% strongly oppose), and 8% of respondents answered they did not know. Once a description of embryonic stem cell research was read, 68% said they favored it (39% strongly favor, and 29% somewhat favor), only 28% opposed the research (11% somewhat oppose, and 16% strongly oppose), and 4% responded they did not know. For therapeutic cloning, 60% of Americans approved the research (27% strongly approved, 33% somewhat approved), whereas 35% disapproved (12% somewhat, and 23% strongly), and 5% of respondents answered they did not know. Once a description of therapeutic cloning research was read, 72% favored it (30% strongly, 42% somewhat), and roughly 23% opposed the research (11% somewhat, 11% strongly), and 6% of respondents answered they did not know.[10]

Interestingly, a different poll focusing on the same issues, done by International Communications Research and commissioned by the United States Conference of Catholic Bishops (USCCB), was released on May 31, 2006, with the results stating that "48% of Americans oppose federal funding of stem cell research that requires destroying human embryos, while only 39% support such funding."[11] In addition, the USCCB Web site states:

> When survey respondents were informed that scientists disagree on whether stem cells from embryos, or from adult tissues and other alternative sources, may end up being most successful in treating diseases, 57% favored funding only the research avenues that do not harm the donor; only 24% favored funding all stem cell research, including the type that involves destroying embryos. . . . The new poll also shows overwhelming opposition to human cloning, whether to provide children for infertile couples (83% against) or to produce embryos that would be destroyed in medical research (81% against).[12]

Because these two polls were a year apart, one might conclude that the public's attitudes had changed during that year. However, one finds earlier polls cited on the USCCB Web site. These polls were done during the previous two years by the same company and showed similar negative responses to human embryonic stem cell research and cloning research.[13] How, then, can two presumably accurate polls reach opposite conclusions? The answer, in part at least, is found in the contradictory descriptions and evaluations of the human embryo.

The current debates surrounding cloning often revolve around the biological and moral realities of human embryos. What was once a seemingly clear concept—a sperm fertilizes an egg and creates an embryo—has now become a convoluted intersection of cutting-edge biological research, ethical reflection, and religious perspective. For instance, some proponents of research cloning will argue that there is no creation or destruction of human embryos in the process of creating cloned stem cells. They base this argument on the fact that there was no sperm used in the cloning procedure, only eggs. Because they define embryos as the result of the union of sperm and egg, cloning cannot produce an embryo.

However, a cloning procedure created Dolly the sheep. No one argues that Dolly was not a sheep. If Dolly was a sheep, then she must have been a lamb at some point. If Dolly was a lamb, then she must have been a fetal sheep before she was born as a lamb. If Dolly was a fetal sheep, then what was she before she was a fetus? In mammalian developmental biology, Dolly must have been an embryo. Hence, cloning produces embryos, and does so without sperm.

Unfortunately, there is even more convolution regarding the embryo definition problem than this issue of whether cloning produces embryos. For example, knowledge of biology indicates that the process of fertilization can create abnormal growths, some of which are cancerous, rather than generating developing organisms. One such growth is a hydatidiform mole.[14] No one argues that a complete hydatidiform mole is an organism or a human being, yet it can arise from the union of sperm and egg. Hence, whereas the processes of fertilization and cloning can both create embryos (i.e., organisms in the earliest stage of development), they can also both create nonorganismal growths that are not embryos. Considering the apparent contradictory results of the two polls just cited, clarification of exactly what one means by the term *embryo* would be crucial when one is arguing for or against the destruction of human embryos in research.

This clarification is crucial because it extends beyond the complexities described previously. Some proponents of cloning research will acknowledge that they accept the creation and destruction of full-fledged human embryos in research because currently the best chance for getting good stem cells comes from creating the best embryos one can. However, these proponents do not consider these embryos to be of the same moral importance or standing as a human fetus, because they are created and developed outside the human body in a Petri dish. As long as there is no transfer of the embryos to a woman's body, they cannot ultimately develop to a stage equivalent to birth. Therefore, proponents argue, embryos created by the cloning process that are intended only for research purposes are not ethically the same as embryos that are developing within a woman's body.

This argument also raises some contentious issues. Presume that a researcher creates two cloned embryos that are equally functional, developing human organisms. This argument asserts that the embryo intended to be destroyed for research is somehow of less value or importance than the embryo that is intended to be transplanted for reproductive purposes. What happens if the two embryos get mixed up in the lab and the one intended for research is transferred to a woman's uterus while the other is destroyed? Has some significant wrong occurred that would not have occurred if there had been no mix-up? What if no one ever finds out about the mistake? Did no wrong occur because people think that there was proper application of their intentions? Can we treat some human organisms as disposable because some people decide that they should be treated as disposable?

Fundamentally, the interpretation of this argument of intentionality is that embryos can be treated similar to property. One can treat one's possessions as precious or not, as one intends. The question is then: Are embryos to be treated the same as property, or does the fact that they are human organisms preclude such treatment?

Some opponents of cloning research argue that embryos must be treated the same as other human beings, at least to the extent that they should not be created and destroyed for research purposes. However, they recognize the potential usefulness that might come from research done on stem cells that have specific disease characteristics. Their proposal is to attempt to create stem cells with such disease characteristics. These stem cells act like embryonic stem cells for research purposes, but do not come from embryos. One way to create these embryonic-like stem cells would be to employ an altered nuclear transfer (ANT) technique. ANT techniques can be done in several different ways.[15] The key point of all the ANT approaches is not to include the destruction of a human embryo in the process of generating the stem cell lines desired for research.

One can place these ANT proposals alongside the iPSC research reviewed earlier, which also pursues the benefits of stem cell research while avoiding the destruction of human embryos. Often all these anti-human-cloning proposals are lumped together in the "adult stem cell research" versus "embryonic stem cell research" choice. This designation of adult versus embryonic is not completely accurate. If the goal of research is to gain understanding of disease and develop better treatments, then opponents of research that destroys human embryos can actually point to all the biomedical research done on diseases and treatments that does not destroy human embryos. Considering that most biomedical research is not specifically stem cell research (either adult or embryonic), it is scientifically quite a stretch to claim that only human cloning research will provide an answer or treatment to a given disease.

Of course, it is part of the nature of scientific research to be unable to predict where and when the breakthroughs will come. Hence, proponents of human cloning research often respond that we need to do all the research we can in order to provide the best chance that we will find answers or treatments as soon as possible. In fact, more recently some proponents have even begun to claim that pursuing human cloning research is a moral obligation because it might help us achieve treatments for those suffering from terrible diseases earlier than we might otherwise.

Although these arguments might appear compelling at first glance, they rest on false assumptions. First, there is already a great deal of human research that is theoretically possible to do and that might readily result in more rapid discoveries and treatments. However, these researchers do not do these studies because they would harm human beings in the process. Because of many past tragedies involving biomedical research that unjustifiably harmed human beings, our society has decided to place limits on human research, regardless of how useful the research might be. Hence, what is good for research is not always what is good for society. The key issue here regarding human cloning research is whether to create and destroy human embryos in research—not whether the research might lead us to treatments sooner.

The second false assumption presented is that we must do human cloning research because it might lead to earlier treatments for those suffering from terrible diseases. This claim assumes that the key aspect of disease treatment is research. In actuality, our world is replete with examples of cures and treatments that exist but are not getting to the people who are in desperate need of them. Hence, if everyone responded fully to the logic of the claim that one needs to do all one can to treat those who are suffering from tragic diseases, then most, if not all, research would have to be stopped.

If the goal to provide treatment for those suffering from terrible diseases trumps all other concerns, then most of the available resources would need to be shifted to healthcare delivery and preventive medicine. After all, what good is a treatment if those who need it cannot get it? In addition, would it not be better to avoid the disease altogether rather than having to treat it once some people get it? Because we are already faced with serious problems in preventing disease and getting the treatments we already have to those who need them, the logical response to the above moral claim about needing to treat people would be to reduce research and do better with the treatments and preventive strategies we already have.

To avoid confusion, there needs to be a clarification of the critique just presented. The critique is not against biomedical research. Biomedical research can be a great good in a society. The critique is against those who would claim that a given type of research is morally obligated based on it possibly resulting in treatments for those suffering from terrible diseases. All health care is oriented toward the prevention and alleviation of suffering, if possible. Decisions regarding what elements of health care should get priority over others depend on many factors. The fact that a particular line of research might bring about good treatments is certainly not by itself a sufficient justification for doing that research, especially when contentious ethical issues of human subject research are involved.

Contentious ethical issues are certainly involved in human cloning research, as has already been demonstrated. However, the ethical issues are not limited to those already described. Another issue that many argue is still not receiving adequate attention involves the acquisition of human eggs for cloning research.

Currently, animal cloning is still a very inefficient process. In addition, as cited previously, no one has provided verifiable evidence of the creation of cloned human embryonic stem cell lines. Combine these two facts and one is faced with the daunting probability that it will require an enormous number of human eggs and embryos to achieve human cloning on a scale that will be adequate for the number and kinds of cloning research programs envisioned by proponents of this research.[16] This probability is daunting because the process of procuring eggs for research involves the hyperstimulation of a woman's ovaries, which involves risks to the woman's health. These risks are of such significance that people from many different perspectives—pro-life and pro-choice, Democrat and Republican, feminist, Green, and social conservatives—have joined in calling for a moratorium on the use of human eggs for cloning research.[17]

Again, society faces the challenge of protecting human beings from harm (i.e., the many young women needed as egg donors) in the face of interest in pursuing research that is seen as desirable to many. Considering the fact that there are many alternative avenues of research that can be pursued without putting women or embryos at risk, the burden of proof should be on those who argue this research is not only good for science but also for society.

When arguing for human cloning research as a good for society, the argument often arises that if our society decides for whatever reason not to pursue this research, we will put ourselves at a disadvantage because other societies or nations will do it. They then will get the benefits and we will lose out. Again, although this argument might seem compelling at first, closer examination reveals that it, too, is flawed. Many historical examples are available to remind us of the harms that may befall a society that too eagerly pursues technological advance at the cost of other societal values and goods. The past catastrophes of eugenic policies pursued both in the United States and Germany should be reminder enough of the harms that can occur in the name of medical advancement.

If one can question research cloning on the grounds of its potential harm to individuals and society, then one can also question reproductive cloning on these grounds. Even if cloning is the only reproductive option an individual or couple might have, should people pursue it? Proposing human cloning to solve reproduction problems depends heavily on the argument that people have the right to have genetically related offspring. When discussing such rights, it is important to distinguish between negative (liberty) rights and positive (welfare) rights.

In 1994, the Ethics Committee of the American Fertility Society (now the American Society of Reproductive Medicine) stated that in the context of procreation, "A liberty right would encompass the moral freedom to reproduce or to assist others in reproducing without violating any countervailing moral obligations. A welfare right to reproduce would morally entitle one to be assisted by another party (or other parties) in achieving the goal of reproduction."[18]

If the ethical problems associated with reproductive cloning trouble society, one can certainly argue that society is not obliged to support it as a welfare right. Additionally, if society concludes that the rights or dignity of the child to be born are violated by reproductive cloning (e.g., to be made as a copy of someone else), then society can also deny even a liberty right to clone oneself because of the countervailing moral obligation to protect the cloned child from harm.

SUMMARY

This chapter has considered several proposals regarding the possibility of human cloning. These range from possible medical interventions for directly treating disease to meeting perceived reproductive needs. In the final analysis, considering the possibility of alternatives both in research and in reproduction, as well as the multitude of ethical problems still plaguing the cloning issue, the burden of proof regarding whether we should pursue human cloning should be on those who desire to clone human embryos—whether for research or reproduction. Currently, the arguments employed by human cloning proponents do not provide enough justifiable reason to apply the recent advances in cloning techniques to human beings.

QUESTIONS FOR DISCUSSION

1. Why do you think there is a renewed interest in human cloning? Does the media attention increase this interest?
2. Do you think science has an ethical obligation to present the public with both the benefits and burdens of cloning research?
3. What is the role of autonomy in cloning research? When evaluating autonomy, how should you consider it?
4. What would be the deontologist's position on cloning?
5. The healthcare community also is concerned about the business aspects of cloning. Do you think cloning will become a good business opportunity?

FOOD FOR THOUGHT

Assuming that technology on cloning increases at its current pace, what are the possibilities for the future? For example, if there are cloned human beings, will they have the same status as noncloned human beings? If a person could clone himself or herself, what would be the limitations on the clone? Apply the principles of ethics to your responses to these issues.

NOTES

1. J. B. Gurdon, R. A. Laskey, and O. R. Reeves, "The Developmental Capacity of Nuclei Transplanted from Keratinized Skin Cells of Adult Frogs," *Journal of Embryology and Experimental Morphology* 34 (1975): 93–112.
2. I. Wilmut, A. E. Schnieke, J. McWhir, A. J. Kind, and K. H. S. Campbell, "Viable Offspring Derived from Fetal and Adult Mammalian Cells," *Nature* 385 (1997): 810–813.
3. For example, see Gregory Pence, *Who's Afraid of Human Cloning?* (Lanham, MD: Rowman & Littlefield, 1998).
4. This perspective against reproductive cloning includes organizations that have taken positions in support of research cloning, such as the National Academies and the National Research Council. For example, see their report *2007 Amendments to the National Academies' Guidelines for Human Embryonic Stem Cell Research* at http://books.nap.edu.
5. D. Normile, G. Vogel, and J. Couzin, "Cloning: South Korean Team's Remaining Human Stem Cell Claim Demolished," *Science* 311 (2006): 156–157.
6. S. Noggle, H-L. Fung, A. Gore, H. Martinez, K. Crumm Satriani, R. Prosser, K. Oum, et al., "Human Oocytes Reprogram Somatic Cells to a Pluripotent State," *Nature* 478 (2011): 70–75. Available at doi:10.1038/nature10397.
7. K. Takahashi and S. Yamanak, "Induction of Pluripotent Stem Cells from Mouse Embryonic and Adult Fibroblast Cultures by Defined Factors," *Cell* 126, no 4 (2006): 663–676.
8. S. Kosuke Yusa, R. Tamir, H. Strick-Marchand, I. Varela, P-Q Liu, D. E. Paschon, E. Miranda, et al., "Targeted Gene Correction of a A1-Antitrypsin Deficiency in Induced Pluripotent Stem Cells," *Nature* 478, no. 7369 (2011): 391–394. Available at doi:10.1038/nature10424. Accessed January 16, 2012.
9. "National Poll Shows Strong Support for Stem Cell and Therapeutic Cloning Research," World Health.net, April 4, 2005. Retrieved from http://www.worldhealth.net/news/national_poll_shows_strong_support_for_s/. Accessed June 6, 2012.
10. Ibid.

11. Office of Media Relations, "New Poll: Americans Continue to Oppose Funding Stem Cell Research That Destroys Human Embryos," United Conference of Catholic Bishops, May 31, 2006. Retrieved from http://old.usccb.org/comm/archives/2006/06-109.shtml. Accessed June 6, 2012.

12. Ibid.

13. Ibid.

14. R. Slim and A. Mehio, "The Genetics of Hydatidiform Moles: New Lights on an Ancient Disease," *Clinical Genetics* 71, no. 1 (2007): 25–34.

15. For a good introduction to ANT, see the President's Council on Bioethics report *Alternative Sources of Human Pluripotent Stem Cells* (Washington, DC: May 2005). Available at http://bioethics.georgetown.edu/pcbe/reports/white_paper/. Accessed June 6, 2012.

16. Currently, there can only be a guess concerning the number of eggs required, because no one has yet succeeded in creating a cloned human embryonic stem cell line. However, considering that hundreds, if not thousands, of eggs already have been used in human cloning research, the number of eggs needed to create the disease-specific cell lines desired by researchers could easily be in the thousands, and possibly much higher.

17. One can find an example of such a group at http://www.handsoffourovaries.com. Accessed June 6, 2012.

18. The Ethics Committee of the American Fertility Society, "Ethical Considerations of Assisted Reproductive Technologies," *Fertility & Sterility* 62, suppl. 1 (1994): 18S.

CHAPTER 7

Competency: What It Is, What It Is Not, and Why It Matters

Byron Chell

INTRODUCTION

A competent adult has the absolute right to refuse medical treatment—even lifesaving medical treatment. Can there be any doubt that this is a correct statement of principle, medical ethics, and law?[1] In spite of this clear and seemingly straightforward declaration, however, when a patient refuses to accept needed medical care, we still find much concern and confusion. This is especially true when the treatment is lifesaving.

The rule that a competent adult has the right to refuse any and all medical treatment emphasizes the importance of the concept of competency. In fact, if we are uneasy about a decision to refuse treatment, we immediately retreat to the thicket of competency.[2] Such a retreat is appropriate, however, because when confronted with a refusal of needed medical care, the first and key question we should ask is whether the patient is competent to make the required decision.

Yet difficulties regarding competency remain, because the concept is confusing. What is a competent adult? What is the definition of competency? Are those who refuse lifesaving treatment on religious grounds competent? How do we find the proper answers to these questions when evaluating patients? Anyone involved in bioethics and medical decision making regularly confronts such questions.

This chapter discusses what competency is and what it is not. It also discusses what we should and should not be doing in making determinations of competency when deciding whether to allow a patient to refuse medical treatment. If we have a clear understanding of what competency is, why we seek it, and why it matters, we will know how to approach and complete the task of determining competency without unnecessary anxiety and confusion.

WHAT COMPETENCY IS AND WHAT IT IS NOT

Competency is not a thing or a fact. It is not something we can look for and find if only we know how. Determinations of competency are not medical judgments. Clinical training is not required. Being competent does not necessarily mean being rational. We find many persons competent to make medical care decisions even though they base their refusal of treatment on irrational beliefs. When we make determinations of competency, we are not seeking truth or facts. We are not assessing the patient in light of a clear and neutral standard upon which we can make a definitive finding. It is not that easy.

Competent is simply a label we apply to persons after we examine various aspects of their physical and mental conditions. Decisions relating to competency are legal and social decisions. They are legal decisions in that they are determinations of an individual's legal capacity to exercise the right to self-determination. No legal education is required, however. They are social decisions in that the statutory definitions we apply in the search are societal decisions. Additionally, when we make determinations of competency, we are doing so with imprecise criteria, vague notions, and personal beliefs and prejudices, all of which affect the outcome.

Considering the importance of the concept of competency in making determinations relating to, respecting, or overriding a patient's refusal, it at first appears necessary that we fix upon a definition of the term *competency*. However, despite our attempt as a society to define it, we have failed to find an adequate definition.

THE SEARCH FOR THE DEFINITION OF COMPETENCY

We do not need to find the definition of competency to fulfill our task. This is fortunate, because there is no preexisting single definition of the term. We can only create a definition—or various definitions. We cannot find a standard definition of competency. No statutory consistency or line of cases can be uncovered that would allow the simple discovery of the meaning of the terms *competent* or *incompetent*. We can find definitions of competency in a number of different and specific situations in which society and the law have always had to deal with the concept. We generally recognize that people can be competent to do one thing and not another or can be competent to some extent and not another. For example, we have laws regulating a person's competency to make a will, to enter into contracts, or to stand trial.

Definitions of *incompetency* have generally fallen into two categories: definitions that emphasize end results and definitions that emphasize thought processes. Both types of definitions, however, have an intimate and necessary relationship in light of what we actually do in making determinations of competency.

Definitions in terms of end results essentially ask us to look at how persons live. What is their condition? What are the consequences or the end results of their thinking? For example, a former definition of the term *incompetent* for mental health commitment purposes is as follows:

> As used in this chapter the word incompetent shall . . . be construed to mean or refer to any adult person who . . . is unable properly to provide for his own personal needs for physical health, food, clothing or shelter, [or who] is substantially unable to manage, his own financial resources.[3]

A definition emphasizing end results tells us to look at what is happening to persons because of their thinking. We must examine the physical consequences that follow from their mental status. An incompetent person is one whose mental processes lead to bad or serious consequences. A competent person simply would not live like that or be in that situation.

Although such definitions are adequate in the context of mental health civil commitment proceedings, they are not very helpful in many cases of refusal of medical care. We question the competency of many persons who refuse medical treatment even though they are quite capable of providing for their own food, clothing, and shelter and can manage their daily affairs very well.

Because definitions in terms of living conditions or end results are not always adequate to the task, we also use definitions of competency that emphasize thought processes. A definition of incompetency in terms of thought processes involves determining whether someone is competent by looking at how he or she relates to and decides things. One essentially tests the person's comprehension of reality, understanding, and ability to make rational judgments. One example of this type of incompetency definition is as follows:

> Several tests of competency might be applied, e.g., patients may be considered competent if (1) they evidence a choice concerning treatment, (2) this choice is "reasonable," (3) this choice is based on "rational" reasons, (4) the patient has a generalized ability to understand, or (5) the patient actually understands the information that has been disclosed. . . . [T]he courts have not settled on any single test of competency; in practice, doctors seem to apply an amalgam of some or all of these tests.[4]

A definition emphasizing thought processes involves listening to the patient and judging whether what is said "makes sense." Is the patient rational? The point is not to examine the physical consequences that follow from the patient's mental state, but rather to examine the mental state itself.

There are currently many competing definitions of competency, which is simply a reflection of the fact that competency can be properly defined in many different ways. The search for a single test of competency is a search for the Holy Grail. Unless one recognizes that there is no magical definition of competency to make decisions about treatment, the search for an acceptable test will never end. "Getting the words just right" is only part of the problem. In practice, judgments of competency go beyond semantics or straightforward applications of legal rules; such judgments reflect social considerations and societal biases as much as they reflect matters of law and medicine.[5]

Competency is, of course, whatever we define it to be. The trick is to define it so that it best helps us to do the job that needs to be done. The job in this context is to make decisions involving decision making. We must decide whether we will allow the patient to decide. Thus, what are the proper considerations we must keep in mind in making our decisions? What is the essence of competency? What criteria should we reflect in creating a proper definition?

THE ESSENCE OF COMPETENCY

Competency is essentially the ability to make a decision. Regardless of the particular definition used, determining competency in a given situation involves answering one question: Should we allow this person to make this decision under these circumstances? Generally, but not always, the answer to this question is yes, and a person is labeled competent if (1) he or she has an understanding of the situation and the consequences of the decision, and (2) the decision is based on rational reasons.

Determining whether the person does or does not understand his or her condition is usually not the troublesome part. Sometimes it is difficult to determine the seriousness of the patient's condition, and sometimes physicians will disagree. However, if the medical conclusion is that intervention is required to prevent death or serious harm, it is normally not too difficult to determine whether the patient understands what the doctors are saying and whether the patient appreciates the consequences of his or her choice. This aspect of determining competency does not create philosophical and conceptual confusion. It can do so, however, in some cases of religious refusals.

Determining whether the patient's decision to refuse treatment is based on rational reasons can cause us much concern. Although the word *rational* might appear redundant, its meaning in this context is "sensible," "sound," "reasonable," or "lucid." We use the term *reasons* in the sense of "reasons why," "motive," or "explanation." Thus, the reason why or the explanation of the decision to refuse treatment is to be considered rational if it is sensible or sound, lucid and not deranged, and conforms to reason. In other words—it makes sense! In lieu of rational reasons, we might require sound explanations, sensible motives, or even reasonable reasons why.

It is not possible to define specifically terms such as *rational reasons*, *sound explanations*, or *sensible motives* or to measure definitively what is rational or reasonable. These determinations will necessarily vary from person to person. We can set out cases in which most persons would conclude that the reasons for the refusal are rational or sensible under the circumstances, and such examples can be instructive.

Suppose, for example, that we inform an older patient that her leg is gangrenous and that an amputation is necessary to save her life. Understanding the situation, she replies, "I refuse the amputation. I am not afraid of death. It is the natural end to life. I am 86 and I have lived a good and full life. I do not want a further operation, nor do I want to live legless. I understand that the consequence of refusing the amputation is death, and I accept that consequence."

This woman understands both her situation and the consequences of her choice. Additionally, her decision is understandable and she bases it on facts and logic. Although we might wish her to choose otherwise (or we might choose otherwise), her reasons and reasoning are sane, sound, and sensible. She is competent.[6]

If she were to say, however, "I understand the consequences but I refuse the operation because the moon is full," it is not likely she would be considered competent. Although she understands her situation and chooses death rather than medical treatment, her decision is not understandable. Her decision does not follow rationally or reasonably from her premise. Her explanation does not make sense. From a medical point of view, she would be labeled incompetent.[7]

A thousand reasons for refusing treatment could be set out. Regarding each, we could ask the question, "Is this a rational or sensible reason?" On some, we might all agree. On others, there would be great disagreement. It is important to recognize that it can be no other way. Understanding this fact relieves the anxiety that accompanies the attempt to find out what competency is or to apply the proper definition of competency or rationality.

The fact that there can be neither a "true" finding of reasonableness nor a single test that will lead to uniform results should not, however, lead us to abandon our responsibility to make these judgments. Yet, when we weigh the reasons for the patient's choice, we many times discard the requirement of reasonableness and label persons competent even though they found their refusals on irrational beliefs. Patients who refuse necessary medical care based on religious beliefs are often given the label of competent even though their beliefs might be quite "irrational."

COMPETENCY IS COMPATIBLE WITH "IRRATIONALITY": RELIGIOUS REFUSALS

We face many difficult questions when we confront a person who is refusing lifesaving medical care based on religious belief.[8] If the patient is going to die because he or she is refusing a readily available medical procedure, we are puzzled, and we necessarily question the patient's competency. We find it difficult to accept that a rational and competent person would die when a simple act would save his or her life.

In considering competency and making judgments regarding those who refuse necessary medical treatment based on religious belief, we can apply the general definition of competency with a slight modification. In cases of religious refusals, a person is competent if (1) he or she has a proper understanding of the situation and the consequences of the decision, and (2) the decision is based on religious beliefs ("irrational" beliefs) that are within our common religious experience or common notions of religion and do not appear to us "crazy" or "nonreligious." If this definition seems vague, it is because it *is* vague.

To demonstrate how to apply this definition of competency, consider the following four examples of religious refusals. In each of these cases, suppose that the patient is refusing a lifesaving blood transfusion. Suppose also that each patient expresses sincerely held beliefs.[9]

Patient A states, "I refuse the blood transfusion because I am a Jehovah's Witness and I believe it is a violation of God's law to accept such blood. I understand that the consequence of my refusal is my death and I accept that result." Patient B states, "I refuse the blood transfusion because I am one of Yoda's Children and, based upon Luke Skywalker's teachings, I believe the acceptance of blood is a violation of Yoda's law and the work of the Dark Side of the Force. I understand that the consequence of my refusal is my death and I accept that result." Because we must make a determination relating to competency in these cases to decide whether we are going to respect or override the patient's refusal, what will be the likely result?

We judge the first patient competent, and he will be allowed to refuse treatment and die. We label the second patient, although a more troubling case, incompetent, and we allow some other person to give substituted consent to the treatment necessary to prevent his death. Now, why is this the case? If we ask, "What is the logical difference between the statement of patient A as opposed to the statement of patient B?" the answer must be "none." Both are identical as statements of "irrational" religious belief or faith.

Belief and faith are irrational in at least one sense. In the context of this discussion, the term *irrational* means not derived logically from facts, data, or circumstances—that is, it is outside the scope of reason. Faith is essentially belief based on that which is incapable of proof. It does not involve logic, facts, or proof; it is trust and belief in a matter empirically unknowable. If it were knowable through facts or proof, we would speak in terms of knowledge and truth and not of faith and belief. Theologians should know this.

A discussion that would attempt to label patient A's belief in Jehovah a religious belief and patient B's belief in Yoda a religious delusion would go nowhere. A conclusion in this situation that A's faith is based on a belief as opposed to a delusion would depend entirely on the beliefs, experiences, and prejudices of the person drawing that conclusion. In these cases, the label applied to the belief and the determination of competency depend on the novelty of the belief and on whether we want to give priority to the individual's continued life or to respecting the individual's choice. If the former, we would conclude that the decision is "crazy" and label the individual incompetent. If the latter, we would conclude that his belief is "religious" and label him competent.

In these two cases, the only difference is that patient A has voiced a religious belief held by organized and recognized groups within our society, whereas patient B has voiced a belief totally outside our common religious experience. The Jehovah's Witness's belief relating to the refusal of blood is now well within our society's general "religious belief experience." Because of our concurrent societal belief in the free exercise of religion, we "respect" the Jehovah's Witness's belief even though it is irrational.[10] We recognize the belief as religious, and we label patient A competent. As far as patient B is concerned, sincere or not, religious or not, we conclude that his belief is too "crazy" to determine a life-and-death decision, and we label him incompetent.

However, what about the protections afforded by the First Amendment? If we do not accept patient B's belief, are we unlawfully discriminating against this Yoda's Child and denying him his right to the free exercise of religion? Although it is true that the U.S. Constitution guarantees certain rights relating to the free exercise of religion, it is emphasized that only "religious beliefs" are protected.[11] In addition, although it is often asserted that the courts will not assess or inquire into the truth or validity of individual religious beliefs,[12] the courts most certainly do decide what constitutes a "religion"[13] and what amounts to a "religious belief."[14] In making such decisions, the courts also apply imprecise criteria and vague notions.

In determining whether a belief is a religious belief that is entitled to protection, the courts have at various times required that the belief be "truly held"[15] or that it be "sincere and meaningful,"[16] and judges have often emphasized the helpful test of orthodoxy.[17] The courts have also noted that some beliefs may simply be "too crazy" to qualify for protection.[18] In sum, the courts do judge the validity of religious beliefs, and they do it in a manner similar to the method of determining competency described earlier. That is, if a belief is "too crazy," there is sufficient room within our law to conclude that the belief is "nonreligious," not "sincere and meaningful," not "truly held," or not sufficiently similar to orthodox religious beliefs. This is the conclusion that ought to be reached about patient B's belief in Yoda.[19] Because his belief is too crazy to consider, we would label him incompetent, and the courts would label his belief as one not entitled to First Amendment protection. In doing so, both the courts and we would be acting properly.[20]

Some might object to making such judgments, but despite objections and difficulties, we ought and will continue to do so.[21] The only alternative to making such distinctions is to accept any statement of belief as consistent with competence and sufficient to support a life-and-death decision regardless of its apparent "craziness." Few would feel comfortable with such a rule.

Next, consider the following patients, who express slightly different reasons for refusing the lifesaving medical care. Patient C states, "I refuse the blood transfusion because the full moon, properly understood, is the source of the human spirit and the key to human happiness and cures all disease. When the moon rises in full next week you shall see that it will cure me without the need of your medical procedure."

This is the easiest case. As with patient B, patient C has based her choice on a belief quite outside our common religious experience. Additionally, she clearly does not appreciate either the nature of the situation or the consequence of her decision. She does not understand that her death is imminent. She fails both tests and is clearly incompetent. Is there any doubt that we would override this patient's refusal and take action to provide the lifesaving care?

Patient D states, "I refuse the blood transfusion because I am a Jehovah's Witness and I believe it is a violation of God's law to accept such blood. God will heal me without the need of your medical procedures." This is a more difficult case. Would you allow this patient to refuse the lifesaving care?

This Jehovah's Witness has based her refusal on a belief within our common religious experience. However, it is also evident that she does not appreciate either the nature of her situation or the consequences of her decision. She does not understand that without the blood transfusion her death is imminent. Although we may accept this patient's belief relating to the prohibition of blood, her religious beliefs go too far. Her belief in a cure without medical intervention in this situation does amount to a religious delusion.

Patient D is similar to the patient in an Ohio case in which treatment was allowed in spite of the patient's "religious refusal." The patient refused to consent to treatment because she believed that she was the wife of a noted evangelist, who would arrive to heal her. The court noted the rule that a patient's honestly held religious belief must be respected, but it decided that when those beliefs amount to a religious delusion, they may be disregarded.[22]

This might appear at first to be a subtle distinction, but it is a very important one. Carefully consider the difference between patient A and patient D. Patient A states, "I believe accepting blood is against God's will, and I will not accept blood even though I will die because of my belief." Patient D states, "I believe accepting blood is against God's will, and I will not accept blood. I also believe God will cure me and I will not die."

In failing to understand and recognize the consequences of her decision, patient D is not making the life-and-death decision required here. She is not deciding between the two, because she does not recognize one as being a consequence of her decision. The decision here is not simply to either accept blood or refuse blood. The decision to be made involves the choice of either accepting blood and living or refusing blood and dying. In Patient D's mind, she is simply choosing between life with treatment as opposed to life without treatment. One cannot freely decide between two choices if one does not understand what the choices actually are. If one cannot freely decide, one is not competent to decide.[23]

Because patient D is in fact not making the required decision between the two alternatives of life and death, in failing to respect her "non-choice" we are denying neither the principle of personal autonomy nor freedom of religious expression. We are obligated only to respect a decision. In refusing treatment, patient D is not making the required decision based on a religious belief. Rather, her religious belief prevents her from understanding that her death is imminent and the decision that we require her to make. Her belief in this situation is a delusion—religious or not—in that it has adversely affected her ability to understand.

In summary, in religious refusal cases and following the general definition of competency just set out, we ought only label a patient competent and respect a refusal of medical treatment when the patient is not deluded and he or she understands the situation and appreciates the consequences of the decision. To respect the patient's refusal, the decision must have a foundation in a religious belief that is within our common religious experience or our common notions of religion. We should not perceive it as extremely unreasonable, crazy, or nonreligious.

Some concepts involved in the issue of competency, the manner in which we should evaluate competency, and the conclusions that should be reached concerning patients A through D can be set out as shown in **Table 7-1**.

Table 7-1   Competency Decisions for Patients A Through D

	Proper Understanding[a]	Accepted Belief[b]	Competence[c]
Patient A (Jehovah's Witness)	Yes	Yes	Yes
Patient B (Yoda's Child)	Yes	Yes	Yes
Patient C (Moon Child)	No	No	No
Patient D (Jehovah's Witness)	No	Yes	No

[a]*Proper understanding:* The patient understands his or her condition and the consequences of the decision. In these cases, the patient understands he or she is going to die without medical intervention. The patient's understanding is not "deluded" by religious belief.
[b]*Acceptable belief:* The person's decision is based on a belief that is within our common religious experience. It is a belief that has been held for a sufficient period of time or is sufficiently similar to other orthodox beliefs so that we label it a religious belief and not nonreligious, unsound, or insane.
[c]*Competent:* The label we apply in the various situations.

CONCLUSIONS RELATING TO COMPETENCY

We can summarize the above view of how to determine competency in cases involving understanding, appreciation, rationality, and religious belief in another fashion. As with the cards used by police officers to assist in giving *Miranda* warnings, a medical decision-making card might state the following:

> *Process for Determining Competency of Patients Who Refuse*
> *Medical Treatment*
> Answer the following questions concerning the patient:
>
> 1. Does the patient understand his or her medical condition?
> 2. Does the patient understand the options and the consequences of his or her decision?
> 3. Does the patient refuse medical treatment based on rational reasons?
> 4. If the patient refuses treatment based on religious beliefs, are the religious beliefs acceptable and entitled to First Amendment protection, i.e., beliefs held by a sufficient number of persons for a sufficient period of time or sufficiently similar to other orthodox beliefs such that we do not label the beliefs crazy or nonreligious?
>
> If the answers to questions 1, 2, 3, and 4 are all yes, then we can respect the patient's refusal. We should label the patient as competent. If the answer to either question 1, 2, 3, or 4 is no, then the patient's refusal should not be respected, and action should be taken to obtain substitute consent. He or she is incompetent.

Using this procedure, one will reach a proper result in all cases, no matter who makes the determination—physician or judge—or what the particular statutory definition might be. If the answer to all four questions is yes, we will fulfill any proper statutory definition of competency. If the answer to any of the four is no, any proper definition of incompetency will be met.[24] This is not to say that in any given case there is a proper conclusion or that different persons asking these same questions will not reach different conclusions. This is also not to say that it is easy to answer such questions in all cases. Sometimes it is easy to answer these questions and we feel quite confident in our conclusions. Sometimes it is terribly difficult. Nevertheless, following this type of procedure will give a proper result simply because these questions are the basis of the concept of competency. They contain the necessary considerations, vague and slippery as they may be, to make the required decision. Such a procedure simply allows us to reach a conclusion in a straightforward manner, and this is all we can hope to do.

WHY IT MATTERS

It is always important to emphasize the significant ethical and moral issues involved in labeling a person incompetent. Such emphasis underscores our need to work hard at making proper determinations. Consider just what it is we are saying when we exercise the power of the state to override a patient's specific refusal of medical care because the patient is incompetent. We are, most assuredly, judging the validity of the patient's reasoning and the truth of the patient's beliefs. We do so without precise criteria or objective standards. We decide which reasons expressed by the patient are acceptable and which are proper religious beliefs entitled to protection.

As a society, we simply think that we should not allow some persons, for one reason or another, to make certain decisions. We reach this conclusion for the same reason that we think that we should not hold certain defendants responsible for otherwise criminal actions. Based on our experience, some persons just do not appear to be rational, responsible, or competent human beings.

In medical decision making, we must distinguish between rational and irrational reasons and between acceptable religious beliefs and craziness (or whatever one wishes to call it). If we do not make such distinctions, then we must allow the refusal of any patient no matter what the basis, even though the patient's beliefs are such that they cloud the patient's understanding of the situation and prevent him or her from making the required decision. What if the patient's beliefs seem clearly senseless and unacceptable, as nonsensical as the beliefs of an acutely psychotic person who chooses death based on "commands" from the television set?

As a further matter, consider this aspect of judging a person incompetent: in spite of the person's stated choice, we make a different choice and force our choice upon the person. We do so claiming that we have the right (and the duty) to force our decision on the person; it is for his or her "own good." We do so because, in spite of the person's choice (an incompetent choice), the person has a right to the benefits of our decision (a competent choice). We reason that the person has a right to the benefits of the choice that he or she would have made if competent. If the person were competent to decide and had reached a different conclusion, he or she would be, in effect, a different person. When you change a person's understanding, beliefs, thoughts, conclusions, and choices, you have changed the person. In forcing our choice upon the patient, we are claiming that the patient has a right to the benefits of being a different person. Indeed, we are insisting that he or she *be* a different person. It is not difficult to understand and appreciate the ethical and moral problems involved in negating personal autonomy under such circumstances and in using power and force, if necessary, to insist that a person be another person.

Of course, most persons are aware that good intentions and the exercise of power for another person's own good can bring about horrendous results. Controversial decisions and disagreements have always and will always result from determinations of competency. Such is our condition; however, the nature and consequences of these decisions simply underscore the weight of our obligations.

SUMMARY

Although there is always more to say, this discussion has attempted to explain what competency is and to set out a straightforward process for making determinations of competency. The patient's competency is the first and foremost question that must be resolved in deciding whether one will respect or override a patient's refusal. There is no single definition of *competency*, and there are many different ways of stating the concepts involved in that term.

The term *competent* is nothing more than a label we place on a person when we conclude that we should allow him or her to make the decision at issue. Generally, we apply the label to the person who understands his or her condition and the consequences of the choices and whose reasons make sense to us. Sometimes, however, especially in cases of religious refusals and First Amendment considerations, we apply the term *competent* to persons who base their refusal on irrational beliefs as long as those beliefs are within our common religious experience and do not seem too strange.

In making determinations of competency and in forcing treatment on others, we are engaging in serious matters. We should not avoid these decisions, however. We must use our experience of the human condition and our best judgment in the attempt to make proper decisions. As long as we make these decisions with proper motives and a proper understanding of the task, we make them properly. Although these decisions might be difficult in individual cases, we should make them without unnecessary concern or doubt, because in doing so we are doing all that can properly be done. We are, after all, simply human beings attempting to make very difficult decisions relating to other human beings.

QUESTIONS FOR DISCUSSION

1. What demographic changes or healthcare practices might increase the need to determine patient competence in the future?
2. How do the principles of patient autonomy and beneficence conflict when making healthcare decisions that run counter to the patient's choice?
3. Why is it important for a healthcare professional to have a guideline for deciding patient competence?
4. In competency cases, how important is it to listen to the patient and clarify his or her wishes? Would you want more than one person to interview the patient?
5. What ethical theories support making a treatment decision for a patient even when he or she does not want treatment?

FOOD FOR THOUGHT

The issue of determining patient competency is never easy and will continue to be challenging to healthcare professionals. Consider the changes that the aging of the American population will bring. After considering this chapter and the principles of ethics you have studied, what is the best advice you can give about determining patient competency in a way that is ethical?

NOTES

1. Judge Cardoza stated it this way: "Every human being of adult years and sound mind has a right to determine what shall be done with his own body." *Schloendorff v. Society of New York Hospital* (1914) 105 N.E. 92, 93. See also *Matter of Spring* (1980) 405 N.E.2d 115; *Superintendent of Belchertown v. Saikewicz* (1977) 370 N.E.2d 417; *Bartling v. Superior Court* (1984) 163 Cal.App.3d 186; and *Barber v. Superior Court* (1983) 147 Cal.App.3d 1006.

2. "On balance, the right to self-determination ordinarily outweighs any countervailing state interests and competent persons generally are permitted to refuse medical treatment, even at the risk of death. Most of the cases that have held otherwise . . . have concerned the patient's competency to make a rational and considered choice of treatment." *Matter of Conroy* (1985) 486 A.2d 1209, 1225.

3. California Welfare and Institutions Code Sec. 1435.2 (repealed Jan. 1, 1981).

4. R. Meisel and L. Meisel, "Toward a Model of the Legal Doctrine of Informed Consent," *American Journal of Psychiatry* 134 (March 1977): 285, 287.

5. R. Meisel and L. Meisel, "Tests of Competency to Consent to Treatment," *American Journal of Psychiatry* 134 (March 1977): 279, 283.

6. See *Lane v. Candura* (1978) 376 N.E.2d 1232 for a decision respecting a patient's refusal of an amputation under similar circumstances.

7. *Matter of Schiller* (1977) 372A.2d 360 is another case in which the court struggled with the refusal of an amputation. In the *Matter of Schiller*, the court found the patient incompetent and a guardian was appointed primarily because Mr. Schiller failed to properly evidence an understanding of his medical condition and the reality of death, the more likely situation in such cases.

8. The First Amendment occasions our additional concern, of course, to the Constitution of the United States: "Congress shall make no law respecting an establishment of religion, or prohibiting the free exercise thereof. . . ."

9. Of course, in making determinations of competency, one would always want to know more and would question the patient carefully and thoroughly.

10. Note that the use of the beliefs of Jehovah's Witnesses is not intended to single out those beliefs as being less rational than or deserving of less respect than any other religious beliefs. The Jehovah's Witness examples are included solely because the beliefs of Jehovah's Witnesses form the most widely known religious basis for the refusal of medical care in this country.

11. "Only beliefs rooted in religion are protected by the Free Exercise Clause, which, by its terms, gives special protection to the exercise of religion." *Thomas v. Review Board* (1981) 450 U.S. 707, 715.

12. "Men may believe what they cannot prove. They may not be put to the proof of their religious doctrines or beliefs. Religious experiences which are as real as life to some may be incomprehensible to others." *United States v. Ballard* (1944) 322 U.S. 78, 86. "[R]eligious beliefs need not be acceptable, logical, consistent, or comprehensible to others in order to merit First Amendment protection." *Thomas v. Review Board* (1981) 450 U.S. 707, 714.

13. See *Engel v. Vitale* (1962) 370 U.S. 421 (school prayer); *Loney v. Scurr* (1979) 474 F. Supp. 1186, 1194; "[T]he Church of the New Song qualifies as a 'religion.'" *Theriault v. Silber* (1978) 453 F. Supp. 254, 260; "The Church of the New Song appears not to be a religion." *Malnik v. Yogi* (1977) 440 F. Supp. 1284 (transcendental meditation).

14. See *Wisconsin v. Yoder* (1972) 406 U.S. 205, which contrasted the "religious beliefs" of the Amish with the "philosophical and personal" beliefs of Thoreau; also, *United States v. Seeger* (1965) 380 U.S. 163, which determined whether or not the beliefs of a conscientious objector qualified as "religious beliefs" to allow an exemption.

15. "[W]hile the 'truth' of a belief is not open to question, there remains the significant question whether it is 'truly held.'" *United States v. Seeger* (1965) 380 U.S. 163, 185.

16. "We believe that . . . the test of belief 'in a relation to a supreme being' is whether a given belief that is sincere and meaningful occupies a place in the life of its possessor parallel to that filled by the orthodox belief in God of one who clearly qualifies for the exemption." *United States v. Seeger* (1965) 380 U.S. 163, 166.

17. "[D]oes the claimed belief occupy the same place in the life of the objector as an orthodox belief in God holds in the life of one clearly qualified for exemption?" *Seeger* supra at 184. "[I]t is at least clear that if a group (or an individual) professes beliefs which are similar to and function like the beliefs of those groups which by societal consensus are recognized as a religion, the First Amendment guarantee of freedom of religion applies." *Loney v. Scurr* (1979) 474 F. Supp. 1186, 1193 citing *Welsh v. United States* (1970) 398 U.S. 333, 340. "While recently acquired religious views are worthy of protection, the history of a religious belief and the length of time it has been held are factors to be utilized in assessing the sincerity with which it is held." In re *Marriage of Gove* (1977) 572 P.2d 458, 461, citing *Wisconsin v. Yoder*.

18. "One can, of course, imagine an asserted claim so bizarre, so clearly nonreligious in motivation, as not to be entitled to protection under the Free Exercise Clause." *Thomas v. Review Board* (1981) 450 U.S. 707, 715.

19. If a professed belief in Star Wars characters and making a life-and-death decision based on faith in Yoda and Luke Skywalker is not sufficiently "crazy" for you, create your own patient. Consider, for example, a refusal by the patient who tells you he is "Serumzat, believer in the teachings of the Prince of Liquids and Tabletops; I believe that accepting blood is wrong and will prevent my passage to the afterlife, which I am destined to rule."

20. As a further example of how courts make these decisions, see *Powell v. Columbian Presbyterian Medical Center* (1966) 267 N.Y.S.2d 450. The facts presented the classic case of the Jehovah's Witness who did not want to die but who refused a lifesaving blood transfusion. In a most candid decision that demonstrated the reality of the difficulty, vagueness, and room for legal discretion involved in these matters, the court stated in part, "This matter generated a barrage of legal niceties, misinformation, and emotional feelings on the part of all concerned—including the Court personnel. . . . Never before had my judicial robe weighed so heavily on my shoulders. . . . I, almost by reflex action, subjected the papers to the test of justiciability, jurisdiction and legality. . . . Yet, ultimately, my decision to act to save this woman's life was rooted in more fundamental precepts. . . . I was reminded of 'The Fall' by Camus, and I knew that no release—no legalistic absolution—would absolve me or the Court from responsibility if I, speaking for the Court, answered 'No' to the question 'Am I my brother's keeper?' This woman wanted to live. I could not let her die!" 267 N.Y.S.2d at 451, 452.

21. It should be noted that in all cases of refusals of medical care, religious or not, as our certainty in the prognosis decreases, our willingness to allow the refusal increases. See, for example, *Petition of Nemser* (1966) 273 N.Y.S.2d 624, which contains an interesting discussion of these issues, although in some areas the court's analysis is incomplete or incorrect.

22. *In re Milton*, 505 N.E. 2d 255 (Ohio 1987). What would we do if this patient was Mrs. Oral Roberts?

23. Consider how terribly subtle these distinctions can be, however. Does it make a difference if the patient says, "I leave my fate to Jehovah," as opposed to "I believe Jehovah will cure me"? Or if the patient states, "God will save me," as opposed to "God may save me"? Again, we would explore this patient's understanding and beliefs carefully.

24. It should be remembered that if the answer to any of these questions is no, the patient also is unable to consent to treatment.

CHAPTER 8

Older People and Issues of Access to Long-Term Care

Janet Gardner-Ray

INTRODUCTION

This chapter presents a historical review of issues concerning access to long-term care and the urgent need for change in the future. Gardner-Ray, an executive in the long-term care industry, assures us that the situation concerning long-term care services has not improved. The issue of access to long-term care promises to be even more critical in the near future given the imminent influx of baby boomers into the Medicare system and their potential need for elder care. The ethical issues posed by Gardner-Ray are certainly not limited to the past, and will challenge our thinking for years to come. In fact, the issue of access to long-term care will loom large on the social, political, and ethical horizon well into the 21st century. Therefore, it is important to understand the current social and political climate as well as the history surrounding elder care before we can adequately address ethical decision making in the long-term care industry.

During the last decades of the 20th century, there was increasing evidence of the public's interest in improving access to humane and appropriate long-term care services in the United States. Opinion polls indicated that a substantial majority of Americans—in all adult age groups—feared the financial, familial, psychological, and social consequences of dependence on long-term care. Most Americans favored the general principle of expanding government financing for such care as the principal means of increasing access.[1] A number of bills to provide new programs of public funding for long-term care were introduced in Congress in the late 1980s and 1990s, with estimated annual price tags ranging up to $60 billion in the first year.

Why did long-term care begin to emerge from the shadows during the 1980s and 1990s? Simply, it was cast into the healthcare arena by the increase in dramatic and aggressive treatments offered by acute-care medicine, which allow the eldest elderly to survive longer with chronic illness and disability. Living longer became a major element in long-term care growth given the enormous growth of our older population; the number of those aged 65 and older doubled from 16 million in 1960 to 32 million in 1990. Persons in this age category are presently 12.5% of our population, and it is expected that they will constitute 71 million, or 20%, in the year 2030.[2]

Another element that precipitated the growth in long-term care was the growing constituency of adult children providing care to elderly parents who understand the importance of long-term care services because of their direct contact with providing or arranging for the care of their aged parents. In 1989, over 13 million adults in the United States who had disabled elderly parents or spouses were potential providers of long-term care, financial assistance, and emotional support; 4.2 million of them provided direct care in home settings.[3] Today, the number of adult caregivers has risen to over 10 million, with an estimated cost of $3 trillion in lost wages, pensions, and Social Security benefits as a result of leaving the workforce early.[4]

Despite the underlying needs and hopes of elder caregivers, enactment of a government program to expand access to long-term care in the immediate future is problematic because of the substantial funds that would be required. Achieving a "balanced budget" is the rhetorical mainstay of contemporary national politics, and containing government expenditures on healthcare costs is one of the major means for balancing the federal and state budgets.

The challenges of ensuring adequate access to long-term care for all who need it are substantial. The number of Americans requiring some form of long-term care is already large and will grow significantly over the next few decades. Financing such care is already very difficult for individuals, their families, and governments. Even with the advent of healthcare reform, indications are that the prices for services and their aggregate national costs will continue to escalate, whereas there could be a curtailment of the role of governments in paying for care of an expanded disabled population.

This chapter focuses on issues of access for older people, although it also considers the need for long-term care for younger disabled persons and the political role they might play in improving access for persons of all ages. First, it provides an overview of the growing population that needs long-term care. Second, it discusses issues of access to care. Third, the chapter briefly recounts how proposals to expand public funding for long-term care rose to the national policy agenda in the early 1990s and then abruptly fell from it. Finally, the chapter presents the political and ethical prospects for improving access in the years ahead.

THE GROWING POPULATION NEEDING CARE

In 2002, the U.S. General Accounting Office reported that more than 14 million Americans required long-term care. *Long-term care need* is defined by being functionally dependent on a long-term basis due to physical or mental limitations, or both. Two broad categories of functional limitations are widely used by clinicians to assess need for care. One category is dependence in basic *activities of daily living* (ADLs)—getting in and out of bed, toileting, bathing, dressing, and eating. (*ADL dependent* is the term used for persons who have cognitive impairments and need cueing from someone else to be able to perform their own ADLs.) The other category is limitations in *instrumental activities of daily living* (IADLs)—taking medications, preparing meals, managing finances, doing light housework and other chores, being able to get in and out of the home, using the telephone, and so on. (Professionals use other criteria to assess children and people with mental illness, such as the ability to attend school or problems in behavior.)

The range of services needed by those who have difficulties in carrying out their ADLs and IADLs, as well as those services needed by their primary caregivers, is extensive. **Table 8-1** presents a list of such services. Almost all of the services can be provided for individuals regardless of where they reside—at home,

Table 8-1   Services That May Be Needed for Disabled Individuals and Their Families

Acute medical care	Homemaker	Personal emergency
Adult day care	Hospice	response system
Audiology	Legal services	Physical therapy
Autopsy	Medication and elimination	Protective services
Chore services	of drugs that cause	Recreation/exercise
Dental care	excess disability	Respite care[a]
Diagnosis	Mental health services	Shopping
Escort service	Multidimensional	Skilled nursing
Family support groups	assessment	Special equipment (ramps,
Family/caregiver counseling	Nutritional counseling	hospital beds, etc.)
Family/caregiver education	Occupational therapy	Speech therapy
and training	Ongoing medical	Telephone reassurance
Financial/benefits	supervision	Transportation
counseling	Paid companion/sitter	Treatment of coexisting
Home health aide	Patient counseling	medical conditions
Home-delivered meals	Personal care	Vision care

[a]*Respite care* includes any service intended to provide temporary relief for the primary caregiver. When used for that purpose, homemaker, paid companion/sitter, adult day care, temporary nursing home care, and other services included on this list constitute respite care.

Adapted from Office of Technology Assessment. *Confused Minds, Burdened Families: Finding Help for People with Alzheimer's and Other Dementias* (Washington, DC: Office of Technology Assessment, 1990).

in a nursing home, or in residential settings such as retirement communities, board-and-care facilities, adult foster homes, assisted-living facilities, and various other forms of sheltered-housing arrangements.

Popular perception is that most of the long-term care population is elderly and resides in nursing homes. However, this is not the case. In 1994, people aged 65 and older composed only 55% of the long-term care population. Working-age adults accounted for 42% of the total, and children the remaining 3%. Moreover, only 22% of the elderly population needing long-term care, and 19% of the total disabled population, resided in nursing homes and other institutions. More recent data indicate that these percentages are changing, partially as a result of the increase in alternatives in elder care.

Although it seems apparent that the number of people needing long-term care will grow substantially in the future, reasonably precise predictions regarding the size of that population and its composition are difficult to generate because of the many factors that are involved. New and improved medical treatments and technological developments could help to prevent, delay, and compensate for various types of functional difficulties. Moreover, health-related lifestyle changes and environmental protection measures could markedly reduce rates of disabling diseases and injuries. To the contrary, medical advances could increase the need for long-term care. Lower death rates from heart disease and stroke, for example, could mean that more people will live longer with disabling conditions and thus enter the pathway of late-onset illnesses such as

Alzheimer's disease. Similarly, improvements in dealing with the complications of acquired immune deficiency syndrome (AIDS) could engender longer periods of care for patients with this condition.

Demographic factors might also affect future needs for providing and financing long-term care at older ages. For instance, the cohorts reaching old age in the next several decades will be better educated than their predecessors. Higher levels of education are associated with lower levels of disability and need for care.[5] Yet, the ethnic composition by 2030 will be 72% white, 10% African American, 11% Hispanic, and 5% Asian, suggesting the need for increased long-term care services and governmental subsidies for financing. From 1990 to 2050, the proportion of nonwhite Americans aged 65 and older is projected to more than double, from 9.8% to 21.3%. When they reach old age, these racial minorities might be highly dependent on public subsidies for their long-term care if present patterns of economic resource distribution among racial and ethnic groups persist throughout the first half of the 21st century. Among persons aged 65 and older who have the lowest household incomes, nearly 40% are racial minorities, and their aggregate net worth is less than one-third that of older white persons.[6] Studies show that health disparities also exist among certain racial and ethnic groups who are disproportionately affected by chronic conditions.[7]

Even though precise projections are difficult, it is clear that there will be enormous increases in the number of disabled older people in the 21st century. When much of the baby boom—a large cohort of 74 million Americans born between 1946 and 1964—reaches the ranks of old age in 2030, the absolute number of people aged 65 and older will have more than doubled, from about 31 million in 1990 to about 71 million. Moreover, the numbers of persons in advanced old-age ranges will also more than double. Those aged 75 and older will grow from 13 million to 30 million between 1990 and 2030, and those aged 85 and older will increase from 3 million to 8 million.[8]

Rates of disability increase markedly at these advanced ages. One reflection of this is in the most currently available data (from 2004) on rates of nursing home use in different old-age categories. Of the 1.4 million residents of nursing homes, about 4.5% are 65 to 74 years old. This compares with 3.6% of persons aged 75 to 84, and 13.9% of persons aged 85 and older.[9] Similarly, disability rates increase in older old-age categories among persons who are not in nursing homes. According to the 2000 U.S. Census Bureau data on the disability of noninstitutionalized populations over age 65 (33,346,626 people), almost 42% demonstrated some degree of disability. The most common form was physical disability (28%), with difficulty going outside the home (20%) and sensory disability (14%) in second and third places.[10]

The tremendous future growth expected in the older population suggests that there will be millions more disabled elderly people in the decades ahead. Whether rates of disability in old age will increase or decline in the future, however, is a matter on which experts disagree, depending on their assumptions and measures. Assuming no changes in age-specific risks of disability, He et al. calculated a 31% increase between 1990 and 2010 in the number of persons aged 65 and older experiencing difficulty with ADLs.[11] Using the same assumption, the Congressional Budget Office projected that the nursing home population will increase 50% between 1990 and 2010, double by 2030, and triple by 2050.[12] Even those researchers who report a decline in the prevalence of disability at older ages emphasize that there will be large absolute increases in the number of older Americans needing long-term care in the decades ahead.

Predicting whether long-term care needs among people younger than 65 will increase or decline is more difficult. One of the principal reasons is that reliable databases for making projections are limited as compared with well-developed national and longitudinal sources available regarding the older population. Data collected on a state basis vary widely with respect to state rates for various types of disabilities.[13] Moreover, the numbers involved with respect to various disabling conditions—such as spinal cord injury, cerebral palsy, and mental retardation—are relatively small and much more susceptible to changing conditions.

Yet, experts agree that the number of younger disabled persons has grown in recent years, and this trend might well persist. New technologies and increased access to medical care continue to enable more people to survive injuries and other conditions that were heretofore fatal, and thereby live for many years with ADL limitations. For example, biomedical advances have enabled many more children with developmental disabilities, as well as low-birth-weight infants, to survive much longer than in the past and to extend the years in which they need long-term care.

ISSUES OF ACCESS

Whether a long-term care patient is in a nursing home, living at home, or in another type of residential setting, there are certain aspects of care that such a person desires. An ideal system of services would be amply available, of high quality, provided by well-trained personnel, easily located and arranged, and readily accessible through private or public funding or both.

The present system, however, is far from ideal. The supply of services is insufficient, service providers lack education and training, and the quality of many services is poor.[14] Moreover, the system is so fragmented that even when high-quality services are sufficiently available, many patients and families do not know about them and require help in defining their service needs and arranging for them to be provided.[15]

Underlying each of these problems is the issue of financing. As is the case with most aspects of the U.S. healthcare delivery system, the nature and extent of policies for funding have substantially shaped the characteristics of long-term care services.

The Costs of Care

Aggregate expenditures for long-term care are sizable and very likely to increase in the decades immediately ahead. The total bill in 1995 was $106.5 billion; of this amount, 73% went to nursing home care and 27% to home- and community-based care.[16] Out-of-pocket payments by individuals and their families accounted for 32.5% of the total. Private insurance benefits paid for 5.5%. Other private funds accounted for 4.6%. Federal, state, and local governments financed the remaining 57.4%. Medicaid paid for 85% of nursing home care. In 2003, the total bill had risen to $183 billion, while the out-of-pocket payments fell to 20% of the total. Paying the costs of long-term care out of pocket can be a catastrophic financial experience for patients and their families. The annual cost of a year's care in a nursing home averages more than $58,000, but can cost well over $100,000.[17] Although the use of a limited number of services in a home- or other community-based setting is less expensive, noninstitutional care for patients who would otherwise be appropriately placed in a nursing home is not cheaper.[18]

For a high percentage of older people, the price of long-term care is simply unaffordable. Among persons aged 65 and older, 40% have a pretax income of less than 200% of the poverty threshold—under $10,458 for an individual and $14,602 for a married couple in which the man is aged 65 or older.[19] The costs of care will undoubtedly grow in the future. Price increases in nursing home and home- and community-based care have consistently exceeded the general rate of inflation. Trends in long-term care labor and overhead costs indicate that this pattern will continue.

Dozens of government programs are sources of funding for long-term care services, including Medicaid, the Veterans' Administration, Social Security's Title XX for social services, and the Older Americans Act.[20] Yet each source regulates the availability of funds through rules regarding eligibility and breadth of service coverage and changes its rules frequently. Consequently, persons needing long-term care and their caregivers often find themselves ineligible for financial help from these programs and unable to pay out of pocket for needed services. In one study, about 75% of the informal, unpaid caregivers of dementia patients reported that their patients did not use formal, paid services because the patients were unable to pay for them.[21]

Recent data on Medicare and Medicaid spending affirms the trends mentioned here. In 2006, these programs cost over $3 billion per day to run. In light of the fact that the first of the baby boomers (a cohort of 77 million) became eligible for Medicare in 2008, the cry for reform is becoming even louder. However, even the 2003 prescription-drug benefit has not slowed down the increase in costs. Healthcare reform will not solve all of these issues: challenges lay ahead.[22]

The Caregiving Role of Families

A number of research efforts have documented that about 80% of the long-term care provided to older persons outside of nursing homes is presently provided on an in-kind basis by family members—spouses, siblings, adult children, and broader kin networks. About 74% of dependent community-based older persons receive all their care from family members or other unpaid sources, about 21% receive both formal and informal services, and about 5% use just formal services.[23] The vast majority of family caregivers are women.[24] The family also plays an important role in obtaining and managing services from paid service providers.

The capacities and willingness of family members to care for disabled older persons may decline, however, because of a broad social trend. The family, as a fundamental unit of social organization, has been undergoing profound transformations that will become more fully manifest over the next few decades as baby boomers reach old age. The striking growth of single-parent households, the growing participation of women in the labor force, and the high incidence of divorce and remarriage (differentially higher for men) all entail complicated changes in the structure of household and kinship roles and relationships. There will be an increasing number of blended families, reflecting multiple lines of descent through multiple marriages and the birth of children outside wedlock through other partners. This growth in the incidence of step- and half-relatives will make for a dramatic new turn in family structure in the coming decades. Already, such blended families constitute about half of all households with children.[25]

One possible implication of these changes is that kinship networks in the near future will become more complex, attenuated, and diffuse,[26] perhaps with a weakened sense of filial obligation. If changes in the intensity of kinship relations significantly erode the capacity and sense of obligation to care for older family members when the baby boom cohort is in the ranks of old age and disability, demands for governmental support to pay for long-term care may increase accordingly.

The Role of Private Insurance

Private, long-term care insurance, a relatively new product, is very expensive for the majority of older persons, and its benefits are limited in scope and duration. The best-quality policies that provide substantial benefits over a reasonable period of time charged premiums in 1991 that averaged $2,525 for persons aged 65 and $7,675 for those aged 79.[27] Only about 4% to 5% of older persons have any private long-term care insurance, and only about 1% of nursing home costs are paid for by private insurance.[28] A number of analyses have suggested that even when the product becomes more refined, no more than 20% of older Americans will be able to afford private insurance.[29]

A variation on the private-insurance-policy approach to financing long-term care is continuing care retirement communities (CCRCs) that promise comprehensive healthcare services—including long-term care—to all members.[30] CCRC customers tend to be middle- and upper-income persons who are relatively healthy when they become residents and pay a substantial entrance charge and monthly fee in return for a promise of "care for life." It has been estimated that about 10% of older people could afford to join such communities.[31] Most of the 1,000 CCRCs in the United States, however, do not provide complete benefit coverage in their contracts, and those that do have faced financial difficulties.[32] Because most older people prefer to remain in their own homes rather than join age-segregated communities, an alternative product termed "life care at home" (LCAH) was developed in the late 1980s and marketed to middle-income customers with lower entry and monthly fees than those of CCRCs.[33] However, only about 500 LCAH policies are in effect.[34]

A relatively new approach for providing long-term care in residential settings is the assisted-living facility. It has been created for moderately disabled persons—including those with dementia—who are not ready for a nursing home and provides them with limited forms of personal care, supervision of medications and other daily routines, and congregate meal and housekeeping services.[35] Assisted living has yet to be tried with a private-insurance approach. The monthly rent in a first-class nonprofit facility averages about $2,400 or higher for a one-bedroom apartment; the rent is even higher in for-profit facilities.

The Role of Medicaid

For those who cannot pay for long-term care out of pocket or through various insurance arrangements and are not eligible for care through programs of the Department of Veterans Affairs, the available sources of payment are Medicaid and other means-tested government programs funded by the Older Americans Act, Social Service block grants (Title XX of the Social Security Act), and state and local governments. The bulk of such financing is through Medicaid, the federal–state program for the poor, which finances the care—at least in part—of about three-fifths of nursing home patients[36] and 28% of home- and community-based services.[37] The program does not pay for the full range of home-care services that are needed for most clients who are functionally dependent. Most state Medicaid programs provide reimbursement only for the most "medicalized" services that are necessary to maintain a long-term care patient in a home environment. Rarely reimbursed are essential supports such as chore services, assistance with food shopping and meal preparation, transportation, companionship, periodic monitoring, and respite programs for family and other unpaid caregivers.

Medicaid does include a special waiver program that allows states to offer a wider range of nonmedical home-care services, if limited to those patients whose services will be no more costly than Medicaid-financed nursing home care. However, the volume of services in these waiver programs—which in some states combine Medicaid with funds from the Older Americans Act, the Social Services block grant program, and other state and local government sources—is small in relation to the overall demand.[38] Although many patients are not poor enough to qualify for Medicaid when they enter a nursing home, a substantial number become poor after they are institutionalized.[39] Persons in this latter group deplete their assets in order to meet their bills and eventually "spend down" and become poor enough to qualify for Medicaid.

Still others become eligible for Medicaid by sheltering their assets—illegally or legally—with the assistance of attorneys who specialize in so-called Medicaid estate planning. Because sheltered assets are not counted in Medicaid eligibility determinations, such persons are able to take advantage of a program for the poor without being poor. Asset sheltering has become a source of considerable concern to the federal and state governments as Medicaid expenditures on nursing homes and home care have been increasing rapidly—nearly doubling from 1990 to 1995. Healthcare reform includes the establishment of a new office under the Centers for Medicare and Medicaid to address this issue and improve access and coordination of services for those who qualify for Medicare and Medicaid. This office is so new that there is no information about how well it is working.[40]

An analysis in Virginia estimated that the aggregate of assets sheltered through the use of legal loopholes in 1991 was equal to more than 10% of what the state spent on nursing home care through Medicaid in that year.[41] A study drawing on interviews with state government staff for Medicaid eligibility determination in four states—California, Florida, Massachusetts, and New York—found a strong relationship between a high level of financial wealth in a geographic area and a high level of Medicaid estate-planning activity. Most of these workers estimated that the range of asset sheltering among single applicants for Medicaid was between 5% and 10%, and for married applicants between 20% and 25%.[42] A law enacted in 1996 made it a federal crime to shelter assets in order to become eligible for Medicaid. However, the law is so vague that, practically speaking, it has been unenforceable. In 2012, these loopholes remain difficult to understand, and changes resulting from healthcare reform do not appear to provide increased clarity for this issue.

FORCES FOR IMPROVING ACCESS

From the mid-1980s until the mid-1990s, a number of national policy makers were sympathetic to these various dilemmas—the inability of individuals and their families to pay for services, the limitations of private insurance, and the anxieties of spending down. Since then, however, the main concern in Washington, D.C., as well as in the states, has been to limit Medicaid expenditures. In this new context, the most likely prospect is that public resources for long-term care will be even less available in relation to the need than they have been to date.

Public recognition of a need to improve access to long-term care has been building over the past two decades. The major initial impetus for this increased awareness has been successful advocacy efforts on behalf of older people, particularly the efforts undertaken by a political coalition formed in the mid-1970s concerned about Alzheimer's disease (AD).[43] This coalition was successful in getting Congress to earmark appropriations for AD research at the National Institute on Aging in the 1980s, and the amount of these funds has been increasing ever since.[44]

Advocates for victims of AD formally coalesced in 1988 with the broader constituency concerned about chronically ill and disabled older persons. The Alzheimer's Association, the American Association for Retired Persons (AARP), and the Families U.S.A. Foundation (a small organization originally established to improve the plight of poor older people) allied during the presidential campaign to undertake a lobbying effort organized under the name Long-Term Care '88.[45] The next year an explicit link was forged between advocates for the disabled and the elderly when Congressman Claude Pepper introduced a bill to provide comprehensive long-term home-care coverage for disabled persons of any age who were dependent in at least two ADLs.[46] Although this bill was not voted on by Congress, it was a milestone in that it was the first major legislative effort to programmatically combine the long-term care needs of younger disabled adults with those of elderly people.

Following the Pepper bill, several dozen long-term care bills were introduced in Congress. The lobbying efforts for long-term care that were launched during the 1988 presidential campaign have broadened to encompass the needs of younger disabled people and have been carried forward by a coalition named the Long-Term Care Campaign. This Washington-based interest group claims to represent nearly 140 national organizations (with more than 60 million members), including religious denominations, organized labor and business groups, nurses, veterans, youth and women's groups, consumer organizations, and racial and ethnic groups, as well as older and younger disabled persons.[47]

In the early l990s, advocates for the elderly and younger disabled persons were optimistic that the federal government would establish a new program for funding long-term care that would not be means tested, as is Medicaid. A number of bills introduced from 1989 to 1994 included some version of such a program, including President Clinton's failed proposal for healthcare reform.[48] None of these proposals became law. The major reason was that any substantial version of such a program would cost tens of billions of dollars each year just at the outset, and far more as the baby boomers reach old age.

By the mid-1990s, there was a squashing of optimism regarding expanded governmental funding for long-term care. A new Republican majority in the 104th Congress reversed the focus on long-term care from expansion to retraction. It proposed to limit federal spending on Medicaid. Advocates for long-term care programs switched from offense to defense.

By 1995, Medicaid's expenditures on long-term care were growing at an annualized rate of 13.2% since 1989.[49] As part of its overall effort to achieve a balanced budget, Congress initially proposed in that year to cap the rate of growth in Medicaid expenditures in order to achieve savings of $182 billion by 2002, to eliminate federal requirements for determining individual eligibility for Medicaid (as an entitlement), and to turn over control of the program to state governments through capped block grants. Such changes were vetoed by President Clinton. They resurfaced in 1996 with proposed reductions totaling $72 billion, but there was no legislation that year. However, in 2005, a report presented as testimony before the Subcommittee on Health and the Committee on Energy and Commerce in the U.S. House of Representatives again addressed reforming long-term care financing referring to Medicare and Medicaid as entitlement programs.

Reduction in Medicare and Medicaid programs remains on the policy agenda at the present, strongly supported by the National Governors Association. According to one analysis, the congressional proposals for limiting Medicaid's growth would have trimmed long-term care funding by as much as 11.4% and meant that 1.74 million Medicaid beneficiaries would have lost or been unable to secure coverage.[50]

In addition, this analysis assumed that states would make their initial reductions in home- and community-based care services (because nursing home residents have nowhere else to go) and concluded that such services would be substantially reduced from their current levels. There was a projection that 5 states would eliminate home- and community-based services by the end of the 1999, and another 19 would cut services by more than half. If provisions to cap and block grant Medicaid do become law, they will almost certainly engender conflict within states regarding the distribution of limited resources for the care of older and younger poor constituencies.

WHAT ARE THE PROSPECTS FOR IMPROVED ACCESS?

Prospects for older people having better access to long-term care seem dim. Out-of-pocket payments for care are becoming larger and increasingly unaffordable for many. Only a minority of older persons—now about 5%, and perhaps 20% in the decades ahead—might be able to afford premiums for private long-term care insurance. Broad societal trends suggest that informal, unpaid care by family members might become less feasible in the future than it is today. Moreover, contemporary federal and state budgetary politics pose a serious threat to the safety net that government programs provide by financing long-term care for the poor.

How might the outlook improve in the future? The most promising seeds for change lie in the enormous projected growth in the number of older persons needing long-term care, outlined at the outset of this chapter. Moreover, leaders of the American Coalition of Citizens with Disabilities, representing 8 million disabled persons, have expressed for some years the hope that they might form a powerful political alliance with organizations representing over 33 million older people to pursue this issue of mutual concern.[51]

As the demand for long-term care, increases while the means for access remain limited or become more restricted, a widespread and deeply felt popular demand for expanded government funding of long-term care could well emerge. Even as organized advocates for long-term care access brought the issue to the public policy agenda in the late 1980s and early 1990s, the entrance of the baby boomers into the ranks of old age may precipitate a grassroots movement that will revitalize political awareness of the issue as a major problem in American society.

However, even if a grassroots movement is able to elevate the principle of expanded government funding for long-term care to the top of the agenda, that general principle masks some basic value questions that, so far, have just begun to surface in public discussion. Widespread debate on and resolution of these questions will be required for a substantial proportion of Americans to understand and support the implications of any law that is to be enacted. Even if enacted, such legislation could be quickly repealed, as was the poorly understood Medicare Catastrophic Coverage Act of 1988.[52] Yet depending on the identity of the primary constituency, seeking support for long-term care (the aged, the disabled, or a broader coalition of the aged, the disabled, and perhaps others), the configurations and primacy of the values involved might be very different, and the likelihood of generating widespread support might vary substantially.

From the perspective of older persons, the view is that long-term care is a problem besetting elderly people, categorically. Economic concern generates the predominant, though not exclusive, element of interest in additional public insurance. That concern is the possibility of becoming poor through spending down—depleting one's assets to pay for long-term care and then becoming dependent on a welfare program, Medicaid, to pay nursing home bills. There is a distinct middle-class fear—both economic and psychological—of using savings and selling a home to finance one's own health care. This anxiety reflects a desire to protect estates, as well as the psychological intertwining of personal self-esteem with one's material worth and independence.

The political weight of this type of concern, however, is not substantial in today's climate of public-policy discourse. The spirit of the late 1970s, the political era in which categorical old-age entitlement programs were created and sustained with relative ease, appears to be gone. The aged have become a scapegoat for a variety of America's problems, and many domestic-policy concerns have been framed as issues of intergenerational equity.[53]

If expanded public long-term care insurance is to be enacted as an old-age entitlement to serve older persons as a buffer against spending down, the American public will need to confront and resolve some fundamental moral and political issues, including the following: Assuming that we can improve laws for protecting spouses of long-term care patients from impoverishment, why shouldn't older people spend their assets and income on their health care? Why should government foot the bill? Why should it be government's responsibility to preserve estates for inheritance? In addition, should government take a more active role than at present in preserving economic-status inequalities from generation to generation? What is the basis for taxing some persons to preserve the inheritances of others? Should the government's taxing power be used to preserve the psychological sense of self-esteem that for so many persons is bound up in their lifetime accumulation of assets—their material worth? Widespread public debate on such issues might very well fail to resolve them in a fashion that supports a major initiative in long-term care to protect older persons from paying for their care.

Even if such questions were satisfactorily resolved, the challenge of bringing together the different perspectives of the elderly and the younger disabled population would remain. In contrast to older persons, younger disabled persons do not perceive long-term care funding as mostly an issue of whether the government or the individual patient or family pays for the care. Their main concern is the issue of whether such funding covers basic access to services, technologies, and environments that will make it feasible to carry forward an active life. They argue that they should have assistance to do much of what they would be able to do if they were not disabled.

The Americans with Disabilities Act of 1990, achieved through vigorous advocacy efforts, has helped to eliminate discriminatory as well as physical barriers to the participation of people with disabilities in employment, public services, public accommodations, transportation, and telecommunications. However, it will not provide the elements of long-term care desired by disabled younger adults, such as paid assistance in the home and for getting in and out of the home, peer counseling, semi-independent modes of transportation, and client control or management of services.

Although the disabled have advocated for long-term care services, they have rejected a "medical model" that emphasizes long-term care as an essential component of health services. This is understandable, given their strong desires for autonomy, independence, and as much "normalization" of daily life as possible. Similarly, disabled people have traditionally eschewed symbolic and political identification with elderly people because of traditional stereotypes of older people as frail, chronically ill, declining, and "marginal" to society.

The efforts of disabled people to advocate on their terms for government long-term care initiatives, however, have made little progress. Rather, previous success in getting expanded public funding for long-term care on the national policy agenda—for persons of all ages—was due largely to advocates for the elderly and to broader concerns about the projected healthcare needs generated by an increasingly larger and, on average, older population of elderly people.

In any grassroots efforts to elevate long-term care funding to the top of the national policy agenda, it is good advice for advocates for the younger disabled to suppress their objections to the healthcare model of long-term care. The challenge of gaining widespread popular support for long-term care funding is to overcome a long-standing cultural perception that long-term care is separate and detached from the arena of health care.

For most of this century, long-term care has been a comparatively neglected backwater in the overall American healthcare scene. Except for occasional nursing home scandals and fires—and subsequent ad hoc activities in response to these events—long-term care has received very little attention from the medical profession and society at large. The glamour and prestige of hospital-based medical care—which is inherently dramatic because it deals with acute episodes of illnesses and trauma—and its relatively high-tech and quick-fix dimensions of diagnosis and intervention eclipse long-term care.

In effect, there is a perception that long-term care is not a part of health care. Long-term care has not been covered through traditional health insurance mechanisms, such as employee benefit plans. An attempt to address this issue was made through the Community Living Assistance Services and Supports (CLASS) Act that was signed into law as part of the Patient Protection and Affordable Care Act on March 23, 2010. Employees would have paid a monthly premium, through payroll deduction, and received benefits after paying for five years.[54] The federal government would have administered the program beginning in January of 2014.

On July 19, 2011 the so-called Gang of Six in the U.S. Senate, a bipartisan group of senators, proposed to repeal the CLASS Act as part of the proposition to balance the budget. On October 14, 2011, the Health and Human Services Secretary announced that the Obama administration was taking the CLASS Act off the table for consideration because they could not "see a viable path forward for CLASS implementation."[55] Thus, when apprehensions are expressed about the fact that 40 million Americans are not covered by health insurance, remember that coverage for the elderly and disabled for long-term care services has ceased to be part of the discussion.

Yet, there are good reasons to believe that long-term care will come to be perceived more widely as part of the continuum of health care that is needed by all of us. As the baby boom cohort begins to approach the ranks of old age, the importance of long-term care, the formidable volume of need for it, the difficulties of financing it, and the challenges of delivering it effectively are likely to become increasingly accepted throughout American society. Such acceptance could bring with it a widespread understanding that long-term care is health care by another name. This perception may enfold long-term care into the shared understanding of justice in health care that dictates that access to long-term care is as much of a fundamental right as is access to other kinds of health care.

UPDATE FROM A PRACTITIONER'S VIEW

In retrospect, although the numbers and percentages may have changed, the trends and issues have not. Long-term care for the elderly and disabled continues to be problematic, and the outlook for the future is bleak. The political climate that controls funding, particularly for minority groups, creates barriers to adequate long-term care, including cultural, social, and economic issues. More specifically, because the elderly and disabled have higher than normal healthcare needs, questionable healthcare status, and anticipated need for increasing services, funding is either capped or so costly that they cannot afford the insurance to cover services. Demand for long-term care will undoubtedly increase as the baby boomers age, but it is questionable whether the relationship between cost and accessibility will maintain its status quo; budget cuts have been proposed for Medicare and Medicaid programs.

Although there was much effort to stall the cuts in Medicare and Medicaid in the 1990s, a rebirth in cost-cutting measures has proliferated since 1998 and significantly escalated throughout the last decade because responsibility for cost containment has been shifted from the federal government to the states. The effects of this shift created a push for alternative delivery methods in elder and disability care. Not surprisingly, alternative methods of care are generally not government funded.

If history judges a culture by how it treats its elderly and disabled, then what legacy do we wish to leave behind? Can we afford to be viewed as a society that values some human lives more than others? If so, where do we draw the line—do we stop at 75 or 80 or what age? Do we make this determination by level and degree of infirmity? Who will make the determination, and what will their criteria be? Ultimately, is limiting or denying access equivalent to selective genocide? If healthcare providers must acquiesce to the political and societal views defined by law and practice, how do they reconcile their internal need for justice within an unjust framework?

Healthcare providers at every level are committed to a wide range of prima facie obligations. The very premise of beneficence is so contrary to the public opinions of the day that nary a healthcare provider will escape unscathed during his or her professional life while attempting to balance beneficence and nonmaleficence to produce net benefit over harm. Finally, one must consider autonomy and equal respect, sometimes described in Kantian terms as valuing others and providing them with the kind of care that you would in turn expect from them. All people are viewed as equal and worthy.[56] Thus, rationing or denying access to health care for the elderly or disabled denies them equal respect and autonomy.

Ultimately the single most important question should be, How do healthcare providers and administrators address these moral and ethical issues in a society driven by the idea of cost containment and make peace with those decisions? The implications are many, and the debate continues. What will public policy dictate and what will society tolerate? These are just a few of the ethical challenges in dealing with the issue of older people and long-term care. The prospect of healthcare reform and cost controls on healthcare spending will only add to these profound challenges.

SUMMARY

With the aging of the baby boomers and the increasing shortage of healthcare professionals, access to long-term care promises to continue to be a significant issue for the 21st century. This chapter identified the population needing care and the type of services that they will need in the future. It presented the issues surrounding access, including cost, the role of insurance, the role of the family, and methods for improving access. Finally, there was a practitioner's view that included challenges to meet in order to address the ethical issues concerning access to long-term care.

QUESTIONS FOR DISCUSSION

1. Access to long-term care seems to be a problem for the elderly in general. However, it is even more difficult for minorities. Why do you think this is true?
2. Why do you think that long-term care insurance lacks popularity among older Americans?
3. How do you think the baby boomer generation will change access to and delivery of long-term care services?
4. What ethical arguments can you make to answer the challenges posed by Gardner-Ray in the last section of this chapter?

FOOD FOR THOUGHT

Long-term care faces additional ethical challenges with the changes proposed by the Patient Protection and Affordable Care Act of 2010 and the approaching retirement of the baby boomer generation. Suppose you are an administrator of a long-term care facility. How would you prepare yourself for the ethical challenges that you will face? What principles or theories would be most useful for your day-to-day decision making?

ADDITIONAL RESOURCES

1. AARP Research Center, http://www.aarp.org/research.
2. Alliance for Aging Research, *Ageism: How Healthcare Fails the Elderly* (Washington, DC: Alliance for Aging Research, 2011). Available at http://www.agingresearch.org/content/article/detail/694/.
3. Consumers for Affordable Healthcare, http://www.mainecahc.org/health-care/healthcareforelderly.htm.

4. National Long-Term Care Ombudsman Resource Center, http://www
.ltcombudsman.org.

5. U.S. Department of Health and Human Services, *CMS Financial Report: Fiscal Year 2000* (Baltimore, MD. Centers for Medicare & Medicaid Services, 2006). Available at http://www.cms.hhs.gov/CFOReport/Downloads/2006_CMS_Financial_Report.pdf.

NOTES

1. S. McConnell, "Who Cares About Long-Term Care?" *Generations* 14, no. 2 (1990): 15–18.

2. "Trends in Aging—United States and Worldwide," *Morbidity and Mortality Weekly Report* 52, no. 6 (2003): 101–106.

3. R. Stone and P. Kemper, "Spouses and Children of Disabled Elders: How Large a Constituency for Long-Term Care Reform?" *The Milbank Quarterly* 67 (1989): 485–506.

4. "MetLife Mature Market Institute Releases Financial Planning Tips for Working Caregivers," *Bloomberg News*, July 12, 2011.

5. S. Crystal, "Economic Status of the Elderly," in *Handbook of Aging and the Social Sciences*, 4th ed., ed. R. H. Binstock and L. K. George (San Diego, CA: Academic Press, 1996), 388–409.

6. G. K. Vincent and V. A. Velkoff, *The Next Four Decades—The Older Population in the United States: 2010 to 2050*, Current Population Reports P25-1138 (Washington, DC: U.S. Census Bureau, May 2010), 1–16.

7. W. He, M. Sengupta, V. A. Velkoff, and K. A. DeBarros, *65+ in the United States*, Current Population Reports P23-209 (Washington, DC: U.S. Census Bureau, December 2005).

8. The Healthy States Initiative, *Keeping the Aging Population Healthy: Legislator Policy Brief* (Washington, DC: U.S. Department of Health and Human Services, August, 2007), 1–12. Retrieved from http://www.healthystates.csg.org. Accessed December 1, 2011.

9. A. L. Jones, L. L. Dwyer, A. R. Bercovitz, and G. W. Strahan, *National Nursing Home Survey: 2004 Overview*, Vital Health Statistics 13, no. 167 (Washington, DC: U.S. Government Printing Office, 2009). Retrieved from http://www.cdc.gov/nchs/data/series/sr_13/sr13_167.pdf. Accessed January 16, 2012. See also J. F. Fries, "The Compression of Morbidity: Near or Far?" *The Milbank Quarterly* 67 (1989): 208–232; K. G. Manton, L. S. Corder, and E. Stallard, "Estimates of Change in Chronic Disability and Institutional Incidence and Prevalence Rates in the U.S. Elderly Population from the 1982, 1984, and 1989 National Long Term Care Survey," *Journal of Gerontology: Social Sciences* 48 (1993): S153–S166; E. L. Schneider and J. M. Guralnik, "The Aging of America: Impact on Health Care Costs," *Journal of the American Medical Association* 263 (1991): 2335–2340; and L. M. Verbrugge, "Recent, Present, and Future Health of American Adults," in *Annual Review of Public Health 10*, ed. L. Breslow, J. E. Fielding, and L. B. Lave (Palo Alto, CA: Annual Reviews, 1989), 333–361.

10. United States Census Bureau, *2009 American Community Survey*. Data available at http://www.census.gov/acs/www/. Accessed January 16, 2012. See also The Healthy States Initiative, *Keeping the Aging Population Healthy*.

11. He et al., *65+ in the United States*.

12. U.S. Congress, Congressional Budget Office, *Policy Choices for Long-Term Care* (Washington, DC: U.S. Government Printing Office, 1991).

13. National Institute on Disability and Rehabilitation Research, *Disability Statistics Report 16* (Washington, DC: U.S. Department of Education, Office of Special Education and Rehabilitative Services, 2001).

14. J. L. Ross, *Long-Term Care: Demography, Dollars, and Dissatisfaction Drive Reform*, U.S. GAO/T-HEHS-94-140 (Washington, DC: Government Printing Office, April 12, 1994).

15. U.S. Congress, Office of Technology Assessment, *Confused Minds, Burdened Families: Finding Help for People with Alzheimer's and Other Dementias* (Washington, DC: U.S. Government Printing Office, 1990).

16. H. R. Levit, H. C. Lazensby, B. R. Braden, et al., "National Health Expenditures," Health Care Financing Review 7 no. 2 (1996): 175-214.

17. U.S. Census Bureau, *Health Care Utilization and National Health Expenditures*, Statistical Abstract Addendums (Washington, DC: U.S. Government Printing Office, 2012), 134–159.

18. K. G. Allen, *Long-Term Care Financing: Growing Demand and Cost of Services Are Straining Federal and State Budgets*, GAO-05-564T (Washington, DC: U.S. Government Printing Office, April 27, 2005).

19. Ibid.

20. C. DeNavas-Walt, B. D. Proctor, and C. H. Lee, *Income, Poverty and Health Insurance Coverage in the United States: 2005*, Current Population Reports, P60-231 (Washington, DC: U.S. Government Printing Office, 2005), 60–194.

21. C. DeNavas-Walt, B. D. Proctor, and J. C. Smith, *Income, Poverty, and Health Insurance Coverage in the United States: 2009*, Current Population Reports P60-238 (Washington, DC: U.S. Government Printing Office, 2010), 61.

22. S. K. Eckert and K. Smyth, *A Case Study of Methods of Locating and Arranging Health and Long-Term Care for Persons with Dementia* (Washington, DC: Office of Technology Assessment, Congress of the United States, 1988).

23. J. Calmes, "Elephant in the Room: Budget Wish Lists Come and Go, but 'Entitlements' Outweigh All," *Wall Street Journal*, February 3, 2006, A-1.

24. K. Liu, K. M. Manton, and B. M. Liu, "Home Care Expenses for the Disabled Elderly," *Health Care Financing Review* 7, no. 2 (1985): 51–58.

25. E. M. Brody, *Women in the Middle: Their Parent-Care Years* (New York: Springer Publishing, 1990); R. Stone, G. L. Cafferta, and J. Sangl, "Caregivers of the Frail Elderly: A National Profile," *Gerontologist* 27 (1989): 616–626.

26. National Academy on Aging, *The State of Aging and Health in America* (Washington, DC: Syracuse University, 2010), 1–46.

27. V. L. Bengston, C. Rosenthal, and L. Burton, "Families and Aging: Diversity and Heterogeneity," in *Handbook of Aging and the Social Sciences*, 3rd ed., ed. R. H. Binstock and L. K. George (San Diego, CA: Academic Press, 1990), 263–287.

28. J. M. Wiener, L. H. Illston, and R. J. Hanley, *Sharing the Burden: Strategies for Public and Private Long-Term Care Insurance* (Washington, DC: The Brookings Institution, 1994).

29. U.S. Congressional Budget Office, *Financing Long-Term Care for the Elderly* (Washington, DC: U.S. Government Printing Office, April 2006).

30. W. H. Crown, J. Capitman, and W. N. Leutz, "Economic Rationality, the Affordability of Private Long-Term Care Insurance, and the Role for Public Policy," *Gerontologist* 32 (1992): 478–485; R. Friedland, *Facing the Costs of Long-Term Care: An EBRI-ERF Policy Study* (Washington, DC: Employee Benefits Research Institute, 1990); A. M. Rivlin and J. M. Wiener, *Caring for the Elderly: Who Will Pay?* (Washington, DC: The Brookings Institution, 1988); Wiener, Illston, and Hanley, *Sharing the Burden*.

31. R. D. Chellis and P. J. Grayson, *Life Care: A Long-Term Solution?* (Lexington, MA: Lexington Books, 1990).

32. M. A. Cohen, "Life Care: New Options for Financing and Delivering Long-Term Care," in *Health Care Financing Review: Annual Supplement* (Thousand Oaks, CA: Sage Publications, 1988), 139–143.

33. T. F. Williams and H. Temkin-Greener, "Older People, Dependency, and Trends in Supportive Care," in *The Future of Long-Term Care: Social and Policy Issues*, ed. R. H. Binstock, L. E. Cluff, and O. von Mering (Baltimore: Johns Hopkins University Press, 1996), 51–74. For an excellent review of the potential changes in health care proposed through the Patient Protection and Affordable Care Act of 2010, see The Henry J. Kaiser Family Foundation, *Focus on Health Reform: Summary of New Health Reform Law* (Menlo Park, CA: The Henry J. Kaiser Family Foundation, 2011). Available at http://www.kff.org.

34. E. J. Tell, M. A. Cohen, and S. S. Wallack, "New Directions in Life Care: Industry in Transit," *The Milbank Quarterly* 65 (1987): 551–574.

35. Williams and Temkin-Greener, "Older People, Dependency, and Trends in Supportive Care."

36. R. A. Kane, and K. B. Wilson, *Assisted Living in the United States: A New Paradigm for Residential Care for Older People?* (Washington, DC: American Association for Retired Persons, 1993); V. Regnier, J. Hamilton, and S. Yatabe, *Assisted Living for the Aged and Frail: Innovations in Design, Management, and Financing* (New York: Columbia University Press, 1995).

37. Wiener, Illston, and Hanley, *Sharing the Burden.*

38. American Association of Retired Persons, Public Policy Institute, *The Costs of Long-Term Care* (Washington, DC: American Association of Retired Persons, 1994).

39. R. B. Hudson, "Social Protection and Services," in *Handbook of Aging and the Social Sciences*, 7th ed., ed. R. H. Binstock and L. K. George (San Diego, CA: Academic Press, 2010).

40. E. K. Adams, M. R. Meiners, and B. O. Burwell, "Asset Spend-Down in Nursing Homes: Methods and Insights," *Medical Care* 31 (1993): 1–23.

41. Levit, Lanzenby, Braden, et al., op cit.

42. B. Burwell, *State Responses to Medicaid Estate Planning* (Cambridge, MA: SysteMetrics, 1993). *For information on healthcare reform and Medicare/Medicaid, see Kaiser Family Foundation, Focus on Health Reform.*

43. B. Burwell and W. H. Crown, *Medicaid Estate Planning in the Aftermath of OBRA '93* (Cambridge, MA: The MEDSTAT Group, 1995).

44. P. Fox, "From Senility to Alzheimer's Disease: The Rise of the Alzheimer's Disease Movement," *The Milbank Quarterly* 67 (1989): 58–102.

45. G. D. Cohen, "Alzheimer's Disease: Current Policy Initiatives," in *Dementia and Aging: Ethics, Values, and Policy Choices*, ed. R. H. Binstock, S. G. Post, and P. J. Whitehouse (Baltimore: Johns Hopkins University Press, 1992).

46. McConnell, "Who Cares About Long-Term Care?"

47. U.S. House of Representatives, Long-Term Care Act of 1989, H.R. 2263, 101st Congress (1989).

48. Long-Term Care Campaign, "Pepper Commission Recommendations Released March 2," *Insiders Update* (January–February 1990): 1.

49. Centers for Disease Control and Prevention and The Merck Company Foundation, *The State of Aging and Health in America 2007* (Whitehouse Station, NJ: The Merck Company Foundation, 2007). Retrieved from http://www.cdc.gov/aging/pdf/saha_2007.pdf. Accessed December 12, 2011.

50. U.S. General Accounting Office, *Long-Term Care: Current Issues and Future Directions* (Washington, D.C.: U. S. Government Printing Office, 1995).

51. E. Kassner, *Long-Term Care: Measuring the Impact of a Medicaid Cap* (Washington, DC: Public Policy Institute, American Association of Retired Persons, 1995).

52. Allen, *Long-Term Care Financing.*

53. R. Himelfarb, *Catastrophic Politics: The Rise and Fall of the Medicare Catastrophic Coverage Act of 1988* (University Park, PA: Pennsylvania State University Press, 1995).

54. R. H. Binstock, L. E. Cluff, and O. von Mering, eds. *The Future of Long-Term Care: Social and Policy Issues* (Baltimore: Johns Hopkins University Press, 1996).

55. California Health Advocates, "Community Living Assistance Services and Supports (CLASS ACT) Summary," March 23, 2010. Retrieved from http://www.cahealthadvocates.org/advocacy/2010/class.html. Accessed January 16, 2012.

56. K. Sebelius, Secretary of Health and Human Services, letter to Speaker of the House John Boehner, October 14, 2011. Retrieved from http://capsules.kaiserhealthnews.org/wp-content/uploads/2011/10/boehner-.pdf.

57. E. Morrison, ed. *Ethics in Health Administration: A Practical Approach for Decision Makers*, 2nd ed. (Sudbury, MA: Jones & Bartlett Publishers, 2011), 8–10.

CHAPTER 9

Assisted Living and Ethics

Rosalee C. Yeaworth

INTRODUCTION

This chapter is a new addition to the third edition of *Health Care Ethics: Critical Issues for the 21st Century*. It discusses assisted living (AL), which primarily developed in the United States in the 1980s. AL is a proprietary answer to the increasing number of elderly people for whom it is not economical to obtain the amount of assistance they need at home. These people do not need or want the 24-hour services of registered nurses (RNs) and the more medical, institutional model of a nursing home. AL has grown rapidly as part of the long-term care continuum because it provides more privacy, independence, and choice than nursing homes. This chapter provides examples of such ethical concerns in AL as access, autonomy, justice, veracity, beneficence/nonmaleficence, and end-of-life decisions.

The United States has a rapidly increasing older population. In 2008, there were 39 million people aged 65 and older, with 5.7 million of these aged 85 and older.[1] The number of Americans at least 90 years old has tripled in recent decades, to 1.9 million people.[2] This is a population with increasing vulnerability and care needs. Eighty percent of all people older than 65 have a chronic condition, and 80.8% of those aged 90 or older have some form of disability. A predicted 70% of all Americans aged 65 and older will need some form of long-term care. Family caregivers have provided and will continue to provide much of that care. For example, one in four American adults help provide care to an older parent, spouse, or other adult relative or loved one. The estimated annual economic value of their unpaid help is approximately $450 billion.[3]

The increasing number of services available in the community, such as meals on wheels, in-home aides, day care, and respite care, can make it easier to provide or receive long-term care in one's home, which is where most people wish to stay. Moves are stressful life change events, but they are less stressful if a person has participated in planning the move and is in agreement with it. Thus, we recognize the ethical principle of autonomy: the ability to make one's own decisions, to make choices, to feel in control. Garrett and colleagues, in their book *Health Care Ethics*, state that the concept of the dignity of the individual is a key issue and stress that this requires that people be allowed to make their own free choices.[4] Many older people choose to participate in planning for needing more assistance by downsizing and moving to an apartment or independent-living retirement setting before their condition absolutely forces it. Decisions such as leaving a long-time home and deciding what to move and what treasured belongings must go during downsizing are very difficult, but they are easier to accept if persons can make these decisions freely instead of having them made for them. Franchised businesses can assist senior citizens in moving. They handle the challenge of sorting through belongings, helping decide what the person needs to move and organizing the rest for sale, donations, and discards.[5]

As older individuals come to need more help with activities of daily living than they are getting at home, they may move to an assisted living facility until their care needs become so great that they require nursing home care. Certainly, not everyone needs this described continuum of care. Some individuals are able to live at home their entire lives. Others may have an accident or catastrophic event such as a severe stroke and go from home to a hospital and be discharged to a nursing home. However, independent living, assisted living, and nursing homes constitute a continuum of care for the expected trajectory of increasing needs. Having as much information about what each choice provides, being able to participate in necessary choices, and deciding which site suits him or her is important to an older person's sense of autonomy.

ASSISTED LIVING DESCRIBED

Assisted living is a more recently licensed long-term care option that primarily developed in the United States in the 1980s. *Assisted living* is the licensure term used by more than two-thirds of the states, but other terms used by some states include *residential care*, *boarding home*, *home for the aged*, *enriched housing program*, *community residence*, *personal care home*, and *basic care facility*.[6] The Assisted Living Federation of America (ALFA) warns that the word *facility*, like *unit* or *patient*, should never be used in relation to AL because these terms sound like a medical model. The federation uses *community*, *apartment*, and *resident*, instead.[7] Representatives of AL stress that it is a social model, not a medical model like a nursing home.

AL provides housing and assistance with activities of daily living (ADLs)—for example, meals, bathing, dressing—and assistance with medications as needed. It offers more independence, privacy, and choice than nursing home care, and people are residents, not patients. Some AL facilities (ALFs) have specialized services such as Alzheimer's units, and others are part of a continuum-of-care campus, which means that there may also be independent living or a nursing home or both as part of the overall facility. Some are actual homes converted to accommodate a group of persons who need the services provided.

The average AL resident is an 80-year-old woman, but men and younger disabled persons may also be among the residents. A study of the population aged 90 and older showed that men were more likely to live with family, whereas women were more likely to live in skilled nursing homes, senior living communities, or alone. The study went on to state that only 2.9% of women aged 90 or older lived in AL or other residential care options. The study noted the high rate of poverty in this age group of women, which may explain why so few live in AL.[8]

The social aspect of AL is important. Many people do well at staying healthy, active, and engaged as they age, but there are losses. Retirement for most people results in less structure and fewer daily contacts. With aging comes loss of friends and, usually, of a spouse. About 6 million 75-plus households are headed by single women.[9] In addition, some older women have been accustomed to their husband doing the driving and give up driving when they become widowed. Other elders have disabilities that limit or prohibit driving.

Families today are smaller and children often live some distance from parents, so there are usually fewer support systems, and some older people become quite isolated. Social support is important to physical and mental health. In AL, social support is increased because there are others with whom to form friendships. Meals are served restaurant style in the dining room, and although, like other groups, elders can form cliques, there is the opportunity to mix and get acquainted. Planned programs and activities are usually available to people. Some residents keep their own cars, but most ALFs have cars or small buses to take residents to appointments, shopping, or other community outings. There thus tends to be many more opportunities for social interaction than when older people are living alone at home.

Although some federal regulations apply, licensure and regulation of ALFs is by individual states, whereas guidance for nursing homes (NHs) comes primarily from federal regulations. Thus, ethical issues that may be uppermost for AL in one state may not apply in another. With different states making regulatory changes at different times, what applies to several states one year may not apply to all or any of them by the next year. For example, the National Center for Assisted Living (NCAL) noted in its 2011 AL *State Regulatory Review*: "[A]t least 18 states reported making statutory, regulatory, or policy changes in 2010 or January 2011. . . . At least six states made major changes including Idaho, Kentucky, Oregon, Pennsylvania, South Carolina, and Texas."[10]

Older people want to preserve their independence and choice as long as possible, and AL offers more of both compared with NHs. In addition, ALFs are considerably less costly than NHs. The Genworth Cost of Care survey found that in 2011, the median annual rate for a private NH room was $77,745, whereas the national median annual rate for a one-bedroom, single-occupancy unit in an ALF was $39,132.[11] The cost of NH care varies somewhat from state to state; however, Reinhard and colleagues point out that it is not "affordable" in any state, because "the national average cost of NH care is 241 percent of the average annual household income of older adults."[12] Even though the national annual median rate for AL is only about half the cost of the median rate for a nursing home, it is still more than 100% of the average annual household income of older adults.

The previously mentioned opportunity for greater independence and choice for residents in AL, and states' interest in reducing Medicaid expenditure growth rates, have created a shift in the supply and utilization of NHs over the past several years. According to Reinhard and colleagues, in 2004, some 1.4 million older people resided in NHs. This represented a 29% reduction in occupancy of NHs since 1989. Considering the cost of NH care compared with older Americans' incomes, it is surprising that only 131,000 of the 1.4 million NH residents are receiving assistance under the Medicaid program.[13]

PROBLEMS WITH ACCESS

Justice and Diversity

Issues of access relate primarily to allocation of resources: the ethical principle of justice or fairness. In a completely fair and just society, AL access would be strictly on the basis of need; however, income, gender, race, language, cultural disparities, and even obesity can affect access to AL altogether or access to what is deemed to be an appropriate facility. For example, patients with Alzheimer's disease frequently display aggressive behavior. In settings in which the Alzheimer's special care unit is usually at capacity, men may have more difficulty being admitted when there is an opening, because men are frequently viewed as more difficult for the predominantly female staff to manage. Many older people are not comfortable being the only one of their gender, race, or culture in a particular unit of a facility. Available food or religious services may not fit with a given person's culture. Many older women become uncomfortable when a young male of a different race or culture tries to help them with toileting. Staff may object to or even be injured by trying to help a very obese person transfer from bed to chair or bath.

Cost of Care

In this country, health care is primarily a for-profit industry. This includes long-term care, whether in the home, in AL, or in a nursing home. Given the national median annual rate of $39,132 for a one-bedroom, single-occupancy unit in an AL and a compound annual inflation rate of 5.99% between 2005 and 2011, cost is a major barrier to access for many people.[14] People who enter a facility under private payment arrangements may find themselves running out of money if they live long enough and do not have an ongoing pension and Social Security benefits that together are sufficient to cover the cost. Many older people who used to count on interest from relatively safe investments such as certificates of deposit or bonds and the cost of living increases to Social Security to cover a sizeable portion of their needs have been left vulnerable by the very low interest rates currently paid on investments and the absence of cost of living increases in Social Security in 2010 and 2011. Some people are fortunate enough to have purchased good long-term care insurance that covers not just nursing homes but assisted living care. Otherwise, all but three states (Alabama, Kentucky, and Pennsylvania) provide Medicaid coverage for AL services.[15] Unfortunately, persons can be served by Medicaid waiver only if they meet the state's criteria for nursing home care.[16]

Mollica's 2009 survey of state Medicaid reimbursement policies and practices in assisted living provided much detail on the use of home- and community-based waivers, state plan services and state general revenue programs, the methods used to determine payment rates, and the marked increase in the numbers of people covered.[17] Only about 12% to 15% of assisted living residents have their services paid for by Medicaid and state-funded programs. Medicaid requires a spend-down and allows a limited personal needs allowance. The rate paid by states for AL services vary by state, as does the personal allowance that the resident can keep. Generally, the payment rate for Medicaid is considerably less than the private payment rate, so some AL facilities will not accept Medicaid.

Most AL facilities limit the number of Medicaid residents by requiring the person to have lived in the facility under private payment for a particular length of time, or they limit their Medicaid exposure to 10% of their units. If these units are filled, they will take no more Medicaid recipients. This may force an AL resident to find a facility that accepts Medicaid and to move against his or her will to a less desirable facility. Once residents have established relationships with other residents and with staff, moves can be very traumatic. Studies have shown that moves of people against their will can be followed closely by falls, illnesses, and even deaths.[18] People who are Medicaid eligible at the time they seek AL may find they are very limited in the facilities that will accept them.

Nursing homes are far more likely to accept Medicaid, but even in this case, a person may not be able to gain access to a nursing home of his or her choice. There does seem to be a relationship between the number of AL and residential care units per 1,000 population aged 65 and older and the percentage of nursing home residents with low care needs. For example, Illinois ranked 45th in state rankings on availability of AL and residential care units and 49th on the percentage of nursing home residents with low care needs.[19] The amount a state pays in Medicaid for an AL resident could influence availability, in that private companies may not be interested in building facilities in states with low Medicaid payments.

Forcing people into a nursing home setting when they do not require that level of care does not respect their dignity and autonomy. Furthermore, it could be interpreted as not in keeping with the Supreme Court's *Olmstead* decision, in which the Court stated that institutional placements of people with disabilities who can live in, and benefit from, community settings perpetuates the unwarranted assumptions that these persons are incapable or unworthy of participating in community life.[20] Many older people with loss of ability in some ADLs or with some dementia still benefit from participating in the more community-like life and activities of an ALF. The *Olmstead* decision was applicable to public facilities, and most ALFs are private operations, but the basic principle remains: people should be able to receive the services, programs, and activities they need in the least restrictive environment. Nebraska's law forcing persons to move if they need RN care seems contrary to the principle on which the *Olmstead* decision was made.[21]

Some AL facilities have been developed for low-income individuals. In these facilities, there is an income cap for admission and a sliding scale based on income for rates. The Rose of Council Bluffs, Iowa, is one such facility, and its staffing is by the Visiting Nurse Association (L. Jenkins, administrator of the Rose of Council Bluffs, personal communication, October 4, 2011).

Most public entities such as cities, counties, or states operate some not-for-profit facilities for low-income individuals, but those that are well operated have scarce resources. Some religious organizations also undertake operating an ALF as a ministry to the elderly. In fact, churches are more and more engaged in helping people access the many resources in the community, and thus helping to avoid the need for an ALF. For example, the block-nursing program, which has been in operation for many years in the Minneapolis/St. Paul area, has a church central to each program.[22] Parish nurses or faith community nurses work not only with church members but also with others in the community to help make care and support available to people in their homes.[23]

HEALTH CARE AND ASSISTED LIVING

The Assisted Living Federation of America defines assisted living as a long-term care option that combines housing, support services, and health care, as needed.[24] The review of regulations provided by the National Center for Assisted Living indicates that the amount of health care provided varies by state.[25] For example, Nebraska does not allow its ALFs to provide any RN care, whereas Alabama requires that an Alzheimer's unit have at least one RN. States that allow for more than one level of care in a facility usually require some RN staffing for the higher levels of care. Some states require an assessment by an RN prior to a resident moving in or if there is a significant change in health status. Kansas requires a licensed pharmacist to conduct a medication regimen review for each resident whose medications are managed by the facility. The facility repeats the review quarterly and each time that the resident has a significant change. There is usually a medical director or some arrangement with a physician. Many states allow the provision of hospice services in ALFs.

Nebraska may be the only state that, by law, prohibits an RN employed by an ALF from providing any complex nursing intervention (defined as any intervention that requires nursing judgment) while on duty.[26] Residents needing nursing care must arrange and pay for that care through an outside agency, or they must move to a nursing home. The lobbyist representing the Nebraska Health Care Association stated that this is the fine line that differentiates ALFs from nursing homes. For the AL industry in Nebraska to use prohibition of RN care in their facilities as a way to differentiate what ALFs offer from a nursing home seems to deny the autonomy of the nursing profession. One wonders if the scope of practice of any other profession would be so limited just to differentiate a setting. License renewal records for RNs in 2008 in Nebraska showed that 123 RNs indicated employment in ALFs, so ALFs *can* employ nurses in their settings, but write into law that these nurses cannot exercise their legal scope of practice. A dilemma is created in the case of licensed practical nurses (LPNs), who can be employed and perform medication administration and supervision. In fact, LPNs may often be in a position that requires them to practice beyond their legal scope of practice. The fact that the Nebraska law states that RNs employed in ALFs cannot perform any intervention that requires nursing judgment would seem to imply that LPNs who do interventions do not employ nursing judgment in their practice.

Although it is true that ALFs are supposed to be homelike and community settings, not institutional settings, and in home life you go to clinics for health care, this is counter to the expectations of the general public as demonstrated in surveys. When people leave their own homes to go to a facility to receive care and assistance, most assume that health care is part of that, especially when they may be paying $3,000 a month or more. The fact that many of the aides tell residents "I am your nurse" reinforces the expectations for health care. In addition, as stated earlier, ALFA defines AL as providing health care.

Veracity

Stating that a facility has a "full time RN" but not stating that that RN is not supposed to provide nursing care relates to the important ethical principle of veracity, or truthfulness. It is a dilemma for an RN who is employed in a setting in which the state law for the setting supersedes the Nurse Practice Act. Who really decides which law takes precedence if the nurse is in a situation in which his or her nursing judgment indicates he or she should act, and the Nurse Practice Act states that he or she is legally qualified to act, yet it is against the state law for an RN to do so in an ALF? Being in an administrative position in an ALF does not absolve an RN from responsibility for the care given in that setting, because Provision 4.3 of the American Nurses Association's Code of Ethics for Nurses (which covers delegation) states, "Nurses in administration . . . share responsibility for care provided by those whom they supervise."[27] Some ALFs in Nebraska advertise that they have an RN on staff, thus leading people to believe that RN care is available. Others advertise that they allow people to age in place, which is not true if residents must move to a nursing home when they need RN care. A study by Phillips and colleagues found that "residents in an ALF employing a full-time RN had less than half the odds of moving to a nursing home compared with residents in facilities that were staffed differently."[28]

Another lack of truthfulness seen in ALF advertising has been in stating that a facility will accept Medicaid, but not revealing that this acceptance may be for only one or two units. If those units are full, a resident who runs out of money and has to rely on Medicaid for payment is required to move out. Nebraska AARP was successful in 2011 in passing legislation requiring that prior to admission written information be provided to applicants to AL, including policies on Medicaid acceptance and reasons that can lead to an involuntary move.

Beneficence and Nonmaleficence

The principles of beneficence and nonmaleficence (doing good or doing no harm) have to be considered concerning staffing. Aides are the primary care-givers for long-term care. If there are inadequate numbers of staff available to meet the needs of residents or if persons are hired for positions for which they have inadequate training and education, the situation may be harmful to the staff as well as to the residents for whom they are providing services. For example, if there are no specified training requirements for aides before they begin working in a setting with residents who have dementia (and studies have shown that 60% to 70% of residents in ALFs have dementia),[29] these aides frequently are frightened or upset by unexpected or confusing behaviors. Some residents with dementia may become aggressive if they misunderstand what is happening. This can lead to high staffing turnover rates at best, and to abuse at worst.

For example, an inexperienced staff member may be hurrying because of the number of residents she or he has to help with baths. As she or he rushes to try to help the resident into the shower, the resident, who has some undiagnosed dementia, believes a total stranger is trying to remove her clothes and begins fighting back. Statistics indicate that persons with dementia are more likely to injure their caregiver than vice versa.[30] Placing persons with little or no knowledge of dementia in positions to care for a population with a high rate of dementia can put them at risk of injury. Likewise, their lack of understanding of persons with dementia can lead to their "punishing" residents, for example, not letting them go to a meal because they soiled themselves.

Aides who have so much responsibility for a frail population with chronic illnesses should be prepared at least at the level of the certified nursing assistant (CNA) and have additional and continuing education in the behaviors of and caring for persons with dementia. Using CNAs would mean that a record is kept of any abuse, neglect, or practice infractions, so that aides cannot go from setting to setting, endangering other residents, if they are fired for a serious infraction. Background checks are required in Nebraska, but in assisted living, employment can occur before the information from that check is available. This could put residents at risk.

Probably one of the most questionable things in an ALF where no RN is employed, or in which an RN is not on duty for a particular shift or is employed only as an administrator, is the use of medication aides or medication assistant technicians (MATs) to give medications. Persons with dementia cannot remember what drugs they are supposed to take when, and whether they have taken them. Barra investigated the program requirements currently used by the 34 states that were using MATs.[31] She found that in some states as few as 10 or 16 hours of training were required for MATs, yet the registered nurse remains ultimately responsible, and thus liable, for delegating to and supervising medication administration assistants. Even states that require 60, 65, or 75 hours of classroom work cannot provide the information in physiology, pharmacology, and pathophysiology or the depth of clinical practice possessed by an RN. The primary idea regarding MATs is to teach them to give the right drug in the right dose by the right route to the right patient at the right time. To assist in this process, there could be a requirement that all drugs be packaged in individual-dose packages, which create additional costs for patients or families. Pictures or bar codes can be used to increase the probability of getting the right drug to the right recipient, but there is much more to medication administration to elderly people than this basic level. Most emergency hospitalizations for recognized adverse drug events in older adults result from a few commonly used medications.[32]

Persons charged with giving medication to the elderly should know about the Beers list, a national guideline and reference guide for prescribing or administering drugs to the elderly. A consensus panel of experts regularly updates this list.[33] Knowing when not to give a prescribed drug because of symptoms, behaviors, or chronic diseases, or recognizing when the drug recipient is not tolerating a drug or is having a drug reaction or interaction from drug combinations, can prevent serious complications or even deaths. Anyone who looks at the warnings in the drug literature knows that physicians prescribe some very potent drugs today, and older people often do not metabolize or tolerate drugs well. How can a nurse be responsible for delegating to and supervising a medication aide in a setting in which he or she is not even employed? The ANA Code of Ethics for Nurses says that nurses in administration share responsibility for the care provided by those whom they supervise. Are the nurses who are employed as administrators in ALFs aware they carry this responsibility?[34]

In considering the principles of doing good or doing no harm, one also has to consider preventing elder abuse and neglect. This statement is not intended to imply that AL is a setting with abuse and neglect, but to raise awareness that elder abuse and neglect can take place in the home, in AL, or in a nursing home. It should be noted that any statistics on elder abuse may be questionable because of serious underreporting and lack of substantiation. Incidents are often unreported by the victim because of mental and physical incapacity, fear, shame, loyalty, or pride. Nationally, Adult Protective Services investigates only two-thirds of complaints received, and it substantiates only half of those investigated as being abuse or neglect. A 2005 publication by the National Center on Elder Abuse, based on 2003 data, showed that 32.5% of the substantiated reports were for caregiver neglect.[35] The fact that a caregiver is involved indicates that people with physical disabilities or dementia or both are more likely to be abused or neglected than well elderly able to live on their own with some assistance with ADLs.

Abuse and violence have a much higher incidence in persons with dementia: 5.4% to 11.9%, compared with 1% to 4% in persons without dementia. A study by Coyne et al. found that 11.9% of caregivers admitted to abusing patients with dementia, and 33.1% indicated that they had received physical abuse from such patients.[36] The importance of training staff to anticipate and avoid situations likely to lead to abuse or violence is apparent, both for their sake, the resident's sake, and the employer's sake. It is also very important for persons who need care to have a good support system so that they have frequent visitors at different times of day, which helps them to be aware of what is happening. Unfortunately, some persons in AL have few visitors.

Financial abuse is a rapidly growing type of abuse of the elderly. Financial abuse, such as misappropriation of property, is reported in actions against nursing staff by state boards of nursing. Medication abuse is another form of abuse (e.g., failing to give insulin or pain medication when needed or using medication as a restraint or for behavior control). Sometimes, spouses or family members may request the discontinuance of insulin because they are running out of money or do not want to see their loved one die in late-stage dementia. Complying with such a request would be contrary to ethical expectations and legal guidelines.

The requirements for state survey visits vary by state. Nebraska, for example, only requires them once every five years unless there is damage to the structure from fire, tornado, or other disaster or enough complaints to require a visit. There are few published, university-based, research-type studies on abuse or neglect incidents in AL and no requirements for a coroner's investigation of deaths. A few newspaper investigations and reports exist. Consequently, elder abuse statistics in AL, like elder abuse statistics in other settings, are very limited.

Almost all the news media focused on the U.S. Census Bureau report on the tripling of the 90-plus population in the recent decades, but it was not to rejoice about the increased life expectancy. The headlines were instead about the "grim picture" for this population and the fact that rising life expectancy meaning rising poverty and disabilities. This, combined with all the campaign rhetoric about doing away with "Obamacare" and the need to cut Medicare to balance the budget, does not seem to bode well for efforts toward the ethical distribution of health care, including long-term care.

SUMMARY

AL is a well-accepted intermediary step between independent living and nursing homes for those with low care needs. AL is less expensive than a nursing home. Given the increasing longevity of the U.S. population, the availability and cost of long-term care will be a continuing part of healthcare policy debate. This chapter focused on describing assisted living, its place in the long-term care continuum, and its rapid growth and popularity. It also included examples of ethical issues commonly encountered in AL settings.

QUESTIONS FOR DISCUSSION

1. If AL is primarily proprietary, with facilities having fireplaces, fancy dining rooms, and other special décor to compete for "tenants," should taxpayers have to pay for these amenities, or should there be facilities with just the plain necessities for those who need this care but cannot pay? Why not just place such people in a nursing home?
2. What are the pros and cons for using medication aides in AL, even in dementia units?
3. What would be the advantages and disadvantages of standardizing AL regulations at the national level (like for nursing homes) rather than having each state legislature enact regulations for its state?
4. What are some arguments for and against requiring all aides who provide personal care in AL facilities to have CNA preparation and background checks before employment?
5. What are the pros and cons of requiring RN oversight in all AL facilities?

FOOD FOR THOUGHT

Your favorite uncle, Uncle Chauncy, has been a bachelor for all of his 90 years. He lives in his own home and still drives his car to church and to the grocery store. Lately, he has become forgetful and seems to be neglecting his grooming. You worry about him and are considering AL as an option for his care. Before you discuss it with him, you want more information.

1. Given what you have learned about ALFs from this chapter, what questions would you ask the owners of the ALFs you are considering?

2. Which of the ethical issues that were discussed relating to AL concern you most? Why are they of concern?

3. What can you do as a healthcare professional to address the current issues related to assisted living?

NOTES

1. Federal Interagency Forum on Aging-Related Statistics, *Older Americans 2010: Key Indicators of Well-Being* (Washington, DC: U.S. Government Printing Office, July 2010). Retrieved from http://www.agingstats.gov/agingstatsdotnet/Main_Site/Data/Data_2010.aspx. Accessed June 9, 2012.

2. "Grim Picture for the Elderly," *Los Angeles Times*, as reprinted in the *Omaha World Herald*, November 18, 2011, 6A.

3. L. Feinberg, S. C. Reinhard, A. Houser, and R. Choula, *Valuing the Invaluable: The Growing Contributions and Costs of Family Caregiving, 2011 Update* (Washington, DC: AARP Public Policy Institute, July 2011).

4. T. M. Garret, H. W. Baillie, and R. M. Garrett, *Health Care Ethics; Principles and Problems*, 5th ed. (Upper Saddle River, NJ: Prentice Hall, 2010), 10.

5. E. Golden, "Aiding the Move of a Lifetime," *Omaha World Herald*, January 8, 2012, 12–13A.

6. K. Polzer, *Assisted Living State Regulatory Review 2011* (Washington, DC: National Center for Assisted Living, 2011), ii.

7. Assisted Living Federation of America, home page, http://www.alfa.org.

8. W. He and M. H. Muenchrath, *90+ in the United States: 2006–2008*, American Community Survey Report ACS-17 (Washington, DC: U.S. Census Bureau, November 2011).

9. A. B. Rand, "New Realities of Aging," *AARP Bulletin*, December 1, 2010.

10. Polzer, *Assisted Living State Regulatory Review 2011*, i.

11. Genworth Financial, *Genworth 2011 Cost of Care Survey* (Richmond, VA: Genworth Financial, 2011). Available at http://www.genworth.com/costofcare.

12. S. C. Reinhard, E. Kassner, A. Houser, and R. Mollica, *Raising Expectations: A State Scorecard on Long-Term Services and Supports for Older Adults, People with Physical Disabilities, and Family Caregivers* (Washington, DC: AARP Public Policy Institute, The Commonwealth Fund, and The SCAN Foundation, 2011), 14.

13. Ibid.

14. Genworth Financial, *2011 Cost of Care Survey*.

15. R. L. Mollica, *State Medicaid Reimbursement Policies, and Practices in Assisted Living*, (Washington, DC: National Center for Assisted Living, American Health Care Association, 2009).

16. Reinhard, Kassner, Houser, and Mollica, *Raising Expectations*.

17. Mollica, *State Medicaid Reimbursement Policies*.

18. M. Thomasma, R. C. Yeaworth, and B. W. McCabe, "Relocation and Anxiety in Institutionalized Elderly," *Journal of Gerontological Nursing* 16, no. 7 (1990): 18–25.

19. Reinhard, Kassner, Houser, and Mollica, *Raising Expectations*.

20. *Olmstead v. L.C.*, 527 U.S. 581, 119 S.Ct. 2176 (1999). See Worksupport.com, "The Olmstead Act? What Is It?" http://www.worksupport.com/resources/printView.cfm/376. Accessed June 9, 2012.

21. Ibid.

22. Living at Home Network, "Block Nurse Program." Retrieved from http://www.elderberry.org. Accessed June 9, 2012.

23. D. L. Patterson, *The Essential Parish Nurse: ABCs for Congregational Health Ministry* (Cleveland, OH: The Pilgrim Press, 2003).

24. Assisted Living Federation of America, home page.

25. Polzer, *Assisted Living State Regulatory Review 2011.*

26. Nebraska Revised Statutes, Section 71-5905. Retrieved from http://nebraskalegislature.gov/laws/statutes.php?statute=71-5905. Accessed June 9, 2012.

27. M. D. M. Fowler, *Guide to the Code of Ethics for Nurses: Interpretation and Application* (Silver Spring, MD: American Nurses Association, 2008).

28. C. D. Phillips, Y. Munoz, M. Sherman, M. Rose, W. Spector, and C. Hawes, "Effects of Facility Characteristics on Departures from Assisted Living: Results from a National Study," *Gerontologist* 43, no. 5 (October 2003): 690–696.

29. H. Magsi and T. Malloy, "Underrecognition of Cognitive Impairment in Assisted Living Facilities," *Journal of the American Geriatric Society* 53, no. 2 (2005): 295–298.

30. G. J. Paveza, D. Cohen, C. Eisdorfer, et al., "Severe Family Violence and Alzheimer's Disease: Prevalence and Risk Factors," *Gerontologist* 32, no. 4 (1992): 493–497.

31. M. Barra, "Nurse Delegation of Medication Pass in Assisted Living Facilities: Not All Medication Assistant Technicians Are Equal," *Journal of Nursing Law* 14, no. 1 (2011): 3–10.

32. D. S. Budnitz., C. M. Lovegrove, N. Shehab, and C. L. Richards, "Emergency Hospitalizations for Adverse Drug Events in Older Americans," *New England Journal of Medicine* 365 (2011): 2002–2012.

33. D. M. Fick, J. W. Cooper, W. E. Wade, J. L. Waller, J. R. Maclean, and M. H. Beers, "Updating the Beers Criteria for Potentially Inappropriate Medication Use in Older Adults: Results of a US Consensus Panel of Experts," *Archives of Internal Medicine* 163 (2003): 2716–2724.

34. Fowler, *Guide to the Code of Ethics for Nurses.*

35. National Center on Elder Abuse, "A Response to the Abuse of Vulnerable Adults: The 2004 Survey of State Adult Protective Services," in *AARP Policy Book 2009–2010* (Washington, DC: AARP, 2009), 12-2.

36. A. C. Coyne, W. E. Reichman, and L. J. Berbig, "The Relationship Between Dementia and Elder Abuse," *American Journal of Psychiatry* 150, no. 4 (1993): 643–646.

CHAPTER 10

Ethical Issues in the Use of Fluids and Nutrition: When Can They Be Withdrawn?

T. Patrick Hill

INTRODUCTION

It has been some time since the landmark decisions regarding Karen Ann Quinlan[1] and Nancy Beth Cruzan[2] were handed down. Since then, it has been reasonable to think that the ethical issues central to these cases and others like them had been resolved and were settled matters. Conceptually that may be the case, but as the more recent case of Terri Schiavo demonstrated, that is not true emotionally. In the Schiavo case, it seemed as though we were confronting the issues for the very first time without any precedents to guide us. And when dealing with a case that had finally exhausted our society's medical capacity to remedy, some tried literally to will a remedy out of conviction, regardless of credible clinical evidence to the contrary.

For this reason the issue of withholding and withdrawing artificial nutrition and hydration from dying and permanently unconscious patients remains contentious, deserving of renewed ethical consideration. It helps to measure the gravity of the problem when we remember that between 10,000 and 60,000 dying or permanently unconscious patients are actually maintained on sustenance supplied artificially by tubes.

In the case of the over one million recovering patients who annually receive artificial nutrition and hydration, no one doubts that artificial sustenance is a boon. But for those patients who, with or without artificially provided sustenance, have no hope of recovering from their illness, supplying nutrition and hydration might be as inappropriate as maintaining a brain-dead body on a ventilator. "Yet, perhaps because of the uniquely symbolic significance of nourishment in the minds of many, artificial feeding appears to be more difficult to discontinue than any other treatment. And this applies both to patients who are expected to die in a relatively short time, and to permanently unconscious and other patients whose death may not occur for months or years unless sustenance by tube is stopped."[3]

Is there something intuitively sound about this symbolism? If so, does it justify the difficulty we feel when we consider discontinuing artificial feeding? Or is it possible on the basis of rational analysis to come to the conclusion that there are indeed sound ethical reasons why we should withhold or withdraw artificial nutrition and hydration? This chapter will attempt to show that in the case of dying and permanently unconscious patients, our intuitive sensitivity to the symbolism of nourishment notwithstanding; there are solid ethical grounds for discontinuing artificial sustenance and permitting death from natural causes to occur.

THE NATURE OF HYDRATION AND NUTRITION

The ethical questions surrounding the withdrawal of fluids and nutrition from a dying patient are more complicated in one significant respect than the withdrawal of any other life-sustaining treatment, such as antibiotics or cardiopulmonary resuscitation. The basic medical justification for the withdrawal of antibiotics, for example, is that under a particular set of clinical circumstances, they can no longer achieve their clinical purpose. When that happens, the fundamental ethical justification for withdrawal would come from the absence of any inherent value—again, under the particular circumstances—in continuing to provide antibiotics. The ensuing death of the patient is medically acceptable on the grounds that it results from an underlying pathology now no longer considered treatable. The death is ethically acceptable as something that has happened in the natural course of events—in this case, the inevitable progress of a fatal illness over which there is now no human control and for which there is no human responsibility. It is regrettable, but regrettable as a nonmoral harm.

Fluids and nutrition used in the care of a dying patient do not fit quite as readily into this line of medical and ethical reasoning because they are not therapeutic, in the strict sense of that term. But if not therapeutic, how are they to be understood? The question is basic and suggests two possible responses. The first, coming from the general perspective of the healthcare provider, is that fluids and nutrition function as a clinical scaffold to provide underlying support to a patient who cannot provide it from his or her own diminished resources. The second, coming from the perspective of family members and friends, is that fluids and nutrition serve as expressions of their instinct to be concerned and to care when hope for loved ones is exhausted. Neither medicine for the nurse and physician, nor food and water for the lay person, fluids and nutrition seem to confound us all and leave, as the cases of Quinlan, Cruzan, and Schiavo illustrate, their recipients at the mercy of an unavoidable ambiguity.

Although public opinion polls suggest that the average person is critical of the continued use of fluids and nutrition in medically hopeless circumstances,[4] that can change when it becomes a personal decision to withhold or withdraw them from a particular individual. Then the inherent ambiguity of fluids and nutrition can assert itself forcefully and painfully. When it does, we have been inclined to respond first by saying that fluids and nutrition embody the natural instinct to care for the most vulnerable population, the dying, when all hope of cure is gone. We can then go on to assert that they can serve to draw the distinction between cure and care in the medical setting. That is, a point might occur in the course of illness beyond which therapeutic treatment is useless and can, as a result, be stopped or withheld; it appears counterintuitive to say the same of care.

There is no medical justification for ceasing to provide care to a dying patient, and because there is always inherent value in providing care, there is no ethical justification for withholding it either. According to this line of reasoning, as long as fluids and nutrition are seen only as being a means of caring for, not curing, a dying patient, there would be no medical or ethical justification for withholding them in some form or another or in some degree or another. However, this line of thinking only confuses matters, because fluids and nutrition can hardly be thought of as therapy, except as a way to correct chemical imbalances in the body caused by malnutrition and dehydration. As far as providing care goes, fluids and nutrition are not by definition care in themselves, but something we choose as an expression of our instinct to provide care. Ample evidence in the coroner's report on Terri Schiavo suggests that the continued provision of fluids and nutrition was more harmful to her than not.[5]

Consequently, it is of paramount importance to determine what fluids and nutrition are and when they can be regarded as having a medical purpose of maintenance in addition to that of providing human care. Beyond that, it is important to determine if and when the provision of fluids and nutrition to a dying patient serves no medical purpose and does not objectively constitute the provision of human care to that patient no matter how much we might subjectively like to think that it does.

To do this, it is necessary to acknowledge the difference between food and drink, on the one hand, and artificial nutrition and hydration, on the other. According to Devine,

> The common forms of eating and drinking are not at issue; this is not a matter of denying a person a lunch. At issue here is a range of medical technologies that vary in complexity, sophistication and, at times, danger. Total parenteral feeding is a world apart from dining on fried chicken, and the difference between them is obvious.[6]

There is a universal need for food and drink to sustain life. There is no such need for artificial nutrition and hydration to sustain life. As a universal need, food and drink might best be seen as a means of human care. Artificial nutrition and hydration, however, because they are designed to address a medical condition, such as a temporary or permanent inability to swallow, are better seen as a form of medical maintenance. Consequently, their use and purposes will be determined by the patient's diagnosis and prognosis.

Understood this way, according to Devine, artificial nutrition and hydration are an integral part of a larger medical effort to restore someone to health or maintain that person at a certain level of human functioning. But when that effort ceases overall to have a medical purpose, nutrition and hydration, as a constitutive part of the effort, also cease to have any purpose.[7] In other words, just as the purposes of the medical treatment plan for the patient justify the decision to provide nutrition and hydration, so, too, any eventual purposelessness of the same medical treatment plan can justify the cessation of treatment, including nutrition and hydration.

The difference between food and water and nutrition and hydration is thus an important consideration when making an ethical decision to withhold the latter. So also is the difference between hunger and thirst and malnutrition and dehydration. A 1987 report by the Hastings Center draws the distinction by describing hunger and thirst as a need felt by the patient and defining malnutrition and dehydration as a chemical condition of the patient's body:

> Medical procedures for supplying nutrition and hydration treat malnutrition and dehydration; they may or may not relieve hunger and thirst. Conversely, hunger and thirst can be treated without necessarily using medical nutrition and hydration techniques, and without necessarily correcting dehydration or malnourishment.[8]

To support the validity of this distinction, the report observes that dehydrated patients, for example, can find relief from thirst by having their lips and mouths moistened with ice chips or a lubricant.[9] This observation gives additional weight to the argument that hunger and thirst are more appropriately the object of interventions to provide care, whereas malnutrition and dehydration are more appropriately the object of interventions to achieve a larger therapeutic goal in which nutrition and hydration play a supportive role. Once the case has been made for nutrition and hydration as a supportive element within a medical intervention, one can assume that the ethical criteria used in deciding to withdraw other medical life-sustaining treatments are applicable in deciding when to withdraw nutrition and hydration.

PATIENTS' BODILY INTEGRITY AND SELF-DETERMINATION

The core criterion around which all the other criteria congregate is the integrity of the patient as a person. Modern medicine operates by isolating symptoms and treating them accordingly. Although this discriminating methodology, which undeniably reflects the sophistication of contemporary medical practice, is highly effective, it runs the serious risk of atomizing the patient, organ by organ, system by system, particularly as a terminal illness runs its course and the body decompensates as a result. Under these circumstances, it is all too easy to lose sight of the person who is the patient and discount the personal control over treatment decisions without which it will be impossible for these decisions to be ethical.

This entails, on the part of those providing medical treatment, the utmost respect for the physical integrity of the body, on which the patient has a fundamental claim. Central to any recognition of the physical integrity of the body as a necessary condition for ethical medical interventions is the patient's informed consent. Hence, there is the need for the patient to consent to be treated and the need to respect the patient's refusal to begin or continue treatment. In other words, it must be a basic working assumption on the part of those responsible for treatment—in this case the provision of nutrition and hydration—that they may not withdraw treatment without the patient's consent.

Even more important, healthcare providers must recognize that the final authority in the patient–physician relationship is the patient. According to J. E. Ruark and T. A. Raffin, "[a]lthough physicians must often be authoritative about the options available to patients, all involved must recognize that the actual authority over the patient never resides with the physician. Patients alone, or their legal surrogates, have the right to control what happens to them."[10]

All the requirements for an ethically satisfactory decision to withdraw or withhold nutrition and hydration will not be found in the patient's subjective preferences alone, significant as they are. Without direct reference to the clinical context, namely, the actual medical condition of the patient and its projected course, it would be ethically unacceptable to withhold life-sustaining treatment such as nutrition and hydration. Although it is true that ethical decisions are guided by principles, they are also rooted in the actual circumstances that suggest those particular principles and provide the justification for their use in a given case.

This observation is important because it illustrates an essential feature of ethical analysis, which, according to one ethicist, "is an exchange between the moral meaning found in the empirical context and the moral meaning found in the several principles contending for application in this concrete case."[11] The moral meaning of the empirical context will be measured in terms of bodily integrity and the extent to which withholding life-sustaining treatment will enhance or diminish that integrity. As we have already seen, bodily integrity is something to which the patient has a claim and something that the physician must respect.

The next question, then, is what is the strength of this claim? How forcefully can the claim to bodily integrity and its corollary, informed consent, be made to justify the decision to withhold or withdraw nutrition and hydration? In responding to this question, ethicists have resorted to the language of rights, saying that bodily integrity is so central to the patient that it can be claimed as a right.

Rights, according to philosophers such as Richard Wasserstrom, are "moral commodities" that automatically create obligations and duties.[12] Similarly, according to Hill, "[i]n other words, a right is a claim, the force of which derives, not from the physical strength or socioeconomic standing of the right holder but the inherent reasonableness of the right being claimed relative to the circumstances under which it is being claimed."[13] Relative to bodily integrity, this implies a patient's claim to discretion over his or her body.

In the context of deciding to withhold or withdraw nutrition and hydration, the implications of such a claim are troublesome, because they create obligations and duties for treatment providers. That could and does result in an adversarial situation as the patient or the physician seeks to control the outcome. In turn, this threatens the moral relationship between the patient and the physician presupposed by the patient's claim and the corresponding responsibilities of the physician.

However, this problem has less to do with the concept of rights than it has to do with how we understand their function. Understood as a prerogative of the patient alone to be exercised against the physician, the right to bodily integrity can make it very difficult to achieve "the kind of joint decision-making of all the concerned parties that is required by a full theory of moral responsibility."[14] For this reason, philosophers such as John Ladd prefer to understand rights as claims *to something* rather than claims *against somebody*. A distinct advantage of this interpretation is that it presupposes cooperation rather than competition. Another is that rather than requiring particular obligations of particular individuals, rights entail collective responsibilities on the part of society at large. Ladd, therefore, refers to rights as ideal and argues that they "relate to things that a society ought to provide for its members so that they will be able to live a good life, that is, a moral life constituted by moral relationships of responsibility and caring."[15]

If we understand the right to bodily integrity as an ideal right on which the decision to withhold nutrition and hydration can be based, thereby permitting the patient to control the circumstances of his or her death, then the manner of the patient's dying becomes a moral enterprise in the same way that the manner of the patient's life has been a moral enterprise. Therefore, the decision to withhold or withdraw life-sustaining treatment, such as nutrition and hydration, might constitute the patient's most profound moral need at that stage in life. As expressed by Hill, "[a]s such it will be a necessary means to pursue whatever moral goals have been directing his life up to this point and should now be directing the circumstances and time of his death, if the two are to be consonant."[16]

However, rights have a habit of conflicting with other rights, and it is particularly important to understand what this might mean in the present context. The patient's claim to bodily integrity and its corollary, informed consent, in relation to the withdrawal of nutrition and hydration can and does, for example, conflict with society's right to preserve life as an interest central to the integrity of society itself. This conflict lies in one form or another at the heart of the decision to withdraw nutrition and hydration from the patient. As a decision taken in the interests of bodily integrity and informed consent on the part of one individual that leads inevitably to death, it is, potentially at least, a threat to the communal interests that society has in the preservation of life in general.

At the same time, both claims can be justified. As a result, neither claim presumably is absolute. It follows, then, that one or the other claim can only be made legitimately when in doing so the individual does not essentially compromise society, and society does not essentially violate the individual. Therefore, any patient decision to withdraw nutrition and hydration, if it is to be ethically acceptable, must not constitute a threat to society's legitimate interests in the preservation of life. The task then becomes one of establishing a working tension between the two claims so that when they do indeed conflict, there is a way to avoid paralysis and achieve a mutually acceptable way of determining which claim, the individual's or society's, should prevail in a given set of circumstances.

In its seminal decision in the case of Karen Ann Quinlan, the New Jersey Supreme Court was acutely conscious of the conflicting claims and of the need to provide a formula by which to resolve the conflict in a way that does justice to both individual and society at the same time: "We think that the State's interests [in the preservation of life] weakens and the individual's right to privacy grows as the degree of bodily invasion increases and the prognosis dims. Ultimately, there comes a point at which the individual's rights overcome the State interest."[17]

In discussing the ethical criteria to be used in withholding nutrition and hydration, this statement is significant in the way it advances self-determination (or "privacy," as the court called it) by protecting bodily integrity from futile medical treatment in the face of an increasingly dim prognosis. Where there is less and less hope that medical interventions will do anything for the well-being of the patient, there is a greater justification, should the patient wish it, to withhold life-sustaining treatment such as nutrition and hydration.

So far, this discussion has attempted to lay the ethical foundation for decisions to withhold or withdraw nutrition and hydration from a patient. When either decision is made, the patient will die eventually, raising the question of whether such an outcome is, on the face of it, ethically acceptable. The assumption is that it is not. Thus, if death has occurred as a result of the decision to withhold or withdraw nutrition and hydration, it becomes necessary to show that someone has the right to make that decision. If someone does make that decision, what is the basis of that right? Assuming there is some basis for such a right, what circumstances and outcomes would justify its exercise?

The discussion, up to this point, has attempted to show that the individual with the rights to bodily integrity and self-determination would logically be able to exercise those rights by making decisions, for example, to withhold or withdraw medical treatment in general and nutrition and hydration in particular. In drawing the distinction between care and cure in order to show that nutrition and hydration have more to do with the latter than the former, it becomes possible to see that under appropriate circumstances nutrition and hydration, like any other medical treatment, could be the object of such a decision. The individual is vested with moral authority to make decisions of this kind, and nutrition and hydration fall within the legitimate range of this authority. Even though this moral authority or right is not absolute, conflicting with a state interest in the preservation of life, in some circumstances the individual right to self-determination can take precedence over the state's interest.

It remains now to look at those circumstances as they appear in the clinical setting. Because nutrition and hydration are considered as a supportive element of a larger medical treatment, the decision to withdraw or withhold them will depend in some measure on whether, given the patient's condition, they can provide sufficient benefit without imposing a burden disproportionate to that benefit. Too frequently in this context the discussion of benefits and burdens is conducted in relation to clinical outcomes. Accordingly, the argument goes, when benefits to the patient's well-being are less than the burdens suffered to obtain those benefits, decisions to forgo such treatment are ethically acceptable, even when they hasten death as a result. This is a cogent argument as presented in terms of outcomes. However, the real strength of the argument is derived from the individual's right to bodily integrity and self-determination. Otherwise, what would ethically justify the opposite decision—to start or continue treatment even though its burdens outweigh the benefits?

This is a critical point, because on it rests the principle of self-determination and the correct relationship between the patient and the physician and the responsibility of the physician to provide for informed consent or refusal on the part of the patient. Independently of the patient, the physician can determine that, given the patient's diagnosis and prognosis, all treatment options entail greater burden than benefit. On the face of it, then, withholding or withdrawing treatment can medically be the right thing to do. However, this would not be the ethically acceptable thing, at least minus any consideration given to the principle of patient bodily integrity and the principle of self-determination. Neither of these principles can be secure in the absence of consent or refusal from the patient, who realistically can only provide one or the other on the basis of an awareness of the treatment options and a clear grasp of their respective benefits and harms. Therefore, what gives ethical sanction to the outcomes of a decision—in this instance, to withdraw nutrition and hydration—is not solely the objective calculation that the burdens of treatment outweigh any benefits. However necessary that calculation is, for ethical purposes it is not sufficient to meet the demands of the bodily integrity and self-determination of the patient. That will come from the patient's consent to or refusal of treatment informed by a calculation of its burden proportionate to the benefits.

PHYSICIANS' PROFESSIONAL INTEGRITY

We have seen that, in this question of withdrawing nutrition and hydration, there is a real and legitimate tension between the rights of the individual and the communal interests of the state. A parallel tension exists between the rights of the patient and the legitimate claims to professional integrity on the part of the treating physician. Arguably, this tension is never as clearly drawn as when decisions to withdraw nutrition and hydration are being considered. The fundamental ethical question is whether physicians should be involved at all. What in the patient–physician relationship could justify such a decision? Is there anything in the nature of this relationship that would sanction, for example, an obligation on the part of physicians to accede to a patient's request to withdraw nutrition and hydration over their better professional judgment?

At stake, from the physician's point of view, are professional obligations to treat the patient in order to further his or her well-being and to avoid doing harm. In this situation, the question for the physician is how, clinically, does withdrawing nutrition and hydration benefit a patient and also avoid doing harm? Far from being an oxymoron, the question is reasonable in itself and has been made answerable, in part, as a result of the argument that nutrition and hydration can be considered an element in a larger medical treatment. As such, they are morally neither good nor bad in themselves, so there can be no presumption that they should or should not be administered. Like the withdrawal of other treatments, then, such as chemotherapy in the case of a patient in the terminal stages of cancer, the withdrawal of nutrition and hydration should be subjected, as we have already said, to a calculation of its benefits proportionate to its burdens in order to provide objective medical reasons why withdrawal not only benefits the patient but also does not cause harm.

Is this possible? One answer to this question is empirical and will tell us what physiologically happens to a patient from whom nutrition and hydration have been withdrawn. The other is ethical and tells us what becomes of the moral standing of the patient from whom this treatment has been withdrawn. Let us consider the empirical answer first. According to Paul C. Rousseau, artificial hydration has long been thought to ease the discomfort of terminal illness.[18] He points out, however, that recent studies suggest something very different:

> As death approaches, dehydration occurs naturally from inadequate oral intake, gastrointestinal and renal losses, and the loss of secretions from the skin and lungs. Transitory thirst, dry mouth and changes in mental status have been found to develop—but the headache, nausea, vomiting or cramps frequently associated with water deprivation rarely occur. The mental changes—while upsetting to relatives—bring relief to patients by lessening their awareness of suffering.[19]

Rousseau adds that although the administration of intravenous fluids can produce a feeling of well-being, the feeling can be of short duration: "In time, artificial hydration is likely to heighten the discomfort of a terminally ill patient, and often exacerbates underlying symptoms."[20] Additional clinical evidence supports the assertion that nutrition and hydration can be harmful to the dying patient. According to Ahronheim and Gasner, "[t]ube feeding itself may produce pain; erosions or hemorrhage of the nasal septum, esophagus, and gastral mucosa have been reported; and nasogastric feeding as well as gastrostomy feeding has been associated with aspiration pneumonia."[21] Ahronheim and Gasner conclude that "withholding or withdrawing artificial feeding and hydration from debilitated patients does not result in gruesome, cruel, or violent death."[22] Indeed, Rousseau would go further on the basis of his clinical evidence: "Accompanied by comfort measures and emotional support, dehydration is a humane therapeutic response to terminal illness."[23] The Hastings Center guidelines arrive at a similar conclusion: "Patients in their last days before death may spontaneously reduce their intake of nutrition and hydration without experiencing hunger or thirst."[24] As a result, decisions to withhold such treatment can meet the physician's twin obligations to do what is in the patient's best interests and to do no harm to the patient.

In her discussion of nutritional support at the end of life, M. Patricia Furman refers to 70 prospective randomized trials of nutrition support in cancer patients.[25] The findings showed no clinical benefit to this patient population. She adds that a comprehensive study of nursing home patients with dementia found, among other things, that the insertion of feeding tubes did not improve survival over those patients who were hand fed. Indeed, according to Furman, another study found that nursing home residents with a feeding tube died 1.44 times sooner than those without a feeding tube.

It is useful here, in addition to considering the physiologic consequences of withdrawing nutrition and hydration, to consider the physiology of dying itself. According to Liz Friedrich,[26] there is substantial evidence from research of a physiologic adaptation, during the dying process, to starvation that prevents any discomfort as a result of the absence of food. The research shows that as someone is dying and stops eating, he or she may experience hunger, but only at the outset. As Friedrich explains it, "When food and fluid intake is poor, dehydration usually occurs before starvation. Dehydration eventually results in hemoconcentration and hyperosmolality, with subsequent azotemia, hypernatremia and hypercalcemia. These metabolic changes are said to produce a sedative effect on the brain just before death."

Dehydration, as R. J. Dunlop and colleagues have pointed out, occurs when someone drinks water at a level insufficient for homeostasis.[27] Typical symptoms of dehydration in someone who in other respects is healthy are thirst, dry mouth, and fatigue, among several others. This is not the case with terminally ill patients. Citing a then-recent prospective study of dying cancer patients with a median time to death of two days, Dunlop stated that the symptoms of dry mouth and thirst did not correlate with the level of hydration. These findings were, according to Dunlop, similar to those of F. I. Burge, who looked at symptoms of dehydration in 51 cancer patients, expected to die in less than six weeks, and found no significant correlation between biochemical markers of dehydration, such as serum osmolality, urea, and sodium, and the symptom of thirst. Given these findings, Dunlop concluded that "giving additional fluid to dying patients in order to alleviate the symptoms of dry mouth and thirst may well be futile." The explanation, he added, was possibly because "the normal homeostatic mechanisms controlling fluid intake and fluid balance are altered in the dying process."[28]

As persuasive as this clinical evidence is, are there ethical reasons as persuasive that would justify a physician withdrawing or withholding nutrition and hydration in order to do what is in the patient's best interests and do no harm to the patient? Essentially, this question is asking what effect the withdrawal of nutrition and hydration has on the moral standing of the patient. If, as some assert, "life is 'the first right of the human person' and 'the condition of all the others,'"[29] what circumstances would justify a decision that would inevitably lead to the death of the patient?

Kevin O'Rourke, a medical ethicist, addresses the same issue when he asserts that "one of the basic ethical assumptions upon which medicine and efforts to nurse and feed people is based is that life should be prolonged because living enables us to pursue the purpose of life."[30] Included in the purpose of life are happiness, fulfillment, and human relationships, which, O'Rourke observes, "imply some ability to function at the cognitive-affective, or spiritual, level."[31]

Despite the theological orientation of these two particular assertions, there is nothing in either of them that the traditional presumption in clinical practice does not affirm, which is to favor life. Implicit in the question under consideration in this chapter is the possibility that now there are clinical circumstances in which the presumption in favor of life is no longer ethically acceptable.

To rephrase the question for purposes of ethical analysis, what becomes of the obligation to prolong life when, despite the continuation of treatment, the patient will remain alive but will not recover sufficiently to be himself or herself physically, mentally, and psychologically? Recover, that is, to resume the central purposes of his or her life knowingly, willingly, and emotionally. That implies at the least that, before the obligation to prolong life ceases, there is a level of purposefulness to which the patient ought to be able to lay claim and to obtain such that the physician can reasonably continue to treat. However, if no such level can be hoped for given the patient's prognosis, we place an impossible burden on the patient by continuing to treat: the expectation of life without the means to appropriate it in any personal sense through mental, volitional, or emotional behavior. Considered in those terms, there seems ample justification to agree with O'Rourke when he concludes that "if efforts to prolong life are useless or result in a severe burden for the patient insofar as pursuing the purpose of life is concerned, then the ethical obligation to prolong life is no longer present."[32]

This is an ethical argument for withholding or withdrawing nutrition and hydration from the patient; it should not be confused with the clinical argument for withholding or withdrawing nutrition and hydration from the patient on the grounds that their use imposes burdens disproportionate to any benefits. However, the basis for making this particular ethical argument rests in part on the clinical calculation that the burdens of treatment will outweigh its benefits. The clinical calculation is necessary but not sufficient to make the ethical argument. It is important to draw this distinction if we are to see the real limitations of the arguments based on clinical data alone and at the same time to see how unsatisfactory it is to make principled ethical arguments that are not informed by clinical data.

The distinction illustrates another critical point. Too frequently, we consider medically supportive interventions such as nutrition and hydration as though they possessed some moral quotient of their own. It would be more accurate, as suggested earlier, to view them as essentially amoral or ethically neutral. Therefore, to be realistic, any ethical analysis of nutrition and hydration should begin with the consequences of their use rather than with nutrition and hydration themselves. Here, the important point is that sustaining life in modern medical practice can and does overreach itself, with consequences for which the medical profession is directly responsible but for which it has no professional ability to determine to be ethically acceptable or unacceptable. Accordingly, from the perspective of the patient receiving such treatment, we can no longer presume that medicine, whatever the intentions of physicians, is a benign exercise, at least as far as its outcomes are concerned. As one commentator has put it, "[d]octors now choose from a vast array of interventions that, when combined with effective therapies for underlying conditions, often greatly prolong survival."[33] However, as the evidence of one intensive care unit after another will verify, "the quality of life so skillfully sought can range from marginally tolerable to positively miserable."[34]

In other words, the distinction between clinical and ethical reasons for withholding life-sustaining treatment shows that there is a difference between judging a clinically supportive intervention, such as nutrition and hydration, to be medically successful in the quantitative, technical sense and judging it to be personally acceptable in relation to the qualitative needs and preferences of the patient. Because of this difference, it is necessary, when making an ethical argument for withholding nutrition and hydration, to acknowledge that the patient's preferences and underlying values will take precedence.

Any decision, therefore, to withhold life-sustaining treatment, such as nutrition and hydration, should be made only after the most careful consideration of the patient's best interests as reflected in his or her preferences and apart from the clinical outcomes. (Because they do not necessarily coincide, they must always be viewed separately.) The natural hesitation we feel in making a decision to withdraw or withhold life-sustaining treatment cannot, however, justify holding the patient hostage to our hesitation on the grounds that its initiation or continuation will be successful in providing the clinical maintenance intended. Rather, armed with the principles laid out in this chapter, we can conclude not only that it is ethically acceptable to withhold or withdraw nutrition and hydration, but also that it might be the only ethical thing to do in the circumstances examined here.

SUMMARY

This chapter dealt with the decision to withhold or withdraw artificial nutrition or hydration or both in end-of-life situations. It is a sensitive ethical issue because food and nutrition are seen as basic to providing care for the patient. Therefore, removing them may seem unethical or even cruel. Hill presented ethical arguments for making the decision to withhold or withdraw artificial nutrition or hydration or both from the patient. He also suggested that such a decision should always be made only after considering the needs of the patient. Further, he posited that this decision may be the only ethical thing to do in certain circumstances.

QUESTIONS FOR DISCUSSION

1. How does the ethical position of the family influence the decision to withhold or withdraw artificial nutrition and hydration?
2. How does the decision to withhold or withdraw artificial nutrition and hydration relate to nonmaleficence?
3. What is the obligation of the physician in determining whether to withhold or withdraw artificial nutrition and hydration?
4. When Hill uses the argument of balancing benefits and burdens, which ethical principles or theories is he using?
5. On what ethical grounds would a practitioner "hold the patient hostage" by hesitating to withdraw artificial nutrition and hydration?

FOOD FOR THOUGHT

The issue of nutrition and hydration at the end of life is more than a purely clinical one. Often the patient's family is in severe emotional distress and sees providing food and hydration as a way to preserve their loved one's life. What ethical duty do you have to the family in these cases? How can you assure the family that the choice to withhold or withdraw nutrition and hydration is the best one clinically and ethically?

NOTES

1. *In re Quinlan*, 70 N.J., 10, 355 A.2d 647.
2. *Cruzan v. Director, Missouri Department of Health*, 497 U.S. 261 (1990).
3. Choice in Dying, *Artificial Nutrition and Hydration and End of Life Decision Making*, pamphlet QA200 (New York: Choice in Dying, September 1990), 1.
4. CNN/USA Today/Gallup poll, April 1–2, 2005.
5. "Autopsy Report—Medical Examiner's Report of Autopsy," April 1, 2005. Available from http://www.co.pinellas.fl.us/forensics.

6. R. J. Devine, "The Amicus Curiae Brief: Public Policy versus Personal Freedom," *America*, April 8, 1989, 323–234.

7. Ibid., 324.

8. Hasting Center, *Guidelines on the Termination of Life-Sustaining Treatment and the Care of the Dying* (Briar Cliff Manor, NY: Hastings Center, 1987), 59–60.

9. Ibid., 60.

10. J. E. Ruark and T. A. Raffin, "Initiating and Withdrawing Life Support," *New England Journal of Medicine* 318 (1988): 25–30.

11. D. C. Maquire, *Death by Choice* (Garden City, NY: Image Books, 1984), 82.

12. R. Wasserstrom, "Rights, Human Rights, and Racial Discrimination," in *Human Rights*, ed. A. I. Melden (Belmont, CA: Wadsworth, 1970), 99.

13. T. P. Hill, "The Right to Die: Legal and Ethical Consideration," *Southern Medical Journal* 85 (1992): 25–57.

14. J. Ladd, "The Definition of Death and the Right to Die," in *Ethical Issues Relating to Life and Death*, ed. J. Ladd (New York: Oxford University Press, 1979), 135.

15. Ibid., 139.

16. Hill, "The Right to Die."

17. *In re Quinlan*, 70 N.J., 10, 355 A.2d 647, at 37.

18. P. C. Rousseau, "How Fluid Deprivation Affects the Terminally Ill," *R.N.* (January 1991): 73–76.

19. Ibid., 73.

20. Ibid., 74.

21. J. C. Ahronheim and M. R. Gasner, "The Sloganism of Starvation," *Lancet* 335 (1990): 279.

22. Ibid.

23. Rousseau, "Fluid Deprivation," 76.

24. Hastings Center, *Guidelines on the Termination of Life-Sustaining Treatment*, 60.

25. M. Patricia Furman, "Nutrition Support at the End of Life: A Critical Decision," *Today's Dietician* 10, no. 9 (2008): 68.

26. L. Friedrich, "PEG Tube Feeding at the End of Life—When It's Appropriate, When It's Not," *Today's Dietician* 12, no. 4 (2010): 42.

27. R. J. Dunlop, J. E. Ellershaw, M. J. Baines, N. Sykes, and C.M. Saunders, "On Withholding Nutrition and Hydration in the Terminally Ill: Has Palliative Medicine Gone Too Far? A Reply," *Journal of Medical Ethics* 21 (1995): 141–143.

28. Ibid.

29. U.S. Bishops' Committee for Pro-Life Activities, "Nutrition and Hydration: Moral and Pastoral Reflections," *Origins* 21, no. 44 (1992): 705–712.

30. K. O'Rourke, "The AMA Statement on Tube Feeding: An Ethical Analysis," *America*, November 22, 1986, 322.

31. Ibid.

32. Ibid.

33. Ruark and Raffin, "Initiating and Withdrawing Life Support," 25.

34. Ibid.

CHAPTER 11

Death, Medicine, and the Moral Significance of Family Decision Making

James Lindemann Nelson

INTRODUCTION

The Death of Ivan Ilych is one of the best-known novellas in literature, a staple of undergraduate curricula.[1] Having access to the title, readers know what's going to happen right from the start: as though to eliminate any possible doubt, we watch the unfolding of Ivan's life, character, and relationships in flashback from his obsequies. Ivan himself, of course, is not positioned so advantageously. A good part of the story's drama consists precisely of his coming to understand that his illness is fatal. This task turns out to be complex and difficult, marked by ambivalence, insight, and denial.

Ivan's story offers us a powerful and particular image of what is involved in coming to grips with dying. It stresses the importance of the jobs we have to do as our lives come to a close and the value of the insights we can then gain. It also offers an equally forceful and vivid image of the place of the family at the end of life, one that highlights the falsity that permeates relationships and the unreliability of those who are closest to us.

Tolstoy wrote *Ivan Ilych* in 1886. We die differently now, many of us in hospitals, many in the aftermath of some deliberation and choice about using, withholding, or withdrawing therapies. Should a very-low-birth-weight, brain-damaged baby be removed from her ventilator, a step that will end her suffering, but also any chance she has at life? Should an elderly man with multiple-organ failure undergo the violence of cardiopulmonary resuscitation if his heart stops, trading a peaceful death for a tiny chance at staying alive long enough to leave the hospital? Contemporary medicine has introduced new complexities into dying, complexities that often force patients and their families into making choices of a sort Ivan did not face. Yet current clinical practice and legal and ethical policy concerning those decisions reflect a very Tolstoyan construction of what is at stake and what is in danger.

The response of Ivan's family to his dying was not notable for its moral insight. This fact is most marked by the translucent curtain of deceit with which his family veils Ivan's descent to death. Ivan is dying, but his dying is a forbidden subject; Ivan in particular must not acknowledge or even allude to it. The terrible consequence is that he must suffer his dying without familial recognition:

> What tormented Ivan Ilych most was the deception, the lie, which for some reason they all accepted, that he was not dying but was simply ill, and that he only need keep quiet and undergo a treatment and then something very good would result . . . this deception tortured him—their not wishing to admit what they all knew and what he knew, but wanting to lie to him concerning his terrible condition and wishing and forcing him to participate in that lie.[2]

In this chapter, I pose a counterimage to Tolstoy, in two parts. My leading idea is that our most intimate connections—which is what I will take "family" to mean here—often have very important constructive roles to play in the tasks we face as our lives come to a close. However, I also underscore the fact that families are often deeply involved in those tasks and significantly affected by the discharge of those tasks. Accordingly, I argue that families ought to have some say in the making of pertinent choices. Both these considerations should enrich and help direct our policy concerning end-of-life decision making.

THE STANDARD APPROACH: ROMANTICIZING DEATH, DEMONIZING FAMILIES

We enjoy a considerable measure of social consensus that we may withhold or withdraw treatment too burdensome for the benefits it promises—even if rejection of treatment is tantamount to acceptance of death. This consensus was perhaps most clearly flagged by the Supreme Court's decision in *Cruzan vs. Director, Missouri Department of Health*, which upheld a patient's right to decide against life-sustaining therapy.[3] There has also been wide agreement that the principle of patient autonomy does not solely authorize such decisions, that is, the moral claim that people enjoy a certain kind of sovereignty over what interventions in their bodies are consistent with their values and which are not.[4]

This consensus has a certain instability packed in it. Economic pressures and a reassertion of the autonomy of healthcare professionals have led some to think that life-prolonging health care can, in principle, be withheld despite patient/family desires, if it is expensive enough,[5] or withdrawn over patient/family objection, if the odds of it working are low enough.[6] But the major practical problem with the patient sovereignty view has been that when people are sick enough to require decision making of this kind, they are often too sick to make any decisions at all. For the past few decades, states have been experimenting with different means of extending a person's decision-making authority regarding health care, a movement that achieved something of a high-water mark in the federal Patient Self-Determination Act of 1990, which mandates that all patients be informed of the procedures approved by their state for directing their health care even if they should become incapacitated.

Practically speaking, what this boils down to is allowing other people to convey a patient's treatment preferences if the patient cannot exercise this authority in his or her own voice at the time a decision is required. Others might assist in the interpretation of "living wills," or, more generally, written treatment directives, which are often both vague and ambiguous. They may simply make a decision as the patient's proxy, trying to judge as the patient would have judged. In either case, the interpreter or proxy decision maker enjoys the position by virtue of relationship to the will of the patient: either because the proxy had been explicitly delegated to fill these roles or, in the absence of an explicit declaration made by the patient, because he or she is assumed to be able to transmit or reproduce the patient's preferences better than anyone else.

The natural assumption is that close relatives will typically be in the best position to decide. However, there is an equally natural objection: family members hardly count as disinterested parties. Because of their very closeness, relatives often have a sizable stake in how treatment decisions go, and if their interests influence the decision making, the orthodox view regards the process as morally contaminated.

This "standard approach" to end-of-life decision making shares the suspicion about intimates found in Tolstoy's depiction of Ivan's decidedly nasty family, in which those who have some kind of relationship to the dying man—his wife and adult daughter—do not love him, and those who do love him—which is to say, his young son—seem to be permitted no relationship to him. Our thinking about end-of-life decision making, particularly concerning patients who cannot make decisions on their own behalf, seems to be haunted by specters closely resembling Ivan's wife and daughter, who saw him largely as a means to fulfilling their own desires. Therefore, we need to guard judgments about starting or stopping life-sustaining therapy carefully to prevent such manipulation of vulnerable people.

Family members, then, have no standing simply as family members, but only as conduits to the preferences that the patient actually has, or would have had. If their interests influence whether medical treatment of various kinds continues or not, then the patient is at great risk of abuse: either suffering the continual burdens of invasive care for an inadequate goal, or forgoing desired care and with it the chance to extend life.

In fact, the picture for families is even darker. Not only are their motives suspect, but also even their readings of the patient's desires are questionable. Several studies of proxy decision making have indicated that families are, as it turns out, not very good at guessing the preferences of their relatives when it comes to the end of life. A recent meta-analysis of the relevant literature by D. I. Shalowitz and colleagues found no better than a two-thirds match between the decisions of family members acting as proxies for their relatives and the decisions those relatives would make on their own behalf.[7] In the standard view, then, their main claim to decision-making authority is undermined. Shalowitz et al., for example, write that their "data undermine the claim that reliance on surrogates is justified by their ability to predict incapacitated patients' treatment preferences," while the main caution against them seems as strong as ever.[8]

The picture for incompetent patients also appears grimmer than has yet been suggested. What they have at stake is not simply the possibility of undergoing extended discomfort or premature death because their families are either mistaken about their preferences or malignantly indifferent to them. Equally significant is the loss of the ability to invest their deaths with the kind of meaning that best comports with their sense of their life overall. *Ivan Ilych* provides us with a hint of this theme. Recall Ivan's painful examination of his life, his insight into how misdirected and trivial he had allowed his life to become, and how his final task is to accept himself, and his suffering, and hence to achieve salvation.

The idea that there is often a "terminal perspective" on life, from which we can get an especially accurate view of our lives, and the idea that how we end our lives is crucial to the success or failure of those lives overall, strike me as at least loosely linked. Together they make up what one might call a romantic view of death, clearly present in Tolstoy, and not at all foreign to contemporary sensibilities. Consider this passage from *Life's Dominion*, by the influential philosopher and legal scholar Ronald Dworkin:

> There is no doubt that most people treat the manner of their deaths as of special, symbolic importance: they want their deaths, if possible, to express and in that way vividly to confirm the values they believe most important to their lives.[9]

Whether or not Dworkin is right about "most people" on this point, he is, I think, surely right about what most ethical and legal theorists think when they take up the issue of how one should make choices at the end of life. We find here another significant reason why our evolving policy on this matter has, since the 1970s, been directed toward empowering patients. It is not simply to defend them from assaults on what Dworkin would call their "experiential" interests, or how things feel to them:[10] it is also to protect their ability to live and die in accordance with their "critical" interests—that is, with their reflective sense of what is truly significant and characteristic about their lives. How we die is of particular significance to whether or not we achieve our critical interest in having lived a good life, and it is crucial to our achieving such a life that our deaths be as much as possible orchestrated according to our own ideas.

A REVISED ACCOUNT: DYING IN INTIMACY

The contemporary context of decision making in the face of death, then, is in very important respects much the same as it was in the late 19th century. We are cynical about families, romantic about death. What is wrong with this standard "Tolstoyan" concept of the significance of death and the suspicious character of families? In my view, pretty much everything.

This is not to say that there are no abusive and otherwise untrustworthy families out there. Nor is it to deny that for some people the process of dying is transformative, offering new and deep insights. Finally, I am not implacably hostile to the idea that the way we die can be crucial to the success or otherwise of our lives overall. Rather, my attitude toward these claims is that they are all overstated; we ought not take them as the predominating feature of either families or death. Many have families who are not decidedly nasty; many die without gaining deep insights into the nature of things. In addition, many can have bad deaths who had quite acceptable lives overall. Many have good deaths who did not achieve that goal because they, personally or through carefully directed proxies, had orchestrated every step. The worst of the overstatement is what we might regard as its cumulative implication: we face death alone most often as "vulnerable adults" whose chief goal is control and whose chief need is protection from rapacious relatives.

General practice, as opposed to policy and theory, indicates that my misgivings about this tableau are not idiosyncratic. Relatively few people avail themselves of formal advance directives, despite the publicity given to the importance of advance healthcare planning; the few who do draw up such directives tend to be disproportionately white, well-off, and well educated.[11] Although there are many possible explanations here, one plausible suggestion is that different subcultures within our nation have different views about how important it is to take a direct hand in end-of-life decision making.

Part of the problem may be that medical practice and legal policy regarding death correctly assume that most people want to die well, but that both practice and policy are confused about what dying well means to many of us. Doing something "well" does not necessarily mean doing it according to our own self-regarding desires; it may mean acting in accord with what strikes us as right, seemly, meet—where these notions guide us in ways that we believe to be good in themselves, and not simply because we happen to accept them. More particularly, many of us may believe that our deaths should cohere with a life lived in important connection with other people. The course of our dying should express concern about their burdens, not because doing so is the crucial task of our lives, nor because death has vouchsafed to us some special moral insight at the end, but because such concern is consistent with long-held views about how to live well, views that need not be abandoned when the job at hand is how to die well.

Data drawn largely from the work of High show that many people feel no need to file a formal document because they think of their families as their advance directives.[12] The medical ethicists Linda and Ezekiel Emanuel have wondered whether High's results do not simply reflect most people's uncritical acceptance of the view that families know best what we ourselves would want, and that this enthusiasm for relatives would not survive the growing evidence to the contrary.[13] However, their critique makes two crucial assumptions. First, it assumes that the kind of medical choices that are open to us as we die are typically such that we have considered preferences about them, preferences expressing something that matters to us deeply. It also assumes, perhaps even more significantly, that our choices should rule the day, no matter how they might affect the interests of those with whom we have been intimate.

However, both these assumptions seem unwarranted. The legal theorist Patricia White, drawing on her experience in the presumably less emotionally charged area of estate planning, has pointed out that "people find it difficult to predict accurately how they would react to some hypothetical future crisis."[14] The idea, then, that the job of a proxy decision maker is to somehow elicit just what the patient would have wanted if the patient could speak in the present situation assumes that there is some one thing he or she would have wanted, and this assumption may well be false.

One of course could simply make determinations about one's future care, rather than predictions. That is, the decision maker would be exerting his autonomy now, reflecting his current preferences, rather than making a guess about what he would want in the future if incapacitated, if, contrary to fact, he could make a considered decision at that time. However, if we are to understand advance decision making as a determination rather than as a prediction, then it is not clear that decision making at the end of life retains the kind of special moral significance the romantic perspective gave it. Dying "romantically"—that is, in a way that reflects something crucially important about your life—might well require not a blunt determination now of how a future event should be handled but fine-grained sensitivity to the details of that future time. How much pain or discomfort is at issue? What are the chances that a medical intervention will achieve its end, and at what cost to the patient or to others for whom the patient cares? It is not implausible that making decisions of this kind could, in principle, allow the decision maker an opportunity to express and even develop her moral character. However, if so, what would best allow her this opportunity is the ability to fit her decision precisely to the circumstances.

The result is that it is far from clear that all, or even many, of the preferences healthy, self-aware people have about hypothetical future crises really count as considered or authoritative in any event. And another point remains to be considered: even if we assume that incompetent patients typically have well-considered and well-ordered preferences that others might put into practice, the interests of their families remain morally relevant to decision making even if those interests run counter to patient preferences.

As John Hardwig has powerfully argued, there is no good reason to think that the ill are totally excused from their moral obligations to their intimates simply because of their illness.[15] Nor is it appropriate to think that family members are required to bear any imaginable burden to further any interest of a relative if that interest happens to be medical. Although it does not explicitly endorse selfishness, the standard approach to decision making at the end of life proceeds as though selfishness—or at least self-absorption—were the appropriate standard for choices worthy of respect. We must serve the patient's needs, and the only way to ensure they are met is to forbid family members to think of anything other than what the patient would want.

However, families quite often have ways of organizing the distribution of caring work that goes on within them that differ from those customary in healthcare settings. Sometimes family organization may be open to moral criticism—as when women are assigned an unequal share of caring labor simply because they are women—but the very fact that they distribute the family's resources in a way that is sensitive to many needs ought not to be regarded as morally questionable simply on its face. Maintaining that proxy decision making by family members is to be censured is particularly ironic in the present context of healthcare delivery, in which the medical interests of patients are sometimes subordinated to the limits of their insurance plan or of the resources their state is willing to make available for Medicaid.

It is on the basis of considerations of this sort that I think that Ivan Ilych's sort of death ought to be seen as unusual—fit to be the subject of an immortal short story—rather than as a good guide to what challenges and choices people will regularly face as they die. We need not construct a policy that assumes families are to be carefully controlled and should be suspected of guilt until proven innocent. We need not think that putting our own stamp on the precise character of our death is a crucial determinant of the quality of our lives. Therefore, we need not be so enamored of systems that rely primarily on explicit advance directives, seeing their authority as stemming solely from the patient and, in effect, disadvantaging the many patients and families without advance directives to whom death will come. It seems to me both more realistic, as well as quite defensible morally, to reverse the burden of proof here. We ought to recognize that families have a certain kind of moral authority to serve as proxies, unless the patient has made an explicit declaration to the contrary or unless that authority is misused to a point that constitutes abuse.

However, this strategy is only part of what should be an overall rethinking of the contexts in which we die, and the assumptions that are prevalent in those contexts—assumptions that tend to undermine the kind of closeness that very ill patients can have with their families. Healthcare institutions should be set up to be as transparent as possible to these connections, which is not now the case. Hospitals, for example, remain places in which certain value commitments are evident and powerful. They are hierarchical, unfamiliar places that separate you from daily routines and common sources of identity affirmation, running all the way from your own clothes to your most intimate connections. Hospitals have their own clear agenda to which they strongly invite patients to subscribe. The notion that patients need to be empowered in such settings is exactly right; the mistake is in thinking this is likely to happen if patients are allowed to be alienated from their own sources of personal affirmation and authority in the name of giving such authority formal protection.[16]

CONCLUSION

One might allege that, the institutional structure of healthcare systems apart, the decision-making system currently in place for incapacitated people is actually very well suited to accommodate just the values sketched out here. Many people have families in which there are people whom they trust. Many people do not think it essential that their death reflect precisely what their own decisions would have been, had they been able to make them directly. Such people can easily execute advance directives that say, in effect, "My spouse gets to decide any feature of my medical care, if I am not able to do so." For those people who either do not trust their families or do not wish to burden them with the task of making end-of-life decisions, appointing nonfamily proxies is possible. For people who think that it is crucial that the circumstances of their deaths fit as closely as possible with some overriding concept of the integrity of their lives, more specific treatment directives are possible.

What does the standard view really leave out? This very reasonable question has a pragmatic answer, to which I have already alluded, and a rather deeper answer. The pragmatic response is simply that the majority of people will, for the foreseeable future, die without a formal advance directive. At the very least, this fact suggests that we need to pay more attention to how to make healthcare decisions for this very large group of people. The most reasonable response would seem to be a system of proxies arranged in descending order of priority: spouse, adult children, parents, siblings, and so on. This system would certainly not be without problems—for instance, understanding what "spouse" means in a society where people often live together without formal marriage, and where some people who share their lives are not legally permitted to become spouses to each other—but it would at least have the right scope and the right slant. Individuals who felt uncomfortable with the ordering or wanted to leave specific instructions to their proxies would be within their rights to execute specific directives to change the hierarchy.

The deeper reason is that the standard approach is not neutral among different views of what a person owes to his or her family, or more broadly, of the nature of intimate connections. It contains a certain expressive force suggesting that our intimate ties are insignificant unless formalized by an explicit exercise of our own sovereign authority. This view is neither self-evidently true nor altogether innocuous with regard to its impact on how we think about family ties generally in this society. Rereading *Ivan Ilych* reminds us that skepticism about the family is not a new phenomenon. However, it should not distract us from the distinct possibility that new forms of defensiveness about intimate connections can make things worse, as well as better.

SUMMARY

In this chapter, Nelson first introduced the romantic view of death that emphasizes the role of choice at the end of life and a cynical view of our intimate relationships that tends to present families in a negative way. He then took the position that that such views are overstated and do not accurately reflect most people's experience when life comes to a close. Instead, he characterized the dying process as one that often importantly includes the family. He also suggested that the ill may even have a moral obligation toward their relatives. Finally, he suggested that the healthcare system should rethink how end-of-life treatment decisions are made and how to honor the role of the family in this process.

QUESTIONS FOR DISCUSSION

1. Consider the issue of autonomy as it applies to end-of-life decisions. Nelson says that decisions do not have to be self-interested to be autonomous. What do you think autonomy means at the end of life?
2. If Nelson continues to be correct about the use of advance directives by only a minority of people, how should an organization handle end-of-life decisions when patients cannot articulate their wishes?
3. Do you agree with Hardwig that the ill have moral obligations to their family members? If so, what obligations do they have?
4. Some have said that we make policy based on the actions of a minority rather than for the majority. Given Nelson's argument, do you think advance directives as a policy are too limited?
5. What is your ethical obligation as a healthcare professional toward those who are at the end of their lives?

FOOD FOR THOUGHT

In this chapter, Nelson increases our knowledge about the process of dying and the issues associated with it. There are certainly ethical considerations from both the family's and the hospital's point of view. In light of the aging baby boomer population, do you think that these considerations will be even more important in the near future than they are now? What ethical issues related to death, medicine, and the family decision-making process will be present as the baby boomers experience the dying process?

NOTES

1. L. Tolstoy, *The Death of Ivan Ilych and Other Stories*, trans. Alymer Maude (1866; reprint, New York: New American Library, 1960).

2. Ibid., 137.

3. *Cruzan v. Director, Missouri Department of Health*, 497 U.S. 261 (1990).

4. R. Faden and T. Beauchamp, *A History and Theory of Informed Consent* (New York: Oxford University Press, 1986); A. Buchanan and D. Brock, *Deciding for Others* (Cambridge: Cambridge University Press, 1989).

5. L. Fleck, "Just Health Care Rationing: A Democratic Decision Making Approach," *University of Pennsylvania Law Review* 140 (1992): 1597–1636.

6. T. Tomlinson and H. Brody, "Futility and the Ethics of Resuscitation," *Journal of the American Medical Association* 264 (1990): 849–860.

7. A. Seckler, D. E. Meier, M. Mulvihill, and B. E. Paris, "Substituted Judgment: How Accurate Are Proxy Predictions?" *Annals of Internal Medicine* 151 (1991): 1276–1280; E. Emanuel and L. Emanuel, "Proxy Decision Making: An Ethical and Empirical Analysis," *Journal of the American Medical Association* 267 (1992): 2067–2071; D. Shalowitz, E. Garret-Mayer, and D. Wendler, "The Accuracy of Surrogate Decision Makers: A Systematic Review," *Archives of Internal Medicine* 166 (2006): 493–497.

8. Shalowitz, Garret-Mayer, and Wendler, "Accuracy of Surrogate Decision Makers," 493.

9. R. Dworkin, *Life's Dominion* (New York: Knopf, 1993), 211.

10. Ibid.

11. Recent data suggest that only 18% to 36% of adult Americans have completed advance directives, and that completion rates differ by race and ethnicity. See U.S. Department of Health and Human Services, *Advance Directives and Advance Care Planning: Report to Congress* (Washington, DC: U.S. Department of Health and Human Services, August 2008). Retrieved from http://aspe.hhs.gov/daltcp/reports/2008/ADCongRpt.pdf. Accessed January 26, 2012.

12. D. High, "All in the Family: Extended Autonomy and Expectations in Surrogate Health Care Decision Making," *Gerontologist* 28 (1988): 46–51; D. High, "Why Are Elderly People Not Using Advance Directives?" *Journal of Aging and Health* 5 (1993): 497–515; D. High, "Families' Roles in Advance Directives," *Hastings Center Report* 24, special suppl. (1994): 516–518.

13. Emanuel and Emanuel, "Proxy Decision Making."

14. P. White, "Appointing a Proxy Under the Best of Circumstances," *Utah Law Review* (1992): 849–860.

15. J. Hardwig, "What About the Family?" *Hastings Center Report* 20 (1990): 5–10.

16. See, for further discussion of this point, H. Lindemann Nelson and J. Lindemann Nelson, *The Patient in the Family* (New York: Routledge, 1995).

CHAPTER 12

Ethical Issues Concerning Physician-Assisted Death

Barbara Supanich

INTRODUCTION

Physician-assisted death is a controversial and challenging concept among the many cultures within U.S. society, which are, in many ways, ambivalent about death and the process of dying. Every day we see death-filled movies, TV serials about doctors, and the evening news showing us film footage of wars, ethnic conflicts, and natural disasters. They all sterilize the death experience, at times making it both surreal and unreal. In contrast are the poignant experiences of our own personal and professional lives that teach us the realities of death and dying—patients, relatives, and friends who have died from acquired immune deficiency syndrome (AIDS), heart disease, cancer, or severe traumatic injuries. It is in this societal, professional, and personal milieu that I ask questions about how people die and how they decide the context of their dying process.[1,2]

Although various faith traditions and ethical guidelines, including those of the American Medical Association Council on Ethical and Judicial Affairs and the American Academy of Hospice and Palliative Medicine, prohibit and oppose assisted suicide and active euthanasia, public opinion polls show that U.S. society is divided into thirds on the issue of assisted death. One-third support it under a wide variety of circumstances; one-third oppose it under any circumstances; and one-third support it in a few cases, but not all.[2,3] It is within this rich and complex societal context that physicians and other health-care professionals need to attain an understanding and an ethical tolerance for these issues and their corresponding controversies and arguments. This chapter reviews some of the major ethical arguments, proposes clinical strategies for responding to a patient's request for death assistance, and discusses the broader context necessary for a deeper understanding of the challenge of assisted death.

KEY DEFINITIONS

I would like to clarify some basic definitions and distinctions regarding assisted death. First, *assisted suicide* refers to when a patient intentionally and willfully ends his or her own life with the assistance of a third party. This assistance may encompass different levels of involvement, from merely providing information about how to commit suicide to providing the means to commit suicide, such as a lethal quantity of pills. It can also include actively participating in the suicide, such as being present at the scene and inserting an intravenous line through which the patient can then administer a lethal dose.[4] The widely publicized actions of doctors Timothy Quill[2,5] and Jack Kevorkian[6] provide examples of the second and third levels of involvement, respectively.

In *voluntary active euthanasia*, patients freely choose to have a lethal agent directly administered to them by another individual with a merciful intent. *Assisted death* is the term I will use in the remainder of the chapter to refer jointly to the practices of voluntary active euthanasia and assisted suicide. Most of the ethics literature has focused on the special problems of the physician's role, and therefore I will most commonly refer to *physician-assisted death*. However, in intensive care units (ICUs), step-down units, cancer units, hospice settings, and long-term care facilities, as well as in the homes of those who choose to die there, the roles of other healthcare professionals and the family are critically important. In many of these settings, patients may actually request assistance in dying from one or more of these individuals as well as (or instead of) from the physician.

It is also important to be clear about what assisted death is not. It is not an assisted death if a competent person decides not to initiate a specific therapy (e.g., antibiotics for a pneumonia or other septic process, artificial nutrition and hydration, further cardiac interventions). Nor is it assisted death to withdraw any of these options from a patient. The use of high doses of opioids, where the intent is to relieve pain and not to hasten death, is not physician-assisted death. Many still believe that high-dose opioids pose a serious risk of fatal respiratory depression. However, palliative specialists know that this very seldom occurs with proper titration of analgesic doses, even when very large doses of opioids are administered in terminal illnesses.[7] Even in the rare case in which respiratory depression is a foreseen (but unintended) consequence of adequate analgesia, administering the analgesic is not considered physician-assisted death. (If, however, the true intent is to cause or hasten death, and analgesia is merely a ruse or a rationalization, then I would classify the case as assisted death.)[8]

Withholding or withdrawing life-sustaining treatment is widely accepted today both in ethics and law as appropriate and compassionate care if the competent patient is fully informed and freely chooses that treatment option. Some philosophers, notably Rachels,[9] have argued that there is no morally relevant difference between this practice and the practice of assisted death. In this chapter, without giving detailed arguments, I will dissent from this view. That is, I will leave open the question of whether assisted death is morally justifiable and will discuss the arguments on both sides of the issue. In addition, I will assume that if assisted death can be justified, it must be justified on its own merits, and not merely because it shares some of the same moral features with the relatively uncontroversial practice of withdrawing and withholding life-sustaining treatment.[10]

ETHICAL ARGUMENTS

The following sections present arguments made by those who support and oppose physician-assisted death. Patient autonomy is an important aspect of ethical consideration. In addition, the concept of compassion plays a significant role in formulating an ethics position on this issue. This section also presents information on consideration regarding safeguards, professional integrity, and the competence level of the patient.

Patient Integrity and Autonomy

When patients with terminal illnesses come to see their primary physicians, multiple issues are on their minds. These issues might include personal image, the ability to maintain control over treatment decisions (including pain management and other treatment issues), family dynamics, personal values, and potential conflicts with family and/or physicians. There also are deeper reflections about life goals and about how to continue living life. Patients want to be able to have conversations about life and the effects that the illness is having on it with their physicians in an open and supportive atmosphere. It is in this type of an atmosphere that patients will be more apt to discuss their concerns and fears about their dying process and options for management of that process, including assisted death.[11]

Those supporting assisted death claim that they are honoring patient integrity by being willing to have conversations with their patients that are open to discussing all treatment options with the patient (and his or her family members, if so desired by the patient), including assisted death. In support of patient integrity and autonomy, proponents argue that only the patient knows what constitutes harm and may decide that continued life with severe interminable suffering is a greater harm than assisted death.[12]

Opponents claim that patient autonomy is not the supreme moral value and is insufficient to justify choosing assisted death. They understand that autonomy is a valid moral value in treatment decisions regarding the withdrawal or withholding of life-sustaining treatments, because in those situations we are respecting personal bodily integrity. However, they do not extend the justification to include a right to demand that others take specific actions to end one's life.

Compassionate Response to Suffering

Proponents of assisted death are supportive of efforts to improve pain and symptom management by physicians and other healthcare professionals; however, they argue that there remain cases in which the best palliative care measures are insufficient to relieve these patients' suffering. They argue, along with Quill and others,[2,13] that a willingness to discuss the option of assisted death with the patient may often act as a suicide preventive. This is true because, during this open conversation, the physician might be able to alleviate the patient's fears and misunderstandings and propose other viable alternatives.[14] Alternatively, if patients do not feel that such a conversation is an option with the physician, they may choose to commit suicide in a manner that is more traumatic for themselves and their families and friends.

In contrast, opponents remind us that suffering is a multifaceted dimension of the human experience. Suffering, in their view, is intimately tied to the individual's values, belief system, and sense of meaning. Therefore, at the end of life, suffering relates to one's unique sense of who one is as a person. It also is about how one experiences an illness in the overall context of one's life journey and personal expectations for the future.[15] To relieve suffering, then, by eliminating the sufferer is always unacceptable. Opponents would argue for physicians and others to more competently attend to the issues of loneliness, fear of death, depression, forgiveness, unresolved family and personal conflicts, anger, and hopelessness. This is a challenging endeavor for the healthcare professional, but ultimately allows for a richer personal resolution for the patient. Attending to these issues is important for another reason—a person might make an assisted death request when the physician or family member is suffering from similar inner turmoil. Rather than actively listening to the reasons and concerns behind the patient's request, the physician or family member might project his or her own suffering onto the patient's request and wrongly conclude that a premature death is a merciful choice for the patient.[16]

Safeguards and the Slippery Slope

Persons on both sides of this issue agree that a policy of assisted death would pose a danger to patients and society.[17] Some physicians might abuse this option at the end of life. **Table 12-1** lists some safeguards and guidelines commonly proposed by supporters of assisted death.[18]

Proponents argue that the safeguards and guidelines presented in Table 12-1 create the structure needed for the appropriate conversations between the patient and physician regarding treatment plans for the control of the patient's pain and suffering. These conversations create the rapport and trust necessary for a truly healing relationship. Proponents strongly support recommendations for a consultation from another physician and that there be clear and accurate documentation that all of the guidelines were followed. Adherence to these

Table 12-1 Safeguards and Guidelines for a Policy of Assisted Death

1. The patient must have a condition that is incurable (not necessarily terminal) and is associated with severe suffering without hope of relief.
2. All reasonable comfort-oriented measures must have been considered or tried.
3. The patient must express a clear and repeated request to die that is not coerced (e.g., emotionally or financially).
4. The physician must ensure that the patient's judgment is not "distorted"; that is, the patient is competent to make rational treatment choices.
5. Physician-assisted death must be carried out only in the context of a meaningful physician–patient relationship.
6. Consultation must be obtained from another physician to ensure that the patient's request is rational and voluntary.
7. There must be clear documentation that the previous six steps have been taken, and a system of reporting, reviewing, and studying such deaths must be established.

guidelines, proponents argue, would adequately guard against the slippery slope that opponents fear.

Opponents believe that the slippery slope is a serious and valid concern. Once there is a dissolution or weakening of the legal protections against physician-assisted death, society will lose interest in protecting the vulnerable against physicians making inappropriate decisions to hasten death. Given the pressures of cost containment and biases toward vulnerable populations such as the poor, the uninsured, minorities, immigrants, and those living with a disability, there is also concern that once the legal constraints are lifted, physicians might feel obligated to provide assisted death.[19]

Opponents view guidelines and safeguards as, at best, a well-intentioned but inadequate protection against these powerful social forces leading to inevitable abuse. At worst, they are a hypocritical façade erected by proponents to win over public opinion. Those in opposition are concerned that when physicians start providing the means of death for their patients, there will be erosion of the patient–physician relationship. Because physicians would be tempted to choose a like-minded physician to serve as a consultant, second opinions would provide dubious safety. Documentation systems could not ensure that physicians are consistent and compassionate and that patients are safeguarded.[20]

The debate over safeguards and the slippery slope comes into sharp focus by examining differing interpretations of the Dutch experience. Proponents point to the Netherlands' history of legally permitted assisted death to support their claim that abuses are minimal and are identified and contained when they occur.[21] Opponents view the Dutch experience as confirming their worst fears of the slippery slope.[22]

Professional Integrity

Opponents of physician-assisted death equate professional integrity with the physician's role as a healer, and thus view physician-assisted death as antithetical to the physician's basic role and moral integrity. Physicians, in their view, are to use their knowledge and skills for healing, restoring, and relieving suffering when possible and to offer comfort always, but never to kill.[23] Similar arguments about integrity can be found in the literature for other healthcare professionals, including nurses and pharmacists.[24]

Many proponents would argue that opponents have narrowly restricted the definition of *physician integrity* to a very traditional understanding of "healing." They would also argue for an expanded understanding of professional integrity, to include relief of suffering, respect for the patient's voluntary choices, and aiding patients to achieve a dignified and peaceful death. For proponents, an exception to the general prohibition against physician-assisted death would be the case of a patient who, despite excellent palliative measures, is still having unremitting suffering. This patient also is making repeated voluntary requests to his or her physician for death assistance. In such a narrowly defined case, a physician of integrity could respond affirmatively to the patient's request, if such an action was not in conflict with his or her personal moral or religious convictions.[25]

Substituted Judgment

The slippery slope argument also raises concerns about extending physician-assisted death to incompetent patients. Presently, proposals for physician-assisted death specifically exclude the option of choosing physician-assisted death by an advance directive. Opponents, however, fear that if a legal right to assisted death were ever accepted, death assistance for now-incompetent patients by advance directive would be a logical and unavoidable extension of any such right.[26] A 1996 United States Court of Appeals ruling stated that patients have a constitutional right to physician-assisted death and left open the possibility that a surrogate on behalf of an incompetent patient might exercise such a right. The final decision in that case, by the United States Supreme Court, was that a patient does not have a "right to die."[27]

CLINICAL MANAGEMENT OF REQUESTS FOR ASSISTED DEATH

As outlined in the previous section, the ethical debate over assisted death seems as intractable as the abortion debate. One might conclude that proponents and opponents would disagree radically about the actual management of individual patients and could not possibly work cooperatively in team settings. However, this is not entirely true.

In my opinion, the apparent irresolvability of the debate masks a broad area of practical convergence. Opponents do not favor merely abandoning the terminally ill to whatever pain and suffering befalls them. Nor do proponents favor assisted death as the first choice for any terminally ill patient. Both share a strong commitment to trying as hard as possible to relieve the patient's distress to the extent that the patient no longer wishes to die. Proponents are committed to this effort so that they can be sure that assisted death is truly a last resort. Opponents are committed to this effort because they believe that such efforts will ultimately remove any serious demands for assisted death. Moreover, neither believes that health professionals should be required to participate in any activity that is against their personal moral or religious convictions.

Table 12-2 outlines suggested steps for the clinical management of a request for assisted death. Some scrutiny of these steps will show that most can be followed equally well by physicians who support and those who oppose the assisted death option.

Listen Openly and Evaluate Underlying Issues

Patients demonstrate both courage and trust when they express a request for assisted death to their primary physician. Such a request might trigger strong feelings in the physician. However, the physician should not allow those feelings to derail the necessary conversations with the patient over the ensuing days, weeks, or months. The physician is encouraged to have multiple supportive conversations with the patient that identify the patient's crucial issues. It is important to let the patient know that he or she is not alone, among those facing a terminal illness, in considering assisted death as a personal option. It is also important for the physician to convey to the patient that the fact that

Table 12-2   Suggested Steps for the Clinical Management of a Request for Assisted Death

1. The provider should listen to the request for assisted death in an open and sympathetic manner and evaluate the issues underlying the request.
2. Providers should share their personal stance with patients in an open and professional manner, always assuring patients that they will be supported throughout this personal decision-making process.
3. All providers should take appropriate steps to process their personal emotional reactions to the patient's request (e.g., hospice team meetings).
4. The provider should have a continuing dialogue with the patient and appropriate family members or support persons concerning the development and implementation of the therapeutic treatment plans, including a request for assisted death, in a manner that is consistent with the provider's moral values and belief system.

the patient chooses to confide in him or her is an honor, and that he or she is prepared for honest discussions about the option of assisted death.

Both the physician and the patient need to seek out support for themselves as they ponder such a significant decision. The patient might want to discuss the request with family members, other members of the healthcare team, clergy, or a close friend. Physicians should not isolate themselves when presented with such a request. They should seek out supportive persons in their personal and professional lives to assist them as they reflect on the implications.

Physicians need to make every effort to understand the reasons that motivate such a patient request and respond appropriately with the information and support that the patient needs. For some patients, this might mean addressing issues of loss of dignity, depression, and feelings of intense loneliness. For these patients, psychological counseling would be an appropriate intervention. Others might have a desire for more information about their disease or specific issues related to the "how" of their dying process. Still others might have concerns about how their illness affects their family and friends, and a social-work consult might be an appropriate intervention. Some might have deep spiritual issues that their terminal illness has brought into sharper focus, and a referral to their religious or spiritual mentor would be a critical next step.

As one can see from these brief examples, an initial request for assisted death, when approached with active listening and sensitivity to the patient's underlying issues, is always more complex that one anticipates. It requires repeated conversations to ensure that the request is both enduring and consistent with the patient's life values and goals.

Share One's Personal Stance with the Patient

It is premature to allow the physician's personal stance on assisted death to disrupt the deep and careful inquiry into the patient's issues and needs. Physicians are obliged to be sincere and candid with patients regarding all aspects of their treatment options, and therefore the next step is for the physician to be transparent regarding his or her stance on assisted death.

Physicians who morally oppose physician-assisted death should couple refusal to provide it with an assurance that they will stand with the patient until the moment of death and will exhaustively search out all appropriate treatment options to ameliorate the patient's suffering. The physician should stress the importance of continuing the dialogue about the patient's perceptions of his or her suffering, so that they can explore mutually acceptable solutions together. Finally, it is important to let the patient know that although the idea of assisted death is morally objectionable to the physician, the person making the request is not.

The physician who is morally willing to be actively involved in assisted death needs to inform the patient of the required procedure for confirming that the patient is making a voluntary and thoughtful choice and that the patient's suffering cannot be relieved by any other accepted means. The actual amount of time to make such determinations varies, and there is a need to negotiate this time with the patient. The physician should also inform the patient that in most cases of this sort, other interventions could improve a person's quality of life and thus might remove the need for death assistance. Before proceeding with a request for assisted death, these interventions should be identified and considered.

At this stage, an occasional patient will break off the dialogue—either because the patient demands death assistance and the physician is not willing to provide it, or because the patient feels entitled to this assistance without going through a long process of exploring alternatives. A few patients might choose to commit suicide without the physician's assistance, perhaps in a way that causes great suffering for both the patient and the survivors. Although such outcomes are tragic, they do not, in my view, count as an argument against the stepwise approach. Safeguards will count for nothing if health care allows patients, in effect, to use a threat of suicide by other means as emotional blackmail to force the physician to circumvent the process. In such cases, the physician's obligation to act out of professional integrity takes priority over any rights or wishes of the patient.

Ensure Adequate Comfort Care

Several reports in the literature document physicians' and other healthcare providers' poor knowledge about appropriate pain management and other comfort measures at the end of life.[28] When a patient makes a request for death assistance, it behooves the physician to ensure that all reasonable comfort measures have been discussed and a trial offered to the patient.

Most patients have concerns and fears regarding suffering. Primarily they fear that they will have unremitting pain with no hope for adequate relief. Frequent discussions about the multiple technologies and techniques available for easing suffering and increasing comfort will help to alleviate their fears. Patients also have concerns about loneliness, abandonment, unresolved family or other personal conflicts, changes to body image, and personal identity issues. Spiritual counseling can help to restore a sense of meaning and hope for patients in the context of their hopes, values, and life-view. Many persons have found that the use of narrative, as a form of life review, is very comforting and can facilitate the restoration of meaning and hope for the patient. I, as well as many other colleagues in palliative medicine, encourage patients to engage in telling or writing stories about their illness, their hopes for survival or their legacy, and the life events and relationships that have enriched their lives and are an expression of their most sacred personal values.

Ensure the Voluntary Nature and Reasonableness of the Request

Using transparent conversations with their patients, physicians should seek a deeper appreciation of the nature of the patient's request and ensure that it is a clear, uncoerced, and voluntary decision. The compassionate and responsible physician will want to ensure that the patient made the request after serious consideration of other treatment alternatives. The physician needs to verify that the patient rationally rejected the alternatives and that he or she was not depressed at the time of the decision for assisted death. Quill and colleagues appropriately emphasized that any sign of ambivalence or uncertainty on the part of the patient should stop the process.[29] The patient's desire for death assistance must be strong, continuous, clear, and convincing.

Just as important, the physician must seek assurance that the patient bases his or her judgment on a clear and accurate understanding of the facts of his or her case. Further, the patient must understand the implications of his or her decision for assisted death. Frequent and compassionate discussions with the patient will facilitate a better understanding of the reasons for the request and ascertain the perseverance of the request. The physician must be especially alert for signs of depression, which could interfere with executive functions as well as add to the patient's suffering. Consultation with a skilled psychiatrist is imperative if there is any suspicion of depression. In some cases, a trial of antidepressant therapy with a rapid-acting drug might be essential before acceding to a request for death assistance.

Patients should be strongly encouraged to share their decision for death assistance with family members. One should not force patients to share their decisions, and they should be able to choose whom to involve and inform, as well as when to share the decision with family members. The primary physician can often function as a facilitator in the discussions between the patient and family members when there are conflicting concerns and opinions.

PLACING THE DEBATE IN CONTEXT

The apparent intractability of the assisted-death debate has done more than obscure the broad area of consensus regarding optimal patient care at the end of life. Reducing the debate to the technical level of "should we or shouldn't we?" distracts us from broader social and spiritual questions. Unless we address those questions, we will be unable to comprehend why our society and our healthcare system are having this particular debate now and why it has assumed the appearance of intractability.

A critical question is whether physicians view their professional obligation as primarily biomedical or whether they include in that obligation the importance of understanding the narrative life journey of the patient. If they choose the latter, then they would describe their profession as one of promoting health and wellness and of sojourning with their patients through all of life, including the dying process—our final journey. Persons who have this viewpoint do not describe death as the enemy, but rather as a part of life's journey. Medicine would finally accept death as a limit that is not able to be overcome and use that limit as an indispensable focal point in thinking about illness and disease.[30] Medicine would change its focus from fighting death at all costs to helping each person live his or her life to its fullest potential.

A key issue often lost in the current intellectual and legal debate is the critical need to improve the quality of care and support for dying patients throughout our healthcare system. My own estimate from the current debate is that only about 3% of patients who might request assisted death have symptoms that are not remediable by current therapeutic options. This means that proponents and opponents of assisted death agree fully on what to do to help 97% of all patients. Yet, the best available evidence is that far too many of that 97% are not served well within our present system. Healthcare professionals in particular have an obligation to provide leadership in reforming the culture of the healthcare system to be more responsive to the needs of terminally ill patients and their families, including better pain and symptom management and coordination of care for the dying.

Many perceive the assisted-death debate as rooted in unrealistic expectations of what technology can offer in the management of disease and the belief that there is a technological cure available for everyone somewhere in the United States. It is a moral obligation of healthcare providers to help all of our patients seek a balance between the technological imperative and the "pursuit of a peaceful death," as described by Daniel Callahan.[31] It is Callahan's observation that the technological imperative becomes oppressive for some patients and their physicians and serves "to make our dying all the more problematic: harder to predict, more difficult to manage, the source of more moral dilemmas and nasty choices, and spiritually more productive of anguish, ambivalence, and uncertainty."[32]

Merely saying that we accept the inevitability of death does not necessarily free us from the seductive power of the technological solution. For some, the "technical fix" might be a "suicide machine." For some, it is the hope that excellent hospice care will allay all suffering and put an end to all requests for death assistance. Both positions represent a failure to grapple with the meaning of suffering and death at the deeper cultural and spiritual levels.

Because physician-assisted death is an issue with serious personal and societal implications, I strongly encourage continuing dialogue on this issue in as many societal arenas as possible. Within this dialogue, the physician–patient relationship and conversations are primary, but not exclusive. Because we, as humans, are communal by our very nature, discussions about life and death demand that we go beyond the individual context and challenge us to contemplate what it means to live together and die well in a compassionate society.

SUMMARY

The chapter began with definitions that are important in understanding the differences in the types of assisted death. Supanich then presented arguments used by those who oppose and favor this action that included respecting patient integrity and practicing compassion. Suggestions for managing requests for assisted death were given, including following steps for clinical management, sharing one's personal view, and ensuring that comfort care will be provided. Finally, Supanich suggested that, because of its significance, we continue the dialogue about this issue and even consider a societal view.

QUESTIONS FOR DISCUSSION

1. Given the aging of baby boomers and the changes in health care, will there be an increase in patient requests for physician-assisted suicides as we move forward in the 21st century? Why or why not?

2. What ethical issues does the physician face when he or she receives a request for assisted suicide?

3. What do you think is the underlying cause of patients making requests for ending their lives with support?

4. Why does technology not hold the complete answer to a "good death"?

5. What principles of ethics should you consider in responding to a patient's request for physician-assisted suicide?

FOOD FOR THOUGHT

This chapter touches on complex and often painful issues. Given the current thinking, how can a physician decide what is the ethical thing to do when asked about assisted suicide? How can the physician respect the patient's wishes and still maintain an ethical practice of medicine?

NOTES

1. D. E. Meier, C. A. Emmons, A. Litke, S. Wallenstein, and R. S. Morrison, "Characteristics of Patients Requesting and Receiving Physician-Assisted Death," *Archives of Internal Medicine* 163 (2003): 1537–1542; E. Emmanuel, "Whose Right to Die?" *The Atlantic Monthly*, March 1997, 73–79.

2. T. E. Quill and J. Greenlaw, "Physician-Assisted Death," in *From Birth to Death and Bench to Clinic: The Hastings Center Bioethics Briefing Book for Journalists, Policymakers, and Campaigns*, ed. Mary Crowley (Garrison, NY: The Hastings Center, 2008), 137–142.

3. D. T. Watts and T. Howell, "Assisted Suicide Is Not Voluntary Active Euthanasia," *Journal of the American Geriatric Society* 40 (1992): 1043.

4. Ibid.

5. T. Quill, "Death and Dignity: A Case of Individualized Decision Making," *New England Journal of Medicine* 324 (1991): 691.

6. J. Kevorkian, *Prescription Medicide: The Goodness of Planned Death* (Buffalo, NY: Prometheus Books, 1991); G. Annas, "Physician-Assisted Suicide: Michigan's Temporary Solution," *New England Journal of Medicine* 328 (1993): 1573.

7. W. C. Wilson, N. G. Smedira, C. Fink, J. A. McDowell, and J. M. Luce, "Ordering and Administration of Sedatives and Analgesics During the Withholding and Withdrawal of Life Support from Critically Ill Patients," *Journal of the American Medical Association* 267 (1992): 949.

8. H. Brody, "Commentary on Billings and Block's 'Slow Euthanasia,'" *Journal of Palliative Care* 12 (1996): 38–41.

9. J. Rachels, *The End of Life: Euthanasia and Morality* (New York: Oxford University Press, 1986).

10. G. Annas, "Death by Prescription: The Oregon Initiative," *New England Journal of Medicine* 331 (1994): 1240; D. Callahan, "Pursuing a Peaceful Death," *Hastings Center Report* (July/ August 1993): 33; California Proposition 161, the Aid-in-Dying Act (1992); A. M. Capron and V. Michel, "Be Sure to Read the Fine Print: Will California Legalize Euthanasia?" *Commonweal*, September 25, 1992; E. J. Emmanuel, "The History of Euthanasia Debates in the United States and Britain," *Annals of Internal Medicine* 121 (1994): 793.

11. J. Peteet, "Treating Patients Who Request Assisted Suicide," *Archives of Family Medicine* 3 (1994): 723; B. Ferrel and M. Rhiner, "High-Tech Comfort: Ethical Issues in Cancer Pain Management for the 1990's," *Journal of Clinical Ethics* (Summer 1991): 108; D. Steinmetz, M. Walsh, L. L. Gabel, and P. T. Williams, "Family Physicians' Involvement with Dying Patients and Their Families: Attitudes, Difficulties, and Strategies," *Archives of Family Medicine* 2 (1993): 753.

12. M. Battin, "Voluntary Euthanasia and the Risks of Abuse: Can We Learn Anything from the Netherlands?" *Law, Medicine, and Healthcare* 20, no. 1–2 (Spring–Summer 1992): 133; J. Davies, "Altruism Towards the End of Life," *Journal of Medical Ethics* 19 (1993): 111.

13. T. Quill, C. K. Cassel, and D. E. Meier, "Care of the Hopelessly Ill: Proposed Clinical Criteria for Physician-Assisted Suicide," *New England Journal of Medicine* 327 (1992): 1380; H. Brody, "Assisted Death: A Compassionate Response to a Medical Failure," *New England Journal of Medicine* 327 (1992): 1384; T. E. Quill, *Death and Dignity: Making Choices and Taking Charge* (New York: W.W. Norton, 1993).

14. T. Quill, "Doctor, I Want to Die, Will You Help Me?" *Journal of the American Medical Association* 270 (1993): 870.

15. E. J. Cassel, "The Nature of Suffering and the Goals of Medicine," *New England Journal of Medicine* 306 (1982): 639; E. J. Cassel, *The Nature of Suffering and the Goals of Medicine* (New York: Oxford University Press, 1991).

16. S. Miles, "Physicians and Their Patients' Suicides," *Journal of the American Medical Association* 27 (1994): 1786.

17. M. Battin, "Voluntary Euthanasia and the Risks of Abuse"; Quill, Cassel, and Meier, "Care of the Hopelessly Ill"; F. Miller, T. E. Quill, H. Brody, J. C. Fletcher, L. O. Gostin, and D. E. Meier, "Regulating Physician-Assisted Death," *New England Journal of Medicine* 331, no. 2 (1994): 119; R. F. Weir, "The Morality of Physician-Assisted Suicide," *Law, Medicine, and Healthcare* 20, no. 1–2 (Spring-Summer 1992): 116.

18. Quill, Cassel, and Meier, "Care of the Hopelessly Ill"; Miller, Quill, Brody, et al., "Regulating Physician-Assisted Death."

19. C. S. Campbell, "'Aid-in-Dying' and the Taking of Human Life," *Journal of Medical Ethics* 18 (1992): 128.

20. D. Callahan and M. White, "The Legalization of Physician-Assisted Suicide: Creating a Regulatory Potemkin Village," *University of Richmond Law Review* 30 (1996): 1–83.

21. G. Van de Wal, J. T. van Eijk, H. J. Leenan, and C. Spreeuwenberg, "Euthanasia and Assisted Suicide, I: How Often Is It Practiced by Family Doctors in the Netherlands?" *Family Practice* 9 (1992): 135–140; Academy of Hospice Physicians, *Position Statement*

(Gainesville, FL: Academy of Hospice Physicians, 1988); National Hospice Organization, *Statement Opposing the Legalization of Euthanasia and Assisted Suicide* (Arlington, VA: National Hospice Organization, 1989).

22. Quill, Cassel, and Meier, "Care of the Hopelessly Ill"; Miller, Quill, Brody, et al., "Regulating Physician-Assisted Death"; G. Van der Wal and R. J. Dillmann, "Euthanasia in the Netherlands," *British Medical Journal* 308 (May 1994): 1346; Van der Wal, van Eijk, Leenan, and Spreeuwenberg, "Euthanasia and Assisted Suicide, I" and "Euthanasia and Assisted Suicide, II: Do Dutch Family Doctors Act Prudently?"

23. W. Gaylin, L. R. Kass, E. D. Pellegrino, and M. Siegler, "Doctors Must Not Kill," *Journal of the American Medical Association* 259 (1998): 2139; L. R. Kass, "Neither for Love Nor Money: Why Doctors Must Not Kill," *The Public Interest* 94 (Winter 1989): 25.

24. C. S. Campbell, J. Hare, and P. Matthews, "Conflicts of Conscience: Hospice and Assisted Suicide," *Hastings Center Report* 25 (1995): 36; A. Haddad, "'Physician-Assisted Suicide: The Impact on Nursing and Pharmacy," *Of Value* (Society for Health and Human Values Newsletter), December 1994; M. T. Rupp and H. L. Isenhower, "Pharmacists' Attitudes Toward Physician-Assisted Suicide," *American Journal of Hospital Pharmacy* 51 (1994): 69; A. Young and D. Volker, "Oncology Nurses' Attitudes Regarding Voluntary, Physician-Assisted Dying for Competent, Terminally Ill Patients," *Oncology Nurse Forum* 20 (1993): 445; S. Kowalski, "Assisted Suicide: Where Do Nurses Draw the Line?" *Nurse Health Care* 14 (1993): 70.

25. F. G. Miller and H. Brody, "Professional Integrity and Physician-Assisted Death," *Hastings Center Report* 25 (1995): 8.

26. California Proposition 161; Capron and Michel, "Be Sure to Read the Fine Print"; D. Callahan, "Aid in Dying: The Social Dimensions," *Commonweal*, August 9, 1991, 476–480.

27. *Vacco v. Quill*, 521 U.S. 793 (1997).

28. "Pain Management: Theological and Ethical Principles Governing the Use of Pain Relief for Dying Patients," *Health Progress* (January/February 1993): 30; Ferrel and Rhiner, "High-Tech Comfort"; Management of Cancer Pain Guidelines Panel, *Management of Cancer Pain*, Clinical Practice Guidelines no. 9 (Rockville, MD: Agency for Health Care Policy and Research, 1994).

29. Quill, Cassel, and Meier, "Care of the Hopelessly Ill."

30. Callahan, "Pursuing a Peaceful Death."

31. Ibid.

32. Ibid., 33.

Critical Issues for Healthcare Organizations

Part III contains information about major changes in the healthcare system and begins to analyze the ethical conundrums these changes can create. Chapter 13 presents a discussion of the differences between ethical issues in a clinical situation and those faced by an organization. This chapter's information will become increasingly important as the changes created by major healthcare reform (i.e., the Patient Protection and Affordable Care Act of 2010, or PPACA) affect healthcare practice. The chapter also shows how organizations must address clinical situations, legislation, and community responsibility and still make money. The author challenges you to think beyond the clinical arena and to consider the broader view held by institutional ethics.

Chapter 14 includes an overview of the institution's response to ethical challenges—the hospital ethics committee (HEC). It gives an update on the function, membership, and future challenges for these committees. The practitioner's view section gives up-to-the-minute examples of issues that HECs face, including having funding connected to patient satisfaction data and the impending influx of the aging baby boomer population.

Chapter 15 examines current and future ethical dilemmas for specific types of healthcare organizations—those that deal with prehospital and emergency care. The chapter suggests that emergency departments (EDs) are struggling to be the safety net for the poor, and that they may continue to struggle even under the PPACA. It acquaints the reader with areas such as paternalism, assisted suicides and emergency room practices, and prehospital do-not-resuscitate (DNR) orders. In addition, the chapter introduces topics that pose unique ethical concerns, such as the need for security for those who work in the ED, the practice of teaching on the newly dead, and the ability to conduct research on critical patients.

Chapter 16 is new to this edition and examines the issues related to medical and information technology and their ethical concerns. Since these technologies dominate practice and fiscal areas in a clinic or hospital setting, this topic is particularly interesting. It includes practical examples of the impact of technology and an analysis of its ethical impact using theory and principles.

Chapter 17 asks the question, What is the role of spirituality in a healthcare organization? Given the whitewater change of PPACA, the issue of spirituality is even more important. This updated chapter connects evidence-based medicine to spirituality and explores why spirituality is important in patient care. It also examines the issue of the relationship between spirituality and the health of healthcare organizations and their employees. An analysis of how ethical theories and principles support spirituality in the healthcare organization is also included.

Part III provides examples of issues that organizations are facing, and will face, as they move through the 21st century. It is also an overview of some of the quandaries faced by specific healthcare organizations, such as home health organizations and the emergency department. In this part of the text, you will need to "think outside of the clinical box" and consider ethics from the organization's view.

CHAPTER 13

Healthcare Institutional Ethics: Broader Than Clinical Ethics

Carrie S. Zoubul

INTRODUCTION

Ethical issues involving healthcare organizations happen at the individual, institutional, and even societal level. For example, individual managers and employees must determine how to act with ethical integrity. Ethical issues also relate to the struggle that institutions face, particularly nonprofit institutions, as they try to provide necessary care (including charity care) to their communities while ensuring that they remain fiscally secure. Finally, the conflicting expectations and demands that American society places upon the healthcare system need to be better understood by healthcare professionals and society in general. Of course, clinical issues also play a major role in the ethics of a healthcare organization.

The development of mechanisms to address bioethical questions, particularly those that arise during the course of clinical care, has dominated much of the ethics-related activity of hospitals and other healthcare institutions for the past 35 years. Clinical issues, such as the termination of treatment, patient autonomy, informed consent, confidentiality, advance directives, and other individual case-based dilemmas, have received much of the attention. However, in the late 1980s and early 1990s, the scope of bioethics began to broaden. With the onset of rapid change in the structure of the healthcare delivery system, many institutions began to recognize and address ethical issues raised by business practices, corporate activity, and managed care. Accordingly, this recognition raised questions about how to expand bioethical inquiry to address institutional structure and the business aspects of health care.

As the healthcare system became increasingly complex, focus on the ethics of clinical and business matters at the institutional level eventually began to give way to network concerns. Networks comprising institutions, physician organizations, financing mechanisms, and other health businesses began to emerge. This change resulted in new and organizationally complex ethical dilemmas that demanded different analytical frameworks and ethical analysis.

In the bioethics literature, this area of inquiry has become known as *organizational ethics*, applicable to both individual healthcare institutions (e.g., hospitals) and to the other entities that make up the modern healthcare system.[1] Several definitions of organizational ethics exist. Some examples include the following: it "aims to enhance the overall ethics of an organization with the goal of changing the climate and then the culture of the organization;"[2] it "deals with an organization's positions and behavior relative to individuals (including patients, providers, and employees), groups, communities served by the organization, and other organizations;"[3] it is "the intentional use of values to guide the decisions of a system;"[4] and it "focuses on the ethical climate of the entire organization . . . which encompasses and integrates all other ethics resources and activities within an organization."⁵

Today, healthcare networks and their member institutions constitute complex, interdependent systems composed of patients, families, professionals, payers, businesses, and communities. These multiple players interact in intricate ways. An organization's daily activities, missions, institutional values, and strategic goals and its impact on society and the community's health status are ethically significant. The bioethical principles of autonomy, beneficence, nonmaleficence, and justice as traditionally formulated may not be sufficient to analyze the related ethical issues that arise. Although these principles have their place, additional notions of justice, social responsibility, and institutional integrity come into play. Furthermore, the principles of business ethics, such as "honesty, truthfulness, and keeping promises"⁶ may also inform the discussion. The questions of organizational ethics often require different considerations and analytical frameworks, as well as additional substantive knowledge to address them appropriately.

Because patient care is still the focus of much of an institution's activity, the need to address clinical bioethical issues remains a necessity. However, this chapter focuses on the ethical issues that healthcare network and institutional administrators, managers, and sometimes trustees need to address from an individual, institutional, and societal perspective. These include justice issues (social, distributive, and commutative), the promotion of the common good, the role of the healthcare system in the community, preservation and support of the workforce, the definition of health, the role of law and government regulation, promoting access to quality health care, management of conflicts of interest, and the allocation of resources, to name a few.

This chapter does not outline a comprehensive theory of justice, argue for a process of allocating or rationing resources, define the concept of health, or advocate for a certain approach to these challenges. Rather, it attempts to outline important considerations, describe potential ethical issues and value conflicts that arise in healthcare institutions and networks at the organizational level, and discuss various principles and frameworks that may be useful in addressing these concerns.

Healthcare organizations play an important public role in their communities, providing medical care, medical education, and significant employment opportunities. Trustees, administrators, and managers confront ethical issues that involve not only clinical matters but also corporate and institutional structure, mission and strategic direction, commitment to their workforce, and the public nature of health care.

MOVING FROM A CLINICAL FOCUS TO INCORPORATE ORGANIZATIONAL CONCERNS

For many years, there has been an expectation that healthcare institutions should be attentive to clinical ethical issues that arise in the context of patient care. Some of the expectations related to patient care are embodied in laws and regulations, for example, the Patient Self-Determination Act, required education for Medicaid recipients, organ donation request laws, EMTALA (the "anti-patient-dumping" statute), HIPAA (the privacy rule), the Patients' Bill of Rights, and laws and regulations governing human subjects research. However, independent accreditation bodies also play a role in defining the requirements for an institution's ethics activities.

In 1995, The Joint Commission (formerly known as the Joint Commission on Accreditation of Healthcare Organizations, or JCAHO) introduced a new accreditation standard in the "Patient Rights and Organizational Ethics" chapter of its accreditation manual, requiring hospitals to "operate according to a code of ethical behavior."[7] In addition to developing processes that provide patients (or their representatives) access to a procedural mechanism designed to address ethical questions and concerns that arise in clinical care, a hospital must address business ethics concerns, including the marketing, billing, admission, transfer, and discharge practices of the hospital and its relationship to "other healthcare providers, educational institutions, and providers."[8] With this standard, The Joint Commission expects hospitals to approach these issues in an ethical manner that reflects their moral responsibility to patients and the community they serve.[9] Soon after, the first edition of standards promulgated by the American Society for Bioethics and Humanities (ASBH) Task Force on Standards for Bioethics Consultation acknowledged the growing importance of organizational ethics issues and the need to develop institutional capabilities to address these issues as part of its ethics consultation service or ethics infrastructure.[10]

A flurry of scholarship in the bioethics literature followed these developments to address the emergence of organizational ethics, including special journal issues, conferences and symposia, and books on the topic.[11] Professional societies also weighed in. For example, the American Medical Association's Institute for Ethics formed an organizational ethics working group,[12] and the American College of Healthcare Executives created a code of ethics setting forth standards to guide the conduct of executives.[13] The discussions focus on questions of what the concept of organizational ethics means for healthcare institutions and how its principles can be successfully implemented and sustained.[14]

The following questions were raised in these discussions: Are business ethics and healthcare ethics compatible?[15] Can healthcare organizations or corporations be considered morally responsible for their actions?[16] Who will do the work—the existing ethics committee, a subcommittee of the ethics committee, a risk management committee, or a new committee or entity focused solely on organizational issues? What additional education or expertise will ethics consultants need to address ethics on the organizational level? What are the differences and similarities between clinical ethics and organizational ethics consultations?[17] What process should be used to address organizational issues?[18] How can an organization build an "ethical culture," and how will the program thrive? How do you ethically negotiate the tension between patient needs and the institution's financial viability?

INTERFACE BETWEEN CLINICAL AND ORGANIZATIONAL ETHICS

Clinical ethics has emerged as a robust and integral aspect of patient care in many institutions. Typically, an institutional ethics committee provides some variation on three services: (1) individual case consultation,

(2) ethics education, and (3) policy formation and analysis. When issues arise in the clinical context, they are often dealt with through traditional ethical principles such as autonomy, beneficence, nonmaleficence, and justice.[19]

Sometimes, a dilemma that arises in the course of patient care is indicative of a broader issue with organizational implications. For example, defining the limits of the principles of autonomy and beneficence might lead health-care institutions to confront ethical issues that reach beyond the clinical setting (e.g., the limits of the institutional or professional obligation to treat a patient who requests "everything"). Therefore, clinical issues may often wind up involving questions of community need,[20] accreditation and government regulation,[21] and organizational structure.[22]

The second edition of the ASBH *Core Competencies for Health Care Ethics Consultation* does not distinguish between clinical and organizational ethics, and instead considers them overlapping "subspecialties" of the broader category of "health care ethics."[23] It lists a number of scenarios to illustrate how the subspecialties might overlap, for instance, "[i]nstitutions eliminating healthcare services that are not sufficiently cost-effective for the institution, but which may be of clinical value (clinical, organizational, and business ethics)."[24] Finding that there is no definite line between clinical and organiza-tional issues, cases with elements of both were described as "hybrids" in one recent article.[25]

Just as new clinical ethical issues arise as medicine and technology continue to develop, so too novel organizational challenges will present themselves as new financial structures emerge that more intimately link hospitals and providers to financial concerns. These issues raise questions as to their effects on the provision of appropriate, quality medical care and their impact on the provider–patient relationship. Related inquiries to consider include the nature of advocacy in the provider–patient relationship,[26] whether physicians are subject to outside influences that might affect care decisions,[27] the potential for financial conflicts of interest,[28] challenges to the traditional fiduciary nature of the physician–patient relationship,[29] and the provision of preventive or primary healthcare services to the community for which the institution might not be reimbursed.

Business ethics theories have been adapted and applied in the healthcare arena. For example, *stakeholder theory*, defined as "an approach to business ethics that takes into account the rights and interests of the broad range of individuals and organizations who interact with it and are affected by business decision making,"[30] is an example of a business ethics theory that has been applied in the healthcare arena. The stakeholders, including but not limited to patients, families, providers, and the community, must be identified and their interests accounted for by the organization.[31]

However, incorporating such principles of business ethics into an existing healthcare ethics program implies expertise in an area not traditionally represented on ethics committees. Effectively addressing organizational issues will often require additional considerations, and in some cases a different skill set or knowledge base.[32] Although some authors suggest that one should view organizational ethics as an additional task for the ethics committee, they recognize that new members must be added or existing members must receive additional training.[33] Clinical ethicists have also acknowledged the gaps in their expertise when it comes to addressing organizational concerns.[34]

Approaches to handling these issues vary from one institution or organization to the next. For example, one institution reports that it restructured its ethics committee to focus primarily on organizational ethics, creating a clinical ethics consultation service that is distinct from the committee to handle clinical matters.[35] Another suggested approach is designating an ethics "mission leader," modeled after a role often utilized in faith-based hospitals, who would draw upon the ethics committee and other resources within an institution to effectuate organizational ethics goals.[36] A health insurance company formed an "ethics advisory group" with representation from a diverse cross section of its stakeholders that provides a consultative service to answer organizational questions brought before it.[37] To many, the goal of an organizational ethics initiative should be to arrive at a system of "integrated ethics," one that combines clinical, organizational, and community goals.[38]

Achieving consensus when addressing organizational concerns—the group of issues that involve an institution's or network's sense of justice, concept of health, or definition of social accountability—is certainly a challenge. However, attention to these issues should lead to better design and implementation of healthcare services that are patient focused and morally sound.

HUMAN RESOURCES AND THE INSTITUTIONAL CLIMATE

Usually there is consensus about an organization's ethical commitment to its human resources. A healthcare organization's greatest resource is its employees, and many would agree that inappropriate or unethical treatment of the workforce could lead to a collapse of the institution's mission and its ability to serve the public. The modern healthcare environment can be extremely challenging for its human resources, as aptly described by a nurse-administrator in a discussion of organizational ethics: "[It] is battered by a perfect storm of revenue production, expense control, regulatory oversight, consumer expectations, and the everyday challenges of providing efficient and effective care."[39]

To address workplace challenges, a list of ethical principles and rules could be developed that, prima facie, seem to be normative. These include treating people as an end, not as a means; providing fair compensation; not being deceitful or manipulative; and instituting mechanisms for participatory decision making and consensus building. They also include ensuring that personnel policies are just and nondiscriminatory, treating employees with dignity and respect, implementing fair disciplinary policies, and protecting against physical or sexual harassment in the workplace.

Surveys of human resources professionals reveal an empirical basis for this normative agreement about what is ethical in the workplace.[40] However, this normative agreement does not necessarily ensure that all people in the workplace act ethically. The temptation might be to dismiss unethical practices as the aberrant behaviors of certain managers or employees, but the root cause might lie in the culture of the organization or its inability to address or control the unethical practices of its employees.

Employees of healthcare organizations have diverse professional back-grounds (e.g., medicine, nursing, social work, administrators), and each individual has a personal sense of what is just or moral, in addition to those values identified in the workplace. Because of these varied perspectives, organizations must focus on building a strong "ethical climate" by identifying core values and beliefs that are visible to both patients and staff, who can then abide by them and expect the organization to live up to them.[41] Hospital staff might also benefit from educational programs that focus on organizational ethics, helping them to learn to identify issues as they present themselves on the job.[42] A review of empirical research exploring management issues found that the creation of an ethical climate is feasible from a management perspective, and concluded that it improves patient care and promotes orga-nizational success.[43] Another review of research studying healthcare worker "burnout" suggests that contributing factors such as "incongruence of values" and "moral strain" occur when providers feel that their personal values do not align with the institution or organization in which they work.[44]

Workers must be provided with organizational support to ensure that they feel comfortable expressing ethical concerns and are able to assert their rights and act on their values. One way to accomplish this is to provide protection for whistle-blowing actions in the workplace.[45] If the organization does not provide protection, employees who witness unethical behavior will be less likely to come forward for fear of retaliation, and, if they do come forward, they may suffer negative consequences for speaking up.[46] It has been proposed that the notion of "psychological safety," which "means that providers are not afraid to speak up to improve work processes or call attention to a potentially dangerous situation," plays an important role in the engagement and commitment of the healthcare workforce.[47] Administrators and managers need to make a commit-ment to the preservation of employee rights and to the inclusion of workers in the process of creating, nurturing, and sustaining the workplace environment.

Trustees or administrators who establish ethical parameters for personnel policies and the managers who implement these policies must think about the factors that contribute to unethical behavior. Furthermore, in order to create an ethical climate they must carefully consider the content of policy manuals, the design of disciplinary procedures, the organization's mission and strategic goals, and other activities that reflect the ethical commitment of the organization. This attention to ethical matters in personnel policies has to be deliberate, ongoing, and public.

Emerging healthcare networks raise additional concerns. Key among them is a potential for change in an institution's commitment to its workforce. In today's healthcare climate, the ethical question is not necessarily about employee loyalty, but rather about an organization's commitment to its human resources that enables workers to learn new skills and respond to rapidly changing work environments. Conversely, employees need to be open to change and be willing to learn and take on new challenges.

Those authors who focus on the question of work, including management-science authors, describe a number of additional "normative" principles that help to create a meaningful work environment, including the principle of *subsidiarity*. Decisions should be made at the level where they have the most impact and involve the owners of work processes. Subsidiarity also includes the principle that decisions, whenever possible, should be based on consensus. This suggests that people who work together, examine the root causes of problems, and seek functional and cross-functional solutions are likely to find effective solutions and to create a respectful work environment.

Involving the healthcare workforce in organizational decision making, particularly with respect to decisions that will directly affect them, is imperative to maintaining a positive workplace climate. Healthcare organizations rely in large part upon physicians and other caregivers to fulfill their mission.[48] Giving caregivers a voice will help them to feel valued, as well as give them a sense of ownership and control over organizational decisions. A study examining the perceptions of healthcare administrators, providers, and ethicists with diverse professional backgrounds found that there is room for improvement in this area: whereas administrators reported that they recognized the value of stakeholder input, the clinicians surveyed did not feel that they had significant influence in organizational decision making with respect to resource allocation.[49]

Finally, although perhaps not purely an ethical commitment, managers need to think about what management style, technique, or process best helps to build a positive and respectful work environment. Furthermore, high-level management must be supportive of creating and affecting the ethical climate of the workplace.[50] It is imperative that the highest levels of administration be committed to organizational ethics for such an effort to succeed.[51] Institutional commitment and management style should be seen as a means to achieve an ethical end—a workplace where employees are respected, are able to assert their rights, and are comfortable expressing their own moral views if they conflict with the practices or policies of the organization.

ORGANIZATIONAL IDENTITY AND STRATEGIC DIRECTION

Another area for ethical reflection for trustees and managers is the mission of the healthcare organization and the means it uses to accomplish this mission. In the late 1980s and early 1990s, issues related to organizational mission came to the forefront when many healthcare institutions saw their nonprofit tax status challenged in state and federal courts.[52] The issue was heightened when proprietary organizations, such as Columbia/HCA, questioned the tax status of community nonprofit organizations. The role of the board in the governance of nonprofit organizations has been the subject of increased scrutiny from the Internal Revenue Service, the United States Congress, and other entities.[53]

What are the ethical duties owed by a healthcare institution to the community it serves? Potter suggests that the incorporation of organizational and community bioethics "will be a time to recover the social responsibility of healthcare institutions."[54] In part, this responsibility arises out of the commitment to meeting the needs of the community. Ideally, managers lead healthcare organizations in an analysis of community needs and develop and design their strategic directions to meet these needs.

For the purposes of this part of the discussion, the focus will be on nonprofit (voluntary) healthcare organizations. Nonprofit institutions must be financially sound, act as appropriate stewards of resources, and generate excess revenues over expenses. Questions about whether an administrator or manager behaves as a responsible steward of these resources or whether the organization acts justly in the "business community" are questions of business ethics. The more specific question here is, what are the organizational ethics concerns of nonprofit healthcare institutions as they provide goods and services to the community?

Paul Starr and Rosemary Stevens each trace the growth of the voluntary healthcare sector.[55] According to Stevens's analysis, this growth involved a shift from voluntary hospitals, whose purpose was to mobilize local resources, to a range of disparate institutions that successfully fought government intervention and organized medicine. By the late 1930s, voluntary hospitals exemplified (in ideal cases) "public responsibility without government compulsion" and "private initiatives untainted by selfish gain."[56]

In time, nonprofit institutions lost touch with the principles of that earlier era. Medicine became increasingly more organized, healthcare institutions became more dependent on federal and state funding, and the government had an increasingly larger role in designing healthcare financing and delivery systems. This was especially evident with the growth of Medicare and Medicaid. Healthcare institutions adjusted their practices to survive and grow in the new environment. As a result, some people looking at health care began to see big business rather than public charitable corporations. The focus has changed again as care has shifted from traditional nonprofit hospitals to community-wide networks that include, for example, proprietary insurance companies and physician networks with equity incentives. The values of the "health system," as described by Stevens and Starr, seem to be long gone.

Municipalities, pressed for tax dollars to maintain other community services, began to question the appropriateness of the tax status of healthcare institutions and emerging networks in light of the amount of "charity" care and community benefit they provide. It has been argued that if things have changed so much, and if the organizations look more like businesses, then perhaps they should pay the same taxes and municipal fees that for-profit enterprises are required to pay. Critical focus on the tax-exempt status of nonprofit healthcare organizations and the provision of charity care has only grown over the last several years. However, an empirical analysis comparing the provision of services by for-profit and nonprofit healthcare organizations found that, comparatively, nonprofit hospitals provide more "private and public goods in the public interest" and that the focus on tax exemption is misplaced because it does not constitute a large percentage of overall public spending.[57]

Complicating this issue, U.S. society has sometimes-conflicting expectations and demands regarding its healthcare institutions. On the one hand, communities expect that healthcare institutions will (1) be close to home; (2) be equipped with the latest technology; (3) abound in expertise; (4) be efficient, high-quality, full-service providers; (5) take care of the poor and uninsured; (6) not be concerned about insurance or payment arrangements; and (7) not be prohibitively expensive. Communities expect that the costs of providing these services will be covered by income derived from the overall activities of the institutions, free from overdependence on public money, and that services should be provided as needed, without addressing questions of the national healthcare budget or allocating resources.

On the other hand, the community also expects that healthcare institutions should (1) not be involved in projects that raise money through non-health-related activities (except for philanthropic fund-raising), (2) be wary of joint ventures and other business practices, and (3) compete openly in the marketplace while not looking like a business. Society balks at the notion that hospitals and other healthcare organizations concern themselves with generating profit at the expense of other considerations. These divergent expectations are also fostered by current law and social policy, which sometimes place inconsistent demands on healthcare organizations.[58]

This is not to suggest that there are not appropriate limits to a nonprofit institution's use of excess revenue, capitalization of proprietary projects, inurement, or executive compensation. However, at the root of these issues are questions about whether healthcare services are public or private goods, whether competition and the marketplace help or hinder the provision of these goods, and how many tiers of healthcare services society really wants.

No clear policy will resolve every issue. Whether or not our society successfully establishes an inclusive national healthcare plan, managers and trustees of voluntary institutions must do their best to create institutions that respond to the needs of the communities they serve. Strategies may differ depending on applicable laws, regulations, and court decisions. Managers and trustees need to develop strategic directions that guide their institutions through the regulatory maze and fiscal challenges while simultaneously meeting the needs of as many people as possible. This is not only sound business strategy but also an ethical imperative if one understands health care as a social good. A recent article makes an argument in support of the ethical imperative that the board members of tax-exempt organizations oversee community-benefit activity as part of their responsibilities, toward the goal of strengthening organizational integrity.[59]

The ethical components of institutional strategy are definitional and procedural. Definitional concerns include defining health. What is health? Should the definition focus on the individual, or should it have a broader community (public health) perspective? What are the goals for which the organization is aiming? Which services benefit individual patients, and which address community health? Increasingly, health benefits are measured in terms of both community and individual gain. Consequently, preventive services, community education programs, primary health care, outreach and advocacy programs, and other activities become part of the institution's mission in the community.[60]

An example of a procedural aspect of strategy is the method by which managers define the process of the allocation of available healthcare resources. Although there may be no ascertainable national healthcare budget to frame spending, each institution or organization has a general sense of an "annual total budget" available to it through implementation of the strategic and financial planning process, its cash reserves, its charitable funds, and its debt capacity. After determining the health needs of the community, managers must allocate the human and fiscal resources necessary to meet these needs. If all health needs cannot be met, the institution must then make decisions about which services it will provide based on the resources available to it.

Therefore, the institution must devise a procedure for allocating resources—
which may entail the denial of possibly beneficial resources to some or all
people—that is publicly defensible, socially accountable, quantitative, and
clear.[61] The procedure for resource allocation is not necessarily clearly defined
or consistent, which has been acknowledged by both managers and clinicians.[62]
Furthermore, transparency in decision making is crucial to the cultivation
of the public trust, particularly with respect to decisions about how and
whether to provide certain services. However, allocation decisions often are
not publicly understood or acknowledged (although one can consider managed
care organizations a very public form of rationing).[63] Society often perceives
managed care rationing as a "denial" of treatment of healthcare consumers,
consequently weakening public confidence and trust in the healthcare system.
In the hospital setting it is an uncomfortable reality, but failure to allocate
care appropriately can lead an institution into fiscal difficulty when services
are provided beyond its resources or without full reimbursement.

Other procedural concerns include ensuring that trustees, administrators,
and managers exhibit integrity[64] and behave ethically. For example, financial
managers must be honest and establish mechanisms that are not illegal or
unscrupulous. Planners must honestly assess the needs of the community
when developing healthcare services and match available financial resources
with the institution's commitment to serve that community. Operations
personnel must make decisions about services and personnel that are aligned
with strategic directions and goals, and the chief executive officer must integrate these activities within the institution and, when necessary, revise them
accordingly as he or she discharges her duties.

THE PUBLIC NATURE OF THE CORPORATION

A healthcare organization's commitment to service is a public statement.
Such a statement is ethically significant because of its contribution to the
community. Trustees and executives must ask basic questions such as "How
will this network or institution make a difference in the future to the community
that it serves?" The fiduciary responsibility of trustees can also be backward-
looking by asking "What was the financial performance of the organization last
month (or last year)?"or "How many goals were achieved last year?" However,
their ethical responsibility is mainly forward-looking, by asking "How will this
organization make a difference in the world tomorrow?" The work of the board
is to plan how the ethical obligations of the organization will be met.[65]

Creating tomorrow's vision demands ethical sensitivity to the public
nature and service orientation of the organization. Generally, this includes
a special concern for vulnerable populations such as the uninsured and the
socioeconomically disadvantaged. The managers and trustees should respond
to community, state, or national demands for social justice, consider the social
determinants of health, work to ameliorate factors that contribute to poor
health, and use their considerable financial and institutional power to help
shape the community's future. These ethical concerns often are addressed
through community networking, by building partnerships between community entities (businesses, educators, etc.), as well as by working with public

and elected officials to promote positive changes that will improve the health status of the community.

The preferential tax treatment of most healthcare organizations, their role in society and the public trust it engenders, and their service mission obligate trustees and managers to work for the public good. At times, this obligation requires an institution to challenge the medicalization of social problems and help eradicate the social determinants of poor health. For example, an organization might take on the causes of lead poisoning (poor housing conditions); the prevalence of malnutrition; the abusive treatment of children, the elderly, and other vulnerable populations; or barriers to access to healthcare services and insurance. If healthcare organizational leadership helps to confront and address these issues, patients will benefit, and the health status of the community will likely benefit from these efforts.

Often, healthcare organizations, whether alone in smaller communities or in groups in larger communities, constitute a leading economic and political force. Leveraging an institution's powerful economic position for community gain should be an ethical requirement flowing from the mission of the institution. A community's trust in and dependence on healthcare institutions, organizations, or networks gives tremendous ethical power to trustees and managers.

The ethical commitment to the common good has implications for other institutional practices as well. For example, why would a healthcare institution not be sensitive to environmental issues? Environmental awareness will lead institutions to consider more closely the appropriate disposal of their wastes and toxins and promote the use of environmentally friendly products. Another example of an area in which many institutions and organizations are taking steps with the common good in mind is disaster preparedness—for instance, attempting to proactively tackle the difficult question of how to provide care in an ethical manner under extreme circumstances such as an influenza pandemic.[66]

Healthcare organizations also need to be self-critical when making strategic decisions. When deciding where to place the newest facility or clinic, they need to consider how a proposed location might affect access to care for the poor and uninsured or contribute to the geographic isolation of the sick. Regarding advocacy, what policies or regulations should institutions promote to increase access, equitable reimbursement, and community support? Sometimes it may seem that there is a tendency for healthcare organizations to advocate for policies that will ensure their own continued existence, rather than those that benefit patients or the community. With ever-increasing external stresses on the healthcare system, one ethical concern for tomorrow is whether healthcare institutions can or will advocate effectively for positive changes that are compatible with patient needs. For example, can there be a redistribution of public dollar commitments to address preventive health needs and decrease institutional and technological use? What social structure improvements will prevent illness and increase the health status of the community? Because healthcare services will always be necessary, healthcare provider organizations will continue to grapple with these issues. There will always be a need for healthcare institutions, and it may be that the most equitable healthcare structure has yet to be identified and will consist of a new and different alignment of institutions, payers, and providers.

CONCLUSION

Healthcare institutions, organizations, and networks are powerful forces in public and political life. The ethical concerns generated by the provision of health care do not end with those that arise in the clinical context, and they are still being defined. Administrators, managers, and trustees of healthcare organizations, if faithful to their mission, identity, and public commitment, must systematically address their role in promoting public welfare and healthy living, protecting employees, influencing the politics and economics of the community, and helping to develop a just public order. Trustees and managers should focus on distinct, but complementary, objectives to achieve these general goals. To accomplish this, there must be ongoing efforts to develop a deliberate and systematic approach to address, implement, and monitor the ethical commitments of healthcare organizations.

SUMMARY

Issues in healthcare ethics are not restricted to those that arise in clinical situations; they are also increasingly difficult for the institutions and organizations that address healthcare needs. This chapter presented some of the areas of concern for these institutions and systems, including their role in clinical concerns, issues surrounding personnel, and the creation of an ethical organizational climate. Because of healthcare organizations' unique mission, a discussion concerning organizational identity and obligation to the community was included. Finally, one should remember the need to be aware of these ethical issues and to continue to address them, now and in the future.

QUESTIONS FOR DISCUSSION

1. Why do you think there has been an interest in ethics with respect to the institutional aspects of healthcare by organizations such as The Joint Commission and others?

2. What is the role of the administrator, manager, or trustee in institutional ethics?

3. Why are healthcare businesses interested in being proactive in meeting the community's healthcare needs?

4. Why do you think Americans seem to have conflicting expectations of the healthcare system?

5. What ethical principles would be most important to institutions as they consider their ethics actions in the future?

FOOD FOR THOUGHT

This chapter provides an excellent overview of the ethical concerns for institutions of health care. Now that you have this overview, do some research and identify at least four ethical issues that may exist for your local hospital or clinic. Are they similar to those discussed in this chapter? What is your role in addressing these issues?

NOTES

1. R. L. Potter, "On Our Way to Integrated Bioethics: Clinical, Organizational, Communal," *Journal of Clinical Ethics* 10, no. 3 (Fall 1999): 171–177.

2. C. F. Thurber, "Assessing Quality in HCO's: A Paradigm for Organizational Ethics," *HEC Forum* 11, no. 4 (1999): 358–363.

3. R. M. Arnold, et al., "Society for Health and Human Values–Society for Bioethics Consultation, Task Force on Standards for Bioethics Consultation," in *Core Competencies for Health Care Ethics Consultation: The Report of the American Society for Bioethics and Humanities* (Glenview, IL: American Society for Bioethics and Humanities, 1998): 24.

4. R. L. Potter, "From Clinical Ethics to Organizational Ethics: The Second Stage of the Evolution of Bioethics," *Bioethics Forum* 12, no. 2 (1996): 3–26.

5. E. Spencer and A. Mills, "Ethics in Healthcare Organizations," *HEC Forum* 11, no. 4 (1999): 323–332.

6. W. Mariner, "Business versus Medical Ethics: Conflicting Standards for Managed Care," *Journal of Law, Medicine and Ethics* 23 (1995): 236–246.

7. Joint Commission on Accreditation of Healthcare Organizations, *Accreditation Manual for Hospitals*, vol. 1 (Oakbrook Terrace, IL: Joint Commission on Accreditation of Healthcare Organizations, 1996), 44–45.

8. Ibid.

9. Ibid.

10. Arnold et al., "Society for Health and Human Values," 24–26.

11. See, for example, *Bioethics Forum* 12, no. 2 (Summer 1996); *HEC Forum* 10, no. 2 (June 1998): 127–229 (the *HEC Forum* regularly features articles in a special section covering organizational ethics); *Journal of Clinical Ethics* 10, no. 3 (Fall 1999); and *Cambridge Quarterly of Healthcare Ethics* 9, no. 2 (Spring 2000): 145–298 (the papers in this issue were generated at a 1998 conference on healthcare organizational ethics, sponsored by the University of Virginia's Center for Biomedical Ethics and the Olson Center for Applied Ethics at the business school). For a comprehensive introduction and literature review, see J. Bishop, et al., *Organizational Ethics and Healthcare: Expanding Bioethics into the Institutional Arena*, Scope Note 36 (Washington, DC: Kennedy Institute of Ethics, 1999), available at http://bioethics.georgetown.edu/publications/scopenotes/sn36.pdf. Accessed June 13, 2012. For books on the topic, see P. J. Boyle, et al., *Organizational Ethics in Healthcare: Principles, Cases, and Practical Solutions* (San Francisco, CA; Jossey-Bass, 2001); R. T. Hall, *An Introduction to Healthcare Organizational Ethics* (New York: Oxford University Press, 2000); M. L. Pava and P. Primeaux, eds., *Symposium on Health Care Ethics*, vol. 2, *Research in Ethical Issues in Organizations* (Cambridge, MA: Emerald Group Publishing, 2000); E. M. Spencer, et al., *Organization Ethics in Health Care* (New York: Oxford University Press, 2000); J. Blustein, L. Farber Post, and N. Dubler, *Ethics for Health Care Organizations: Theory, Case Studies, and Tools* (New York: United Hospital Fund, 2002); S. D. Pearson, et al., *No Margin, No Mission: Health Care Organizations and the Quest for Ethical Excellence* (New York: Oxford University Press, 2003); A. S. Iltis, *Institutional Integrity in Health Care* (New York: Springer, 2003); E. E. Morrison, *Ethics in Health Administration: A Practical Approach for Decision-Makers*, 2nd ed. (Sudbury, MA: Jones and Bartlett, 2011); and N. Borkowski, *Organizational Behavior in Healthcare*, 2nd ed. (Sudbury, MA: Jones and Bartlett, 2009).

12. American Medical Association, Institute for Ethics, *Organizational Ethics in Healthcare: Toward a Model for Ethical Decision-Making by Provider Organizations* (Chicago, IL: American Medical Association, 2000). The document is limited in scope in that it only addresses organizations that provide "direct patient care"; therefore, it does not extend to entities such as insurance companies or managed care.

13. American College of Healthcare Executives, "Code of Ethics," November 10, 2003. Available at http://www.ache.org/ABT_ACHE/CodeofEthics.pdf. The code of ethics was updated on November 14, 2011; the most recent version is available at http://www.ache.org/abt_ache/code.cfm. Accessed June 13, 2012.

14. G. Khushf, "Struggling to Understand the Nature of Organizational Ethics," *HEC Forum* 11, no. 4 (1999): 285–287.

15. J. Andre, "The Alleged Incompatibility of Business and Medical Ethics," *HEC Forum* 11, no. 4 (1999): 288–293.

16. L. L. Emanuel, "Ethics and the Structures of Healthcare," *Cambridge Quarterly of Healthcare Ethics* 9 (2000): 151–168.

17. N. J. Hirsch, "All in the Family—Siblings but Not Twins: The Relationship of Clinical and Organizational Ethics Analysis," *Journal of Clinical Ethics* 10, no. 3 (Fall 1999): 210–215.

18. S. Dorr Goold, et al., "Outline of a Process for Organizational Ethics Consultation," *HEC Forum* 12, no. 1 (2000): 69–77.

19. See generally T. L. Beauchamp and J. Childress, *Principles of Biomedical Ethics*, 6th ed. (New York: Oxford University Press, 2008).

20. See D. Seay and R. Sigmond, "The Future of Tax Exempt Status for Hospitals," *Frontiers of Health Services Management* 5, no. 3 (1989): 3–39.

21. C. Mackelvie and B. Sandborn, "Mooring in Safe Harbours," *Health Progress* 70 (1989): 32–36; J. Inglehart, "The Recommendations of the Physician Payment Review Committee," *New England Journal of Medicine* 320 (1989): 1156–1160; D. Kinzer, "The Decline and Fall of Deregulation," *New England Journal of Medicine* 318 (1988): 112–116.

22. See, for example, A. Enthoven and R. Kronick, "A Consumer-Choice Health Plan for the 1990s," *New England Journal of Medicine* 320 (1989): 29–37; and U. Reinhardt, "Whither Private Health Insurance? Self Destruction or Rebirth?" *Frontiers of Health Services Management* 9, no. 1 (1992): 5–31.

23. R. M. Arnold, et al., *Core Competencies for Health Care Ethics Consultation: The Report of the American Society for Bioethics and Humanities*, 2nd ed. (Glenview, IL: American Society for Bioethics and Humanities, 2010): 2–3.

24. Ibid.

25. S. Bean, "Navigating the Murky Intersection Between Clinical and Organizational Ethics: A Hybrid Case Taxonomy," *Bioethics* 25, no. 6 (2011): 320–325.

26. E. Howe, "How Should Careproviders Respond When the Medical System Leaves a Patient Short?" *Journal of Clinical Ethics* 18, no. 3 (Fall 2007): 195–205.

27. A. Regan, "Regulating the Business of Medicine: Models for Integrating Ethics and Managed Care," *Columbia Journal of Law and Social Problems* 30 (1997): 635–684.

28. M. Rorty, "Ethics and Economics in Healthcare: The Role of Organizational Ethics," *HEC Forum* 12, no. 1 (2000): 57–68.

29. G. J. Agich and H. Forster, "Conflicts of Interest and Management in Managed Care," *Cambridge Quarterly of Healthcare Ethics* 9, no. 2 (2000): 189–204; S. Wolf, "Toward a Systemic Theory of Informed Consent in Managed Care," *Houston Law Review* 35 (1999): 1631–1681.

30. P. H. Werhane, "Business Ethics, Stakeholder Theory, and the Ethics of Healthcare Organizations," *Cambridge Quarterly of Healthcare Ethics* 9 (2000): 169–181.

31. American Medical Association, Institute of Ethics, *Organizational Ethics in Healthcare*, 5–6.

32. M. Lanoix, "Understanding the Scope of Clinical Ethics," *American Journal of Bioethics* 9, no. 4 (2009): 45–46 (noting that ethics committees may need additional training to address questions with long-term implications, such as those regarding resource allocation).

33. E. M. Spencer, "A New Role for Institutional Ethics Committees: Organizational Ethics," *Journal of Clinical Ethics* 8, no. 4 (Winter 1997): 372–376.

34. D. S. Silva, et al., "Clinical Ethicist's Perspectives on Organizational Ethics in Healthcare Organizations," *Journal of Medical Ethics* 34 (2008): 320–323.

35. F. McDonald, C. Simpson, and F. O'Brian, "Including Organizational Ethics in Policy Review Processes in Healthcare Institutions: A View from Canada," *HEC Forum* 20, no. 2 (2008): 137–153.

36. P. McCruden and M. Kuczewski, "Is Organizational Ethics the Remedy for Failure to Thrive? Toward an Understanding of Mission Leadership," *HEC Forum* 18, no. 4 (2006): 342–348.

37. J. E. Sabin and D. Cochran, "Confronting Trade-offs in Health Care: Harvard Pilgrim Health Care's Organizational Ethics Program," *Health Affairs* 26, no. 4 (2007): 1129–1134.

38. Potter, "On Our Way to Integrated Bioethics"; C. R. Seeley and S. L. Goldberger, "Integrated Ethics: Synecdoche in Healthcare," *Journal of Clinical Ethics* 10, no. 3 (Fall 1999): 202–209.

39. L. Marsh, et al., "The Words on the Wall: Nurse Leaders' Perspectives on Organizational Ethics in Health Care," Bioethics Forum Blog, November 20, 2008. Retrieved from http://www.thehastingscenter.org/Bioethicsforum/Post.aspx?id=2934&blogid=140.

40. A survey of human resource management personnel indicates that the 10 most serious ethical situations are as follows: (1) hiring, training, or promotion based on favoritism; (2) allowing differences in pay, discipline, promotion, and so on, because of friendships with top management; (3) permitting sexual harassment; (4) yielding to sexual discrimination in promotion; (4) using discipline for managerial and nonmanagerial personnel inconsistently; (5) not maintaining confidentiality; (6) tolerating sex discrimination in compensation; (7) using nonperformance factors in appraisals; (8) arranging with vendors or consulting agencies; (9) situations leading to personal gain; and (10) acquiescing to sex discrimination in recruitment and hiring. For example, 22.6% of those surveyed indicated that sex discrimination in recruitment and hiring was an ethical issue they confronted, and nearly 31% indicated that the hiring, training, or promotion of personnel based on favoritism was an issue. See Society of Human Resources Management, *Human Resources Management: 1991 SHRM/CCH Survey* (Chicago: Commerce Clearing House, June 26, 1991), 1–12.

41. J. Fletcher, J. Sorrell, and M. Cipriano Silva, "Whistle-blowing as a Failure of Organizational Ethics," *Online Journal of Issues in Nursing* 3, no. 3 (1998). Retrieved from http://www.nursingworld.org/MainMenuCategories/ANAMarketplace/ANAPeriodicals/OJIN/TableofContents/Vol31998/No3Dec1998/Whistleblowing.html. Accessed June 12, 2012.

42. Seeley and Goldberger, "Integrated Ethics," 206.

43. R. Suhonen, et al., "Organizational Ethics: A Literature Review," *Nursing Ethics* 18, no 3 (2011): 285–303.

44. S. Gabel, "Ethics and Values in Clinical Practice: Whom Do They Help?" *Mayo Clinic Proceedings* 86, no. 5 (May 2011): 421–424.

45. Fletcher, Sorrell, and Cipriano Silva, "Whistle-blowing."

46. Ibid.

47. C. Rathart, G. Ishqaidef, and D. R. May, "Improving Work Environments in Health Care: Test of a Theoretical Framework," *Health Care Management Review* 34, no. 4 (2009): 334–343.

48. S. Wall, "Organizational Ethics, Change, and Stakeholder Involvement: A Survey of Physicians," *HEC Forum* 19, no. 3 (2007): 222–243.

49. M. B. Foglia, et al., "Ethical Challenges Within Veterans Administration Healthcare Facilities: Perspectives of Managers, Clinicians, Patients, and Ethics Committee Chairpersons," *American Journal of Bioethics* 9, no. 4 (2009): 28–36.

50. A. E. Mills and E. M. Spencer, "Organization Ethics or Compliance: Which Will Articulate Values for the United States Healthcare System?" *HEC Forum* 13, no. 4 (December 2001): 329–343.

51. J. L. Gibson, "Organizational Ethics and the Management of Health Care Organizations," *Healthcare Management Forum* (Spring 2007): 32–34. See also D. T. Chen and A. E. Mills, "Symposium: Ethics Across the Professions: Professional Ethics and Corporate Conduct: Addressing Ethical Commitments When Professionals Partner with Organizations," *McGeorge Law Review* 39 (2008): 719–735.

52. Seay and Sigmond, "The Future of Tax Exempt Status"; D. Pellegrini, "Hospital Tax Exemption: A Municipal Perspective," *Frontiers of Health Services Management* 5, no. 2 (1989): 44–46.

53. G. Magill and L. D. Prybil, "Board Oversight of Community Benefit: An Ethical Imperative," *Kennedy Institute of Ethics Journal* 21, no. 1 (2011): 25–50.

54. Potter, "On Our Way to Integrated Bioethics," 171–177.

55. P. Starr, *The Social Transformation of American Medicine* (New York: Basic Books, 1982); R. Stevens, *In Sickness and in Wealth: American Hospitals in the Twentieth Century* (New York: Basic Books, 1989).

56. Stevens, *In Sickness*, 141.

57. J. R. Horwitz, "Why We Need the Independent Sector: The Behavior, Law, and Ethics of Not-for-Profit Hospitals," *UCLA Law Review* 50 (2003): 1345–1347.

58. R. S. Loewy, "Symposium: Across the Professions: Professional Ethics and Corporate Conduct: The 'Ethics' of Organizational/Institutional Ethics in a Pluralistic Setting: Conflicts of Interests, Values, and Goals," *McGeorge Law Review* 39 (2008): 703–718.

59. Magill and Prybil, "Board Oversight," 30.

60. See American Hospital Association, *Community Benefit and Tax Exempt Status: A Self-Assessment Guide for Hospitals* (Chicago: American Hospital Association, 1988); and Catholic Health Association, *Social Accountability Budget: A Process for Planning and Reporting Community Service in a Time of Fiscal Constraint* (St. Louis, MO: Catholic Health Association, 1989).

61. One suggested approach is presented in Catholic Health Association, *With Justice for All? The Ethics of Health Care Rationing* (St. Louis, MO: Catholic Health Association, 1991).

62. Foglia, et al., "Ethical Challenges," 33.

63. S. Wolf. "Toward a Systemic Theory of Informed Consent in Managed Care," *Houston Law Review* 35 (1999): 1631.

64. For a discussion of integrity in today's healthcare market, see R. Dell'Oro, "The Market Ethos and the Integrity of Health Care," *Journal of Contemporary Health Law and Policy* 18 (2002): 641–647.

65. J. Carver, *Boards That Make a Difference: A New Design for Leadership in Non-Profit and Public Organizations* (San Francisco: Jossey-Bass, 1991), 1–23, 40–55.

66. See, for example, A. K. Thompson, et al., "Pandemic Influenza Preparedness: an Ethical Framework to Guide Decision-Making," *BMC Medical Ethics* 7, no. 12 (2006).

CHAPTER 14

Hospital Ethics Committees: Roles, Memberships, Structure, and Difficulties

Michael P. West and Eileen E. Morrison

INTRODUCTION

Hospitals face many challenges in their mission of providing quality care for the communities that they serve. This mission may be made even more difficult because of the need to remain profitable in order to pay for the care provided, and in the case of for-profit hospitals, the need to provide dividends to investors. The tug of war between deontology and utilitarian decision-making creates tension and profound ethical dilemmas.

In addition, it has become commonplace for technological growth to outstrip the hospital's ability to make ethical decisions about its use. Ethics committees will face new conundrums as they respond to a public, educated by television and the popular press, that expects technology to perform miracles. However, in a practical sense, the lifesaving equipment and techniques may preserve a semblance of life but not provide quality of life. Physicians cannot predict what a treatment will achieve in an individual case; they apply the best treatment available in emergencies. They also cannot predict the future technology needed to meet the demands of aging baby boomers.

Hospitals are places where practitioners must make difficult decisions, often at a moment's notice. They are also places where policies affect the lives of patients and staff members. Because of this environment, there is an expectation that hospitals will hire and maintain staff members who are educated in ethics and practice it on a daily basis. Hospitals respond to the challenges of patient care and policy changes through their ethics committees. As healthcare reform advances, these committees will become increasingly more important and face increasingly more political and ethical challenges.

THE ROLE OF ETHICS COMMITTEES

A brief overview of the history of ethics committees is helpful in understanding this issue. Ethics committees in the United States began as a response to difficult patient issues. For example, in the 1970s, when hemodialysis was restricted by a shortage of the dialysis machines, ethics committees (sometimes called "God squads") were convened to determine which patients would receive treatment.[1] In recent years, there has been an emphasis on the role of case consulting and policy development to assist practitioners. In 1992, The Joint Commission determined that there was a need for hospitals to have a formal mechanism to deal with ethical conflicts. A recent national survey determined that 95% of hospitals had some form of ethics consultation capabilities.[2]

In addition, nonacute settings such as nursing facilities and managed care organizations are beginning to use ethics committees for assistance with a growing number of patient-centered and financial issues.[3]

In the 21st century, hospital ethics committees (HECs) serve three main functions: developing standards and policies, educating staff, and conducting clinical consultations. Clinical consultations allow HECs to assist with the resolution of often-difficult decisions on ethical patient care and staff needs. In addition, ethics committees are becoming increasingly more involved in resource allocation decisions. A brief explanation of these functions follows.

Developing Standards and Policy

There is a constant need to review and update hospital standards and policies in light of major changes in health law, including the Patient Protection and Affordable Care Act (PPACA) of 2010,[4] the almost daily changes in technology, and the requirements of regulatory agencies. The charge of HECs includes conducting reviews of existing policies and evaluating new policies with respect to their compliance with the mission of the organization and their foundation in ethical practice. Some of the standards and policies reflect recurrent ethical issues, such as advance directives, care of terminal patients, and patient competency guidelines. In addition, HECs may be involved in policy reviews on issues such as allocation of resources, community outreach, and fund-raising.[5] HECs review policies for consistency, conflict of interest, and consistency with the mission of the organization.[6,7]

Education

Another function commonly assigned to ethics committees is education. This function includes setting the appropriate goals for ethics education, including who should receive ethics education, how to deliver education, and what content it should have.[8] Ethics committees can provide education through guest speakers, workshops, and as part of a new employee's orientation to the facility. Case discussions with a process structure and the support of ethics experts can provide additional information to practitioners. This model is especially appropriate for teaching hospitals.

Ethics committee members must also be educated on the issues that they may face and on methods of decision making in ethics consultations. Although there is some evidence concerning the lack of agreement on universal content of moral reasoning and theory for ethics committees, there is recognition that HEC members should be educated on the issues that hospitals face. This includes traditional medical ethics, bioethics, and organizational healthcare ethics.[9,10]

Clinical Consultation

Ethics consultation is perhaps the most common function of ethics committees. In this role, the committee provides assistance with resolving issues surrounding a number of patient-centered dilemmas and organizational problems.[11] Clinical consultations can be conducted by the committee as a whole or by small groups within the committee. Because ethical issues concerning patients are often time-sensitive, these small groups can expedite the process of consultation. In addition, ethics committees can conduct retrospective case reviews to assess how the handling of issues and to serve as a learning tool for the organization.[12] These reviews also allow for multidisciplinary discussions that enrich the understanding of all staff and administrative personnel and are especially helpful in teaching hospitals.

Resource Allocation

The provision of patient care involves a myriad of decisions, many of which go beyond the boundaries of the care itself. With the increase in the number of aging baby boomers and the cost and availability of technology, resource allocation is becoming an increasingly critical ethical decision and a challenge for ethics committees. Committees can be involved with policy construction and review on issues of macroallocation, or "who gets what and when do they get it?"[13] The committees must examine the mission of the organization and its ethical position to formulate recommendations on the purchase and use of resources such as high-technology services, the provision of charity care, and other cost/benefit issues. Recent proposed changes in healthcare insurance coverage, Medicare and Medicaid provisions, and documentation included in PPACA 2010 promise to add even more complexity to this issue and to ethics committees' responsibilities.[14]

Addressing issues involving the microallocation of resources is also part of the current and future duties of the ethics committee. The center for these issues is often the individual patient and the use of scarce resources needed by that individual. Cases may involve decisions about who gets the only available bed in an intensive care unit, intervention in near-futile cases, and conflicts between patient desires (expressed in advanced directives and do-not-resuscitate orders) and those of family members. These microallocation issues involve both policy development and clinical consultations. Of course, changes in health laws will add to the complexity and intensity of this resource issue.[15]

In the near future, the luxury of dealing with individual cases for which payments can be received will almost completely cease, replaced by the hardship of being no longer able to provide expensive services for which little or no payment will be received. Cost will become an essential ingredient in the ethical decisions regarding allocation of scarce resources unless the necessary funds are available. The claim to necessary but expensive health care will be weighed in the balance of resource allocation and funding.

As outside entities establish even greater control over reimbursement for specific diseases, each institution will face a major ethical question: "Can we balance cost containment and institutional survival with quality of care?" If it is the responsibility of a hospital to fulfill its stated mission, philosophy, identity, and image, then particular judgments regarding allocation should be appropriate discussion matter for relevant administrators, staff, and community members. Ethics committees will serve as a forum for this discussion.

Each hospital employee ostensibly commits himself or herself to the aims of the institution, and individual determinations and actions should further these aims. When the achievement of these aims is in jeopardy, there will be an even greater need to seek consensus on how to maintain the best possible balance of values. The consensus that is achieved can then be conveyed to the community that the hospital serves. The HEC can be central to this effort to renew and communicate the hospital's aims and the community's values and choices.

ETHICS COMMITTEE MEMBERSHIP

According to Monagle, the traditional membership of HECs represents a broad range of value perspectives, professional expertise, and community representation. The committee should include the following:[16]

- *Medical staff.* Staff from specialty areas such as obstetrics, neurosurgery, neurology, nephrology, oncology, psychiatry, and so forth. Physicians are the most commonly represented group on an ethics committee.[17]
- *Nursing staff.* The director of nursing, operating room supervising nurse, emergency department supervising nurse, etc.
- *An administrator.* A high-level, qualified administrative person who is interested in ethical issues, sensitive to medical staff responsibilities, patient and employee rights, financial realities, and community concerns.
- *A social services representative.* A person knowledgeable about what the hospital, as well as the larger community, can provide in the way of care for patients.
- *Clergy or bioethicist.* Having at least one such person is essential for multidisciplinary discussions. Candidates should have training not only in moral theology but also in the formal discipline of philosophical ethics in order to present the ethical theories and principles that can be applied to the individual case. Some clergy do not have these credentials. Although they can bring important and essential insight to the committee, such insight cannot replace the formal discipline of ethics.
- *A member of the hospital board.* Because the hospital board represents the community, the person selected should be knowledgeable about the larger community's concerns as to the kinds of medical procedures and treatments that are needed in the demographic area that the hospital serves. In addition, because all of the hospital's services are ultimately the responsibility of the hospital board, the governing-body representative should participate in and have knowledge of the hospital ethics committee's discussions and decisions.

In addition, hospitals often include a patient representative or ombudsman who can add information from the patient or family perspective. Ethnic and cultural diversity of membership is also a current issue for ethics committees. Patient-centered ethical issues may involve cultural or religious issues, and diversity can add to effective decision making when this is the case.[18]

An interdisciplinary approach both to the makeup of HECs and to proposed ethical discussions in hospitals is essential for several reasons. It should be noted that ethical dilemmas are not confined to the physician–patient relationship; they occur with respect to many other healthcare professionals, institutional demands, and social factors. The increased specialization of health care demands "defragmentation" of staff during attempts to resolve ethical issues. Communication across disciplines regarding difficult emotional issues (often involved in ethically complex cases) tends to minimize disruptions that could damage healthcare delivery.

For example, a patient's wife requests that the physician remove her husband from a respirator. Does the request represent the wishes of the patient or of the family? Sometimes the nurses (or the significant attending nurse) know the answer better than the attending physicians, who in many hospital situations might not know the family well. In such cases, a sound decision cannot be reached without involving the nursing staff (or the significant nurse) and other relatives who know the patient's lifestyle, desires, and requests.

A second consideration is the effect that the decision will have on the caregivers. Staff members often form emotional bonds with patients, especially when the patient is so helpless as to need ventilator support. A physician's order to wean the patient off the respirator, when this action may result in death, requires at the very least some discussion with the attending nurses and respiratory specialists who have been providing the care. Nurses often ask hospital ethicists to approach physicians about such determinations—not in a spirit of rebellion, but with a simple request that they be part of the discussion on the decision. Any attempt to avoid such interdisciplinary discussion at the specific case level not only ignores the emotional dimensions of ethical issues but also causes new ethical issues to arise for those who must carry out the orders. As one nurse stated privately years ago, the most fundamental ethical issue for nurses concerns the expectations that they will remain silent and "get used to" being excluded from the decision-making process.

Multidisciplinary discussion does not merely address the emotional aspects of ethical issues; the inherently multidisciplinary nature of the ethical dilemmas that occur today requires it. The federal government is directly involved in promulgating guidelines on research and on the care of defective newborns. State authorities are involved in executing prospective payment policies that might prevent some persons from receiving the care they need. Insurance companies are involved, especially through preferred provider organizations (PPOs) and health maintenance organizations (HMOs), because they reward physicians who keep their patients away from expensive care. Hospital administrators are involved in determining who will receive expensive care that is not reimbursable. In addition, physicians and consultants are involved in day-to-day decisions to which they bring legal, moral, and professional standards. It becomes impossible to resolve some clinical ethical problems without considering the involvement of all these participants.

THE ETHICS COMMITTEE'S BACKGROUND AND EDUCATION

Hospital and other organizations should choose ethics committee members carefully because of their responsibility for decisions that affect lives, care, and utilization of resources. Although there is some discussion about what "expertise in ethics" means, knowledge of ethical theory and principles and the ability to analyze a problem and determine its issues are essential.[19] In addition, committee members must be skilled in communication, conflict mediation, and "big picture" thinking. Lachman suggests that committee members:

- Be competent in their areas of expertise
- Commit to preparing for meetings (including perusing materials)
- Be up-to-date on the organization's ethical position, including its mission, vision, and code of conduct statements
- Be known for their high moral principles[20]

Because decisions in consultations are often emotional, HEC members need training in the process of decision making to provide a rational and consistent process. The first step in the training process should be to select a model. There are several available; the organization should select a model based on agreed-upon criteria. This model must be concise and easily understood so it does not become an obstacle to decision making. Once this model is chosen, current ethics committee members should be trained in its use so that it becomes a well-used part of the decision process. As the committee adds new members, in-service education must be provided to maintain consistency and efficiency.

Nelson discusses the need for ethics committees to have a foundation in a procedural justice approach that involves the use of a clearly understood model to increase the fairness of decisions.[21] His multistep model helps to clarify the conflict and to move to resolution with efficiency. A summary of the steps in this model includes the following:

1. Be clear about the conflict and its ethical question.
2. Determine those affected by the conflict.
3. Research the facts of the conflict, including its implications.
4. Decide what ethical principles and theories apply.
5. Discuss possible alternatives to address the conflict.
6. Evaluate each of the identified alternatives.
7. Select the best alternative and communicate it appropriately.
8. Evaluate the decision to determine if it resolved the issue.[22]

Training in this model, or another like it, would allow ethics committees to provide fairness in their treatment of often-emotional issues and better communicate both the decision process and the result.

INSTITUTIONAL COMMITMENT

Hospitals provide a good that people cannot obtain on their own using their own resources. This good is not like most consumer products, which in some sense are luxuries. To reduce it to mathematical or economic analysis alone is to diminish its vast importance. Every hospital governing body has the duty to ensure that the institution reflects the mission and philosophy stated in its charter and developed in its traditions. Staff turnover and a natural tendency, especially in institutions, for ideals to decay over time make it desirable to establish perdurable policies regarding ethical decision making. In effect, such policies are a form of prescriptive or directive ethics.

Ethics committees need leadership and support from the top levels of administration in order to make a difference in the operation of a hospital or other healthcare facility. The committee chair needs to be someone who is well respected in the organization and who has expertise in ethics. In addition, this person needs to understand the clinical side of hospital practice and be able to communicate well with clinical and administrative professionals. It would also be helpful for the committee chair to demonstrate good judgment, practical political knowledge, and solid mediation skills.[23]

The ethics committee's effectiveness and accountability is linked to its reporting structure within the facility. Ideally, it should report directly to senior management, such as the chief executive officer or chief operating officer. This direct report mechanism not only demonstrates a commitment by the institution but also gives the committee a source a support and finances. However, the committee's position on the organizational chart is not sufficient in itself. Members must work to obtain commitment from department directors, clinical staff, and colleagues. To increase this support, committee members must be able to explain the service provided by their committee and its goals and provide easily available expertise on ethics. However, these support-generating activities must not intrude on the business of health care— service to patients.[24]

STRUCTURES FOR ETHICS COMMITTEES

Ethics committees can be structured in terms of their philosophical orientation or their organizational design within an institution. Darr addresses the philosophical structure of ethics committees by suggesting that they use models that address their accountability and emphasis.[25] For example, if an ethics committee is based on the principle of autonomy, it will stress decision making based on the concerns and expressed wishes of competent patients. If the committee uses social justice as its ethical foundation, it will stress accountability to the community and to the organization and discuss issues of policy, resources, and cost. Finally, if an ethics committee uses a model that stresses overall benefit to patients, it will be particularly concerned with bioethical issues and with advocating for patients who are unable to make their own healthcare decisions.

From a organizational design view, three structures are possible for an ethics committee. The part of the hospital that has authority over the ethics committee's operations determines the overall structure of the committee.

These structures include an ethics committee as part of the hospital's governing board, as a committee that reports to the hospital's chief executive officer, and as a committee responsible to the hospital medical staff executive committee. Each committee's structure and membership, authority and responsibility, charge and scope of activity, and limits of purpose and authority are defined according to the particular needs of each hospital.

Under the governing board model, the ethics committee uncovers, discusses, and clarifies ethical concerns or problems. In consultation with the medical staff executive committee and the hospital administration, it forms an ethical policy subcommittee to analyze the available information on the subject. The ethics committee reviews the subcommittee's policy recommendations and forwards the approved recommendations for adoption by the governing board as hospital policy. When a case involving these issues arises, those policies serve as guidelines to ethics advisory groups formed to help families and physicians understand the ethical choices involved.

The flow of information and development of hospital policies is similar in the other two models, but in those models the hospital's administration or the medical staff executive committee has more or less direct authority for final review and approval of policies. One of the differences among the governing board, administration, and medical staff organizational models is the level of public disclosure each affords. Because the ethics committee's primary focus is on patients' rights and hospital and community education in bioethical issues, it might not be advisable to seek the protection from discovery in legal action that state law gives to the deliberations of medical staff quality-care review committees. To the extent that the discussions and recommendations about or solutions to ethical concerns, issues, and dilemmas are shared openly, the medical staff members' and the institution's assumption of ethical responsibility for policies and actions will be visible and recognized. Furthermore, if there is a challenge to the hospital's ethical practices through civil or criminal suit, summary documentation of the ethics committee's proceedings may well serve as a defense for the physicians and the hospital.

Under the medical staff organizational model, the ethics committee might seek protection from discovery for the records and proceedings of its ethical policy subcommittees because these committees report to the ethics committee of the medical staff. Likewise, ethics advisory groups might be protected from discovery under either the medical staff or governing board organizational models. The governing board structure might be the most amenable to openness of information, discussion, and recommendations, while at the same time protecting records and proceedings related to individual case discussions of the ethics advisory groups.

The administration model, although unable to seek protection from discovery under quality-assurance confidentiality statutes, might be more responsive to management control of cost-effectiveness and to evaluating risk-management and professional liability implications of hospital ethical policies. The medical staff model, although fully protected from disclosure of discussions, must guard against domination by physicians and lack of interaction with the community.

DIFFICULTIES AND NEEDS FOR ETHICS COMMITTEES

The following areas represent areas of difficulty for most ethics committees and ethicists. They exist in a variety of current healthcare environments. They also promise to be problems for committees in the future.

- The necessary funding and time to address present and future ethical issues is a continuing issue for ethics committees. It takes time and expert personnel to develop and implement a single ethical policy. If a committee has only one or two hours a month to discuss, formulate, and prepare to implement an ethical policy, only one or two policies can be produced in a year. In light of the policies that will be required for PPACA implementation, this pace of creation is unacceptable. In addition, a national network of healthcare committees willing to share policies does not exist.
- Some money-strapped healthcare institutions find it difficult to justify expenditures on ethicists or ethics committees because upper management may consider them unnecessary for direct patient care. This lack of support promises to be an increasing problem as health care becomes even more complex because of the dramatic changes it must make to accommodate new laws and changes in populations served.
- Ongoing issues such as abortion, sterilization, surrogate motherhood, transplants, euthanasia, and assisted suicide have not been resolved successfully by any universally applicable solutions to benefit the care of patients. In addition, technological advances such as cyber surgery, robotics, cloning, and genetics present new ethical issues. Ethics committees will not have a frame of reference for these emerging issues, but they still will need to find patient-centered and fiscally responsible solutions.
- Physician survival has forced more professionals into managed care organizations. Regulations and policies for insurance companies are changing under the new healthcare legislation. The quality of patient care may become a secondary consideration in order to meet the requirements, thereby increasing ethical issues. Ethics committees in these organizations will struggle with protecting patient needs and ensuring fiscal survival when the prime directive is reduction of managed care costs.
- Most ethicists and ethics committees are not educated in business practice or managed care ethics. Ethicists come more readily from a humanities background and are not corporate business practitioners. They do not easily deal with enforced government rationing, as demonstrated by Medicare and Medicaid. In general, ethicists are not financially experienced regarding the cost of personnel staffing requirements. They also do not have training in business marketing and health service plans. In addition, most ethicists are not able to contribute to the ethical and financial issues involved in healthcare mergers, joint ventures, corporate restructuring, and the financial limitations of institutions in providing uncompensated care. Consequently, ethics committees may not fully understand ethical demands in the context of financially based insurance

policies limiting or denying certain options of coverage. Given the prospect of increased ethical challenges from healthcare reform legislation and its impact on healthcare organizations, the issue of under education in the business aspects of ethics needs to be resolved.

- Bioethics has reached a crisis in its young adulthood. It needs to identify (1) who its practitioners are, what their qualifications are, and what their training and experience should be; and (2) what problems and issues they handle from a professional standpoint. In addition, it must address (3) in what areas ethicists need to educate themselves and contextualize their views, and (4) to what extent they need to adopt a financial or Wall Street approach to health legislation and managed care.

- Most of the bioethicists who will survive and progress in the new millennium will be those who become involved in the administrative, financial, and clinical functions of managed care organizations, healthcare facilities, and socially responsible entities. These organizations will deal with comprehensive ethical issues that may include environmental concerns, including hazardous waste, and issues involving the homeless, the disabled, home care, and hospice efforts. A focus on these efforts will be necessary if bioethicists want to be active participants in change and valued in both the administrative and public views of the healthcare system.

- There has been reluctance in the past, as there undoubtedly will be in the future, by some bioethicists to become involved in "the dirty business of finance." Unless so fortunate as to have an endowed academic or clinical chair, an ethicist will quickly realize the necessity for knowledge of healthcare financing as he or she becomes involved in the financial concerns pervading the healthcare industry, because these concerns influence ethical issues and decisions constantly. Otherwise, some might come to consider bioethicists and ethics committees as parasitic to the financial efficiency of healthcare entities.

- Gaudine, Lamb, LeFort, and Thorne found that clinical staff had barriers to using the ethics committee. These barriers included the following:
  - Not enough information about what ethics committees actually do
  - Not enough experience in dealing with ethics committees
  - Fear of the reaction of others in their work culture
  - A personal attitude of avoiding asking for assistance[26]

- Given the American love affair with technology, it would not be unusual to find that its use is beginning to affect the functions of ethics committees. Smith and Barnosksy found the use of web-based ethics consults for situations involving adults to be effective in a large hospital system.[27] They report that technology can expedite the process of receiving assistance with patient care decisions. In the healthcare system they studied, a website provided information about the service of ethics consultation. Practitioners could add case information to the site by typing information on the website. This entry would then trigger an automated email to the on-call ethics committee member. The member could then respond to the case. Facilities still use face-to-face meetings for difficult cases, but the use of the new web-based system has increased. As with other aspects of health care, technology promises both changes and challenges for ethics committees.

CONCLUSION

Ethical issues are not going to diminish in frequency or complexity. The individual treatment dilemmas raised by new technology are difficult enough. However, dilemmas that are even more agonizing have surfaced with the introduction of healthcare reform, the aging of the baby boomers, changes in technology, and other societal issues. Challenges and changes will make ethics committees even more important to the success of health care in the 21st century. Members of these committees will have to be educated in ethical principles, decision making, business practices, and many other areas as they face issues that would test the wisdom of Solomon.

UPDATE FROM A PRACTITIONER'S POINT OF VIEW

The following section presents the results of West's current research on hospital ethics committees. Given the changes in healthcare law and the population, it suggests issues that these committees may face in the future. There appears to be a struggle with social justice, or balancing the benefits of care with the burdens of financing that care. It is important that committees do not forget ethics in this struggle.

Ethics committees will face new challenges because the delivery of healthcare is in transition. The passage of the PPACA will certainly create new challenges for hospital ethics committees. Features of the law such as increasing the number of insured people, expanding care for early retirees, increasing efforts to control costs, and others promise many ethical dilemmas for HECs.[28] The media and politicians have conjured up nightmares of death panels and patients suffering because they cannot get care, which are certainly extreme scenarios. However, given increased demand and a not necessarily increased supply of services, hospital ethics committees will spend many hours on resource allocation issues.

For example, one of the issues that HECs face is that the numbers of baby boomers entering the entitlement programs of Medicare and Social Security are the highest in U.S. history. The prediction of 11,000 applicants per day had already become a reality by the end of the third quarter of 2011.[29] There is no question that as 78 million Americans reach age 65, they will utilize higher levels of healthcare services both as elective choices and as nonelective aging-associated clinical management.[30] This surge in utilization will force the healthcare system to develop new methods and technology to manage and monitor larger numbers of patients per provider. The definition of "provider" will expand to cover the unquestionable shortage of physicians, nurses, and allied health professionals. The level and intensity of care that allied healthcare professionals will provide in the future will extend to primary care practices historically limited to physicians.

This shifting paradigm will also have consequences for the hospital and its ability to monitor ethical practice, including its use of ethics committees.

The current ethical monitoring system has developed based on the complex medical staff governing process. Some of the positive aspects of this process are credentialing standards, license verification, malpractice notification, and peer review. One negative aspect has been economic credentialing, in which a large group of physicians can deny or limit practice privileges, through the committee review process, to competitive groups or individual practitioners. Adding the increasing demand for physicians and allied health practitioners to this mix will require extensive changes to the medical staff governance model and a drastic change in the monitoring of ethical behavior and practice.

Simultaneously, the Centers for Medicare and Medicaid Services (CMS) is transforming from being a passive payer of healthcare claims into an active purchaser of healthcare value through the establishment of value-based purchasing (VBP).[31] Performance achievement and improvement will determine total hospital reimbursement. CMS will base 30% of hospital reimbursement on the Hospital Consumer Assessment of Healthcare Providers and Systems (HCAHPS) standardized patient survey process. Comparable data across acute care hospitals will use evidence-based questions to judge the patient's view of quality care. Initially, the six composite categories will include nurse communication, doctor communication, responsiveness of hospital staff, pain management, communication about medication, and discharge information. There will also be two environmental questions: how often rooms/bathrooms are cleaned and how often rooms are quiet at night. Two global questions are also included: overall rating of hospital, and willingness to recommend hospital.[32]

There are ethical issues with the survey itself. According to the HCAHPS Fact Sheet,[33] the survey is used with a random sample of recently discharged patients (between 48 hours and 6 weeks after discharge). It contains 18 items that address the issues described earlier. Hospitals must survey patients throughout the year and must have a minimum of 300 surveys in four calendar quarters. When one examines the nature of the questions, one can see that they are subjective and influenced by a multitude of factors, including patient acuity, private room versus double occupancy, family input, and so forth. In addition, the potential for ethical abuse exists within data collection. For example, will patients feel coerced to answer the survey either through the way data is collected or for fear of retribution if they complain? Given the monetary connection, will staff members be tempted to alter the comments made by patients?

The use of survey data to set reimbursement rates also has the potential of creating serious ethical issues and potential violations for the hospital and its ethics committee, including the increased costs for training staff members, administering surveys, compiling data, and writing reports. Overall, this practitioner's experience with the patient survey process has generally been positive. However, there have been occasions on which he witnessed data manipulation to enhance positive outcomes through the submission of false surveys. This practice occurred in settings where executives and managers had monetary incentives tied to positive survey results. When there is a tie between a large portion of reimbursement and easily manipulated data, the potential for this type of aberrant behavior is greatly increased. Ethically, this should be a major concern for hospitals, and they should take steps to avoid data abuse. Ethics committees can play an active role in prevention.

The changes in the VBP system also create new challenges for HECs, which will have increased importance, input, and visibility. A parallel to this increasing importance can be seen in the change in the value of medical records coders that occurred with the implementation of the diagnosis-related group (DRG) payment system. Ethics committees should add prospective surveillance and monitoring to their current retrospective-based review process to meet the challenges posed by subjective quality judgments by patients. In addition, they will have to increase their continuing education efforts to be more aware of potential issues that can occur when there is a connection between hospital reimbursement and survey measures.

Since 1992, when The Joint Commission mandated that hospitals address ethical concerns, HECs have had increasingly more difficult and diverse ethical issues on their agendas. In a national survey of 1,000 hospitals in the United States, end-of-life issues were cited as the most important clinical issue for HECs. Given the nature of the patient census, this finding was not surprising. However, the respondents reported that financial issues were the next most important issue. Financial issues included rationing, cost containment, and managed care. Ethics committees had the highest rate (33%) of not being successful in dealing with this issue category.[34] In light of the imminent changes in health care for hospitals, it seems certain that HECs will continue to have more and different kinds of responsibilities and greater challenges in the 21st century.

SUMMARY

Ethics committees are the primary way in which healthcare institutions address increasingly difficult institutional and patient ethical issues. This chapter reviewed the roles of these committees and detailed the duties of ethics subcommittees. In addition, current and future issues for these committees were presented. Finally, through his research on practicing hospital ethics committees, West suggested that they may face even more difficult issues in the future, including the challenge of providing clinically sound, cost-effective care that is also socially just.

QUESTIONS FOR DISCUSSION

1. How do you think ethics committees can contribute to an organization's commitment to ethics-based practice?
2. Do you think that patient advocates or community members should be included on ethics committees?
3. What effect will the continuing progress of technology have on the job of the ethics committee?
4. If you were an ethics committee member, how would you address the following statement: "Patient surveys are the best way to create value-based purchasing"?

FOOD FOR THOUGHT

You are a newly appointed member of a hospital ethics committee in your community. You will be attending a new member's orientation meeting next week.

1. What concerns do you have about serving on an HEC?
2. What additional training or information would you like your hospital to provide?
3. What ethical principles will be most useful to you as you serve on this committee?

NOTES

1. V. D. Lachman, "Clinical Ethics Committees: Organizational Support for Ethical Practice," *Medsurg Nursing* 19 (November/December 2010): 351–353.
2. Ibid., 351.
3. K. Darr, *Ethics in Health Services Management*, 5th ed. (Baltimore, MD: Health Professions Press, 2011).
4. For a concise summary of health reform law, see The Henry Kaiser Family Foundation, *Focus on Health Reform: Summary of New Health Reform Law* (Menlo Park, CA: The Henry Kaiser Family Foundation, 2011). Available on the Kaiser Family Foundation's website: http://www.kff.org.
5. E. E. Morrison, *Ethics in Health Administration: A Practical Approach for Decision Makers*, 2nd ed. (Sudbury, MA: Jones and Bartlett Learning, 2011).
6. Darr, *Ethics in Health Services Management*, 101
7. V. D. Lachman, *Ethical Challenges in Health Care* (New York: Springer Publishing, 2009).
8. L. F. Post, J. Blustein, and N. N. Bubler, *Handbook for Health Care Ethics Committees* (Baltimore, MD: The Johns Hopkins University Press, 2007).
9. A. Bardon, "Ethics Education and Values Prioritization Among Members of U.S. Hospital Ethics Committees," *Kennedy Institute of Ethics Journal* 14, no. 4 (2004): 395–406.
10. R. E. Thompson, "The Hospital Ethics Committee—Then and Now," *The Physician Executive* 32, no. 3 (May–June 2006): 60–62.
11. Darr, *Ethics in Health Services Management*, 101.
12. The Joint Commission, "Forming an Ethics Committee," Joint Commission Resources. Retrieved from http://www.jcrinc.com/Ethics-Committee/Organizational-Ethics-Issues/Forming-an-Ethics-Committee. Accessed February 27, 2012.
13. Darr, *Ethics in Health Services Management*, 309–339.
14. Kaiser Family Foundation, *Focus on Health Reform*.
15. Darr, *Ethics in Health Services Management*, 309–339.
16. J. F. Monagle, "Blueprints for Hospital Ethics Committees," *CHA Insight* 8, no. 20 (1984): 1–4.
17. Darr, *Ethics in Health Services Management*, 103.
18. Post, Blustein, and Bubler, *Handbook for Health Care Ethics Committees*, 19–20.
19. Ibid., 21–22.
20. Lachman, *Ethical Challenges in Health Care*, 202.
21. W. A. Nelson, "An Organizational Ethics Decision-Making Process," *Healthcare Executive* 20, no. 4 (July/August 2005): 8–14.
22. Ibid.

23. Post, Blustein, and Bubler, *Handbook for Health Care Ethics Committees*, 22–23.

24. Ibid.

25. Darr, *Ethics in Health Services Management*, 95-96.

26. A. Gaudine, M. Lamb, S. M. LeFort, and L. Thorne, "Barriers and Facilitators to Consulting Hospital Ethics Committees," *Nursing Ethics* 18, no. 6 (2011): 767–780.

27. L. B. Smith and A. Barnosky, "Web-Based Clinical Ethics Consultation: A Model for Hospital-Based Practice," *Physician Executive Journal* 37, no. 6 (November–December, 2011): 62–64.

28. U.S. Department of Health and Human Services, "Key Features of the Affordable Care Act, By Year," HealthCare.gov. Available at http://www.healthcare.gov/law/timeline/full.html. Accessed June 14, 2012.

29. T. Dennis, "Patient Experience Leadership Panel Discussion," Beryl Institute Patient Experience Conference 2011, April 13–15, Southlake, Texas.

30. J. Walker Smith and A. Clurman, *Generation Ageless: How Baby Boomers Are Changing the Way We Live Today . . . And They're Just Getting Started* (New York: Collins, 2007).

31. J. Meyer, L. Rybowski, and R. Eichler, *Theory and Reality of Value-Based Purchasing: Lessons from the Pioneers*, AHCPR Publication 98-0094 (Gaithersburg, MD: Agency for Healthcare Policy and Research, November 1997). Retrieved from http://www.ahrq.gov/qual/meyerrpt.htm. Accessed June 14, 2012.

32. Dennis, "Patient Experience Leadership Panel."

33. Hospital Consumer Assessment of Healthcare Providers and Systems, "HCAHPS Fact Sheet." Retrieved from http://www.hcahpsonline.org/files/HCAHPS%20Fact%20Sheet,%20 revised1,%203-31-09.pdf. Accessed June 14, 2012.

34. G. M. McGhee, J. P. Spanogle, A. L. Caplan, D. Perry, and D. A. Aasch, "Successes and Failures of Hospital Ethics Committees: A National Survey of Ethics Committee Chairs," *Cambridge Quarterly of Healthcare Ethics* 11, no.1 (January 2002): 87–93. Retrieved from http://responsitory.upenn.edu/bioethics_papers/4. Accessed June 27, 2012.

CHAPTER 15

Bioethical Dilemmas in Emergency Medicine and Prehospital Care

Kenneth V. Iserson

INTRODUCTION

Emergency medicine is at once the oldest and the newest of medical specialties. Stemming from soldiers helping their wounded comrades in the field, the modern domain of emergency medicine includes care provided in hospital emergency departments (EDs), urgent-care centers, and areas outside of medical facilities via ambulance and medically trained flight crews (i.e., prehospital care). Emergency medical practitioners, physicians, nurses, and prehospital personnel face not only the traditional ethical dilemmas common to all healthcare providers, but also new ethical challenges arising from their added responsibilities in the health treatment system and the unique demands of emergency medical care.

These relatively new ethical dilemmas stem from the changing nature of the health treatment system and the technical practice of medicine. The U.S. health system increasingly fails to meet the needs of the medically indigent, and EDs have attempted to take up this slack; however, they often lack the resources to perform both this task and their primary duty to treat the acutely ill and injured. Emergency medical practitioners face 10 key ethical issues.[1] These issues are as follows, and are discussed in this chapter:

1. How to continue to care for the critically ill and injured while also acting as a medical safety net for the medically indigent
2. How to aggressively treat critical patients and yet avoid paternalism toward those who can participate in their own healthcare decisions
3. How to preserve patient autonomy while implementing prehospital advance directives
4. How to respond to failed physician-assisted suicides
5. How to best break bad news and provide end-of-life care
6. How to evaluate patients' decision-making capacity and work with surrogate decision makers
7. How to keep emergency medical providers safe while caring for patients
8. How to approach triage/disaster ethics
9. How to respect both the living and the dead while staying current in necessary lifesaving skills
10. How to ethically perform research to advance the field of emergency care while safeguarding patients

THE SAFETY NET AND OVERCROWDING

The U.S. health treatment system is in need of resuscitation. EDs, which have been described as the system's safety net, are losing their ability to provide this service.[2] Medically indigent patients often access health care through EDs because they cannot access the health treatment system in any other way.[3] EDs have taken up the slack, but they often lack the resources to perform both this task and their primary role of treating the acutely ill and injured. Serious ED overcrowding has been a national problem for more than 20 years and is a result of decreasing hospital capacities, the closure of many EDs, increased numbers of patients, and decreasing reimbursement as the number of uninsured patients seeking treatment in EDs has proportionately increased.[4] Additionally, hospital EDs and trauma centers are "the only providers required by federal law to accept, evaluate, and stabilize all who present for care, regardless of their ability to pay. An unintended but predictable consequence of this legal duty is a system that is overloaded and underfunded to carry out its mission."[5] This last situation poses a significant dilemma: whether to focus on emergency medicine's primary duty to treat the acutely ill and injured or to provide a major source of care to medically indigent patients.

Paradoxically, as EDs see increasing numbers of patients for a wider spectrum of problems (many of which are non-emergent), they are also targeted as a convenient site to access socially underserved populations. Emergency medical personnel find themselves castigated for not providing general medical screenings, preventive care, and public medical education programs. Social problems are being "medicalized," putting the onus of the remedy for multifactorial problems on medicine—and, increasingly, on emergency medicine. In part, this is due to crumbling social supports as well as confusion about how to solve serious social ills. The ethical dilemma facing emergency medicine is whether to assume these various social roles and dilute (or change) its primary mission, or to take a hard line and ignore these ills—as have most others in our society.

Unfortunately, studies now show that as an ED becomes overwhelmed with patients and the waiting times increase, ED patient mortality increases.[6] Thus, the results of ED overcrowding are not simply a matter of longer wait times or even increased illness, but sometimes a matter of life and death. What are emergency medicine providers to do?

PATERNALISM

Paternalism, in the medical context, denotes the belief that "the doctor knows best." A physician with a paternalistic attitude intervenes to do what he or she believes will be beneficial, whether or not the patient desires an intervention.[7] Although paternalistic behavior has long characterized physicians in cultures around the world, it is beginning to be replaced in many Western settings by increased patient autonomy.

In the emergency medical care setting, paternalism often results from the constant pressure to use time and resources optimally to aid critically ill or injured patients who often lack decision-making capacity. Time pressures to make critical decisions are nowhere as intense or as constant as in emergency medicine. Simply doing something without asking often saves time, which is the major resource in emergency medical services (EMS). However, this paternalistic attitude may put practitioners' values and their patients' desire to exercise autonomy in direct conflict.

Emergency medicine in its most basic form, as practiced during wars and disasters, is the immediate decision of one provider. He or she decides who receives treatment and who he or she allows to die. In the common hospital and prehospital scenario, this translates into rapid unilateral decisions to intervene to save lives or limbs with tubes, fluids, medications, electric shocks, and surgery. Many patients desire such actions, and they are considered beneficial rather than paternalistic. Patients want and expect aggressive and immediate action by emergency medical teams. Too easily, however, this aggressive behavior can become paternalistic when applied to the patient who is not critically ill. ED and prehospital patients commonly complain that "things are done to them" without prior discussion or acquiescence when they enter the emergency medical system. Significantly, these "things" often commit patients to large expenses for tests or procedures. In cases in which patients lack decision-making capacity but the patient can expect benefit from the medical team's actions, aggressive intervention is not only reasonable but also essential. Transferring this attitude to other patients who maintain decision-making capacity, however, is problematic.

Paternalism can also arise in the guise of "futility." In emergency medicine and prehospital care, there are two questions that are closely linked: What constitutes futility for the emergency patient? When should one withhold or withdraw life-sustaining measures? Even as advanced cardiopulmonary life support and other techniques in trauma resuscitation increase practitioners' capacity to extend biological life, the patient benefits remain uncertain. Few guidelines exist to aid either prehospital or ED practitioners regarding the decision to abandon therapeutic interventions other than their lack of success in a "reasonable" amount of time. Prehospital advance directive orders are, unfortunately, still rarely seen. Clinicians in these situations are therefore forced to make unilateral decisions regarding further care—and they often choose unwanted treatments.

PREHOSPITAL ADVANCE DIRECTIVES VERSUS DO-NOT-RESUSCITATE ORDERS

Most EMS systems still mandate that ambulance personnel called to the scene of a patient in cardiac arrest must attempt resuscitation unless it is physiologically futile (generally meaning rigor mortis, decomposition, burned beyond recognition, or other situations incompatible with life). Over the past decade, an increasing number of systems have adopted rules or state laws whereby patients (or their surrogates) can opt out of resuscitation if they request an ambulance erroneously. Ethicists and emergency medical personnel have jointly helped to address the tragedy of unwanted resuscitations through the development of prehospital advance directives (PHADs). A danger, however, has arisen.

Although some states have successfully maintained patient autonomy by using patient- or surrogate-initiated PHADs, others have rigidly attempted to preserve physician prerogatives by changing the nature of these laws and rules to mimic in-hospital do-not-resuscitate (DNR) orders.[8] Prehospital DNR (PHDNR) orders, although requested by (or at least discussed with) patients or their surrogate decision makers, must be approved and signed by physicians.[9] This eliminates patients' autonomous decisions regarding what is perhaps the most important decision of their lives—deciding how they will die. Occasionally, patients try to use their own forms of PHAD, such as tattoos or jewelry, but physicians or EMS personnel fear the risk of incorrectly interpreting the messages, so they are rarely followed.[10]

Although initially the laws and EMS rules governing PHDNR orders stemmed from concerns about the misuse of and possible criminal activity associated with using patient-initiated forms, experience with patient-initiated PHADs has shown that these concerns are unwarranted. Although physicians espouse patient autonomy, the widespread continued use of physician-initiated PHDNR rules belies this attitude.

Emergency medicine has three significant challenges regarding prehospital directives: (1) increasing the locales where these programs are available, (2) increasing patient awareness of how to best use these programs, and (3) ensuring that patient autonomy is preserved. The American College of Emergency Physicians, among other groups, is attempting to correct this situation.[11]

PHYSICIAN-ASSISTED SUICIDES AND EMERGENCY DEPARTMENT RESUSCITATIONS

As assisted suicide laws spread throughout the United States over the next decades, experience shows that the number of failed suicides will increase—perhaps dramatically. Will this change the role of the entire EMS system and that of emergency physicians in particular?

At present, all emergency medical personnel operate under the general rule of "when in doubt, preserve life." This rule stems from their frequent lack of information about the patient, the circumstances surrounding the incident bringing the patient to the ED, and any wishes or values the patient might have. The rule includes committing to psychiatric hospitals those patients who pose a danger to themselves. Although this is, in fact, at odds with patient autonomy, both legal and ethical theorists agree that protecting suicidal patients is a necessary medical function.

In situations in which physicians (and sometimes EMS personnel through a PHAD or PHDNR order) know that a patient does not want resuscitation, the patient's wishes are generally followed.[12] Yet, when the need for resuscitation arises from a failed assisted-suicide attempt, how will ED physicians respond? What if there is an underlying condition that also precipitated signing a PHAD? (Patients without a serious medical illness generally will not fall under current assisted-suicide statutes, although it may be difficult for EMS or ED personnel to determine initially whether the patient has such a condition.) Such cases of failed assisted suicides have already appeared in the bioethics literature.[13] These cases indicate that another complicating factor might be interference (perhaps self-motivated) from the physician who prescribed the almost-lethal drugs.

Emergency medical personnel are often caught between several less-than-optimal options—maximal resuscitative efforts, no resuscitative efforts, or providing temporizing measures while gathering information. The only indication of how emergency physicians will respond is an Oregon study that suggests that many emergency physicians will abstain from aggressively resuscitating such patients only if they have clear proof that the patient desired and tried to die.[14] This result suggests the need to increase the use of PHADs by terminally ill patients.

An ethical analysis of the issue suggested that, whenever possible, emergency physicians should gather as much relevant information as they can and originate life-sustaining treatment to buy time to gather the information. If valid information indicates that physician-assisted suicide was the patient's competent and informed choice in response to a terminal illness, life-sustaining treatments can be withdrawn or not instituted. If such circumstances are not clear, treatment should continue. However, the authors concluded that emergency physicians should not provide direct assistance to patients who have attempted physician-assisted suicide by giving them a lethal drug to ingest or by administering a lethal injection.[15]

BREAKING BAD NEWS AND PROVIDING END-OF-LIFE CARE

One of the most difficult tasks emergency physicians perform is delivering the news of sudden, unexpected deaths. Similarly, they often must break bad news to patients and families about critical conditions and devastating illnesses. How to do this with sensitivity and professionalism is the ethical issue in which emergency medicine residents and ED nurses feel they need the most education.[16]

Coupled with end-of-life care, which is often difficult in a stressful ED environment with relatively few appropriate resources, emergency medicine personnel often feel overwhelmed by the need to communicate bad news. The key element is to respect and understand recipients' feelings, which can be more difficult if they speak a different language, are from a different culture, or often both. Teaching physicians rarely teach notification of sudden death because they often fear that they are mishandling the process and thus are reluctant to have trainees observe them. Physicians pass down this attitude through generations of physicians.

The key to performing this task with survivors, who are now considered patients, is to prepare in advance to deliver the news; inform them using nontechnical language, appropriate phrases, and active listening; be ready to answer their questions, especially about organ and tissue donation and autopsies;[17] and provide support in whatever manner possible.[18]

The delivery of bad news in the ED is much more difficult when the primary physician has not provided adequate information to the patient or family prior to a critical illness. Even though impending death might be a difficult topic, resources are available to make that discussion easier.[19] No doubt newer generations of physicians will become more comfortable with performing these tasks as emphasis on these educational topics becomes more common.

DECISION-MAKING CAPACITY AND SURROGATE DECISION MAKERS

Frequently troublesome to ED and EMS providers is the question of whether an individual has the capacity to consent to (or refuse) medical treatment, how to assess that capacity, and who makes the decision if the individual cannot. People often assume, incorrectly, that minors and inebriated or psychiatric patients lack decision-making capacity. Minors can be emancipated (treated as adults) under numerous conditions, or may simply fall under the "emergency treatment" category, such as when they present alone or with a nonguardian adult for treatment and then assent to sutures, radiographs, or intravenous hydration. The principle for minors is that one should not deny them what would otherwise be the standard of care for emergencies because of their age.

Inebriated and psychiatric patients, unless they have no contact with reality, usually retain some elements of decision-making capacity, although possibly not enough to make important medical decisions. The rule is that the more serious the decision, the higher the level of capacity a person must have. For example, the person might be able to decide what he wants to eat, but not have the capacity to decide whether he needs (or can refuse) a chest tube for a collapsed lung.

In the ED setting, to have decision-making capacity for a particular decision, patients must show an understanding of (1) the treatment options that have been described to them, (2) the risks and benefits to them of each option, and (3) how their decision relates to their normal value system.[20] This last question can be put as simply as, "Why did you make that decision?" If patients retain decision-making capacity, not only can they select treatments, but they can also refuse them, even if to do so might be life threatening.[21] This often causes consternation among ED and EMS providers, who are, by nature, "rescuers."

If adult patients lack decision-making capacity, both their advance directives and any surrogate list in state law come into play. Generally, if a patient has a durable power of attorney for health care (DPAH), it names a surrogate decision maker, who then takes precedence over anyone other than a court-appointed guardian.[22] If no DPAH exists, decisions can be made by individuals named in the state's surrogate list.[23] In all cases, if a surrogate declines to assume the decision-making position, the next person on the list can assume the role. Having an excellent advance directive law and a substantive surrogate list in state law is an example of proactive ethics, which greatly assists ED and EMS patients and practitioners.

PROVIDER SAFETY AND SECURITY

Increasingly, EMS and ED healthcare providers must concern themselves with safety issues. Gang-affiliated and other violent individuals no longer think of the EMS and ED as sanctuaries or "neutral zones" but rather as sources of additional victims. Ethical dilemmas arise when the provider's desire to be beneficent conflicts with the innate need to be safe. This safety concern starts with access to the system. Should EMS personnel enter unsecured (no police) scenes to provide aid to victims of violence, or wait and possibly jeopardize their patients' well-being?[24] Similar, but not as obvious, are the restrictions on ED entry (or entry to patient-care areas) that have become much more common. Self-preservation can be justified both because it is a natural instinct that professionalism does not abolish and because the ED health provider is a valuable societal resource and should not be endangered in a frivolous manner.

The underlying theme is that EMS personnel must guard their own safety first. This includes refusing to "play cop" in the ED with violent patients. (Such behavior also distorts physicians' roles, so that patients see them as security guards and may no longer willingly trust them as physicians.) Next, emergency medical practitioners must, whenever possible, safeguard their coworkers' well-being by ensuring that they are not put in harm's way. Only once that is accomplished can emergency medical providers protect their patients.[25] Ideally, this situation rarely arises, but in a crisis, the ethics of resource conservation, if nothing else, dictates this order of priorities.

RESOURCE ALLOCATION: TRIAGE, DISASTERS, AND GLOBAL MEDICINE

Emergency medicine clinicians frequently need to allocate resources when current demands outstrip the available resources for current medical treatment. Several terms, including *triage*, *rationing*, and *allocation*, are used to refer to the distribution of scarce resources in different healthcare contexts.[26] Formal or informal triage determines which patients receive the resources that do exist, including time (i.e., treatment priority).

Triage is necessary in the prehospital setting (multiple-casualty incidents), in emergency departments (routine prioritization for diagnostic and therapeutic interventions and inpatient bed assignment), and in resource-poor environments (developing countries, battlefields, and disasters). Decisions about distributing scarce healthcare resources can arise at all levels, from societal choices within a national healthcare system (macroallocation) to individuals allocating immediate emergency treatment and transport among the multiple, severely injured survivors of a motor vehicle crash or industrial accident (microallocation).

Numerous theories of distributive justice (fair resource allocation) abound. But in the practical sense, as long as resources exist, experienced emergency medicine personnel, both in the ED and the EMS, will continue to use the utilitarian concept of providing the most good for the most people to determine who receives limited resources.[27] Of the possible triage models, the most common is to treat the most serious, or potentially serious, illnesses and injuries first. Everyone receives necessary treatment, although those who are less ill must wait longer. Triage procedures, following the concept of equity, provide equivalent treatment for those with equivalent needs—that is, they treat similar patients similarly. There is an application of the concept of social worth primarily when the individual can help many others if returned to functioning (the multiplier effect). Based on utilitarian principles, a patient's best prognosis applies only to instances of severe resource limitation, such as battlefield and post-catastrophe triage, sometimes called "lifeboat" or "nightmare" situations.[28]

When triage officers do not understand the ethical basis for their decisions, they may be indecisive. Failing to act due to moral uncertainty is unacceptable, however, because inaction is often the worst of the available options. In multiple-casualty incidents, triage criteria may demand that, contrary to their normal practice of devoting maximum time and resources to the sickest patients, clinicians must first evacuate ambulatory patients and then those not dependent on high-intensity care or advanced technology.[29]

To maximize understanding of the methods and reasoning for triage decisions in situations of widespread severe resource scarcity, we must engage in proactive bioethical decision making to develop a broad-based consensus on triage guidance policies or protocols. Those involved should include ED and prehospital clinicians, hospital administrators, religious leaders, bioethics committees, and community leaders.[30]

One often-overlooked element is that most disaster plans depend on using the regular hospital and out-of-hospital emergency personnel to maintain the healthcare system's front line during crises. However, this often involves personal risk to themselves or their families. Although there are moral arguments for a duty to treat during disasters and social crises, the decision to stay or leave will ultimately depend on individuals' risk assessments and value systems. Preparations for the next pandemic or disaster should include policies that encourage emergency personnel to "stay and fight."[31]

In sum, whereas nearly every discussion of disaster plans calls for an ethical basis for resource allocation decisions, few specific suggestions have been offered. What appears to be essential is to make hard decisions about resource allocation before, rather than during, disasters. Based on sound ethical principles, disaster/triage plans must (1) include equitable (not equal) distribution of resources, (2) prioritize patients based on fairness and utility, (3) have an individual ultimately responsible for implementing resource allocation decisions, and (4) both the medical and potential patient communities (stakeholders) must be aware of these plans and buy into them through community focus groups.[32]

PRACTICING AND TEACHING ON THE NEWLY DEAD

The public demands and expects all emergency practitioners to be skilled in critical lifesaving procedures and to teach these procedures to new practitioners. The most efficient and practical way for them to remain proficient in these sometimes little-used, technically difficult skills is for them to practice and teach on the newly dead. For many years, physicians learned technical skills such as intubation and central-line placement on patients who had recently died. Recently, however, there has been a suggestion that postmortem procedures are only permissible if there is prior consent from relatives. This position, however, ignores the nature of and purpose of informed consent, contravenes patient altruism, and disregards society's interest in having an optimal number of medical care providers experienced in lifesaving techniques.[32]

The process of obtaining informed consent stems from the concept of patient autonomy and, ultimately, a respect for others. In theory, the process increases communication between the physician and patient prior to dangerous, disfiguring, or seriously invasive procedures. Requiring emergency medical personnel to obtain prior consent to practice or teach lifesaving procedures on the newly dead, however, misapplies informed consent and misrepresents the concept of patient autonomy.

The dead, of course, have no autonomy claim. Autonomy, based on the principles of freedom and liberty, is a function of personhood. However, the dead are no longer persons, although by societal consent they can still implement their wishes for the disposition of their bodies through advance directives or a legal will—neither of which are normally available in the ED. Nevertheless, the former patients' wishes should be respected, which generally means respecting an altruism not found as readily in their relatives.[33] The relatives' "quasi-property rights" to a corpse are strictly limited and do not give them either moral or legal authority to counteract stronger competing claims.

Society also has a substantial interest in these procedures. That interest is the need to maintain an optimal number of ED and EMS personnel proficient in lifesaving procedures. The medical professions recognize that both primary instruction and continued practice is necessary for proficiency in lifesaving skills. This instruction and practice is best on fresh cadavers, because the available alternatives are not adequate. However, although they recognize that unreasonable barriers to this training should not exist, limits are equally important. These limits should include the respectful treatment of the body, limiting the training to those who must use these procedures, and eliminating from use any corpses of persons who had an available document declining use as an organ or tissue donor or who was from a culture that does not permit this. One academic emergency medicine organization suggests that hospitals develop a policy on such practices and recommends asking for consent from next of kin.[34] (Interestingly, the same organization firmly supports resuscitation research on living patients without consent. See next section.)

Alternatives to using fresh cadavers are inadequate—or dangerous. Although models, animals, and donated embalmed cadavers are useful ways to learn or practice some aspects of critical-care techniques, they poorly simulate the critical patient. The use of animals, aside from being logistically ever more difficult, is itself ethically problematic. Donated, preserved cadavers and models are less realistic, are expensive, and have limited availability. (Eventually, we will use virtual reality models at larger training centers, and this discussion will be moot.) The commonly used alternatives to cadavers are to use patients who are undergoing anesthesia or to prolong resuscitations beyond the point where the clinicians know it to be futile so that training procedures can be done.[35]

If a legal or ethical requirement for consent exists prior to postmortem ED instruction, it decreases the number of clinical personnel trained in lifesaving procedures. A need to request this permission from distraught relatives raises significant emotional barriers for clinicians to overcome in order to practice and teach the procedures. In a survey of medical personnel involved in organ harvesting, a dislike of "adding to relatives' distress by asking permission for donation" was the single greatest barrier to organ procurement.[36] This barrier is unlikely to be breached, especially for the seemingly more trivial request to teach or practice procedures. The stringent time limitations imposed by the onset of rigor mortis, the rapid transport of bodies to the morgue, and the press of duties for the ED staff once a resuscitation attempt has ended further compound impediments to organ harvesting.

In summary, patient autonomy plays an appropriate and vital role in keeping modern medicine from overstepping individual interests. However, its inappropriate extension to requiring consent for ED postmortem practice and teaching cannot be justified. The concept of autonomy is not advanced, and future patients, the medical profession, and society would be harmed.[37]

RESUSCITATION RESEARCH WITHOUT CONSENT

Finally, emergency medicine cannot remain static. Research on the treatment of critical patients in the prehospital arena and the ED is essential if the field is to progress. Despite the benefit to society, societal strictures on informed consent increasingly have prohibited much of this research in the United States.[38]

Research in acute care is a troubling area for institutional review board (IRB) approval and informed consent. Confusion about ethical and legal requirements has hampered research efforts and subsequent patient benefits. The acute care patients commonly seen in EDs and prehospital care are the relatively few patients who have suffered unexpected events that carry a high probability of mortality or severe morbidity unless there is immediate medical intervention. Because of the lack of substantive research on their medical and surgical problems and the difficulty in implementing research protocols, thousands of individuals receive care that is at best untested, and at worst inappropriate, each day in the United States. They deserve better. Acute care research can be implemented more widely and still satisfy both bureaucratic mandates and the ethical requirements to protect patients and research subjects.

There is an argument that acute care research is justified if the usual ethical requirements for research are modified to reflect the uniqueness of the situation. The recommendations are (1) to use an explicit definition of acute care as distinct from other modes of critical care, (2) to eliminate the requirement for informed consent (as usually understood), and (3) to require stringent IRB oversight regarding the unique ethical problems raised by this research. It has been further suggested that IRB oversight include review of the protocol by a panel of individuals who represent possible enrollees in the proposed study.[39]

Yet, in 1993, the Food and Drug Administration (FDA), the governing body for individual IRBs, placed a moratorium on resuscitation research.[40] The Office of Protection from Research Risks (now called the Office for Human Research Protection) halted all human resuscitation research, including studies using alternative consenting mechanisms, such as deferred consent, implied consent, and two-tiered consent.[41]

Toward the end of 1996, the National Institutes of Health (NIH), the FDA, and other government agencies loosened a few of their restrictions on critical care research, publishing the "Final Rule" that permitted limited critical care research without prior informed consent. The restrictions have resulted in a significant decrease in the number of published clinical cardiac arrest trials—and, by implication, other resuscitation research. In contrast, the European Union has significantly increased the number of such studies published since 1993.[42]

In part, this situation led to a 2005 consensus conference held by the Society for Academic Emergency Medicine. There was not only consensus that this research was vital, but also that systematically excluding any subgroups from such studies would be inappropriate. The group also recommended that a risk/benefit determination for inclusion of vulnerable populations in research without consent should be added to standard IRB deliberations, and that various methods for the difficult, but required, IRB consultation with representative members of the community be tested.[43] In fact, by 2005, almost all medical school IRBs were willing to review minimal-risk waiver studies, with about half of them already having approved at least one.[44] One participant summarized the issue as follows: "The societal value of minimizing future morbidity and mortality may conflict with individuals' right of self-determination. In allowing research to take place without informed consent, the current regulations resolve this conflict in favor of the societal benefit."[45] The one part of this review process not worked out is how to obtain valid community consultation. One suggestion that may work well is to use a random-dialing survey.[46]

In spite of these regulatory changes, some aspects of clinical research and research oversight fall short of meeting the ethical standards of safety and patient benefit. The availability of funds still largely drives research agendas. Many patient groups are omitted or are sorely underrepresented as research subjects, most notably those that are critically ill and injured, especially children.[47]

In sum, despite regulation changes and widespread professional approval, our society remains conflicted about proceeding with research in critical situations when one cannot obtain consent. We also have yet to implement a research agenda that follows needs rather than funding and includes all patient classes. How our society will resolve these questions is still undecided.

OTHER TROUBLESOME AREAS

Although the dilemmas described in this chapter epitomize some of emergency medicine's unique ethical conundrums, many other ethical dilemmas exist. In the ED, the basic beneficent value of alleviating pain runs up against two other values—to the patient's detriment. The physician's stricture against doing harm keeps adequate analgesia from many patients whom professionals suspect of "drug-seeking" behavior. This includes many patients with migraines and back pain, and some with kidney stones (all classic complaints of drug seekers). The majority of patients with these complaints are simply seeking relief for an acute problem. In addition, inadequate treatment can be accorded, although for different reasons, to patients who need pain relief before they are taken to operating or procedure rooms. Many physicians want patients to be coherent rather than comfortable when they sign an operative or procedure permit. Therefore, patients may wait hours without adequate analgesia, especially those with fractures and abdominal catastrophes requiring surgery, due to an ethical (or more likely legal) requirement for the patient's signature on an operative permit.

A common part of emergency care is the communication that occurs with ambulances, other physicians and EDs, and sometimes providers in remote locations (e.g., airplanes, ships, and field stations). These communications, generally referred to as *telemedicine*, often strain confidentiality but may become more common as more sophisticated systems and electronic recordkeeping become more common. At this point, emergency medicine clinicians must join the national and global discussions to ensure that we set ethical standards to guide our use of these powerful technologies.[48]

Emergency physicians commonly face another dilemma for which there does not seem to be an adequate answer. In most clinical situations, a patient's decision-making capacity is easily determined. If there is a question, clinicians test the patient's understanding. There is a significant question about decision-making capacity under the severe stress of an acute and unexpected illness, compounded by the strange surroundings of the ED. Patient autonomy governs much of modern U.S. biomedical ethics. It is unclear, however, what it takes to be autonomous in a crisis. The patient gasping for breath who refuses intubation, the acquired immune deficiency syndrome (AIDS) patient who at the last moment verbally changes a well-thought-out advance directive, or the patient agreeing to take a risky medication or undergo a major operative procedure under these circumstances might be exhibiting panic behavior rather than autonomy in any accepted sense. Even in these scenarios, many patients continue to want to make their own healthcare decisions. Is this appropriate? We just do not know.

SUMMARY

Emergency medicine faces ethical challenges as it enters the 21st century and struggles to meet its mission in a changing healthcare environment. In this chapter, Iserson presented 10 dilemmas that are critical for those who provide prehospital or emergency care. Emergency medicine practitioners must be prepared to address such issues as their status as a safety net, paternalism versus patient autonomy, prehospital advance directives, and failed physician-assisted suicides, while maintaining the emotionally and physically grueling pace of emergency care. The challenges of end-of-life care, disaster ethics, and research and training on the newly dead pose additional ethical problems. Finally, these practitioners must be aware of their own safety as they provide quality care to all who enter their systems.

QUESTIONS FOR DISCUSSION

1. How does the overcrowding in EDs affect patient autonomy?
2. What ethical issues does the lack of implementation of PHADs create for emergency medicine staff? What issues does it create for the healthcare system itself?

3. When emergency medicine physicians do not receive training on how to deliver bad news, does that lack of training present ethical issues for the patients and their families?

4. How does the theory of utilitarianism relate to the safety of emergency medicine practitioners?

5. What is the relationship between autonomy and the ethical dilemmas faced by emergency medicine practitioners?

FOOD FOR THOUGHT

Of all the procedures that you can do in emergency medicine, which ones should you do—for which patients and in which circumstances? How can you use ethics to make these decisions? When there is a shortage of medications, supplies, or beds within your own institution, how do you ethically determine who receives the available resources?

NOTES

1. K. V. Iserson and C. E. Heine, "Bioethics," in *Rosen's Emergency Medicine: Concepts and Clinical Practice*, 7th ed., eds. J. A. Marx, R. S. Hockberger, R. M. Walls, et al. (Philadelphia: Elsevier/Mosby, 2012).

2. G. D. Velianoff, "Overcrowding and Diversion in the Emergency Department: The Health Care Safety Net Unravels," *Nursing Clinics of North America* 37, no. 1 (2002): 59–66.

3. K. V. Iserson and T. Kastre, "Are Emergency Departments a 'Safety Net' for the Medically Indigent?" *American Journal of Emergency Medicine* 14, no. 1 (1996): 1–5; Committee on the Future of Emergency Care in the United States Health System, Institute of Medicine of the National Academies, *Emergency Medical Services at the Crossroads*, Future of Emergency Care Series (Washington, DC: National Academies Press, 2006), xii.

4. J. S. Olshaker and N. K. Rathlev, "Emergency Department Overcrowding and Ambulance Diversion: The Impact and Potential Solutions of Extended Boarding of Admitted Patients in the Emergency Department," *Journal of Emergency Medicine* 3 (2006): 351–356.

5. Committee on the Future of Emergency Care, *Emergency Medical Services at the Crossroads*.

6. P. C. Sprivulis, J. A. DaSilva, I. G. Jacobs, et al., "The Association Between Hospital Overcrowding and Mortality Among Patients Admitted via Western Australian Emergency Departments," *Medical Journal of Australia* 184, no. 5 (2006): 208–212; D. B. Richardson, "Increase in Patient Mortality at 10 Days Associated with Emergency Department Overcrowding," *Medical Journal of Australia* 184, no. 5 (2006): 213–216.

7. P. T. Hershey, "A Definition for Paternalism," *Journal of Medical Philosophy* 10, no. 2 (1985): 171–182.

8. K. V. Iserson, "A Simplified Prehospital Advance Directive Law: Arizona's Approach," *Annals of Emergency Medicine* 22, no. 11 (1993): 1703–1710.

9. K. V. Iserson, "Prehospital Advance Directives—A Better Way," *Journal of Emergency Medicine* 23, no. 11 (2002): 419–420.

10. K. V. Iserson, "Nonstandard Advance Directives: A Pseudoethical Dilemma," *Journal of Trauma* 44, no.1 (1998): 139–142; K. V. Iserson, "The 'No Code' Tattoo: An Ethical Dilemma," *Western Journal of Medicine* 156, no. 3 (1992): 309–312.

11. R. M. Schears, C. A. Marco, and K. V. Iserson, "'Do-Not-Attempt Resuscitation' (DNAR) Policy in the Out-of-Hospital Setting," *Annals of Emergency Medicine* 44, no. 1 (2004): 68–70.

12. R. Byock, "A Slight Postmortem Disagreement," in *Ethics in Emergency Medicine*, 2nd ed., eds. K. V. Iserson, A. B. Sanders, and D. R. Mathieu (Tucson, AZ: Galen Press, 1995), 80–87.

13. K. V. Iserson, D. R. Gregory, K. Christensen, and M. R. Ofstein, "Willful Death and Painful Decisions: A Failed Assisted Suicide," *Cambridge Quarterly of Healthcare Ethics* 1, no. 2 (1992): 147–158.

14. T. A Schmidt, "Oregon Emergency Physicians' Experiences, Attitudes, and Concerns About Physician-Assisted Suicide," *Academy of Emergency Medicine* 3, no. 5 (1996): 490.

15. J. Moskop and K. V. Iserson, "Emergency Physicians and Physician-Assisted Suicide, Part I: A Review of the Physician-Assisted Suicide Debate," *Annals of Emergency Medicine* 38, no. 5 (2001): 570–575; J. Moskop and K. V. Iserson, "Emergency Physicians and Physician-Assisted Suicide, Part II: Emergency Care for Patients Who Have Attempted Physician-Assisted Suicide," *Annals of Emergency Medicine* 38, no. 5 (2001): 576–582.

16. M. A. Pauls and S. Ackroyd-Stolarz, "Identifying Bioethics Learning Needs: A Survey of Canadian Emergency Medicine Residents," *Academy of Emergency Medicine* 13, no. 6 (2006): 645–652.

17. K. V. Iserson, *Death to Dust: What Happens to Dead Bodies?* 2nd ed. (Tucson, AZ: Galen Press, 2001).

18. K. V. Iserson, *Grave Words: Notifying Survivors About Sudden Unexpected Deaths* (Tucson, AZ: Galen Press, 1999); American College of Emergency Physicians, "Ethical Issues in Emergency Department Care at the End of Life," *Annals of Emergency Medicine* 47, no. 3 (2006): 303; K. V. Iserson, "Bereavement and Grief Reactions," in *Harwood-Nuss' Clinical Practice of Emergency Medicine*, 4th ed., eds. A. B. Wolfson, G. W. Hendey, P. L. Henry, et al. (Philadelphia: Lippincott Williams & Wilkins, 2005), 649–653.

19. K. V. Iserson, *After-Death Planner*, 2nd ed. (Tucson, AZ: Galen Press, 2001).

20. A. E. Buchanan, "The Question of Competence," in *Ethics in Emergency Medicine*, 2nd ed., 61–65.

21. A. R. Derse, "What Part of 'No' Don't You Understand? Patient Refusal of Recommended Treatment in the Emergency Department," *Mount Sinai Journal of Medicine* 72, no. 4 (2005): 221–227.

22. See http://www.galenpress.com/extras/extra1.htm for Arizona's extremely useable and often-copied advance directives. Accessed July 6, 2012.

23. Arizona's list, one of the most extensive in the nation, cites the following surrogate decision makers, in order: spouse, adult children, parents (of an adult), domestic partner, adult sibling, close friend, and attending physician in consultation with a bioethics committee.

24. R. A. Lazar, "Prehospital Personnel's Safety Versus a Duty to Treat," in *Ethics in Emergency Medicine*, 2nd ed., 412–416.

25. K. V. Iserson and C. Heine, "Ethics in Wilderness Medicine," in *Wilderness Medicine: Management of Wilderness and Environmental Emergencies*, 6th ed., ed. P. Auerbach (Philadelphia: Elsevier/Mosby, 2012).

26. K. V. Iserson and J. C. Moskop, "Triage in Medicine, Part I: Concept, History, and Types," *Annals of Emergency Medicine* 49, no. 3 (2007): 275–281.

27. Ibid.; J. C. Moskop and K. V. Iserson, "Triage in Medicine, Part II: Underlying Values and Principles," *Annals of Emergency Medicine* 49, no. 3 (2007): 282–287.

28. K. V. Iserson and N. Pesik, "Ethical Resource Distribution After Biological, Chemical or Radiological Terrorism," *Cambridge Quarterly of Healthcare Ethics* 12, no. 4 (2003): 455–465.

29. Moskop and Iserson, "Triage in Medicine, Part II"; K. V. Iserson, "The Rapid Ethical Decision-Making Model: Critical Medical Interventions in Resource-Poor Environments," *Cambridge Quarterly of Healthcare Ethics* 20, no. 1 (2011): 108–114.

30. N. Pesik, M. E. Keim, and K. V. Iserson, "Terrorism and the Ethics of Emergency Medical Care," *Annals of Emergency Medicine* 37, no. 6 (2001): 642–646.

31. K. V. Iserson, C. E. Heine, G. L. Larkin, et al., "Fight or Flight: The Ethics of Emergency Physician Disaster Response," *Annals of Emergency Medicine* 51 no. 4 (2008): 345–353.

32. K. V. Iserson, "The Most Difficult Healthcare Decisions, Part 1: Resource Allocation—Ethical Justification" (video, 10:35 min), 2007; "The Most Difficult Healthcare Decisions, Part 2: How to Ration Healthcare Resources" (video, 10:40 min), 2007; and "The Most Difficult Healthcare Decisions, Part 3: Who Allocates Scarce Healthcare Resources?" (video, 13:15 min), 2007; all available at http://www.crestaznm.org. Accessed July 6, 2012. Also see K. V. Iserson,

"Teaching Without Harming the Living: Performing Minimally Invasive Procedures on the Newly Dead," *Journal of Health Care Law and Policy* 8, no. 2 (2005): 216–231.

33. R. M. Oswalt, "A Review of Blood Donor Motivation and Recruitment," *Transfusion* 17 (1977): 123–135.

34. T. A. Schmidt, J. T. Abbott, J. M. Geiderman, et al., "Ethics Seminars: The Ethical Debate on Practicing Procedures on the Newly Dead," *Academy of Emergency Medicine* 11, no. 9 (2004): 962–966.

35. Iserson, *Death to Dust.*

36. Iserson, "Teaching Without Harming the Living."

37. K. V. Iserson and D. L. Lindsey, "Research on Critically Ill and Injured Patients: Rules, Reality, and Ethics," *Journal of Emergency Medicine* 13, no. 4 (1995): 563–567.

38. K. V. Iserson and M. Mahowald, "Acute Care Research: Is It Ethical?" *Critical Care Medicine* 20 (1992): 1032–1037.

39. G. B. Ellis, "'Dear Colleague' Letter: Human Subjects' Protection," *OPRR Report* 93, no. 3 (August 12, 1993).

40. U.S. Food and Drug Administration, "Protection of Human Subjects: Informed Consent and Waiver of Informed Consent Requirements in Certain Emergency Circumstances," *Federal Register* 61, no. 192 (1996): 51497–51531.

41. K. M. Hiller, J. S. Haukoos, K. Heard, et al., "Impact of the Final Rule on the Rate of Clinical Cardiac Arrest Research in the United States," *Academy of Emergency Medicine* 12, no. 11 (2005): 1091–1098.

42. J. M. Baren and S. S. Fish, "Resuscitation Research Involving Vulnerable Populations: Are Additional Protections Needed for Emergency Exception from Informed Consent?" *Academy of Emergency Medicine* 12, no. 11 (2005): 1071–1077.

43. M. C. Morris, "An Ethical Analysis of Exception from Informed Consent Regulations," *Academy of Emergency Medicine* 12, no. 11 (2005): 1113–1119.

44. A. Ernst, S. J. Weiss, T. G. Nick, K. V. Iserson, and M. Biros, "Minimal-Risk Waiver of Informed Consent (Final Rule) Studies at Institutional Review Boards Nationwide," *Academic Emergency Medicine* 12 (2005): 1134–1137.

45. Morris, "An Ethical Analysis of Exception from Informed Consent."

46. E. M. Bulger, T. A. Schmidt, A. J. Cook, et al., "The Random Dialing Survey as a Tool for Community Consultation for Research Involving the Emergency Medicine Exception from Informed Consent," *Annals of Emergency Medicine* 53, no 3 (2009): 341–350.

47. K. V. Iserson, "Has Emergency Medicine Research Benefited Patients? An Ethical Question," *Science and Engineering Ethics* 13 (2007): 289–295.

48. K. V. Iserson, "Ethics of Clinical Telemedicine," in *Health Care Ethics: Core and Emergency Issues*, eds. R. Chadwick, H. ten Have, and E. M. Meslin (Cardiff, UK: Sage Publications, 2011), 379–391.

CHAPTER 16

Technological Advances in Health Care: Blessing or Ethics Nightmare?

Cristian H. Lieneck

INTRODUCTION

Currently there is a strong emphasis on increasing the prevalence and effective utilization of medical and health information technology within all types of healthcare organizations. Hospitals and ambulatory care facilities are facing extreme marketing and economic pressures to employ technology in their current clinical and administrative processes in an attempt to meet quality demands as well as prescribed regulatory requirements and associated financial incentives. These attempts at technology implementation leave several basic questions unanswered: What is the overall benefit? Will quality of care improve? What potential harm may result? Is it possible to sustain equity and efficiency of care across all patient populations?

As a result of the forthcoming ramifications of healthcare reform in the United States, it would appear that healthcare organizations must do more with fewer resources. This includes experiencing cuts in government and private payer reimbursements, increased shortages in several types of healthcare providers, as well as an ever-increasing Medicare and Medicaid population. These changes will continue to inflict strain on the system as they progress. Consequently, organizations are turning to medical and health information technology in an attempt to increase productivity and the quality of care provided. It is hoped that the result will be a positive influence on overall patient outcomes. However, serious ethical implications may arise throughout the concurrent advances in medical and health information technologies as these outcome-based reimbursement models and related healthcare reform ideals become reality.

The field of health care encompasses many complex processes and protocols, which are in a state of constant fluctuation. Healthcare organizational leaders experience internal and external organizational influences that affect the decisions that are to be made affecting the well-being of all stakeholders involved, most importantly the external customer in health care: the patient. Often these decisions involve the procurement and implementation of technology in an attempt to further organizational productivity, process improvement, and quality of care. The discussion in this chapter focuses on several aspects of the healthcare technology front with regard to critical issues and ethical challenges, presented from an overall industry level. It also presents a distinctive view of the medical group practice perspective. The goals of the chapter are to accomplish the following:

1. *Define medical and health information technology and discuss their close relationship with advances in medical science and accountable care.* This section segregates and defines the types of technology utilized in the healthcare context to set the framework for further discussion.

2. *Assess ethical challenges related to recent advances in medical technology and medical science.* This section presents a selection of complex medical innovations in which technology facilitates advancement of the medical field and quality patient care, while simultaneously questioning several ethical principles.

3. *Assess health information technology developments within the medical group practice, including ethical challenges related to recent and upcoming healthcare reform requirements.* This section provides a realistic view of several ethical challenges as medical group practices undergo pressure regarding the implementation and meaningful use of medical technology and health information technology in order to meet legislative mandates, economic goals, and market pressures.

MEDICAL AND HEALTH INFORMATION TECHNOLOGY DEFINED

The field of medical technology, broadly defined, relates to a series of products designed to advance patient care while simultaneously working to increase both the efficiency and effectiveness of the healthcare organization, its medical providers, and medical staff. More specifically, this chapter addresses these advances using the two following classifications for healthcare technology.

- *Medical technology* is defined as that which is intended to assist with proper diagnosis and further the quality of medical care by offering less invasive treatment options through the technological advancement of medical products, equipment, processes, and procedures.

- *Health information technology (HIT)* includes a series of computer hardware, software, administrative databases, and network systems designed to assist medical providers in providing quality care using the electronic medical record (EMR). The associated interoperability of peripheral electronic medical support systems is also part of this definition. Examples of these additional support systems may include computerized physician order entry (CPOE); data warehousing; database backup, mining, and reporting platforms; and other computer-assisted management-of-care products such as clinical decision support systems (CDSS).

Although both categories define several aspects of technological resources, this chapter focuses on these two classifications and their contributions to the medical field from several ethical perspectives. A challenge exists for healthcare leaders, providers, and administrators to continue to research ethical implications as technological resources are implemented into current, everyday healthcare processes. This ongoing awareness will help ensure an effective implementation and utilization of such innovations for all stakeholders involved.

THE ETHICAL OBLIGATION

Developments in medical technology often aid or mediate advancements in both medical science and healthcare administrative processes. As a result, the healthcare field is becoming increasingly dependent on technological developments to ensure organizational success, as quality outcomes and reimbursement for medical services become further concomitant with continuous advancements in the technological realm. Almost overnight, the healthcare industry's primary purpose has been altered to not only involve the constant provision of safe, quality medical services, but also the need to become highly proficient in the accumulation and communication of patient data and related patient care outcomes.

Given a new assembly of healthcare terminology dedicated to increasing the quality of care provided (and identified by a multitude of acronyms), the healthcare leader's challenge is to make sense of it all as this movement influences his or her medical organization. Examples of these acronyms include ACOs (accountable care organizations), P4P (pay for performance), and VBP (value-based purchasing). Healthcare systems and their internal processes are being adapted to include technology at various levels in an attempt to meet this challenge. This almost overwhelming reliance on medical technology and HIT must be continuously evaluated by healthcare leaders for its potential ethical implications from all healthcare stakeholder perspectives to ensure that the legal and fiduciary duties of the medical researchers, providers, and healthcare executives hold to the highest standards of our industry.

SCIENCE AND TECHNOLOGY INNOVATIONS
AND ETHICAL CONCERNS

The development of new technological resources in the field of medicine requires thorough due diligence with regard to the quality, efficiency, efficacy, and safety of the research and implementation process for an innovation. Thorough research with documented outcomes is necessary to establish the value of new procedures, treatments, and medical equipment prior to mar-ketwide adoption of the innovation as an established industry best practice. Although several regulatory and licensing agencies exist to evaluate these continuous technological advances, the focus remains primarily on patient safety and the overall effectiveness of the technology and equipment in treatment of a disease or condition. Subsequently, a disregard for overall healthcare equity and other unintentional, yet important, ethical implications continues to exist, even before a new innovation is approved and accepted into patient care protocols. The use of medical technology and its contribution toward the research and development of medical innovations in the United States demonstrates a disassociation and lack of attentiveness regarding medical ethics and intended innovation outcomes or benefits.

Exploitation of Research Subjects During Research and Development

Prior to the actual approval and implementation of technological advances in medicine, several ethical principles come into question from the genesis and development of the innovation itself. Additionally, as new diseases and disabling conditions continue to surface, civilization becomes more dependent on advances in medical science and technology to assist in the control of these conditions' unpleasant side effects or in the cure of life-threatening conditions altogether. This dependence on technology often allows for a false sense of plausible deniability to occur, particularly as a disassociation between researchers and the research itself. This particular mind-set enables the researcher to focus directly on the study results for only those who may receive direct benefit from the study outcomes. The public thinks that this situation, enabled by technological advances in science and medicine, has happened only in remote instances throughout the history of United States medical research and development processes. Recently, however, researchers and historians have discovered that these ethical blemishes, once believed to be isolated incidents in our country's medical research history, existed much more frequently than originally thought.

The Tuskegee Syphilis Study and the Willowbrook Hepatitis Study are two primary, well-documented incidents of unethical medical research on human subjects, characterized by a lack of informed consent and complete disregard for the ethical principle of patient autonomy. To assist in the evaluation of these studies' methodologies and their disregard for ethical principles, Morrison[1] discusses the following elements, which we must consider to avoid the negation of autonomy as demonstrated by informed consent:

- *Competence:* Patients must understand the treatment involved with the research study. Do patients understand potential side effects, as well as the probability of receiving possible outcomes, properly?
- *Voluntariness:* Patients must have the opportunity to decide whether to participate in the study based on their own terms, beliefs, and feelings. Do they have the opportunity to say "no" to those individuals conducting the study without remorse or follow-on judgment if such declination occurs?
- *Disclosure:* Potential study participants must have knowledge of all legal and ethical aspects of the research, so they may use this information to aid in the decision whether to participate. Is the study and all of its details transparent to all stakeholders involved?
- *Authorization:* Patients must agree with the study's treatment plan and agree to proceed as a research participant. Does the subject actually know he or she is part of a research study, and if so, has he or she signed a written (informed) consent form documenting agreement to participate?

The Tuskegee study (1932–1972) involved 200 African American males serving as study control subjects, while another 200 African American males were used as the experimental group.[2] Researchers conducting the study purposely inoculated the experimental group with active syphilis. The individuals exposed to the syphilis disease (the experimental, noncontrol group) were told they were receiving the medical interventions as treatment for a rare and deadly blood disease. In return for their participation in the study, all the men received compensation with food, medical care, and burial insurance.

Although an individual's actions often imply autonomous consent,[3] this was certainly not the case for the Tuskegee study. On several levels, the competence, voluntariness, disclosure, and authorization requirements for consent failed to be addressed or adhered to prior to these study participants entering into the study. Moreover, there was further corruption of patient autonomy when the researchers manipulated the potential study participants and influenced them into participating in the study by offering compensation methods that were highly attractive to this disadvantaged population of potential subjects.

Researchers conducted the Willowbrook study (1963–1966) in an attempt to understand further the progression of the hepatitis virus and the effects of treatment for the disease using gamma globulin.[4] A similar research and control group methodology as in the Tuskegee study existed, except that the subjects in the Willowbrook study were all children attending the Willowbrook State School, an institution for adolescents with mental disabilities. When compared with the Tuskegee study, there were similar autonomy issue challenges, yet the Willowbrook methodology also failed to address the study participants' competency on two additional and unembellished levels.

We are often unable to deem adolescents (minors) competent when presented with medical decisions regarding their personal health. It was this acknowledgment of the inability for an adolescent patient to provide proper informed consent that eventually led to the establishment of the patient-centered medical home (PCMH) concept, which was born out of the pediatric specialty and is now being utilized in several other medical specialties today.[5] Furthermore, these children were mentally challenged and not able to make regular decisions by themselves in everyday situations, much less regarding the question of whether to participate in a research study that included the potential to become selected into an experimental group that was to be purposely infected with the deadly hepatitis virus.

Collective review of the Tuskegee and Willowbrook studies demonstrated the ability of researchers to become intellectually intrigued and personally invested in the methodology and potential outcome of their studies, with complete disregard of the ethical implications that continued throughout the research. More specifically, this lack of transparency failed to afford the study participants their individual autonomy by failing to disclose methodology related to the potential side effects and permanent treatment outcomes, which included the possible contraction of syphilis and hepatitis. Although these two occurrences in U.S. medical research history are both concerning and horrific, it has been recently determined that instances involving similar flawed research methodology with regard to ethical principles were more prevalent in U.S. history than originally identified.

In August 2010, Susan Reverby, a professor of history and women's and gender studies at Wellesley College, announced further evidence of unethical medical research. Her efforts of diving through the dusty coffers of medical archives in Pittsburgh resulted in the discovery and confirmation that the

U.S. Public Health Service funded and conducted a syphilis-inoculation program on over 5,500 Guatemalan prisoners, mental patients, and soldiers between 1946 and 1948.[6] Although similar to Tuskegee and Willowbrook in that these study participants also did not provide consent, in this case the Guatemalan authorities supposedly authorized the experiment on their own citizens even though the United States funded the study and it occurred outside of U.S. territory. Reverby's research findings spread like wildfire, gaining political attention in both countries. On September 30, 2010, President Barack Obama personally contacted President Alvaro Colom of Guatemala to apologize for the ethically unacceptable event and to offer his regrets for all those affected.[7] Further apologetic efforts were conducted by Secretary of State Hillary Clinton and by Health and Human Services head Kathleen Sebelius.[8]

Advancements in science and medicine are not possible without technology resources, and this technology requires thorough research and development initiatives. Moreover, new advancements in medicine often require approval by several regulatory or licensing authorities or both prior to acceptance and use in the U.S. healthcare industry. Researchers must complete these research and development steps in an ethical manner with complete transparency among all stakeholders involved, especially the research subjects. Ethical committees and review boards are necessary to offer third-party evaluation of proposed research studies, the subjects involved, and overall research methodologies. It is not just for a few uninformed or disadvantaged individuals to participate in an innovation's research and development process even if a large population of beneficiaries may exist upon successful completion of such a study.

RECENT INNOVATIONS INVOLVING TECHNOLOGY AND THEIR ETHICAL CONCERNS

As new technological advances develop in the field of medicine, their availability, method of implementation, and even their existence itself often motivate questions regarding ethics and societal concerns. The initial research and development phases, as well as a controlled implementation, require attentive healthcare leaders and ethics committees to ensure there is no violation of ethical principles. To demonstrate the potential ethical issues, selected advances in health care are discussed in this section. Although several ethical principles are addressed for each innovation, the author challenges the reader to identify additional principles that may apply to various situations involving these technological innovations.

Synthetic Biology

One of the most recent and prominent fields that has developed from advances in both science and technology is that of synthetic biology. Posited from research studies involving molecular biology, this new genetic science builds on the initial discovery of the configuration of recombinant DNA molecules. It now allows scientists to replace the natural genetic material within a simple bacterial cell with synthetic (human-made), genetically copied material that is capable of self-replicating.[9] In other words, scientists have created nongenetic raw materials as a substitute for genetic material within a living organism (synthesized organism genes).

Since the May 20, 2010, announcement from the J. Craig Venter Institute, mixed opinions of this advance have surfaced, entailing both excitement and concern. The field of synthetic biology holds the promise of future advances in products related to several industries, including environmental pollution control, agriculture and food engineering, and the field of medicine.[10] On the other hand, because the fabrication of genetic materials from natural resources is a field still in its infancy, speculations and criticisms continue to surface, primarily as a result of the unknown future applications and consequences associated with this form of bioengineering. As a result, several ethics-based questions challenge the hastily growing science. These include the following:

- What agencies will be trusted with the oversight and regulation of this advancing science?
- Will unsupervised or nonaffiliated organizations begin to replicate various organisms with synthetic genetic material for purposes that may pose harm to others?
- How does one regulate such an advanced, yet specialized, industry to ensure its purposeful use while maintaining ethical research standards?
- As a more outrageous perspective, what will prevent the household biologist/chemist from fabricating his or her own genetic material in the secrecy of his or her private residence solely for individual motivations that do not match those of current regulatory standards?

Since the successful materialization of synthesized genetic biology, President Barack Obama requested that the Presidential Commission for the Study of Bioethical Issues investigate the field of synthetic biology and identify any ethical implications of the advancing science. A broad panel of experts, including science and engineering professionals, as well as faith-based and other secular ethicists, conducted a wide range of reviews.[11] Working to serve in a proactive manner by evaluating the ethical ramifications of the field while it is still in the developmental stages, the commission successfully identified and used five ethical principles to guide its investigation into the potential social implication of the emerging science: public beneficence, responsible stewardship, intellectual freedom, democratic deliberation, and justice and fairness.[12] The following is a brief explanation of each identified principle.

Public beneficence calls for the capitalization of overall public benefits from the science, while continuing to focus efforts on minimizing harm to the public. Similar to the main ethical principle of beneficence, public beneficence concerns the overall masses or the public populations who stand a chance to experience the gains or losses from the emerging science. These gains or losses may result from either a direct or an indirect nature. Therefore, the presidential commission has urged governments and scientific organizations to further the research and development of synthetic biology while continuing to be increasingly aware of unintended consequences and potential harm to the public. The commission also recommended reviewing techniques for reducing research risks and the ethical implications of the science and publication of the results.[13] Support of future research and ensuring collaboration among professional organizations (e.g., the National Institutes of Health, the Department of Energy, academia, and other industrial groups) were deemed mandatory to help support public beneficence.[14] As a result, there is an intention of cooperation and transparency among all stakeholders involved to assist with protection of the masses.

Responsible stewardship directs ethical efforts toward ensuring that there is consideration of those unable to represent themselves throughout the emergence of future research studies and utilization of synthetically generated cellular material. Focusing specifically on future generations for both global and domestic communities, requirements of clarity, coordination, and account-ability across governmental authorities were determined necessary to fulfill this ethical principle.[15] Therefore, all advances of the field must be clearly communicated to oversight committees and other invested stakeholders.

Furthermore, the coordinated effort should not include isolated, or lone-wolf, scientific efforts, but rather a more collaborative and mission-centered effort. This will allow for continuous monitoring of the field's hurdles and achievements, as well as containment and prevention of ethical quandaries. In conclusion, the presidential commission also described strong recommendations related to ongoing ethics education for scientists and student researchers in synthetic biology, as well as ongoing evaluation and reassessment of objections to the field itself.[16]

To assist in furthering the field of synthetic biology, the presidential commission called for *freedom of intellectual efforts*, while also ensuring the responsibility of all parties involved.[17] Specifically describing a moratorium on synthetic biology research as an inappropriate action, a compromise was suggested by the commission, therefore ensuring ongoing accountability through the use of periodic assessments and oversight controls.[18] As a result, the presidential commission called for a cautious freedom of study, to neither limit research efforts nor allow for unmonitored, uncontrolled research agendas. Allowing for debate among differing views, it suggested that *democratic deliberation* ensures representation from all societal groups and that they should be heard so that monitoring practices and policy making may reflect the support of the public majority.

Finally, the commission addressed the promotion of *justice* and *fairness*, with regard to those exposed to risks in synthetic biology research, as well as regarding commercial production and distribution efforts.[19] Following the main ethical principle of justice, certain individuals, groups, or communities are not to be subjected to research risks in an unfair manner. The same concept applies for the production or commercialization of synthetic products necessary to promote research in the field of synthetic biology.

Computer-Assisted and Robotic-Assisted Surgery

An area of medicine that continues to grow exponentially involves the use of technology, specifically computers and specialized peripherals, to assist medical providers during certain types of advanced surgical procedures. Computer-assisted technology, in addition to a central computer, may also include image-guided systems to allow the provider increased visibility and access to difficult procedural sites. Additionally, robotic surgery employs actual robotic equipment that functions as surgical assistants to the medical provider during surgical interventions. Virtually every field of medicine is implementing technological advances, with varying levels of utilization. The following are examples of surgical specialties now performing procedures with heightened levels of computer-assisted or robotic-assisted surgeries:

- *Stereotactic radiosurgery.* Within the field of neurology/neurosurgery, physicians conduct this image-guided surgical procedure using various radiotherapy devices that strategically guide various levels of radiation at precise measurements into the brain to target both malignant and benign brain metastases.[20] Real-time radiography is typically used throughout the procedure to accurately position the instrument delivering the radiation. A device named the gamma knife delivers over 200 radiation beams into deep levels of the brain that are often inaccessible and unfeasible using conventional surgery techniques.[21]

- *Computer-aided maxillofacial surgery.* Medical providers are now realizing the increased benefits of computer-aided navigation systems, including three-dimensional (3D) systems, which allow for more accurate diagnosis and virtual planning. These systems provide increased intraoperative surgical navigation for orthognathic and temporomandibular (TMJ) surgeries.[22] This technology enables dental surgical providers to better visualize oral characteristics to ensure proper implant technique and ultimately enhanced patient outcomes. Recently, this technology created 3D images of the limited-view sinus cavities within the nasal cavity and those nerves and vessels within the cavity to assist providers during complicated sinus surgeries.[23]

- *Robotic-assisted visceral surgery.* Researchers describe surgical laparoscopy of the abdomen as a more difficult procedure for the surgeon with regard to instrument maneuverability, as well as limited, two-dimensional vision.[24] Robot-assisted abdominal surgery, also known as telemanipulation, has allowed the surgeon to overcome these disadvantages of conventional laparoscopy. Additionally, these types of surgeries are often physically demanding for the medical providers involved. The use of robotics during surgery improves the surgeon's ergonomics during the procedure, as well as relieving other physical demands on the surgical staff members.[25]

Whereas the benefits of computer-assisted and robotic-assisted surgeries are evident, access to these highly technological devices remains quite limited. Often, healthcare facilities face challenges regarding the capital required to procure such equipment. Organizations may not be able to meet this cost and are therefore unable to provide such advanced procedures to their surrounding populations, affecting the potential for beneficent treatment for the community they serve. Additionally, the ethical principle of justice becomes important when evaluating access to these potentially scarce health resources. Is it fair that only those patients capable of affording time away from work and of traveling to a remote site that offers such technology will benefit from its advantages over conventional surgical procedures? Furthermore, each procedure using computer-assisted or robotic-assisted surgery technology carries higher costs for the organization in an attempt to recover initial capital investment costs.

Often organizations pass this extravagant cost through to the patient, the patient's medical insurance carrier, or both. The result is inequality, because only those patients with ample financial resources or sufficient medical coverage may be able to afford these advanced surgical resources.

Continuous Advancements in Magnetic Resonance Imaging

Discoveries in diagnostic radiology have allowed physicians to identify disease and anatomic abnormalities within the body at a much more effective rate and accuracy than previously possible. One continuous drive for technological innovation to assist clinical diagnoses and medical outcomes persists within the field of magnetic resonance imaging (MRI). MRI innovations have consistently centered on the device's magnetic field strength, often termed *signal* and measured in tesla (T) units. Over the years, MRI equipment has progressed in signal strengths from 0.3T devices, to 1.5T and 3T. Emerging research is striving to increase the signal strength to 7T and even to as much as 9.4T.[26] As signal strength increases, the image quality is enhanced, and there is a possibility for shorter exam times. Although this increased signal strength may seem advantageous to the patient and assist the diagnostic effectiveness of the physician, several ethical concerns regarding the significantly expensive capital investment required for these devices remain present for both hospital and ambulatory radiology facilities. As a result, the decision to acquire such an advanced imaging device, as well as ethical use of the enhanced technology, requires assessment at multiple levels.

The decision for a healthcare organization to invest in an advanced MRI machine is not a simple one. It involves extensive due diligence and market research by organizational leadership to ensure that the capital investment fits directly into the organization's strategic plan. Currently, a 3T MRI is the most advanced magnetic resonance imaging equipment approved for the medical treatment of humans. Higher-tesla MRI machines do exist, demonstrating faster, increased quality images, but these devices are still in the testing and research phases and are not yet available for routine use in the medical treatment of patients. However, the 3T MRI does possess advantages over its predecessor and medical imaging workhorse, the 1.5T MRI.

Enter "3T MRI" into any Internet search engine and the results will include several healthcare organizations advertising the advanced imaging capabilities now available with their newly procured 3T MRI machine. These boasted advantages are often compared with competitors' 1.5 MRI machines, which remain the current industry standard in MRI procedures. Comments such as "better-quality images" and "faster, more accurate diagnoses" are also often displayed. As a result, the decision to acquire a 3T MRI may be highly influenced by an organization's marketing strategy, primarily to elevate one organization's medical technology and promote its increased diagnostic capabilities over local market competition.

Although market position is a vital component in the strategic plan of most organizations, should the decision to invest in new medical equipment rely so heavily on the desire of an organization to stand out as a more technologically advanced institution? Given continually shrinking operational revenue margins for both the profit and not-for-profit sectors, would this capital investment (often $1 to $1.5 million more expensive than the standard 1.5T MRI) truly benefit the surrounding community? Many medical providers will base such decisions on the premise of deontology, believing that there is an obligation or duty for medical providers to be able to provide the best medical care possible, even if it is only benefiting patients with a specific diagnosis. Conversely, many healthcare administrators will assess this situation from a utilitarian viewpoint, deciding whether to invest in the new MRI technology based on the overall benefit to the community and which decision would help provide ample imaging services to the most patients.[27]

The 3T MRI is capable of generating lower, 1.5T-quality images, but in a shorter time than the regular 1.5T machine requires. As a result, the possibility of increased patient throughput exists when the 3T MRI is used to generate images at the 1.5T signal strength.[28] Although the actual time difference in image generation between the 3T and 1.5T MRI is marginal in an individual instance, over time this increased patient throughput will ultimately result in increased operational revenue for the organization, which aids in covering the additional expense of the advanced 3T technology.[29] The decision regarding whether to use the 1.5T or 3T imaging capability rests with the medical provider ordering the MRI for the patient, as well as the radiologist's expertise.

However, one must question the motivations of medical providers when using this new imaging technology in such a manner. For example, the decision to generate a reduced-quality image on the 3T MRI machine for purposes of increasing patient throughput creates ethical dilemmas with regard to quality of care, especially if the patient or referring medical provider picked that facility to perform the original MRI because of its advertised 3T advanced imaging capability (therefore potentially becoming a bait-and-switch technique). Furthermore, those patients who receive a 1.5T MRI exam that does not provide an image capable for diagnosis may then require a second, duplicate MRI procedure at the 3T image quality level. Questions of cost-effectiveness and the efficient use of medical resources arise when the same medical organization conducts repeat exams.

At the current time, most healthcare payers, including Medicare and commercial insurance, are contemplating reimbursement for MRI procedures based on the signal strength utilized. Some commercial healthcare payers may provide slightly higher reimbursement for a 3T MRI versus the standard 1.5T MRI procedure. This reimbursement difference depends on the medical provider's individual contract with any specific managed care organization, as well as the state in which the procedure was performed.[30] However, with no specific medical coding method exists to document the signal strength used for an MRI procedure, the possibility exists for a medical provider to perform a 1.5T exam and inadvertently receive the 3T image reimbursement. This occurrence will result in an overpayment to the provider, which still experiences increased patient throughput by performing the lower-level, 1.5T MRI procedure.

Finally, those payers who do not reimburse more for the 3T MRI may influence medical providers to perform more 1.5T images on the 3T machine to take advantage of the quicker exam time and increased patient throughput.[31] This technique was often used in order to make up the lost radiology revenue that resulted from the Deficit Reduction Act of 2005, which included strict cuts to radiology procedures.[32] In this instance, it is highly unethical for the 1.5T MRI exam to be used if the 3T MRI was initially deemed necessary to properly diagnose the patient and the lower-quality exam was simply used to increase patient throughput to enhance overall operational revenue from the 3T machine. As demonstrated, one must question ethics when one makes clinical decisions such as which MRI processes to use based solely on operational and financial incentives.

HEALTH INFORMATION TECHNOLOGY AND THE MEDICAL GROUP PRACTICE

It is an understatement to say that the field of health information technology is growing at a rapid pace. With medical hardware and software becoming outdated or obsolete in months, or even days, after its clinical procurement and implementation, the HIT industry continues to focus on adapting computers and associated technology for increasing productivity, ease of reporting mechanisms, and improvement of quality outcomes for patients at an unimaginable rate. To further this rush toward technological implementation in our hospitals, clinics, and other healthcare organizations, recent legislation has added an increased pressure to establish HIT use within the organization.

The Rush to Electronic Health Record Implementation

The enactment of the Health Information Technology for Economic and Clinical Health (HITECH) Act occurred as part of the American Recovery and Reinvestment Act (ARRA) of 2009. This was an attempt by the U.S. government to ensure the technological adoption of electronic health records (EHRs) by healthcare organizations.[33] Furthermore, "meaningful use" is required of this technology, mandating that medical providers and organizations (eligible professionals, or EPs) not only invest in these clinical and administrative technologies but also demonstrate applicable use of the new systems, as outlined by the ARRA of 2009. The criteria include the following:

- Use of certified EHR technology for the electronic exchange of health information (interoperability)
- Use of certified EHR technology to collect and report on quality improvement measures

HITECH established financial incentives for healthcare organizations to adopt and properly implement this technology within specific timelines.[34] For example, those EPs who invested in EHR technology and implemented its use properly prior to May 2011 were eligible for an incentive payment on all Medicare services provided. However, the incentive payments were altered based on the time of successful implementation by the EP. To receive the maximum incentive reimbursement by Medicare for this program, providers must have successfully implemented their technology prior to 2012. Additionally, those providers who fail to successfully demonstrate meaningful use of an EHR by 2015 will receive an adjustment (payment deduction) for each Medicare service provided until successful implementation of an EHR is established. This legislative mandate, intended to further quality outcomes and process improvement in the medical industry, has raised concerns regarding organizational implementation of the EHR and underlying motivations, specifically the financial incentives.

There is also an ethical concern regarding beneficence, with critics citing the risk associated with small to medium-sized healthcare organizations rushing to meet EHR incentive timelines.[35] Although the selection, purchase, and establishment of an EHR within an organization seems to be the correct first step toward meeting the legislation's objectives, it is the safe and diligent implementation period that is most vital in ensuring success of this advanced workflow technology. Therefore, regardless of HITECH incentive timelines and even the 2015 penalty deadline, medical organizations must focus on the quality of care provided to each individual patient, whether utilizing paper or electronic medical record systems. Additionally, the implementation period must include sufficient education on the new EHR technology for all stakeholders involved, including the patient, to ensure quality outcomes during this hybrid period of concurrent paper and electronic medical record systems. Whereas the implementation of the EHR directs itself toward benefiting patients and improving the quality of care provided in the long run, the healthcare organization also has a moral obligation to act for the benefit and well-being of its current patient populations. One must uphold this principle throughout the paper-to-EHR transition process, while also not allowing the incentive timelines of Medicare and other healthcare payers to influence operational decisions that affect quality of care.

The Decision to Forego Electronic Health Records

The legislative and financial pressures to implement the use of EHR technology within the medical group practice are often enough to allow this process to become a line item on the agenda for organizational strategic planning meetings. However, as important and necessary as EHRs are, as the Centers for Medicare and Medicaid Services (CMS) has established, some medical providers have made the decision to opt out of the Medicare EHR incentive program, foregoing incentive payments and making plans to accept the upcoming payment reductions as a normal business expense. In other words, they have chosen not to invest in an EHR, thus remaining with paper medical records throughout their tenure as medical professionals. This decision is often made by medical providers concerned with their individual competencies regarding computers and technology; the overwhelming capital expense of EHR purchase, follow-on training, and implementation expenses; and the potential retirement perspective of the physician owner. As a result, many medical practices have yet to implement EHR technology into their patient care processes and do not intend to do so, regardless of the financial disincentives to come.

As a result, quality-of-care concerns have surfaced, questioning medical providers' ability to access, organize, successfully document, and report on patient care quality without an EHR system.[36] Additional advantages of an

EHR system are also sacrificed, such as clinical decision support systems (CDSS) and e-prescribing (e-Rx). The following are examples of issues that may occur in the medical practice when it does not implement an EHR:[37]

- Patient allergy information is less accessible, and lack of e-Rx capability may result in prescribing of incorrect medications, as well as contradictory medications.

- There can be illegible physician orders, leading to dosing errors or other medical errors.

- It is possible to overlook important information within a large paper medical record that could have easily been alerted to the provider within an appropriately utilized EHR system.

Whereas the rush to EHR implementation primarily involves a question of the principle of beneficence, the decision to forego EHR implementation in its entirety may contradict the principle of nonmaleficence. There may be harm to those patients receiving care from a medical provider utilizing paper medical records, committing one of the example errors mentioned above. Additionally, this omission of technology closely relates to negligence on behalf of the medical provider and organizational leadership. Regardless of the reasons for deciding against EHR adoption and implementation soon, or at all, the medical provider must consider the ethical principles of beneficence and nonmaleficence when choosing to disregard the proven quality-of-care benefits received from this technology.

Privacy Implications of Health Information Technology

Coincidentally, one of the primary benefits of HIT and EHRs can actually be a severe disadvantage and legal liability for the healthcare organization. Since the inception of the EHR, several data breaches have occurred, allowing inappropriate individuals to access individual, confidential, private health information (PHI). In some cases, there was purposeful leaking of this information into the public's view. Instead of being a single and tangible paper medical record that can be physically secured via lock and key, an EHR often allows access through several information technology (IT) resources, including desktops, laptops, tablet computers, and smart phone devices. This increased accessibility of PHI has allowed the following HIPAA (Health Information Portability and Accountability Act) violations to occur:

- A theft of a password-protected, but nonencrypted, desktop computer containing the PHI for over 4.24 million patients from a Sutter Health medical office occurred in Sacramento, California, in November 2011.[38] As a result, a suit was filed against the organization for over $1,000 per patient record leaked, primarily because Sutter failed to notify the patients of the occurrence.[39]

- University of California–Los Angeles (UCLA) hospitals were sued and required to pay close to $1 million in penalties for the breach of over six celebrity medical record files, including those of the late Farrah Fawcett and Michael Jackson.[40] This case did not involve a missing computer, but rather forensic IT research within the EHR system, providing documentation that UCLA Medical Center employees with no medical reason to access these specific patients' medical records did so without proper authorization.

- Fifteen Kaiser Permanente employees were fired and eight others underwent disciplinary and training actions when the medical records of Nadya Suleman (the "Octomom") were accessed without medical need or authorization.[41] Afterward, it was claimed that the media frenzy that resulted was highly influenced by these employees sneaking peeks at this patient's medical records and relaying this PHI to unauthorized parties.

Regardless whether an EHR system exists or the medical organization continues to rely on paper medical records, patients should not have to worry about the proper security and access of their PHI by the appropriate medical providers and administrative staff. It is the organization's fiduciary duty to uphold the highest security precautions, while also providing continuous education for all employees regarding the protection and limited access of patients' PHI.

An individual's medical history is a highly sensitive topic and should be limited to only those who need to know. Most EHR systems will allow records to be locked from all employees, minus a select few. This option can help protect privacy by limiting access to those medical records of high interest, such as the "Octomom's," but this does not fully prevent the abuse of privacy if those leaders with continuous access abuse the system in an unethical manner. Confidentiality has been a huge criticism, even a black eye, of HIT developments and implementations over the last couple of years. Further security innovations are required as more electronic devices allow the capability for providers to access such information through remote networks. Additionally, ethical leadership and ongoing training of providers and staff continues to remain a mandatory requirement during the use of this technological resource.

SUMMARY

Technological resources have allowed the medical industry to treat more medical diseases and ailments at a much more effective level, while also ensuring earlier diagnoses and less complicated treatment processes with quicker recovery periods. The overall benefits of implementing technology into medicine have easily outweighed any disadvantages, although it has not been without the negation of various ethical principles along the way. Learning from these previous, failed methodologies will allow the medical researcher to not only establish beneficial technological resources but also to do so in an appropriate manner, respecting individual autonomy.

Questions immediately arise regarding ethics and medical-related technology: Where does the common ground exist between the medical provider's deontological viewpoints and the healthcare administrator's utilitarian beliefs? What communities, and even individuals within each community, are to benefit from such technology? How are those individuals whose providers use new technology to be protected from privacy breaches and other PHI implications? It is the ethics committee's responsibility to evaluate all of these processes and potential outcomes to ensure that future ethical ramifications are not on tomorrow's front page. Although healthcare revenues are currently incapable of covering additional liability expenses related to ethical implications, the organization cannot afford to fail to uphold its fiduciary duty to address ethics before, during, and throughout all technology implementations. Simply laying technological advances over existing healthcare processes will not work, and process redesign must involve a fresh look at ethics to ensure the highest respect for all stakeholders involved.

QUESTIONS FOR REVIEW

1. Describe two classifications of healthcare technology addressed in this chapter and provide two examples of each. What corruption of ethical principles can occur with each technological resource? What actions should healthcare leaders take to prevent such negative implications?

2. Discuss how healthcare administrators and healthcare providers may view investment, access, and implementation of healthcare technology from differing viewpoints. What ethical theories can administrators use to describe these potential perspectives? Which theory or viewpoint is correct?

3. Review a time when you or a close family member utilized healthcare resources involving technological advances. Were any of the actions (or lack thereof) by the healthcare organization or medical provider in conflict with ethical principles? If so, what could they have done differently to circumvent the dilemma or dilemmas?

FOOD FOR THOUGHT

Technology, coupled with the Internet, has allowed for increased access to medical information that was once never accessible to prior patient generations. As a result, healthcare consumers of today are well informed and much more involved in the decision-making process concerning their care. Additionally, these same patients are also using the power of the Internet to evaluate the quality of medical providers and healthcare organizations prior to undergoing any treatment or procedures. The following are examples of professional websites that are consistently used by patients and their representatives to evaluate levels of quality for medical providers and healthcare organizations:

- http://www.healthgrades.com/
- http://www.hcahpsonline.org/home.aspx
- http://www.hospitalcompare.hhs.gov/

Although some quality-rating systems and surveys in health care are not anonymous and specifically require patient identification during the survey process, several are not. Note that both methods introduce bias into the survey method. However, an ethical issue exists when medical providers, or their representatives, use the various anonymous quality-rating websites to their advantage. Examples of this may include completing their own surveys and giving themselves high marks to increase their average quality scores, as well as providing positive commentary about themselves, acting as if they were an actual patient. Such a dishonest medical provider with strong local competition could even go so far as to provide negative commentary and feedback on his or her competitors' websites, with the intention of directing patients away from the local competition and, it is hoped, toward his or her healthcare organization.

What kind of ethical implications are created by such actions? If dishonest medical providers participate in skewing online representations of quality, how does this affect the various ethical principles associated with medicine and patient care previously discussed in this chapter? What technological resources could be developed or used to prohibit such dishonesty?

NOTES

1. E. E. Morrison, *Ethics in Health Administration*, 2nd ed. (Sudbury, MA: Jones and Bartlett, 2011).
2. Centers for Disease Control and Prevention, "U.S. Public Health Service Syphilis Study at Tuskegee," June 15, 2011. Retrieved from http://www.cdc.gov/tuskegee/timeline.htm.
3. Morrison, *Ethics in Health Administration*.
4. Education Development Center, "Willowbrook Hepatitis Experiments," in *Exploring Bioethics* (Richmond, VA: Educational Development Center, 2009). Retrieved from http://science.education.nih.gov/supplements/nih9/bioethics/guide/pdf/Master_5-4.pdf.
5. C. Sia, T. Tonniges, E. Osterhus, and S. Taba, "History of the Medical Home Concept," *Pediatrics* 113, no. 4 (2004): 1473–1478.
6. L. Kasdon, "Presidential Panel Slams 1940s Guatemalan STD Study: Alum's Research Leads to International Condemnation of Experiments," *BU Today*, August 31, 2011. Retrieved from http://www.bu.edu/today/2011/presidential-panel-slams-guatemalan-sdt-study/.
7. Ibid.
8. Ibid.
9. J. Craig Venter Institute, "First Self-Replicating Synthetic Bacterial Cell." Retrieved from http://www.jcvi.org/cms/research/projects/first-self-replicating-synthetic-bacterial-cell/overview/. Accessed July 6, 2012.
10. Presidential Commission for the Study of Bioethical Issues, *New Directions: The Ethics of Synthetic Biology and Emerging Technologies* (Washington, DC: Presidential Commission for the Study of Bioethical Issues, December 2010). Available at http://bioethics.gov/cms/synthetic-biology-report.
11. Ibid.
12. Ibid.
13. Ibid.
14. Ibid.
15. Ibid.
16. Ibid.
17. Ibid.
18. Ibid.
19. Ibid.

20. Johns Hopkins Medicine, "Stereotactic Radiosurgery." Retrieved from http://www.radonc .jhmi.edu/radiosurgery/treatmentoptions/stereotacticradiosurgery.html. Accessed July 6, 2012.

21. Johns Hopkins Medicine, "What Is the Gamma Knife?" Retrieved from http://www.hopkins-medicine.org/neurology_neurosurgery/specialty_areas/brain_tumor/treatment/gamma-knife.html. Accessed July 6, 2012.

22. Y. Jayaratne, R. Zwahlen, L. Lo, S. Tam, and L. Cheung, "Computer-Aided Maxillofacial Surgery: An Update," *Surgical Innovation* 17, no. 3 (2010): 217–225.

23. New York University, "Sinus Surgery at NYU Otolaryngology." Retrieved from http://ent.med .nyu.edu/patient-services/rhinology/sinus_surgery. Accessed July 6, 2012.

24. C. N. Gutt, T. Oniu, A. Mehrabi, A. Kashfi, P. Schemmer, and M. W. Buchler, "Robot-Assisted Abdominal Surgery," *British Journal of Surgery* 91 (2004): 1390–1397.

25. Ibid.

26. R. Bell, "The Quest for Improved Image Quality, the Need for Efficiency, and Declining Reimbursement Will Shape the Burgeoning MRI Market Well into the Future," *Imaging Economics*, December 2004. Retrieved from http://www.imagingeconomics.com/issues/ articles/2004-12_02.asp. Accessed November 22, 2011.

27. A. Montagnolo, "The Imaging Question: Are Advances in MRI Technology and CT Scanners Worth the Investment?" *Trustee*, June 2011, 25–26.

28. D. Harvey, "3T: It's in the Way That You Use It," *Imaging Economics*, November 2004. Retrieved from http://www.imagingeconomics.com/issues/articles/MI_2004-11_06.asp. Accessed November 22, 2011.

29. D. Hinesly, "Expanding Business and Clinical Options Using 3T MRI," *Imaging Economics*, December 2006. Retrieved from http://www.imagingeconomics.com/issues/articles/ 2006-12_15.asp.

30. Harvey, "3T."

31. S. Wallask, "Higher-Quality MRIs Raise Questions About Costs and Reimbursement," HealthLeaders Media, July 14, 2009. Retrieved from http://www.healthleadersmedia.com/ content/235903/topic/WS_HLM2_TEC/Higherquality-MRIs-Raise-Questions-about-Costs-and-Reimbursement.html##. Accessed November 22, 2011.

32. Hinesly, "Expanding Business and Clinical Options."

33. Centers for Medicare and Medicaid Services, "Medicare and Medicaid Programs; EHR Incentive Program; Final Rule," *Federal Register* 75, no. 144 (2010): 44313–44588. Retrieved from http://edocket.access.gpo.gov/2010/pdf/2010-17207.pdf. Accessed November 22, 2011.

34. Centers for Medicare and Medicaid Services, "CMS Medicare and Medicaid EHR Incentive Programs: Milestone Timeline." Retrieved from https://www.cms.gov/EHRIncentive-Programs/Downloads/EHRIncentProgtimeline508V1.pdf.

35. E. Weaver, "Will the Rush to EHRs Harm Patients? Small-, Medium-Size Groups at Most Risk," *MGMA Connexion* 11, no. 7 (2011): 21–22.

36. R. Yates "Is it Unethical Not to Use an EHR?" *MGMA Connexion* 9, no. 10 (2009): 23–24.

37. Ibid.

38. K. Robertson, "Sutter Health Says Patient Data Was Stolen," *Sacramento Business Journal*, November 16, 2011. Retrieved from http://www.bizjournals.com/sacramento/news/2011/11/16/ sutter-heatlh-laptop-patient-data-stolen.html. Accessed November 22, 2012.

39. D. Smith, "Sutter Health Sued over Theft of Computer Containing Patient Data," *The Sacramento Bee*, November 23, 2011. Retrieved from http://www.mercurynews.com/breaking-news/ci_19398492. Accessed November 22, 2012.

40. C. Clark, "Six Major Patient Record Breaches Draw $675,000 in Penalties," HealthLeaders Media, June 11, 2010. Retrieved from http://www.healthleadersmedia.com/page-1/LED-252360/ Six-Major-Patient-Record-Breaches-Draw-675000-In-Penalties##. Accessed November 22, 2012.

41. B. Monegain, "Breach into 'Octuplet Mom's' Medical Records Highlights Privacy Issues Again," *HealthCare IT News*, March 31, 2009. Retrieved from http://www.healthcareitnews. com/news/breach-octuplet-moms-medical-records-highlights-privacy-issues-again. Accessed November 22, 2012.

CHAPTER 17

Spirituality and Healthcare Organizations

Dexter R. Freeman and Eileen E. Morrison

INTRODUCTION

The 21st century has seen a resurgence in the recognition of the importance of responding to the holistic needs of patients and providers within the medical healthcare system. The interesting thing about this spiritual and religious transformation is that the same factors that moved the healthcare industry away from religion and spirituality—namely, empiricism and concerns about professionalism—have brought religion and spirituality back to the healthcare industry. The healthcare industry abandoned its connection to religion and spirituality during the 20th century in an attempt to emphasize medical care that was reliable, scientifically sound, and effective in meeting the patient's needs. This focus on identifying clinical practices that consistently provide successful outcomes and that are scientifically sound is commonly referred to as *evidence-based practice*. Evidence-based practice (EBP), a concept that was introduced to medicine and health care in 1992,[1] has become a consistent screening criterion for selecting clinical practice approaches within the healthcare industry.[2]

Prior to the current era in health care, the focus was on curing illnesses and controlling the spread of disease. Now the emphasis is on developing hospitals that promote healing while maintaining accountability and professionalism. Erie Chapman, author of *Radical Loving Care*, put it this way:

> How would you like to be part of a hospital that: 1) is in the top one percent in patient satisfaction, 2) has outstanding employee morale, 3) has low turnover, 4) has exceptional clinical care, 5) has a high evaluation score from the Joint Commission on Accreditation of Healthcare Organizations, 6) demonstrates good financial performance, and 7) is characterized as a loving and caring environment?[3]

The supposition is that no hospital or healthcare organization will be able to experience the aforementioned accomplishments unless it is willing to incorporate evidence-based practices that also acknowledge the holistic needs of patients, providers, and other members of the healthcare team.

This chapter provides information about the role of spirituality in healthcare work settings. Patients are no longer satisfied with reductionist views of curing. Furthermore, professionals are desperately seeking a sense of fulfillment that is greater than their paycheck. Even The Joint Commission has responded by mandating that healthcare institutions incorporate spiritual assessments into their medical practice.[4] With such a change in emphasis, one must question whether it is unethical not to incorporate spirituality into the healthcare work environment.

The current belief is that the essence of quality health care in the 21st century is EBP, which is deemed economically beneficial and lowers the risk of litigation. Therefore, insurance companies, policy makers, government regulators, and healthcare providers are pursuing EBP as the gold standard for success in healthcare practice.[5] However, the transition to a healthcare system that emphasizes services driven by empirical data and financial success risks another danger—that is, creating a medical system that promotes paternalistic medical care driven by research outcomes at the expense of emphasizing healing. Chapman states, "The great unfinished business of healthcare is not curing but healing."[6] Curing focuses on relieving and treating patients' symptoms, whereas healing requires acknowledging the holistic needs of healthcare customers by tapping into the yearnings of their minds, bodies, and spirits.

Prior to the 20th century, an interweaving of religion and spirituality existed within the practice of physical and mental health.[7] However, the 20th century ushered in a new perspective toward religion and spirituality in the delivery of physical and mental healthcare. During this period, healthcare professionals viewed those professions that embraced religiousness and spirituality as unprofessional, irrational, and unscientific.[8]

However, the same focus on empiricism that caused many healthcare professionals to abandon religion and spirituality in the middle of the 20th century caused them to reconsider in the late 20th century. The empirical data was clear and consistent—religion and spirituality were not just important; they were making a difference in the health and well-being of patients. As a result, many healthcare organizations called for greater sensitivity and better training of clinicians on how to integrate religious and spiritual issues in the assessment and treatment of patients.[9] Today, even though spirituality has been deemed an essential ingredient for helping patients in the healthcare system find meaning and purpose in their pain and suffering, many healthcare providers still view spiritual care as contrary to competent EBP[10] and antithetical to what a professional healthcare organization should emulate.

This conflict exists within the healthcare environment even though Americans typically value selfless and compassionate healthcare service that evolves from spiritual care.[11] Thus, a question that one must ask is, Given the changes that have occurred in the national healthcare system, do healthcare personnel have time to address the holistic needs of patients and employees? If we believe that patients seek quality medical treatment, and that providers enter the healthcare system to learn how to alleviate the pain of those suffering, how important is it to show loving care? Finally, is meeting the nebulous spiritual needs of healthcare customers still relevant in today's transient and technology-driven society?

There is a continual struggle within the healthcare system regarding what is most important—empiricism or relationships. Wesorick and Doebbeling point out health care's desperate need for transformation when they highlight the system's resistance to change, resulting in dissatisfaction on the behalf of many customers.[12] They state, "Large gaps exist between evidence and practice, suboptimal quality, inequitable patterns of utilization, poor safety, and unsustainable cost increases." What can help revive this system that some perceive as being out of control and at risk of going under? Some view EBP as the answer to the problem for both the system and the customers who are being affected by long waits and rising costs.[13-15]

EVIDENCE-BASED PRACTICE: THE ANSWER AND THE CHALLENGE

Over the past 30 years, the International Consortium of the Clinical Practice Model Resource Center (CPMRC), a conglomeration of 23 healthcare systems that meet on a regular basis to serve as a think tank and resource center for healthcare transformation, has developed six core practice models that provide the framework for healthcare transformation. These practice models are all evidence-based strategies that incorporate interdisciplinarian partnerships, reduce redundancy through each member of the healthcare team clearly articulating its scope of practice, and effectively use health informatics to capitalize on evidence-based clinical knowledge to affect healthcare processes for the future. In addition, they are designed to ensure that organizations promote a health and healing environment for those who give and receive care; finally, they emphasize that patients should receive care based on the best scientific knowledge available.[16] The practice models that have been developed by the CPMRC clearly demonstrate the belief that EBP is the means to developing a credible and viable healthcare system that will be equipped to meet the challenges of the 21st century.

Fineout-Overholt and Melnyk defined EBP as "[a] problem-solving approach to clinical practice that integrates a systematic search for, and critical appraisal of, the most relevant evidence to answer burning clinical questions, based upon one's clinical expertise, and the patient's preferences and values."[17] This definition refutes the perception that EBP advocates and promotes inflexible, paternalistic medical care that is driven by research and the needs of the healthcare system, without consideration of the needs of the client, customer, or patient. Furthermore, EBP is based on the belief and assumption that healthcare customers not only desire but also expect to receive medical care that has been proven effective.[18]

There is no doubt that EBP will continue to be a central part of the healthcare transformation that will occur throughout the 21st century. The need to identify health care that is cost-effective and that efficiently utilizes personnel is more important today than it has ever been. In fact, the CPMRC developed its healthcare practice models and beliefs about healthcare transformation in the expectation that EBP would be at the core of every practice model. The CPMRC believes that (1) every person has the right to safe, individualized health care, which promotes wholeness of body, mind, and spirit; (2) a healthy culture requires interaction and a partnership between all systems involved; (3) there must be continuous feedback and learning for a healthcare system to maintain and improve its effectiveness; (4) partnerships are essential to the proper coordination, delivery, and evaluation of health care across the continuum; (5) each individual must commit to being accountable to the system; and (6) quality will occur where there is a shared purpose, vision, and values.[19]

As one examines the importance of EBP in the transformation of the healthcare system, it is also evident that another factor, spirituality, can be viewed as a significant vehicle that would be able to promote healing in the 21st century healthcare system. However, what do we mean by spirituality? Is there evidence to support its incorporation into the healthcare system? Is it ethical to incorporate spirituality into health care, or would it be ethical to leave spirituality out?

THIS THING CALLED SPIRITUALITY

Carl Jung said, "Called or not called, God is present."[20] A spiritual ethos often serves as the impetus for many people entering healthcare professions. Dr. Rachel Remen, a clinical professor of family and community medicine at the University of California in the San Francisco School of Medicine, identified why countless numbers of scientifically competent students pursue careers in medicine: "Filled with gratitude, they choose this field and have an overwhelming desire to help others."[21] She goes on to explain that although these future physicians are scientifically gifted, they are spiritually inspired.

However, over the years, many physicians and healthcare administrators have stopped seeing themselves as facilitators of healing. Many entered the profession with idealistic hopes and dreams of being able to make a difference. Yet, the indoctrination they received in institutions of higher education and their work environments taught them that "real professionals" do not have time for matters as abstract and obtuse as exploring their patients' sense of existence or spirituality. As a result, we now have spiritless healthcare organizations and professionals who are seeking to help patients and customers who desire not only physical but also spiritual transformation.

Over the past three decades, a transition has been occurring in the healthcare industry; people are starting to express an interest in healing again. Of course, when we discuss *healing*, we are referring to it in its Old English sense, "to make whole," acknowledging that healing cannot occur without recognizing it as a spiritual process.[22] Because of this renewed interest, attitudes toward spirituality in the workplace appear to be changing. Although today's information-age culture, with its emphasis on facts, brevity, and the security of depersonalization, continues to be prevalent, a transition to a deeper calling is becoming apparent. This is reflected in patients' desires. Research suggests that patients desire and feel more comfortable with physicians who are not only open to their own humanity but who also are willing to allow patients to discuss their spiritual proclivities.[23]

The past two decades have revealed a resurrection of the need to embrace the whole patient in health care, and all types of organizations are beginning to recognize the importance of addressing their workers' spiritual needs. Books such as Briskin's *Stirring of Soul in the Workplace*, Bolman and Deal's *Leading with Soul*, and, more recently, Benefiel's *Soul at Work* affirm that the business world has recognized people's need to pursue a profession for more than a salary or prestige.[24]

Ashmos and Duchon associate this amplified interest in spirituality in the workplace with several factors.[25] First, the spread of worker demoralization, brought about by massive layoffs, downsizing, and workplace reengineering, has left employees empty and apathetic. Second, baby boomers are aging and beginning to recognize their impending mortality, generating greater interest in the meaning of life. Third, social isolation and the decline in neighborhood organizations have increased the need for workers to feel connected in their work environment. These social conditions support spirituality as not just something that makes people feel good, but rather as an aspect of people's lives that is essential to acknowledge in order to promote the well-being of everyone.

A Review of Definitions

There is a universal force that compels humanity to express compassion for the helpless and to search for a more complete state of existence. This force is so multifaceted, dynamic, and unique that it is nearly impossible to completely describe, measure, or define. Our best efforts to define it, which some refer to as *spirit* or *soul*, often are feeble and inadequate; nevertheless, no one can ever doubt the reality of its existence.

Carl Jung said, "I do not hold myself responsible for the fact that man has, everywhere and always, spontaneously developed religious [spiritual] forms of expression, and the human psyche from time immemorial has been shot through with religious [spiritual] feelings and ideas."[26] No one can truly explain where this universal force originates or how to control it; however, research is beginning to show that its presence has a positive effect on recovery from illness, on organizational performance, and on the relationship between healthcare practitioners and their patients. Yet, how do we define this nebulous force that we call *spirit* or *spirituality*?

McBride and colleagues define spirituality as an intrinsic experience that goes beyond a belief in God or a higher power. It is an internal perspective that inspires one to believe in a force greater than one's self, and it serves as a guide for providing meaning to one's life.[27] Ashmos and Duchon describe the spiritual dimension as a universal state of human existence that involves a search for the experience of a sense of meaning and purpose.[28] Neck and Milliman define spirituality as an expression of one's desire to find meaning and purpose in life. It is a process of living out one's deeply held personal values.[29] Handzo and Koenig state that it is a personal quest for understanding answers to ultimate questions about life, its meaning, and one's relationship to the transcendent.[30] In summary, although spirituality can incorporate the practice of one's religious faith, it includes much more than religion. In fact, one can be religious and not spiritual, as well as be spiritual and not religious.

Spirit or spirituality is the force or source that inspires an individual, community, or organization to seek its meaning, purpose, and a connection with all things. When an individual or an organization is open to its spiritual potential, that individual or organization is multidimensional and capable of embracing a sense of duality. Conger defined spirituality as the source of one's values and meaning—a way of understanding the world, an awareness of one's inner self, and a means of integrating the various aspects of oneself into a whole.[31] If an individual or organization is estranged from the spirit, that organization or individual becomes estranged from values, meaning, and a sense of humanity. Although this may seem theoretically understandable, there must be empirical research in order for modern-day healthcare organizations to truly integrate spirituality into their clinical practice.

Spirituality and Healthcare-Related Empirical Evidence

The clinical practice guidelines promulgated by the CPMRC emphasized the importance of transforming healthcare organizations into healing hospitals in which everyone plays a vital role in promoting holistic healing for patients and the interventions used are based on evidence-based practices.[32] Even though there may be dispute over the research designs and the quality of the research conducted to examine the effects that spirituality and religion have on health care, one cannot dispute the volume of encouraging findings as they relate to the impact that religion and spirituality have on patients within the health-care system.

For example, research in religion and spirituality in health care has discovered that faith and intercessory prayer can reduce the mortality of cardiology patients.[33] Patients who had an active religious faith recovered quicker from significant burn injuries,[34] and patients who report a high sense of spiritual well-being tend to experience less end-of-life despair in relation to terminal conditions.[35] Furthermore, a great deal of literature also supports the idea that individuals who view faith or their spirituality as an active resource in their lives suffer fewer physical health problems, recover from illnesses sooner, and experience less stress during serious illnesses.[36,37] Whether an individual or healthcare organization chooses to believe that spirituality is significant or not, it is difficult for one to refute the evidence. The following case scenario depicts the spiritual transformation that often occurs in patients when confronted with a medical crisis that compels them to connect with their own conception of spirituality.

Sharon's Story: Finding Peace Living in the In-Between

Sharon is a 53-year-old African American female who has relied on hard work and determination to combat fear, helplessness, skepticism, and social injustice. Despite the resounding complaints of those around her, she has never used her birth in poverty, the illiteracy of her parents, or the existence of racial injustice as an excuse for not achieving her goals in life. In fact, Sharon frequently used these ostensible barriers as motivations to work harder. She was the first member of her family to receive a college education and a master's degree; now people call her "Dr. Sharon" because she has her PhD. However, it was shortly after Sharon reached the ultimate goal in her life that her world came crashing down.

Sharon suffered from headaches, high blood pressure, and fluid retention in her legs while she was finishing her PhD. Visits to her doctor resulted in the use of medication to lower her blood pressure, and she was encouraged to modify her diet. Sharon attributed her symptoms to the stress of working a full-time job while trying to complete her dissertation—a feat that many of her family, friends, and so-called well-wishers said was impossible. She assumed that once she completed her studies, she would be back to normal. This did not prove to be the case; within a couple of months after she received her doctoral degree, she received the diagnosis of chronic kidney disease.

She now receives dialysis three days a week, is on a strict diet, is waiting for a suitable kidney donor, and is filled with countless questions. She asks herself,

"Why did this happen to me?" "How did this happen to me?" "How can I have a quality life when I am always hooked up to this machine?" "Will I ever be free from this pain?" Each time Sharon goes into the dialysis center, she confronts the harsh, cold reality of her current condition. Her endless questions follow her everywhere she goes.

However, no one in the bastion of compassion and hope, better known as the dialysis clinic, asks her about her day. No one asks her questions about her apprehensions or what she relies on to make it through the day. She even wonders if they would notice if she did not show up. As she observes the robotic manner in which many of the technicians, nurses, and social workers perform their duties, she wonders if these people even believe in what they are doing. One part of Sharon would like to believe that the doctors and providers are working hard and really care about what is happening to her. Another part of her says that she is only a body, an insurance claim, and a name waiting on a list. Yet, Sharon has always been the eternal optimist, and she hates to see things this way. She has never had much patience for whiners, and her greatest fear is that people will view her as a whiner.

Sharon has worked most of her life to be free to pursue the life she desires. In most cases, every goal that she sought she has accomplished—that is, until now. The pain she feels is more than physical—it is the pain that comes from acknowledging the presence of two worlds, neither of which she can totally embrace. For years, she chose to believe in the value of hard work, commitment, and dedication. She felt that if people were willing to dedicate themselves to succeed, there was nothing that they could not overcome. She refused to believe that oppressors and social injustice could hold her down. She refused to be part of a world of oppression and victimization filled with pain, hopelessness, and feelings of personal and social inadequacy.

However, Sharon now is feeling oppressed and victimized by this disease that she cannot conquer. She desperately needs the assistance of someone, or to go someplace where she can recapture her hope, joy, and passion for life again. She is living between hope and despair, fear and certainty, and anger and faithfulness.

Spirituality and Living in the In-Between

Many people and organizations are like Sharon, in the process of transformation; however, most are not even aware of it. People, organizations, and societies invariably grapple with who they really are, what is most important, and what is the best way to satisfy the mutual needs of everyone involved. Does one rely on policies and programs devised according to empirical wisdom? Does one allow one's conscious self to be his or her guide? Is it best to do that which is most expedient? Does one do that which is the most cost-efficient? In the case of Sharon, does she continue to work hard and do what she has always done? Should a healthcare organization, physician, or administrator be concerned with helping Sharon answer her questions? Carol Pearson and Sharon Seivert described the transition from one paradigm, or personal perspective, to another perspective as a time of living in the "in-between."[38]

During times of living in the in-between, individuals, organizations, and communities begin to uncover their deepest truths. For individuals who have always been in control, their moment of living in-between occurs when they become aware of their helplessness. Other individuals may have lived their entire lives nurturing and serving others; their time of living in-between occurs when they must seek the assistance of others and allow others to see their pain. Living in the in-between demands that individuals embrace the shadowy aspects of their souls. In the case of Sharon, she must learn to acknowledge her sense of helplessness as as much a part of herself as her belief that she can control her fate through hard work. When she learns to acknowledge that she is weak as well as strong, initially she may feel more vulnerable. However, eventually she will develop a greater sense of completeness.

Nurturing the Whole Person

William Miller and Carl Thoresen discuss the perpetual pendulum that swings from science based secularism to spiritually based holistic treatment in health care.[39] They describe how, long before the proliferation of subspecialties and the emergence of the medical-technological model, healthcare delivery systems used culturally defined healers who incorporated spiritualism to promote health. During this time in history, a lack of scientific knowledge about the disease process resulted in more reliance on spiritual and religious resources. It would not have been uncommon to rely on a shaman, curandero, priest, or pastor to assist, or in some cases serve as, the primary healthcare provider. However, as the healthcare system became more specialized, knowledgeable, and focused on understanding the organic origins of diseases and illnesses, it became more dichotomous. In an effort to become more scientifically grounded and medically proficient, many healthcare delivery systems have thrown out the spiritual baby with the bathwater. As a result, we have people who work, manage, and seek services in healthcare delivery systems who only recognize part of the person.

Whether one is addressing the needs of people with cancer, AIDS, chronic kidney disease, diabetes, the death of a loved one, or a multitude of medical problems, the literature consistently confirms that illness is fraught with spiritual concerns and issues.[40] In her book *My Grandfather's Blessings*, Rachel Ramen notes the following:

> Through illness, people may come to know themselves for the first time and recognize not only who they genuinely are but also what really matters to them. As a physician, I have accompanied many people as they have discovered in themselves an unexpected strength, courage beyond what they would have thought possible, an unsuspected sense of compassion or a capacity for love deeper than they had ever dreamed. I have watched people abandon values that they have never questioned before and find the courage to live in new ways.[41]

The research, anecdotal accounts, and literature all agree that it is impossible to treat the whole person without acknowledging the spiritual aspects of the healthcare consumer. Larimore, Parker, and Crowther examined the literature pertinent to incorporating spirituality into medical practice and discovered the following: (1) a positive relationship frequently exists between spirituality and physical and mental well-being; (2) most patients desire to discuss and be offered basic spiritual care by their healthcare provider; (3) most healthcare providers believe that spiritual interventions would help healthcare consumers, but they feel inadequately trained to deliver such care; and (4) most healthcare consumers (patients) censure healthcare delivery systems for ignoring their spiritual needs.[42]

Moreover, a plethora of data supports the idea that individuals who are spiritually connected have fewer physical health problems, recover from illness quicker, and experience less stress during serious illness than those who are not.[43] Thus, it is clear that providing appropriate, competent, effective, and ethical care to consumers of healthcare delivery systems demands that the spiritual aspects of the healing process be incorporated. Moore and Casper conclude that caring for the whole person begins with the organization—in this case, the healthcare delivery system—recognizing that those who deliver care have an inner life that needs to be incorporated into the work they do.[44] The next section of this chapter addresses the importance of having a spiritually oriented organization that enables consumers, workers, leaders, and communities to reach their ultimate goal in life. This discussion begins with an overview of the business of health care and a history of work in America.

THE HEALTHCARE WORKPLACE: A PLACE OF SPIRITUALITY IN ACTION?

Health care has become a business. Like any other business, it is concerned with efficiency, effectiveness, productivity, and profit. The business of health care employs a variety of personnel who provide services ranging from highly skilled surgical procedures to quality room and ground maintenance. It requires management personnel to address quality assurance, financial planning, marketing, and growth. However, it is not like any other business.

The customers for this business are unique. When they enter the business of health care, they receive a new name—patients. When these "customers" enter this business, they are not thinking about profitability, efficiency, or procedures. They are seeking help with their health concerns and problems. Patients are often worried, in pain, or in fear. Although the cost of health care may be of concern, their immediate goal is for healing as they define it. To achieve this goal, they are willing to experience embarrassment, pain, and loss of privacy. Patients also assume that those who care for them are people who choose to be part of a healing profession and who will demonstrate a level of competent and compassionate care.

For patients, health care is a business that is there for them at the beginning of their lives and at the end of their lives. Healthcare personnel see them at their worst moments, and they must trust these professionals with deeply personal and often embarrassing information in order to be treated. Certainly, this highly sensitive work and profound responsibility would lend itself to attracting and maintaining employees with a deeper commitment to being present to people and exercising compassion. However, to demonstrate the expected compassionate quality care on a consistent basis, healthcare staff members need more than incentive plans and bonuses. They need a type of intrinsic motivation centered in spirituality.

Part of the spiritual center is the ability to find meaning and purpose in one's work. The nature of working in health care should provide ample opportunities to experience this meaning and an affirmation of purpose. However, finding meaningful work is not always easy in many healthcare facilities. There is always an ever-present need to balance efficiency, effectiveness, and profitability with the needs of patients. The famous "No margin, no mission" phrase is a truism in this business. In addition, healthcare facilities need to hire, retain, and compensate highly educated healthcare personnel who are willing to provide services on a 24/7/365 basis in many cases. In addition, technology has become a way to increase efficiency and provide quality care, but it is often costly and can decrease the personal level of patient care.

This business also needs to prove its merit to a plethora of regulators who oversee both the clinical and financial aspects of its product. In light of this complexity, the need to be efficient and provide procedures that can be documented may overwhelm the needs of the healthcare customer—the patients. When this happens, healthcare practitioners can forget the patients entirely or just practice detached concern for them. Practitioners become efficient, but often find their work meaningless and devoid of the elements that called them to their professions in the first place.

Is it possible to exercise one's spirituality as a healthcare professional and still meet health care's business demands? Can health care meet its customers' needs and still make a profit? The following sections address these questions, beginning with a brief history of attitudes toward work and an explanation of why these attitudes are changing. In addition, there is discussion about the role of leadership in spirituality in the workplace. Using examples, the section contains a description of how to better integrate spirituality in health care and the benefits of this integration for both patients and caregivers. The final section addresses the ethical implications of spirituality in the workplace.

A Brief History of Attitudes Toward Work

Researchers trace attitudes toward work in America to the Industrial Revolution and the development of Taylor's Scientific Management.[45] During the Industrial Revolution, the United States transitioned from a primarily agrarian and cottage-industry culture to an industrial model. In response to this change, Frederick Taylor sought to make the workplace more efficient and profitable. In his view of efficiency, people worked the same way machines did, producing the same quality work through standardization of the work process. Therefore, there was no difference between a person and machine.

Managers achieved harmony in the work setting by organizing workers and enforcing workers' adherence to the rules. If workers deviated from the prescribed best way to approach a task, there was a decrease in efficiency and productivity. In short, companies paid workers to work, not think. Thinking was the role of the manager.

Taylor believed that the ideal employee was one who conformed to instructions and submitted to regulations. He (gender selection deliberate) was an employee who could control himself and his emotions. He acquired self-control by maintaining diligence when completing tedious work. In addition, Taylor expressed paternalistic attitudes toward the worker. He believed that those who had knowledge (management) should manage the poor for the poor's own good. Individuals should be willing to sacrifice for the corporation and accept a day's pay for a day's work as determined by managerial formulas.

The legacy of Taylor's work is alive and well in today's workplaces. Management often speaks of reengineering to increase the clockwork order of the work process and to remove human interference. There is an increasing need to standardize and to pay for performance, even in healthcare delivery systems. Management laments that it cannot get employees to "think right" or that employees are "not paid to think, just to get the work done." This thinking is also evident when bonuses are given to employees based on the number of procedures completed in any given day.

The idea of employees as machines is also alive and well. Employees still work to the limits of their resiliency, through 12- to 15-hour daily work schedules. Although the workplace has become increasingly stressful because of its requirements for high-level performance, increased pace, and intensity of work, management often discourages time off and time-outs. Taylor's idea of a day's pay for a day's work has evolved into the idea that bonuses and higher pay will keep employees' efficiency high for tedious or even dangerous jobs. The human element is ignored in order to get the work accomplished, and money is used to "rent souls."[46] Employees are finding that their jobs are increasingly regimented, less in tune with who they are as human beings, and require that they sacrifice who they are. The organization's definition of proficiency often conflicts with the reason why employees were called to become a part of the healthcare system.

Taylor is not the only influence on the American attitude toward work. As early as 1933, Eton Mayo offered a different idea of how to view work.[47] Based on his research at Harvard and the now famous Hawthorne Studies, he postulated that one could influence work and productivity through humane variables such as job satisfaction and teamwork. The nature of work came to include psychological factors, and the field of industrial psychology took on new meaning. The new field of industrial psychology attempted to understand the balance between these humane factors and work itself.

One can see the legacy of Mayo's work in the 21st-century workplace. Influential writers such as Peter Drucker and Peters and Waterman have explored the humane side of work, including how feelings affect morale. This side of work is linked with productivity and the need to find meaning in life. There has been exploration of the tension between working for money and finding the passion in work. Researchers began to seek strategies for blending the soft, or humane, side of management with the hard side of productivity and efficiency.

Research on organizations conducted over the past 20 years shows that blending the two paradigms is not only a good idea but also has a positive impact on organizational performance. Jurkiewicz and Giacalone found that organizations that embrace spirituality grow faster, have larger increases in efficiency, and have higher rates of return than those that do not embrace spirituality.[48] Rick Chamiec-Case and Michael Sherr noted that, even though there remains a strong bias against organizational leaders incorporating their spiritual beliefs and values into the workplace, the literature has clearly identified benefits in three areas of organizational growth when spirituality is incorporated: (1) increased productivity, worker motivation, and creativity; (2) increased overall performance of the organization and the likelihood of developing a more ethical organization; and (3) increased job satisfaction and level of worker commitment.[49] These findings and other factors have increased receptivity toward incorporating spirituality into the workplace.

Why a Change in Attitude for Health Care?

With the passage of the Patient Protection and Affordable Care Act (PPACA) of 2010, healthcare has entered a period of extraordinary change. This change requires the business of health care to examine many of its practices that it used to take for granted. To be successful in this changing environment, healthcare organizations must hire and retain employees who are willing to be effective, efficient, and caring. These employees are part of patient-centered care, which started as a movement and has now become part of the healthcare vocabulary.

Patient-centered care began with the work of Angelica Thieriot, founder of the Planetree Movement. She proposed a model for patient care that supported the human side of health care and the need for patients to be participants in their own care.[50] Her model stressed the need for human interaction, information, partnerships with patients, and a healing environment. Spirituality for patients and for caregivers was also part of her model.

Frampton, Gilpin, and Charmel conducted further research and development of Thieriot's model.[51] Their work included information on how to involve staff members in providing the kind of care described in the model. A business case was made for patient-centered care, including that such practices would decrease length of stay, improve image and marketing prospects, and decrease malpractice issues. In addition, the authors discussed the issue of staff shortages. They found that patient-centered care improved retention and satisfaction in both patients and the workforce.

The idea of patient-centered care has gone far beyond its initial efforts as a movement to improve the quality of care that patients received. It has become part of the vocabulary of the healthcare industry and of its practice standards. For example, the Institute of Medicine issued a report on the need for a patient-centered care treatment plan when dealing with oncology patients. It identifies the advantages and challenges faced in making this addition to oncology care the norm.[52]

In 2010, The Joint Commission published a guide entitled *Advancing Effective Communication, Cultural Competence, and Patient- and Family-Centered Care: A Roadmap for Hospitals*.[53] This 102-page guide provided advice to healthcare institutions on how to provide patient-centered care, beginning with admission and extending to assessment and treatment. The Joint

Commission provided checklists and support materials for addressing issues such as patient communication, culture, spiritual beliefs, and other patient issues. Patient-centered care is now a requirement under several areas of The Joint Commission standards, such as human resources, patient safety, and quality of care.

In addition to the discussion of patient-centered care, the healthcare industry must face the expanding demands of a new patient group. This group, the boomer generation, changed American institutions as it proceeded through its life process. As the boomer generation ages, it will require more healthcare services and promises to change healthcare delivery as well. In addition, members of this group differ from other generations in their response to health care. For example, in the past, patients viewed physicians and other healthcare professionals in a god-like status. One "did what the doctor said" with very little questioning. Compliance with medical professionals' instructions was necessary for health. The boomer generation has a different view of health care. They want to be "partners" in their own health, ask questions about their treatment, and may question the physician's decisions. In addition, many of them want patient-centered care in all their interactions with the healthcare system. As they age, the boomer patients will expect more than detached concern from those who provide their care.

How does patient-centered care and the boomers relate to spirituality for healthcare providers? If the healthcare system is to successfully address the great changes of recent legislation and the need to provide patient-centered care, it will need employees who find health care more than the way to earn a paycheck. This type of employee needs more than bonuses or other external motivation techniques to be successful and productive in the new healthcare environment. Such employees find health care a source of meaning and purpose in their lives, are resilient, and are deeply committed to their vocations. These employees serve as role models. In addition, organizations must reduce turnover to maintain consistent-quality, efficient, and compassionate patient care. Given these challenges, health care needs to assess its ability to influence intrinsic motivation, including employees' spirituality at work.

INTEGRATION OF SPIRITUALITY INTO HEALTHCARE WORKPLACES

The first step in integrating spirituality into the healthcare workplace is to create an operational definition of spirituality. There is often confusion between the ideas of spirituality and religion. Whereas religion holds a place in faith-based facilities, secular organizations are often uncomfortable with the idea of religion unless it relates to chaplaincy. Therefore, it is necessary to definite spirituality in a way that clearly differentiates it from religion.[54] Although there are several possible definitions for spirituality in the workplace, the one that appears most plausible for healthcare application can be based on the work of Viktor Frankl in *The Doctor and the Soul*.[55] Frankl believed that having meaning and purpose in life is essential for full human function. Work, because of its ability to allow people to apply their unique talents, is one of the main ways that humans can find meaning in life. Using Frankl's extensive research, one could operationally define spirituality at work as the ability to find meaning and purpose in the work that one does. This ability also serves as an intrinsic motivation for the employee to provide the services needed by the organization.[56] This definition is supported by researchers, including Ashmos and Duchon,[57] and is applied in Pattakos's *Prisoners of Our Thoughts*.[58]

Spirituality and Leadership

Once a definition of spirituality is reached, there is a need for commitment from leadership for a change to or enhancement of spirituality in the workplace. To paraphrase Gandhi, leaders must be the change that they want their organizations to have. This is true whether the change is a more meaningful workplace or meeting the high-level challenges of PPACA. Because of their influence through both title and personal example, leaders should demonstrate their own commitment to spirituality in the workplace in their words and actions.

Leaders need to decide whether fostering spirituality is beneficial to the organization and its mission. The mission of health care involves more than procedures and cost-effective care. From the patient's view, it also includes compassionate behavior that respects individual dignity. Can spirituality in terms of meaningful work assist in this mission and improve the bottom line of healthcare facilities? If so, then it is worth the effort needed to create an environment in which there is meaningful work and spirituality.

It is not enough to talk about mission and finding meaning and purpose in work. Leaders must demonstrate their own commitment to the organization in their attitudes and behaviors. To begin the process, leaders need to conduct a self-assessment and identify why they work for their organization.[59] Once they identify their own meaning and purpose in work, they need to create a vision for how the workplace would exhibit this spirituality in compliance with its operational definition. Of course, an effective leader does not work alone; appropriate staff members would work toward this applied vision statement.

Organizational change happens through people. Therefore, healthcare leaders who seek to have spirituality in their workplaces need to develop mechanisms for achieving this goal. Teamwork and communication are essential for achieving any level of change, particularly one in which spirituality can be part of the work that is accomplished. Recognition that spirituality is part of the culture of health care needs reinforcement on many levels, including day-to-day interactions with patients and coworkers. Although this should be an easy change because of the nature of the industry, it is easy to overlook spirituality when the pressure for fiscal responsibility increases. Therefore, it is necessary for leaders to include the concept of spirituality in their daily interactions. Dan Wilford, the one-time CEO of Memorial Hermann Healthcare Systems, said, "[T]he essence of trust is spiritual, and requires faith."[60] Given the current environment of whitewater change in health care, trust is a critical element for both employees and patients.

Practicing Spirituality in the Healthcare Workplace

Once the definition of spirituality has been determined and the leadership demonstrates commitment, the next step in integration is to begin making the change to a more spiritually centered workplace. Given the current challenges to health care, this may be the best time or the worst time to move the organization toward spirituality. It may be the best time because change is already happening and the door is open to new practices and procedures. It may be the worst time because employees do not even want to hear the word "change." Regardless of the position taken, there is a need to address workplace spirituality. The following is a list of practical ways to address the issue.

1. *Look at what already exists.* Chapman discussed the need to have employees with a "servant's heart."[61] Such employees find work meaningful and demonstrate their value through high performance. They also have personal values that are examples for others. These employees should be honored and form the basis of a spirituality-centered culture.

2. *Think about the culture.* Cultural change in healthcare organizations should occur slowly so patients are a part of increasing spirituality. Persistence and focus on the mission, vision, and values of the organization can assist in making this change. In addition, leaders should exemplify spiritually centered behaviors and be open to criticism and suggestions for change.[62]

3. *The human resources department is important.* It is not enough simply to encourage employees to find meaning in their work in a healthcare setting. Because there are connections between workplace spirituality and organizational interests, it is important for there to be active engagement from human relations departments in the process of any change that relates to this issue. Giacalone and Jurkiewicz found that the process of building workplace spirituality begins with recruitment.[63] Chapman supported their work and suggested that employees be recruited not only for their clinical competence but also for their commitment to meaningful and spiritually centered work.[64] In addition, the human resource department is significant in helping with the development of motivational and reward systems, measuring job satisfaction, and dealing with group dynamics as they relate to workplace spirituality.

4. *There will be challenges.* Chapman notes that the process of creating meaningful, spirituality-centered workplaces is not without challenges.[65] In a post–healthcare reform era, there will be the concerns about doing more with less and still maintaining profitability. In addition, the way in which health care is provided may increase the emphasis on bureaucracy rather than on compassionate care. A degree of cynicism may also prevail throughout systems because, in times of change, employees cling to what is comfortable and reject areas that seem to require more than business as usual. However, it should be remembered that the reason most employees seek a career in health care is not solely for financial gain. Although salaries and benefits are important, there is also a vocation or calling to this work. Increasing the emphasis on meaning in work through its focus on patient care may actually improve the bottom line.

If employees are engaged in work that they perceive to be meaningful, there can be an increase in morale and a decrease in absenteeism and turnover, thereby decreasing the cost of providing care. In addition, the potential for medical error, employee theft, and other systemic difficulties may decrease, which also improves the bottom line.

ETHICAL THEORIES AND SPIRITUALITY

What is the relationship between respecting, and even encouraging, spirituality in the healthcare workplace and theories of ethics? Certainly, elements of each ethical theory support this practice. For example, if one were a proponent of natural law, one could argue that ignoring spirituality could limit a person's ability to achieve his or her highest potential. This is especially true when considering that part of an employee's potential is to seek wisdom and to know God. Therefore, to diminish the spiritual component of a person or an organization could be an unethical practice.

Sheep proposed two spiritually laden questions that every healthcare administrator should consider when creating a work environment that is conducive to nurturing the whole worker: (1) Would this organization be more productive, innovative, and the people feel more satisfied if the workers felt a greater sense of connection to their work? (2) Does this organization have an ethical responsibility to seek to improve the quality of life of its workers as members of society?[66] If an administrator supports Kantian deontology, he or she could use the categorical imperative to state that respecting and allowing one to pursue spiritual growth is a moral and ethical duty. Alternatively, one might consider that allowing people to find meaning in their work and life is a universal law. As such, healthcare leaders and administrators have an ethical duty to provide environments in which both patients and workers can examine their spiritual needs and desires.

The practical utilitarian view might also consider the ethics of incorporating spirituality into the healthcare workplace. Unlike the deontological approach, which determines the appropriateness of an action based on duty, utilitarian theories of ethical decision making often are based on theory developed by Jeremy Bentham and John Stuart Mill.[67] These writers suggested that an action or behavior might be justified if it yields the greatest good for the greatest number. Therefore, a utilitarian could support spirituality in the workplace if incorporating this practice resulted in increased worker productivity, decreased worker turnover, increased patient confidence in the provider, and a greater sense of connectedness between administrators and staff. Studies by Lloyd,[68] Jurkiewicz and Giacalone,[69] and Mitroff and Denton,[70] among others, have confirmed that spirituality in the workplace does more than meet the existential desires of workers and patients. It positively affects worker performance, organizational growth, and creativity. For example, Mitroff and Denton conducted a study of spirituality in the workplace by interviewing managers and executives.[71] They discovered that the more spiritual an organization was, the more profitable it was. In addition, the more workers were able to include themselves in their work, the more creative, emotionally stable, and productive the worker was in the workplace.

Finally, one should consider the concept of Aristotle's virtue ethics.[72] Aristotle believed that ethical people are capable of working toward their highest level of excellence and desire to live virtuous lives. The community and patients expect healthcare professionals to have high moral character and practical wisdom in their daily practice. Certainly, developing this discernment comes from a work setting that allows for meaningful work and honoring a calling to serve. Including spirituality in the healthcare workplace can facilitate and even honor this practice. If professionals actually demonstrate Aristotle's practical wisdom and high moral character in their practice, they should be better able to assist patients when they are experiencing moments of in-between. They also add value to their organization as examples of caring professionals who find purpose in their work.

ETHICAL PRINCIPLES AND SPIRITUALITY

Health care calls for the application of ethical principles in day-to-day practice at the patient and organizational level. For example, first one must practice nonmaleficence, or not doing harm to patients or employees. The story of Sharon comes to mind as an example. The lack of spiritual connection between her and the professionals who were supposed to be serving her needs caused her harm. Simple and cost-free acts, such as asking the appropriate questions and really listening to her responses, could have avoided this harm. In addition, small acts of kindness (beneficence) could have made her life-changing illness easier for her to bear.

Nonmaleficence and beneficence are not limited to patient spirituality. Think of how much more positive and less stressful a healthcare environment can be when professionals truly care about each other and the work that they do. Again, small actions and well-chosen words can provide a refurbishing of the spirit that can only lead to greater-quality health care and an increase in organizational loyalty. In addition, employees' view of work would be vastly different. Patient encounters would be more than just another procedure; they would be opportunities to find meaning and to honor the sacredness of health care.[73]

Respect for autonomy also relates to spirituality at work. It is impossible to imagine engaging in respect for persons without acknowledging that the spirit is part of who they are. It would seem incredibly disrespectful to do so (Kant would not be happy at all). The same is true for the autonomy of an organization. If one does not feel that one is part of something larger or that the work that one does is valued, then it would be easy to be disloyal to the organization. Imagine the financial and quality implications of the potential lack of commitment, low morale, and high turnover rates stemming from a lack of respect for employee autonomy.

It is impossible to ignore the relationship between ethics and spirituality in the healthcare workplace. To ensure just treatment, healthcare delivery systems must be willing to nurture the whole person, whether the patient or the worker. This includes more than just responding the physical needs of the patient or the monetary needs of the worker; healthcare systems must acknowledge their spirit as well. Just treatment might require a few more minutes of listening, even when you are tired, or asking questions to determine hidden issues or concerns. It is helpful to think about the Kantian question, "How would I like to be treated if I were in this situation?"

Practicing justice that acknowledges an employee's spirituality can take many forms. Perhaps justice means making sure that breaks are a part of the workday or respecting time for renewal. It can also be honoring employees' quests for understanding their purpose and meaning in life by providing them a quiet place to think. Again, acting with justice does not have to add to the cost of health care, but it can positively affect the bottom line.

Embracing the spirit in the workplace begins with spiritual leadership that results in the transformation of the organization and community. Wolf identified several principles that spirit-focused healthcare leaders should use to promote transformation in their organizations.[74] First, the spirit-focused leader is primarily concerned with creating an environment that recognizes and respects the importance of strong moral and ethical values throughout the organization. Second, spirit-focused leaders recognize that healthcare providers enter the field in response to a calling; therefore, they give employees the opportunity to discover and examine their sense of purpose and meaning for the work they have chosen to pursue. Third, spirit-focused leaders recognize the importance of connectedness at both the vertical (with a divine being) and horizontal (between workers and those outside the organization) levels. As a result, spiritual leaders typically plan and encourage community involvement via joint programs and community-oriented activities. These leaders help to create work environments in which ethics and spirituality are the norm and in which work provides meaning and purpose to employees.

SUMMARY

This chapter examined the ethics of spirituality in the workplace. The literature available has expanded from the previous edition and even more strongly suggests that not only is excluding spirituality unethical, impractical, and counterproductive, but also that it is impossible to exclude spirituality from health care. The process of providing care for people is inherently spiritual. Therefore, spirituality will always be paramount to the services provided via healthcare delivery systems, as long as the people who pursue careers in the healthcare arena do so in response to a spiritual calling. It will also be significant as long as people seek care because they desire healing (wholeness or a sense of completeness) and not just relief from physical symptoms.

The ultimate role of the worker in the healthcare delivery system is to help communities reconcile the dichotomous thoughts, feelings, emotions, and experiences they encounter during the time of in-between. These times of in-between often occur during physical crises; however, to help communities experience healing, the organization must recognize its spiritual calling, employ spirit-focused leadership, and value spirituality at every level of operation.

Although spirituality is multifaceted—and some say nebulous and impossible to define—this chapter provided a brief overview of just how important and relevant it is to the delivery of health care. The chapter presented a number of definitions of spirituality and offered information on how to recognize its influence in the workplace. Even though some might insist that spirituality is antithetical to professional medical care or the healthcare delivery system, this position is contrary to the expressed needs of those who work in health care and those who seek care in healthcare systems. It is clear that healthcare organizations that embrace spirituality tend to be ethically sound and maintain a healthy balance between the needs of the individual and the organization. They also are efficient, productive, and create an environment that connects with patients.

QUESTIONS FOR REVIEW

1. What is the connection between spirituality in health care and evidence-based practice?
2. How do you define the term *spirituality*?
3. How do Pearson and Sievert define "living in the in-between," and how does this concept relate to spirituality in healthcare organizations?
4. What are some common factors in the ability to express spirituality in the workplace?
5. What is the role of leadership in workplace spirituality?
6. How does spirituality in the workplace contribute to profitability?
7. How does deontology support spirituality in healthcare organizations? How does the utilitarian perspective support spirituality in healthcare organizations?

FOOD FOR THOUGHT

You are the office manager of a four-dentist clinical practice. Morale has been low and turnover high. One of the dentists just returned from a workshop on spirituality in the workplace. He is convinced that increasing spirituality will increase the bottom line and improve morale. He gives you the assignment to make spirituality happen among the employees of this clinic. What do you do? How do you prove that your efforts made a difference?

NOTES

1. Evidence-Based Medicine Working Group, "Evidence-Based Medicine: A New Approach to Teaching the Practice of Medicine," *Journal of the American Medical Association* 268 (1992): 2420–2425.
2. B. Wesorick and B. Doebbeling, "Lessons from the Field: The Essential Elements for Point-of-Care Transformation," *Medical Care* 49, suppl. (December 2001): S49–58.
3. E. Chapman, *Radical Loving Care: Building the Healing Hospital* (Nashville, TN: Erie Chapman Foundation, 2011), 11.
4. Joint Commission on the Accreditation of Healthcare Organizations, *Comprehensive Accreditation Manual for Healthcare Organizations: The Official Handbook* (Chicago: Joint Commission on the Accreditation of Healthcare Organizations, 2003).

5. H. McKenzie, "What Does the Healthcare Patient Want?" *Home Healthcare Nurse* 28, no. 9 (2010): 575–576.

6. Chapman, *Radical Loving Care*, 4.

7. H. Koenig, M. E. McCullogh, and D. B. Larson, *Handbook of Religion and Health* (New York: Oxford University Press, 2001).

8. W. L. Larimore, M. Parker, and M. Crowther, "Should Clinicians Incorporate Positive Spirituality into Their Practices? What Does the Evidence Say?" *Annals of Behavioral Medicine* 24, no. 1 (2002): 69–73.

9. Ibid.

10. P. Speck, "The Evidence Base for Spiritual Care," *Nursing Management* 12, no. 6 (2005): 28–31.

11. D. Garber, "Spirituality and Healthcare Organizations," *Journal of Healthcare Management* 46 (2001): 39–52.

12. Wesorick and Doebbeling, "Lessons from the Field."

13. R. F. Levin, J. M. Keefer, J. Marren, M. Vetter, B. Lauder, and S. Sobolewski, "Evidence-Based Practice Improvement: Merging 2 Paradigms," *Journal of Nursing Care* 25, no. 2 (2010): 117–126.

14. T. Leufer and J. Cleary-Holdforth, "Evidence-Based Practice: Improving Patient Outcomes," *Nursing Standard* 23, no. 32 (2009): 35–39.

15. McKenzie, "What Does the Healthcare Patient Want?"

16. Wesorick and Doebbeling, "Lessons from the Field."

17. E. Fineout-Overholt and B. M. Melnyk, "Transforming Healthcare from the Inside Out: Advancing Evidence-Based Practice in the 21st Century," *Journal of Professional Nursing* 21, no. 6 (2005): 335–344.

18. Leufer and Cleary-Holdforth, "Evidence-Based Practice."

19. Wesorick and Doebbeling, "Lessons from the Field."

20. C. Jung, cited in Chapman, *Radical Loving Care*, 4.

21. R. Remen, "Clueing Doctors in on the Art of Healing," *Science and Theology News*, July–August 2004, 32.

22. M. Burkhardt, "After All: Reintegrating Spirituality into Healthcare," *Alternative Therapies in Health and Medicines* 4 (1998): 2.

23. M. Donnelly, "Faith Boosts Cognitive Management of Cancer and HIV," *Science and Theology News*, June 15, 2006.

24. A. Briskin, *The Stirring of Soul in the Workplace* (San Francisco: Jossey-Bass, 1996); L. G. Bolman and T. E. Deal, *Leading with Soul: An Uncommon Journey of Spirit* (San Francisco: Jossey-Bass, 1995); M. Benefiel, *Soul at Work: Spiritual Leadership in Organizations* (New York: Seabury, 2005)

25. D. Ashmos and D. Duchon, "Spirituality at Work: A Conceptualization and Measure," *Journal of Management Inquiry* 9 (2000): 134–145.

26. C. G. Jung, *Modern Man in Search of a Soul* (Orlando, FL: Harcourt Brace Jovanovich, 1933), 122.

27. J. L. McBride, G. Arthur, R. Brooks, and L. Pilkington, "The Relationship Between a Patient's Spirituality and Health Experience," *Family Medicine* 30 (1998): 122.

28. Ashmos and Duchon, "Spirituality at Work."

29. C. Neck and J. Milliman, "Thought Self-Leadership: Finding Spiritual Fulfillment in Organizational Life," *Journal of Managerial Psychology* 9 (1994): 9.

30. G. Handzo and H. Koenig, "Spiritual Care: Whose Job Is It Anyway?" *Southern Medical Journal* 97 (2004): 1242.

31. J. A. Conger, *Spirit at Work: Discovering the Spirituality of Leadership* (San Francisco: Jossey-Bass, 1994).

32. Wesorick and Doebbeling, "Lessons from the Field."

33. R. C. Byrd, "Positive Therapeutic Effects of Intercessory Prayer in a Coronary Care Unit Population," *Southern Medical Journal* 81 (1988): 826–829.

34. Speck, "The Evidence Base for Spiritual Care."

35. J. T. Chibnall, S. D. Videen, O. N. Duckro, and D. K. Miller, "Psychosocial-Spiritual Correlates of Death Distress in Patients with Life-Threatening Medical Conditions," *Palliative Medicine* 16, no. 4 (2002): 331–338.

36. H. G. Koenig and H. J. Cohen, *The Link Between Religion and Health: Psychoneuroimmunology and the Faith Factor* (London: Oxford University Press, 2002).

37. C. E. Thoresen, "Spirituality and Health: Is There a Relationship?" *Journal of Health Psychology* 4, no. 3 (1999): 291–300.

38. C. Pearson and S. Sievert, *Magic at Work: A Guide to Releasing Your Highest Creative Powers* (New York, NY: Doubleday, 1995).

39. W. Miller and C. Thoresen, "Spirituality and Health," in *Integrating Spirituality into Treatment*, ed. William Miller (Washington, DC: American Psychological Association, 1999), 3–18.

40. R. Dunphy, "Helping Persons with AIDS Find Meaning and Hope," *Health Progress* 68 (1987): 58–63; E. J. Taylor, "Why and Wherefores: Adult Patient Perspectives of the Meaning of Cancer," *Seminars in Oncology Nursing* 11 (1995): 32–40; Garber, "Spirituality and Healthcare Organizations," 42.

41. R. Remen, *My Grandfather's Blessings* (New York: Riverhead Books, 2000), 29.

42. Larimore, Parker, and Crowther, "Should Clinicians Incorporate Positive Spirituality into Their Practice?"

43. Koenig and Cohen, *The Link Between Religion and Health*.

44. T. Moore and W. Casper, "An Examination of Proxy Measures of Workplace Spirituality: A Profile Model of Multidimensional Constructs," *Journal of Leadership and Organizational Studies* 12 (2006): 111.

45. Briskin, *Stirring of Soul*.

46. Ibid., 155.

47. Ibid.

48. C. L. Jurkiewicz and R. A. Giacalone, "A Values Framework for Measuring the Impact of Workplace Spirituality on Organizational Performance," *Journal of Business Ethics* 49 (2004): 129–142.

49. R. Chamiec-Case and M. Sherr, "Exploring How Social Work Administrators Integrate Spirituality in the Workplace," *Social Work and Christianity* 33 (2006): 270.

50. S. B. Frampton, L. Gilpin, and P. A. Charmel, eds., *Putting Patients First: Designing and Practicing Patient-Centered Care*, 2nd ed. (San Francisco: John Wiley & Sons, 2009).

51. Ibid.

52. Institute of Medicine, *Patient-Centered Cancer Treatment Planning: Improving the Quality of Oncology Care—A Summary of a Workshop* (Washington, DC: The National Academy of Sciences, 2011).

53. The Joint Commission, *Advancing Effective Communication, Cultural Competence, and Patient- and Family-Centered Care: A Roadmap for Hospitals* (Chicago: The Joint Commission, 2010).

54. R. A. Giacalone and C. L. Jurkiewicz, *Handbook of Workplace Spirituality and Organizational Performance*, 2nd ed. (New York: M. E. Sharpe, 2011).

55. V. Frankl, *The Doctor and the Soul: From Psychotherapy to Logotherapy* (New York: Random House, 1986), 117–131.

56. For additional reading about Frankl's work on meaning and meaning in work, consult the 2006 edition of his *Man's Search for Meaning* (Boston, MA; Beacon Publishing), and the 2000 edition of *Man's Search for Ultimate Meaning* (New York, NY: Perseus Publishing).

57. Ashmos and Duchon, "Spirituality at Work."

58. A. Pattakos, *Prisoners of Our Thoughts: Viktor Frankl's Principles at Work* (San Francisco: Berrett-Koehler, 2004).

59. W. A. Guillory, *The Living Organization: Spirituality in the Workplace* (Salt Lake City, UT: Innovations International, 2000).

60. M. H. Annison and D. S. Wilford, *Trust Matters: New Directions in Health Care* (San Francisco: Jossey-Bass, 1998), 14.

61. Chapman, *Radical Loving Care*, 155.

62. D. R. Marques, S. Dhiman, and R. King, eds., *The Workplace and Spirituality: New Perspectives on Research and Practice* (Woodstock, CA: Skylight Paths Publishing, 2009).

63. Giacalone and Jurkiewicz, *Handbook of Workplace Spirituality*.

64. Chapman, *Radical Loving Care*.

65. Ibid.

66. M. Sheep, "Nurturing the Whole Person: The Ethics of Workplace Spirituality in Society of Organizations," *Journal of Business Ethics* 66 (2006): 357.

67. F. Reamer, ed., *Ethical Dilemmas in Social Service* (New York: Columbia University Press, 1990), 15.

68. T. Lloyd, *The Nice Company* (London: Bloomsbury, 1990).

69. Jurkiewicz and Giacalone, "A Values Framework."

70. I. Mitroff and E. Denton, "A Study of Spirituality in the Workplace," *Sloan Management Review* 40 (1999): 86.

71. Ibid.

72. J. Summers, "Theory of Health Care Ethics," in *Health Care Ethics: Critical Issues for the 21st Century*, 3rd ed., eds. E. E. Morrison and E. Furlough (Sudbury, MA: Jones and Bartlett Learning, 2013).

73. Chapman, *Radical Loving Care*, 3–23.

74. E. Wolf, "Spiritual Leadership: A New Model," *Healthcare Executive*, March–April 2004, 23.

PART IV

Critical Issues for Society's Health

Americans face monumental issues as a nation, including the economy, crime and crime prevention, education, and poverty. Because the scope of these issues is so great, this section will only discuss representative examples of these issues and their ethical implications. One major example for health care is the change in healthcare policy represented by the Patient Protection and Affordable Care Act (PPACA), which affects more than organizations and professional staff. Policy changes will also have major effects on the society as a whole. Two chapters in this section present the changes in healthcare policy and their ethical impact.

Chapter 18 presents a discussion of the equality and inequality of the current healthcare system. In light of PPACA, this chapter is even more relevant than in previous editions. It defines the concepts of healthcare equality and inequality and their measurement. It also establishes the ethical positions on which Americans base their assessment of health inequalities and inequities. Finally, the author poses some ideas about dealing with inequalities and inequities when they occur.

In Chapter 19, Hackler presents information about rationing health care and discusses its ethical ramifications. After defining healthcare rationing, he gives arguments for situations in which this action is ethically defensible. He also presents a mechanism for making morally sound healthcare rationing decisions. Given the major changes proposed through PPACA, this knowledge is essential to ethics-based decision making.

In Chapter 20, Warshaw writes about an issue that continues to affect individuals, the community, and health care—namely, domestic violence. She presents information on how clinical practitioners address this issue and the limitations in their ability to do so effectively. She also discusses ethical dilemmas faced by these clinicians and the need for society to continue their efforts to address this societal problem.

Chapter 21 is especially germane in light of recent events, including mass shootings. It provides an overview of the government, the healthcare system, and the individual's response to both human-caused and natural disasters. New information on planning and response to these events is included. There is also discussion of problems in relationship to ethical theory and principles.

Chapters 22 and 23 are new to this edition and present a discussion of ethics and PPACA. In Chapter 22, O'Brien provides a context for the current legislation with a brief history of past efforts at universal health care. Through a timeline, he presents the features of the legislation and then gives an analysis related to ethical principles. In Chapter 23, Furlong examines the populations that PPACA may not cover: (1) immigrants who are not documented, (2) individuals eligible for Medicaid but who are not enrolled, and (3) those exempted from purchasing insurance because of the financial burden. Through case studies and discussion, she presents a principle-based ethical analysis and ideas for advocacy.

The final chapter (Chapter 24) begins with a brief summary of all four sections of the text. Morrison and Furlong then present emerging issues in both ethical theory and society. Furlong discusses how thinking about the theory of ethics is evolving through her introduction to the Ethic of Care model and the Narrative Ethics model. She describes how these models appeal to healthcare professionals. Morrison discusses the increased use of complementary and alternative medicine (CAM) among Americans and the reasons for the increase. She analyzes ethical issues for society and for healthcare professionals using the four principles. In addition, Morrison introduces the issue of the aging Baby Boomer population and its impact on society and on health care. She gives an analysis of ethical issues for the Baby Boomers and for health care in her section of the chapter.

CHAPTER 18

Health Inequalities
and Health Inequities

Nicholas B. King

INTRODUCTION

People have long recognized that some individuals lead longer and healthier lives than others, and that often these differences are closely associated with social characteristics such as race, ethnicity, gender, location, and socioeconomic status. The introduction of the regular collection of vital statistics by European states in the 19th century enabled Edwin Chadwick and other social reformers to quantify and compare the health and living conditions of different social classes. More recently, epidemiologists, sociologists, geographers, and other researchers have used advanced qualitative and quantitative methods not only to identify and track a wide variety of health inequalities but also to produce increasingly sophisticated models to explain their causes and consequences.

As knowledge and understanding of health inequalities has increased, so too has the political will to reduce or eliminate them. One of the two goals of the U.S. Healthy People 2020 initiative is to "achieve health equity, eliminate disparities, and improve the health of all groups."[1] In the United Kingdom, the release of successive government reports on socioeconomic inequalities in health in 1980 (the Black Report) and 1987 (the *Health Divide* report) stimulated increased scrutiny of the National Health Service. Other countries and nongovernmental organizations have undertaken major initiatives to address health inequalities both within and between nations. As the World Health Organization's Commission on Social Determinants of Health's 2008 final report notes:

> Within countries, the differences in life chances are dramatic and are seen worldwide. The poorest of the poor have high levels of illness and premature mortality. But poor health is not confined to those worst off. In countries at all levels of income, health and illness follow a social gradient: the lower the socioeconomic position, the worse the health. . . . Putting right these inequities—the huge and remediable differences in health between and within countries—is a matter of social justice.[2]

This chapter reviews the central ethical issues raised by the existence of health inequalities, their study, and attempts to reduce or eliminate them. One can summarize the chapter's concepts in a series of basic questions: What are health inequalities? Why are some health inequalities also health inequities? How are health inequalities measured? What is the best way to reduce or eliminate health inequities?

WHAT ARE HEALTH INEQUALITIES?

Understanding and assessing health inequalities requires us to answer three subsidiary questions: What is health? What is a health inequality? What is the difference between a health inequality and a health inequity?

Health

What is *health*? The answers vary considerably, from narrow definitions focusing on the absence of disease to broader ones encompassing a wide range of measures of subjective and objective characteristics. At one end of the spectrum, bioethicist Norman Daniels offers a narrow definition of health as "normal functioning, that is, the absence of pathology, mental or physical."[3] By contrast, the constitution of the World Health Organization defines it as "a state of complete physical, mental, and social well-being and not merely the absence of disease or infirmity."[4] More expansive definitions of health might include happiness, freedom from disability, quality of life, and the capacity to lead a socially meaningful and economically productive life. Narrow definitions have the benefit of being objectively measurable by biological and physiologic characteristics, but fail to capture aspects of human experience that might be more relevant to ensuring social justice, such as happiness, well-being, or capabilities. Broader definitions rectify this limitation but often involve highly subjective judgments by researchers or patients and thus are more difficult to adequately measure and compare.

Researchers assess health status in many ways. Under a narrow definition of health, the most common health indicators are mortality, survival, life expectancy, disease incidence, and disease prevalence. Definitions that are more expansive might include physiologic indicators of overall health (e.g., height, weight, body mass index, and blood pressure), symptoms, self-rated health status, sense of well-being, social connectedness, and productivity. Different kinds of health problems have different classification schemes. The *International Classification of Diseases* (ICD) *Manual* provides standard definitions of physical illness based around etiopathies that alter organ function and produce symptoms. ICD classifications are widely accepted and used in clinical diagnosis and health research. By contrast, the American Psychiatric Association's *Diagnostic and Statistical Manual of Mental Disorders* (DSM) defines mental health problems in terms of symptoms rather than etiology, which has been subject to considerable criticism.[5]

Because different populations can have radically different health belief systems, definitions of health, or subjective experience of symptoms, comparing populations to determine the levels of inequality between them can be difficult. This is particularly true when trying to compare rates of mental illness, symptoms, or self-reported health status between nations with widely disparate cultures. For this reason, authors often express international health inequalities in terms of adult or infant mortality, or life expectancy, which—although collected haphazardly in some locations—they think are the most objective indicators of health status available.

Assessments of health inequalities might also use measures of health care, including rates of diagnosis, treatment, cost, insurance coverage, quality, survival, symptom reduction, or some other health outcome measure. Strictly speaking, one should distinguish *health inequalities* from inequalities in *health care*. Linkage can exist between the two; however, this not always the case. Some inequalities in health care do not necessarily lead to health inequalities, whereas many health inequalities occur in the context of healthcare equality.

Inequality

Health inequality is a descriptive term that can refer either to the total variation in health status across individuals within a population or to a difference in average or total health between two or more populations. In **Table 18–1**, the average body mass index (BMI) of populations A and B are identical, but the variation within population A is clearly larger than that within population B. Thus, we may say that there is greater total inequality within population A than population B, but that there is relative equality *between* the two populations. Although there is some debate over which is a more scientifically rigorous measurement,[6] most scholarly work on the topic defines health inequalities as differences in health between populations.

Because health inequalities generally involve the comparison of population averages (although one can use other measures), one must take great care in making inferences regarding individuals. In **Table 18–2**, the average BMI of population A is lower than that of population B. However, the two individuals with the highest BMI are in population A, and the individual with the lowest BMI is in population B. Thus, we cannot infer that any particular individual in a group with better health will be any healthier than an individual in a group with worse health. Inequality is a property of populations rather than individuals.[7]

WHY ARE SOME HEALTH INEQUALITIES ALSO HEALTH INEQUITIES?

In contrast to the descriptive term *health inequality*, *health inequity* is a normative term that refers to a difference that society judges to be morally unacceptable.[8] Although almost all health inequities are, by definition, health inequalities, not all health inequalities are health inequities. For example, because society does not consider elective cosmetic surgery a necessity for good health and functioning, society would not consider unequal access to such surgery to be an inequity. Similarly, because society considers skydiving to be

Table 18–1   Average Body Mass Index: Example 1

	Population A	Population B
	40	30
	38	29
	18	27
	16	26
Average	**28**	**28**

Table 18–2 Average Body Mass Index: Example 2

	Population A	Population B
	35	33
	34	32
	22	31
	21	20
Average	**28**	**29**

a freely chosen behavior, it would not consider the fact that the mortality rate for falls from great heights is much higher among skydivers than the general population to be a health inequity.

Determining whether a particular inequality (or class of inequalities) constitutes an inequity requires a moral judgment based on a priori beliefs about justice, fairness, and the distribution of social resources, and thus is one of the primary areas in which ethical analysis plays a role. One commonly defines *health inequities* by referring to either the populations affected by inequalities or the causes and consequences of inequalities.

One way of determining whether a health inequality qualifies as an inequity is through reference to the relative social position of different populations. If a health inequality benefits a population that is in some way already socially or economically advantaged, then we may deem that inequality unjust through its association with a prior distributive injustice. This "egalitarian liberal" perspective judges health inequalities morally wrong primarily because they suggest that some individuals' or groups' rights are being violated, thus negatively affecting their health.[9] For example, Paul Farmer argues that ill health, and health inequalities in particular, is evidence of injustice or structural inequity in the world "even though it may be manifest in the patient."[10] More specifically, Paula Braveman argues that

> [a] health disparity between more and less advantaged population groups constitutes an inequity *not* because we know the proximate causes of that disparity and judge them to be unjust, but rather because the disparity is strongly associated with unjust social structures; those structures systematically put disadvantaged groups at generally increased risk of ill health and also generally compound the social and economic consequences of ill health.[11]

The existence of health inequalities might indicate that a given population has disproportionately suffered international military and economic exploitation,[12] inequitable distribution of economic resources,[13] or historical patterns of race-based economic and social injustice.[14] This definition of health inequity accords with John Rawls's "difference principle" of distributive justice: any inequalities in the distribution of an important resource should benefit the least-advantaged members of a society.[15] It also has the benefit of using a priori judgments about social or economic inequity as the foundation for adjudicating claims of health inequity. Thus, for example, disadvantaged populations do not have to prove repeatedly that every health inequality adversely affecting them constitutes an inequity.

However, this definition also suffers from significant drawbacks. First, the a priori identification of disadvantaged populations can be contentious or arbitrary in some situations. For example, would a health inequality favoring those with annual incomes of $5 million over those with annual incomes of $2 million constitute an inequity, or do both of these groups qualify as "advantaged"? Another example: in most countries, despite their lesser social status, women enjoy a longer lifespan than men do. This is possibly because of genetic factors, but also possibly because of lower rates of risky behaviors, such as smoking and alcohol use. Few observers identify this longer lifespan as a health inequity.

At the same time, many observers argue that the dramatically higher rates of morbidity and mortality from HIV/AIDS among women in a number of countries[16] are evidence of serious health and social inequities.[17] By contrast, higher rates of HIV/AIDS among men in richer nations, such as the United States, have seldom been identified as a gendered health inequity (although the delay in devoting health resources to the disease during the 1980s was frequently cited as evidence of a sexual-orientation health inequity). In addition, how might this definition account for novel forms of sociological categorization that may be accurate but do not lend themselves easily to judgments of relative disadvantage? An example of such a categorization might be race–county combinations that indicate that low-income rural blacks who live in the South have a lower life expectancy than low-income whites in Appalachia and the Mississippi Valley.[18]

This definition also neglects situations in which a genuinely unjust distribution of health might happen to benefit those in socially superior positions—as, for example, when a major pollutant happens to disproportionately affect a nearby wealthy community. Finally, if other social inequities exist and one deems them (rightly or wrongly) as socially acceptable, does this mean that the resultant health inequalities cannot qualify as unjust? Many American cities tolerate a certain level of homelessness as socially acceptable. Are higher rates of tuberculosis and mental illness among the homeless therefore socially acceptable as well?

Another common definition of health inequity focuses on the *causes and consequences* of a given health inequality, rather than the specific populations that it affects.[19] From this point of view, a health inequality is inequitable if it is systematic, avoidable, and unjust.[20] A *systematic* health inequality is one that consistently affects two or more populations and is not the result of random variation. For example, some so-called cancer clusters (elevated incidence of cancer in a community) are in fact the transient result of random variation. This has led to conflicts between community members who feel victimized by an apparent health inequity and health officials who argue that no such inequity exists.[21]

The criterion of *avoidability* has several components.[22] Health inequities must be *technically avoidable*—that is, a successful means of reducing the inequality must exist. They must be *financially avoidable*—that is, sufficient resources exist to rectify the inequality. Finally, they must be *morally avoidable*—that is, rectifying the inequality must not violate some other social value, such as liberty or distributive justice.

The third criterion is an *unjust cause*. Whitehead lists the following determinants of inequality: [23]

1. Natural, biological variation
2. Freely chosen health-damaging behavior, such as participation in certain sports and pastimes
3. The transient health advantage of one group over another when that group is first to adopt a health-promoting behavior (as long as other groups have the means to catch up fairly soon)
4. Health-damaging behavior where the degree of choice of lifestyles is severely restricted
5. Exposure to unhealthy, stressful living and working conditions
6. Inadequate access to essential health and other public services
7. Natural selection or health-related social mobility involving the tendency for sick people to move down the social scale

Whitehead argues that health inequalities resulting from the first three determinants are neither unjust nor unfair, and he would not consider them health inequities. By contrast, health inequalities arising from the latter four determinants are unjust and unfair, and thus qualify as health inequities. Examples of inequalities that would not qualify as inequitable under this definition might include the following: Ashkenazi Jews' elevated risk of developing breast cancer because of their slightly higher rates of carrying the BRCA1 and BRCA2 mutations;[24] the previously mentioned example of skydivers, whose freely chosen behavior elevates their risk of death; the higher rates of some communicable diseases among people living in temperate climates, because the insect vectors for those diseases are more prevalent than in colder climates; and early recipients of a new vaccination campaign.

This definition of health inequity avoids the criticisms leveled at the first definition, and it accords with Iris Marion Young's observation that, in general, it is not patterns of inequality per se that are morally wrong, but rather those whose causes and consequences we deem to be unjust.[25] However, like the previous definition, it suffers from some significant drawbacks. First, the degree to which many high-risk health behaviors are "freely chosen" is a topic of considerable debate. Three of the top nine "actual causes of death" in the United States—consumption of tobacco, alcohol, and illegal drugs—involve the use of substances that are highly addictive,[26] which might significantly diminish the element of free choice. In addition, many "freely chosen" health behaviors exhibit strong socioeconomic gradients. For example, both lung cancer rates and cigarette consumption (a primary risk factor for lung cancer) increase as socioeconomic status diminishes.[27] Many argue that the existence of a socioeconomic gradient in smoking is evidence that these behaviors are not freely chosen—for example, they may be mechanisms for coping with social or occupational stressors—and thus the resulting health inequalities are inequitable.

A second problem with this definition is that, by favoring cause over population as the deciding factor, health inequalities that benefit otherwise socially advantaged populations would be deemed inequitable and thus ostensibly in need of social remedy. This contradicts most peoples' intuition that social justice by definition involves redistributing social resources to the disadvantaged, rather than the other way around.

Perhaps the most significant problem with this definition is that many health problems have multicausal etiologies, and it is difficult or impossible to isolate a single, overriding causal factor. Diseases of the heart and cardiovascular system result from a complex combination of "just" causes, such as genetic predisposition and health behaviors (diet, exercise, smoking, etc.), as well as "unjust" causes, such as stressful living and working conditions and inadequate access to preventive health care. In some cases, it might be possible to quantify the relative contribution of each determinant to a population's health through sophisticated regression analyses. Yet this leaves open the question of whether moral judgments of inequity should be entirely dependent on the outcome of statistical analyses.

Finally, a health inequality might be judged to be morally wrong not because there is something inherently bad about health inequality, but rather because it is evidence of, or a contributing factor to, some other morally unacceptable situation. A health inequality thus "acts as a signpost—indicating that something is wrong."[28] For example, from an "objective utilitarian" perspective, a health inequality between two subpopulations might be judged bad because it indicates that the sum total of health in the entire population is not being maximized.[29] In this case, one does not see inequality per se as morally wrong, and the rectification of the health inequality would simply be a means toward the end of maximizing overall population health.

Similarly, some researchers argue that pervasive health inequalities across the entire socioeconomic spectrum are indications not of injustices directed at particular subpopulations but of fundamental social problems that adversely affect the health of all but those at the absolute top of the social hierarchy. Michael Marmot argues that socioeconomic gradients in chronic disease and life expectancy result from comparatively low levels of autonomy, social engagement, and social gradient.[30] Similarly, Richard Wilkinson argues that low social cohesion and pervasive psychosocial stress in societies with greater income inequality lead to shorter life expectancy.[31] If these authors are correct that almost every member of a society is in some way subject to health inequality, then attempts to encourage health equity could appeal to self-interest rather than social injustice.

HOW CAN WE MEASURE HEALTH INEQUALITIES?

Regardless of which definition of health inequity one uses, determining whether a specific situation is inequitable requires the measurement and comparison of the status of at least two populations. To do this, one must determine which *populations* it is most appropriate to compare and which *measures* are most appropriate to use in comparing these populations. Although one bases these determinations primarily on technical judgments to ensure the most statistically valid measurement and data analysis, they also require ethical judgment regarding the appropriate focus of description and intervention.[32]

Populations

By definition, inequalities are differences between groups of people. Specifying the composition of these groups is vital and involves important ethical decisions. First, the populations chosen should differ from one another in some way that is socially or morally important. We would thus expect that health inequalities among socially important groups based on factors such as race/ethnicity, gender, education level, or socioeconomic status would deserve scrutiny, whereas health inequalities among groups with different hair or eye color—distinctions that carry little social or moral weight—would be of less interest. In general, there is significant overlap between commonly accepted social and political distinctions and populations of interest to health inequalities researchers. However, the moral relevance of some distinctions—for example, health inequalities between U.S. states, counties, or census tracts—are more ambiguous.

Second, health inequalities generally involve establishing a *comparison group* that serves explicitly as a reference against which one can compare one or more populations, and implicitly as an ideal achievable target by all groups. A number of choices of comparison groups exist, any one of which is technically sound, but each of which carries different ethical implications. Consider the hypothetical example shown in **Table 18–3**. Clearly, significant health inequalities exist among the different racial/ethnic groups. However, the *amount* of inequality depends on the choice of comparison group. Which is the most appropriate in this case? Several answers are possible:

- We might choose the *total population average* as the reference group. Intuitively, it seems most just to consider the average of the general population as the standard of fairness against which to judge any particular subpopulation, much as we might consider a fair distribution of income to be one in which everyone clustered closely around the average.[33] In this example, the relative risk of the worst-off group (Hispanics) when compared with the total average is 1.75.

- We might choose the *best-off population* as the reference group. Many argue that every group in a society should enjoy the best possible level of health. Indeed, in some cases—for example, life expectancy, immunization

Table 18–3 Disease Prevalence, per 100,000

Subgroup	Disease Prevalence
Non-Hispanic White	7.6
Black	12.4
Hispanic	16.8
American Indian/Alaskan Native	6.9
Asian/Pacific Islander	10.2
Total	**9.6**

coverage, or access to lifesaving HIV medications—it is difficult to justify expecting anything less than the best possible health status as a fair and just outcome. In this example, the relative risk of the worst-off group (Hispanics) when compared with the best-off group (American Indians/Alaskan natives) is 2.44.

- We might choose the *most socially advantaged population* as the reference group. Under the first criterion, a health inequity is by *definition* a difference that favors a more (or most) socially advantaged population over a less socially disadvantaged one, and we would be less concerned with comparisons between relatively disadvantaged populations. In this example, the relative risk of the worst-off group (Hispanics) when compared with the most socially advantaged group (Non-Hispanic whites, the majority population) is 2.21.

- Finally, we might choose some *independently defined target rate* as a reference category. Many common health indicators, including blood pressure, body mass index, and total cholesterol level, have widely accepted thresholds separating high and low risk. It might be most just to expect all groups to pass that threshold, regardless of the relative rates of other groups. (The example in Table 18–3 is not pertinent to this choice.) Moreover, using this reference category would ensure that all groups use a medically justifiable amount of some healthcare resource, which is useful in cases where some subpopulations "overutilize" that resource.

Measurement

Wide varieties of statistical measures of inequality are available, from simple averages to sophisticated measures of total inequality. A comprehensive review of these measures is beyond the scope of this chapter. Instead, it will use the example of absolute and relative measures to illustrate the ethical issues often involved in choosing between different measurement strategies.[34]

Two of the simplest measures of health inequality are the rate difference and the rate ratio. The *rate difference* (RD) is a number resulting from subtraction of the numeric measure of one group's health status from another. The *rate ratio* (RR) is a ratio resulting from division of the numeric measure of one group's health status from another. Consider the example shown in **Table 18–4**.

Clearly, inequalities exist and favor population B for both conditions. Suppose one could fund efforts to reduce only one of these inequalities. Absent other considerations, one might reasonably decide to fund the larger inequality, but which one is larger? In absolute terms, the inequality in cancer rates is twice as large as that in heart disease (40 vs. 20), but in relative terms, the

Table 18–4   Mortality Rate, per 100,000

	Population A	*Population B*	*RD*	*RR*
Heart disease	80	60	20	1.333333
Cancer	270	230	40	1.173913

RD, rate difference; RR, rate ratio.

Table 18–5 U.S. Infant Mortality Rate, per 100,000 Live Births

	Black	*White*	*RD*	*RR*
1950	43.9	26.8	17.1	1.6
1998	13.8	6	7.8	2.3
Change	**30.1**	**20.8**	**−9.3**	**1.5**

RD, rate difference; RR, rate ratio.

inequality in heart disease rates is almost twice as large (33% vs. 17% higher for population A). There is no consistent standard for judging which measure is more appropriate in this case. One could make a reasonable case that the RD is more important because eliminating it would save more lives in absolute terms, and thus cancer should receive funding. Conversely, one might reasonably argue that the RR better represents the "true" inequity because the number of cases involved does not affect it, and thus there should be funding for heart disease.

The choice of the appropriate measure is particularly important when assessing health inequalities over time, as well as the relationship between *distributive* considerations (in this case, health inequalities) and *aggregative* ones (in this case, overall health). In some cases, measures that improve aggregate health in an entire population and all of its subpopulations might simultaneously increase inequalities between the more and less advantaged members of the population. Consider **Table 18–5**.

Between 1950 and 1998, overall infant mortality in the United States declined precipitously for all racial groups. The absolute reduction in infant deaths during this period was almost 50% higher among blacks than whites (30.1 vs. 20.8), and the rate difference decreased (from 17.1 to 7.8), which indicates that blacks benefited *more* than whites did from reductions in infant mortality during this time period. However, during the same period the rate ratio between the two groups increased (from 1.6 to 2.3), indicating that blacks benefited less. So, were racial inequalities in infant mortality better or worse in 1998 than in 1950? Did improvements in infant mortality disproportionately benefit whites or not? Was there a trade-off between overall population health and health inequalities or not?

WHAT IS THE BEST WAY TO REDUCE OR ELIMINATE HEALTH INEQUALITIES?

Even if we can reach agreement that a measurable health inequality exists, that it constitutes an inequity, and that we need to address it, there is no single rationale for determining the most ethically sound way to reduce or eliminate that inequity. Several ethical considerations play a role in deciding among possible interventions.

The first consideration concerns the relationship between equality of *treatment* and equality of *outcomes*, embodied in the principles of horizontal and vertical equity. *Horizontal equity* refers to the equal allocation of resources (in this case, health care) across a population. Universal health care accords with this principle on the grounds that everyone needs health care, and no individual or group should receive disproportionately better or worse care than another.

Vertical equity refers to the allocation of different resources for different levels of need. Healthcare or public health programs that target a disadvantaged social group accord with this principle, on the grounds that unequal allocation of resources might be necessary to achieve equal health outcomes. An extreme emphasis on vertical equity is liberation theology's injunction that the poorest members of a society should always be accorded preferential treatment, because they bear the greatest burden of social inequality.[35] In choosing between these two principles, it is worth asking, If everyone receives the same treatment, are unequal outcomes ethically problematic? If everyone has the same outcome, are unequal treatments ethically problematic?

A second issue is the aforementioned relationship between distributive and aggregative considerations, and the cases of "leveling up" or "leveling down" to achieve the goal of equity. Consider the four situations shown in Figure 18–1 through Figure 18–4. Assume that the measured rate in these charts is something beneficial, such as access to lifesaving medications. Figure 18–1 represents the current situation, in which the total population rate is 27.5, and a simple index of total inequality[36] is 5. Suppose that we wish to *both* improve overall access to lifesaving medication *and* reduce the total inequality of access in this population. In Figure 18–2, the total population rate is better (higher), and each subpopulation has benefited, but the total inequality is worse (also higher).

In Figure 18–3, there is a great reduction in the total inequality, but there is a slight reduction in overall inequality; the access rate of the two best-off populations has decreased, but that of the worst-off has increased. Finally, in Figure 18–4, total inequality has been reduced to zero, and overall access has dropped slightly, The access of the top two populations has decreased,

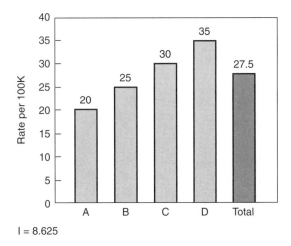

I = 8.625

Figure 18–1

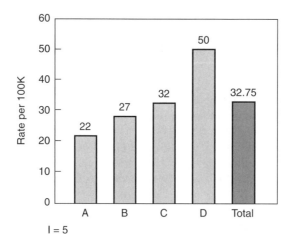

Figure 18–2

while that of the bottom two has increased. Which of the other three situations represents the best trade-off between reducing inequity and improving overall health?

Many other considerations regarding the appropriate distribution of social resources play a role in determining the best approach to reducing health inequities. Given a number of different subpopulations (e.g., multiple racial or ethnic groups or education levels), are some subpopulations more or less "deserving" of direct intervention to reduce health inequalities? Consider a final example. Epidemiologic evidence indicates that differences in socioeconomic status, nutrition, exposure to pathogens and toxic substances, and health care very early in life can have a profound impact on health status and inequalities later in life.[37] This raises the possibility that the best way to reduce (adult) health inequalities in the long term might be to invest as heavily as possible in pre- and postnatal health care, perhaps at the expense of health care much later in life, when reducing inequalities might be prohibitively expensive. Is this an acceptable triaging of social resources?

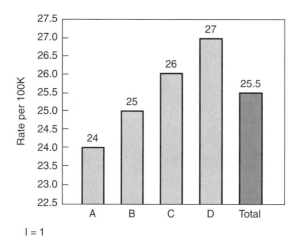

Figure 18–3

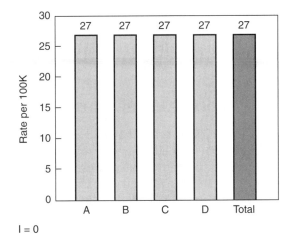

$I = 0$

Figure 18–4

CONCLUSION

Despite repeated calls for and considerable resources devoted to their elimination, dramatic health inequities persist and in some cases are increasing. This review might make the task of addressing health inequities seem daunting or even insurmountable. In some cases, the task is indeed complex. However, the existence and persistence of significant gaps in health and longevity between the most- and least-advantaged populations worldwide compels us to take action, no matter how challenging the task.

SUMMARY

This chapter began by defining the essential concepts for understanding the ethical problem posed in the chapter. It also explored the ethical difference between an inequality and an inequity. It further explained how inequalities are measured and the issues associated with defining populations and measurement standards. Finally, it presented areas to consider in reducing or eliminating health inequalities.

QUESTIONS FOR DISCUSSION

1. What is the difference between health inequalities and inequities in health care?
2. What ethical theories help to define whether a health inequality is truly an inequity?
3. How are health inequalities indicators of larger social problems for socioeconomic groups?

4. How do researchers apply ethics to specify populations when studying health inequalities?

5. In the author's view, what is the best way to decrease health inequality?

FOOD FOR THOUGHT

From the viewpoint of ethics, the number and degree of health inequities that exist in a wealthy nation such as America is not acceptable. However, as this chapter suggests, correcting health inequities is not a simple task. Think of an area of health inequity in your community. Using what you have learned about ethics and health care, answer the following questions:

1. Why is this health inequity also an ethical issue?
2. What are the current efforts, if any, to address this concern?
3. Who needs to be a part of addressing this concern?
4. What else could be done to address this concern?

NOTES

1. U.S. Department of Health and Human Services, "About Healthy People," HealthyPeople.gov, para. 5. Retrieved from http://www.healthypeople.gov/2020/about/default.aspx. Accessed January 28, 2012.

2. World Health Organization Commission on Social Determinants of Health, *Closing the Gap in a Generation: Health Equity Through Action on the Social Determinants of Health. Final Report of the Commission on the Social Determinants of Health* (Geneva, Switzerland: World Health Organization, 2008), 1.

3. N. Daniels, "Equity and Population Health: Toward a Broader Bioethics Agenda," *Hastings Center Report* 36, no. 4 (2006): 22–35.

4. World Health Organization, "Preamble to the Constitution of the World Health Organization," *Official Records of the World Health Organization* 2 (1946).

5. P. R. McHugh, "Striving for Coherence," *Journal of the American Medical Association* 293, no. 20 (2005): 2526–2528.

6. See C. J. L. Murray, E. E. Gakidou, and J. Frenk, "Health Inequalities and Social Group Differences: What Should We Measure?" *Bulletin of the World Health Organization* 77, no. 7 (1999): 537–543; and P. Braveman and S. Gruskin, "Defining Equity in Health," *Journal of Epidemiology and Community Health* 57 (2003): 254–258.

7. Making inferences about the properties of individuals from aggregate group statistics is commonly referred to as the *ecological fallacy*.

8. Authors use the term *health disparity* interchangeably with *health inequities*, particularly in the United States, but it also is used interchangeably with *health inequality* in other countries. For this reason, I will use the terms *health inequality* and *health inequity* throughout this chapter.

9. M. J. Roberts and M. R. Reich, "Ethical Analysis in Public Health," *Lancet* 359, no. 9311 (2002): 1055–1059.

10. P. Farmer, *Pathologies of Power: Health, Human Rights, and the New War on the Poor* (Berkeley: University of California Press, 2003), 153.

11. P. A. Braveman, "Measuring Health Inequalities: The Politics of the World Health Report 2000," in *Health and Social Justice: Politics, Ideology, and Inequity in the Distribution of Disease*, ed. Richard Hofrichter (San Francisco: Jossey-Bass, 2003).

12. S. Benatar, "Global Disparities in Health and Human Rights: A Critical Commentary," *American Journal of Public Health* 88, no. 2 (1998): 295–300.

13. N. Daniels, B. Kennedy, and I. Kawachi, *Is Inequality Bad for Our Health?* (Boston: Beacon Press, 2000).

14. J. S. House and D. R. Williams, "Understanding and Reducing Socioeconomic and Racial/Ethnic Disparities in Health," in Hofrichter, *Health and Social Justice.*

15. J. Rawls, *A Theory of Justice* (Cambridge, MA: Harvard University Press, 1971).

16. T. C. Quinn and J. Overbaugh, "HIV/AIDS in Women—An Expanding Epidemic," *Science* 308 (2005): 1582–1583.

17. S. Zierler and N. Krieger, "Reframing Women's Risk: Social Inequalities and HIV Infection," *Annual Review of Public Health* 18 (1997): 401–436.

18. C. J. L. Murray, S. C. Kulkarni, C. Michaud, N. Tomijima, M. T. Bulzacchelli, T. J. Iandiorido, and M. Ezzati, "Eight Americas: Investigating Mortality Disparities Across Races, Counties, and Race-Counties in the United States," *PLoS Medicine* 3, no. 9 (2006): 1513–1524.

19. M. Whitehead, "The Concepts and Principles of Equity and Health," *Health Promotion International* 6, no. 3 (1991): 217–228; O. Carter-Pokras and C. Baquet, "What Is a 'Health Disparity'?" *Public Health Reports* 117, no. 5 (2002): 426–434.

20. M. Whitehead, *The Concepts and Principles of Equity and Health* (Copenhagen, Denmark: The World Health Organization, 2000), 5.

21. P. Brown, "Popular Epidemiology and Toxic Waste Contamination: Lay and Professional Ways of Knowing," *Journal of Health and Social Behavior* 33, no. 3 (1992): 267–281; A. Gawande, "The Cancer-Cluster Myth," *The New Yorker*, February 8, 1999, 34–37.

22. A. Bambas and J. A. Casas, "Assessing Equity in Health: Conceptual Criteria," in Hofrichter, *Health and Social Justice.*

23. Whitehead, *Concepts and Principles of Equity and Health.*

24. J. P. Struewing, P. Hartge, S. Wacholder, S. M. Baker, M. Berlin, M. McAdams, M. M. Timmerman, L. C. Brody, and M. A. Tucker, "The Risk of Cancer Associated with Specific Mutations of BRCA1 and BRCA2 Among Ashkenazi Jews," *New England Journal of Medicine* 336, no. 20 (1997): 1401–1408.

25. I. Marion Young, "Equality of Whom? Social Groups and Judgments of Injustice," *Journal of Political Philosophy* 9, no. 1 (2001): 1–18.

26. J. M. McGinnis and W. H. Foege, "Actual Causes of Death in the United States," *Journal of the American Medical Association* 270, no. 18 (1993): 2207–2212; A. H. Mokdad, J. S. Marks, D. F. Stroup, and J. L. Gerberding, "Actual Causes of Death in the United States, 2000," *Journal of the American Medical Association* 291, no. 10 (2004): 1238–1245.

27. C. R. Baquet, J. W. Horm, T. Gibbs, et al. "Socioeconomic Factors and Cancer Incidence Among Blacks and Whites," *Journal of the National Cancer Institute* 83 (1991): 551–557.

28. Carter-Pokras and Baquet, "What Is a 'Health Disparity'?", 432.

29. Roberts and Reich, "Ethical Analysis in Public Health."

30. M. Marmot, "Health in an Unequal World," *Lancet* 368 (2006): 2081–2094.

31. R. Wilkinson, *Unhealthy Societies: The Afflictions of Inequality* (London: Routledge, 1996). Also note that the apparent connection between income inequality and life expectancy has been the subject of much debate; see J. P. Mackenbach, "Income Inequality and Population Health," *British Medical Journal* 324 (2002): 1–2; J. W. Lynch, G. D. Smith, G. A. Kaplan, and J. S. House, "Income Inequality and Mortality: Importance to Health of Individual Income, Psychosocial Environment, or Material Conditions," in Hofrichter, *Health and Social Justice;* and J. Lynch, G. D. Smith, S. Harper, M. Hillemeier, N, Ross, G. A. Kaplan, and M. Wolfson, "Is Income Inequality a Determinant of Population Health? Part 1: A Systematic Review," *Milbank Quarterly* 82, no. 1 (2004): 5–99.

32. Material in this section draws heavily on S. Harper and J. Lynch, "Measuring Health Inequalities," in *Methods in Social Epidemiology*, eds. J. M. Oakes and J. S. Kaufman (San Francisco: Jossey-Bass, 2006).

33. A related problem concerns whether to include the subpopulation of interest in the total population average.

34. S. Harper, N. B King, S. C. Meersman, M. E. Reichman, N. Breen, and J. Lynch, "Implicit Value Judgments in the Measurement of Health Inequalities," *Milbank Quarterly* 88, no. 1 (2010): 4–29.

35. Ibid.

36. Average deviation from the total population rate, given by

$$I = [\,|(A - T)| + |(B - T)| + |(C - T)| + |(D - T)|\,]/4$$

Subtract the number from Column A from the total, the number from column B from the total, the number from Column C from the total, and the number from Column D from the total. The sum of these individual results are then divided by four. This gives the average deviation from the total population.

37. E. D. A. Hyppönen, L. M. G. Kenward, and H. Lithell, Prenatal Growth and Risk of Occlusive and Haemorrhagic Stroke in Swedish Men and Women Born 1915–1929: Historical Cohort Study," *British Medical Journal* 323 (2001): 1033–1034; A. Case, A. Fertig, and C. Paxson, "The Lasting Impact of Childhood Health and Circumstance," *Journal of Health Economics* 24, no. 2 (2005): 365–389.

CHAPTER 19

Is Rationing of Health Care Ethically Defensible?

Chris Hackler

INTRODUCTION

Expenditures for health care constitute a significant portion of the budgets of all industrialized nations. In the absence of cost-control measures, medical spending tends to grow more rapidly than the general rate of economic growth. Increasing demand and the high cost of new medical technologies are only two factors driving healthcare inflation. In several countries, including the United States, substantial portions of the population face difficulty in obtaining medical care. Correcting this situation will mean even greater demand for healthcare services. In these countries, it would seem that the only way to expand coverage while holding costs near current levels would be to reduce per-capita spending.

The problem in the United States becomes more acute year by year, as increasing numbers of citizens from the post–World War II baby boom become eligible for Social Security and Medicare. As we proceed through the second decade of the 21st century, the average age of the population will continue to increase dramatically, placing formidable pressure on both healthcare and retirement programs. With inflation and the demand for services increasing yearly, spending on health care will consume a larger and larger portion of the national budget. Unless we find some way to reduce the level of healthcare spending, or at least government healthcare spending through Medicare and Medicaid, we might have little left to fund other essential social services. Thus, healthcare spending is a serious and growing problem for which we must find a solution that is both economically sound and ethically just.

The most difficult, painful, and divisive debates about this problem today, at least in the United States, revolve around the issue of rationing. Some say we must never ration health care and that physicians certainly must not do such a thing. Others maintain that soaring health expenditures require us to place significant limits on medical spending, and that means denying some medical services that are both beneficial and desired. Still others claim that we are already rationing health care, either by market forces or by denying inclusion or coverage in public programs for the poor. This debate certainly involves serious substantive issues, but some of it also results from lack of clarity about the term *rationing*.

WHAT IS RATIONING?

In the strict sense of the term, we are not rationing health care, and we never have. To ration generally means to give equal portions of a scarce good to everybody. A clear example of rationing is the allotment of goods such as rubber, sugar, gasoline, or gunpowder in wartime. The amount needed by the military is set aside, and the remainder is allocated to citizens in equal shares. Another use of the term is for the fixed (and equal) amounts of food given to soldiers in battle. Rationing in this sense, which is the common or dictionary definition, does not apply to health care. We have never considered giving our citizens fixed allotments of health care—so many days of hospitalization, so many visits to the doctor, a fixed amount of money to spend on health care, or any such thing.

An essential point is that we do not practice rationing in the ordinary sense as a way to save money or decrease expenditures. Rather, it is a response to a real physical scarcity of goods for consumption. The shortage might be the result of a diversion to war efforts or to exports for foreign capital, or it may result from natural events such as crop failures or earthquakes. There is no comparable shortage of medical goods or services in the United States or western Europe, so it is not obvious why *rationing* would be the term chosen to refer to some of our attempts to limit healthcare spending.

Rationing is essentially a method of distributing resources outside the market system. We, in the United States, are ambivalent about the status of health care. We think of it both as a market commodity and as a social good that we ought to supply to those unable to procure it. The result is a complex patchwork of a "system" that leaves many without adequate access to care. That millions of our citizens are not getting the health care they need because they cannot afford it is a deplorable fact and a serious ethical and political problem, but it might be confusing to describe the situation, as many do, as "rationing by price."[1]

One of the first uses of the term *rationing* in the context of health care was by Aaron and Schwartz.[2] In their view, rationing occurs when "not all care expected to be beneficial is provided to all patients." This is surely too broad a definition of rationing. If this is the meaning of the term, then we ration almost everything. Most of us would benefit from a new automobile, a new suit of clothes, and perhaps even from extensive cosmetic surgery. Patients who cannot pay for it rarely receive treatment for infertility by in vitro fertilization, but it seems odd to say it is being rationed. Aaron and Schwartz claim that denying any potentially beneficial care means that "the value of care is being weighed against its costs, explicitly or implicitly."[3] This seems to equate rationing with cost-benefit analysis, that is, basing the decision whether to provide a certain treatment not just on whether it would be of any benefit, but also on whether the benefits would be proportional to the cost of the treatment.[4] Cost-benefit analysis is certainly a potential strategy to reduce healthcare spending, but it is not rationing in the customary sense.

A number of practices resemble rationing and are frequently so labeled. Three of these are distribution of scarce goods, prioritization of services, and allocation of financial resources. Distribution of organs for transplantation is a clear example of the first. Transplantable organs are an absolutely scarce resource (i.e., there is no way to produce enough to satisfy all needs). We must make choices concerning who will get a given organ and who will not. We all agree that it is ethically acceptable that we deny someone the organ; only one person can have it, and it is better that someone gets it than that no one gets it. It is not possible for all to share equally in the limited resources, which is the ordinary sense of rationing, but it is possible and ethically necessary to distribute organs fairly. Because we deny someone access to the organ, some will call it rationing, but the expression "just distribution of scarce goods" is quite adequate and less misleading.

The practice of triage in the emergency room is an example of prioritizing access to care. A scarce resource—in this case, physician and staff time—is distributed according to urgency of need. We sometimes refer to this as rationing, although it bears almost no resemblance to ordinary rationing. Everybody gets service; it is only the order in which it is given that is at issue. *Prioritizing* is a perfectly serviceable term and more accurate in describing the practice than *rationing*. Again, nobody questions the ethical propriety of this practice, because the alternative policy of "first come, first served" would lead to much poorer aggregate outcomes.

We also refer to allocation of scarce resources as rationing. *Allocating* resources means dividing or apportioning them among competing interests. When there is a scarcity of a given resource, then we must devise a scheme to allocate among potential recipients in a way that is efficient, fair, and socially desirable. Rationing in the usual sense—that is, handing out equal shares—is one possible scheme, but not necessarily the best, certainly not in health care.

Money is a scarce resource, although not in the same way as transplantable organs. As a society, we can always find more money to meet the needs of a given group, but we do so at the expense of competing interests. There is a growing consensus that we are spending too much on health care and neglecting other important social needs, and that we must find ethically acceptable ways to limit healthcare spending. We can try to reduce waste and inefficiency, reduce the level of compensation for services, and so on. However, the most direct way to limit spending is to limit consumption or utilization. There are roughly two strategies for limiting utilization: eliminating some of the kinds of services offered or limiting access to the services (or both).

If access is to be limited, the next step is to find an acceptable way to determine who will gain access to the available services. One way to do this is by chance: either first come, first served, or by some kind of lottery. Another way is to identify criteria that will be used to determine when access will be granted. It might be the urgency of the medical need, the potential for medical benefit, the potential for quantity or quality of life, or any combination of factors. It is here that we are most inclined to speak of rationing, but notice that the situation is quite similar to the distribution of transplantable organs: we have too little to go around, and must distribute what we have on the basis of criteria that are fair to all. The big difference, and one that calls for ethical justification, is that the scarcity is a matter of policy, a deliberate choice we have made regarding the allocation of social resources. If the services that are no longer available are ineffective or are of little benefit, then the policy will be relatively easy to justify. If the services are of significant benefit, however, the task of justification will be more difficult.

Although it should be understood as a special use of the phrase, let us use *rationing of health care* in this chapter to refer to policies and procedures that result in individuals being denied services that would be of significant medical benefit to them for reasons other than absolute scarcity or inability to pay. Again, lack of access because of inability to pay is also a serious ethical issue, but a different one both conceptually and ethically. There are two aspects to rationing so understood: (1) policies that restrict the availability of services and (2) the implementation of those policies by individual gatekeepers who deny patients access to particular services. We turn now to the ethical justification of rationing so understood.

IS RATIONING ETHICALLY JUSTIFIABLE?

The case for the general possibility of rationing health care is quite simple. Life and health are basic goods, and we have a very strong social claim on the means necessary to sustain them. However strong the claim, life and health must compete with other social goods that in the end might be more important to the flourishing of the community. Under certain circumstances, discussed below, we may limit the funds devoted to health care in order to invest in such things as education and cultural enrichment, without which life and health would be hollow possessions, as well as such things as prisons and police activities, which are necessary to the very preservation of the community. To deny that rationing could ever be justified, it would seem necessary to hold that health (or life) is an absolute good, or that our moral claim on the means to health is always stronger that any competing claim or need. One could view a compromise of that claim for essentially economic reasons as putting a price on human life, thus contradicting the Kantian maxim. This posits that a life has not a price but a dignity, that is, an inner value that takes it out of the realm of things to which we can assign a comparative value or price. We will return to this issue later.

The case for rationing of health care in principle is simple, but that does not mean it will be easy to justify particular rationing schemes. What would be the important considerations in deciding whether a given proposal to ration health care is justifiable? Let us attempt to answer that question by trying to construct an ideal set of conditions sufficient to justify rationing. After surveying the following list, we shall consider how we might realize these ideal conditions in the real world.

1. There are other equally important needs competing for scarce resources.
2. There are no alternative ways to produce equivalent savings.
3. Savings from denied services will benefit other patients or be invested in equally important social needs.
4. Policies and procedures for limiting access to treatment are applied equitably to all.
5. Limits are self-imposed through democratic processes.

If we met all these conditions, then rationing of health care would clearly be justifiable. The trouble is that we only imperfectly meet them in the real world, and the degree of approximation varies from place to place. We will have to decide in each case how close to the ideal we must be before a given rationing scheme would be justifiable. There are real budget pressures and competing needs that we must somehow resolve. It is not helpful to insist on the perfect realization of ideal conditions before adopting a policy to deal with a pressing problem. With this in mind, let us examine the criteria in detail and discuss briefly the problems in satisfying them under various social arrangements.

JUSTIFYING RATIONING IN THE REAL WORLD

First, there must be equally important needs competing for scarce resources. We will need to address the appropriate level of funding for such things as education, housing, and national defense in concrete terms in a given social context. Is the military budget too big? Are we wasting money on inefficient administrative programs? These are important questions, but, in the end, I believe we will still find far more needs than we can fulfill at current budget levels. In addition, the constant development of new and expensive medical technologies and the aging of the population will continue to increase both the demand for health care and the cost of providing it.

Rationing of care is by no means the only way to control healthcare costs. Before we implement rationing, we should make every reasonable effort to reduce waste and inefficiency within the system. We should eliminate unnecessary services and minimize the duplication of resources. This is surely easier in more centrally organized systems such as those of Great Britain and Canada than in the fragmented system of the United States. For example, in the United States, there is far more expensive equipment than necessary because of competition among hospitals. Each institution has its own magnetic resonance imaging machine, though it sits unused much of the time. Because the hospital must pay for the machine, the charge for the procedure is artificially high. A study published in 1990 indicated there were 10,000 mammogram machines in the United States, four times the number needed to satisfy current demand and double that needed to satisfy all potential demand if everyone for whom it is recommended had the procedure.[5] More current data is not available, but there is no reason to think that the proportions have changed. Inefficient deployment of resources is a serious structural problem that is difficult to attack in a decentralized and fragmented system.

Another structural problem for the justification of rationing within the U.S. system concerns the proper transfer of savings. The justice of the practice of distributing organs for transplantation is apparent because we can see that someone benefits from the organ even when it is denied to someone else. It is likewise important in the justification of healthcare rationing that savings stay within the system and benefit other patients, although the trade-offs might be less visible. The trade-offs are much easier to accomplish and to demonstrate in a unified system than in a fragmented one. It is quite possible for savings to be directed to the salaries of healthcare or insurance company executives or to corporate profits. As private hospitals and health maintenance organizations increase their share of the U.S. healthcare system, the potential for misdirection of savings grows. Where we have insufficient guarantees against such results, we have a strong argument against rationing measures.

The fourth item on the list of ideal conditions for rationing is the equitable application of rationing policies. If one person sacrifices a beneficial and desired treatment, then others in the same situation should make the same sacrifice. Once again, this criterion is much more easily satisfied within a unified system than a fragmented one. If there is a unified system, then the same policies should apply to everyone. In our current system of many separate and independent units, there is no assurance that policies will be similar. Similarity of policies among units, however, is not the only issue. The application of policies should also be similar among individual physicians within the same system. Because the traditional role of the physician is as the patient's advocate, an understandable temptation will be to game the system for one's own patients, that is, to bend, manipulate, or bypass rules that deny a needed resource. Because clinical judgment is necessary in any rationing scheme, we probably will have to live with this problem and just try to minimize it.

The fifth ideal condition for rationing is that we freely adopt limits to health care rather than have them imposed. Clearly, it is better to deny a service because of a policy one has adopted rather than because of a policy imposed by others. Limits can be self-imposed in two ways: by participating in the formation of policies and by accepting the results of the process. Direct citizen participation in policy making can be cumbersome, but it was an important element in the development of Oregon's prioritized list of healthcare procedures.[6] Rationing policies developed openly by politically accountable representatives would also carry a presumptive legitimacy that secretly developed plans would lack.

In addition to the process of development, the fairness of the result is of great importance. If we freely adopt limits in the sense that they are accepted, those who are affected must perceive them as fair. It will be no small task to create policies that society universally perceives as just, especially in nations with diverse populations and historic inequities.

It would be difficult enough if there were general agreement on the criteria for making rationing decisions, but the American philosopher Norman Daniels has argued persuasively that there is no consensus on this matter and that none is likely.[7] In distributing organs for transplantation, for example, should we favor those who will live longest and thus benefit most, or should we give each individual a fair chance by means of a lottery? We have neither consensus nor a demonstrable theory that would yield a convincing answer to the question. Nor is there consensus on the matter of aggregating benefits. Prolonging a life for a year has a higher priority than providing routine dental care for one person, but if the funds saved by allowing the person to die can provide dental care for 600 people during that year, is that an appropriate trade-off? We do not now have answers to these questions, and there is no good reason to think a philosophical theory is about to be produced that will enable us to resolve such issues with confidence.

It is unfortunate that such fundamental issues are unresolved, but it need not paralyze public policy. We do not have a theory that guides our trade-offs in other areas of social policy either, but we manage to make difficult decisions nonetheless. We should not expect a system that everyone agrees is perfectly just. What we should expect is a system that we create openly; that tries to be fair, and succeeds in large measure; and that is open to continual improvement. Designing a workable system that is "just enough"[8] is a matter not only of ethics but also of economics, history, psychology, and politics.

WHO MAKES RATIONING DECISIONS?

The realization that we do not have an adequate and agreed-upon theoretical basis for rationing decisions makes more poignant the issue of who is making the decisions and how they make them. The previous section suggests that open procedures that are broadly inclusive are best. However, an opposite view also deserves consideration. In their book *Tragic Choices*, Guido Calabresi and Philip Bobbit argue that public involvement in rationing decisions would be unwise.[9] Every open society adheres to a set of fundamental values that is not internally consistent; that is, the values may come into conflict with one another. Tragic choices are those that bare the inconsistencies and force us to choose between cherished values, thus eroding our commitment to the dishonored value.

Rationing decisions are among the most dangerous of tragic choices because they expose our willingness to make trade-offs with human life and in some sense to set a price on it. Thus, these decisions compromise our commitment to the Kantian principle that human life does not have a price, but rather a dignity that gives it inestimable value and incomparable worth.

Of course, we regularly make public policy decisions that in effect price human life, but only if they are the lives of unknown future individuals. We may refuse to invest in mine safety, knowing that lives will be lost as a result, but we will pay whatever it takes to rescue a trapped miner. To do otherwise would be to acknowledge our willingness to price life. That is the essence of rationing decisions, so the argument goes. These decisions expose the conditional nature of our commitment to the sanctity and equality of human life.

In addition to being psychologically painful to individuals, there may be two truly serious consequences of rationing decisions. We may become too willing to price and trade in human life, and social cohesion might suffer. Our shared values provide the moral foundation of social collaboration. As tragic choices expose the contradictions among our values and erode our commitments to them, the foundation will begin to crumble. To preserve social cohesion, according to Calabresi and Bobbit, societies must mask their tragic choices. A policy-making elite should make rationing decisions. Such an elite will be sophisticated enough to realize that necessary compromises do not truly diminish the value of life, whereas the larger group "may not be able to make such nice distinctions."[10]

Although the possibility that public participation in rationing decisions might produce moral and political decay should sober us, it is by no means clear that this would be the result. It is an empirical claim for which evidence is scant. In fact, we have no more evidence for this pessimistic and anti-utopian vision than we do for the idealistic strain in Rousseau's view of democracy in *The Social Contract* (Rousseau was, characteristically, capable of deep pessimism at the same time).

The primary value of democracy for Rousseau was not what it does for us (by producing good laws), but what it does *to* us. By participating as a member of the Sovereign, an individual's "faculties so unfold themselves by being exercised, his ideas are so extended, his sentiments so exalted, and his whole mind so enlarged and refined" that he is transformed "from a circumscribed and stupid animal into an intelligent being and a man."[11]

Surely the truth lies somewhere between the deep skepticism of Calabresi and Bobbit and the soaring faith of Rousseau in human reason. It would be wrong to rely solely on any one source for rationing policies. We should employ open and democratic procedures, although their exact nature and role in the overall process is not clear. We should take citizen opinions and preferences into account, although policy experts must do the actual formulation of policies (a point acknowledged by Rousseau as well, in the figure of the Legislator). The potential role of citizen groups is very much an open question that deserves further study.

An important lesson to learn from Calabresi and Bobbit, however, is that we should frame the debate in such a way that allegiance to the basic conflicting values is preserved as much as possible, consistent with effective and responsible decision making.[12] Although choices might need to be formulated in terms of monetary value, this does not mean that the ultimate trade is lives for money. Money is only the medium of exchange that allows us to purchase one good at the expense of another. The real trade is, for example, the last two remaining months of a person's life, which would cost $200,000 to prolong, for the chance to save many infant lives by a citywide inoculation program that would cost $200,000. Thus understood, it is not life for money, but life for life, which is still in a sense a tragic choice, but one that is perhaps not so ethically suspect or socially corrosive.

CONCLUSION

Rapidly increasing spending on health care can threaten a society's economic and cultural vitality by decreasing savings and investment and draining funds from other social services. Governments are seeking to limit the growth of health spending by promoting greater efficiency and limiting reimbursement for physician and hospital services. A further step is to limit utilization of services, first by discouraging marginally beneficial treatments, and then, if necessary, by denying some costly treatments that would be of substantial benefit. We commonly call adopting policies that limit access to treatments of significant medical benefit *rationing of health care*, although this use is somewhat at odds with the ordinary meaning of the term.

Rationing will be defensible to the extent that funding is truly needed for other essential social goods and services, that alternative ways of limiting medical spending have been attempted, that the money saved will be directed to more compelling needs, and that the limits are applied equitably to everyone. It is also important that limits be self-imposed in the sense that they are openly developed and generally accepted as fair. Accepting rationing will be painful because it calls into question our conviction that human life is priceless. We must guard against the potentially corrosive effects of overtly making comparative judgments about human lives.

SUMMARY

As the cost of healthcare delivery increases and healthcare reform makes major changes in the business of health care, the issue of rationing will become more important and increasingly difficult. In his consideration of this issue, Hackler defined the concept of rationing and argued that it may be ethically justified under certain conditions. He also discussed the ideal conditions for rationing in the real world and provided cautions about who should make decisions about this practice. Finally, he stressed that whereas rationing of healthcare spending may be necessary and defensible, trading lives for money is not.

QUESTIONS FOR DISCUSSION

1. How does Hackler define rationing when it concerns healthcare products and services?
2. What is the impact of a market-driven economy on the rationing arguments presented in this chapter?
3. How does a fragmented healthcare system negatively affect the ethical and procedural decisions in a rationing plan?
4. How can having a foundation in Kantian ethics help to limit the potential for making tragic choices in rationing health care?
5. Given the changes that are projected in the 21st century for America (including the Patient Protection and Affordable Care Act [PPACA] and the increasing numbers of elderly people), do you think rationing of health care will be inevitable?

FOOD FOR THOUGHT

PPACA promises great changes in the healthcare system. Coupled with the rapidly aging baby boomer generation, this change may lead to an increased demand for services without an accompanying supply of providers. Do you think that rationing as defined in this chapter will be part of the post-PPACA future? How can you justify rationing in a universal healthcare environment?

NOTES

1. For example, L. Churchill uses this terminology in his excellent book *Rationing Health Care in America* (Notre Dame, IN: University of Notre Dame Press, 1987), 14.
2. H. J. Aaron and W. B. Schwartz, *The Painful Prescription: Rationing Hospital Care* (Washington, DC: The Brookings Institution, 1984).
3. Ibid.

4. M. D. Reagan, "Health Care Rationing: What Does It Mean?" *New England Journal of Medicine* 319, no. 17 (1988): 1150.

5. M. L. Brown, L. G. Kessler, and F. G. Rueter, "Is the Supply of Mammography Machines Outstripping Need and Demand? An Economic Analysis," *Annals of Internal Medicine* 113 (1990): 547–552.

6. M. Brannigan, "Oregon's Experiment," *Health Care Analysis* 1, no. 1 (1993): 15–28.

7. N. Daniels, "Rationing Fairly: Programmatic Considerations," *Bioethics* 7, no. 2–3 (1993): 224–232.

8. I borrow this term from L. M. Fleck, who has used it in a number of works. See, for example, "Just Caring: Lessons from Oregon and Canada" in *Health Care for an Aging Population*, ed. C. Hackler (Albany: State University of New York Press, 1994), 193.

9. G. Calabresi and P. Bobbit, *Tragic Choices* (New York: W. W. Norton, 1978).

10. Ibid, 69.

11. J. J. Rousseau, *The Social Contract* (New York: E.P. Dutton, 1913).

12. J. L. Nelson, "Publicity and Pricelessness," *Journal of Medicine and Philosophy* 19, no. 4 (1994): 340.

CHAPTER 20

Domestic Violence: Changing Theory, Changing Practice

Carole Warshaw

INTRODUCTION

Despite widespread recognition of domestic violence as a public health problem, many clinicians still have difficulty integrating routine intervention into their day-to-day work with patients. This is in part because domestic violence raises a distinct set of challenges for both providers and the institutions that shape clinical practice. Domestic violence is a complex social problem rather than a biomedical one; addressing it means asking clinicians to step beyond a traditional medical paradigm to confront the personal feelings and social beliefs that shape their responses to patients and to work in partnership with community groups committed to ending domestic violence. In addition, addressing domestic violence raises important challenges to the healthcare system itself—to its theoretical models, to the nature of medical training, and to the structure of funding and service delivery. If, as healthcare providers, we truly want to play a role in preventing domestic violence rather than just treating its consequences, we also need to play a role in broader community efforts to transform the social conditions that create and support this kind of violence in the first place.[1]

Over the past 30 years, it has become increasingly clear that domestic violence carries not only serious health consequences for women, but also many hidden social costs as well. As clinicians, we see the profound effects of this violence on a daily basis.[2] We often are deeply affected when we allow ourselves to listen, understand, and grapple with issues that require far more than our medical expertise.

However, society is making efforts to address domestic violence. For example, standard guidelines now exist because of the combined efforts of the domestic violence advocacy community, individual practitioners, and numerous professional societies. Major initiatives have been launched to increase provider awareness, establish and distribute clinical guidelines, and offer strategies for improving institutional responses to domestic violence, including recommendations for screening.[3] Innovative hospital-based advocacy programs have increased in number, and over 60% of medical schools, over 80% of family practice residencies, and approximately 70% of obstetrics/gynecology residencies have incorporated training on family violence into their standard curricula.[4] Yet despite widespread recognition of domestic violence as a public health problem, many clinicians still have difficulty integrating routine inquiry about domestic violence into their day-to-day clinical work.[5] Understanding the difficulties faced by healthcare providers as they attempt to address this issue can help not only to improve the practice of medicine but also to develop more realistic strategies for prevention and social change.[6]

Addressing domestic violence requires more than simply adding new diagnostic categories to differential diagnoses or new technical skills to clinical repertoires. As noted previously, it means asking clinicians to step beyond a traditional medical paradigm to confront the personal feelings and social beliefs that shape their responses to patients, which presents a difficult barrier. In addition, the healthcare system itself, through its theoretical framework, the nature of its training process, and the changing structure of clinical practice, presents another set of barriers that profoundly affect the ability of individual providers to respond to women (or men) who have been abused.[7]

PERSONAL AND SOCIAL BARRIERS

As Holtz et al. have reported, the majority of healthcare providers have not learned about domestic violence during their training. Although more recent trainees have been exposed to the topic during their graduate and postgraduate years, the amount of time devoted to it is limited.[8] As a result, "clinical" responses often are shaped by an interplay of the physician's own personal experiences and social, cultural, and religious beliefs.[9] Many factors combine to shape the ways we interpret and respond to life events, including our individual experiences and the social contexts in which they take place.

Koss et al.,[10] Johnson,[11] Brown,[12] Rieker and Carmen,[13] and Miller[14] have described the psychological impact of gender socialization, the traumatic effects of social disenfranchisement, and the ways in which the denial of intolerable feelings can shape our perceptions and lead to protectively rationalized ways of viewing ourselves, other people, and the world. For instance, the psychological need to protect ourselves from certain feelings in order to ensure psychic survival combined with social or cultural explanations of our experiences can solidify into beliefs and values that may then appear to us as "givens."[15] Clinicians absorb a range of societal views regarding gender and power, around which their own identities are constructed. Assumptions about gender, race, and class so permeate our culture that they often provide an unconscious backdrop through which we come to understand our own experiences and interpret those of others.

In addition, listening to people describe the violence in their lives can have a significant psychological impact on providers.[16] When physicians are not specifically trained to deal with psychological trauma, they are forced to rely on their own capacities to address painful and potentially overwhelming issues. In addition, given the prevalence of violence against women in this society, a significant number of physicians will have experienced or witnessed abuse in their own lives.[17] These issues touch too close to home for many healthcare providers, who may be understandably reluctant to have their own painful experiences evoked while trying to function in a professional capacity.[18]

SYSTEMIC BARRIERS

Impact of Medical Training

Once they enter the healthcare arena, clinicians are faced with a new set of forces that shape their perceptions and responses.[19] A number of authors have described the gaps in medical education that influence psychosocial aspects of care.[20] Not only is medical training often lax in equipping physicians to deal with difficult social and personal issues, but also, more insidiously, the process of professional socialization can actually diminish the capacities individuals already have. Pain, anger, frustration, and sadness are common responses to hearing about abuse. Without specific training and support, many clinicians find themselves dealing with these situations through a variety of techniques designed to protect and distance themselves from potentially distressing encounters.

In a field where competence and mastery are highly valued, it is difficult to risk venturing into areas that make clinicians feel less competent. They may find it easier to focus on problems for which interventions lead to outcomes that are more predictable or for which it is possible to retain a greater sense of control. Time-pressured working conditions only magnify these difficulties.[21]

Professional Socialization and the Intergenerational Transmission of Abuse

Extrapolating from the work of Richman et al.,[22] Baldwin et al.,[23] and others,[24] we can see how abusive training environments might also affect clinicians' abilities to deal with abuse among the women they see as patients. Medical training can be physically punishing, emotionally draining, and socially isolating. Trainees often report feeling humiliated and controlled as well as anxious, exhausted, depressed, overwhelmed, and traumatized.[25] Over time, both students and house staff begin to reorient their identities in terms of medicine's values, to internalize its constructs and judge themselves by its terms. Thus, medical training itself can create some of the same dynamics as abuse. In addition, the structure of medicine is hierarchical and, as such, reflects the gendered power arrangements of the larger society.

In their review of the sexual harassment literature, Schiffman and Frank found that sexual harassment and gender discrimination were common experiences among women physicians, adding yet another layer of abuse for women working within that system.[26] Clinicians' inabilities to recognize abuse in their own lives, whether personal, social, or professional, or to tolerate acknowledging their own vulnerability, make it more difficult for them to empathize with a woman who is struggling in an abusive relationship. The need to maintain a sense of power and control in order to be recognized as competent within that system and the pressure to avoid feelings that might arise when one cannot do so reinforce this dynamic on both individual and systemic levels. Although there has been much discussion about how abuse is transmitted intergenerationally within families, the process of professional socialization within the current structure of medicine can also serve as a vehicle for the intergenerational transmission of abuse.[27]

IMPACT OF THEORY ON CLINICAL PRACTICE

The theoretical foundations of medical education also affect the physician's ability to treat patients affected by domestic violence. For example, there is often a connection between social problems and clinical diagnoses, even though they are much more complex than any clinical label. In addition, traditional mental health models may be limited as clinical models in providing a framework for recognizing and treating domestic violence. In fact, the mental health system may actually retraumatize the patient. The healthcare system is beginning to understand that a new paradigm may be necessary for addressing this critical problem.

Medicalization of Social Problems

One aspect of medicalization involves the reduction of complex social problems into distinct clinical diagnoses.[28] One of the clearest illustrations of the need to shift from a standard problem-oriented framework to a more comprehensive model involves our evolving understanding of the role domestic violence plays in the lives of women with human immunodeficiency virus (HIV). Several studies have reported that many HIV-positive women either are or have been abused by partners.[29] Many "discrete" medical problems are, in fact, intimately connected to domestic violence, but because we think of them as separate issues, their interrelationships are more likely to be missed. For instance, one might easily generate a problem list that includes HIV infection, substance abuse, pregnancy, depression, post-traumatic stress disorder (PTSD), and domestic violence without necessarily seeing the connections among them.

Initial recognition of domestic violence among HIV-positive women led to appropriate concerns about reducing the risk for further violence, particularly regarding partner notification.[30] It took longer for the incorporation of domestic violence education and intervention into risk reduction counseling for HIV, pregnancy, and substance abuse. There are significant implications for funding, education, and prevention given that coerced sex within the context of an abusive relationship is a risk factor for HIV transmission and the other consequences of unprotected sex. In addition, substance abuse among women, the other major risk factor for HIV, increases in the context of domestic violence.[31] In fact, recognition of these connections has led a number of comprehensive HIV programs to integrate screening and counseling for domestic violence into the preventive as well as treatment services they provide.[32] In addition, reproductive coercion is now considered to be a key issue to be addressed in obstetrics/gynecology and family planning settings.[33]

Limitations of Mental Health Models

The process of stripping away context and transforming lived experience into disorders also occurs within the major mental health models and affects the nature of both diagnosis and intervention. For example, clinicians who work within a purely biological or disorder-specific framework run risks similar to their medical and surgical colleagues of failing to recognize and respond to the ongoing violence in a patient's life. They may also see the abuse as being caused by a particular woman's increased vulnerability or as only a secondary problem—a social stressor affecting the course of her primary biological or developmental disorder.

Traditional psychoanalytic theory historically has presented a different set of limitations. The context of ongoing violence and danger that creates and perpetuates a woman's symptoms might not be addressed or might be regarded as symptomatic rather than etiologic. In addition, a clinician bound by the constraints of remaining true to the neutrality of a psychodynamic framework might find it difficult to play a more active role in advocating for safety and in helping women gain access to community resources. Of course, other models— both feminist and psychodynamic—do recognize the importance of social and intersubjective contexts.[34]

When domestic violence is framed solely under the rubric of "family violence," the gendered aspects of this problem are obscured and are more likely to be seen in terms of dysfunctional couple or family dynamics. In doing so, clinicians can lose sight of the larger social dynamics that shape gendered behaviors in families, and are thus less able to help women to gain perspective or mobilize necessary resources. A family systems approach can present even greater dangers to battered women. Assuming equal power within and responsibility for relationship dynamics, it inadvertently holds a battered woman responsible for her partner's criminal behavior and keeps her engaged in the countertherapeutic task of trying to change herself in order to get him to change. In addition, counseling sessions often precipitate further threats or violence.

Andersen and colleagues[35] and Walker[36] described the dynamics of battering in terms of ongoing domestic terrorism, akin to hostage situations. In that kind of setting, particularly when her partner continues to engage in violence, controlling behavior, or threats, it is not safe for a woman to be honest or to assert herself. Nor is she likely to be free to make her own choices.[37] Again, newer models of family and couples therapy are being developed that specifically address domestic violence.[38] However, limited data is available on the effectiveness or safety of these treatment modalities, and they have been studied in couples where the level of violence is low.[39]

The emergence of trauma theory over the past three decades has created a significant shift in the conceptualization of mental health symptoms and in our understanding of the role abuse and violence play in the development of psychological distress and mental health conditions. Arising out of the experiences of survivors of civilian and combat trauma, it views symptoms as survival strategies. They are adaptations to potentially life-shattering situations that one makes when real protection is unavailable and normal coping mechanisms are overwhelmed. Trauma models, although immensely helpful in understanding the impact of domestic violence and other types of victimization, also have limitations in the context of ongoing domestic violence. For many women, symptoms are not "post"; rather, they reflect survival strategies needed in the face of ongoing danger. In addition, therapies that focus on helping survivors understand why they unconsciously "chose" an abusive partner, that label them as "codependent" or "enabling," or that hold them responsible for their partner's abusive behavior and for stopping it could be undermining and potentially endangering to someone who is currently entrapped or unsafe.[40]

These models are limited precisely because they are clinical models. They do not provide a framework for recognizing that it is the combination of the abuser's use of violence, threats, and intimidation with the social conditions that support gender inequality and limit options for safety that keeps partners trapped in abusive situations and restricts their possibilities for change.[41] These same gender biases also contribute to the reduced likelihood that the small percentage of men abused by a female partner will receive services and to the homophobia that impedes recognition of domestic violence in LGBTQI (lesbian, gay, bisexual, transgender, queer, questioning, and intersex) relationships.

Inadvertent Retraumatization

Inadvertent retraumatization of patients through disempowering interactions within the health and mental health system is another crucial issue. The pressure in current practice arrangements, particularly in managed care or underresourced public sector environments, to make rapid assessments, diagnoses, and treatment recommendations can push clinicians into taking a more controlling stance in their clinical encounters. For someone whose life is already controlled by another person, the subtly disempowering quality of many clinical interactions can serve to reinforce the idea that adapting to another's controlling behavior is both expected and necessary for survival. Guidelines for implementing trauma-informed services address these concerns.[42]

Changing Theory and Incorporating Context

Clearly, a purely clinical framework limits our ability to respond to abuse. In fact, maintaining such a stance would require that we "diagnose" and find ways to "treat" a pervasive, long-standing form of normative social pathology characterized by a gender socialization process. This process (in its most polarized form) has taught women to focus their identities on meeting men's needs and on maintaining relationships at all costs. It also teaches men that it is both necessary and legitimate to sustain their sense of self at the expense of those with less power, often women and children.[43] This belief is produced within the context of a socioeconomic system that frequently leaves women, particularly those with small children, increasingly fewer options for living independent lives[44] and a criminal justice system that often fails to protect or does so in discriminatory ways.

Although the healthcare system is finally beginning to face the consequences of a problem rooted in centuries of social and legal tradition, it is important for us to address the more difficult task of transforming gender socialization patterns and to recognize that gender equality is an essential component of primary prevention.[45]

We also stretch the boundaries of the healthcare system when we work with the domestic violence advocacy and criminal justice systems. For example, many women are in danger at the time they seek health care, yet the danger itself is not something amenable to medical intervention. By becoming informed of options available in their communities for increasing women's safety, clinicians can help women get the services they need and begin to understand the complexity of their situations. Will a woman risk losing her children in a custody battle? Will she risk losing her means of providing for them? Will she risk deportation if she seeks help? Does she qualify for immigration remedies under the Violence Against Women Act? Will she risk losing someone she loves and who might act lovingly toward her much of the time? Will she risk the possibility of being killed if she leaves? A more comprehensive model provides a framework for understanding responses to not only trauma, but also, more significantly, to ongoing danger, and for mobilizing the social and legal resources that can increase safety, expand options, and ultimately prevent further violence.[46]

STRUCTURAL CONSTRAINTS

Healthcare providers face a number of structural constraints that affect their ability to provide appropriate care to women dealing with ongoing abuse. In the current healthcare climate, cost containment often is achieved at the expense of care, and clinicians' needs are placed in conflict with those of patients for access to diminishing resources.[47] This is a problem particularly for primary care providers, who often are penalized for spending too much time with patients and for making too many referrals. This is even more problematic for patients, however, at a time when reimbursement for social and mental health services continues to shrink.

Micromanagement strategies devised by insurance companies to reduce "unnecessary" mental healthcare utilization (e.g., continuous intrusive demands to justify treatment) can be disruptive and traumatic in themselves. They create an environment in which short-term medication management or potentially retraumatizing directive treatments focused on symptom reduction rather than healing have become the standard of care, making the consistency and safety required for long-term trauma recovery less likely to be reimbursed.

It is unfortunate that, just when an expanding body of research is clearly delineating the impact of trauma on the human psyche and the need for more intensive treatment for many survivors,[48] market forces are decreasing the likelihood that these kinds of services will be available. This becomes increasingly true as managed care further erodes the possibility of choosing one's provider and type of treatment, removing even the consumer-based economic power from individuals seeking care. For low-income women whose only access to services has been through the public mental health system, this lack of choice has been the norm.[49]

Although providing short-term cost reductions, these policies do not address the long-term personal, financial, and, ultimately, social costs of failing to provide appropriate intervention.[50] In this type of setup, cost containment is seen only in terms of direct individual costs to a given healthcare corporation or system, whereas the exponential, but indirect, personal and social costs that could be prevented by early intervention are not considered part of the relevant financial equation.

A diagnosis-driven reimbursement system poses yet another set of problems for battered women. In order for a woman to use mental health services, she must be given a diagnosis. But for battered women, the very diagnosis itself can create new dangers.[51] Batterers often use their victims' psychiatric diagnoses to "prove" that they are right, that the problems are her fault, that she is crazy, or that she is an unfit mother. In seeking treatment, a battered woman potentially risks losing her children in custody battles and losing her credibility in court. However, appropriate documentation of the mental health impact of domestic violence can help a survivor to build her legal case. For some women, "psychiatric" symptoms disappear once they are out of danger, but many women continue to be threatened and stalked long after they have left the relationship.[52] For others, symptoms of PTSD may not begin until they are relatively safe.[53]

In the past, women were refused health insurance for having the preexisting condition of being battered and were refused disability or life insurance because they were considered at higher risk for injury and death.[54] In addition, if a woman was insured on her husband's policy and the bills were sent to him, she was likely to be placed in further jeopardy when he discovered she was seeking outside help. There have been strides in both of these areas. Since 1994, 41 states have enacted legislation prohibiting discrimination against victims of domestic violence, and HIPAA (Health Information Portability and Accountability Act) regulations allow the sending of bills to a safe address at a patient's request.[55]

In some states, laws that require mandatory reporting of domestic violence can again place the clinician's legal obligations in conflict with the wishes and the safety of his or her patients. Not only do these policies potentially destroy the ability of clinicians to provide a safe place for women to discuss their most pressing concerns, but also they violate women's rights to choose what they feel will be safest and most helpful to themselves and their children. Under these conditions, both clinicians and patients may avoid raising concerns about abuse, thus losing important opportunities for intervention.[56]

Listening to patients, learning about the repercussions of our interventions, and working to prevent revictimization within the system's survivors are important components of our roles as healthcare professionals practicing preventive medicine. Without a clear institutional commitment to address these issues, however, the pressures to continue practice as usual may be greater than the ability to change.

IMPLICATIONS FOR TRAINING AND PRACTICE

Experience has led many clinician-educators to realize that new training strategies must be developed in order to change attitudes and behavior on the scale that is required to address domestic violence.[57] Standard didactic formats, for example, do not provide sufficient opportunity to address the attitudes and feelings that might interfere with a clinician's ability to provide appropriate care, nor do they offer room to acquire the interviewing skills necessary for an optimal response. Training environments that offer the emotional safety to explore personal and cultural responses to abuse and the opportunities to discuss individual, professional, and institutional obstacles can provide a vehicle for generating change within the healthcare community. Although one-time trainings might raise awareness, ongoing feedback and support are necessary to sustain provider response.[58]

Providing quality health care involves integrating routine inquiry about domestic violence into ongoing clinical practice. This means asking all patients about abuse and violence in their lives. Whether or not a person chooses to use services or leave her or his partner, our intervention is very important. People often return to violent partners many times before they feel safe enough to leave, feel that they can survive on their own, or can accept that the person they love will not change. When we fail to ask about abuse, we inadvertently isolate people who are living in danger.[59] Just by inquiring and expressing concern, we begin to build bridges, decrease isolation, and create hope.

For a person who lives in an atmosphere of ongoing threats, intimidation, and violence, being treated with respect, being taken seriously, and feeling free to make her or his own choices lets that individual know that supportive experiences are possible. By asking women to describe the pattern of their abuse and level of danger and to discuss their options for safety, we provide a place for women to reflect on their situations and consider their choices. By providing access to resources and by facilitating a woman's own decision-making process rather than attempting to direct her to change, we help her shift the balance of power in her life. When we work collaboratively with other members of our communities, we not only help individual survivors rebuild their lives, but also help to change the conditions that allow domestic violence to exist.

For clinicians to develop and sustain appropriate responses to domestic violence, however, they must have the support of the institutions in which they practice. Thus, addressing this issue requires some fundamental changes in the nature of most medical training and in the culture of medical institutions. Creating practice environments and policies that model nonabusive ways of interacting, that support clinicians' efforts to address complex issues with skill and compassion, and that reimburse the more labor-intensive tasks of listening and advocating for change are important components of institutionalizing effective responses to domestic violence.[60] Refocusing our priorities is particularly important in a healthcare climate in which administrators, insurers, and those who influence healthcare policy must begin to recognize that the long-term consequences of nonintervention far exceed the costs of investing in appropriate intervention and prevention.[61]

In addition, providers acting alone, no matter how motivated, cannot meet all the needs of battered women and their children. An optimal response requires the efforts of all members of the community. Developing interdisciplinary teams within the healthcare setting and creating collaborative partnerships among the domestic violence advocacy community, the mental health and healthcare systems, the child protective system, and the legal system serves a number of functions. It not only provides referral networks for patients but also creates support networks for providers. More important, it is only by working together that we can begin to develop the kinds of intervention strategies that will be appropriate for and respectful to all victims of domestic violence, while laying the groundwork to develop effective prevention strategies as well.

CONCLUSION

When we ask what survivors of domestic violence need from individual providers, we must also ask what providers need from their training institutions and practice environments in order to respond to those needs. When we do not address the denial of intolerable feelings at a personal level, we are in danger of recreating them not only in individual relationships but also on social and political levels. Further, when socially sanctioned abuses of power are not acknowledged, they often are internalized and reproduced through individual interactions. If we truly want to play a role in preventing domestic violence, rather than just treating its consequences, it is important to work together to address the social conditions that create and support this kind of violence in the first place.

SUMMARY

Domestic violence is widely recognized as a social problem that affects both the family and the community. Clinicians deal with the effects of this issue on an almost daily basis, but often find it beyond their medical expertise. This chapter presented a discussion of why physicians may not be prepared to address the needs of those affected by domestic violence and the need for changes in physician training and practice. In addition, it suggested strategies for institutions' and communities' engagement in better addressing the challenges of this significant social issue.

QUESTIONS FOR DISCUSSION

1. How does the training environment influence future physicians' position on responding to survivors of domestic violence? How does it influence how they address domestic violence?
2. What is the connection between social justice and the treatment of the traumatic effects of domestic violence?
3. What is the moral duty of physicians to the victims of domestic violence? How will the Patient Protection and Affordable Care Act (PPACA) affect this duty?
4. Does a utilitarian approach help or hinder treatment for victims of domestic violence?
5. How do the principles of beneficence and nonmaleficence relate to the issue of dealing with domestic violence?

FOOD FOR THOUGHT

You are a physician in a busy family practice. Even though you are busy, you want to comply with guidelines for addressing domestic violence issues in your practice. Your next patient is Jesse, a 14-year-old girl whose complaint is severe headaches. While you are doing your physical examination, you notice bruising on Jesse's arms and legs. She also has a bruise that resembles a handprint on her face.

1. What would you do?
2. What ethical principles support your action?
3. If Jesse does not have a logical explanation for her bruises, but denies abuse, what is your next step?

NOTES

1. N. A. Kapur and D. M. Windish, "Optimal Methods to Screen Men and Women for Intimate Partner Violence: Results from an Internal Medicine Residency Continuity Clinic," *Journal of Interpersonal Violence* 26, no. 2 (2011): 2335–2352.

2. M. A. Black, K. C. Basile, M. J. Breiding, S. G. Smith, et al., *National Intimate Partner and Sexual Violence Survey 2010: Executive Summary* (Atlanta, GA: National Center for Injury Prevention and Control, Centers for Disease Control, 2011). Retrieved from http://www.cdc.gov/ViolencePrevention/pdf/NISVS_Executive_Summary-a.pdf. Accessed June 25, 2012; E. Stark and A. Flitcraft, "Violence Among Intimates: An Epidemiologic Review," in *Handbook of Family Violence*, eds. V. N. Van Hasselt et al. (New York: Plenum, 1988), 293–317; D. Drossman, J. Leserman, G. Nachman, et al., "Sexual and Physical Abuse in Women with Functional or Organic Gastrointestinal Disorders," *Annals of Internal Medicine* 113 (1990): 828–833; J. Domino and J. Haber, "Prior Physical and Sexual Abuse in Women with Chronic Headache: Clinical Correlates," *Headache* 27 (1987): 310–314; M. Koss and I. Heise, "Somatic Consequences of Violence Against Women," *Archives of Family Medicine* 1 (1992): 53–59; M. P. Koss, P. G. Koss, and W. J. Woodruff, "Deleterious Effects of Criminal Victimization on Women's Health and Medical Utilization," *Archives of Internal Medicine* 151 (1991): 342–347; J. Fildes, L. Reed, N. Jones, et al., "Trauma: The Leading Cause of Maternal Death," *Journal of Trauma* 32 (1992): 43–45; L. McKibben, E. De Vos, and E. H. Newberger, "Victimization of Mothers of Abused Children: A Controlled Study," *Pediatrics* 84 (1989): 531–535; E. Stark and A. Flitcraft, "Women and Children at Risk: A Feminist Perspective on Child Abuse," *International Journal of Health Services* 18 (1988): 97–118; E. Stark and A. Flitcraft, "Killing the Beast Within: Woman Battering and Female Suicidality," *International Journal of Health Services* 25 (1995): 43–64; A. Jacobsen and B. Richardson, "Assault Experiences of 100 Psychiatric Inpatients: Evidence of the Need for Routine Inquiry," *American Journal of Psychiatry* 144 (1987): 908–913; L. S. Brown, "The Contribution of Victimization as a Risk Factor for the Development of Depressive Symptomatology in Women" (paper presented at the 97th Annual Convention of the American Psychological Association, New Orleans, Louisiana, August 1989); J. A. Hamilton and M. Jensvold, "Personality, Psychopathology and Depression in Women," in *Personality and Psychopathology: Feminist Reappraisals*, eds. L. S. Brown and M. Ballou (New York: Guilford Press, 1992); J. Herman, *The Aftermath of Violence: From Domestic Abuse to Political Theory* (New York: Basic Books, 1992); B. M. Houskamp and D. Foy, "The Assessment of Posttraumatic Stress Disorder in Battered Women," *Journal of Interpersonal Violence* 6 (1991): 367–375; A. Kemp, E. I. Rawlings, and B. L. Green, "Post-traumatic Stress Disorder (PTSD) in Battered Women: A Shelter Sample," *Journal of Traumatic Stress* 4 (1991): 137–148; L. E. Walker, "Post-traumatic Stress Disorder in Women: Diagnosis and Treatment of Battered Woman Syndrome," *Psychotherapy* 28 (1991): 21–29; J. C. Campbell, "Battered Woman Syndrome: A Critical Review," *Violence Update*, December 1990, 1, 4, 10–11; J. C. Campbell, "Post-traumatic Stress in Battered Women: Does the Diagnosis Fit?" *Issues in Mental Health Nursing* 14 (1993): 173–186; C. R. Figley, "Posttraumatic Stress Disorder, Part 2: Relationships with Various Traumatic Events," *Violence Update*, May 1992; C. Warshaw and S. Poirier, "Case and Commentary: Hidden Stories of Women," *Second Opinion* 17 (1991): 48–61.

3. Institute of Medicine, *Clinical Services for Women: Closing the Gaps* (Washington, DC: National Academies Press, 2011). Retrieved from http://www.iom.edu/Reports/2011/Clinical-Preventive-Services-for-Women-Closing-the-Gaps.aspx. Accessed June 29, 2012; Health Resources and Services Administration, "Women's Preventive Services: Required Health Plan Coverage Guidelines," http://www.hrsa.gov/womensguidelines/. Accessed June 29, 2012; H. D. Nelson, C. Bougatsos, and I. Blazina, "Screening Women for Intimate Partner Violence: A Systematic Review to Update the U.S. Preventive Screening Task Force Recommendation," *Annals of Internal Medicine* 156, no 11 (2012): 796–808; American College of Obstetricians and Gynecologists, Committee on Health Care for Underserved Women, "Intimate Partner Violence," *Obstetrics and Gynecology* 119 (2012): 412–417. Retrieved from http://www.acog.org/Resources_And_Publications/Committee_Opinions/Committee_on_Health_Care_for_Underserved_Women/Intimate_Partner_Violence. Accessed June 25, 2012; A. Flitcraft et al., *Diagnostic and Treatment Guidelines on Domestic Violence* (Chicago: American Medical Association, 1992); C. Warshaw et al., *Improving the Health Care Response to Domestic*

Violence: A Resource Manual for Health Care Providers (San Francisco: Family Violence Prevention Fund and Pennsylvania Coalition Against Domestic Violence, 1995); C. J. Scott and N. Matricciani, "Joint Commission on Accreditation of Health Care Organizations Standards to Improve Care for Victims of Abuse," *Maryland Medical Journal* 43 (1994): 891–898; W. K. Taylor and J. C. Campbell, "Treatment Protocols for Battered Women," *Response* (1992): 1–21; A. Flitcraft, "Physicians and Domestic Abuse: Challenges for Prevention," *Health Affairs* 12 (1993): 156–161.

4. L. K. Hamberger, "Preparing the Next Generation of Physicians: Medical School and Residency-Based Intimate Partner Violence Curriculum and Evaluation," *Trauma, Violence, and Abuse* 8 (2007): 214–225; E. J. Alpert, "Family Violence Curricula in U.S. Medical Schools," *American Journal of Preventive Medicine* 14 (1998): 273–282; S. Rovi and C. P. Mouton, "Domestic Violence Education in Family Practice Residencies," *Family Medicine* 31 (1999): 398–403; R. A. Chez and D. L. Horan, "Response of Obstetrics and Gynecology Program Directors to a Domestic Violence Lecture Model," *American Journal of Obstetrics and Gynecology* 180 (1999): 496–498; *Curricular Principles for Addressing Family Violence: Conference Report* (Oklahoma City, OK: Robert Wood Johnson Foundation, 1995); S. Hadley, "Working with Battered Women in the Emergency Department: A Model Program," *Journal of Emergency Nursing* 18 (1992): 18–23; C. Warshaw et al., "An Advocacy-Based Medical School Elective on Domestic Violence" (class offered at the National Conference on Cultural Competence and Women's Health, Curricular in Medical Education, Washington, DC, October 1995).

5. L. R. Chambliss, R. C. Bay, and R. F. Jones III, "Domestic Violence: An Educational Imperative?" *American Journal of Obstetrics and Gynecology* 172 (1995): 1035–1038; L. S. Friedman, J. H. Samet, M. S. Roberts, et al., "Inquiry About Victimization Experiences: A Survey of Patient Preferences and Physician Practices," *Archives of Internal Medicine* 152 (1992): 1186–1190; E. Gondolf, *Psychiatric Responses to Family Violence: Identifying and Confronting Neglected Danger* (Lexington, MA: Lexington Books, 1990).

6. N. K. Sugg and T. Inui, "Primary Care Physician's Response to Domestic Violence: Opening Pandora's Box," *Journal of the American Medical Association* 267 (1991): 3157–3160; D. H. Gremillion and G. Evins, "Why Don't Doctors Identify and Refer Victims of Domestic Violence?" *North Carolina Medical Journal* 55 (1994): 428–432; C. Warshaw, "Limitations of the Medical Model in the Care of Battered Women," *Gender and Society* 3 (1989): 506–517; C. Warshaw, "Domestic Violence: Challenges to Medical Practice," *Journal of Women's Health* 2 (1993): 73–80.

7. Warshaw, "Domestic Violence."

8. B. Gerbert, J. Moe, N. Caspers, et al., "Simplifying Physicians' Response to Domestic Violence," *Western Journal of Medicine* 172 no. 5 (2000): 329–331; H. A. Holtz, et al., "Education about Domestic Violence in U.S. and Canadian Medical Schools: 1987–1988," *Morbidity and Mortality Weekly Report* 38 (1989): 17–19; E. J. Alpert, "Family Violence Curricula in U.S. Medical Schools," *America Journal of Preventive Medicine* 14 (1998): 273–282.

9. S. K. Burge, "Violence Against Women as a Health Care Issue," *Family Medicine* 21 (1989): 368–373; A. Kramer, "Attitudes of Emergency Nurses and Physicians About Women and Wife Beating: Implications for Emergency Care," *Journal of Emergency Nursing* 19 (1993): 549; D. R. Langford, "Consortia: A Strategy for Improving the Provision of Health Care to Domestic Violence Survivors," *Response to the Victimization of Women and Children* 13 (1990): 7–18; N. S. Jecker, "Privacy Beliefs and the Violent Family: Extending the Ethical Argument for Physician Intervention," *Journal of the American Medical Association* 269 (1993): 776–780; D. Kurz and E. Stark, "Not-so-Benign Neglect," in *Feminist Perspectives on Wife Abuse*, eds. K. Yllo and M. Bograd (Newbury Park, CA: Sage, 1988), 249–266.

10. M. P. Koss et al., *No Safe Haven: Male Violence Against Women at Home, at Work and in the Community* (Washington, DC: American Psychological Association, 1994).

11. K. Johnson, *Treating Ourselves: The Complete Guide to Emotional Well-Being for Women* (New York: Atlantic Monthly Press, 1990).

12. L. S. Brown, "A Feminist Critique of Personality Disorders," in *Personality and Psychopathology: Feminist Reappraisals*, eds. L. S. Brown and M. Ballou (New York: Guilford Press, 1992).

13. P. Rieker and E. Carmen, "The Victim-to-Patient Process: The Disconfirmation and Transformation of Abuse," *American Journal of Orthopsychiatry* 56 (1986): 360–370.

14. A. Miller, *Prisoners of Childhood: The Drama of the Gifted Child and the Search for the True Self* (New York: Basic Books, 1981); A. Miller, *Thou Shalt Not Be Aware: Society's Betrayal of the Child* (New York: Farrar, Straus & Giroux, 1984).

15. Rieker and Carmen, "The Victim-to-Patient Process"; Miller, *Prisoners of Childhood*; Miller, *Thou Shalt Not Be Aware.*

16. E. Arledge and R. Wolfson, "Care of the Clinician," in *Using Trauma Theory to Design Service Systems*, eds. M. Harris and R. Fallot (San Francisco: Jossey-Bass, 2001), 91–98; K. Baird and A. Kracen, "Vicarious Traumatization and Secondary Traumatic Stress: A Research Synthesis," *Counseling Psychology Quarterly* 19 (2006): 181–188; I. Way, K. M. vanDeusen, G. Martin, et al., "Vicarious Trauma: A Comparison of Clinicians Who Treat Survivors of Sexual Abuse and Sexual Offenders," *Journal of Interpersonal Violence* 19 (2004): 49–71; L. H. Madsen, L. V. Blitz, D. McCorkle, and P. G. Panzer, "Sanctuary in a Domestic Violence Shelter: A Team Approach to Healing," *Psychiatric Quarterly* 72 (2003): 155–171; B. Bride, "Prevalence of Secondary Traumatic Stress Among Social Workers," *Social Work* 52 (2007): 63–70; C. R. Figley, "Compassion Fatigue: Toward a New Understanding of the Costs of Caring," in *Secondary Traumatic Stress: Self-care Issues for Clinicians, Researchers, and Educators*, ed. B. H. Stamm (Lutherville, MD: Sidran Press), 3–28; S. R. Jenkins and S. Baird, "Secondary Traumatic Stress and Vicarious Trauma: A Validational Study," *Journal of Traumatic Stress* 15 (2002): 423–433; G. Iliffe, "Exploring the Counselor's Experience of Working with Perpetrators and Survivors of Domestic Violence," *Journal of Interpersonal Violence* 15 (2000): 393–413; J. L. Herman, *Trauma and Recovery*, rev. ed. (New York: BasicBooks, 1997); M. A. Dutton, *Empowering and Healing the Battered Woman: A Model for Assessment and Intervention* (New York: Springer, 1992); M. P. Koss, "The Women's Mental Health Research Agenda: Violence Against Women," *American Psychologist* 45 (1990): 374–380; L. Goldman et al., *American Medical Association Diagnostic and Treatment Guidelines on Mental Health Effects of Family Violence* (Chicago: American Medical Association, 1995).

17. Sugg and Inui, "Primary Care Physician's Response to Domestic Violence."

18. Warshaw, "Domestic Violence"; Koss et al., *No Safe Haven*; Johnson, *Treating Ourselves*; Brown, "A Feminist Critique of Personality Disorders."

19. Warshaw, "Domestic Violence."

20. P. D. Connor, S. S. Nouer, S. N. Mackey, M. S. Banet, and N. G. Tipton, "Intimate Partner Violence Education for Medical Students: Toward a Comprehensive Curriculum Revision," *Southern Medical Journal* 105, no. 4 (2012): 211–215; P. Williamson, B. D. Beitman, and W. Katon, "Beliefs That Foster Physician Avoidance of Psychosocial Aspects of Health Care," *Journal of Family Practice* 13 (1981): 999–1003; R. Fox, "Training in Caring Competence: The Perennial Problem in North American Medical Education," in *Education: Competent and Humane Physicians*, eds. H. C. Hendrie and C. Lloyd (Bloomington, IN: Indiana University Press, 1990), 199–216.

21. Warshaw, "Domestic Violence."

22. J. A. Richman, J. A. Flaherty, K. M. Rospenda, and M. L. Christensen, "Mental Health Consequences and Correlates of Reported Medical Student Abuse," *Journal of the American Medical Association* 167 (1992): 692–694.

23. D. Baldwin Jr., S. R. Daugherty, and E. J. Eckenfels, "Student Perceptions of Mistreatment and Harassment During Medical School: A Survey of Ten United States Schools," *Western Journal of Medicine* 155 (1991): 140–145.

24. E. Frank, L. Elon, L. E. Saltzman, D. Houry, P. McMahon, and J. Doyle, "Clinical and Personal Intimate Partner Violence Training Experiences of U.S. Medical Students," *Journal of Women's Health* 15 (2006): 1071–1079; P. Babaria, S. Abedin, D. Berg, and M. Nunez-Smith, "'I'm Too Used to It': A Longitudinal Qualitative Study of Third Year Female Medical Students' Experiences of Gendered Encounters in Medical School," *Social Science and Medicine* 7, no. 7 (2012): 1013–1020; B. J. Tepper, "Consequences of Abusive Supervision," *Academic Management Journal* 43 (2000): 178–190; D. M. Elnicki, R. H. Curry, M. Fagan, et al., "Medical Students' Perspectives on and Responses to Abuse During the Internal Medicine Clerkship," *Teaching and Learning Medicine* 14 (2002): 92–97; T. J. Wilkinson, D. J. Gill, J. Fitzjohn, et al., "The Impact on Students of Adverse Experiences During Medical School," *Medical Teaching* 28 (2006): 129–135; L. N. Dyrbye, M. R. Thomas, and T. D. Shanafelt, "Systematic Review of Depression, Anxiety, and Other

Indicators of Psychological Distress Among U.S. and Canadian Medical Students," *Academic Medicine* 81 (2006): 354–373; L. N. Dyrbye, M. R. Thomas, and T. D. Shanafelt, "Medical Student Distress: Causes, Consequences, and Proposed Solutions," *Mayo Clinic Proceedings* 80 (2005): 1613–1622; M. Seabrook, "Intimidation in Medical Education: Students' and Teachers' Perspectives," *Studies in Higher Education* 29 (2004): 59–74; D. G. Kassebaum and E. R. Cutler, "On the Culture of Student Abuse in Medical School," *Academic Medicine* 73 (1998): 1149–1158; T. M. Wolf, H. M. Randall, K. von Almen, and L. L. Tynes, "Perceived Mistreatment and Attitude Change by Graduating Medical Students: A Retrospective Study," *Medical Education* 25 (1991): 182–189.

25. Warshaw, "Domestic Violence"; Richman et al., "Mental Health Consequences and Correlates of Reported Medical Student Abuse."

26. D. Wear, J. Aultman, and N. Borges, "Retheorizing Sexual Harassment in Medical Education: Women Students' Perceptions at Five U.S. Medical Schools," *Teaching and Learning Medicine* 19 (2007): 20–29; F. M. Witte, T. D. Stratton, and L. M. Nora, "Stories from the Field: Students' Descriptions of Gender Discrimination and Sexual Harassment During Medical School," *Academic Medicine* 81 (2006): 648–654; T. D. Stratton, M. A. McLaughlin, F. M. Witte, and L. M. Nora, "Does Students' Exposure to Gender Discrimination and Sexual Harassment in Medical School Affect Specialty Choice and Residency Program Selection?" *Academic Medicine* 80 (2005): 400–408; S. A. Shinsako, J. A. Richman, and K. M. Rospenda, "Training-Related Harassment and Drinking Outcomes in Medical Residents Versus Graduate Students," *Substance Use and Misuse* 36 (2001): 2043–2063; J. Bickel, "Gender Equity in Undergraduate Medical Education: A Status Report," *Journal of Women's Health* Gen-B 10 (2001): 261–270; Richman et al., "Mental Health Consequences and Correlates of Reported Medical Student Abuse"; Baldwin et al., "Student Perceptions of Mistreatment and Harassment During Medical School"; Wolf et al., "Perceived Mistreatment and Attitude Change by Graduating Medical Students"; M. Schiffman and E. Frank, "Harassment of Women Physicians," *Journal of the American Medical Women's Association* 50 (1995): 207–211; D. A. Charney and R. C. Russell, "An Overview of Sexual Harassment," *American Journal of Psychiatry* 151 (1994): 10–17; M. Komaromy, A. B. Bindman, R. J. Haber, and M. A. Sande, "Sexual Harassment in Medical Training," *New England Journal of Medicine* 328 (1993): 322–336.

27. Warshaw, "Domestic Violence"; Kurz and Stark, "Not-so-Benign Neglect"; Koss et al., *No Safe Haven*; Johnson, *Treating Ourselves*; Brown, "A Feminist Critique of Personality Disorders"; Fox, "Training in Caring Competence"; C. S. Widom, "Does Violence Beget Violence? A Critical Examination of the Literature," *Psychology Bulletin* 106 (1989): 437–447.

28. K. Johnson and E. Hoffman, "Women's Health and Curriculum Transformation: The Role of Medical Specialization," in *Reframing Women's Health: Multidisciplinary Research and Practice,* ed. A. Dan (Thousand Oaks, CA: Sage, 1994), 27–39.

29. A. C. Gielen, R. M. Ghandour, J. G. Burke, et al., "HIV/AIDS and Intimate Partner Violence," *Trauma, Violence, and Abuse* 8 (2007): 178–198; S. Maman, J. Campbell, M. D Sweat, and A. C. Gielen, "The Intersections of HIV and Violence: Directions for Future Research and Interventions," *Social Science and Medicine* 50 (2000): 459–478; A. Raj, C. Santana, A. La Marche, et al., "Perpetration of Intimate Partner Violence Associated with Sexual Risk Behaviors Among Young Adult Men," *American Journal of Public Health* 96 (2006): 1873–1878; B. Lichtenstein, "Domestic Violence, Sexual Ownership, and HIV Risk in Women in the American Deep South," *Social Science and Medicine* 60 (2005): 701–714; A. J. Heintz and R. Melendez, "Intimate Partner Violence and HIV/STD Risk Among Lesbian, Gay, Bisexual, and Transgender Individuals," *Journal of Interpersonal Violence* 21 (2006): 193–208; G. Wyatt et al., "Does History of Trauma Contribute to HIV Risk for Women of Color? Implications for Prevention and Policy," *American Journal of Public Health* 92 (2002): 660–665; A. Raj, J. G. Silverman, and H. Amaro, "Abused Women Report Greater Male Partner Risk and Gender-Based Risk for HIV: Findings from a Community-Based Study with Hispanic Women," *AIDS Care* 16 (2004): 519–529; N. El-Bassel, L. Gilbert, E. Wu, et al., "HIV and Intimate Partner Violence Among Methadone-Maintained Women in New York City," *Social Science and Medicine* 61 (2005): 171–183; J. M. Simoni and M. T. Ng, "Trauma, Coping, and Depression Among Women with HIV/AIDS in New York City," *AIDS Care* 12 (2000): 567–580; S. C. Kalicharan, E. A. Williams, C. Cherry, et al., "Sexual Coercion, Domestic Violence, and Negotiating Condom Use Among Low-Income African American Women," *Journal of Women's Health* 7 (1998): 371–379; M. Cohen et al., "Prevalence of Domestic Violence in Women with

HIV" (paper presented at the Midwest Society of General Internal Medicine, Chicago, October 1995); K. Rothenberg, S. J. Paskey, M. M. Reuland, et al., "Domestic Violence and Partner Notification: Implications for Treatment and Counseling of Women with HIV," *Journal of the American Medical Women's Association* 50 (1995): 87–93.

30. Rothenberg et al., "Domestic Violence and Partner Notification."

31. Stark and Flitcraft, "Violence Among Intimates."

32. New York State Department of Health, "Guidelines for Integrating Domestic Violence Screening into HIV Counseling, Testing, Referral, and Partner Notification." Retrieved from http//www/health.ny.gov/nydoh/rfa/hiv/guide.htm. Accessed June 29, 2012; S. J. Klein, "Screening for Risk of Domestic Violence Within HIV Partner Notification: Evolving Practice and Emerging Issues," *Journal of Public Health Management* 7 (2001): 46–50; R. Wolfe, J. Lobozzo, V. Frye, and V. Sharp, "Screening for Substance Use, Sexual Practices, Mental Illness, and Domestic Violence in HIV Primary Care," *Journal of Acquired Immune Deficiency Syndromes* 33 (2003): 548–550; Maman et al., "Intersections of HIV and Violence"; J. E. Maher et al., "Partner Violence, Partner Notification, and Women's Decisions to Have an HIV Test," *Journal of Acquired Immune Deficiency Syndromes* 25 (2000): 276–282; S. J. Klein, M. L. SanAntonio-Gaddy, E. L. Berberian, and G. S. Birkhead, "Implementation of Domestic Violence Screening as a Component of HIV Partner Notification in New York State" (paper presented at the National HIV Prevention Conference, Atlanta, Georgia, 1999); Cohen et al., "Prevalence of Domestic Violence in Women with HIV"; Rothenberg et al., "Domestic Violence and Partner Notification"; V. Breitbert, C. Layton, W. Chavkin, et al., "Model Programs Addressing Perinatal Drug Exposure and HIV Infection: Integrating Women's and Children's Needs," *Bulletin of the New York Academy of Medicine* 71 (1994): 236–251.

33. E. Miller, M. R. Decker, H. L. McCauley, et al., "A Family Planning Clinic Partner Violence Intervention to Reduce Risk Associated with Reproductive Coercion," *Contraception* 83 (2011): 274–280.

34. Miller, *Thou Shalt Not Be Aware*; G. Atwood and R. Stolorow, *Structures of Subjectivity: Explorations in Psychoanalytic Phenomenology* (Hillsdale, NJ: The Analytic Press, 1984); L. Brown, *Subversive Dialogues: Theory in Feminist Therapy* (New York: Basic Books, 1994).

35. S. Andersen et al., "Psychological Maltreatment of Spouses," in *Case Studies in Family Violence*, eds. R. Ammerman and M. Hersen (New York: Plenum, 1991): 293–328.

36. L. Walker, "The Battered Woman Syndrome," in *Family Abuse and Its Consequences*, eds. G. T. Hotaling et al. (Beverly Hills, CA: Sage, 1988), 139–148.

37. Brown, "A Feminist Critique of Personality Disorders"; M. Bograd, "Family Systems Approaches to Wife Battering: A Feminist Critique," *American Journal of Orthopsychiatry* 54 (1984): 558–568.

38. M. Hansen, "Feminism and Family Therapy: A Review of Feminist Critiques of Approaches to Family Violence," in *Battering and Family Therapy: A Feminist Perspective*, eds. M. Hansen and M. Harway (Thousand Oaks, CA: Sage, 1993); M. Harway and M. Hansen, "Treatment of Spouse Abuse," in *Spouse Abuse: Assessing and Treating Battered Women, Batterers, and Their Children*, eds. M. Harway and M. Hansen (Sarasota, FL: Professional Resource Press, 1994), 57–88; V. Goldner, "Morality and Multiplicity: Perspectives on the Treatment of Violence in Intimate Life," *Journal of Marital and Family Therapy* 25, no 3 (1999): 325–336.

39. K. O'Leary, R. Heyman, and P. Neidig, "Treatment of Wife Abuse: A Comparison of Gender-Specific and Conjoint Approaches," *Behavior Therapy* 30 (1999): 475–505.

40. Focusing on how a client should change herself may reinforce a perpetrator's controlling tactics (i.e., "you are the one with the problem") and further undermine her ability to gain perspective on her situation or to take steps that would increase the safety of herself and her children. This may be of particular concern for clinicians who conduct couples or family therapy. See C. Warshaw, "Women and Violence," in *Psychological Aspects of Women's Health Care: The Interface Between Psychiatry and Obstetrics and Gynecology*, eds. D. Stewart and N. Stotland (Washington, DC: American Psychiatric Association Press, 2001).

41. A. Jones and S. Schechter, *When Love Goes Wrong: What to Do When You Can't Do Anything Right* (New York: Harper, 1993); A. Ganley, "Understanding Domestic Violence," in *Improving the Health Care Response to Domestic Violence: A Resource Manual for Health Care Providers*, eds. C. Warshaw et al. (San Francisco: Family Violence Prevention Fund and Pennsylvania Coalition Against Domestic Violence, 1995), 15–45.

42. M. Harris and R. Fallot, "Envisioning a Trauma-Informed Service System: A Vital Paradigm Shift," *New Directions for Mental Health Services* 89 (2001): 3–22.

43. Miller, *Prisoners of Childhood*.

44. A. Brown, "Violence, Poverty, and Minority Races in the Lives of Women and Children: Implications for Violence Prevention" (paper presented at the Centers for Disease Control Violence Prevention Conference, Des Moines, Iowa, October 1995).

45. Other forms of inequality also contribute to abusive power dynamics, and eradicating those are important aspects of primary prevention.

46. P. F. Cronholm, C. T. Fogerty, B. Ambuel, and S. Leonard Harrison, "Intimate Partner Violence," *American Family Physician* 83, no. 10 (2011): 1165–1172; D. S. Morse, R. Lafleur, C. T. Fogarty, and C. Cerculli, "They Told Me to Leave: How Health Care Providers Address Intimate Partner Violence," *Journal of the American Board of Family Medicine* 25, no. 3 (2012): 333–342; Jones and Schechter, *When Loves Goes Wrong*; A. Ganley, "Understanding Domestic Violence," in C. Warshaw and A. Ganley, *Improving the Health Care Response to Domestic Violence: A Resource Manual for Health Care Providers* (San Francisco: The Family Violence Prevention Fund, 1998); "VAWA Laws for Abuse Victims," WomensLaw.org, http://www.womenslaw.org/immigrantsVAWA.htm. Accessed June 21, 2012.

47. S. Woodhandler and D. Himmelstein, "Extreme Risk—The New Corporate Proposition for Physicians," *New England Journal of Medicine* 33 (1995): 1706–1708; S. Glied and S. Kofman, *Women and Mental Health Reform* (New York: Commission on Women's Health, Commonwealth Fund, 1995).

48. L. Mellman and R. Bell, "Consequences of Violence Against Women," in *Violence Against Women in the United States: A Comprehensive Background Paper* (New York: The Commonwealth Fund Commission on Women's Health, 1995), 33–40; L. Innes and L. Mellman, "Treatment for Victims of Violence," in *Violence Against Women in the United States*, 41–54.

49. E. Carmen, "Inner-City Community Mental Health: The Interplay of Abuse and Race in Chronically Mentally Ill Women," in *Mental Health, Racism, and Sexism*, eds. C. Willie, B. Kramer and B. Brown (Pittsburgh: University of Pittsburgh, 1995).

50. T. Miller, M. A. Cohen, and B. Wiersema, *Crime in the United States: Victim Costs and Consequences* (Washington, DC.: National Institute of Justice, 1995).

51. C. Warshaw, "Women and Violence," in *Psychosocial Aspects of Women's Health Care: The Interface Between Psychiatry and Obstetrics and Gynecology*, 2nd ed., eds. N. L. Stotland and D. E. Steward (Washington, DC: American Psychiatric Press, 2001), 477–548; D. Markham, "2003 Mental Illness and Domestic Violence: Implications for Family Law Litigations," *Journal of Poverty Law and Policy* (May–June, 2003): 23–35.

52. Walker, "The Battered Woman Syndrome"; Jones and Schechter, *When Love Goes Wrong*; Ganley, "Understanding Domestic Violence."

53. Warshaw, "Domestic Violence"; Burge, "Violence Against Women as a Health Care Issue."

54. Women's Law Project and Pennsylvania Coalition Against Domestic Violence, *Insurance Discrimination Against Victims of Domestic Violence* (Harrisburg, PA: Coalition Against Domestic Violence, 1995); L. Kaiser, *Survey of Accident and Health and Life Insurance Relating to Insurance Coverage for Victims of Domestic Violence* (Harrisburg, PA: Pennsylvania Insurance Department, 1995).

55. See also the Women's Law Project website, http://www.womenslawproject.org/New-Pages/wkImpact_litigation.html. In 1994, in partnership with the Pennsylvania Coalition Against Domestic Violence, the Law Project began its ongoing effort to stop insurers from discriminating against victims of domestic violence. The impetus for this work was the denial of health, life, and mortgage disability insurance to a Pennsylvania woman because of medical records revealing an incident of domestic violence. The advocacy began with administrative and legislative efforts to stop such discrimination in Pennsylvania and expanded to assuming a leading role in efforts nationwide to stop discrimination against victims of domestic violence. At present, 41 states have legislation prohibiting insurance discrimination against victims of abuse, and efforts continue to ensure comprehensive legislation at the state and federal level.

56. A. Hymes, D. Schillinger, and B. Lo, "Laws Mandating Reporting of Domestic Violence: Do They Promote Patient Well-Being?" *Journal of the American Medical Association* 272 (1995): 1781–1787. For more information, see the American Association of Orthopaedic Surgeon's

website, http://www.aaos.org/about/abuse/ststatut.asp. See also the National Center for Domestic and Sexual Violence's website, http://www.ncdsv.org/.

57. Warshaw et al., *Improving the Health Care Response to Domestic Violence*; Hadley, "Working with Battered Women in the Emergency Department"; S. V. McLeer, R. A. Anwar, S. Herman, and K. Maquiling, "Education Is Not Enough: A Systems Failure in Protecting Battered Women," *Annals of Emergency Medicine* 18 (1989): 651–653.

58. N. E. Allen, A. Lehrner, E. Mattison, et al., "Promoting Systems Change in the Health Care Response to Domestic Violence," *Journal of Community Psychology* 35 (2007): 103–120; D. Minsky-Kelly, L. K. Hamberger, D. A. Paper, and M. Wolff, "We've Had Training, Now What? Qualitative Analysis of Barriers to Domestic Violence Screening and Referral in a Health Care Setting," *Journal of Interpersonal Violence* 20 (2005): 1288–1309; M. J. Zachary, C. B. Schechter, M. L. Kaplan, and M. N. Mulvihill, "Provider Evaluation of a Multifaceted System of Care to Improve Recognition and Management of Pregnant Women Experiencing Domestic Violence," *Women's Health Issues* 12 (2002): 5–15; J. C. Campbell, J. H. Coben, E. McLaughlin, et al., "An Evaluation of a System-Change Training Model to Improve Emergency Department Response to Battered Women," *Academic Emergency Medicine* 8 (2001): 131–138; G. L. Larkin, S. Rolniak, K. B. Hyman, et al., "Effect of an Administrative Intervention on Rates of Screening for Domestic Violence in an Urban Emergency Department," *American Journal of Public Health* 90 (2000): 1444–1448; Warshaw et al., *Improving the Health Care Response to Domestic Violence*; McLeer et al., "Education Is Not Enough."

59. Jones and Schechter, *When Loves Goes Wrong*.

60. Warshaw et al., *Improving the Health Care Response to Domestic Violence*.

61. S. R. Dube, V. J. Felitti, M. Dong, et al., "The Impact of Adverse Childhood Experiences on Health Problems: Evidence from Four Birth Cohorts Dating Back to 1900," *Prevention Medicine* 37 (2003): 268–277; V. J. Felitti, "The Relationship Between Adverse Childhood Experiences and Adult Health," *The Permanente Journal* 6 (2002): 44–47; C. L. Whitfield, "Adverse Childhood Experiences and Trauma," *American Journal of Preventive Medicine* 14 (1998): 245–258; V. J. Felitti, R. F. Anda, D. Nordenberg, et al., "The Relationship of Adult Health Status to Childhood Abuse and Household Dysfunction," *American Journal of Preventive Medicine* (1998): 245–258; Warshaw et al., *Improving the Health Care Response to Domestic Violence*.

CHAPTER 21

Ethics of Disaster Planning and Response

Eileen E. Morrison and Karen J. Bawel-Brinkley

INTRODUCTION

A *disaster* is any incident that overwhelms our emergency response systems and creates an imbalance between needs and resources locally, regionally, or nationally. Americans have experienced a number of disaster situations resulting from natural events, such as fires, floods, tornados, and hurricanes. There have also been an increasing number of human-made events (anthropogenic hazards), such as terrorist bombings, structural collapse, and school shootings. Any of these events can occur without warning, affecting individuals, families, and communities.[1] Regardless of the form of the disaster, the individual, organization, and community have the responsibility to be proactive and develop contingency plans that address the known risks, from natural disasters to terrorism.[2] In addition, the plans should address both the logistical and ethical dilemmas following the disaster and postrecovery phases.[3]

All information indicates that the United States will continue to face disasters from various sources throughout the 21st century. This chapter presents examples of how government, healthcare organizations, and individuals plan for and respond to disaster situations. Although not all-inclusive, these examples provide a framework for a discussion of the ethical issues that relate to disaster preparedness.

The chapter begins by reviewing examples of recent efforts by the federal government to prepare for and respond to disasters. The scope of the chapter will not allow a thorough examination of every effort made by governments, including those of state or local entities. However, it will highlight examples of agencies that are attempting to prepare the nation for disasters and to respond when they occur. Examples are included from the Department of Homeland Security, the Centers for Disease Control and Prevention, the Federal Emergency Management Agency, and the American Red Cross. Following this presentation, there is a discussion of the ethical issues surrounding disaster preparedness. Using both theories and principles, the authors analyze ethical dilemmas related to logistical problems, loss of privacy and autonomy, and social justice.

Next, the chapter moves to efforts made by the healthcare system to prepare and respond to disasters. Again, examples highlight the system's ability to prepare for natural or human-caused disasters. These examples include information from The Joint Commission, the Office of the Assistant Secretary for Preparedness Response, and hospital systems. These examples lead to a discussion of ethical issues regarding resource allocation, the obligations of first responders, and social justice.

Finally, there is a review of the obligation of individuals to prepare for disasters. This section also begins the discussion of the ethical issues faced by individuals concerning their preparation for and response to disasters. The chapter concludes with a summary of the critical ethical issues for disaster planning and response in the 21st century.

DISASTER RESPONSE AND DISASTERS IN U.S. HISTORY

The healthcare industry and its providers have a daily operational framework of treating individuals based on time, survival resources, and supplies. In one respect, healthcare providers plan, develop, implement, and evaluate services for caring for individuals based on the theory of supply and demand. Therefore, the daily operational framework of the organization must be able to adapt to an unexpected crisis leading to chaos. For example, in an emergency, the goal for healthcare facilities would be to treat the most severely injured patients first while providing the highest level of care. The time frame, resources, and services would also have to be adequate to meet the needs of the situation. Therefore, treating and providing the highest level of care depends on time, resources, and supplies.[4]

In a disaster situation, the goal is to provide care for the greatest number of potential survivors without depleting resources or services. An unexpected catastrophic event or situation that depletes an organization's survival resources and supplies in a relatively short time frame increases the individual survivor's vulnerability and decreases the chance for survival.[5] Therefore, in the event of a disaster, healthcare providers must have a contingency plan that addresses the spectrum of known risks. They must be able to shift from a daily operational framework to one that includes providing care for the greatest number of potential survivors involved in the disaster in an efficient and effective manner.[6] Healthcare organizations must plan both for what exists and for what might exist.

Disasters are categorized in two ways: natural or human-caused. This means that their causation comes either from natural external events or from human choices. These types of disasters have occurred throughout American history and have not only influenced the environment and U.S. society but also the human experience in general.

In the past, the United States has experienced natural disasters such as severe tornados, hurricanes (Betsy, Camille, and Ivan), floods (Johnstown, Pennsylvania, in 1889 and the Mississippi River flood in 1993), and fires (Chicago in 1871 and San Francisco in 1906). Recent examples of disasters include Hurricane Katrina, which claimed at least 1,833 lives in the states of Louisiana, Mississippi, Florida, Georgia, and Alabama. In 2012, Hurricane Sandy hit and promises to be the second most expensive storm in the United States. In 2011, over 300 tornados (ranking high on the tornado severity scale) rampaged through the Southeast, demolishing whole towns and killing hundreds of people. On May 22, 2011, this unprecedented tornado outbreak was followed by another level 5 tornado in Joplin, Missouri, that wiped out the town and killed 158 people. The National Weather Service and emergency managers reported that this was the most deadly storm in modern times, with damage to 75% of Joplin.[7]

Finally, the year ended with the blizzards of 2011 leaving a 2,000-mile-long trail of snow and ice from the Midwest to the Northeast. This situation created an impact on electrical power, transportation, businesses, activities of daily living, and emergency medical services. Individuals not only sustained injuries but also, in some situations, death as a result of this natural disaster. Survivors found themselves without shelter and facing financial ruin.

In 2012, the National Weather Service said that the four tornados that hit Kentucky were the worst in the region in 24 years. In Indiana, an EF-4 tornado (second-highest on the Fujita scale) packing 175-mph winds hit the town of Henryville and stayed on the ground for more than 50 miles. In April 2012, 688 tornado warnings were issued and 757 severe thunderstorm warnings from Texas to New York.

Human-made disasters also have caused devastation and costs in lives and property. Americans now remember where they were on September 11, 2001, and many must live with the loss of life caused by the choices made on that day. It will also not be easy to forget the billions of dollars of damage and the environmental impact of the Deepwater Horizon oil spill in the Gulf of Mexico in 2010. In addition, on the 100th anniversary year of the *Titanic* disaster, cruise ships were still involved in accidents that threaten passenger lives and safety.[8]

Disasters happen, and preparation for them is necessary. Without adequate disaster planning, chaos can proliferate, leading to poor decision making and unethical behaviors. To have both an ethical and efficient response to a disaster, order needs to be reestablished and chaos eliminated as soon as possible.[9]

DISASTER PLANNING AND RESPONSE BY THE FEDERAL GOVERNMENT

According to Redlener, the events of September 11, 2001, spurred efforts to upgrade America's ability to plan for disasters.[10] However, as of 2012, we remained vulnerable to the effects of major disasters. To be proactive, governments will have to invest in long-term programs that might not provide a return on investment for decades. In addition, these programs will require partnerships among the government (federal, regional, state, and local); nonprofit organizations; healthcare systems, including first responders; and individual citizens. As a nation, America responds well in crises; we work together to diminish suffering when we see it or hear about it. However, we are also a nation based on individual autonomy; therefore, the idea of long-range disaster planning and budgets for "what if" scenarios, teamwork, and shared burdens may not be politically attractive.

The Department of Homeland Security

One response to the events of 9/11 has been the creation of the Department of Homeland Security (DHS). Any American who has traveled since 9/11 is aware of the many changes in security that are part of the duties of this organization. The DHS is responsible for preventing terrorist attacks and providing aircraft security, including for crew, cargo, and passengers.[11] It employs professional screeners at airports and advanced imaging technology to mitigate the possibilities of terrorist activity.

However, airport security is only one small part of how the DHS uses its $57.7 billion budget.[12] The DHS includes the Federal Emergency Management Agency, the U.S. Immigration and Customs Enforcement Agency, and the U.S. Coast Guard among its agencies. The DHS is now responsible for preparedness, response, and recovery for all types of emergencies, from natural disasters to anthropogenic hazards.

In addition, the National Center for Educational Statistics (NCES) and the National Academic Consortium for Homeland Security (NACHS) have evolved in conjunction with the Homeland Security and Defense Education Consortium (HSDEC) to support and provide education regarding homeland security. Both organizations have proposed standardized curriculum-based programs and core competencies for professionals.[13]

The Federal Emergency Management Agency

The Federal Emergency Management Agency (FEMA) responds to both local and national disaster situations. It is now part of the DHS Preparedness, Response and Recovery mission and works to coordinate efforts of governments (regional, state, and local branches), volunteer organizations, and healthcare systems to increase the nation's resilience to disasters. Examples of FEMA's efforts include the coordination of the federal government's response to the 2010 Gulf Coast oil spill and its response to the tornados of 2011.[14]

FEMA's website contains a plethora of information concerning its mission. For example, under "Preparing Your Family," there is information about FEMA's Citizen Corps, which prepares individuals for disasters. There is also information about how to prepare families for disasters, including developing emergency plans and kits. The "Disaster Response" section provides information about federal disaster declarations, applying for FEMA assistance, and urban search and rescue teams. Extensive information on providing safety after a disaster, dealing with the emotional aftermath of a disaster, and assisting children who are survivors is also available, as well as a section on rebuilding homes and businesses after a disaster.[15]

FEMA provides direct assistance to qualified disaster survivors to help rebuild their homes and businesses. This assistance helps with temporary housing, rebuilding or replacing homes, and other disaster-related expenses. It is generally for those survivors who do not have insurance. FEMA also includes the National Flood Insurance Program, which provides flood insurance and flood hazard mapping.[16]

The Centers for Disease Control and Prevention

Other federal agencies also are involved in planning and responding to natural and human-caused disasters. One such agency is the Centers for Disease Control and Prevention (CDC), which includes the Health Alert Network and public and community health systems.[17] According to the CDC website, this agency is the primary source for providing information on natural and human-caused disasters.[18] The CDC's website contains information on hazards from A to Z and is available in many languages.

The CDC now also includes programs such as the Public Health Emergency Preparedness Research Program (PHEP), which was formerly part of the Agency for Healthcare Research and Quality.[19] CDC-based programs conduct research on ways to respond to the aftermath of adverse events. In 1999, the CDC established the Laboratory Response Network, involving a network of laboratories to identify, communicate, and provide a quick response to outbreaks of disease and implement the appropriate protocols. The CDC also has developed a national pharmaceutical stockpile of "push packages" that can be delivered within 12 hours anywhere in the United States.[20] This ability is critical in responding to both human-made and natural disasters.

Education is a priority in disaster preparedness, so the CDC provides training opportunities to both professionals and the public for disaster planning and response. It also offers guides specifically designed for healthcare facilities, businesses, and individuals. This guidance includes fact sheets, tool kits, and research reports on many areas, including mass-casualty event preparation and response.[21]

The American Red Cross

Although not a government agency, the American Red Cross (ARC) is a major resource for disaster-response information.[22] Inspired by the Swiss International Red Cross movement, the ARC is a humanitarian organization founded in 1881. Since that time, the ARC has provided relief and served as a mode of communication between members of the American armed forces and their families. It also provides national and international disaster relief.

According to its charter, established by Congress in 1905, the mission of the American Red Cross is to relieve suffering, particularly when disaster strikes, which includes education of the public and training. Initially, the ARC established first aid, water safety, and public health nursing programs. As the ARC has grown throughout the years, its services have expanded to include educational programs, such as safety training, HIV education, and more. During wartime, it has provided services for military personnel, civilian war victims, and prisoners of war. It maintains the civilian blood program and provides disaster relief.

The ARC is famous for its use of volunteers from both the medical and nonmedical communities. Volunteers trained by the American Red Cross provide services in a variety of disaster situations. Although volunteers are more noted for their efforts in major disasters such as floods and fires, they actually assist in over 70,000 disasters per year.[23] The ARC also has a matching program that coordinates a volunteer's expertise with a particular American Red Cross need. Volunteers are an integral part of the success of the disaster relief efforts provided by the Red Cross organization.

The Red Cross disaster relief programs provide for the *immediate* needs of individuals and families affected by a disaster. When a disaster strikes, the ARC provides shelter and food and assists with healthcare issues and mental health services. It also offers support services for those who are part of the disaster relief efforts, including emergency workers.

The ARC is a great proponent of education. It provides an ample amount of educational information on disaster and disaster preparedness. Its website includes articles on family disaster planning, animal safety, helping children cope with disasters, and the special needs of the elderly. In addition, information on what to include in a disaster preparation kit and information sheets on how to prepare for a variety of disaster situations are provided. Businesses can also find resources on how to prepare for disasters on the ARC website.

IMPROVING DISASTER PREPAREDNESS AND RESPONSE

These organizations constitute only a small portion of how the U.S. government prepares for catastrophic events. They have certainly helped to increase the public's awareness of the potential for such events. However, Redlener has suggested that there is still much more to do in preparing the nation for future disasters.[24] He offered a plan that included setting benchmarks, correcting methods of overseeing disaster planning, creating accountability standards, and making the reduction of threats a priority. In addition, he supported changing how disaster responses occur. He suggested increasing the influence of the U.S. Surgeon General, changing FEMA's reporting system, and clarifying the role of the military in a disaster situation. Even though there have been improvements in response capability, the government must continue improving its plans for responding to natural and human-caused disasters.

ETHICAL ISSUES AND GOVERNMENT DISASTER PLANNING AND RESPONSE

Government agencies have contributed a great deal of information, plans, and funding to assist in disaster planning and response. However, reports by the media and by the government agencies themselves reveal that major issues still exist with both the planning for and response to disasters. Many of these issues stem from ethical considerations, including aspects of social justice. Even though there may be extensive planning for a disaster, the actual implementation of these plans will be challenging. The unexpected can always occur. In addition, the postrecovery situation is at best complicated and complex, often resulting in chaos; as a result, ethical principles can be violated.

Roberts and DeRenzo suggested that ethical responsibility begins with the plan itself.[25] Because there is a need to make serious ethical decisions once a disaster happens, it is necessary to be prepared *ethically* as well as *logistically* in the event of a disaster. This means that planners need to make ethics part of the plan's guiding principles and foundation. For example, the very nature of a disaster presents conflicts of interest that will require discussion and the formulation of standards that account for the community's interest as well as of those who respond to the disaster.

A consistent theme in Roberts and DeRenzo's work is the necessity of balancing utilitarian and deontological views. In a disaster situation, many feel that the "greatest good for the greatest number" is the most logical approach, maximizing the benefits for as many people as possible. Typically, the definition of this benefit is the number of lives saved. When healthcare providers are presented with the challenge of caring for the acutely sick and injured and managing those with chronic illnesses and special needs, they may use the utilitarian approach. In this case, triage provides a strategy for healthcare providers to offer the greatest good for the greatest number of disaster victims. The goal is to minimize risks, maximize resources, and simplify administrative processes to facilitate aid to survivors, especially the most vulnerable ones.[26]

Mass-casualty triaging was a wartime innovation that has evolved into grouping individuals based on medical need to achieve greater survival rates. Baker contends that real-time events, the healthcare setting, and management options drive triage as it is used in the healthcare facility.[27] Situational awareness, decisiveness, and clinical expertise are required in triaging disaster victims. However, lack of preparation and training can negatively influence the outcomes of a disaster and postrecovery efforts. Therefore, each healthcare facility should develop and practice rigorous decision-making criteria for triaging.

One type of triage system used in disaster responses places casualties into the following groups: (1) those with nonsurvivable injuries, (2) those who would benefit from immediate lifesaving interventions, (3) those who do not need immediate care, and (4) those who have negligible injuries. However, this is only one of several ways to group casualties for disaster response. Systems for triage are based on evidence-based research, and their ethical basis can be found in the utilitarian theory of ethics. Triage becomes Mill's theory in action and affects survival rates for those affected by disasters.[28]

However, utilitarianism has a number of limitations when one considers the viewpoint of the individual and the community. For example, after Hurricane Katrina and the 2011 tornados, much effort and money was expended on recovery of the remains of the dead. Although strict utilitarianism would find this to be unacceptable because the dead do not offer much benefit to the living, the families and the community involved found this action and expense to be appropriate. Even though the dead could no longer create benefit, the moral obligation to honor their lives justified the recovery efforts.

In the case of response to a disaster, utilitarianism needs to be balanced with concerns for Kantian, or duty-based, ethics. In this approach to ethics, all humans have worth. Therefore, it would be inappropriate to sacrifice some individuals over others, even if it means ignoring the rule of the greatest good for the greatest number. For example, duty explains the use of the greater resources needed to assist those who are elderly, ill, or otherwise vulnerable. Duty to our fellow human beings would not allow us to leave these people behind because they lacked resources to respond to a disaster.

Another ethical issue that might emerge during a disaster is respect for autonomy. Individual freedom, which is part of the principle of autonomy, can often come into question. For example, should an individual have the right to build a home on a flood plain and not have flood insurance? If an individual decides to ignore disaster warnings or cannot take action when disasters occur, what is the government's responsibility? What if there is evidence of exposure to a highly infectious disease? Does the community have the right to quarantine an individual against his or her will in an effort to protect itself? Where does autonomy stop and community protection begin?

In addition, the concept of social justice is a major ethical consideration with respect to the government's response to disasters. When a disaster occurs, Americans expect that the government will do whatever it can to respond to the situation and to relieve the suffering of its citizens. Historically, Americans have been both compassionate and generous when disasters have occurred. They expect coordinated action that protects both individual lives and community property. When communication and coordination between government entities are lacking, there can be tragic consequences. Communities react with moral outrage and demand investigation.

An example of this expectation and lack of coordination occurred during the response to Hurricane Katrina, which led to an investigation and the publication of *A Failure of Initiative: Final Report of the Select Bipartisan Committee to Investigate the Preparation for and Response to Hurricane Katrina*.[29] This report provides an extensive review of the human and ethical impact of disaster responses. It also details recommendations that can improve disaster response on both a government and community level.

The ethical issues related to disaster response go beyond preparation and response to events. When large amounts of capital (in the billions of dollars) are involved in these efforts, the potential for fraud, abuse, and corruption exists. Such actions are not only illegal, but also violate many ethical principles, including beneficence, nonmaleficence, and justice. When these violations are part of government actions, the level of trust in government is undermined, and people believe that those in government increase their own wealth by trading on the suffering of others. Ethics must be part of every agency's disaster plan—from its development to implementation and evaluation—in an effort to prevent fraud, abuse, and a loss of trust. Once disaster plans are developed, there needs to be a review not just in terms of resources but also with an eye toward ethics and community acceptability.

Once an agency has its disaster plan and it is determined to be congruent with corporate values and ethics, the next step is to communicate the plan's ethical foundation. Application of the plan through training is necessary to ensure that the ethical principles articulated in the plan are practiced. Clinical simulations can provide practice, experiential learning, and ethics-based discussion. For example, local branches of the ARC periodically hold disaster drills. Volunteers from the community are actively encouraged to participate. This allows them not only to practice logistics, but also to experience and discuss potential ethical issues in a nondisaster situation.

HEALTHCARE ORGANIZATIONS AND DISASTER PLANNING

Society entrusts certain professionals (doctors, nurses, paramedics, emergency medical technicians, firemen, police, and military) with the responsibility to act in ways that facilitate the whole society's ability to overcome or recover from a disaster. Regardless of what they encounter in a disaster, the guidelines for these professionals must be common principles of nonmaleficence, justice, autonomy, and beneficence. Therefore, they and their respective organizations have the responsibility to be prepared for natural and human-made events. In addition, they must have a contingency plan that incorporates strategies with clear priorities, an organized but flexible plan of action, and effective communications at the various levels. In addition, a response plan must include resources that can move quickly from location to location to reduce the amount of chaos during a complex and complicated situation.[30]

The United States has over 7,500 hospitals, which represent the front line when a disaster occurs. Therefore, it is necessary for hospitals and the entire healthcare system to be prepared to respond effectively and efficiently when a crisis occurs. Although it is not possible to discuss all of the efforts that hospitals and the healthcare system make with regard to disaster planning and response, examples will provide a helpful background. Information from The Joint Commission provides some information on disaster planning and preparedness training in the nation's hospitals.

The Joint Commission

The Joint Commission is one of the more prominent forces in establishing minimum standards for acceptable practice for hospitals and many other healthcare facilities.[31] In this role, it mandates that all organizations must have an emergency management program. The standards for hospitals are frequently updated and address effectiveness of care during an emergency or disaster situation. The program should address the kind of disasters that may occur based on a hazardous vulnerability analysis. Based on probabilities, natural disasters such as hurricanes, tornados, landslides, and earthquakes may be included in the emergency plan. In addition, human-made disasters such as riots, airplane crashes, terrorist acts, and fires can be included in the hospital's emergency planning.[32]

The Joint Commission's emergency management planning includes many standards that span different divisions of a hospital or facility. An example of one such standard is EM.02.01.01, which requires a hospital to have an action plan for the first 96 hours after a disaster. The hospital must assess its capabilities in six areas: communications, resources, security and safety, staff, utilities, and patient care. Based on this assessment, the hospital must design procedures for how it will respond in these areas if there is no community support for 96 hours.[33,34]

The Joint Commission is concerned with providing health care for those in need even when the unexpected and unwanted occurs. Therefore, one can imagine that its standards for hospital disaster preparedness are quite extensive and exacting. The California Hospital Association has an excellent website that provides resources to assist in meeting Joint Commission standards. This site includes a resource for preparing the Emergency Operations Plan (EOP) that is just one aspect of The Joint Commission's overall emergency management program. Their checklist for program components includes a mechanism for assessing and evaluating the response process, beginning with the program description and ending with an event evaluation after a disaster response. Disaster preparation drills, exercises, and essential functions assessments are included, as are details about specific response plans, surge plans, and 96-hour capacity information.[35]

The Office of the Assistant Secretary for Preparedness and Response

The Joint Commission is not the only organization that provides guidelines to assist hospitals in disaster planning and response efforts. The Office of the Assistant Secretary for Preparedness and Response (ASPR), which is part of the U.S. Department of Health and Human Services, provides guidance for implementing the Hospital Preparedness Program (HPP).[36] Through this program, public health departments receive funds to work with hospitals and other healthcare facilities to develop plans for disaster readiness. The ASPR has identified eight capabilities needed for preparation: [37]

1. Healthcare system preparedness
2. Healthcare system recovery
3. Emergency operations coordination
4. Fatality management
5. Information sharing
6. Medical surge
7. Responder safety and health
8. Volunteer management

Using FEMA preparedness methods and public health planning models, the ASPR provides a mechanism to assist hospitals and healthcare organizations in assessing and improving their disaster response capabilities. Its planning assistance focuses on the eight health preparedness capabilities, and the organization provides detailed information on each area. Each capacity has a series of functions, tasks, recommendations, and resources to assist organizations in being better prepared for both natural and human-made disasters.

For example, Capability 4 (fatality management) begins with an operational definition of the capability. It then identifies three functions that need to coordinate with all agencies that are responsible for fatality management, including morgue space and disposal options for human remains. This capability also includes information on dealing with the large groups of citizens who may be affected by the mass casualties, and on coordinating support for mental health responders, survivors, and family members.[38] The guide provides detailed information on tasks to be accomplished under each of these functions.

ETHICAL ISSUES AND HEALTH ORGANIZATION DISASTER PLANNING AND RESPONSE

Development of a systematic infrastructure and superstructure that links healthcare agencies, government entities, and the community together is a complex and complicated task. This task challenges agencies strategically, fiscally, and ethically. Organizations must devote time and resources to developing plans, conducting emergency drills and exercises, and budgeting for needed technology and other resources. Although such plans are certainly worth the effort because of health care's commitment to human life, they do take time and resources from other areas of the organizations and require ethical analysis.

The ethical question of balancing the duty toward the individual (Kant) with the need to provide the greatest good for the greatest number affected in a disaster (Mill) should always be part of the planning considerations for healthcare organizations. It would be wise for disaster response planners to consider the ethical issues that might occur when they must ration resources and how they can avoid them. In addition, planners have to be aware of the issue of justice or fairness as they decide how to best provide their response to a disaster situation. They should consider that there is no universal definition of fairness, so what seems just in a preparedness plan may not seem just to the community. Discussion and planning for ethical issues is important not only for the organization but also for maintaining community trust—an element that is essential in times of disaster.[39]

In addition, hospitals must decide the best use of scarce resources while remembering to honor the worth of all people. For example, consider a rescue situation. First responders must decide who to save and in what order. Often, this heartrending and difficult decision happens in an instant. Responders rescue those who are mobile first, because they require fewer resources. The elderly, ill, handicapped, or otherwise disabled are rescued later. Although this is an attempt to provide the greatest good for the greatest number when using a scarce resource, it can create situations in which professionals are tempted to assist in the death of patients rather than watch them suffer. Planners should remember that "what if" situations need to be discussed before they occur so that first responders are prepared emotionally and ethically.

Another major ethical dilemma that might occur for first responders and hospital staff is the conflict between their duty to the community versus their duty to their families. In a disaster situation, their profession and professional ethics require these individuals to care for the needs of the community even when their own safety or that of their loved ones is endangered. However, they also are human and are concerned about what might be happening to their own families. This causes a conflict and a sense of moral ambiguity. Should they stay and care for the needs of the community, or leave and take care of their own families? One way a hospital or other agency can assist with this dilemma is to include plans for the families of those who respond to emergencies in their overall disaster response plans. In this way, necessary staff members can be where they are most needed with the knowledge that their families are receiving attention and care. Such assurance would make it less likely that those charged with disaster response would leave their assignments in order to protect the needs of their families.

The areas discussed here are just a few examples of why it is important to include ethics in disaster planning. Jennings suggested seven ethics goals that should be part of a facilities response for disasters.[40] Nonmaleficence in the form of prevention and reduction of harm and protection of safety should be an ethics-based goal for disaster planning. In addition, plans should respect individual autonomy and dignity and try to balance the burdens and effects of the event with the benefits provided (distributive justice). There is also an ethical obligation to strengthen communities so that they are better prepared to deal with disasters. This action includes support systems and education about disaster prevention. Finally, he recommended that professionals recognize their obligations in disaster response and maintain their competence and sense of personal responsibility.

INDIVIDUAL RESPONSE TO DISASTERS

Despite the extensive media coverage of disasters and mass-casualty events, most individuals do not think that they will have to deal with such unfortunate circumstances. Perhaps it is part of human nature not to want to prepare for the worst, but it is necessary. Studies indicate that some of the most vulnerable people, such as low-income families, are the least prepared to deal with emergencies. Others simply do not feel that it is necessary or are too busy to make the effort.[41]

What should individuals do to be better prepared for emergencies? According to the American Red Cross, people should be "Red Cross Ready" in the event of an emergency.[42] This readiness includes preparing an emergency first aid kit that will enable people to care for their own emergencies. This is especially important because, in the event of a major disaster, government assistance might not be immediate. Preparedness also includes having at least a three days' worth of supplies for survival. This means having at least one gallon of water and 1,600 calories of food that does not require cooking per person per day. These survival materials should be stored in containers that are easily accessible. The Red Cross also asks individuals to include money, a flashlight, a battery-operated radio, and prescription medicines in the emergency kit.

Preparedness requires that individuals develop a disaster plan. This plan should contain information about what they would do in an emergency. It should identify where they would go and who they would need to contact. The American Red Cross encourages individuals to communicate their plan to family members and friends and even to conduct practice sessions so that they are prepared in an emergency. Finally, individuals should know about the types of disasters that could occur in their area and how to get accurate information pertaining to them. The ARC also encourages everyone to learn first aid and cardiopulmonary resuscitation (CPR) because it may take time for emergency medical staff to reach everyone in a major disaster.

The CDC notes that individuals might have to shelter in place when a disaster occurs.[43] This means that people must be able to prevent contamination if a chemical or radiological disaster occurs. The CDC suggests choosing a room in the home to prepare as a shelter. This room would contain a disaster supply kit, food, and sufficient water supply for the family. Businesses should have an emergency plan to get employees to a designated shelter. This shelter should have first aid kits, food, and water. Police or fire departments should have the ability to issue warnings whenever a shelter-in-place policy is necessary.

Redlener has noted that publically available materials do not emphasize the most important disaster-planning principles.[44] Not only must citizens be physically prepared, but also they must be mentally ready for disasters and for survival. People must be physically fit to survive in a disaster situation. They also need to consider what they would do in an emergency and how they would survive. This may require devising a plan and practicing it.

Redlener also suggested that citizens receive CPR and first aid training through either the American Red Cross or another entity. It also is important to be aware of one's situation at work, home, or in the community. This might include knowing how to exit buildings, being aware of people in one's surroundings, and anticipating any dangers in one's environment. To be truly disaster-ready, Americans need information about their own communities and the potential for disasters.

In accordance with the ARC's suggestions, Redlener urges individuals to have a family plan for emergencies.[45] This would include how to care for family members who are elderly, neighbors who might be disabled, or coworkers who might need additional assistance. Plans should also address situations that require rapid evacuation or shelter-in-place situations. In addition, communication is essential during an emergency, so individuals must prepare for situations in which traditional telephone services might not be operational. In such cases, two-way communication devices such as cell phones might become lifelines because they can be battery operated. In an age when nature and humankind can cause disasters, citizens and families need to be able to control their disaster responses by being prepared.

ETHICAL IMPLICATIONS FOR INDIVIDUAL RESPONSE TO DISASTERS

When a disaster strikes, individuals might face a number of ethical problems. Fear and injury can cause individuals to enter into a survival mode that might not respect the rights and dignity of others. Panic might cause some to harm individuals or property. In fact, disaster survival might cause people to change their behaviors on many levels.

In the United States, individuals tend to expect the government to respond in a timely manner whenever any type of emergency occurs. Because of the country's history of responding to disasters, they put great faith in the ability of American citizens and the government to handle emergencies. However, individuals also have an ethical responsibility to be prepared to handle emergencies on their own because government help may not be imminent. There can be a feeling of injustice when citizens pay for services through their tax dollars and these services are not readily available or adequate for the situation. As seen in reactions toward the government response in Hurricane Katrina and other events, individuals can lose trust in their government and begin to question its ability when its response does not meet their needs.

Autonomy is another ethical issue for individuals. As government and organizations begin to use high-tech tools to prevent potential disasters, individuals are beginning to question how much of their privacy and autonomy is being lost versus the benefits gained. For example, more and more cities are adding camera surveillance on streets to protect against potential terrorist acts or other crimes. Recently, Congress approved the use of drones for surveillance in American cities under the FAA Reauthorization Act. This technology is to be used to fight terrorism, provide support for disaster relief, and fight fires. The testing and licensing of this technology must be developed by 2015.[46] Although surveillance technology has benefits for safety, some question its value in light of the loss of personal freedom. Others believe that such surveillance is the beginning of a slippery slope in which all citizens can be a target and autonomy is nonexistent.

Beneficence also is an issue for individuals in both planning and responding to disasters. Without acts of beneficence, many will not survive in a disaster situation. Citizens often become even more altruistic and compassionate in times of disaster and widespread suffering. However, in planning for disasters, individuals have to consider how far their responsibility goes. Are they going to be responsible for all the elderly in their neighborhood, or just for their immediate family members? Who will be responsible for those in the community who might require extra relief during a disaster? What is the gap between individual beneficence and the government's responsibility? These questions will be troubling for individuals who wish to live an ethical life. They also pose a challenge to an individual's concept of duty (deontology) and make for deep levels of discussions in both ethics courses and family dinner tables.

SUMMARY

There is much to say about the relationship between disaster response and ethics. This chapter is just the beginning of a discussion that should be part of the disaster planning process for healthcare organizations, responders, and individuals. It provided an overview of some of the efforts made by government and healthcare organizations and discussed the ethical issues they raise. In addition, it included information about an individual's responsibility to prepare for the event of a disaster. Even though Americans have survived many natural and human-made disasters, it is not possible to anticipate all potential sources for events in the 21st century. It is only possible to prepare for these events organizationally, individually, and ethically and to hope that we need never put into action the plans that we have made.

QUESTIONS FOR DISCUSSION

1. What ethical theories apply to the use of scarce resources in a disaster situation?

2. How can individual healthcare professionals prepare themselves to deal with potential disaster situations?

3. Do you think the funds spent on disaster drills and exercises are worth the expenditure? How can you defend your answer from an ethics standpoint?

4. Who should be responsible for what happens during a disaster: the individual or the government?

5. Review a disaster plan for a healthcare facility. What is the focus of this disaster plan? On what type of ethical principles is this disaster plan based?

6. When a major disaster happens, can one expect others to demonstrate ethical decision-making abilities? Why or why not?

FOOD FOR THOUGHT

Suppose you are part of a physician–nurse team that owns a small medical clinic in Bastrop, Texas. Your clinic provides a major part of the medical services to the Bastrop community, and your patients' average age is 60. It is Labor Day weekend, and your clinic is in the center of a fire zone. You are not sure it will even exist in the future.

1. What is your first plan of action?
2. What is your long-term plan?
3. What ethical issues do you face in the immediate future?
4. What ethical issues do you face as your community recovers from the fires?

NOTES

1. H. H. Soliman and M. E. Rogge, "Ethical Considerations in Disaster Services: A Social Work Perspective," *Electronic Journal of Social Work* 1, no. 1 (2002): 1–23. Retrieved from http://www.centerforurbanstudies.com/documents/electronic_library/disaster_planning/ethics_in_disasterplanning.pdf. Accessed April 15, 2012.

2. A. Adu-Oppong, G. R. Ledlow, M. A. Cwiek, J. A. Johnson, and M. N. Coppola, "Organization Development for Terrorism and Natural Disasters," in *Health Care Organizations: Theory, Behavior, and Development*, ed. J. J. Johnson (Sudbury, MA: Jones and Bartlett, 2009).

3. Soliman and Rogge, "Ethical Considerations in Disaster Services."

4. M. Baker, "Creating Order from Chaos, Part I: Triage, Initial Care, and Tactical Considerations in Mass Casualty and Disaster Response," *Military Medicine* 172 (2007): 232–236.

5. Ibid.; S. Sasser, "Field Triage in Disasters," *Prehospital Emergency Care* 10 (2006): 322–323; B. Rogers and E. Lawhorn, "Disaster Preparedness: Occupational and Environmental Health Professionals' Response to Hurricanes Katrina and Rita," *American Association of Occupational Health Nurses* 5, no. 5 (2007): 197–207.

6. J. A. Johnson and D. J. Breckon, *Managing Health Education and Promotion Programs: Leadership Skills for the 21st Century* (Sudbury, MA: Jones and Bartlett, 2006).

7. National Weather Service, "Joplin Tornado Event Summary: May 2, 2011." Retrieved from http://www.crh.Noaa.gov/sgf/?m=event_2011may22_summary. Accessed April 14, 2012.

8. R. A. Klein, "Stop Rearranging Deck Chairs: Cruise Industry Needs Big Changes," *The Seattle Times*, April 10, 2012. Retrieved from http://seattletimes.nwsource.com/html/travel/2017948779_webcruiseships11.html. Accessed April 15, 2012.

9. Baker, "Creating Order from Chaos, Part I."

10. I. Redlener, *Americans at Risk* (New York: Albert A. Knopf, 2006).

11. Department of Homeland Security, "Prevent Terrorism and Enhance Security." Retrieved from http://www.dhs.gov/xabout/ge_1240598490142.shtm. Accessed April 13, 2012.

12. See the Department of Homeland Security website, http://www.dhs.gov/index.shtm. Accessed April 15, 2012.

13. Adu-Oppong et al., "Organization Development for Terrorism and Natural Disasters."

14. Department of Homeland Security, "Ensure Resilience to Disasters." Retrieved from http://www.dhs.gov/about/xabout/gc_12961607526000.shtm. Accessed April 15, 2012.

15. Department of Homeland Security, "Preparedness, Response, and Recovery." Retrieved from http://www.dhs.gov/files/prepresprecovery.shtm. Accessed April 15, 2012.

16. See the FEMA website, http://www.fema.gov/index.shtm. Accessed April 15, 2012.

17. D. A. Henderson, "Bioterrorism," *International Journal of Clinical Practice Supplement* 115 (2000): 32–36.

18. See http://www.cdc.gov/. Accessed April 15, 2012.

19. Agency for Healthcare Research and Quality, "Public Health Emergency Preparedness." Retrieved from http://www.ahrq.gov/prep/. Accessed April 22, 2012.

20. Adu-Oppong et al., "Organization Development for Terrorism and Natural Disasters."

21. Centers for Disease Control and Prevention, "Training and Education." Retrieved from http://www.bt.cdc.gov/training/. Accessed April 22, 2012

22. See the American Red Cross website, http://www.redcross.org/. Accessed April 15, 2012.

23. American Red Cross, "Who We Are." Retrieved from http://www.redcross.org/about-us. Accessed April 15, 2012.

24. Redlener, *Americans at Risk.*

25. M. Roberts and E. G. DeRenzo, "Ethical Considerations in Community Disaster Planning," in *Mass Medical Care with Scarce Resources: A Community Planning Guide*, eds. S. J. Phillips and A. Knebel (Rockville, MD: Agency for Health Research and Quality, 2007), 9–23.

26. Soliman and Rogge, "Ethical Considerations in Disaster Services."

27. Baker, "Creating Order from Chaos, Part I." For more information, see also J. T. Ihlenfeld, "A Primer on Triage and Mass Casualty Events," *Dimensions of Critical Care Nursing* 22, no. 5 (2003): 204–207; R. Lanoix, D. E. Wiener, and V. D. Zayas, "Concepts in Disaster Triage in the Wake of the World Trade Center Terrorist Attack," *Topics in Emergency Medicine* 24, no. 2 (2002): 60–70; and M. E. Sheeley and N. Mahoney, "A New Reality: Mass Casualty Teams," *Nursing Management* (April 2007): 39B–40H.

28. Baker, "Creating Order from Chaos, Part I."

29. Select Bipartisan Committee to Investigate the Preparation for and Response to Hurricane Katrina, *A Failure of Initiative: Final Report of the Select Bipartisan Committee to Investigate the Preparation for and Response to Hurricane Katrina*, House Report 109-377 (Washington, DC: U.S. Government Printing Office, 2006). Available at http://biotech.law.lsu.edu/katrina/govdocs/109-377/katrina.html. Accessed April 22, 2012.

30. Adu-Oppong et al., "Organization Development for Terrorism and Natural Disasters."

31. See The Joint Commission's website, http://www.jointcommission.org/, for information about the functions of this organization. Accessed April 22, 2012.

32. The Joint Commission, "Standards FAQ: Emergency Management (CAMH/Hospitals)." Retrieved from http://www.jointcommission.org/standards_information/jcfaqdetails.aspx?StandardsFAQId=392&StandardsFAQChapterId=63. Accessed April 26, 2012.

33. L. M. Gehring, "Emergency Management and the 96-Hour Capability Planning Requirement," Joint Commission Resources. Retrieved from http://www.jcrinc.com/. Accessed April 26, 2012.

34. For more detailed information about The Joint Commission's emergency management plans, see D. Manley, *Emergency Management in Health Care: An All Hazards Approach*, 2nd ed. (Oakbrook Terrace, IL: The Joint Commission, 2012).

35. California Hospital Association, "Hospital Emergency Management Checklist." Retrieved from http://www.calhospitalprepare.org/emergency-operations-plan. Accessed April 27, 2012. This site also has a wealth of practical information on disaster planning for hospitals.

36. Office of the Assistant Secretary for Preparedness and Response, *Healthcare Preparedness Capabilities* (Washington, DC: U.S. Department of Health and Human Services, 2012).

37. Ibid., vii.

38. Ibid., 21–23.

39. B. Jennings, "Disaster Planning and Public Health," in *From Birth to Death and Bench to Clinic: The Hastings Center Bioethics Briefing Book for Journalists, Policymakers, and Campaigns*, ed. M. C. Crowley (Garrison, NY: The Hastings Center, 2008), 41–44.

40. Ibid, 43.

41. American Red Cross and Wirthlin Worldwide, "U.S. Public Unprepared," *The Wirthlin Report* 13, no. 5 (2004).

42. American Red Cross, "Prepare your Home and Family." Retrieved from http://www.redcross.org/prepare/location/home-family. Accessed April 27, 2012.

43. Centers for Disease Control, "Learn How to Shelter in Place." Retrieved from http://emergency.cdc.gov/preparedness/shelter/. Accessed April 27, 2012.

44. Redlener, *Americans at Risk*.

45. Ibid.

46. S. Waterman, "Drones over U.S. Get OK by Congress," *The Washington Times*, February 7, 2012. Retrieved from http://www.washingtontimes.com/news/2012/feb/7/coming-to-a-sky-near-you/?page=all. Accessed April 27, 2012.

CHAPTER 22

A New Era of Health Care: The Ethics of Healthcare Reform

Richard L. O'Brien

INTRODUCTION

The U.S. healthcare system is facing its most dramatic change in over 48 years. Full implementation of the Patient Protection and Affordable Care Act (PPACA) and H.R. 4872, the Health Care and Education Reconciliation Act, will create changes that will challenge the current healthcare system in its delivery of and reimbursement for health care and its ability to balance ethical practice and profitability. This chapter presents the history of the current legislation for healthcare reform and the ethical considerations that underlie this action. It also delineates the major features of this new reform legislation and discusses its ability to address the expectations of making American health care more just. It will assist the reader in understanding how ethics relates to PPACA.

HEALTHCARE REFORM IN THE UNITED STATES

In 2010 Congress passed and President Obama signed H.R. 3590, the Patient Protection and Affordable Care Act, and H.R. 4872, the Health Care and Education Reconciliation Act. Together these constitute healthcare reform legislation that represents the culmination of more than a century of efforts to ensure access to high-quality affordable health care for all or most Americans. For most of the 20th century, a desire to ensure access to care for all Americans drove efforts and proposals to reform the healthcare system in the United States. However, in recent decades the problems of quality and cost have assumed equal importance. Thus, access, quality, and cost control constitute the triumvirate mantra of healthcare reform and the intentions of the 2010 legislation, as well as many of the efforts to reform U.S. health care during the past quarter of a century.

There are essentially three ways to provide universal coverage for a population.[1]

- Require private insurance coverage for all by individual or employer mandate (Bismarck model)
- Government owns and provides all required medical services (Beveridge or National Health Service model)
- Government provides health insurance (National Health Insurance model)

The U.S. system is a mixture of these three. Massachusetts has individual and employer mandates to have or provide health insurance; the Veterans Administration, military, and Indian Health Services are government-owned and -operated; and Medicare and Medicaid constitute government-provided insurance.

HEALTH SYSTEM REFORM IN THE 20TH CENTURY

Otto von Bismarck introduced universal health insurance in Germany in 1883. By the early 20th century, essentially all European democracies had "sickness insurance," provided either by government or mandated and provided by labor organizations or guilds, frequently with government subsidy. These plans were primarily intended to protect against wage loss rather than pay the costs of health care. Health care was not very expensive, and if wages were protected, it was affordable. Most of these plans were not truly universal in coverage; they covered workers and, in some instances, those with incomes below a certain level. A few countries, such as Germany, had (nearly) universal coverage.

In Britain, Germany, and Russia, the motives were less altruistic than in some other nations. In those countries, the motive of very conservative governments was to co-opt political positions held by labor, socialist, and communist parties. As medical costs rose and became more difficult to manage on the incomes of most persons during the first half of the 20th century, most European nations evolved from wage protection plans to universal insurance that pays for medical and hospital costs.

Theodore Roosevelt was the first U.S. president to support the concept of universal health insurance. However, no legislation was introduced into Congress during his term (1901–1909). In 1912, he attempted to recapture the presidency as the candidate of the Progressive (Bull Moose) Party. That party's platform included a plank calling for national health insurance, and it was an important part of Roosevelt's presidential campaign. He was not elected.

In 1912, the American Association of Labor Legislation (AALL) created a committee on social welfare, which concentrated on health insurance. In 1914, it recruited physicians to help draft model legislation, which the American Medical Association (AMA) House of Delegates endorsed in 1917. Several states (and one Canadian province) introduced bills based on the model; it was defeated in all with intense opposition from the American Federation of Labor (AFL), state medical societies, the insurance industry, and business interests. Much of the opposition expressed their positions in ideological terms, characterizing the proposed legislation as socialism, socialized medicine, Bolshevism, or Prussian. For many in opposition, the real motives were the threat to income, fear of government controls, or, in the case of the AFL, fear of losing its power to control what benefits its members had. In 1920, the AMA reversed its position from support to opposition, marking the beginning of its opposition to all efforts at reform until the 1990s.

The impetus to provide universal coverage stalled during the 1920s and early 1930s. It was excluded from the Social Security Act (1935) because President Roosevelt was convinced it would cause the defeat of the pension portion of the bill. The Senate introduced a bill that would have enacted government health insurance in 1935, but it went nowhere.

In 1939, Senator Robert Wagner introduced S. 1620, the National Health Act, to create national compulsory health insurance for all employees and their dependents. Benefits were to include physician's services, hospitalization, drugs, and laboratory diagnostic services. Employer and employee contributions, deposited in a health insurance fund, covered the cost of insurance.

If enacted, the plan would have been administered by the states. The bill died in committee. It did not have the full support of President Roosevelt and was strongly opposed by a conservative Congress elected in 1938. World War II also diverted attention from the issue.

The Wagner-Murray-Dingell Bill was introduced in 1943. It would have provided comprehensive medical insurance for people covered by the Social Security program, both working and retired, and needy persons. The plan would have covered doctors' visits, hospital costs, and nursing, laboratory, and dental services. This bill was introduced, with modifications, repeatedly during the next several Congresses, but it never passed.

In 1945, President Truman proposed, in a special message to Congress, a single comprehensive, universal national health insurance plan. In 1946, Senator Wagner introduced a bill to establish national health insurance, but the Republicans had gained control of Congress and the committee killed the bill.

In 1948, universal health insurance was part of the Democratic Party platform and one of the issues on which Truman campaigned most strongly. Public opinion polls at the time showed that 71% of Americans favored universal national health insurance. Truman won and proposed compulsory national health insurance for persons of all ages, financed by a federal payroll tax. Once again, a bill was introduced but never passed. It was opposed by the insurance industry, organized medicine, and political conservatives, the last of which used it to attack the bill's supporters with charges of fostering socialism or communism. Organized medicine compared it to the "socialized medicine" of the United Kingdom. This was misleading. Truman did *not* propose a National Health Service as in the United Kingdom.

The efforts of reformers probably also faltered because of the rapid and pervasive rise of employment-based health insurance. During and in the aftermath of World War II, as employers scrambled for workers in a labor-short market, unions made health insurance one of the most important parts of contract negotiations. At the beginning of World War II, fewer than 10% of Americans had employment-based health insurance. This rose to nearly 50% by 1952. In 1954, premiums became tax deductible. This reduced broad concern for expanding coverage. By 1980, employer coverage had risen to 80%.

In 1960, incremental increases in coverage of the uninsured began, supported by a new set of allies who vote: the elderly. The Kerr-Mills Act, authorizing the federal government to make grants to states to subsidize costs for the elderly "medically indigent," became law. It took another five years and President Johnson's formidable persuasive skills for Medicare, covering all Americans over 65, to be enacted into law. The legislation was vehemently opposed by the AMA, the insurance industry (both commercial carriers and Blue Cross), and politically conservative ideologues. The elderly, organized labor and, interestingly, a segment of the business community that probably saw it as a way to reduce the cost of providing health care for retirees, all supported the legislation. Medicaid, designed to provide care for needy children, was passed in the same Social Security Act of 1965.

Although bitterly opposed by the AMA and the insurance industry, Medicare soon became a boon to both. Physicians were reimbursed for their "usual and customary fees" for providing care for the elderly, hospitals were reimbursed on a cost-plus basis, and insurers were contracted to be fiscal intermediaries for processing and paying provider claims for a population they would have had great difficulty selling insurance to because of risk rating. In spite of these extensions of health coverage, significant fractions of Americans remained uninsured.

In 1971, President Nixon proposed a plan of compulsory employment-based health insurance for all workers and their dependents. It died a quick death when opposed by business and political conservatives who objected to a mandate and by liberals who believed it was not comprehensive enough. From then until the Clinton administration, the main government healthcare agenda was cost control, not access. In 1991 and 1992, Congress introduced a few bills that would have enacted a single-payer universal health insurance or an all-payer system. None received much attention, and none of the bills was reported out of committee.

In 1993, the Clinton administration rolled out the Clinton National Health Security Plan. It mandated employer coverage through purchasing alliances, defined a standard benefits package, relied on premium price competition among private health insurers to control costs, and subsidized premiums for those under 150% of the federal poverty level. Early in the process of development, it had the support of 71% of the public. Immediately after the completed plan was announced, it was supported by about 60% of the public, but by April 1994, public support had dropped to 43%, largely because of the insurance industry's advertising against it.

It was endorsed by several physician groups, including the American Academy of Family Practice, American College of Physicians, American Academy of Pediatrics, American College of Obstetrics and Gynecology, and American Society of Internal Medicine. The AMA supported parts of the plan, objected to others, and neither endorsed nor condemned the plan as a whole. The American College of Surgeons debated and concluded that universal coverage was a good thing but neither endorsed nor opposed the plan. The American Hospital Association also endorsed it. Organized labor was supportive. Some leaders of large corporations expressed support, but the National Association of Manufacturers and the Chamber of Commerce denounced the plan. Intense opposition came from the insurance industry. The bill died in committee in August 1994.[2] In subsequent years, several representatives and senators introduced numerous reform bills, but none was successful.

By 2010, the fraction of the population lacking health insurance had reached more than 16%, a number that has increased steadily since the Census Bureau first began to gather this data in 1980.[3] Employment-based coverage had fallen from a high of 80% in 1980 to about 55% in 2010, largely because rising costs have made it less affordable for employers and employees, and the fraction of the population eligible for Medicare has increased substantially.[4]

Access to health care is compromised by shortages of professionals in many rural areas and inner cities. The Bureau of Health Professions publishes lists of health professional shortage areas.[5] Costs have continued to rise at a rate far surpassing the growth of the economy and family incomes.[6] The United States has the most expensive health care of all OECD (Organization for Economic Cooperation and Development) nations, both in terms of per capita expense and as a share of GDP (gross domestic product). The United States spends more than twice as much per capita as the OECD median.[7] This high expenditure does not buy high-quality care. Numerous studies show significant lapses in the quality of care delivered.[8–11]

Rising numbers of the uninsured, quality lapses, and rising costs have given impetus to recent efforts to reform the system with three goals in mind:

- Greater access to care
- Improved quality
- Cost control

Early in 2009, the 111th Congress of the United States began to consider a number of healthcare reform bills introduced by both the House and the Senate. After a great deal of debate and a number of compromises, Congress passed H.R. 3590 (Public Law 111-148), the Patient Protection and Affordable Care Act (PPACA), and H.R. 4872 (Public Law 111-152), the Health Care and Education Reconciliation Act, in March 2010. The bulk of the legislation is contained in PPACA, and that is the reform legislation discussed later in this chapter.

ETHICAL CONSIDERATIONS UNDERLYING HEALTHCARE REFORM

What underlying ethical assumptions have driven healthcare reform efforts for the last 100 years? Most persons and societies have concluded that there is a fundamental right to health care. This is declared in a number of international agreements, including the Universal Declaration of Human Rights (Article 25),[12] the Constitution of the World Health Organization (p. 1),[13] the American Declaration of the Rights and Duties of Man (Article 11),[14] the International Covenant on Economic, Social and Cultural Rights (Article 12),[15] the UNESCO Declaration on Bioethics and Human Rights (Article 14),[16] the Convention on the Rights of the Child (Article 24),[17] and the Convention on the Rights of Persons with Disabilities (Article 25).[18]

The preamble of the U.S. Declaration of Independence begins with the sentence "We hold these truths to be self-evident, that all men are created equal, that they are endowed by their Creator with certain unalienable Rights, that among these are Life, Liberty and the pursuit of Happiness."[19] The interpretation of this sentence is usually that access to health care is a right because it is necessary to attain the declared rights of "Life, Liberty and the pursuit of Happiness."[20] Further, the American public generally subscribes to such a right. Public opinion polls have found that 70% to 89% of Americans have supported universal health insurance coverage or health care at least since 1948. However, not everyone subscribes to the view that health care is a right.[21] Various religious traditions, including Roman Catholics, Anglican/Episcopalians, Baptists, Methodists, Jews, and Muslims, also hold health care as a right.[22–28]

Some argue that health and health care are social goods, that is, that the health of individuals is good for society and all of its members. This is a kind of contractarianism[29] or communitarianism.[30] A social contract binds us because we live in a communal society in which the good of individuals is beneficial for society as a whole. Healthy people contribute to a good society and a sound economy.

As a nation we have made a compact with each other to strive to create an environment that is in the best interests of each of us and all of us. If we believe that health and health care are good for us, then we have a duty to provide it for all. Thus, it is reasonable to expect that a well-structured healthcare system will provide access to affordable, high-quality care for all.[31]

KEY PROVISIONS OF THE HEALTHCARE REFORM LEGISLATION OF 2010 (PPACA)

The following list provides a summary of the key provisions of PPACA as it currently exists.[32]

- There is a requirement for all Americans and legal immigrants to have health insurance coverage or pay a penalty (with some exemptions for financial hardship and religious belief). Businesses are also required to provide health insurance coverage or pay a penalty (businesses with 50 or fewer employees are exempted). Households with incomes of up to 400% of the poverty level are provided subsidies for premium support and out-of-pocket expenses. Small businesses will receive tax credits to offset the costs of employee coverage.

- There is an extension of Medicaid eligibility to all persons, including childless adults, with incomes at or below 133% of the federal poverty level.

- It improves Medicare benefits by providing preventive care with no copayments and lower drug prices for Medicare Drug Plan (Part D) participants, and there will be a gradual elimination of the Part D coverage gap.

- There is substantial insurance reform. Insurers are required to offer a federally defined benefit plan and guarantee issue and renewal with limited risk rating; coverage cannot be denied to anyone. There can be no annual or lifetime limits on benefits. In addition, insurers must provide preventive care with no copayment. Insurers are also required to have minimum loss ratios of 80% for individual and small group coverage and 85% for large group coverage. States can receive financial assistance to set up state-based insurance exchanges where individuals and small businesses may shop for insurance offered by private insurers. If any states decline to set up exchanges, the federal government will provide one.

- There is substantial support for efforts to improve quality, including support of comparative effectiveness research, support for the integration and coordination of healthcare services, and incentive payments to providers based on quality measures.

- To provide a balanced health professions workforce, to ensure adequate numbers of primary care providers, and to induce providers to practice in underserved areas, substantial incentives in the form of scholarships, loan forgiveness, bonus payments, and higher Medicare and Medicaid payments are offered.

- A combination of new taxes, savings, and penalties assessed on those who choose not to comply with the law will provide funding. There will be a tax assessment on high-cost "Cadillac" health plans. Increased Medicare taxes are assessed on individuals with incomes more than $200,000 and families with incomes higher than $250,000. Insurers, pharmaceutical companies, and medical device companies are also assessed taxes. Savings will be achieved by special efforts to enforce laws against fraud and abuse, especially in Medicare and Medicaid, by reduction of hospital readmissions, and by administrative efficiencies in claims processing. Additional savings will come from reduction of payments to Medicare Advantage Plans to bring them more in line with the costs of regular Medicare and from reduction of disproportionate share payments because there will be fewer uninsured. Because of increased revenues and reduced expenditures, the Congressional Budget Office has estimated that PPACA will reduce the deficit by $143 billion over the first 10 years after enactment.[33]

The following are the changes scheduled to be phased in gradually from 2010 to 2020. For purposes of clarity, the year of enactment is used for their presentation.

- 2010: Insurers may not deny children coverage because of preexisting conditions. In addition, young adults up to age 26 can be covered by their parents' health plans. By late 2011, this had resulted in 2.5 million newly covered young adults. Insurers may not rescind health insurance coverage except in cases of intentional fraud. There can be no annual or lifetime limits on coverage. Insurance companies cannot charge copayments for preventive care. Tax credits are available to small employers providing employee health coverage. Participants are provided with rebates of $250 in the Medicare Part D Drug Benefit program if they fall into the coverage gap. A number of incentives are provided to improve healthcare workforce makeup and location. These include scholarships and loan forgiveness programs for health professionals choosing primary care, as well as other health professions training grants for professionals providing services to underserved populations. Grants are also established to support comparative effectiveness and prevention research and service.

- 2011: Copayments for Medicare preventive services, including an annual comprehensive risk assessment and prevention plan, are phased out. There is a 50% discount on brand-name prescriptions filled during the Part D coverage gap. Primary care physicians and general surgeons practicing in health professions shortage areas receive a 10% Medicare and Medicaid bonus. Funding for community health centers increases. Insurers must have minimum loss ratios of 80% (small group and nongroup) to 85% (large group). There will be an institution of increased primary care training opportunities for health professionals, including grants for nurse practitioner training. Wellness program grants are available to small employers.

- 2012: Performance- and efficiency-based Medicare payments to providers are begun. There will be bonus payments to high-quality Medicare Advantage plans.

- 2013: Simplified and uniform insurance claims processing and payment are introduced. There is a phase-in of federal subsidies to close the Part D coverage gap. In addition, there is an increased Medicaid payment for primary care.

- 2014: All citizens and legal residents are required to have health coverage through employers, individually purchased plans, Medicaid, or Medicare or pay a penalty (phased in over several years). State-based health benefit exchanges for individuals and small business (fewer than 100 employees) are established. All insurers are required to offer the essential benefits package. Insurers are required to guarantee issue and renewal. Insurers' differences in premiums based on age are limited to 3:1; tobacco users may be charged 50% higher premiums than nonusers. Deductibles are limited to $2,000 per individual or $4,000 per family. Subsidies for premiums are provided to those with incomes from 133% to 400% of the federal poverty level, and subsidies for out-of-pocket expenses are provided for those with incomes of up to 400% of the federal poverty level. Employers with more than 50 employees are required to offer coverage at least equivalent to the prescribed benefit plan or to pay into a pool to help subsidize individual insurance purchases from the exchanges. Employers of more than 200 employees are required to enroll employees automatically in employer-provided coverage (although employees may opt out and buy coverage on the exchanges). Medicaid eligibility expands to everyone under 65 with incomes up to 133% of the federal poverty level. The size of the coverage gap in Medicare Part D is reduced (the coverage gap should be eliminated in 2020).
- 2016: States may form interstate compacts allowing insurers to sell across state lines.
- 2018: Taxes are imposed on "Cadillac" health care plans with annual costs of more than $10,200 for individual coverage and $27,500 for family coverage (indexed to 2010-dollar purchasing power).
- 2020: There is a phase-out of the Medicare Part D coverage gap (doughnut hole).

HOW WELL DO THE REFORMS MEET THE EXPECTATIONS OF A JUST HEALTHCARE SYSTEM?

If a just healthcare system provides access to high-quality affordable care for all in need of it, how well does PPACA fare in increasing access, improving quality, and controlling costs? It is expected to do all of these, at least in part. The reforms address access by greatly increasing the number of Americans who have health insurance. More than 30 million persons without health insurance will acquire coverage. It also establishes means to increase the supply and professional distribution of healthcare providers to meet the needs of the newly insured and to deliver services in underserved areas. In addition, it addresses the quality of care by supporting comparative effectiveness research, providing incentives for organized delivery systems to ensure integration and coordination of care, and rewarding providers based on the quality of care provided.

PPACA addresses affordability by insurance reform (80% and 85% minimum loss ratios), subsidies for low- and middle-income persons and families, support of prevention efforts, increased system efficiencies, and enhanced efforts to reduce fraud and abuse. It is reasonably anticipated that at least some health professional shortage areas will see increased numbers of providers and that community health centers will be able to serve more persons. In addition, it is reasonable to expect that incentives for quality and comparative effectiveness research will have some impact on the quality of care.

However, PPACA clearly falls short in some areas. It will still leave approximately 18 to 20 million Americans uninsured, including about 5 million undocumented immigrants, about 3 million persons exempted from the requirement to buy insurance because of financial hardship, and about 7 million low-income adults eligible for Medicaid but not enrolled. The remainder are likely to have chosen to pay the penalty for not having coverage rather than pay the premiums.[34]

Only time will tell if other of its initiatives will be as effective as desired. It remains to be seen how effective the workforce incentives and quality initiatives will be. PPACA is projected to slow the cost growth of health care, but costs are projected to continue to rise faster than the GDP and inflation in general.[35] Although it delays the date at which the Medicare Hospital Trust fund is depleted (which would be 2017 without reform), the fund is still projected to be depleted by 2024.[36] Thus, it seems likely that we will be revisiting and fine-tuning healthcare reform efforts for some time to come. In June 2012, the Supreme Court handed down its decision finding the mandate constitutional under Congress's taxing power and upholding the expansion of Medicaid but not permitting the imposition of penalties on the states by the federal government if they did not comply with such expansion.

SUMMARY

Health care will change on many levels because of the enactment of the Patient Protection and Affordable Care Act and H.R. 4872, the Health Care and Education Reconciliation Act. Almost every part of the healthcare system will be examining how it provides patient care and addresses the costs of this care. This chapter provided an important look at the history of healthcare reform so that we can better understand why there was a need for this monumental change. It also reviewed the key features of PPACA (the primary legislation) to foster understanding. Finally, it began to address the critical issue of justice and healthcare reform—an issue that will be part of health care as the PPACA era continues.

QUESTIONS FOR DISCUSSION

1. The history of health care is very different in the United States than it is in Europe. What ethical principles apply to reform efforts in the United States prior to Medicare/Medicaid?

2. What principles of ethics are evident in the Medicare/Medicaid laws?

3. Justice is often viewed differently by different groups of people. Consider PPACA. How is justice defined by the following: physicians, insurance companies, the currently uninsured, well-insured Americans, and those who are in poor health?

FOOD FOR THOUGHT

It is 2014 and you are a physician with a small practice in Blueberry Hill, Texas. Many of your patients are now Medicaid recipients, and you have a growing Medicare patient group. The community of Blueberry Hill respects you as a physician with great integrity. Given the PPACA changes, answer the following questions:

1. What practice issues do you face?

2. What ethical concerns do you have with respect to PPACA and your practice?

3. How will you keep your status as an ethics-based physician in the community?

NOTES

1. T. R. Reid, *The Healing of America: A Global Quest for Better, Cheaper, and Fairer Health Care* (New York: Penguin Press, 2009), 16–27.

2. The author used the following sources to compile the history recounted in this chapter: R. A. Stevens, "History and Health Policy in the United States, 1948–2008," *Social History of Medicine* 21, no 3 (2008): 461–483; J. S. Ross, "The Committee on the Costs of Medical Care and the History of Health Insurance in the United States," *Einstein Quarterly Journal of Biology and Medicine* 19 (2002): 129–134; and K. A. Palmer, "A Brief History: Universal Health Care Efforts in the US," *Physicians for a National Health Program* (Spring, 1999). Retrieved from http://www.pnhp.org/facts/a_brief_history_universal_health_care_efforts_in_the_us.php?page=all. Accessed May 14, 2012.

3. C. DeNavas-Walt, B. D. Proctor, and J. C. Smith, *Income Poverty and Insurance Coverage in the United States: 2010*, Current Population Reports P60-239 (Washington, DC: U.S. Government Printing Office, 2011).

4. Ibid.

5. Health Resources and Service Administration, "Shortage Designation: Health Professional Shortage Areas and Medically Underserved Areas/Populations." Retrieved from http://bhpr.hrsa.gov/shortage/index.html.

6. C. J. Truffer, S. Keehan, S. Smith, et al., "Health Spending Projections Through 2019," *Health Affairs* 29, no. 3 (2010): 1–8.

7. Organization for Economic Cooperation and Development, "OECD Health Data 2011." Retrieved from http://www.oecd-ilibrary.org/social-issues-migration-health/public-health-spending_20743904-table4. Accessed May 14, 2012. The OECD is a group of 34 mostly developed countries with the goal "to promote policies that will improve the economic and social well-being of people around the world." It collects extensive statistical data from its members.

8. L. T. Kohn, J. M. Corrigan, and M. S. Donaldson, *To Err Is Human* (Washington, DC: National Academy Press, 1999).

9. E. A. McGlynn, S. M. Asch, J. Adams, et al., "Quality of Care Delivered to Adults in the United States," *New England Journal of Medicine* 348, no. 26 (2003): 2635–2645.

10. S. C. Williams, S. P. Schmaltz, D. J. Morton, R. G. Koss, and J. M. Loeb, "Quality of Care in U.S. Hospitals as Reflected by Standardized Measures," *New England Journal of Medicine* 353, no. 3 (2005): 255–264.

11. R. Mangione-Smith, A. H. DeCristofaro, C. M. Setodji, et al., "Quality of Ambulatory Care Delivered to Children in the United States," *New England Journal of Medicine* 357, no. 15 (2007): 1515–1523.

12. The United Nations, "Universal Declaration of Human Rights." Adopted by the General Assembly of the United Nations, resolution 217 A (III), 10 December 1948. Retrieved from http://www.un.org/en/documents/udhr/index.shtml. Accessed May 14, 2012.

13. The World Health Organization, "Constitution of the World Health Organization," *American Journal of Public Health Nations Health* 36, no. 11 (1948): 1315–1323.

14. The Organization of American States, *American Declaration of the Rights and Duties of Man* (Bogota, Columbia: The Organization of American States, 1948). Retrieved from http://www .hrcr.org/docs/OAS_Declaration/oasrights.html. Accessed May 14, 2012.

15. The General Assembly of the United Nations, *International Covenant on Economic, Social, and Cultural Rights* (New York: The United Nations, 1966).

16. United Nations Educational, Scientific, and Cultural Organization, *Universal Declaration on Bioethics and Human Rights* (Paris, France: United Nations Educational, Scientific, and Cultural Organization, 2005). Retrieved from http://unesdoc.unesco.org/images/0014/ 001461/146180E.pdf. Accessed May 14, 2012.

17. The General Assembly of the United Nations, *Convention on the Rights of the Child* (New York: The United Nations, 1989).

18. The General Assembly of the United Nations, *Convention on the Rights of Persons with Disabilities* (New York: The United Nations, 2006).

19. See *The Declaration of Independence: A Transcription*. Retrieved from http://www.archives .gov/exhibits/charters/declaration_transcript.html. Accessed May 6, 2012.

20. Ibid.

21. B. H. Baumrin, "Why There Is No Right to Health Care," in *Medicine and Social Justice*, eds. R. Rhodes, M. P. Battin, and A. Silvers (New York: Oxford University Press, 2002), 78–83.

22. General Board of the Baptist Churches, "American Baptist Policy Statement on Human Rights," 1976; modified 1992. Retrieved from http://www.abc-usa.org/LinkClick.aspx?filetic ket=8gLU4H3BXuE%3d&tabid=199. Accessed May 14, 2012.

23. The United Methodist Church, "Social Principles of the United Methodist Church, 2009–2012." Retrieved from http://www.umcsc.org/PDF/boards/SocialPrinciples.pdf. Accessed May 14, 2012.

24. United State Catholic Conference, *Health and Health Care. A Pastoral Letter of the American Catholic Bishops* (Washington, DC: United States Catholic Conference, 1981). Retrieved from http://old.usccb.org/sdwp/national/HEALTH.PDF. Accessed May 14, 2012.

25. R. T. Alpert, "The Jewish Tradition and the Right to Health Care," *Reconstructionist* (April–May 1984): 15–20.

26. Union for Reform Judaism, "59th General Assembly Resolution on Health Care," 1987. Retrieved from http://urj.org//about/union/governance/reso//?syspage=article&item_id=2081. Accessed May 14, 2012.

27. Episcopal Church USA, "Right of All Persons to Comprehensive Health Care," General Convention (A010) and (A099) Resolution, 1991.

28. M. H. Al-Khayat, *Health as a Human Right in Islam* (Cairo, Egypt: Regional Office for the Eastern Mediterranean, World Health Organization, 2004).

29. A. Cudd, "Contractarianism," Stanford Encyclopedia of Philosophy, 2008. Retrieved from http://plato.stanford.edu/entries/contractarianism/. Accessed December 2, 2012.

30. D. Bell, "Communitarianism," Stanford Encyclopedia of Philosophy, 2010. Retrieved from http://plato.stanford.edu/entries/communitarianism/. Accessed December 2, 2012.

31. For a more detailed description of ethicists' consensus about what healthcare reform legislation should do, see M. A. Levine, M. K. Wynia, P. M. Schyve, et al., "Improving Access to Health Care: A Consensus Ethical Framework to Guide Proposal for Reform," *Hastings Center Report* 37 (September–October, 2007): 14–19.

32. A very good, more extensive summary of the legislation can be found at the Kaiser Family Foundation Health Reform website, at http://www.kff.org/healthreform/upload/8061.pdf .

33. Congressional Budget Office, letter to Speaker Pelosi, March 20, 2010. Retrieved from http:// www.cbo.gov/ftpdocs/113xx/doc11379/AmendReconProp.pdf. Accessed January 10, 2012.

34. M. Buettgens and M. A. Hall, "Who Will Be Uninsured After Health Insurance Reform?" March 2011. Retrieved from http://www.urban.org/UploadedPDF/1001520-Uninsured-After-Health-Insurance-Reform.pdf.

35. Truffer et al., "Health Spending Projections Through 2019."

36. The Board of Trustees of the Federal Hospital Insurance and Federal Supplementary Medical Insurance Trust Funds, *2011 Annual Report of the Board of Trustees of the Federal Hospital Insurance and Federal Supplementary Medical Insurance Trust Funds* (Washington, DC: Federal Hospital Insurance and Federal Supplementary Medical Insurance Trust Funds, 2011). Retrieved from http://heartland.org/sites/all/modules/custom/heartland_migration/files/pdfs/30102.pdf. Accessed May 14, 2012.

CHAPTER 23

Healthcare Reform: What About Those Left Behind?

Beth Furlong

INTRODUCTION

This chapter examines the populations not covered in healthcare reform and analyzes the ethical issues related to these omissions. The relevant populations are (1) immigrants who are not documented, (2) individuals who are eligible for Medicaid but who may not be enrolled, and (3) those exempted from purchasing insurance because of the financial burden it poses. It is the stance of this author that the lack of healthcare access for these populations is unjust and unethical. Disparities and inequalities in healthcare access remain, and these disparities affect the most vulnerable populations in the United States. This author's stance strongly reflects an evaluation of ethical theories applied to a population's health status, her four decades of public health nursing, a commitment to the Code of Ethics of the American Nurses Association (ANA) and the Standards of Practice of the ANA, as well as a commitment to the advocacy role of professional nurses (with special emphasis on advocacy for the vulnerable).[1,2] The author invites readers from nursing and other health professions to evaluate her arguments in the context of their analysis of ethical theories, particular education, socialization, lived experiences, professional codes of ethics, and standards of practice.

It is the evaluation of this author that nurses and health professionals have an ethical obligation to be policy advocates for vulnerable populations. In particular, the three populations addressed in this chapter are the three groups identified by O'Brien as the populations who will not or may not receive coverage through health insurance reform.[3] In addition, this chapter discusses the differences in states' Medicaid policies and how they affect individuals. Thus, this chapter will discuss three aspects of the author's thesis. The first aspect is that noncoverage is unethical. This discussion is followed by ethical analyses of this stance and examples of policy advocacy that apply such ethical analyses.

The chapter includes several case studies that exemplify some of the populations not covered by access to health insurance. A caveat in reading this chapter is that it was written in fall 2011 and winter of early 2012, knowing that the Supreme Court would make decisions on all or part of the Patient Protection and Affordable Care Act (PPACA) of 2010 in early summer 2012. Healthcare legislation and policy may change by the time of the publication of this book. Regardless whether there is a policy change in later 2012 or in 2013 because of the Supreme Court decision or because of national elections, this chapter lays a foundational context that enables the reader to reflect and evaluate his or her stance on these issues.

ETHICAL ANALYSIS BY FOUR MAJOR PRINCIPLES

The four principles of ethics articulated by Beauchamp and Childress—namely, nonmaleficence, beneficence, autonomy versus paternalism, and distributive justice—are applied in the analysis in this section.[4,5]

Nonmaleficence

The analysis begins with the concept of nonmaleficence, or the necessity of avoiding harm, which could be considered to be the highest priority ethical principle of the healthcare system. A system that does not provide health insurance coverage for people who cannot afford it does harm to those individuals. Many indicators illustrate the increased morbidity, mortality, and decreased quality of living experienced by such individuals.[6] This is harm.

One theoretical way of understanding this is using the systemic advantage/disadvantage theory.[7] The essence of this theory is that some populations and some individuals, in a systemic manner, receive either more advantages or disadvantages over their lives than other populations and individuals. Included in this system is whether one receives or does not receive a quality education, a job, health insurance with a job, and so on. This, then, has either a positive or a negative synergistic effect on a person's quality of life. A current exemplar case study follows, which is reflective of some of the individuals to whom O'Brien referred.[8]

An educated, middle-class, Caucasian citizen in her early 60s with several major chronic illnesses, a need for two major orthopedic surgeries, and with an unemployment history only in recent years, is relieved that she will become age-eligible for Medicare in March 2012 so she can better address her health needs and needed surgeries (R. Ramaley, personal communication, January 15, 2012). Her individual story of now being poor (having used up her savings because of recent years' unemployment), without a job, and without health insurance will be repeated by some future individuals who will remain without healthcare access. Although she became age-eligible for Medicare in March 2012, there are others who mirror her story and are part of the 3 million population O'Brien discussed, that is, those who are exempt from the requirement to buy insurance because of financial hardship.[9] In summary, the PPACA (because it does not provide coverage for all) is doing harm to those individuals and populations who are not able to access health insurance. Besides the ethical precept of avoiding harm, another principle to evaluate is that of beneficence.

Beneficence

When the three populations are not covered, the ethical principle of beneficence cannot be met. There is no benefit for those populations, who are poor and already at social, economic, and educational disadvantage. A major population that does not receive coverage is that of undocumented immigrants. One can evaluate the concept of beneficence and extend the analysis beyond the individual who is not documented to the larger population of the United States.

For example, in addition to vulnerable populations not being benefited, it can be argued that the total U.S. population is not benefited. There are three arguments that one can raise that relate to (1) prevention of communicable diseases, (2) cost control of the healthcare system, and (3) the economic development of the society.

In making arguments for the first variable, that of prevention of communicable diseases, one notes that immigrants come from many parts of the world and have had varied life, health, and illness experiences before they arrive in this country. Many have lived for years in refugee camps. Some of these experiences could include having communicable diseases and being at risk of transmitting these diseases to the larger general U.S. population. The countries from whence they came may also have endemic infectious diseases not normally seen in the United States. Thus, in this communicable disease example, both from beneficence and nonmaleficence arguments, neither the individual immigrants nor the U.S. population as a whole benefits by denying health care to individuals who are undocumented. In addition, one can argue that additional harm is caused to both the individuals affected and the general U.S. population. Thus, for one set of illnesses, communicable diseases, not providing access to health care causes harm to the undocumented patient, his or her family, and the community in which he or she lives.

When a population does not have healthcare access, the cost to the health system is most likely increased. For example, in some situations, an ill undocumented individual will present at a health system setting and be treated, and the incurred costs and expenses will have to be paid by someone. Because of EMTALA (the Emergency Medical Treatment and Active Labor Act) legislation, which governs legal authority over care in emergency rooms, patients must receive care. The cost to individual health systems and to the aggregate U.S. healthcare system may well be more expensive with this "later model" of health service delivery. Therefore, such a policy also includes a second variable (lack of cost control of the health system) when it excludes certain people.

In reference to the third variable mentioned earlier, economic development, there is an argument that a healthy population and workforce enhances economic development. Individuals who are not documented contribute to the economic sector of society; they, like any other workers, are able to contribute more productively to a society if they are healthy and able to work. Thus, all three variables further a stance calling for the availability of health insurance access for all populations, including those who are not documented.

However, even more importantly for the population of individuals who are labeled and framed as "undocumented individuals," this author believes that harm is done to such individuals by the very categorization. Beneficence is lacking because there is a basic nonrespect of the individual when a person is evaluated, labeled, and framed by a "paper status." In this example, as in other aspects of global phenomena, first a person becomes an object, and then he or she experiences violence. In this case, the violence is related to a total evaluation of objectifying "who a person is" by his or her documentation status. The violence is extended when access is denied to what some people see as a basic life necessity. This is a lack of basic respect for another individual. No one (including this chapter's reader) wants to be labeled, characterized, and judged on just one aspect of his or her life, such as documentation status. The author will analyze this demonstration of nonrespect to another individual from other ethical perspectives in other sections of this chapter.

Case Study Analysis: A Population In Need of Renal Dialysis

The following case study example presents a very current ethical concern in the United States regarding one subset of the undocumented population, namely, those who need renal dialysis. When this population is not covered, the principle of beneficence is violated because of the negative illness status of these undocumented individuals who have need for consistent renal dialysis. In addition, there is harm to these individuals. Thus, there is a lack of practice of both of these ethical concerns with this particular population of ill individuals. The issue discussed here is a major healthcare system issue that is unresolved, and it will continue that way under current PPACA policy.

Individuals with kidney disease need dialysis three times weekly.[10] Although some hospitals and their respective departments will donate twice-weekly dialysis, this decreased schedule results in increased morbidity, increased cost to the healthcare system because of the deteriorating health of the patient, illness consequences, increased hospitalizations, and so on.[11] Campbell, Sanoff, and Rosner have characterized these concerns for this population of patients as delivery of substandard care, along with illness care expenditures that exceed those for parallel-case U.S. citizens receiving standard renal care.[12] In addition, health providers are not taking opportunities to administer cost-saving and life-extending interventions; there is cost shifting that affects selected, but not all, health providers and health systems; and there are the ethical dilemmas of nonmaleficence, beneficence, social justice, and truth telling by health providers, among others.[13] This case is an example of these concerns in several ways. Further concerns include the following: (1) an estimated population of 5,500 individuals affected, (2) an estimated total cost of $383 million, (3) inconsistent state Medicaid policies for reimbursement, (4) inconsistent case law rulings that leave health providers unable to do future planning, and (5) worse morbidity, quality of life, and mortality outcomes for this population compared with the parallel citizen population.[14]

Case Study Analysis: A Population of Women Who Are Pregnant and Undocumented

For this author, another policy of concern is her state's policy of denial of Medicaid reimbursement for health care to women who are pregnant and undocumented. This change in policy occurred two years ago. However, in spring 2012, the Nebraska unicameral passed legislation to again provide prenatal reimbursement. One important variable was the intense lobbying by a coalition of organizations.

In November 2009, the Nebraska Health and Human Services was notified by the U.S. Health and Human Services of a needed Medicaid reimbursement change. Utilization of the State Children's Insurance Program reimbursement account could have easily satisfied the required change—this was how other states had addressed a similar problem. However, based on the governor's wishes, this was not the way that the change was made. Instead, in March 2010, Medicaid no longer paid reimbursement of health care of women who were pregnant and undocumented. In spring 2010, 2011, and again in 2012, a bill was introduced in the Nebraska unicameral to provide Medicaid reimbursement for such women. The bill did not pass in 2010 or 2011, but, as noted previously, was successful in 2012.

The outcomes of this 2010 policy change were as follows: (1) 1,600 women were denied payment of prenatal care, (2) there were five infant deaths, (3) women reported delaying or not seeking prenatal health care, (4) women reported increased seeking of abortions, (5) care of some of these women was provided by physicians and nurse practitioners in federally funded community health centers and private practices, and (6) the need for private donations to the health services to pay expenses for such patients increased. This policy was not an isolated occurrence. For example, in spring 2010 anti-immigrant legislation was introduced in the state unicameral, and an anti-immigrant ordinance was introduced in a small town. Both of these initiatives related to housing, employment, and identification policies.

These case examples are a few of the many concerns of populations without health insurance. The major discussion needs to be why and how the exclusion of 18 to 20 million individuals from access to health insurance coverage does not result in benefits to the affected population or to the total U.S. population. Besides the ethical precepts of nonmaleficence and beneficence, one must consider the ethical precept of autonomy versus paternalism. The following section addresses this important precept.

Autonomy versus Paternalism

The third basic principle discussed by Beauchamp and Childress is whether one practices autonomy or paternalism in one's relationship with a patient.[15] Although generally this tension traditionally has been between the physician, health provider, or health organization and the individual patient or family, one can extend the same concept to the tension between a policy maker and the individual patient. The tension could also include a health provider who is an advocate for the patient. Policy makers have taken on a paternalistic role in their decisions about who has access to health insurance coverage and who does not. This author is one of many health providers and lay individuals who argue against such paternalism when the decisions harm or do not benefit the patient and family.

The author acknowledges that some health providers do not implement such paternalistic policy decisions, but rather provide health care for individuals. Such health providers implement health care in the face of negative policy directives and with no financial reimbursement. They recognize that to be true to the ethics of their practices, they must deliver health care. Some physicians and nurse practitioners in community health centers and in private clinics in Nebraska provided access to health care for the undocumented women denied access by state law and intentionally countered the state's barrier directives. The health providers did this by using donated funds to their organizations and other strategies.

In such cases (with the Nebraska case study as only one exemplar), health providers responded to what they understood as their professional and ethical mandates rather than following strict policy directives. Thus, when policy directives mandate certain stances, a health provider's socialization, professional education, standards of practice, and code of ethics will cause some (although certainly not all) health providers to provide care. This author furthers the argument that evaluation of ethical theories should include an analysis of the ethical precept of autonomy. In summary, the paternalism of policy makers can be problematic for patients' health status and for the ethical choices of health providers.

Distributive Justice

Finally, the fourth ethical principle of Beauchamp and Childress is that of distributive justice.[16] Noncoverage of the three major populations outlined by O'Brien does not meet the principle of distributive justice.[17] Some vulnerable populations are excluded. Further, the reader is encouraged to note the major indicators O'Brien listed regarding global comparisons of coverage and health indicators among the United States and other countries.[18] In essence, the non-inclusion of these three populations is the opposite of distributive justice. The justice question becomes even more acute when one considers that the United States is not only a First World country but also a global economic leader and a country that is far richer than many other countries. One could argue that with such economic resources, one has even a greater capacity for commitment to caring for the most vulnerable populations.

ETHICAL CODES

One reason denial of healthcare access for some populations is not ethical is because it violates the codes of ethics for many health providers. Because this author is a nurse, she will analyze the code of ethics formulated by the ANA. Student readers of other health professions are encouraged to read their codes and to do similar reflective analyses. It is the evaluation and strong conviction of this author that health providers' socialization, professional education, and living of their professional code of ethics and standards of practice will take priority for them as they practice their profession and care for patients. At the minimum, policy directives that result in nonaccess cause great tension for health providers in practicing their profession, following their code of ethics, and applying standards of practice.

There are three important guidelines for the professional nurse: the ANA Code of Ethics, ANA's Social Policy Statement, and the ANA and other specialty associations' standards of practice.[19,20] Nurses are held responsible for following these three guidelines. If a nurse were liable in either a civil or a criminal law situation, these are the basic guidelines to which the nurse would be held legally, professionally, and ethically liable and accountable. The Social Policy Statement reminds nurses of their accountability to the social concerns that permeate both health care and nursing.[21] Nurses are also held to a responsibility of care for all individuals and to be a part of solving problems that result in lack of healthcare access for all.

Ethical Analysis Using a Code of Ethics

Five of the nine provisions of the ANA Code of Ethics relate to a professional nurse's ethical responsibility to promote access to health care for all individuals. The eighth provision states, "The nurse collaborates with other health professionals and the public in promoting community, national, and international efforts to meet health needs."[22] Each provision is followed by interpretative statements. Of specific concern to this chapter and the stances that this author promotes is the following interpretative statement: "The nursing profession is committed to promoting the health, welfare, and safety of all people."[23] The author directs the reader to the last two words of this statement: "all people." This inclusivity is the antithesis of not being committed to caring for vulnerable populations such as those with undocumented status or certain populations who are low income and will not be covered by Medicaid in the future.

An interpretative statement for this provision further notes the responsibility of the professional nurse to not only care for an individual patient but also to be educated on the larger health concerns of the world; one of these concerns is the lack of access to health care. Following such awareness and education, nurses then have the responsibility of participating in strategies (cross-disciplinary planning and collaborative partnerships) to address problems for which a solution is needed. Again, nurses' strategies address the issue of nurses working for all patients (as opposed to only certain patients). If nurses plan to meet this provision of their code of ethics, they have an ethical responsibility to ensure access for all.

The ninth provision of the ANA Code of Ethics promotes such responsibility from a different perspective: "The profession of nursing, as represented by associations and their members, is responsible for articulating nursing values, for maintaining the integrity of the profession and its practice, and for shaping social policy."[24] The important point related to this chapter is that of the nurse's role in shaping social policy. This chapter includes some case studies and content relative to policy interventions by nurses (by implication, things all health professionals could do) because this author considers this to be a professional responsibility of all health professionals.

One interpretative statement notes that nurses affect social policy as individuals, through their professional nursing associations, and through civic, policy, and political actions. This statement reminds nurses that the definition of health involves more than the individual patient and more than delivery and financial systems; it also includes such issues as the violation of human rights. This author promotes the stance that labeling patients by their immigration status violates a basic human right, objectifies a person, and constitutes a type of interpersonal violence.

A third provision that relates to this chapter's content is provision 7: "The nurse participates in the advancement of the profession through contributions to practice, education, administration, and knowledge development."[25] An interpretative statement for this provision again emphasizes the nurse's responsibility in shaping policy.

Another applicable provision is provision 2: "The nurse's primary commitment is to the patient, whether an individual, family, group, or community."[26]

This commitment does not exclude certain patients because of their immigration status or income level. Finally, provision 1 states that "[t]he nurse, in all professional relationships, practices with compassion and respect for the inherent dignity, worth, and uniqueness of every individual, unrestricted by considerations of social or economic status, personal attributes, or the nature of health problems."[27] The first interpretative statement supporting this provision reinforces a basic element of this provision, namely, a respect for the inherent dignity of each individual. This is parallel to the basic concept of deontology. This author advances the argument that if one is committed to practicing respect for the inherent dignity of each individual, then one should work for access to health care for all. A nurse does not give care to only some populations, but to all populations.

ETHICAL ANALYSIS USING DEONTOLOGIC THEORY

The previous analysis of healthcare reform used the four main ethical principles as articulated by Beauchamp and Childress and the health provider's professional code of ethics. Another ethical theory to use for such an analysis is deontologic theory.[28] Again, the denial of access to health insurance for any individual—particularly a vulnerable individual or vulnerable populations—demonstrates a basic nonrespect for the dignity of the human being. One aspect of Kant's categorical imperative is that one should have equal respect for both someone else and oneself and should never use another person or treat another person as a means to one's end.[29] This author argues that to be respectful to another human being, one cannot label and deny services to people based on their immigration documentation. Further, one conclusion is that immigrants who are not documented are being used for their economic contributions to a society but are not being respected and assisted with health services. From this author's analysis, application of the deontologic concept of following a moral duty means that health care should be provided for the population of undocumented individuals.

ETHICAL ANALYSIS USING UTILITARIAN THEORY

Some will argue for insurance coverage for the three uncovered populations by using a utilitarian argument. The most concise statement of this ethical theory is to practice behavior that results in the greatest good for the largest population. Opposing arguments can be made as to what constitutes the greatest good and the largest population. For example, some might argue that undocumented and low-income individuals should not receive care because there is not enough money to pay for the health care of the total U.S. population. The argument could be made that the healthcare access needs of the larger number of the U.S. population are currently being met; thus, one might argue that the "greatest good for the greatest number" has been met.

However, this author argues against that point of view because of the populations involved—namely, vulnerable versus nonvulnerable populations. The greatest good is not being met for populations who are very vulnerable. Further, one could extend this argument to state that, in a longer perspective, the "greatest good" is not being served because costs to the health system are higher for emergency care when ill noninsured patients present themselves in emergency rooms and when there are consequences from illnesses that could have been prevented. This state of affairs does not benefit the general population and the general economy. Extending an argument from earlier in the chapter, a less than healthy workforce does not enhance the general population of the United States. Thus, this author argues that there has not been an accomplishment of the greater good for the larger U.S. population with these three populations not being covered. She also argues that insurance coverage for all would best meet this ethical theory.

ETHICAL ANALYSIS USING RELIGIOUS ETHICS

Another perspective for analysis is how health professionals ethically respond to practicing in their particular health organizations. Health providers, very pragmatically, must meet a mission statement, vision, and commitment of a health organization toward certain beliefs. When the basis for such an organization is religious beliefs, then Pierce and Randels note the application of religious ethics.[30]

For example, health providers working in some Catholic organizations are well aware of and knowledgeable about Catholic social teaching that might permeate those particular health institutions.[31] In such a setting, health providers would follow practices that promote health care for all. For example, emphasis on this inclusive access has been more focused in the decades following the 1963 encyclical written by Pope John XXIII titled *Pacem in Terris*.[32] The following are some basic principles of Catholic social teaching that have repercussions for one's stance toward the delivery of health care:

1. Health care is viewed as a basic right of a human being.

2. Priority is given to meeting the needs of the poor.

3. There is a commitment to solidarity among all community members.

This example focuses on one religious denomination and how it affects the policies of its health organizations. One could conduct a similar analysis of other religious denominations and examine how their beliefs are reflected in the mission statements and practices of their health organizations.

This concludes the ethical analysis of the three populations who do not have health insurance coverage. The following case study describes concerns of those individuals who will receive coverage by Medicaid. The reader will note that there may well be discrepancies among individuals reimbursed by Medicaid depending on the state in which they live. Following the case study, the author finishes this chapter by applying an ethical analysis to specific policy advocacy interventions and initiatives.

CASE STUDY ON STATE DIFFERENCES REGARDING MEDICAID

This case study concerns the population of individuals in Nebraska who have health care reimbursed by Medicaid and has implications for both current and future individuals who are Medicaid enrollees. This case study is being used as indicative of the concerns faced by many states in managing their budgets and of the populations who are not covered by Medicaid or who have parts of their care that are no longer reimbursed by Medicaid.

The Nebraska unicameral passed LB 709, the Medicaid Reform Act, in 2005. "The act mandated the preparation of a Medicaid reform plan to make specific recommendations for 'fundamental reform' of the Nebraska Medicaid Program" (Vivian Chaumont, Blue Ribbon Task Force letter to the Nebraska senators, personal communication, December 27, 2011). The Nebraska Division of Medicaid and Long-Term Care proposed legislation during the spring 2012 unicameral session for six major changes in Medicaid that would save millions of dollars and affect thousands of persons and would affect many health providers and health organizations.

The national economic downturn since 2008 is a major societal variable affecting the health system. In the Nebraska Medicaid Annual Report, Chaumont noted the increase in people who applied for Medicaid (Chaumont, 2011). There was a significant increase in 2009, which continued into 2010 and 2011. Although there has been much media coverage of one aspect of the PPACA—namely, that Medicaid would be expanded to include more people in need—there will still be some people who are low income who, although eligible, will not be enrolled. Although some health services are mandated by the federal government and there will be a minimum services package, other services are optional. Thus, there is currently great diversity in availability of services, and that will continue. Thus, individuals who are poor or have low incomes may not receive all the services that similar individuals may receive in other states.

The proposed changes for 2012 in the Nebraska legislation regarding those who have health care reimbursed by Medicaid were as follows (Chaumont, 2011):

1. There will be an increase in copayments for physical, speech, and occupational therapies; dental services for those in Medicaid Managed Care; and nonemergency visits to the emergency room.

2. Home health services will be limited to 240 hours per year.

3. Private-duty nursing will be eliminated.

4. Personal assistance services will be restricted and eliminated for some clients.

5. Some nutritional supplements will be eliminated.

6. Behavioral therapy visits will be limited to 60 per year to match the number of physical therapy visits.

If states receive less money from the federal budget because of concerns about the federal budget, Chaumont noted, the following policies would become effective:

1. The elimination of coverage of dental and chiropractic services, physical therapy, occupational therapy, speech therapy, dentures, eyeglasses, and hearing aids for adults.

2. Limited coverage of prescription drugs (10 monthly for adults), limited hospital days, and limited physician visits (12 yearly, excluding pregnancy).

All of the above policies would become effective in Nebraska on July 1, 2012, if this proposed legislation passed the unicameral. One can see from this one case study that for a person receiving Medicaid-reimbursed health care, there will be a varied spectrum of access to healthcare services dependent on the state in which one lives. Thus, even though the PPACA expands the Medicaid program to cover more individuals, the structure of the program still creates nonavailability of some health services for some individuals. One can evaluate each of the above-proposed changes as problematic for the person with minimal to no money.

For the population of seven million individuals who are low income and eligible for Medicaid but for whom enrollment is not predicted, several reasons have been suggested for such lack of enrollment. They may not have knowledge about enrollment, there may be onerous barriers to Medicaid enrollment, or the person may think it is not necessary. This author noted a parallel example many years ago when there was an expansion of children's health services with Medicaid reimbursement in states throughout the country. The director of the advocacy organization in Nebraska, Voices for Children, noted the difficulty of reaching all families, of educating them, of the barriers against enrollment, and of enrolling them (K. Moore, personal communication, 2000). To combat barriers, many states consciously and intentionally used state culturally sensitive program titles so that parents would not be concerned about using a government Medicaid program. In Nebraska, for example, the service was called "Kids Connection"; in Iowa it was called "hawk-i," an acronym for Healthy and Well Kids in Iowa that also suggested Iowa's Hawkeye sports teams. Thus, two contiguous states initiated interventions to decrease some barriers against enrollment. Health providers need to remain alert to initiatives they can take to further eligible patients' enrollment into Medicaid.

POLICY ADVOCACY OF ETHICAL STANCES

It is the evaluation of this author that health providers and health provider students have professional and ethical responsibilities and obligations to further policies that best meet the ethical needs of patients in the healthcare area. For this author, that means furthering those policies that enhance the health status of others and opposing those policies that decrease access to care. This section of the chapter addresses examples of policy interventions based on ethical analyses. The use of exemplar case studies assists the reader in analyzing how to best become involved in policy change.

Several Advocacy Strategies

The first case study is that of involvement with one's professional association at a state level to be active regarding state policy for one's profession and for the health of the state's population. Examples of such activity include the following: (1) working on campaigns to elect one's state constituent representatives,

(2) developing a relationship with one's state senators, (3) educating oneself on policy issues and the legislative process, (4) implementing best practice lobby efforts to either support or oppose policies, (5) involving oneself in one's state professional association through time, money, and energy, and (6) taking a leadership role in advocacy in one's state professional association. For example, this author intentionally practices the above policy behaviors because of a commitment to her ethical responsibility as articulated in the ANA Code of Ethics and in the ANA Standards of Practice. Concomitant with this policy, the author uses ethical theories to reflect, analyze, and evaluate how best to respond in each particular situation that arises relative to access issues for patients.

The focus of this chapter has been on the lack of access to health care for certain vulnerable populations. In parallel with the above interventions, which this author promotes, she did the following:

1.   Intentionally invested time, money, and energy into the campaign of candidate Burke Harr to be the state senator from Legislative District 8 in Nebraska. One of many examples was hosting a house party to both educate others and to facilitate fund-raising.

2.   Once candidate Harr was elected as a state senator, the author ensured a continued relationship with him, educating him on issues relative to vulnerable patients and lobbying him on specific proposed bills. For example, in fall 2011 as soon as this writer knew the date of the annual day at the unicameral of the Nebraska Nurses Association (NNA) for 2012, she contacted Senator Harr to be her guest at the luncheon for that event.

3.   Educated herself on policy issues and the legislative process with consistent intention, using many venues for such learning.

4.   Implemented best practice lobby behaviors to maximize the writer's concerns and, it was hoped, realize the desired policy outcomes.

5.   Although this author has consistently been active with the NNA in a variety of ways to promote selective proposed bills, starting in 2012 she will be practicing leadership as chair of the NNA Commission on Advocacy and Representation for two years. This particular commission is working for prioritization of the health access issues that the NNA will be supporting.

Professional associations (at the global, national, state, and local levels) are important venues for practicing ethical behaviors for advocacy of increasing populations' access to health care. Readers of this chapter, both health professionals and health professional students, are encouraged to evaluate their professional association behaviors. This author believes that such active professional association interventions constitute responsible ethical behavior by health professionals.

State Professional Associations

One way health professionals can advocate for the affected populations discussed in this chapter is via their state professional association. This section relates a case study example involving the author and other nurses in Nebraska relative to these concerns. The author serves as chair of the NNA's Commission on Advocacy and Representation. She, along with nine other elected nurse members representing the entire state, the association's executive director, and a paid lobbyist, met weekly by telephone for two months during the early part of the 2012 unicameral session to evaluate proposed legislation. Almost 1,200 bills were introduced during the 2011 and the 2012 two-year unicameral session. The ten commission nurse members divided the bills among themselves and read and evaluated each bill. If a bill related to the practice of nursing or the health of the Nebraska population, they discussed the bill and made a decision concerning support, opposition, or a neutral stance on the bill.

For the bills introduced during the first ten days of the 2012 session, the commission members prioritized their work according to two populations: nurses and patients. Bills were evaluated in language similar to the language of ethics—that is, does this bill harm or benefit nurses and patients? The members defined patients as current or potential patients (including family members) and as individuals or populations of patients. As noted earlier in this chapter, several bills related to projected cuts and changes in Medicaid were introduced. Commission members took stances on selected bills that reflected the advocacy role of the professional nurse and that enabled the registered nurse to best apply the ANA Code of Ethics.

This author, as well as other commission members, wrote testimony for many of the bills. Whether for writing the NNA's testimony or for testifying physically at the public hearing for every bill proposed in the Nebraska unicameral, the commission recruited the most appropriate commission members or other NNA members. All members were knowledgeable and informed of the importance of selecting those nurses with the most lived experiences that related to each bill. Such nurses could inform state senators of the lived patient experiences they had seen and what it meant in a patient's life when health care was not available. They, of course, told patient stories in general terms, as they were all cognizant and respectful of HIPAA boundaries.

In the weekly telephone commission meetings, nurses shared their lived clinical knowledge with each other, articulated their knowledge of evidence-based practice (EBP) behaviors relative to the projected Medicaid cuts and their evaluation of ethical theories as applied to the projected cuts, and were moved to action to advocate for vulnerable patients being reimbursed by Medicaid. In addition, during the first two months of 2012 when some of these nurses testified, they were doing so because they had immediate particular knowledge of those adult family members negatively affected by Medicaid cuts. They did not rely solely on their assigned clinical patient stories. One example of applying EBP was to argue against the proposed denial of dental care to patients who are poor; this does not follow the best practices of health care, given the research over the past decade on the interaction of dental health with cardiac health.

Advocacy by Civic Engagement

In the fall of 2011, a county commissioner appointed this author to be one of 14 members of the Douglas County ad hoc Blue Ribbon Task Force to evaluate four health services that the county provides for the poor in the county as a last resort of health care: primary health care, a mental health center, a long-term care facility, and an assisted living facility. The county commissioners were expecting a $5 million gap in the budget for 2012 and noted the $12 million dollars annually that the county needed to subsidize these four services and keep them operational. Seeking an outside community members' task force was one of their strategies to evaluate their potential future actions. The task force completed its work in February 2012.

The author shares this example because much of her verbal voice at meetings and construction of a report in early 2012 with another task force member reflected her data collection, ethical analysis of recommendations for vulnerable poor patients in her county, and policy advocacy. There was no consensus among the 14 members for the recommendations they gave to the county commissioners. Rather, there were three separate reports. For this author, the basis for the voice that she transmitted in this task force setting—whether verbally at meeting after meeting or in her and a colleague's final report of recommendations—was language from the ANA Code of Ethics. In addition, such language integrates with one of the four ethical principles, that is, to do no harm.

Some practices to take from this particular example are the following:

1. Health providers can, by their history, be known to policy makers as patient advocates.

2. Health providers can choose to respond to serve on such short-term civic committees that have major impacts on policy for vulnerable populations in their county or city.

3. Health providers can share information and knowledge with non-health-providers who bring other perspectives to the discussion.

4. Civic engagement is one more venue for advocacy by health providers.

SUMMARY

This chapter has done the following: (1) identified the populations who will be left uninsured if the health reform bill stays as it is now written, (2) proposed why it is unethical for these populations not to have access to health care, (3) used several ethical theories for these arguments, and (4) discussed and promoted policy interventions that this author evaluates as necessary for the health provider, the health provider student, or the policy maker reading this chapter and book.

Hillel, a Jewish rabbi and scholar, summarizes this author's stance on the need for policy and practice behaviors that promote health care for vulnerable populations: "If I am not for myself, then who will be for me? And, if am only for myself, then what am I? And, if not now, when?"[33] This author believes that it is not ethical to fail to meet the health needs of vulnerable populations. Purtilo and colleagues have studied the concept of moral courage.[34] The author argues that those health providers who provide health care in environments with barriers or who promote policy for vulnerable populations also demonstrate degrees of moral courage. The reader is encouraged to study these issues, evaluate the concerns raised and the ethical arguments proposed, and to reach a conclusion for one's self based on one's reasoning, life experiences, and value systems.

QUESTIONS FOR DISCUSSION

1. Who are the populations of concern (i.e., those without access to health care)?

2. What are the ethical arguments for advocacy of health care for all?

3. How does a professional association's ethical code obligate the clinical and advocacy practices of a health professional?

4. What are current case studies in the student's geographic area that have parallel concerns to the case studies discussed in this chapter?

5. What policy advocacy behaviors do students envision themselves taking for patients without access to health care?

FOOD FOR THOUGHT

Think about each of the following roles: a patient without healthcare access, a family member of that patient, a nurse, a taxpayer opposed to provision of health care for all, an ethicist, a patient with health insurance who opposes healthcare access for all, and a physician. Then think about this statement: "The patient should have access to health care." Choose at least one or two of the roles and present your arguments to support this statement using ethical theories or principles.

NOTES

1. M. D. M. Fowler, *Guide to the Code of Ethics for Nurses* (Silver Spring, MD: American Nurses Association, 2008).

2. American Nurses Association, *Nursing's Social Policy Statement* (Silver Spring, MD: American Nurses Association, 2010).

3. R. L. O'Brien, "A New Era of Health Care: The Ethics of Healthcare Reform," in *Health Care Ethics*, 3rd ed., eds. E. E. Morrison and E. A. Furlong (Burlington, MA: Jones & Bartlett Learning, 2013).

4. T. L. Beauchamp and J. F. Childress, *Principles of Biomedical Ethics* (New York: Oxford University Press, 1994).

5. J. Pierce and G. Randels, "Bioethics: An Introduction to the Discipline," in *Contemporary Bioethics*, eds. J. Pierce and G. Randels (New York: Oxford University Press, 2010), 1–28.

6. S. Kosoko-Lasaki, C. T. Cook, and R. L. O'Brien, *Cultural Proficiency in Addressing Health Disparities* (Sudbury, MA: Jones and Bartlett, 2009).

7. S. Crystal and D. Shea, "Cumulative Advantage and Inequality Among Elderly People," *Gerontologist* 30, no. 4 (1990): 527–537.

8. O'Brien, "A New Era of Health Care."

9. Ibid.

10. G. A. Campbell, S. Sanoff, and M. H. Rosner, "Care of the Undocumented Immigrant in the United States with ESRD," *American Journal of Kidney Diseases* 55, no. 1 (2010): 181–191.

11. Ibid.

12. Ibid.

13. Ibid.

14. Beauchamp and Childress, *Principles of Biomedical Ethics*.

15. Ibid.

16. Ibid.

17. O'Brien, "A New Era of Health Care."

18. Ibid.

19. Fowler, *Guide to the Code of Ethics for Nurses*.

20. American Nurses Association, *Nursing's Social Policy Statement*.

21. Ibid.

22. Fowler, *Guide to the Code of Ethics for Nurses*, 103.

23. American Nurses Association, *Code of Ethics for Nurses with Interpretative Statements* (Silver Spring, MD: American Nurses Association, 2001), 23.

24. Fowler, *Guide to the Code of Ethics for Nurses*, 121.

25. Ibid., 89.

26. Ibid., 11.

27. Ibid., 1.

28. Pierce and Randels, "Bioethics."

29. Ibid.

30. Ibid.

31. M. L. Coulter, S. M. Krason, R. S. Myers, and J. A. Varacalli, "Health Care Policy," in *Encyclopedia of Catholic Social Thought, Social Science, and Social Policy* (Lanham, MD: Scarecrow Press, 2007), 495–497.

32. To read the full text of this encyclical, see http://www.vatican.va/holy_father/john_xxiii/encyclicals/documents/hf_j-xxiii_enc_11041963_pacem_en.html. Accessed June 22, 2012.

33. The Hillel quote is available at http://www.jewishvirtuallibrary.org/jsource/Quote/hille l2.html. Accessed June 22, 2012.

34. R. B. Purtilo, G. M. Jensen, and C. B. Royeen, *Educating for Moral Action* (Philadelphia: F.A. Davis, 2005).

CHAPTER 24

Looking Toward the Future

Beth Furlong and Eileen E. Morrison

INTRODUCTION

This chapter summarizes the themes encountered in the previous four sections of the text. In addition to this summary, it discusses additional areas of ethical theory and examples of emergent issues that were not previously addressed. Furlong discusses the Ethic of Care and the narrative models of ethics, and Morrison presents a discussion of the ethical ramifications of complementary and alternative medicine (CAM), which is also called integrated medicine (IM). In addition, she discusses ethical issues related to the aging of the baby boomer generation.

SUMMARY OF SECTION THEMES

Part I, "Foundations in Theory," provided an overview of the most commonly held ethical theories and principles used in the American healthcare system. Summers (who holds three degrees in philosophy) presented a scholarly but understandable overview of these ethical theories and principles. This foundation helps the reader to better understand the complex ethical issues that are presented in subsequent chapters. The following themes emerged from this part of the text:

- There is no one theory of ethics that will apply to every situation. Each theory has strengths and limitations.
- Knowledge of the ethical theories is useful in practice because it allows critical thinking concerning issues faced in healthcare situations.
- As you build your expertise and practice, consider the concept of virtue. It is about your character and your professional presence in the world.
- The principles of ethics derive from theory and are useful in making decisions that benefit the individual and the community as a whole.
- Patients expect you to practice beneficence and nonmaleficence. However, the practice of autonomy and justice often poses difficult choices.
- The reflective equilibrium model provides a tool for making difficult ethical decisions.

Part II, "Critical Issues for Individuals," included an exploration of the complexity of the ethical issues faced by individuals who use the healthcare system. The chapters were presented in life-cycle order, beginning with the unborn facing the challenge of just how they come to be. You will be able to explore the concept of whether those who have not yet been born have rights and the impact of technology on their existence.

After conception, there are continuing ethical issues. Chapters 6 and 7 considered the ethical implications of being able to diagnose diseases before birth and the impact of this ability on the existence of the individual. You will also be able to consider finding a middle ground on the abortion debate. These controversial areas will most certainly continue to be among those you face as you practice in the 21st century.

Additional ethical issues arise once a person becomes an adult. Chapter 7, "Competency," presented an overview of what it means to be competent and to make your own healthcare decisions. Although this might appear simple on the surface, it becomes increasingly difficult when you consider all of the variables that can affect competency. Chapters 8 and 9 presented issues related to the elderly and long-term care. The issues presented in these chapters will certainly be of concern in healthcare practice in the future given the potential increase for the need for long-term care services. The aging of the baby boomer generation alone should call your attention to the ethical issues raised in these two chapters.

The last three chapters in Part II dealt with end-of-life issues. These chapters provided both information and ethical challenges. These challenges are sure to be part of the future of health care as the provisions of the Patient Protection and Affordable Care Act (PPACA) become part of the business of health care. In addition, the increasing numbers of people facing the end of their lives each year can add ethical as well as financial pressure to the healthcare system.

Part III, "Critical Issues for Healthcare Organizations," presented several topics among the many ethical issues faced by healthcare organizations. For example, Chapters 14 and 15 were concerned with ethical issues faced by hospitals and hospital systems. These chapters attempted to clarify the differences between institutional ethical positions and clinical ones. In addition, the nature of ethics committees, their decision-making processes, and the current and future issues they face were part of the presentation in Chapter 15. If you plan to practice in a hospital setting, you should find these chapters particularly helpful.

One chapter (Chapter 16) stressed the power of technology in health care and the organizational issues it creates. More importantly, it challenges you to examine the ethical issues that this rapidly evolving field can create. Certainly medical technology and health information technology will be an increasing part of healthcare practice in the 21st century.

Another chapter (Chapter 17) revisited a concept that has been at the core of healthcare organizations—spirituality. In this edition, spirituality is tied to evidence-based medicine practices. In addition, the chapter shows how spirituality in the workplace can increase both productivity and staff member morale. It also discussed considerations about the ethics involved in this issue for healthcare practice.

Part IV, "Critical Issues for Society's Health," featured examples of issues that affect more than the individual or the organization. The issues of equality and inequality and of rationing are even more important now because of the profound changes in health care promised in the 21st century. In addition, the societal issues of domestic violence and disaster relief continue to affect lives and our ability to provide compassionate, ethics-based care for our communities. Finally, two new chapters in this edition provided an overview of the most profound current healthcare issue for our society—the implementation of PPACA. Not only did these chapters present the history and implementation of this system-changing law, but also they presented its ethical challenges. One chapter (Chapter 23) gave practical advice about how to deal with the ethical issues faced by those left uncovered by the legislation. Finally, the current chapter presented two ways to view ethics that are different from those presented by Summers—namely, the Ethic of Care and the narrative ethics models. It also discusses the emerging issues of the growing use of CAM in health care and the ethical ramifications of the influx of aging baby boomers into the healthcare system.

NEW CONSIDERATIONS IN ETHICAL THEORY

Ethic of Care Model

Whereas some health providers have utilized and applied such ethical theories as deontology, utilitarianism, virtue ethics, and principlism (autonomy, beneficence, nonmaleficence, and justice), other health providers, notably women and nurses, have also incorporated an Ethic of Care model.[1,2] This theory, which evolved from the moral development research of feminist Carol Gilligan in the 1980s, focused on the importance of relationships and context in decision making. This model is attentive to the needs of all. Lachman wrote that this theory "has a focus on the context of the situation versus impartial deliberation of the ethical issue. Impartial reflection is an element of justice-based moral deliberation and does not take into consideration the level of caring or closeness in the relationship."[3]

Gilligan noted in her previous research that women never reached the highest levels of moral decision making. Her research showed the difference between some men and women's approaches to decision making, namely, men were more justice-oriented, and women were more oriented to the complex of relationships, caring, and the context of a situation in arriving at an ethical decision.[4,5] Whereas men might resolve ethical dilemmas with black-and-white rules, women did not. Women were concerned about the particular situation and the current and future interpersonal connections and relationships of those involved. Because women dominate the nursing profession, nurses embrace this model more than other health provider professions.

Volker argued that using an Ethic of Care model is not unique to nurses.[6] She acknowledged that a core theme of nursing, recognized by nurses, other health providers, society, and the media, is that of the caring relationship between patients and nurses. However, such a dynamic also applies to other patient–health provider relationships. For nurses, the model's accompanying traits of empathy, compassion, and connectedness resonate in their daily care of patients and their families, 24 hours daily, seven days weekly. Given nurses' intensity of care of patients in vulnerable, intimate situations, the Ethic of Care model has integrated easily with their lived reality.

Edwards asserted that the history of medicine and nursing, with the differentiation of "curing" and "caring" between them as their major distinctive goals and functions, resulted in the four principles approach being used by physicians, whereas the Ethic of Care seemed more appropriate to the women-dominated nursing profession.[7]

Several authors have furthered this ethical model for nursing.[8,9] Their arguments are based on the strong assertion of the importance of the caring theme to nursing practice. These authors proposed that the Ethic of Care be used as the dominant model versus the principlism model. Volker noted that the latter model "is intuitively attractive to many nurses" because it integrates well with how nurses have been educated, socialized, and perceived by society.[10]

However, research to date does not demonstrate a clear picture. One can cite research showing nurses who apply a justice orientation, whereas other research shows nurses using a care orientation.[11,12] Pinch critiqued some use of the Ethic of Care model because of concerns that it furthers oppression of nurses.[13] Edwards summarized the evolvement of Gilligan's work by categorizing her work in the early 1980s as the first version of an ethic of care. Tronto's work a decade later represented the second version, and work by Little in 1998 and Gastmans in 2006 constituted the third version.[14] Tronto differentiated between an ethics of responsibility and an ethics of obligation. Further, she proposed four elements of care (attentiveness, responsibility, competence, and responsiveness) and four phases. Finally, the third version can be summarized by Gastmans's following words: "[C]are ethics is more a stance from which we can theorize ethically rather than a full-blown ethical theory in itself."[15]

Although the literature provides no definitive answer to the soundness of the Ethic of Care model or the extent of its usage by nurses, this author (Furlong) will end this section by citing a group of authors who advocate for this model for nurses. They note the particularity of specific situations and respectful relationships between patients and nurses, and provide evidence of the value of a caring relationship to the healing process of patients.[16] They argue that an ethic of care, versus other theories, is the one needed. In particular, they directly address some conflicts between being caring and providing justice for a nurse's assigned group of patients; they conclude that "in some cases individual exceptions must be allowed."[17]

In summary, for the past 30 years, Gilligan's work, which evolved into the Ethic of Care model, has been an important model for nurses, other health providers, and those in other disciplines. The utility of this model is being studied and critiqued.

Narrative Ethics Model

A second emerging model is the narrative ethics model, which has gained increased proponents in the last two decades. McCarthy broadly described narrative ethics' tenets in the following way: (1) because every moral situation is unique, no one universal law or principle applies, (2) any healthcare decision can be justified given an individual's life story, and (3) the dialogue for justification of a decision is to be open and the tensions explored.[18] A narrative is "a first person narrative, personal story . . . for qualitative data about the unique lives of individual people."[19]

Another way of perceiving, understanding, and analyzing the difference between narrative ethics and other theories is McCarthy's statement of this difference "as one between those theorists who see principles at the heart of moral life and those who see communication at its core."[20] The former group is composed of those theorists who promote principlism, and the latter of those who advocate the use of narrative ethics. On a personal and professional note, author Furlong has recognized the value of the latter when assigning a narrative, "Procedures," as an assignment in a graduate healthcare ethics program. Student response is quite compelling when reading this first-person patient account of a woman's experience with the healthcare system.[21] McCarthy noted that principlism has dominated health providers' approach to bioethics for the last two decades.[22] It is the opinion of author Furlong that narrative ethics may better resonate with health providers at this time because the first-person patient story provides learning and reflection at a time when all health providers are concerned about the provision of safety and avoidance of errors in the health system. Hearing, reading, and understanding the communication gaps that are occurring among patients, family members, and health providers provides insights into how to better the health system. Analyzing narratives facilitates this reflective understanding.

Those who advance the use of narrative ethics note the importance of storytelling by the patient.[23] Further, this model honors an individual's life story and how one makes an ethical decision at a point in time. McCarthy noted that the following skills are necessary to promote narrative ethics with a patient: (1) literary skills to understand and interpret someone's story, (2) an ability to construct metaphors and recognize the bigger picture, (3) an ability to be reflective, and (4) compassionate communication skills.[24]

Adams[25] expanded on some of the analysis by McCarthy. One of his critiques of principlism is that it is a preformed set of rules that can do violence to a person's singular experience. A colloquial phrase in U.S. society, "Been there, done that," is not accurate because every situation is different. An inability to reflect on and recognize this has some parallel to a nonrecognition of the value of narrative ethics. This is furthered by Ellis, who noted that there are no universal principles that apply to all situations except the general premise of doing no harm.[26] In summary, those interested in ethical analysis of individual, clinical, and population concerns can enhance their understanding by using this method. A review of its strengths and limitations is beyond the purview of this chapter.

EMERGENT ISSUES AND ETHICS

There is no doubt that the future practice of health care will continue to struggle with a plethora of ethical issues and difficult decisions. There will be a continuing call for practitioners to provide patient services that are evidence based, safe, cost-effective, and ethically sound. This action will be conducted in the world of PPACA, which is currently full of uncertainty and white-water change.

Although it is not within the scope of this chapter to examine every one of the changes in the future of health care, it will address two areas of interest.

The first is a discussion of the growing interest in CAM (or IM) among both patients and conventional medical practitioners, including the reasons for its growth. In addition, this section discusses the ethical ramifications of these practices for professionals and patients. The second area is a discussion of the effects the aging baby boomers will have on health care. It addresses the ethical issues caused by the increasing needs of this population group.

Complementary and Alternative Medicine and Ethics

Complementary and alternative medicine is not new. In fact, its roots are thousands of years old, and it is used all over the world as a healing practice.[27] Despite its lack of acceptability for some members of the allopathic medical system, its use and acceptance is growing in the United States among both patients and conventional medicine practitioners. Consumer choice and increased education on CAM have driven the use of these practices. Because of the proposed changes through PPACA and the increasing number of aging baby boomers, CAM promises to be an even greater part of health care in the future. This section briefly explains the practice of CAM and the reasons for concern regarding it by allopathic medicine. It also presents some of the potential ethical issues associated with CAM from both the patient and provider views.

Defining CAM

Creating a simple definition for CAM is not easy because, much like conventional medicine, it includes diverse elements of practice. The National Center for Complementary and Alternative Medicine (NCCAM), part of the National Institutes of Health (NIH), defines CAM as "a group of diverse medical and health care systems, practices that are not generally part of conventional medicine."[28]

This definition explains what CAM is not, but does not explain what it is.

Therefore, NCCAM further defines CAM by providing a typology and descriptions of the categories. Categories of CAM are as follows: [29]

- *Natural products*, including herbal medicine, dietary supplements, and natural substances such as probiotics.
- *Mind/body medicine*, including practices that stress the connections between the brain and physical health. Examples of this category are meditation in its many forms, yoga, tai chi, and hypnotherapy.
- *Manipulation/body-based practices*, including chiropractic medicine and the many forms of massage.
- *Whole medical systems*, including areas of medicine based on different cultural beliefs and orientations than that of Western medicine. This category includes Ayurvedic, traditional Chinese, and Native American medicine.

Micozzi noted that CAM has a different paradigm from that of contemporary medicine.[30] For example, new discoveries in physics and studying other medical systems form a foundation for CAM practitioners' thinking about and practices of healing. He also notes that CAM emphasizes areas such as wellness, self-healing, nutrition, plants, and individuality.

Regardless of its definition, an increasing number of Americans use CAM as part of their healthcare practice. The most recent available national statistics (from 2008) indicate that over 4 of every 10 Americans have used CAM therapies, with the most popular being natural products, meditation, chiropractic manipulation, and massage.[31] National and international research has been conducted to determine why individuals seek out CAM practices. Because many people use this form of health care in addition to that provided by conventional practitioners, the explanation is linked to the practices of medicine.[32] The use of CAM appears to be closely linked to the patient's experience of illness and not solely to the scientific knowledge base used to treat it in conventional medicine. Patients are looking for a way to address the components of health and healing not found in traditional treatments.

Research has also found that people who use CAM have certain common elements. They tend to be female, highly educated, and have higher income levels. In addition, these patients suffer from chronic illnesses that affect their daily lives in negative ways. They seek CAM treatments that improve their quality of life, including their ability to sleep and deal effectively with pain and other discomforts. Even though these patients suffer from chronic conditions, they tend to be in better health than the general population.[33]

People who use CAM tend to have a different value system than those who do not. They tend to feel responsibility for their own health, and want a more holistic-type treatment than is typically found in conventional medicine. Although still using conventional medicine, they "wish to multiply their preventive and therapeutic options, they have reasons to believe these therapies may be useful, and/or they have philosophical and experiential reasons to find an attractive and reasonable choices."[34] CAM practitioners offer advice on improving life, including diet, exercise, and spiritual practices. Conventional medicine provides these practices only in a limited way.[35] In addition, those who use CAM treatments often recommend them to their friends and family, hence the consumer-driven nature of these treatments. Although conventional physicians may consider the choice to use CAM practices as coming from ignorance and irrational behavior, CAM users find these treatments to be helpful and use them in addition to those offered by scientific medicine.

Concerns About CAM

Although CAM is increasing in use and popularity among patients, the medical community has concerns about its use in practice. Conventional medicine bases treatment on its definition of scientific principles, including Newtonian physics. These practitioners base their values on what they consider to be verifiable scientific knowledge about the body and its functions. They also base their actions on the diagnostic criteria of a disease or diseases and the ability to treat those conditions.[36] This biomedical model tends to view the patient in a way that focuses on his or her physical body, and treatments address observed or verified physical problems. These treatments tend to favor "surgery, injection or ingestion of pharmaceuticals."[37]

The basis of CAM practice comes from a very different model from that of conventional medicine. This model integrates the physical, spiritual, psychosocial, and energy aspects of human beings into practice modalities. It offers treatments that combine these aspects to treat the whole person. It is easy to see the paradigm conflict and the foundation of concern from conventional medicine's viewpoint. One of the arguments of conventional medicine against CAM is that there is no proof of the efficacy of CAM practices by research (specifically randomized, double-blind, control group studies, which are the gold standard of research). This claim ignores the current research conducted at medical schools (including Harvard University) and through research grant funding provided through the NCCAM. In fact, this division of the NIH offers research-based information about everything from acupuncture to zinc on its website.[38]

In 2005, Shelle and colleagues found challenges in assessing the quality of studies involving CAM practices.[39] Their concerns were that presentation of negative results of CAM studies most often occurred in mainstream medical journals. In contrast, CAM journals most often featured positive results. In addition, indexing of CAM journals was incomplete or improperly done. Therefore, publication biases existed. In addition, there were issues regarding the internal validity and reliability of the studies reviewed because of the need to provide replication and still conduct a study on applied CAM practices. They noted the lack of analogues in Western medicine, the inability to blind some of the CAM practices, and the inability to mask the placebo effect. Finally, there was concern about how to assess the rare-event side effects of CAM treatments through databases and other sources.

There is also concern about CAM practices that has a historical base. In the early history of U.S. medicine, medical school graduates were an elite minority, and healers, midwives, and an assortment of non-medical-school-trained practitioners provided most patient care.[40] Over time, medical schools became increasingly science based, and the medical profession extended its authority. This change caused increasing conflict between orthodox medicine and those who provided other ways of treatment, including the establishment of the AMA's Committee on Quackery.[41] This long-standing concern with quackery and fraudulent practices has continued to affect attitudes toward CAM practices in the 21st century.

However, a new dialogue has begun recently based on a different direction in the medical community, which has become more open to examining diversity, dissatisfaction with the existing medical system, and the impersonal nature of medical technology. In addition, the economic forces of consumer-driven CAM practices have caused the medical community to begin to consider CAM and its impact. CAM practitioners are also becoming less adversarial and acting more in partnership with conventional practices. In addition, the practitioners of many CAM therapies (such as acupuncture and massage) have become licensed or registered professionals. This external validation of standards adds greater quality assurance in the eyes of conventional medicine. Although issues remain, there is certainly movement toward cooperation in the medical pluralism of the 21st century.[42]

Patient-Centered Ethical Issues

Those who wish to make CAM part of their practice of health care want to experience a truly patient-centered, holistic form of medicine. Their intent is not to avoid what they perceive as the technology- and body-parts-centered system so aptly described by Geisel,[43] but to enhance that care by using the many available CAM options. Making this choice involves ethical issues that well-informed patients must consider. For the sake of brevity, the following discussion centers on the four principles of ethics: autonomy, beneficence, nonmaleficence, and justice.

Autonomy

Issues of autonomy, or the freedom of self-rule, would appear to be the most obvious for patients. In commenting on autonomy, Mertz found that the use of the practice of CAM was ethical.[44] However, having the freedom to select the practitioners for one's health care carries with it the responsibility for researching the practices and qualifications of those chosen. In addition, because health insurance does not always cover the costs of CAM services, patients must be vigilant to understand both the treatment procedures and the cost of each visit. Patient responsibility is part of exercising one's autonomy.

Informed consent is an expression of autonomy in health care. This issue is also part of CAM practices. CAM professionals must provide accurate information about their services and the risks involved in using them. In addition, they must gather medical information from patients in order to formulate the best treatment plans. The patient also has an ethical obligation to provide accurate information to the CAM provider.

An ethical issue also exists with respect to informed consent and CAM for conventional health providers. Patients might feel that their conventional health providers do not accept their use of CAM practices. The basis of the perception may be comments that have been made or even nonverbal cues. Regardless of the reason, patients often take a "don't ask and don't tell" strategy about CAM use. Conventional practitioners could be in the dark, and this lack of knowledge could jeopardize treatment. The responsibility for dealing with this issue lies with both the patient and the practitioner. Currently, conventional medicine practices have added the use of CAM to their consent forms and have begun to ask about this use. In addition, patients need to be forthcoming about what health practices they use, without fear, so that treatment can be optimal.

Beneficence and Nonmaleficence

One should also consider the principles of beneficence and nonmaleficence when thinking about patients becoming partners in their health care through the selection of CAM practices. Because of the holistic nature of CAM, beneficence, acting in charity and kindness, appears to be a consistent part of this practice. Patients feel that CAM practitioners listen, allow them to be partners in treatment, treat them with respect, and give compassionate care. From the patient point of view, CAM practitioners have a broader view of healing than contemporary medical providers do and respect their experience of illness, including its spiritual aspects.[45]

From the patient perspective, nonmaleficence is more complicated. Some CAM practices have the potential to cause harm. Although licensed or registered practitioners provide most of the commonly used CAM practices, there are certainly practitioners who do not have such credentials. In addition, some

CAM practices may have more risks than benefits or may even be fraudulent. Patients have the responsibility to protect themselves from harm by researching the credentials of CAM practitioners and the efficacy of CAM practices themselves. Although word-of-mouth is often the source of referral to CAM practitioners, patients should be diligent in selecting a CAM provider.

Justice

The patient's right to choose CAM in addition to conventional medicine can demonstrate the principle of justice. Patients have their own belief systems about their illness, spirituality, and treatment of their conditions and need to be treated fairly even when this system is different from conventional medicine. Fairness and respect for patients translates into feeling comfortable discussing the use of CAM with those who practice conventional medicine. Although the physician, nurse practitioner, dentist, or so forth may not agree, he or she should consider diversity of belief systems as part of the provision of patient-centered care.

Practitioner-Centered Ethical Issues

Ethical concerns are not limited to the patient. Practitioners should also think about their ethical duty where CAM is concerned. Part of this duty is to understand what CAM really is and why patients seek its services. Physicians and medical schools are becoming more interested in this area because of the increase in patient use of CAM services. Medical schools such as the University of San Francisco, University of Arizona, University of Maryland, and Harvard University have courses on or centers for the study of CAM.[46] Workshops and online courses are also available as part of continuing medical education for physicians, nurses, physical therapists, and other healthcare practitioners. In addition to knowledge about CAM and its practices, conventional medicine practitioners should consider potential ethical issues, including those concerning autonomy, beneficence, nonmaleficence, and justice.

Autonomy

Most practitioners of conventional medicine entered the field because they wanted to make a difference and to assist patients to be well. They spent many difficult years learning the science and art of medicine and are appropriately proud of their accomplishments. In this education process, they learned the concept of paternalism. This means that, given their superior knowledge in the field, the authority of those who are educated in medicine is greater than the rights of patients to make their own decisions about health issues.[47] Given this view, CAM practices threaten the autonomy of practitioners because they go against their orientation to care for their patients. Further, CAM practitioners are viewed as having knowledge and credentials that are not in any way equivalent to those of conventional medicine practitioners. In addition, some may see CAM practices as not scientifically based and do not want to risk their autonomy by endorsing what they see as "quackery."

Beneficence and Nonmaleficence

With respect to beneficence, conventional medicine often has a concept of healing that differs from that of CAM. Given this difference, conventional medicine may question whether CAM provides benefit to patients. In fact, there may be generalizations in some practitioners' minds that all CAM practices are fraudulent and do not create patient benefit. However, conventional practitioners may be changing this view, based on the trend toward understanding the patient experience and moving beyond disease care. If CAM provides benefit to patients, should conventional medicine consider CAM in its lexicon of acceptable treatments? Discussions will continue on this matter.

"First do no harm" is part of the core of conventional medical practice. Given this foundation, practitioners question whether CAM causes harm to patients by what it does and does not do. If the practice of CAM makes patients' condition worse, then conventional medicine cannot support it. This is part of the reason for requiring evidence-based proof of effectiveness beyond the placebo effect. Of even greater concern is the fear that patients will use CAM in place of conventional medicine, thereby causing them harm by not employing verified conventional treatments. Although most Americans use both systems, there are cases where this situation does occur, and it is of concern to ethics-based conventional practitioners.[48]

Justice

The concept of justice also poses ethical issues for conventional practitioners. On the one hand, justice calls for the patient's right to choose a treatment or procedure and to be treated fairly while making this choice. Therefore, patients must have the right to choose CAM options as well as those of conventional medicine. However, conventional medicine, with its emphasis on the scientific model, does not always accept CAM as a treatment or procedure. Therefore, the possibility of supporting CAM, educating patients on its use, or offering it as a part of healthcare insurance does not appeal to many on the conventional side of medicine. Certainly, there is a need for future research, education, and dialogue before conventional medicine could support the justice of including CAM in its treatment protocols.[49]

The Future

At the writing of this chapter, there is a challenge for some aspects of PPACA before the U.S. Supreme Court, and the healthcare system continues to be in a time of change. Therefore, it is difficult to predict the future of the entire system. With respect to CAM, there are indicators of movement toward greater acceptance of its practices. For example, the widespread use of technology has led to greater understanding of CAM practices on the part of both patients and conventional practitioners. In addition, a model for integrating CAM with conventional medical practice that is used in behavioral health is available for consideration.[50] This model could be a first step in creating a healthcare system that addresses the whole patient and the connections between mind, body, spirit, and healing. In the future, this more holistic approach to patient care may find a place in the evolving patient-centered medical home (PCMH) model designed to improve medical outcomes, reduce healthcare costs, and provide comprehensive care in partnership with the patient.[51]

Here Come the Boomers!

It is not surprising that the homecomings after World War II triggered the existence of the worldwide population change known as the baby boom. Today this group represents 78 million people—approximately 29% of the U.S. population, or 3 of every 10 Americans—and they are aging.[52] Even though they are a diverse group, the generational cohort called the boomers will matter to the health care system and can shape its future in dramatic ways.

It is important to recognize that the population increase represented by the boomer generation influenced each social institution that the boomers encountered. Their numbers continue to dominate markets and influence social institutions.[53] For example, when the boomers entered the elementary school system, the system was not prepared for their numbers. There was an expansion of classrooms and increased hiring of teachers to meet the boomers' educational needs. The decade of the 1960s helped to define the boomer generation. These turbulent times saw civil rights protests; assassinations of presidents, presidential candidates, and civil rights leaders; and Woodstock's celebration of rock and roll. The Viet Nam War was also a major influence on the boomers' attitudes toward the federal government. The 1960s were a rollercoaster of hope and despair for the early boomers (1946–1957) and influenced American culture on many levels.[54]

The boomer generation's experiences influenced their outlook on life and on their futures. Although one cannot assign a specific attitude set to individuals, certain attitudes tend to be prevalent in the boomer population. These include the desire not to get old (maintaining youthfulness), to make a difference, and to be empowered.[55] In addition, the boomer generation tends to have greater financial power than previous aging populations.[56] These attitudes and the boomers' financial power shape their vision of the aging process and can greatly influence markets.

Dychtwald devotes several chapters of his work to the market influence of the boomer generation and to how they perceive aging.[57] Boomers are redefining the traditional attitudes toward this process. This attitude change has opened up a large market for anti-aging products, from makeup with serum included to gene therapy and bionics. In addition, boomer retirement is not about sitting in a rocking chair and waiting to die. For the boomers, it is about continuing to be productive even as they age, making a difference and having meaningful employment, and having second careers.[58]

The Boomers' Ethical View

According to Smith and Clurman, the boomer generation has its own moral focus that will continue to be important to them as they age.[59] They have moved from an orientation of self-expression and abundance to one dominated by concern for moral issues. The last section of Smith and Clurman's book focuses on the aging boomers' moral agenda, which includes continuing to have a sense of purpose, concern about maintaining health and avoiding frailty, and reconnecting with community. In addition, boomers expect that they can take charge of their health and that the healthcare system will be able to provide adequate insurance coverage, fix their problems, and provide quality care.

Impact of the Boomers on Future Healthcare Practice

As one can imagine, the aging boomers promise to have a tremendous impact on the healthcare market. On the positive side, Dychtwald lists over 50 areas for new markets to meet the needs of this emerging demographic.[60] Some of these areas include business opportunities for services to maintain health and independence, such as companies that coordinate care, Internet-based medical systems, and financial services. Creativity will be needed to find out what the boomers want and then providing the required services. One can create profitable businesses by assisting boomers to remain active as long as possible.

However, there are also serious concerns about the adequacy of services to meet the needs of aging boomers. With the baby boomers turning 65 in record numbers, there is a major concern about the ability of current healthcare benefit plans (Medicare, Medicaid, etc.) to meet the care needs of this population and maintain their fiscal viability.[61] Many predict massive changes in these plans—changes that will not please the politically powerful boomers. Dychtwald stressed that healthcare systems need to be ready for the chronic diseases that will accompany the aging of the baby boomers.[62] Healthcare systems must also address the shortage of long-term care facilities, from nursing homes to adult day care centers. In addition, there will be a lack of caregivers, including professionals such as geriatricians, nurses, physical therapists, and others. There will also be a need for nonprofessional caregivers who can provide homemaker services, home repair services, and transportation. Since the goal of the boomers is to remain in their homes as long as possible, these providers are essential.

Not all of the boomer generation is financially ready for retirement and the aging process. Dychtwald points out that "as much as one-third (and a group disproportionally female)—has no savings, no investments, no pensions."[63] This group may not be able to survive on Social Security alone (assuming that it is continued) and face dependency on their children, charities, or other sources of survival. There is a great need for financial planning for all boomers, including increasing their savings, reducing credit card debt, and reviewing their current pension plans. From the healthcare standpoint, providing affordable long-term care insurance products may assist boomers in coping with potential reductions in Medicare services.

Ethical Issues for the Healthcare System

The boomers have a moral position on aging, and so should the healthcare system. In reality, the ethics of caring for the aging boomer population could be a book of its own. For brevity's sake, one could apply the four principles of ethics—autonomy, beneficence, nonmaleficence, and justice—as a focal point for discussion.

Autonomy

The issue of autonomy is an important one for the individual boomer in that he or she wants to be in charge of his or her health as much as possible. This means that the healthcare system must do a better job attending to patient needs (patient-centered care) and communicating with patients. In addition, there will be a greater need to maintain high standards of quality in terms of facility appearance and patient safety. Thinking from an economic point of view, the boomers' need to spend money to maintain their autonomy can be a boon to healthcare businesses. New enterprises have the potential of being extremely profitable, but ethics must be part of the planning to avoid exploitation. These and other boomer-related issues are currently under study as part of healthcare reform, and they will continue to be important in dealing with the boomers.

In addition to boomers as patients, healthcare facilities must deal with the aging of their employee base. Because many boomers have not planned well for retirement, they may remain part of the workforce longer than they intended. Although they may provide great experience and wisdom, it may be necessary to adapt their work routine to accommodate their diminishing physical abilities. Whether this is a problem for health care in the future remains to be seen.

Beneficence

Patients who enter the healthcare system expect treatment based on charity and kindness. This is certainly true for the boomer generation. However, their mere numbers may cause violations of this basic premise for health care. When staff members have too many patients and too little time, patients can become just another "head in a bed." This lack of compassionate care will not be acceptable to boomer patients. Therefore, healthcare systems must continue to evaluate processes and procedures to not only increase efficiency but also increase the emphasis on human-to-human interaction. This effort will pay off not only in terms of patient satisfaction but also in increased organizational image and business potential.

Nonmaleficence

A key element in all health care is to "first do no harm." Because boomers do not want to age, they may be attracted to businesses and services that feature anti-aging products and procedures. Although these services may be highly profitable, it is important to consider the benefit to the patient versus the harm. Minimally, patients need to be informed about the risks and the benefits of any anti-aging procedures so that an informed decision can be made.

Health care as a system also needs to practice vigilance to avoid errors and safety violations that can cause harm to the patient and to the reputation of the organization. This requires continuous evaluation, staff education, and diligence. Of course, as healthcare reform progresses, more attention will be drawn to these issues, linked not just to ethics, but also to financial compensation.

Justice

Justice is perhaps the most difficult ethical area to address with respect to the boomers. One needs to ask, "What is just?" and "To whom is it just?" The boomer generation has a highly focused sense of justice, which includes fair treatment of their needs. Fairness, in their mind, centers on getting what they need and what they feel they deserve. In addition, this conception of fairness is linked to effective communication. In other words, if the patient understands why something has occurred, he or she will be less likely to see it as an injustice.

There are also justice issues for staff members working in a high-boomer-population situation. Healthcare systems may ask their employees to do more with less on a consistent basis. Although this makes economic sense, it creates feelings of being treated unfairly, which can lead to high turnover and poor morale. Lower employee morale can then lead to robotic, uncompassionate patient care and the continuation of an undesirable and unprofitable business cycle. Finding solutions to avoid this cycle requires attention to detail, creativity, training, and evaluation.

SUMMARY

Although this chapter gives examples of trends in thinking about ethics and in healthcare issues, it does not give a clairvoyant picture of the future. However, we do know that challenges to health care will continue in the 21st century. This means that you must always be "ethics ready" to address them. This ability is essential to building an ethics-based career and maintaining your professional integrity.

QUESTIONS FOR DISCUSSION

1. What are the most important ethical lessons you learned from reading this text?

2. Does the Ethic of Care model change the way that you think about ethics?

3. How does the narrative ethics model compare with the theories presented by Summers?

4. What are the key ethical issues for healthcare practitioners who use or recommend CAM practices?

5. How will the aging of the baby boomers affect your future practice of health care?

FOOD FOR THOUGHT

It is now 2020, and your career in health care is highly successful. Using your imagination and the knowledge gained through this text, answer the following questions.

1. How important is the application of ethics to your career success?

2. How has your knowledge of ethics assisted you in your career?

3. What ethical challenges do you face in your future?

NOTES

1. D. L. Volker, "Is There a Unique Nursing Ethic?" *Nursing Science Quarterly* 16, no. 207 (2003): 207–211.

2. S. D. Edwards, "Three Versions of an Ethic of Care," *Nursing Philosophy* 10 (2009): 231–240.

3. V. D. Lachman, "Applying the Ethics of Care to Your Nursing Practice," *Medsurg Nursing* 21, no. 2 (2012): 112.

4. Volker, "Unique Nursing Ethic?"

5. Edwards, "Three Versions of an Ethic of Care."

6. Volker, "Unique Nursing Ethic?"

7. Edwards, "Three Versions of an Ethic of Care."

8. D. C. Thomasma, "Toward a New Medical Ethics: Implications for Ethics in Nursing," in *Interpretative Phenomenology: Embodiment, Caring, and Ethics in Health and Illness*, ed. P. Benner (Thousand Oaks, CA: Sage, 1994).

9. A. Bishop and J. Scudder, *Nursing Ethics: Therapeutic Caring Presence* (Sudbury, MA: Jones and Bartlett, 2001).

10. Volker, "Unique Nursing Ethic?" 209.

11. M. Corley and P. Selig, "Prevalence of Principled Thinking by Critical Care Nurses," *Dimensions of Critical Care Nursing* 3 (1994): 96–103.

12. A. Gaul, "Casuistry, Care, Compassion, and Ethics Data Analysis," *Advances in Nursing Science* 17, no. 3 (1995): 47–57.

13. W. J. Pinch, "Is Caring a Moral Trap?" *Nursing Outlook* 44 (1996): 84–88.

14. Edwards, "Three Versions of an Ethic of Care."

15. C. Gastmans, "The Care Perspective in Health Care Ethics," in *Essentials of Teaching and Learning in Nursing Ethics: Perspectives and Methods*, eds. A. J. Davis, V. Tschudin, and L. de Raeve (London: Churchill Livingston): 146.

16. P. Nortvedt, M. H. Hem, and H. Skirbekk, "The Ethics of Care: Role Obligations and Moderate Partiality in Health Care," *Nursing Ethics* 18, no. 2 (2011): 192–200.

17. Ibid., 197.

18. J. McCarthy, "Principlism or Narrative Ethics: Must We Choose Between Them?" *British Medical Journal* 29 (2003): 67.

19. Ibid., 67.

20. Ibid., 65.

21. K. Dayton, "Procedures," in *An Arduous Touch: Women's Voices in Health Care*, eds. A. M. Haddad and K. H. Brown (West Lafayette, IN: Purdue University Press, 1999), 12–20.

22. McCarthy, "Principlism or Narrative Ethics," 66.

23. Ibid., 65–71.

24. Ibid., 70.

25. T. E. Adams, "A Review of Narrative Ethics," *Qualitative Inquiry* 14 (2008): 179.

26. C. Ellis, "Telling Secrets, Revealing Lives: Relational Ethics in Research with Intimate Others," *Qualitative Inquiry* 13 (2007): 3–29.

27. For excellent resources on the history and practice of CAM/IM, see M. S. Micozzi, *Fundamentals of Complementary and Alternative Medicine*, 4th ed. (St. Louis, MO: Saunders, 2011).

28. National Center for Complementary and Alternative Medicine, "What Is Complementary and Alternative Medicine?" para. 2. Retrieved from http://nccam.nih.gov/health/whatiscam. Accessed March 14, 2012.

29. Ibid., para. 4–24.

30. Micozzi, *Fundamentals of Complementary and Alternative Medicine*.

31. P. M. Barnes, B. B. Bloom, and R. L. Nahin, "Complementary and Alternative Medicine Use Among Adults and Children: United States, 2007," *National Health Statistics Reports* 12 (December 2008): 1–24.

32. M. Clark-Grill, "When Listening to the People: Lessons from Complementary and Alternative Medicine (CAM) for Bioethics," *Bioethical Inquiry* 7 (2010): 71–81.

33. Ibid., 73–74.

34. Ibid., 74.

35. S. Tyremann, "Values in Complementary and Alternative Medicine," *Medical Health Care and Philosophy* 14 (2011): 209–217.

36. Ibid., 209–217.

37. Micozzi, *Fundamentals of Complementary and Alternative Medicine*, 50.

38. National Center for Complementary and Alternative Medicine, "What Is Complementary and Alternative Medicine?"

39. P. G. Shelle, S. C. Morton, M. J. Suttorp, N. Buscemi, and C. Friesen, "Challenges in Systematic Reviews of Complementary and Alternative Medicine Topic," *Annals of Internal Medicine* 142, no. 12 (2005): 1042–1047.

40. T. J. Kaptchuk and D. M. Eisenberg, "Varieties of Healing, 1: Medical Pluralism in the United States," *Annals of Internal Medicine* 135, no. 3 (2001): 189–195.

41. Ibid., 190.

42. Ibid., 192–193.

43. T. S. Geisel, *You're Only Old Once: A Book for Obsolete Children* (New York: Random House, 1986). Note: This is a "must read" to understand the patient experience.

44. M. Mertz, "Complementary and Alternative Medicine: The Challenges of Ethical Justification," *Medicine, Health Care, and Philosophy* 10 (2007): 329–345.

45. Ibid., 334.

46. M. D. Landau, "Medical Schools Embrace Alternative Medicine," *U.S. News and World Report*, April 12, 2011.

47. Mertz, "Complementary and Alternative Medicine," 333–334.

48. Ibid., 337–341.

49. C. L. Ross, "Integral Healthcare: The Benefits and Challenges of Integrating Complementary and Alternative Medicine with a Conventional Medical Practice," *Integrative Medicine Insights* 4 (2009): 13–20.

50. A. C. Essary, "The PCMH: A Model for Primary Care," *Journal of the American Academy of Physician Assistants* (September 2009). Retrieved from http://www.jaapa.com/the-pchm-a-model-for primary-care/article/148332/. Accessed March 31, 2012.

51. Ibid.

52. J. W. Smith and A. Clurman, *Generation Ageless: How Baby Boomers Are Changing the Way We Live Today . . . And They're Just Getting Started* (New York: Harper Collins, 2007), xv.

53. Get Involved! "Baby Boomer Facts." Retrieved from http://www.getinvolved.gov/newsroom/programs/factsheet_boomers.asp. Accessed May 16, 2012.

54. Smith and Clurman, *Generation Ageless*, 10.

55. Ibid., 30.

56. K. Dychtwald, *Age Power: How the 21st Century Will Be Ruled by the New Old* (New York: Jeremy P. Archer/Putnam, 1999), 15–19.

57. United States History, "Baby Boomer Generation." Retrieved from http://www.u-s-history.com/pages/h2061.html. Accessed May 15, 2012.

58. Dychtwald, *Age Power*, chapters 2 and 4.

59. Smith and Clurman, *Generation Ageless*, chapters 6–8.

60. Dychtwald, *Age Power*, 70–78.

61. R. Schwartz, "Baby Boomers, Agents, and Health Care," *Florida Underwriter*, September 2010, 14–15.

62. Dychtwald, *Age Power*, chapter 6.

63. Ibid., 173.

Glossary

a priori   Experience-based knowledge.

absolute difference (AD)   A number obtained by subtracting the numeric measure of the health status of one group from that of another group.

accountable care organization   A group of providers who provide coordinated care for patients. There is a link between their reimbursement for this service and their quality care goals.

act utility   In utilitarianism, the tenet that one should judge each act on its own overall benefit. This version of utilitarianism is not conducive to health care.

activities of daily living (ADLs)   Basic needs and activities of life, such as getting in and out of bed, toileting, bathing, dressing, and eating.

adult protective services (APS)   Agencies that have the task of assisting older adults when they are not able to meet their needs or are abused, neglected, or exploited.

advance directive   A document that allows a patient to express his or her wishes about end-of-life issues and treatment. Hospitals and others also use the term *living will* for this legal document.

altered nuclear transfer technique (ANT)   A technique scientists use to generate embryonic stem cells without first creating an embryo. Researchers propose this technique as an ethical way to create stem cell lines.

alternative fuel source   A non-fossil-fuel-based source of energy, such as wind, hydrodynamic, hydrogen, and solar power.

altruism   Acting unselfishly or in the belief that one's actions benefit others.

amniocentesis A procedure for taking a sample of amniotic fluid from the uterus. Based on this sample, physicians can order genetic screening for the detection of health conditions.

anthropogenic hazard An event or action that results from the interaction of human beings with the world.

antinomies Two statements that appear to be correct, but do not agree, creating a paradox.

artificial nutrition A form of feeding used for medical maintenance. It is a temporary form of providing nutrients in cases when a person cannot swallow.

artificially inseminated by donor (AID) children Children created by joining sperm and egg outside the womb and then inserting the fertilized eggs into a natural or surrogate mother.

assisted death The generic term for practices of voluntary active euthanasia and assisted suicide.

assisted living facility (ALF) A recent addition to long-term care options that provides assistance with activities of daily living, greater privacy, and independence, primarily for seniors.

assisted reproduction The use of technologies, such as in vitro fertilization, artificial insemination, and cloning, to facilitate procreation.

assisted reproductive technology (ART) Any of a number of alternative ways to reproduce children. Cloning is one example of ART.

assisted suicide Intentionally ending one's life through the assistance of a third party.

authority-based ethics Theories of ethics that use faith or ideology as the focal point for making ethical decisions.

autonomy In healthcare ethics, the ability to act independently and to make decisions about actions, treatment, and health practices.

azotemia A form of blood poisoning that occurs when waste products, normally eliminated in the urine, accumulate in the blood. It is also known as uremia.

beneficence In ethics, to act with charity and kindness. It applies to both professionals and organizations.

best-off population A method of computing the amount of inequality in populations. In the case of health care, those who are the best off in terms of health serve as the reference group for comparisons with the worst-off group.

biological reductionism A view that reduces human beings to the cellular level and assumes that one human can replace another.

blastocyst An embryo ready for implantation in the wall of the uterus.

boomer generation A group of people who were born in the period following World War II (baby boomers). Because of their numbers, this group has changed American culture in many ways.

bureaucratic parsimony An organization's unwillingness to spend money or resources on programs.

categorical imperative Kant's tool for making ethical decisions. It includes the ideas of a decision being able to become a universal law and of respect for humankind. If both of these concepts apply, then the action can be truly moral.

chorionic villus sampling (CVS) The process of inserting a catheter into the uterus to collect a sample of tissue from the developing placenta.

clinical decision-support system (CDSS) A type of health information technology that gives physicians information for making patient treatment decisions.

clinical practice guidelines Recommendations for medical practice developed by experts in the field and based on evidence-based treatment practices.

cloning The process of creating a plant or animal that is genetically identical to its parent through asexual reproduction.

clouded genetic heritage A situation that occurs when reproductive technologies are used and the genetic identity of the produced child is unknown.

collaborative reproduction The use of surrogates, cloning, and other alternative reproductive options to produce a child.

competency The ability to understand a situation and make choices based on understood logic. This term has many definitions, and is applied to persons based on their physical and mental condition.

computer-assisted maxillofacial surgery The use of computer-aided navigation systems in order to better conduct dental surgery and other procedures with fewer complications.

computer-assisted surgery The use of computers and specialized equipment to assist physicians in advanced surgical procedures.

consequentialism Basing decisions about the nature of ethical decisions on their consequences and not on the intent of the agent. A part of teleological ethical theories.

curing   Bringing an end to illness or injury through medical treatment.

decisional capacity   The ability to make decisions about one's personal life, including where one lives and receives care and about the type of care received.

decisional incapacity   The level of inability to make decisions about one's personal life, including where one lives and receives care and about the type of care received.

dehydration   A lack of water in the body as the result of inadequate intake of fluids or excessive loss of fluids.

deontology   A theory of ethics, largely attributed to Emmanuel Kant, that uses the concept of duty and respect for persons to define appropriate ethical action.

disease experience   How patients see the disease process, which can be vastly different from the way professionals view it.

disenfranchisement   A circumstance in which a person's rights to full participation in society appear to be limited; the individual does not feel that he or she has the right to benefits that others receive.

distributive justice   The subset of justice that addresses the balancing of benefits and burdens and the appropriate sharing of those benefits and burdens.

domestic violence   A complex social problem that carries serious health-care consequences, especially for intimate partners and others in society.

electronic medical record (EMR)   A generic term for the creation, maintenance, and storage of a patient's medical record on a computer system.

ensoulment   Part of the beginning of moral personhood, conceptualized as the moment when a fetus gains a soul. The mother feels it as "quickening."

environmental sustainability   The ability of the local or global environment to maintain life for all species.

empiricism   The philosophical position that all knowledge comes from observed information and experimentation.

EMTALA   An acronym for the Emergency Medical Treatment and Active Labor Act of 1986, also known informally as the patient anti-dumping act.

ethical analysis   The application of ethical theory and principles to concrete clinical situations.

ethical climate   The overall culture of an organization with respect to ethics. The climate for the application of ethics to decision making can be favorable or unfavorable.

ethical egoism An ethical position that maintains that people should act only for their own self-interest or benefit. This position does not fit well in the healthcare context because healing requires putting the patient's interests before those of the healer.

ethical relativism The theory that because every situation is different, there is no appropriate ethical theory or set of theories. Ethical decisions would depend on the situation. Because of the nature of health care, this position is not appropriate.

ethicist A professional who typically has a doctoral degree in ethics, bioethics, and sometimes theology. He or she serves as a consultant on ethical issues for a hospital or ethics committee.

ethics committee A group of people who serve in an advisory capacity for ethical issues in a hospital or major clinic; membership varies depending on the committee's function.

ethics toolbox The knowledge and application of ethical theory and principles to everyday issues in health care. If one has a full ethics toolbox, one can better choose the appropriate ethics-based action.

etiopathy The scientific study of determining the causes of pathological changes in the body.

eudaimonia The translation of this term is "happiness" or "well-being." However, in Aristotle's philosophy, eudaimonia is different from mere pleasure in that it occurs when a person lives a rational life.

evidence-based practice (EBP) Providing medical care based on treatments and procedures found to be scientifically sound practices that produce successful outcomes.

family systems approach An approach to psychotherapy that views the family as a unit and addresses problems within the system of the family.

fetal biopsy An invasive procedure for diagnosing disease or problems with fetal development.

fiduciary relationship A situation in which trust must be present for an appropriate interaction to occur. An example is the physician–patient encounter.

financially avoidable inequity A classification of inequities in health care, meaning that there are enough funds available to correct or avoid the inequity.

freedom of intellectual effort The need for a balance between limiting research efforts and allowing unmonitored and uncontrolled research.

fungible The ability to be interchanged or substitutable.

futility   In general contexts, a term meaning an action that does not produce a valuable effect or that is useless. In medical situations, this is often difficult to determine, because it includes the definition of the medical limits of care.

gender socialization   The process by which males and females learn their identities and roles in society.

genetic mother   The woman who provides the germ cells (egg) for the creation of a child; she may or may not be the gestational mother.

genetic therapy   An intervention that includes gene testing and counseling of prospective parents about genetic-related disease.

gestational mother   The woman who carries the fertilized egg in her uterus; she may or may not be the genetic mother.

gourmet children   Children who are special ordered for their genetic attributes (gender, height, intellect); also known as designer children.

hacker   An individual who uses his or her expertise to break into a computer system; can be done for illegal purposes or just for the hacker's own amusement.

harm   In a clinical setting, harm is something that makes the situation worse for the patient. Harm can be physical, emotional, financial, or spiritual.

harm as negligence   Situations in which healthcare personnel have failed to protect patients, families, or communities from injury, damage, or impairment caused through encounters with the healthcare system.

hazard vulnerability analysis   A process involved in evaluating potential emergencies and their effect on hospitals and communities. Several areas are included in such an analysis, including mitigation, response, and recovery operations.

healing   The process of treating the patient beyond his or her symptoms, using the mind, body, and spirit.

health inequality   Variations of health status across individuals within a population or a difference in the average or total health between two or more populations.

health inequity   A difference in the health status of populations or individuals within populations that society or individuals find morally unacceptable.

health information technology (HIT)   The computer hardware, software, databases, and systems that support quality care through the electronic medical record.

Health Information Technology for Economic and Clinical Health Act (HITECH)   Part of the American Recovery and Reinvestment Act of 2009; this law is an attempt to ensure the adoption of electronic medical records.

Healthy People 2020   The title of a government program addressing prevention strategies for many diseases and health conditions.

hemoconcentration   An increase in the concentration of cells or solids in the blood resulting from a decrease in its fluid content.

horizontal equity   The equal allocation of a resource across a population.

human-caused disaster   A situation of loss of life, property, or sense of safety created by the actions of humans rather than by nature.

human cloning   The process of creating a human being from a cell or other living tissue. Clones would have genetic makeup identical to that of their donors.

hydatidiform mole   A tumor-like mass in the uterus that is often mistaken for a pregnancy.

hydration   In health care, the act of giving fluids artificially to support medical treatment when a patient is unable to swallow.

hypercalcemia   The medical term for an unusually high amount of calcium in the blood.

hypernatremia   The medical term used to describes an abnormal concentration of sodium in the blood.

hyperosmolality   The medical term used to describe an abnormal increase in the concentration of the blood.

in vitro fertilization   A procedure that involves the fertilization of the ovum by the sperm outside the human body. In cases where conception is affected by low fertility, couples can use in vitro fertilization for conception.

incompetency   This term has many definitions. Medical practice defines it in terms of the end results of a decision and in terms of the thought processes used to make decisions.

induced pluripotent stem cell (iPSC)   The result of a technique that causes adult cells to act like embryonic stem cells; the cells are pluripotent, which means they are able to make all the various tissues and cells that are present in the human body after birth.

inerrant   A person who is incapable of making a mistake or a thing that contains no mistakes.

institutional review board (IRB)   A committee made up of experts and concerned individuals whose mission is to ensure protection of human subjects in research.

instrumental activities of daily living (IADLs) A category of functional capabilities that includes taking medications appropriately, managing finances, using the telephone, and being able to get in and out of the home.

integrated ethics An approach to ethics whereby ethics is part of the "business as usual" workings of an organization, rather than solely the responsibility of an ethics committee or the chaplaincy.

intergenerational problem A situation in which a problem or condition affects patients of two or more generations. An example of an intergenerational problem is domestic violence or alcoholism.

intergenerational transmission of abuse The process of passing the culture of abuse from one generation to another in families.

intimate partner violence (IPV) Any type of harm caused by a current or past partner of a person; also known as domestic violence. Remember that this issue is not limited to women.

Joint Commission An agency that accredits or certifies thousands of healthcare facilities in the United States. Its mission is to improve the quality of health care.

justice A principle of ethics that includes actions that provide fairness or that address the perception of what a person or community deserves.

LGBTQI An abbreviation for lesbian, gay, bisexual, transgender, queer, questioning, and intersex. It attempts to be inclusive when defining intimate partners.

legal right The existence of legislation that grants a person an entitlement.

libertarianism The position, taken by Robert Nozick and others, that freedom or liberty is the central moral principle. Therefore, individual autonomy is critical to moral action.

long-term care The use of health care on a long-term basis as required by an individual's physical or mental limitations.

mass prophylaxis Efforts for community preparedness for and prevention of natural or human-caused disasters.

mass-casualty event A natural or human-caused occurrence in which more than the expected number of deaths and injuries occur. Such events challenge hospitals and other healthcare systems.

meaningful use As used in the HITECH Act, the requirement to demonstrate the application of computer systems to patient care and quality improvement.

medical paradigm The logic used in traditional medical practice to assess and diagnose the patient's problems.

medical technology A general term for medical products and equipment used to provide less invasive treatment and diagnostic options.

medicalization of social problems Converting areas viewed as social problems into medical ones. For example, society now recognizes alcoholism as a disease and not just a social failing.

metaethics The study of ethical concepts and definitions. Think of this as the macro study of ethics itself.

mitigation Organizational and individual efforts to lessen the impact of a disaster. Disaster planning is part of mitigation efforts.

moral community The group of people with whom we feel a moral affinity and for whom we assume an ethical obligation. Perceptions of who is a member and who is not establish the boundaries of the moral community.

morally avoidable inequity An inequity that can be corrected. When society corrects an inequity, the correction must not violate other social values, such as liberty or distributive justice.

morning-after pill A contraceptive designed for use after sexual intercourse to prevent pregnancy. Plan B is a brand name for this type of contraceptive.

most socially advantaged population A method of computing the amount of inequality in a population. In this case, the most socially advantaged group serves as a referent for comparison with other groups in the population.

natural disaster A situation in which there is loss of life, property, or sense of safety that is caused by natural events such as floods, hurricanes, fires, and tornados.

natural law theory A branch of ethics based on the tradition of St. Thomas Aquinas. It uses the rationality of God and the idea of conscience to determine ethically appropriate actions.

natural right Respect for attributes that contribute to a human being's highest good and that come from nature. An example of a natural right is the right to the pursuit of happiness.

negative right This term means that a person has a right to do anything not defined by the law. Examples of negative rights are found in the Bill of Rights and include the right to assembly and to free speech.

neonatal intensive care unit (NICU) Specialized area of a hospital designed to meet the needs of premature and severely ill infants. NICUs require specialized technology and highly specialized professionals.

network In the healthcare system, a cooperative relationship among various types of healthcare organizations, including hospitals, clinics, long-term care facilities, and combinations of organizations.

nonconsenting third party   With regard to reproductive technologies, the potential child created by these technologies. The potential child cannot give consent for the treatment that initiates its existence.

nonmaleficence   The ethical principle of refraining from causing harm or preventing intentional harm from occurring.

nonmarital third party   With regard to reproductive technologies, individuals who contribute to the procreation of a child but who will not be the parents of the child. Examples include egg and sperm donors.

normative ethics   The application of ethics in determining what is right or wrong in a certain situation, such as the provision of health care.

noumenal world   For Kant, the world as it exists within itself and not as we interpret it.

original position   Part of Rawls's hypothetical model to assist in determining what is just. In this hypothetical position, all people are equal and are not aware of personal circumstances (the veil of ignorance).

palliative specialist   A healthcare professional who specializes in providing care that reduces pain and suffering without eliminating the cause. Such expertise is particularly important for end-of-life care.

partial-birth abortion   A form of ending a pregnancy that involves conducting procedures at the latest possible stage before live birth. The United States bans this procedure except when it is necessary to save the mother's life.

paternalism   An action or attitude taken by one person (usually a health professional) that limits the autonomy of another person. The intent is to benefit the person or to protect him or her from harm. For example, paternalism occurs when a physician does not tell the patient the complete truth about his or her condition.

Patient Self-Determination Act (PSDA)   A law that requires Medicare and Medicaid providers to provide written information about a person's rights to make healthcare decisions, including rights for accepting or refusing treatment.

patient-focused care   The delivery of healthcare services with the patient as the center of care. Elements of this type of care include providing information, patient-friendly environments, open medical records, and the use of care partners. Also known as patient-centered care.

pay-for-performance (P4P)   A payment system that rewards providers who meet certain predetermined standards and goals. It is also known as value-based purchasing.

pediatric intensive care unit (PICU)   An area of a hospital designed to treat severely ill infants and pediatric patients. PICUs often employ sophisticated technology and specialized medical care professionals.

person   An entity who can maintain social relationships with other persons. It involves a social role and not just a biological one.

physician order entry (POE)   A specific type of health information technology that facilitates communication between a physician and his or her office. It enhances the ability to place patient orders and update patient files.

physician-assisted death   Active or passive euthanasia involving physician practice. In active euthanasia, the physician directly causes the death. In passive euthanasia, he or she avoids practices that would prolong life. The physician might also use practices that would increase comfort but hasten death.

pluripotent   Cells that are able to make all of the tissues and cells in the human body.

PPACA   An abbreviation for H.R. 3590, the Patient Protection and Affordable Care Act of 2010. Some sources use the abbreviation ACA.

practical wisdom   In Aristotle's virtue ethics, the process of using one's character, education, and experience to decide correct action in a situation.

prehospital advance directive (PHAD)   A document prepared by an individual before he or she becomes a patient. It specifies actions for end-of-life situations, including the actions of emergency medical technicians and emergency department personnel. It can also designate who can speak for the patient if he or she is unable to speak for him or herself. States vary in their laws regarding PHADs. Also called a living will.

prehospital do-not-resuscitate order (PHDNR)   A document, prepared before one is a patient, that specifies actions in the event of a life-threatening or end-of-life situation. It spells out the patient's desire or lack of desire for cardiopulmonary resuscitation by emergency medical technicians or emergency department staff.

prenatal diagnosis   The diagnosis of conditions or disease before birth.

presymptomatic diagnosis   The ability to determine the presence of disease before actual symptoms are present; one of the potential benefits of genetic testing.

prima facie   A legal term indicating the assumption that something exists on initial examination.

principle of double effect   An ethical principle used when there is a conflict between the good and evil effects of one action.

procedural justice   Due process. Violations of due process can occur with healthcare employees and the use of procedures for decision making.

psychic survival   The denial of feelings and formation of values in order to protect oneself from psychological harm.

public beneficence Similar to the ethical principle of beneficence. However, it involves decisions concerning the public's ability to experience gains from emerging scientific discoveries.

radical loving care A term, coined by Chapman, that describes a way of treating patients that is effective, holistic, and respects their spirituality.

reflective equilibrium A decision-making model for dealing with ethical concerns that involves considered judgment and ethical intuition.

relative difference (RD) A number obtained by the division of the numeric measure of the health status of one group by that of another group.

religious refusal When a person does not allow treatment based on his or her religious practices. Healthcare practitioners determine the competency of a person to make this decision based on whether he or she understands the situation and its consequences and whether the basis for his or her decision is a common religious belief.

research cloning The use of cloning technology to advance the study of disease prevention and treatment.

responsible stewardship A concept dealing with the ethical efforts to ensure that those persons unable to represent themselves receive consideration in the practice of future research studies.

retraumatization Trauma created after a person suffers a trauma, such as domestic violence, by virtue of the process used to gain information required for treatment. The patient must relive the pain and psychological damage in order to obtain treatment. Retraumatization also occurs if the individual decides to press charges against the abuser.

robotic-assisted surgery Procedures that employ actual robots to provide greater visibility and accessibility in different procedural sites and to reduce fatigue for surgeons.

RU-486 The FDA-approved drug Mifepristone, used in nonsurgical abortion.

rule utility Part of the theory of utilitarianism; the concept that the person making a decision should consider the greatest benefit (or good) for the greatest number. Rule utility can assist with policy decisions.

safety net In health care, the institutions that provide treatment to medically indigent patients who cannot obtain care from other sources. The emergency departments of hospitals and public health clinics are examples of safety nets.

scientific-based secularism An orientation to medical practice that excludes religion or spirituality as a consideration of diagnosis or treatment practice.

second-trimester abortion   The ending of a pregnancy during the second trimester, a process that requires a modified surgical procedure, such as vacuum aspiration.

selective abortion   Abortion performed for a special reason, such as when the fetus has the potential of a genetic disease, or when one or more fetuses from a multiple pregnancy are terminated to enhance the odds of survival of the remaining fetuses.

self-identity   The process of knowing who one is and of perceiving one's uniqueness.

sex-selective abortion   The termination of a pregnancy based on the preference for a particular gender, usually male.

shelter in place   The policy of remaining in one's home, school, or place of business until help is available in an emergency or natural disaster.

sine qua non   A legal term meaning an essential condition or prerequisite.

social mother   The woman who cares for a child after birth; she may or may not be the genetic or gestational mother.

stakeholder theory   Used in healthcare management to describe the involvement of those who have an investment in the mission of an organization, including employees, board members, physicians, and others.

stem cell   A special type of cell that can develop into any kind of human tissue.

stereotactic radiosurgery   An image-guided procedure using radiotherapy devices and precise measurements in the brain. Surgeons use this procedure in treating malignant and benign brain tumors.

stewardship   A management philosophy whereby one recognizes that one does not own resources. The manager, instead, protects the use of these resources in trust for the community or other stakeholders. Such a philosophy implies a high level of ethical awareness and application.

subacute care   Healthcare treatment for conditions that are less severe than acute situations.

substantive right   Something that is morally appropriate, such as food, housing, or a minimum wage. Substantive rights may be legal rights or not depending on the government structure.

substituted judgment   A situation that occurs when a person is not competent to make healthcare decisions and has not indicated a preference for those decisions. The decision maker uses knowledge of the patient's wishes when he or she was competent to make current decisions.

Summa Theologica   The title of one of the primary works of St. Thomas Aquinas, which includes his discourse on ethics.

surrogate   In healthcare situations, one who makes decision for another, such as a relative who makes decisions for a nursing home resident.

surrogate mother   With respect to reproductive technology, a woman who carries another woman's child in her womb. This process is known as surrogacy.

surveillance reports   In disaster planning, documents that provide information on potential natural or human-caused disasters. Planners use several methods to obtain this information, including weather reports, telephone monitoring, and tracking of suspicious individuals.

synthetic biology   A new genetic science that allows scientists to replace natural genetic material with genetically copied material.

systematic health inequality   A difference in health that consistently affects two or more populations and is not caused by random variation.

technology diffusion   When a technology becomes so common in a culture that it helps to define that culture.

telemanipulation   Robot-assisted surgical procedures that allow surgeons improved ergonomics during the procedure.

telemedicine   A general term for the use of email, video links, computers, and other telecommunications to send information about the patient to medical staff members.

teleology   The collection of ethical theories based on explanations of ethics as related to a goal or result.

tesla signal strength   A measurement of the magnetic field strength of a magnetic resonance imaging machine.

third-party donor   A person who contributes sperm or ova in a collaborative reproduction effort.

total institution   A type of facility that meets of the needs of an individual and where the meeting of those needs comes with restrictions; for example, a long-term care facility.

total population average   A method of computing the amount of inequality in a population; it examines the average of healthcare events in the population as a reference group to compare the same event with subpopulations.

totipotent   Cells that can access all the genes that are needed to make different types of cells and tissues.

trauma theory A recent addition to psychological theories, this research attempts to explain the effects of trauma as survival strategies or adaptations to life-shattering situations.

triage The setting of priorities for the treatment of sick or injured people using the seriousness of their condition as the criteria. It is often necessary in war or disaster situations.

unjust cause One of the criteria for judging health inequities; health inequities that result from severe restrictions to lifestyle choices, unhealthy working conditions, and inadequate access to health services fall into this category.

usual and customary fee A government method for reimbursement for physicians in the early stages of Medicare/Medicaid.

utilitarianism Often seen as a synonym for consequentialism, this term actually means that actions are ethical when they produce the greatest happiness, or utility. The reverse is also true. Actions are good when they avoid producing the greatest harm.

value-based purchasing See *pay-for-performance*.

vertical equity The allocation of different resources for different needs.

virtue ethics Part of authority-based ethics, theories of virtue ethics seek to determine the proper behavior for human beings. In other words, "How does an ethical person live his or her life?"

voluntary active euthanasia The situation in which patients freely choose to have a lethal agent directly administered to them by another individual, with a merciful intent.

Index